T0215773

Communications in Computer and Information Science   906

Commenced Publication in 2007
Founding and Former Series Editors:
Phoebe Chen, Alfredo Cuzzocrea, Xiaoyong Du, Orhun Kara, Ting Liu,
Dominik Ślęzak, and Xiaokang Yang

More information about this series at http://www.springer.com/series/7899

Mayank Singh · P. K. Gupta
Vipin Tyagi · Jan Flusser
Tuncer Ören (Eds.)

Advances in Computing and Data Sciences

Second International Conference, ICACDS 2018
Dehradun, India, April 20–21, 2018
Revised Selected Papers, Part II

 Springer

Editors
Mayank Singh
University of KwaZulu-Natal
Durban, South Africa

P. K. Gupta
Jaypee University of Information
Technology
Solan, India

Vipin Tyagi
Jaypee University of Engineering
and Technology
Guna, Madhya Pradesh, India

Jan Flusser
Institute of Information Theory
and Automation
Prague 8, Czech Republic

Tuncer Ören
University of Ottawa
Ottawa, Canada

ISSN 1865-0929   ISSN 1865-0937 (electronic)
Communications in Computer and Information Science
ISBN 978-981-13-1812-2   ISBN 978-981-13-1813-9 (eBook)
https://doi.org/10.1007/978-981-13-1813-9

Library of Congress Control Number: 2018909291

This Springer imprint is published by the registered company Springer Nature Singapore Pte Ltd.
The registered company address is: 152 Beach Road, #21-01/04 Gateway East, Singapore 189721, Singapore

Preface

Computing techniques like big data, cloud computing, machine learning, Internet of Things etc. are playing a key role in processing of data and retrieving of advanced information. Several state-of-art techniques and computing paradigms have been proposed based on these techniques. This volume contains the papers presented at the Second International Conference on Advances in Computing and Data Sciences (ICACDS 2018) held during April 20–21, 2018, at the Uttaranchal Institute of Technology, Uttaranchal University, Dehradun, Uttarakhand, India. The conference was organized specifically to help bring together researchers, academics, scientists, and industry and to derive benefits from the advances of the next generation of computing technologies in the areas of advanced computing and data sciences (ACDS).

The Program Committee of ICACDS 2018 is extremely grateful to the authors who showed an overwhelming response to the call for papers, with over 598 papers being submitted in two tracks in "Advanced Computing" and "Data Sciences." All submitted papers went through a peer review process and, finally, 110 papers were accepted for publication in two volumes of Springer's CCIS series. The first volume is devoted to advanced computing and the second deals with data sciences. We are very grateful to our reviewers for their efforts in finalizing the high-quality papers.

The conference featured many distinguished personalities like Prof. Ling Tok Wang, National University of Singapore, Singapore; Prof. Viranjay M. Srivastava, University of KwaZulu-Natal, Durban, South Africa; Prof. Parteek Bhatia, Thapar Institute of Engineering and Technology, Patiala, India; Prof. S. K. Mishra, Majmaah University, Saudi Arabia; Prof. Arun Sharma, Indira Gandhi Delhi Technical University for Women, India; Dr. Anup Girdhar, CEO and Founder, Sedulity Solutions and Technology, India, among many others. We are very grateful for the participation of these speakers in making this conference a memorable event.

The Organizing Committee of ICACDS 2018 is indebted to Sh. Jitendra Joshi, Chancellor Uttaranchal University, and Dr. N. K. Joshi, Vice Chancellor, Uttaranchal University for the confidence that they have invested in us for organizing this international conference, and all faculty members and staff of UIT, Uttaranchal University, Dehradun, for their support in organizing the conference and making it a grand success.

We would also like to thank the authors of all submitted papers for their hard work, adherence to the deadlines, and patience with the review process. Our sincere thanks to CSI, CSI SIG on Cyber Forensics, Consilio Intelligence Research Lab, and LWT India for sponsoring the event.

September 2018

Mayank Singh
P. K. Gupta
Vipin Tyagi
Jan Flusser
Tuncer Ören

Organization

Steering Committee

Chief Patron
Jitender Joshi
(Chancellor)

Uttaranchal University, Dehradun, India

Patron
N. K. Joshi (Vice
Chancellor)

Uttaranchal University, Dehradun, India

Honorary Chair
Arun Sharma

Indira Gandhi Delhi Technical University for Women,
Delhi, India

General Chair
Mayank Singh

University of KwaZulu-Natal, Durban, South Africa

Program Chairs
Shailendra Mishra

Majmaah University, Kingdom of Saudi Arabia

Viranjay M. Srivastava

University of KwaZulu-Natal, Durban, South Africa

Convener
Pradeep Kumar Gupta

Jaypee University of Information Technology, Solan, India

Co-convener
Vipin Tyagi

Jaypee University of Engineering and Technology, Guna,
India

Advisory Board Chair
Tuncer Ören

University of Ottawa, Canada

Technical Program Committee Chairs
Jan Flusser

Institute of Information Theory and Automation,
Czech Republic

Dirk Draheim

Tallinn University of Technology, Estonia

Conference Chairs

Manoj Diwakar	Uttaranchal University, Dehradun, India
Sandhaya Tarar	Gautham Buddha University, Greater Noida, India

Conference Co-chairs

Anand Sharma	Mody University of Science and Technology, Sikar, India
Vibhash Yadav	Rajkiya Engeering College, Banda, India
Purnendu S. Pandey	THDC Institute of Hydropower Engineering and Technology, Tehri, India
D. K. Chauhan	Noida International University, Greater Noida, India

Organizing Chairs

Devendra Singh	Uttaranchal University, Dehradun, India
Amit Kumar Sharma	Uttaranchal University, Dehradun, India
Sumita Lamba	Uttaranchal University, Dehradun, India
Niranjan Lal Verma	Mody University of Science and Technology, Sikar, India

Organizing Secretariat

Kapil Joshi	Uttaranchal University, Dehradun, India
Punit Sharma	Uttaranchal University, Dehradun, India
Vipin Dewal	Krishna Engineering College, Ghaziabad, India
Krista Chaudhary	Krishna Engineering College, Ghaziabad, India
Umang Kant	Krishna Engineering College, Ghaziabad, India

Finance Chair

Tarun Kumar	Uttaranchal University, Dehradun, India

Creative Head

Deepak Singh	MadeEasy Education, Delhi, India

Organizing Committee

Registration

Ugra Mohan	Uttaranchal University, Dehradun, India
Vivek John	Uttaranchal University, Dehradun, India
Meenakshi	Uttaranchal University, Dehradun, India
Vinay Negi	Uttaranchal University, Dehradun, India

Publication

Sumita Lamba	Uttaranchal University, Dehradun, India
Prashant Chaudhary	Uttaranchal University, Dehradun, India

Cultural

Shivani Pandey	Uttaranchal University, Dehradun, India
Rubi Pant	Uttaranchal University, Dehradun, India

Transportation

Pankaj Punia	Uttaranchal University, Dehradun, India
Arvind Singh Rawat	Uttaranchal University, Dehradun, India
Avneesh Kumar	Uttaranchal University, Dehradun, India

Hospitality

Sonam Rai	Uttaranchal University, Dehradun, India
Shruti Sharma	Uttaranchal University, Dehradun, India
Nitin Duklan	Uttaranchal University, Dehradun, India

Stage Management

Punit Sharma	Uttaranchal University, Dehradun, India
Arti Rana	Uttaranchal University, Dehradun, India
Musheer Vaqar	Uttaranchal University, Dehradun, India

Technical Session

Mudit Baurai	Uttaranchal University, Dehradun, India
Manish Singh Bisht	Uttaranchal University, Dehradun, India
Sunil Ghildiyal	Uttaranchal University, Dehradun, India
Ravi Batra	Uttaranchal University, Dehradun, India

Finance

Sanjeev Sharma	Uttaranchal University, Dehradun, India
Amit Kumar Pal	Uttaranchal University, Dehradun, India
Sudhir Jugran	Uttaranchal University, Dehradun, India

Food

Sourabh Agarwal	Uttaranchal University, Dehradun, India
Arpit Verma	Uttaranchal University, Dehradun, India
Ankur Jaiswal	Uttaranchal University, Dehradun, India
Gaurav Singh Negi	Uttaranchal University, Dehradun, India

Advertising

Kapil Joshi	Uttaranchal University, Dehradun, India
Himanshu Gupta	Uttaranchal University, Dehradun, India
Ravi Dhaundiyal	Uttaranchal University, Dehradun, India

Press and Media

Shreya Goyal   Uttaranchal University, Dehradun, India
Rachna Juyal   Uttaranchal University, Dehradun, India

Editorial

Parichay Durga   Uttaranchal University, Dehradun, India
Nishi Chachra   Uttaranchal University, Dehradun, India

Technical Sponsorship

Computer Society of India, Dehradun Chapter
Special Interest Group – Cyber Forensics, Computer Society of India

Financial Sponsorship

Consilio Intelligence Research Lab
LWT India Private Limited

Contents – Part II

Unsupervised Time Series Data Analysis for Error Pattern Extraction
for Predictive Maintenance. 1
    Vidya Ravi and Ravindra Patil

Glacier Terminus Position Monitoring and Modelling Using Remote
Sensing Data 11
    Rahul Nijhawan and Kanupriya Jain

Multiple Imputation Inference for Missing Values in Distributed
Datasets Using Apache Spark. 24
    Sathish Kaliamoorthy and S. Mary Saira Bhanu

Optimal Threshold Coverage Area (OTCA) Algorithm for Random
Deployment of Sensor Nodes in Large Asymmetrical Terrain 34
    Anamika Sharma and Siddhartha Chauhan

Dataset Expansion and Accelerated Computation for Image Classification:
A Practical Approach. 43
    Aditya Mohan and Nafisuddin Khan

Resilient Algorithm Solution for MongoDB Applications 55
    Ayush Jindal, Pavi Saraswat, Chandan Kapoor, and Punit Gupta

An Automatic Annotation Scheme for Scene Text Archival Applications 66
    Ayatullah Faruk Mollah, Subhadip Basu, and Mita Nasipuri

FDSS: Fuzzy Based Decision Support System for Aspect Based Sentiment
Analysis in Big Data. 77
    A. Jenifer Jothi Mary and L. Arockiam

Load Adaptive and Priority Based MAC Protocol for Body Sensors
and Consumer Electronic (CE) Devices 88
    Deepshikha and Siddhartha Chauhan

ProRank-Product Ranking on the Basis of Twitter Sentiment Analysis. 98
    Aysha Khan and Rashid Ali

Parallelization of Protein Clustering Algorithm Using OpenMP. 108
    Dhruv Dhar, Lakshana Hegde, Mahesh S. Patil,
    and Satyadhyan Chickerur

Intelligent Face Recognition System for Visually Impaired. 119
    Riya Goyal, Karan Kalra, Parteek Kumar, and Sanmeet Kaur

Ranking of Cancer Mediating Genes: A Novel Approach Using Genetic
Algorithm in DNA Microarray Gene Expression Dataset   129
   Sujay Saha, Priyojit Das, Anupam Ghosh, and Kashi Nath Dey

Hand Gesture Recognition Using Gaussian Threshold and Different
SVM Kernels   138
   *Shifali Sharma, Shatrughan Modi, Prashant Singh Rana,
   and Jhilik Bhattacharya*

Using Concept Map Network Based CLE for Teaching Learning
and Evaluating the Knowledge Acquired by Learners   148
   Sharma Minakshi and Chawla Sonal

Go-Park: A Parking Lot Allocation System in Smart Cities   158
   *Tanmoy Mukherjee, Shayon Gupta, Poulomi Sen, Vijay Pandey,
   and Kamalesh Karmakar*

A Question Answering Model Based on Semantic Matcher
for Support Ticketing System   167
   *Suyog Trivedi, Gopichand Agnihotram, Balaji Jagan,
   and Pandurang Naik*

Multiple CAs Based Framework to Provide Remote Palliative Care
for Patients Undergoing Chemotherapy   177
   *H. Lathashree, Niveditha J. Moka Katte, K. P. Pooja, K. Bhargavi,
   and B. Sathish Babu*

A Collaborative Filtering Approach for Movies Recommendation Based
on User Clustering and Item Clustering   187
   Shristi, Alok Kumar Jagadev, and Sachi Nandan Mohanty

Investigations of Optimized Optical Network Performance Under Different
Traffic Models   197
   Himanshi Saini and Amit Kumar Garg

Deployment Consideration on Secure Computation for Radix-16
Scalar Multiplication   205
   Gautam Kumar, Hemraj Saini, and U. M. Fernandes Dimlo

Clustering of Social Networking Data Using SparkR in Big Data   217
   Navneet Kaur and Niranjan Lal

Impact of Disruptive Technology on Juvenile Disruptive Behavior
in Classroom   227
   Vani Ramesh

Learners' Satisfaction Analysis Using Machine Learning Approaches   239
   Maksud Ahamad and Nesar Ahmad

Data Analysis: Opinion Mining and Sentiment Analysis of Opinionated
Unstructured Data   249
Harshi Garg and Niranjan Lal

Mobile Handset Selection Using Evolutionary Multi-objective
Optimization Considering the Cost and Quality Parameters.   259
Anurag Tiwari, Vivek Kumar Singh, and Praveen Kumar Shukla

An Adaptive Feature Dimensionality Reduction Technique Based
on Random Forest on Employee Turnover Prediction Model   269
*Md. Kabirul Islam, Mirza Mohtashim Alam, Md. Baharul Islam,
Karishma Mohiuddin, Amit Kishor Das, and Md. Shamsul Kaonain*

A Comparative Evolution of Unsupervised Techniques for Effective
Network Intrusion Detection in Hadoop   279
Priyanka Dahiya and Devesh Kumar Srivastava

Effective Traffic Management to Avoid Traffic Congestion
Using Recursive Re-routing Algorithm   288
K. Geetha, N. Sasikaladevi, and G. T. Dhayaleni

A Normalized Cosine Distance Based Regression Model for Data
Prediction in WSN   298
Arun Agarwal and Amita Dev

Comparative Study of Regression Models Towards Performance Estimation
in Soil Moisture Prediction.   309
Amarendra Goap, Deepak Sharma, A. K. Shukla, and C. Rama Krishna

Dynamics of Modified Leslie-Gower Model with Stochastic Influences   317
V. Nagaraju, B. R. Tapas Bapu, S. Pradeep, and V. Madhusudanan

Electricity Consumption Forecasting Using Time Series Analysis   327
Praphula Kumar Jain, Waris Quamer, and Rajendra Pamula

A Comparative Analysis of Fuzzy Logic Based Query Expansion
Approaches for Document Retrieval   336
Dilip Kumar Sharma, Rajendra Pamula, and D. S. Chauhan

Trends and Macro-economic Determinants of FDI Inflows to India   346
Jyoti Gupta

A Technical Evaluation of Neo4j and Elasticsearch for Mining
Twitter Data.   359
Janet Zhu, Sreenivas Sremath Tirumala, and G. Anjan Babu

Visibility Prediction in Urban Localities Using Clustering   370
Apeksha Aggarwal and Durga Toshniwal

Handling Web Spamming Using Logic Approach 380
  Laxmi Ahuja

Spider Monkey Optimization Algorithm with Enhanced Learning 388
  Bhagwanti, Harish Sharma, and Nirmala Sharma

Performance Evaluation of Wavelet Based Image Compression for Wireless
Multimedia Sensor Network 402
  Addisalem Genta and D. K. Lobiyal

NavIC Relative Positioning with Smoothing Filter and Comparison
with Standalone NavIC 413
  Ashish K. Shukla, Pooja K. Thakkar, and Saurabh Bhalla

Extended Kalman Filter Based User Position Algorithm for Terrestrial
Navigation System 423
  Ashish K. Shukla, Komal G. Bansal, and Saurabh Bhalla

Investigation of Iterative and Direct Strategies with Recurrent Neural
Networks for Short-Term Traffic Flow Forecasting 433
  Armando Fandango and Amita Kapoor

Comparative Analysis of Pre- and Post-Classification Ensemble Methods
for Android Malware Detection. 442
  Shikha Badhani and Sunil K. Muttoo

Design and Implementation of a New Model for Privacy Preserving
Classification of Data Streams 454
  Aradhana Nyati, Shashi Kant Dargar, and Sandeep Sharda

Partial Confirmatory Factor Analysis for E-Service Delivery Outcomes
Using E-Tools Provided by the Government. 463
  Seema Sahai and Gurinder Singh

Finding Association Between Genes by Applying Filtering Mechanism
on Microarray Dataset 471
  Gauri Bhanegaonkar, Rakhi Wajgi, and Dipak Wajg

Comparitive Study of Bergman and Augmented Minimal Model
with Conventional Controller for Type 1 Diabetes. 479
  Surekha Kamath, Cifha Crecil Dias, K. Pawan Kumar,
  and Meenal Budhiraja

Performance Comparison of Machine Learning Classification Algorithms. . . . 489
  K. M. Veena, K. Manjula Shenoy, and K. B. Ajitha Shenoy

Deep Learning and GPU Based Approaches to Protein Secondary
Structure Prediction.   498
   Maulika S. Patel

J-PAKE and ECC Based Authentication Protocol for Smart Grid Network . . .   507
   Aarti Agarkar and Himanshu Agrawal

Motion Detection for Video Surveillance System   523
   Aditi Kumbhar and P. C. Bhaskar

An Android Based Smart Environmental Monitoring System Using IoT.   535
   Sangeeta Kumari, Manasi H. Kasliwal, and Nandakishor D. Valakunde

Detection of Fruit Ripeness Using Image Processing   545
   Anuprita Mande, Gayatri Gurav, Kanchan Ajgaonkar, Pooja Ombase,
   and Vaishali Bagul

Comparative Study of Different Approaches to Inverse Kinematics   556
   Ayush Gupta, Prasham Bhargava, Sankalp Agrawal, Ankur Deshmukh,
   and Bhakti Kadam

Semitransparency Effect in a Video Using Deep Learning Approach   564
   Pavan Dongare and M. Sridevi

Author Index   575

Contents – Part I

Two Stage Histogram Enhancement Schemes to Improve Visual Quality
of Fundus Images   1
    Farha Fatina Wahid, K. Sugandhi, and G. Raju

A Secure and Efficient Computation Outsourcing Scheme for Multi-users . . .   12
    V. Sudarsan Rao and N. Satyanarayana

Detecting the Common Biomarkers for Early Stage Parkinson's Disease
and Early Stage Alzheimer's Disease Associated with Intrinsically
Disordered Protein   25
    Sagnik Sen and Ujjwal Maulik

Assamese Named Entity Recognition System Using Naive
Bayes Classifier   35
    Gitimoni Talukdar, Pranjal Protim Borah, and Arup Baruah

Medical Image Multiple Watermarking Scheme Based on Integer Wavelet
Transform and Extraction Using ICA.   44
    R. Nanmaran, G. Thirugnanam, and P. Mangaiyarkarasi

Recognizing Real Time ECG Anomalies Using Arduino, AD8232
and Java   54
    Pratik Kanani and Mamta Padole

Interpretation of Indian Sign Language Using Optimal HOG
Feature Vector   65
    Garima Joshi, Anu Gaur, and Sheenu

Stable Reduced Link Break Routing Technique in Mobile
Ad Hoc Network   74
    Bhagyashri R. Hanji and Rajashree Shettar

Disguised Public Key for Anonymity and Enforced Confidentiality
in Summative E-Examinations   84
    Kissan G. Gauns Dessai and Venkatesh V. Kamat

Early Diabetes Prediction Using Voting Based Ensemble Learning   95
    Adil Husain and Muneeb H. Khan

A System that Performs Data Distribution and Manages Frequent Itemsets
Generation of Incremental Data in a Distributed Environment.   104
    Vinaya Sawant and Ketan Shah

Assessing Autonomic Level for Self-managed Systems – FAHP
Based Approach   114
  Arun Sharma, Deepika Sharma, and Mayank Singh

Bounded Paths for LCR Queries in Labeled Weighted Directed Graphs   124
  B. Bhargavi and K. Swarupa Rani

An Efficient Image Fusion Technique Based on DTCWT   134
  Sonam and Manoj Kumar

Low-Delay Channel Access Technique for Critical Data Transmission
in Wireless Body Area Network   144
  M. Ambigavathi and D. Sridharan

Lexicon-Based Approach to Sentiment Analysis of Tweets Using
R Language   154
  Nitika Nigam and Divakar Yadav

Twitter Based Event Summarization   165
  Amrah Maryam and Rashid Ali

Comparative Analysis of Fixed Valued Impulse Noise Removal Techniques
for Image Enhancement   175
  Rashmi Bisht, Ritu Vijay, and Shweta Singh

A Novel Load Balancing Algorithm Based on the Capacity of
the Virtual Machines   185
  S. B. Kshama and K. R. Shobha

A Hybrid Approach for Privacy-Preserving Data Mining   196
  NagaPrasanthi Kundeti, M. V. P. Chandra Sekhara Rao,
  Naga Raju Devarakonda, and Suresh Thommandru

Network Traffic Classification Using Multiclass Classifier   208
  Prabhjot Kaur, Prashant Chaudhary, Anchit Bijalwan,
  and Amit Awasthi

An Efficient Hybrid Approach Using Misuse Detection
and Genetic Algorithm for Network Intrusion Detection   218
  Rohini Rajpal and Sanmeet Kaur

Ensemble Technique Based on Supervised and Unsupervised Learning
Approach for Intrusion Detection   228
  Sanmeet Kaur and Ishan Garg

Recognition of Handwritten Digits Using DNN, CNN, and RNN   239
  Subhi Jain and Rahul Chauhan

Evaluating Effectiveness of Color Information for Face Image Retrieval
and Classification Using SVD Feature.   249
    Junali Jasmine Jena, G. Girish, and Manisha Patro

PDD Algorithm for Balancing Medical Data.   260
    Karan Kalra, Riya Goyal, Sanmeet Kaur, and Parteek Kumar

Digital Mammogram Classification Using Compound Local Binary Pattern
Features with Principal Component Analysis Based Feature Reduction
Approach.   270
    Menaxi J. Bagchi, Figlu Mohanty, Suvendu Rup, Bodhisattva Dash,
    and Banshidhar Majhi

Assessing the Performance of CMOS Amplifiers Using High-k Dielectric
with Metal Gate on High Mobility Substrate.   279
    Deepa Anand, M. Swathi, A. Purushothaman,
    and Sundararaman Gopalan

The Impact of Picture Splicing Operation for Picture Forgery Detection.   290
    Rachna Mehta and Navneet Agrawal

LEACH- Genus 2 Hyper Elliptic Curve Based Secured Light-Weight
Visual Cryptography for Highly Sensitive Images.   302
    N. Sasikaladevi, N. Mahalakshmi, and N. Archana

HEAP- Genus 2 HyperElliptic Curve Based Biometric
Audio Template Protection.   312
    N. Sasikaladevi, A. Revathi, N. Mahalakshmi, and N. Archana

Greedy WOA for Travelling Salesman Problem   321
    Rishab Gupta, Nilay Shrivastava, Mohit Jain, Vijander Singh,
    and Asha Rani

Deterministic Task Scheduling Method in Multiprocessor Environment   331
    Ranjit Rajak

Performance Comparison of Measurement Matrices in
Compressive Sensing.   342
    Kankanala Srinivas, Nagapuri Srinivas, Puli Kishore Kumar,
    and Gayadhar Pradhan

A Novel Approach by Cooperative Multiagent Fault Pair
Learning (CMFPL)   352
    Deepak A. Vidhate and Parag Kulkarni

Novel Technique for the Test Case Prioritization in Regression Testing.   362
    Mampi Kerani and Sharmila

Extreme Gradient Boosting Based Tuning for Classification in Intrusion
Detection Systems.   372
    Ashu Bansal and Sanmeet Kaur

Relative Direction: Location Path Providing Method for Allied
Intelligent Agent.   381
    *S. Rayhan Kabir, Mirza Mohtashim Alam, Shaikh Muhammad Allayear,
    Md Tahsir Ahmed Munna, Syeda Sumbul Hossain,
    and Sheikh Shah Mohammad Motiur Rahman*

FPGA Implementation for Real-Time Epoch Extraction in Speech Signal. . . .   392
    *Nagapuri Srinivas, Kankanala Srinivas, Gayadhar Pradhan,
    and Puli Kishore Kumar*

Privacy-Preserving Random Permutation of Image Pixels Enciphered
Model from Cyber Attacks for Covert Operations   401
    *Amit Kumar Shakya, Ayushman Ramola, Akhilesh Kandwal,
    and Vivek Chamoli*

MIDS: Metaheuristic Based Intrusion Detection System for Cloud
Using k-NN and MGWO.   411
    Jitendra Kumar Seth and Satish Chandra

An Improved RDH Model for Medical Images with a Novel EPR
Embedding Technique.   421
    Jayanta Mondal, Debabala Swain, and Devee Darshani Panda

Machine Learning Based Adaptive Framework for Logistic Planning
in Industry 4.0   431
    *Krista Chaudhary, Mayank Singh, Sandhya Tarar, D. K. Chauhan,
    and Viranjay M. Srivastava*

An Analysis of Key Challenges for Adopting the Cloud Computing
in Indian Education Sector   439
    Mayank Singh and Viranjay M. Srivastava

Texture Image Retrieval Based on Block Level Directional Local Extrema
Patterns Using Tetrolet Transform.   449
    Ghanshyam Raghuwanshi and Vipin Tyagi

Development of Transformer-Less Inverter System
for Photovoltaic Application.   461
    Shamkumar B. Chavan, Umesh A. Kshirsagar, and Mahesh S. Chavan

English Text to Speech Synthesizer Using Concatenation Technique   471
    Sai Sawant and Mangesh Deshpande

Text Translation from Hindi to English   481
 Ira Natu, Sahasra Iyer, Anagha Kulkarni, Kajol Patil, and Pooja Patil

Optical Character Recognition (OCR) of Marathi Printed Documents Using
Statistical Approach.   489
 Pritish Mahendra Vibhute and Mangesh Sudhir Deshpande

Multi View Human Action Recognition Using HODD.   499
 Siddharth Bhorge and Deepak Bedase

Segmental Analysis of Speech Signal for Robust Speaker
Recognition System.   509
 Rupali V. Pawar, R. M. Jalnekar, and J. S. Chitode

Multimicrophone Based Speech Dereverberation.   520
 Seema Vitthal Arote and Mangesh Sudhir Deshpande

Modeling Nonlinear Dynamic Textures Using Isomap with GPU   530
 Premanand Ghadekar

Exploration of Apache Hadoop Techniques: Mapreduce and Hive
for Big Data.   543
 Poonam Rana, Vineet Sharma, and P. K. Gupta

Author Index   553

Unsupervised Time Series Data Analysis for Error Pattern Extraction for Predictive Maintenance

Vidya Ravi[(✉)] and Ravindra Patil

Philips Research, Bangalore, India
{vidya.ravi, patil.ravindra}@philips.com

Abstract. With large amount of machine log data at our disposal, predictive maintenance has come into play in many avenues. A key component in predictive modelling is to identify and track error patterns that are indicative of underlying component failure. Subject matter experts (SME) or system experts who know internals of the said component and its interaction with overall system usually define the error patterns. However, this opinion is biased and prone to human error. Subjectivity in defining error patterns can result in omission of certain error patterns. Here, we introduce an approach to identify probable error patterns in an unsupervised manner on MR machine log data, which allows us to automate this task with high efficiency and without need of subject matter expert and bias. This automation also reduces the time taken to analyse large volumes of log data and create meaningful machine learning models for predicting possible failure of components.

Keywords: Time series · Error pattern · Unsupervised pattern extraction
Predictive maintenance

1 Introduction

Predictive maintenance is the key to resolving issues that affect machine behavior and is a potential solution to reduce system downtime and maintain its performance. Understanding error logs and extracting meaningful information is a very active area with many methods to tackle different kinds of logs [5]. There are many industries which are adopting this principle such as automotive industry [1], telecommunication sector [3], and healthcare industry [2, 6] to name a few. As the large systems in these industries are made up of many subcomponents that need to be maintained in good order, component level failure prediction has become the norm [7]. In order to successfully predict component failures; errors and error patterns need to be identified and models need to be built that can trigger alerts before the failure events occur.

In the context of predictive maintenance of large commercial machines with many sub components, there is a need to identify possible system failure and indicate the component that needs correction. In order to achieve this, quite often, expertise in understanding the system functions are of paramount importance. The traditional approach in predictive maintenance is depicted in Fig. 1. Once the system experts

© Springer Nature Singapore Pte Ltd. 2018
M. Singh et al. (Eds.): ICACDS 2018, CCIS 906, pp. 1–10, 2018.
https://doi.org/10.1007/978-981-13-1813-9_1

indicate the errors to identify and the corresponding issues, a model can be created and deployed [2]. However, the current approach has following drawbacks.

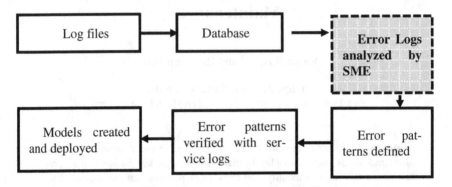

Fig. 1. Block diagram of traditional approach

The need of system expert is often necessary to consult before a model can be created and executed, hence availability of system experts for legacy systems is difficult. There are also differences in the machine configurations across geographies with systems customized with certain settings. Involving experts to cover these differences and working across geographies is an added challenge.

The second issue is an inherent bias present with individual experts in defining the occurrence of these error patterns. Due to this bias, often certain error patterns go unnoticed which might be crucial to predict the failure of components.

The third issue being the sheer time it might take to comb through the log files manually to identify error occurrences and verify if their presence truly is indicative of a component failure. The time necessary for this can be in the order of days.

In this paper, an approach is proposed to automatically detect error patterns in an unsupervised manner. This approach is depicted in Fig. 2. Further, a system expert can validate this, and a decision can be made if the error pattern found can be exploited in creating a component failure prediction model [2]. This method has proved to be efficient in identifying error patterns that recur across different machines of the same type across geographies, without the aid of system experts and also reduces the time for building and deployment of the models. It has also resulted in more models being created with higher quality and higher predictive ability. The rest of the paper is organized as follows: Sect. 2 contains the various steps of the algorithm, Sect. 3 contains the results and points of discussion while Sect. 4 concludes the paper.

2 Experimental and Computational Details

The approach adopted to arrive at the error patterns that determine the creation of predictive models is depicted in the flow chart depicted in Fig. 3.

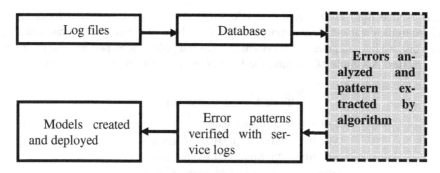

Fig. 2. Block diagram of proposed approach

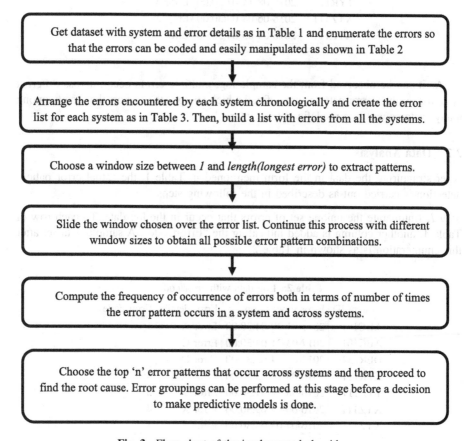

Fig. 3. Flow chart of the implemented algorithm

2.1 Data Aggregation

The source of data for the current experiment was obtained from the connected MR systems of Philips, where in every day operational log files from each of the systems are converted from unstructured data into structured using Extract, Transform, Load and fed to the database. Furthermore, queries were built to extract the relevant data. In this work, we have targeted a component that has multiple subcomponents and multiple error modes. A sample of the machine log that was used is as shown in Table 1.

Table 1. Sample error data

System ID	Error time stamp	Error details
ABC101	2017-01-20 04:30:00	Error A
ABC101	2017-03-21 04:30:00	Error C
DER234	2017-04-14 03:30:00	Error D
TYR111	2016-08-16 03:30:00	Error X
TYR111	2016-08-14 07:30:00	Error Y
XYZ111	2016-06-04 09:30:00	Error X
XYZ111	2016-04-03 04:30:00	Error A

As it can be observed from the sample log, multiple errors occur, across different systems. Further, error patterns are defined which comprises of errors that occur among many systems within a predefined time interval.

2.2   Data Analysis

After structuring the data in the form mentioned in Table 1, the actual error pattern detection is carried out as described in the following steps:

Step 1. Enumerate the unique set of errors that occur in the log data. To each row of Table 1, another column is added indicating the "ErrorCode". A sample data set after this enumeration is as shown in Table 2.

Table 2. Log data with error codes

System ID	Error time stamp	Error details	Error code
ABC101	2017-01-20 04:30:00	Error A	1
ABC101	2017-03-21 04:30:00	Error C	2
DER234	2017-04-14 03:30:00	Error D	3
TYR111	2016-08-16 03:30:00	Error X	4
TYR111	2016-08-14 07:30:00	Error Y	5
XYZ111	2016-06-04 09:30:00	Error X	4
XYZ111	2016-04-03 04:30:00	Error A	1

Step 2. Next step is to aggregate the data chronologically so that for each system the sequence of occurrence of errors becomes available as a single field. An aggregation of the sample data set of Table 2 is shown in Table 3.

Table 3. Error code aggregation

System ID	Pattern code
ABC101	12
DER234	3
TYR111	54
XYZ111	514
PYU213	1

A more realistic aggregation comprises of many more error codes and is much longer if the error logs used for the analysis comprises of many months of data. A sample snippet of the kind of data used in this paper is as shown in Table 4.

Table 4. Error code aggregation-2

System ID	Pattern code
ABC101	1234355111233545141233551142335542113355
DER234	33333333333333333333
TYR111	78491011121314156161718192022115816422010
XYZ111	1335151135531133553355511113553
PYU213	1616161616161616161616161616161616161616

Step 3. To extract all the possible combination of errors that might occur in the component considered of the system, a moving window method is adopted. The length of the window determines the number of errors that needs to be grouped that will indicate a pattern. For example, if we consider the length of the group of errors to be 5, then for the case with system ID ABC101 where the errors are: E: 1234355111233545141233551142335542113355, the following list of patterns are extracted (Table 5).

Table 5. Patterns for a given list of errors

Patterns	Pattern code
P1	12343
P2	23435
P3	34355
P4	43551
P5	35511
…	…

In the same manner, exhaustive lists of errors in groups of five are found across all the systems. The length of the group of errors to be found is an iterative process. Once, these error patterns are found for all the systems, there might be cases where multiple systems have the same set of errors. Hence to obtain unique errors patterns duplicates on the exhaustive list can be removed.

Step 4. With the distinct patterns in place, the next step adopted was to identify the occurrence of each of these patterns across all the systems considered in our input log data. To perform this, an iterative procedure is employed wherein each pattern is compared to the error listed by all the systems. The start and end positions of the error pattern in the error list is recorded. This in turn helps in extracting unique data points. Consider the following example: Pattern (P) is '12335' and we need to identify the systems this occurs in and the number of times it occurs. If the error list upon which this search happens is as before:

E: 12343551112335451412335511142335542113355, then we can identify the locations 'P' occurs in 'E'. P in E: 1234355111**12335**4514**12335**51142335542113355

The Brute-force pseudo code for the above implementation is as follows:

```
do
if (text letter == pattern letter)
    compare next letter of pattern to next
    letter of text
else
    move pattern down text by one letter
while (entire pattern found or end of text)
```

However, the above brute force approach was optimized using the Rabin-Karp algorithm [4] which is a string searching algorithm that uses hashing to find patterns in strings. This optimization technique is implemented to reduce the time complexity of the approach. Similar optimization techniques can be used to reduce the complexity and increase the performance of the algorithm based on the nature of error patterns that are being handled. From the above analysis, we know that in one system, the pattern occurs twice in the course of a specified duration. Like wise, the same pattern is searched across all the systems and the occurrences are mapped to following metrics: number of times the error occurs and the number of systems in which it occurs.

Step 5. If we denote the number of error patterns by 'i', and the number of error lists by 'n', then the frequency of occurrence of error patterns (EP) is denoted by the following equation. The frequency of occurrence of errors is mapped as shown in Table 6.

$$\text{Freqeuncy}(i) = \sum_{k=1}^{n} \text{EP}(i)_k \tag{1}$$

Subsequently, the frequency of occurrence of an error is computed across systems and we considered the top 'n' errors based on the occurrences and the model to be constructed.

Table 6. Error pattern frequency

Error pattern	Frequency
12343	15
23435	12
34355	10
43551	9
12335	9

3 Discussion

Magnetic Resonance Imaging systems are the focus of this work. Data has been col-lected from around 3000 systems and over a period of 3 years. The log data thus collected has been parsed and accumulated in a database, which is queried to form the input data set for this work. Here, it is important to note that the log data that has been queried must be exhaustive enough to extract patterns, also it must be cohesive enough for the error patterns to make sense. Hence, it has to be ensured that related sub-components are being considered and not unrelated parts of the system. If unrelated parts of the system are considered in the logs, then the error patterns will not be effective in helping us identify root causes and perform predictive maintenance.

The error patterns shown as an example in the previous section are of a fixed length. However, it is not necessary to use a fixed length. The length parameter can be iteratively incremented to a known value if we are aware of the distinct error modes the component of interest has, or we can set the upper limit of the length to the longest length of the error list we have in our input data. Thus encompassing all possible error combinations of all possible lengths.

With all possible combinations obtained, the important decision that needs to be taken is which of the error patterns are of interest to us. This depends on two metrics:

- The number of times this particular error patterns repeats in a system before a fault is noticed
- The number of times this error pattern manifests among multiple systems in the dataset that is under consideration.

Both of the above measures lead us to choosing the most indicative error pattern. Among the above two metrics, the first priority is assigned to the second metric which decides if this error pattern is common and can be used as a distinguishing feature while building predictive models. The first metric is also important as it allows us to remove those patterns, which occur multiple times in one system, but fail to occur in other systems. This gives us a potential indication of a fault in a particular system but not a generic fault behavior across systems.

Once the error patterns that most commonly manifest across multiple systems are detected, then using their frequency of occurrence, the top 'p' errors can be picked up and further validation can be performed on them. The actual value of 'p' can be set by adopting some rules depending on the criticality of the subcomponents being analyzed.

For example, using the following rule, we can pick out all the error patterns whose frequency is more than a set threshold (th).

$$Select\ EP(i)\ if\ Frequency(EP(i)) > th \tag{2}$$

It has been observed that in some cases there is a strict need for errors to occur in a particular sequence for a fault to be detected, but in other cases, the errors themselves are indicators and not their order of occurrence. For example, consider the error sequence e1: 35511 and another error sequence e2: 15153. Both the sequences contain the same errors but they occur in a different order. By using some prior knowledge about the component or after consultation with subject expert, it is known that the presence of errors 1, 3, 5 indicates that a component has some fault. In such scenarios, we need to be able to combine error patterns that are similar as permutation ambiguity is of no consequence. This assumption has in fact been validated for the use case that we implemented. So, a grouping technique can be added as a last step and similar error patterns can be combined together.

To perform the grouping of error patterns, one of the most effective ways is to compute the hamming distance between pairs of error patterns that have been extracted. Hamming distance provides us the number of positions that the two patterns differ in. For example, 1234 and 1235 differ in just 1 location, but 1234 and 1243 differ in 2 locations. Hence, we can easily see that by placing an appropriate threshold on the hamming distance that is acceptable to us, we can group errors together. Let A and B denote vectors containing error patterns that need to be tested for grouping.

$$A = [a_1, a_2, a_3, \ldots, a_n], \quad B = [b_1, b_2, b_3, \ldots, b_n] \tag{3}$$

For every $b \in B$ the following minimum hamming distance is computed where

$$min\{\forall x_y \in A : hamming\_dist(x_y, b)\} \tag{4}$$

An obvious point to be noted is that while hamming distance is perfectly well suited to identify patterns that need to occur in a particular order, it is of little use if it has to detect the presence of certain errors regardless of its position of occurrence in the pattern. For example, if we need to group 1234 and 2143, into a single group, hamming distance will not help as the result of computing hamming distance will be 4, which is the length of the error pattern itself. This value indicates total dissimilarity, which is not the intended objective. In order to group error patterns for this purpose, we can use other techniques depending on the need of the predictive model to be created. For instance, if the intent is to find errors where their order does not matter but only their presence matters, then cosine similarity is a good candidate. Cosine similarity for two vectors A and B as denoted in Eq. (5) is defined as

$$cosine\ similarity = \frac{\sum_{i=1}^{n} a_i b_i}{\sqrt{\sum_{i=1}^{n} a_i^2}\sqrt{\sum_{i=1}^{n} b_i^2}} \tag{5}$$

Cosine similarity has values ranging from −1 to 1 where −1 indicates complete dissimilarity and 1 indicates identical vectors. Let us consider a case where we are interested in grouping errors 1234 and 2314 in the same group. This cannot be done using hamming distance as Hamming_dist (1234, 2314) = 3, which will be rejected immediately by any set threshold for similarity. But if cosine measure were to be computed, the result would be Cosine_similarity (1234, 2314) = 0.9. As cosine similarity for identical data is 1, a score of 0.9 indicates high correlation between the error patterns which is the intent.

Simple clustering techniques will enable us to find clusters of similar error patterns which in turn will lead us to a single root cause. Further, this root cause can then be addressed using predictive models.

Results. To validate the error patterns that were extracted by this method, we used the log data of a particular component of the system, which contained other related sub components. Error patterns of all possible length can be found, but for the system that this algorithm was deployed on worked best with error groups of size 3, 4 and 5. Out of entire, space of possible error patterns that were computed, we extracted the top five most frequently occurring error patterns across different machines. The top 10 errors that we observed are shown in Table 7.

Table 7. Observed error pattern frequency

Error pattern	Frequency (# of machines)
1111	16
11111	15
3333	13
13355	10
3355	10
11335	9
33333	8
3551	7
33551	6
5555	6

Here we had considered error pattern to be of two different lengths – a set of 4 errors and a set of 5 errors. From these, we can observe that error 1 occurred in 16 distinct machines in sets of 4 and in 15 different machines in sets of 5. When we looked up these systems, it was found that in 13 of the 16 systems service work orders related to the component resulted in actual incident. Similarly, we grouped errors 11335, 33551 and 3551 into a single group as here order of errors was not important. For these two sets of errors, models were created and an alert was set up to indicate probable failure of the component.

We then looked into the service records for these systems to check if the presence of these error patterns in a time window of 30 days resulted in any issues being raised. We were able to determine that the presence of the top 5 error patterns resulted in system faults that were attended to by service engineers and also that using these patterns, a predictive model could be created and alerts could be raised to prevent unplanned downtime of the system. We were able to identify multiple error patterns that were related to different subsystems of this component and hence multiple failure modes could be addressed by creating suitable predictive models.

4   Conclusions

In this paper we have addressed three issues that are inherent in the process of developing models for predictive maintenance from error logs. First is to automate the process of extracting the possible error patterns that occur in a significant number of systems. Secondly, by doing this, we reduce the chance of missing any crucial information in the error pattern and a comprehensive search is done and is not subject to human bias. Thirdly, this is a time efficient implementation that has resulted in successfully developing models that have helped reduce system downtime by allowing planned maintenance of systems. This is a generic approach on how to automate log extraction for a given environment that has been shown using MR systems as a case study.

References

1. Simoncicova, V., Hrcka, L., Spendla, L., Tanuska, P., Vazan, P.: Pattern recognition for predictive analysis in automotive industry. In: Silhavy, R., Senkerik, R., Kominkova Oplatkova, Z., Prokopova, Z., Silhavy, P. (eds.) CSOC 2017. AISC, vol. 574, pp. 311–318. Springer, Cham (2017). https://doi.org/10.1007/978-3-319-57264-2_32
2. Sipos, R., Fradkin, D., Moerchen, F., Wang, Z.: Log-based predictive maintenance. In: Proceedings of the 20th ACM SIGKDD International Conference on Knowledge Discovery and Data Mining, pp. 1867–1876. ACM (2014)
3. Fan, X., Wang, F., Liu, J.: Boosting service availability for base stations of cellular networks by event-driven battery profiling. ACM SIGMETRICS Perform. Eval. Rev. 44(2), 88–93 (2016)
4. Rabin-Karp Algorithm: Brilliant.org. https://brilliant.org/wiki/rabin-karp-algorithm/. Accessed 12:17, 22 Aug 2017
5. Aharon, M., Barash, G., Cohen, I., Mordechai, E.: One graph is worth a thousand logs: uncovering hidden structures in massive system event logs. In: Buntine, W., Grobelnik, M., Mladenić, D., Shawe-Taylor, J. (eds.) ECML PKDD 2009. LNCS, vol. 5781, pp. 227–243. Springer, Heidelberg (2009). https://doi.org/10.1007/978-3-642-04180-8_32
6. Patil, R.B., Patil, M.A., Ravi, V., Naik, S.: Predictive modeling for corrective maintenance of imaging devices from machine logs. In: 2017 39th Annual International Conference of the IEEE Engineering in Medicine and Biology Society, EMBC, Jeju, Korea (2017)
7. Zheng, Z., Lan, Z., Park, B.H., Geist, A.: System log pre-processing to improve failure prediction. In: 2009 IEEE/IFIP International Conference on Dependable Systems & Networks, Lisbon, pp. 572–577 (2009)

Glacier Terminus Position Monitoring and Modelling Using Remote Sensing Data

Rahul Nijhawan[1] and Kanupriya Jain[2(✉)]

[1] Indian Institute of Technology Roorkee, Roorkee 247667, India
[2] Computer Science Engineering, Graphic Era University,
Dehradun 248002, India
kanupriya.kj.96su@gmail.com

Abstract. This study basically deals with the identification of glacier terminus position. The data used include Toposheets, Landsat TM, MSS, ETM+ and OLI/TIRS sensors. Firstly, converts the Landsat DN images are converted into Reflectance images using formulae from Landsat Handbook. The formulae were implemented using Raster calculator following the ARC GIS 10.2 software. Secondly, the NDVI and NDWI images were created and used for the identification of glacier terminus positions for a period 1990–2012 for a glacier in Alaknanda basin, while for the glacier in Indus basin an analysis was made for the period 1963–2013. Glacier terminus is considered as the starting point of the river from it. Further, the altitude of snout position was marked, and elevation value was obtained using Cartosat DEM. In addition, the retreat rate of glaciers was determined per year. A linear regression model was derived for the altitude position of glacier terminus, which gave a good value of coefficient of determination. A comparison was made on the predicted value of 2013, altitude position from ANN and linear regression model. It was observed that the ANN predicted results with a better accuracy. Further analysis was made on future affect of such a glacier retreat on cold water habitat, on crop irrigation and on the fisheries.

Keywords: Glacier · Terminus · Snout · Outburst · Flood · Moraines
Glacier retreat · Global warming · Climate change · Thematic Mapper (TM)
Enhanced Thematic Mapper Plus (ETM+) · Operational Land Imager (OLI)
Thermal Infra-Red Scanner (TIRS)
Normalized Difference Vegetation Index (NDVI)
Normalized Difference Water Index (NDWI) · Digital Elevation Model (DEM)
The Artificial Neural Network (ANN)

1 Introduction

Glaciers are a way to demonstrate the changes in the climate [1]. The influence of climate recast on glaciers of world has been a topic of active concern in recent times [2]. Recasting in the huge natural balance also signifies the redesigning in the clamorous conditions. The variations in the situation of muzzle over the particular time span

© Springer Nature Singapore Pte Ltd. 2018
M. Singh et al. (Eds.): ICACDS 2018, CCIS 906, pp. 11–23, 2018.
https://doi.org/10.1007/978-981-13-1813-9_2

indicate the influence on Glacier due to reshape in the climatic and atmospheric indisposition. The profane recasting in huge natural balance of the Glacier is being crooked as well [3]. For evaluating the corporeal variation with the atmospheric change, continuous monitoring of Glacier is the necessitate demand. Several of Himalaya glaciers are retreating. Their remote access brings remote sensing into picture. Global warming and clamorous change is the two major anchors for Glacier recession studies in the higher altitudes of the Indian Himalaya [4]. This study is an initiative or an attempt to witness the variations in the snout altitude. The recoil rates were computed for different time periods using satellite images.

Glaciers of the Himalaya are one of the largest ice deposits outside the polar region, covering an area of 35,110 km^2 with total ice reserves as one of the largest 3,734.5 km^3 [5]. As an effect to increase in global warming, the temperature of Himalaya is increasing rapidly. Increase in the temperature is also causing the increase in the amount of melt in glaciers, which further would increase the water flow in river temporarily. Current studies about the Himalayan Glaciers by remote sensor observatory (ground-based and satellite-based observations), stipulate the clamorous or climate change which has accelerated the momentum of the unfreezing of the higher altitudes of the Himalayan Glaciers [6]. This has resulted in decreased ice/snow mass balance. It will decrease the water flow in the river. Raise in the warmth temperature has reduced the tenacity in form of snow [7]. The accumulation of the snow and the ice has reduced. This would reduce the volume of the water and the speed by which the Glaciers are withdrawing in the Himalaya region [8]. The resulting of this fact has lead the Glaciers over the high altitudes of the Himalaya are at a considerable risk. This fact could even lead to the disappearing of the Himalayan prosperity in the future. This enhances the possibilities of threatening out-bursting flood which can affect the large mass of population, which can further damage the economic infrastructure, social infrastructure, glory and assets of the Himalayan belt. The situation in downstream area would be adverse by the impact on the climatic and environmental factors in the Himalayan region.

2 Study Area and Data Used

The study is performed in the two areas; the Alaknanda basin and the Indus basin, over the Himalayan range, as shown in Fig. 1. Figure 2 represents the glacier terminus position in the Alaknanda basin, while Fig. 3 represents that in the Indus basin. Data was collected free from Cloud for this study. The images of the Landsat are used for snout demarcation are given in Table 1.

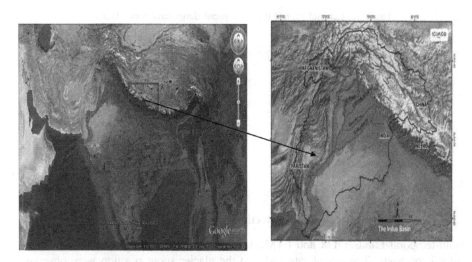

Fig. 1. Landsat satellite imagery of study area Indus basin (Source, International Centre for Integrated Mountain Development (ICIMOD))

Fig. 2. Glacier terminus represented in Google Earth

Fig. 3. Glacier terminus represented in Google Earth

Table 1. Landsat scenes used for snout demarcation of glacier

S. no.	Year of pass	Landsat sensor	Basin
1.	1990, 2002, 2005, 2007, 2009 and 2012	Landsat TM	Alaknanda
2.	1998 and 2000	Landsat ETM+	
3.	1963	Toposheets	Indus
4.	1976, 1990, 2009, 2011	Landsat TM	
5.	1999 and 2001	Landsat ETM+	
6.	2013	Landsat 8	

3   Methodology

3.1   Glacier Terminus Position Detection

Multi-temporal Landsat TM and ETM+ images were used along with the Survey of India Toposheets. The retreat rate and also the glacier snout position were observed over a period of 22 years (1990–2012) in Alaknanda basin and for a period of 50 years in Indus basin (1963–2013). For year 1963, the glacial expansion was available from the survey of India, Dehardun. Remote sensing images were used for snout demarcation. Basically, images prior to winters were used for glacier retreat and demarcating the snout. As the glaciers contain some amount of debris so the snout position was considered same as the point of the origin of the river water. So for its identification, both NDVI (Normalized Difference Vegetation Index) and NDWI (Normalized difference water Index) were computed and used. These images gave a clear interpretation of snout position in different years. Before calculating NDVI and NDWI images, the Landsat DN images were converted into reflectance images using formulae from Landsat Handbook [9]. The formulae were computed using Raster Calculator in Arc GIS 9.3 Software. Formulae for Landsat 5 (Conversion to radiance using spectral radiance scaling method):

The formula used in this process is:

$$L\lambda = \left(\frac{LMAX\lambda - LMIN\lambda}{QCALMAX - QCALMIN} \right) * (QCAL - QCALMIN) + LMIN$$

Where:

$L\lambda$ is the cell value as radiance
QCAL = Digital Number
$LMIN\lambda$ = Spectral Radiance Scales to QCALMIN
$LMAX\lambda$ = Spectral Radiance Scales to QCALMAX
QCALMIN = the quantized calibrated pixel value which is minimum (typically = 1)
QCALMAX = the quantized calibrated pixel value which is maximum (typically = 255).

Formulae to Covert Radiance to TOA (Top of Atmosphere) Reflectance

$$P\lambda = \left(\pi * L\lambda * d^2\right)/\left(ESUN\lambda * \cos(\theta s)\right)$$

Where:

$\rho\lambda$ = Unitless Planetary Reflectance
$L\lambda$ = Spectral Radiance (from earlier step)
d = Earth-Sun distance in astronomical units
$ESUN\lambda$ = Mean Solar Exo-atmospheric Irradiances
Θs = Solar Zenith Angle.

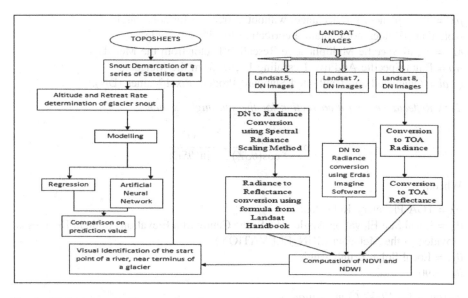

Fig. 4. Methodology for Demarcation of snout position of glacier in Alaknanda and Indus basin

Formulae for Landsat 8

Conversion to TOA (Top of Atmosphere) Radiance
The band data of Operational Land Imager (OLI) and Thermal Infrared sensor (TIRS) can be changed or converted to TOA (Top of Atmosphere) Spectral Radiance by using the Radiance rescaling factors provided in the metadata file:

$$L\lambda = ML * Qcal + AL$$

Where:

$L\lambda$ = Spectral Radiance for TOA
ML = Band-Specific Multiplicative Rescaling factor from the metadata

AL = Band-Specific Additive Rescaling factor from the metadata
$Qcal$ = Quantized and Calibrated Standard Product Pixel Values (DN).

Conversion to TOA (Top of Atmosphere) Reflectance
Band data by OLI can also be converted to TOA planetary reflectance using reflectance rescaling coefficients provided in the product MTL file (metadata file). To convert DN values to TOA reflectance for OLI data as follows, the given below equation is used:

$$\rho\lambda' = M\rho * Qcal + A\rho$$

Where:

$\rho\lambda'$ = TOA planetary reflectance, without correction for solar angle.
Note that $\rho\lambda'$ does not contain a correction for the sun angle.
$M\rho$ = Band-Specific Multiplicative Rescaling Factor from the Metadata
$A\rho$ = Band-Specific Additive Rescaling Factor from the Metadata
$Qcal$ = Quantized and Calibrated Standard Product Pixel Values (DN).

TOA Reflectance with a correction for the sun angle is then:

$$\rho\lambda = \frac{\rho\lambda'}{\cos(\theta SZ)} = \frac{\rho\lambda'}{\sin(\theta SE)}$$

Where:

$\rho\lambda$ = TOA Planetary Reflectance
θ_{se} = Local Sun Elevation Angle. The Scene Centre Sun Elevation Angle in Degrees is provided in the Metadata (SUN_ELEVATION)
θ_{SZ} = Local Solar Zenith Angle
$\theta_{SZ} = 90° - \theta_{SE}$.

Formula for NDVI Computation is:

$$NDVI = \frac{NIR - RED}{NIR + RED}$$

NDVI of Landsat Images was used as water absorbs the radiations in NIR band. Hence these water pixels appear darker and could be easily identified. NDWI was computed by first converting the DN values into reflectance of the image. Then applying the formula.

$$NDWI = \frac{Green - NIR}{Green + NIR}$$

This index is used as it maximizes the water's reflectance by the green wavelength, minimizes the NIR smutty reflectance by the water characteristics and takes the benefit of NIR's high reflectance by the soil features. Conclusion of this process have positive results on the water features and this enhanced the soil which usually has negative values or zero values that had been before suppressed are now in the figure [10].

3.2 Glacier Terminus Position Monitoring and Modelling

Linear regression analysis is defined as the method to determine the relationship between the variables. There are two types of regression relations; (1) Linear and Non linear and (2) Simple and Multiple. In this study, linear regression was carried out. Linear relation finds out whether the relationship between the variables is linear or not.

Artificial Neural Network (ANN) is defined as a biological computational model containing several single units, neurons and weights which represents the neural structure. They process the information, hence called the processing elements. Basically, the processing elements constitute the weighted inputs, transfer function and one output. Even a single neuron is capable to perform some information processing functions. But when the neurons are connected together the whole system becomes very powerful. Generally, ANNs have a few hundred to thousands of processing elements. ANNs have the capability to process large amount of data. They are capable of giving the results which are very accurate. There are several designs of neural network based on the transfer functions, the learning rule and the connection formula.

Basically the ANN is designed, of which the building component is artificial neuron. The inputs are multiplied with the weights and are summed and further inputted to the transfer function, in order to produce the output for that particular neuron. Figure 5 represents the design of ANN.

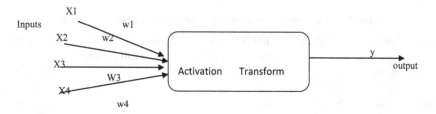

Fig. 5. Working of Artificial Neural Network

This study performs the regression modelling on the series of observed values of altitudes (from Cartosat DEM) corresponding to the year. The model predicted the pattern of increase in the altitude of snout position. An ANN was designed for the same in which the input parameters used were aspect, slope and elevation values. The accuracies of the predicted values were compared by using regression and ANN model. The altitude values for the year 2013 were already observed from the discussed methodology. Here, we have used the regression equation to compute the altitude of year 2013. The same was done by ANN. For this, we first trained ANN for a set of input and output values till year 2011, and then predicted the value for year 2013. Figure 4 represents the methodology.

4   Results and Conclusions

It was observed that the changes in altitude and retreat of snout position in glacier situated in Alaknanda basin and Indus basin follow a linear path. The results are shown in Tables 2 and 3 respectively. Shift in glacier snout position is shown in Figs. 6 and 7 respectively. On performing linear regression analysis, it was observed that the value of regression coefficient of determination (R^2) for altitude of snout position for Alaknanda basin is 0.907 and that for Indus basin is 0.905. The equation obtained after computing the linear regression analysis for Alaknanda basin and Indus basin are (1) and (2) respectively.

$$y = 5.973 * x - 8086 \tag{1}$$

$$y = 2.181 * x - 771.0 \tag{2}$$

The results, after applying NDVI and NDWI for glacier in Alaknanda basin (Figs. 8 and 10) and Indus basin (Figs. 9 and 11) are computed. The glacier terminus position could easily be identified in both the images. This study also computes the glacier retreat rate of the area, as shown in Figs. 12 and 13. The bar graph and results of linear regression model are shown in Figs. 14, 15, 16 and 17 respectively.

Table 2. Glacier snout positions and retreat rate in Alaknanda basin

Year	Latitude	Longitude	Altitude (m)	Rate of retreating (m/y), b/w previous and current reading	Reference
1990	30°46' 42.11"	79°24' 50.26"	3805	-	Landsat TM
1998	30°46' 34.42"	79°24' 44.48"	3859	23.5	Landsat ETM+
2000	30°46' 28.74"	79°24' 42.07"	3861	34	Landsat ETM+
2002	30°46' 23.45"	79°24' 39.49"	3867	32.98	Landsat TM
2005	30°46' 19.15"	79°24' 37.76"	3873	26.75	Landsat TM
2007	30°46' 15.59"	79°24' 36.46"	3885	28.5	Landsat TM
2009	30°46' 12.57"	79°24' 33.30"	3934	31.1	Landsat TM
2012	30°46' 09.46"	79°24' 30.23"	3942	35.2	Landsat TM

Table 3. Glacier snout positions and retreat rate in Indus basin

Year	Latitude	Longitude	Altitude (m)	Rate of retreating (m/y), b/w previous and current reading	Reference
1963	31°03′ 08.25″	79°36′ 47.83″	5069	–	Toposheet
1976	31°04′ 06.95″	79°36′ 48.36″	5074	22.55	Landsat MSS
1990	31°04′ 00.97″	79°36′ 48.34″	5107	23.71	Landsat TM
1999	31°03′ 58.39″	79°36′ 48.60″	5120	26.95	Landsat ETM+
2001	31°03′ 53.53″	79°36′ 49.22″	5129	29	Landsat ETM+
2009	31°03′ 43.29″	79°36′ 49.64″	5149	18.1	Landsat TM
2011	31°03′ 35.57″	79°36′ 49.92″	5162	28.5	Landsat TM
2013	31°03′ 27.68″	79°36′ 50.92″	5186	30.5	Landsat 8

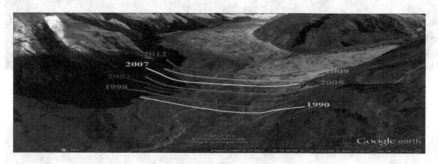

Fig. 6. Google earth image representing shift in position of glacier snout in Alaknanda basin

Fig. 7. Google earth image representing shift in position of glacier snout in Indus basin

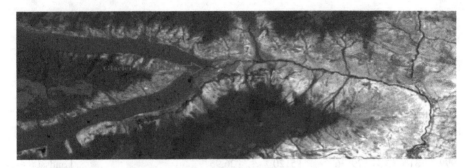

Fig. 8. NDVI image representing Glacier Terminus position of Alaknanda basin

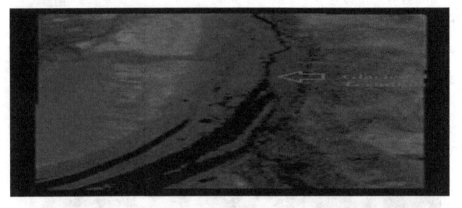

Fig. 9. NDVI image representing Glacier Terminus position of Indus basin

Fig. 10. Glacier Terminus identification using NDWI of Alaknanda basin

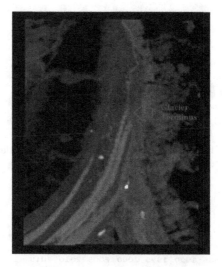

Fig. 11. Glacier Terminus identification using NDWI of Indus basin

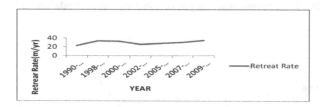

Fig. 12. Retreat rates for the glacier in Alaknanda basin

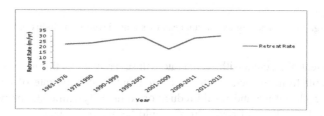

Fig. 13. Retreat rates for the glacier in Indus basin

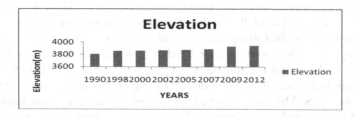

Fig. 14. Changes in elevation of snout position of Alaknanda basin

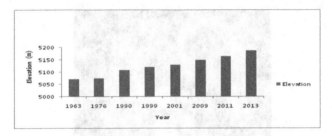

Fig. 15. Changes in elevation of snout position of Indus basin

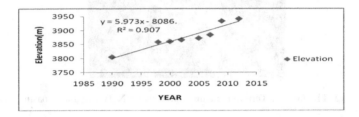

Fig. 16. Linear regression analysis of snout elevation of Alaknanda basin

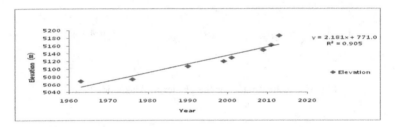

Fig. 17. Linear regression analysis of snout elevation of Indus basin

Due to retreat of glaciers with such a rate will severely affect the areas dependent on the water runoff from glaciers in the summer months. As this rate of retreat would remove off the glacial ice and would reduce or completely eliminate the runoff. With this reduction the ability to irrigate crops would be greatly affected.

Also the summer streams would be reduced which are required to keep dam and reservoir replenished. Some amount of glacier melt water is also used for keeping drinking supplies. Several cold water habitat species depend on glacier water to ensure their survival. Like some of the fresh water species fishes require cold water to reproduce and also for their living. Reduced glacial runoff leads to insufficient stream flow, which prevents their survival. Also, the change in the ocean currents as a result of the increase in the freshwater coming as a result of glacier melt affects the human survival depends. Further, this study compares the prediction value by linear regression model and by ANN. The results showed that the error in the prediction value is less using the ANN approach as compared to linear regression model. ANN predicted the altitude value of 2013 with an error of 2%, while linear regression analyzer predicted it with an error of 5%.

References

1. Paul, F., Kaab, A., et al.: Rapid disintegration of Alpine Glaciers observed with satellite data. Geophys. Res. Lett. **31**(21), L21402 (2004)
2. Syed, T.H., Famiglietti, J.S., Zlotnicki, V., Rodell, M.: Contemporary estimates of Arctic freshwater discharge from GRACE and reanalysis. Geophys. Res. Lett. **34**, L19404 (2007). https://doi.org/10.1029/2007GL031254
3. Elsberg, D.H.: Quantifying the effects of climate and surface change on glacier mass balance. J. Glaciol. **47**(159), 649–658 (2001)
4. Kulkarni, A.V.: Effect of global warming on snow ablation pattern in the Himalayas. Curr. Sci. **83**(2), 120–123 (2002)
5. Jianchu, X., Shrestha, A., Vaidya, R., Eriksson, M., Hewitt, K.: The melting Himalayas: regional challenges and local impacts of climate change on mountain ecosystems and livelihoods, 14 p. ICIMOD Technical Paper, Kathmandu, Nepal (2007)
6. Negi, H.S., Saravana, G., Rout, R., Snehmani, R.: Monitoring of great Himalayan glaciers in Patsio region, India using remote sensing and climatic observations. Curr. Sci. **105**(10), 1383–1392 (2013)
7. Racoviteanu, A.E., Williams, M.W., Barry, R.G.: Optical remote sensing of glacier characteristics: a review with focus on the Himalaya. Sensors **8**, 3355–3383 (2008). https://doi.org/10.3390/s8053355
8. Dyurgerov, M.D., Meier, M.F.: Glaciers and changing earth system: a 2004 snapshot, 117 p. Institute of Arctic and Alpine Research, University of Colorado, Boulder (Colorado) (2005)
9. Landsat handbook. http://landsathandbook.gsfc.nasa.gov/
10. Mcfeeters, S.K.: The use of normalized difference water index (NDWI) in the delineation of open water features. Int. J. Remote Sens. **17**, 1425–1432 (1996)

Multiple Imputation Inference for Missing Values in Distributed Datasets Using Apache Spark

Sathish Kaliamoorthy$^{(\boxtimes)}$ and S. Mary Saira Bhanu

The Department of Computer Science and Engineering, National Institute of
Technology, Tiruchirappalli 620015, Tamil Nadu, India
sathishbourne@gmail.com, msb@nitt.edu

Abstract. Big data is a term that describes the large volume of data, both
structured and unstructured. Due to its huge quantity, big data are stored by
partitioning and distributing into smaller chunks of data in multiple machines for
quick and efficient analysis, because it is not possible for a single machine to
hold all of the big data by itself. However, these datasets are generally
incomplete because it contains many instances of missing values. Missing
values are a serious impediment to data analysis, and Multiple Imputation is a
preferred method for handling missing values. All existing multiple imputation
implementations in statistical software packages are all based on the in-memory
processing of data and are unsuitable if the data is distributed. So there is a need
for handling missing values using multiple imputation if the data is distributed.
The goal of this work is to implement a multiple imputation algorithm for
missing values using fuzzy clustering on a distributed computing system built
with Apache Spark. The results show that the multiple imputation algorithm
outperforms traditional imputation techniques for missing values in a distributed
computing system in terms of imputation accuracy.

Keywords: Apache Spark · Big data · Data pre-processing
Distributed datasets · Fuzzy clustering · Missing values · Multiple imputation

1 Introduction

Today huge amount of data being generated everywhere from various sources. The act
of gathering and storing information for eventual analysis is ages old, but it had never
been based on such a large amount of data, which is there today. But it is not the
amount of data that is important; it is what organizations do with the data that matters.

Big data analytics is the process of examining large and varied data sets, i.e., big
data - to uncover hidden patterns, unknown correlations, market trends, customer
preferences and other useful information that can help organizations make more-
informed business decisions.

© Springer Nature Singapore Pte Ltd. 2018
M. Singh et al. (Eds.): ICACDS 2018, CCIS 906, pp. 24–33, 2018.
https://doi.org/10.1007/978-981-13-1813-9_3

1.1 Missing Values

Data quality is considered important and concerned as big role in Data Analytics and other correlated areas. Missing values are highly undesirable in data mining, machine learning and other information systems [10, 11]. The presence of missing value is the common problem for all type research. Many datasets have a large percentage of missing values.

Missing values directly impacts the big data sets' usefulness in yielding high accuracy while doing big data analytics [1, 10]. It also impacts classifiers when used for training in supervised machine learning and other unsupervised machine learning algorithms like clustering.

1.2 Imputation

There are several methods for handling missing data [4, 5, 10]. One of the methods to handle missing values is to ignore cases with missing values. But this method may introduce bias or affect the representativeness of the results. Imputation of missing values is another approach which involves the replacement of missing value with some value that has been estimated based on the available information in the dataset [3, 10]. Imputation is seen as a way to avoid pitfalls involved with missing data ignoring techniques because missing data can create problems for analyzing data. The preferred method for doing imputation of missing values is multiple imputation.

1.3 Apache Spark

A wide variety of computing frameworks have been developed for analyzing Big Data. One of the most used frameworks being Hadoop MapReduce. This framework is widely used because of its simplicity, generality, and maturity. However, MapReduce does not perform well for iterative algorithms.

Apache Spark [2, 13] is a distributed computing model and can overcome the drawbacks of MapReduce. Apache Spark can perform up to 100 times faster than Hadoop MapReduce and works well for iterative algorithms. Thus, this paper focuses on the design and implementation of multiple imputation algorithm for distributed datasets based on Apache Spark framework.

The remainder of the paper is organized as follows: Sect. 2 introduces multiple imputation and existing software libraries for multiple imputation procedure. Section 3 presents the proposed methodology to handle missing values when the data is distributed using Apache Spark. The experiment and results are presented in Sect. 4. Section 5 provides the conclusion and future work.

2 Multiple Imputation

To deal with the problem of increased noise due to imputation, multiple imputation methods were developed, and it works by averaging the outcomes across multiple imputed data sets to account for the increased noise problem [3, 7].

2.1 Existing Software Libraries

Multiple imputation [7] is the preferred method for imputing missing values because it decreases the noise due to imputation. Hence many statistical software packages [5, 6, 12] have their multiple imputation implementations for handling missing values. Some of the most common multiple imputation implementations in software packages include:

- **SAS:** SAS/STAT has the Procedure MI. PROC MI implements multiple imputation. However, SAS ends up being the most expensive option because it is proprietary software.
- **IBM SPSS Statistics:** IBM SPSS statistics software has multiple imputation implementations which can be used if missing data is present. Like SAS, IBM SPSS is also proprietary software.
- **R:** R is the Open source counterpart of SAS, which has traditionally been used in academics and research. R supports libraries like "mice" and "mi" that implement multiple imputation procedures.
- **Python:** Python supports many libraries that implement multiple imputations for missing values. Some of them are "SASPy" (used to access SAS via Python), "fancyimpute" and "statsmodel".

All software libraries mentioned above for multiple imputation only supports in-memory processing because they are not built for a distributed environment.

2.2 Multiple Imputation Algorithm for a Distributed Environment

Fuzzy possibilistic c-means clustering algorithm, based on fuzzy c-means clustering, is a single imputation algorithm introduced in [11]. Iterative Fuzzy Clustering (IFC) algorithm is a multiple algorithm also based on fuzzy c-means clustering. IFC introduced in [8], helps to impute missing values in datasets. Both these algorithms, fuzzy c-means clustering (FCM) algorithm is used to cluster the datasets and update the imputed values. In Fuzzy clustering, a data point can belong to multiple clusters with varying degrees of membership. In IFC multiple imputation algorithm, missing values are updated in multiple iterations. Both these imputation algorithms cannot be used when the datasets are distributed or partitioned among multiple machines.

3 Methodology

The goal of the work is to handle missing values for datasets that are partitioned among multiple nodes using multiple imputation and Fig. 1 illustrates the proposed approach with Apache Spark. A modified version of IFC multiple imputation algorithm [8] is used to impute missing values.

Data Frame. A Data Frame is a dataset organized into named columns. Data Frames in Apache Spark supports a wide array data formats [13], and in this proposed work the format of the dataset files are comma separated files (CSV), and it will be used to

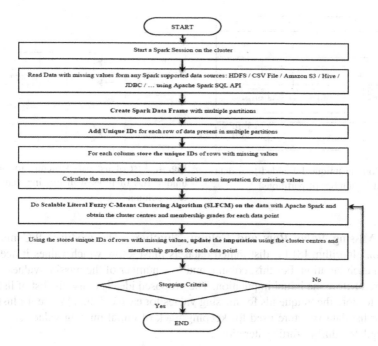

Fig. 1. Proposed methodology

construct the data frame. Figure 2 illustrates the data frame creation process from a Comma-Separated Value (CSV) source data file.

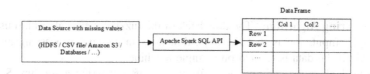

Fig. 2. Creating a Data Frame from a data source using Apache Spark SQL API

Unique IDs. The Distributed IFC for multiple imputation algorithm works by updating the imputed missing value iteratively. For this, there is a need to keep track of rows for each column in data frame where there was a missing value before the initial imputation.

Apache Spark data frame method 'monotonically increasing Id' [13] is used to create a unique ID column to the data frame which will be used to identify each row uniquely. As Fig. 3 illustrates the generated ID is guaranteed to be monotonically increasing and unique, but not consecutive. The unique ID is a 64-bit integer with upper 31-bits has the partition ID and the record number within each partition in the lower 33 bits [13].

Partitions	Data Frame			
		Col 1	Col 2	...	Unique ID
1	Row 1				1
	Row 2				2
	...				...
2	Row k				8589934592
	Row k+1				8589934593
	...				...
...					
p	Row m				1767829211
	Row m+1				1767829212
	...				...

Fig. 3. Column unique ID added to a data frame with p number of partitions

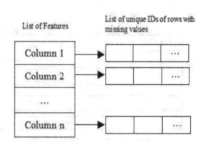

Fig. 4. List of list data structure for storing unique IDs of rows with missing values for each column

Storing Missing Value Row and Column Numbers. The modified IFC multiple imputation algorithm [8] for distributed datasets must know which values it needs to update in each iteration. For this, column and row number of the missing values needs to be stored before the initial imputation. The proposed idea is to use the list of list data structure to store the unique ids for missing values for each column. Figure 4 illustrates the list of list data structure used for keeping track of initial missing values so that, it can be updated during further iterations.

Initial Mean Imputation. Mean imputation is done as the initial imputation of missing values [8].

- For all the columns, mean values are calculated using Pyspark API [13].
- Then all missing values in each column are replaced with their respective mean values.

Fuzzy Clustering Algorithm. The drawback of the fuzzy c-means algorithm used for IFC multiple imputation is that the algorithm does in-memory processing and will execute only if the data is located on a single machine.

So instead of applying in-memory fuzzy c-means clustering algorithm, Scalable Literal Fuzzy c-Means (SLFCM) algorithm [9] a fuzzy based clustering algorithm implemented on Apache Spark has been adopted. As the data is distributed on multiple nodes, for the fuzzy clustering of data SLFCM is used.

For SLFCM on Apache Spark [9], complete data set will be partitioned and are distributed on the worker nodes. Then randomly initialize the cluster centers. In each worker node, do fuzzy clustering and obtain cluster centers and membership degrees for the partition of data present in those worker nodes. Then SLFCM updates the cluster centers on the master node and then again the updated cluster centers will be passed on to the worker nodes to do clustering. This process is repeated until the deviation of current cluster centers from previous cluster centers meets a predefined threshold [8]. Finally, the membership degree and cluster centroid information are obtained.

New Value Estimation and Stopping Criterion. Both new value estimation for missing value and stopping criterion for iterations are adopted from [8]. The new values are estimated as the weighted average of the membership degree and the cluster centers, which is obtained by applying the scalable literal fuzzy c-means (SLFCM) algorithm [9] on complete dataset. Once the new values are estimated, the stored unique IDs information is used to update the missing values.

The algorithm stops when one of the two conditions becomes true:

1. Number of iterations > Maximum number of iterations (or)
2. Average total variation < Specified threshold.

Here average total variation is calculated for imputing missing values in consecutive iterations.

4 Experiment Results

For the experiments, Apache Spark cluster is configured with three nodes with one node as a master, and the other two are worker nodes using Apache Spark version 2.2.0. Experiments are performed on three datasets downloaded from Indian government's Open Government Data (OGD) Platform [14]. Table 1 depicts three datasets that were chosen for the experiment with different attribute data types.

Table 1. Datasets for the experiment

Dataset name	No. of columns	Data types
Economy Indicator 1999–2013	14	– Floating point – Negative values
Annual Rainfall 1901–2015	12	– Floating point
Tourism Statistics of India 2001–2015	15	– Integer values

From each dataset one, three and five percent values were artificially removed at random. Performance analysis is done by comparing imputation accuracy of three imputation algorithms: mean imputation algorithm, imputation using k-means clustering (missing value of a data point is replaced using its cluster center) and the proposed multiple imputation algorithm using distributed iterative fuzzy clustering algorithm. The imputation accuracy was compared with the actual values from the original complete dataset. For experiments done for this work, the assumed number of clusters for all the datasets is considered to be five.

Root Mean Square Error (RMSE): The measure RMSE is used in this experiment to calculate how much the imputation of missing values is far from the actual values in the original dataset. RMSE is calculated as per (1).

$$RMSE_i = \sqrt{\sum_{j=1}^{n_i} \frac{NV_{ij} - AV_{ij}}{n_i}} \qquad (1)$$

Where $RMSE_i$ is the Root Mean Square Error for column(attribute) i and n_i is the total number of missing values for column i. IV_{ij} and AV_{ij} are imputed value and actual value for column i and row j.

Dataset 1: Economy Indicator 1999–2013. The Economy Indicator dataset [14] contains the economy indicator values of India for 14 years.

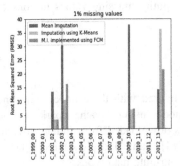

Fig. 5. Imputation evaluation for economy indicator dataset with 1% missing values

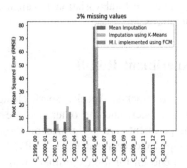

Fig. 6. Imputation evaluation for economy indicator dataset with 3% missing values

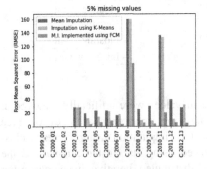

Fig. 7. Imputation evaluation for economy indicator dataset with 5% missing values

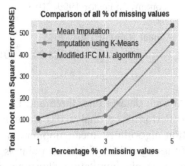

Fig. 8. Complete imputation accuracy comparison for economy indicator dataset

Figures 5, 6 and 7 are the imputation accuracy results with one, three and five percent missing values from the whole dataset and Fig. 8 shows the results for complete imputation accuracy for all percentages of missing values.

Dataset 2: Tourism Statistics of India 2001–2015. The Tourism statistics of India dataset [14] contains the number of tourists visited India from various countries. The dataset had 15 columns (for 15 years) and made up of integer values. Figures 9, 10 and 11 are for one, three and five percent missing values from the entire dataset and Fig. 12 shows the results for complete imputation accuracy.

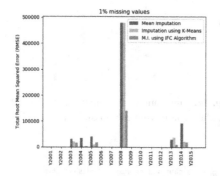

Fig. 9. Imputation evaluation for Tourism statistics dataset with 1% missing values

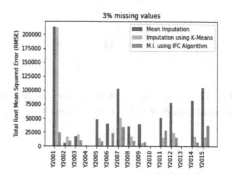

Fig. 10. Imputation evaluation for Tourism statistics dataset with 3% missing values

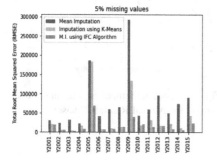

Fig. 11. Imputation evaluation for Tourism statistics dataset with 5% missing values

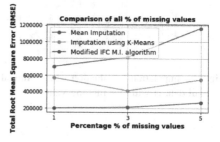

Fig. 12. Complete imputation accuracy comparison for Tourism statistics dataset

Dataset 3: Annual Rainfall 1901–2015. The Annual Rainfall of India dataset [14] holds the records of the total received rainfall in centimeters for each month from 1901 to 2015, i.e. 115 years. The dataset had 12 columns (Jan to Dec) and made up of float values. Figures 13, 14 and 15 are the imputation accuracy results with one percent, three percent, and five percent missing values from the whole dataset and Fig. 16 shows the results for complete imputation accuracy for all percentages of missing values in Annual Rainfall dataset.

From the result graphs, it can be visualized that, the proposed approach in this paper for handling missing values in distributed datasets using the modified iterative

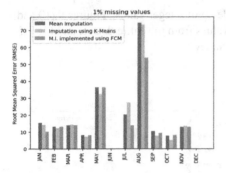

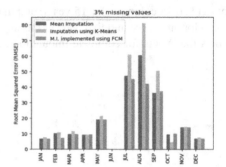

Fig. 13. Imputation evaluation for Annual Rainfall dataset with 1% missing values

Fig. 14. Imputation evaluation for Annual Rainfall dataset with 3% missing values

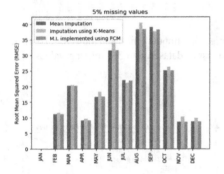

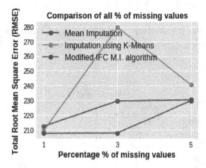

Fig. 15. Imputation evaluation for Annual Rainfall dataset with 5% missing values

Fig. 16. Complete imputation accuracy comparison for Annual Rainfall Dataset

fuzzy clustering multiple imputation algorithm has better accuracy than traditional mean imputation and imputation based on k-means clustering.

5   Conclusions and Future Work

Handling missing values in big data is very important for data analytics and machine learning applications. The problem of missing values exists in the distributed datasets. In this paper, a modified version of iterative fuzzy clustering multiple imputation algorithm was implemented successfully for handling missing values in the dataset that is distributed over multiple machines using Apache Spark computational framework. The results show the total RMSE for imputing missing values using multiple imputation algorithm is low compared to traditional mean imputation for handling missing values using Apache Spark.

For clustering on complete dataset, there is a need to get a good priori estimate of the number of clusters. So the estimation of the number of clusters before applying fuzzy clustering algorithm on distributed datasets can be taken up as future work.

References

1. Kang, H.: The prevention and handling of the missing data. Korean J. Anesthesiol. **64**(5), 402–406 (2013)
2. Zaharia, M., et al.: Resilient distributed datasets: a fault-tolerant abstraction for in-memory cluster computing. In: USENIX Symposium on Networked Systems Design and Implementation (2012)
3. Azur, M.J., Stuart, E.A., Frangakis, C., Leaf, P.J.: Multiple imputation by chained equations: what is it and how does it work? Int. J. Methods Psychiatr. Res. **20**(1), 40–49 (2011)
4. Houari, R., Bounceur, A., Tari, A., Kechadi, M.T.: Handling missing data problems with sampling methods. In: International Conference on Advanced Distributed Systems and Applications (2014)
5. Ye, H.: Missing data analysis using multiple imputation: getting to the heart of the matter. Circ. Cardiovasc. Qual. Outcomes **3**(1), 98–105 (2010)
6. Harel, O., Zhou, X.H.: Multiple imputation - review of theory, implementation and software. Stat. Med. **26**(16), 3057–3077 (2007)
7. Rubin, D.B.: Basic ideas of multiple imputation for nonresponse. Stat. Can. **12**(1), 37–47 (1986)
8. Nikfalazar, S., Khorshidi, H.A., Bedingfield, S., Yeh, C.-H.: A new iterative fuzzy clustering algorithm for multiple imputation of missing data. In: IEEE International Conference on Fuzzy Systems, Fuzzy Systems, FUZZ-IEEE, Naples (2017)
9. Bharill, N., Tiwari, A., Malviya, A.: Fuzzy based clustering algorithms to handle big data with implementation on Apache Spark. In: IEEE Second International Conference on Big Data Computing Service and Applications, Exeter College, Oxford, UK, pp. 95–104 (2016)
10. Armina, R., Zain, A.M., Ali, N.A., Sallehuddin, R.: A review on missing value estimation using imputation algorithm. J. Phys. Conf. Ser. (JPCS) **892**(1), 4 (2017)
11. Saravanan, P., Sailakshmi, P.: Missing value imputation using fuzzy possibilistic C means optimized with support vector regression and genetic algorithm. J. Theoret. Appl. Inf. Technol. **72**(1), 34–39 (2015)
12. Software for Multiple Imputation. http://multiple-imputation.com/software.html
13. Apache Spark. https://spark.apache.org
14. Open Government Data Platform (OGD) India. https://data.gov.in

Optimal Threshold Coverage Area (OTCA) Algorithm for Random Deployment of Sensor Nodes in Large Asymmetrical Terrain

Anamika Sharma[✉] and Siddhartha Chauhan

Computer Science and Engineering Department, National Institute of
Technology, Hamirpur, Hamirpur, Himachal Pradesh, India
anamika@nith.ac.in

Abstract. Random deployment of sensor nodes cause coverage problems due
to unbalanced deployment. This includes both coverage area overlapping among
the nodes and coverage holes in the terrain. Actual coverage area computations
are partial and unreliable without considering these irregularities. The purpose of
this paper is to compute the minimum number of sensor nodes that increase the
probability for achieving Optimal Threshold Coverage Area (OTCA) for a given
terrain in random deployment strategy. The analytical and simulation results
show that OTCA is efficient in calculating the minimum number of sensor nodes
required to achieve threshold coverage level for a given terrain.

Keywords: Asymmetrical terrain · Coverage area · Overlapped coverage area
Random deployment

1 Introduction

In wireless sensor networks, coverage is vital performance metric for reliable results, as
it reflects how efficiently an area is being monitored. Coverage represents the proportion of the terrain that is covered under the sensing range of deployed sensor nodes.
It is one to one mapping between spatial points of sensing area and sensor nodes of a
sensor network [1].

One important criterion in WSN is to compute the minimum number of sensor
nodes for maximal coverage. These computations are done to reduce the overall network cost in terms of sensor count. However, it becomes more beneficial, when
deployment strategy is random. This deployment strategy is very much efficient in
hostile regions, where physical placement of nodes is difficult, such as harsh border
area surveillance [2], battlefields [3] and disaster relief missions [4]. In such applications lack of topographical information also disrupts the deployment of sensor nodes.
The network designers must have prior estimate of required minimum number of
nodes.

Random deployment can never guarantee full coverage, due to its stochastic nature.
It does not have any pre-determined topology. This causes unbalanced deployment, as
some parts of terrain have densely deployed nodes while others suffer from scarcity of

© Springer Nature Singapore Pte Ltd. 2018
M. Singh et al. (Eds.): ICACDS 2018, CCIS 906, pp. 34–42, 2018.
https://doi.org/10.1007/978-981-13-1813-9_4

nodes. Therefore the computations for required minimum number of sensor nodes have become more important for optimal threshold coverage level.

Balister et al. [5] have proposed a Trap Coverage model for large scale random deployments. According to this model full coverage is neither cost effective nor required for such deployment in hostile regions due to the presence of obstacles or sensor nodes' positioning. For random deployment, network designer must maintain a proper trade-off between coverage level, number of sensor nodes and network lifetime in terms of network cost [6].

k-coverage [7, 8] and path exposure [9] are some common methods in the literature used for calculating the coverage area. Total coverage area computations are different for both deterministic and random deployments. Coverage Rate Calculation (CRC) protocol is proposed in [10] for random deployment. This protocol calculates precise and approximate coverage rates using unit disk graph (UDG) and probabilistic coverage model (PCM). CRC calculates coverage rate and area of coverage holes but does not provide any solution to mitigate these coverage holes. Moreover, CRC does not optimize the network cost. A lot of research has been done to solve the problem of maximal coverage by detecting coverage holes and then deploy extra nodes to mitigate these coverage holes [11].

Coverage area calculations are complex due to the presence of irregularities and biased deployment of sensor nodes. Total coverage area computations must include coverage area overlapping, sparse deployment and coverage holes. Moreover, if sensors are randomly deployed, it is not possible to guarantee with any number of sensor nodes that some coverage will be reached. It is only possible to increase the probability of coverage. The main focus of this paper is to compute the minimum number of sensor nodes need to be deployed randomly to increase the probability of Optimal Threshold Coverage Area (OTCA). The trade-off lies between the terrain size, sensor count and coverage area.

The analytical and simulation evaluations show that our proposed scheme efficiently calculates the minimum number of sensor nodes for increasing the probability of threshold coverage level. Our proposed scheme is efficient for computing optimum coverage level. Results also show that OTCA is cost effective and performs well in hostile regions.

2 Network Architecture

A WSN cannot work efficiently with biased deployment and coverage issues. Optimum Threshold Coverage Area (OTCA) protocol has been designed to compute the coverage area provided by a set of randomly deployed $N_{minimum}$ sensor nodes in a given terrain and compare it with the coverage threshold value, T_{value}. If the computed coverage area is equal to or above the coverage threshold value, then this zone is considered as optimally covered, otherwise more nodes will be deployed. Following assumptions were considered while designing OTCA.

1. A 2-dimensional asymmetrical terrain of area A_T, is sensed by $N_{minimum}$, minimum number of sensor nodes, where each sensor S_i has a sensing range ξ and sensing coverage area A_s that is randomly and independently distributed within A_T.
2. The proportion of communication range is considered twice to that of sensing range [12] for better network connectivity.
3. The nodes have been deployed densely and sparsely, in the given terrain because of random deployment. These nodes initialized and localized themselves using efficient localization algorithm [13]. Each node has accurately computed its coordinates in 2-dimensional plane.

The pictorial representation of network architecture is as shown in Fig. 1.

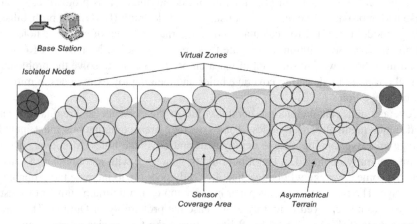

Fig. 1. Randomly deployed sensor nodes in asymmetrical terrain

The deployment site is large asymmetrical terrain and coverage computations have been done by applying divide-and-conquer approach. This approach minimizes the complexity of computation for large problems. Using divide-and-conquer, the base station has segregated the deployment site into Z equal virtual zones for accurate coverage computations.

The main advantage of applying divide-and-conquer is to identify coverage holes in each zone. This provides an estimate about the locations of coverage holes present in large terrain for deploying extra nodes. The base station has maintained a record of each zones' dimensions and number of sensor nodes, S_{vz} lie inside it along with their coverage area.

3 Proposed Protocol: OTCA

OTCA has been designed to compute the minimum number of sensor nodes $N_{minimum}$, required for random deployment strategy that increases the probability in achieving optimal threshold coverage level. Coverage area is computed by capturing the geometrical relation between sensing area and sensor nodes. To compute the solution for OTCA, Theorem 1 is introduced for computing the minimum number of sensor nodes Theorem 2 for optimum threshold coverage area.

3.1 Minimum Sensor Count

This computation is done for minimum number of sensor nodes that will be deployed in given asymmetrical terrain, whose area A_T is already known. The total number of $N_{minimum}$ sensor nodes for this terrain is given by Eq. (1).

Theorem 1: *For optimal threshold coverage, the minimum number of sensor nodes, $N_{minimum}$ required for random deployment in an asymmetrical terrain.*

$$N_{minimum} \geq \frac{T_{value} \times A_T}{A_s} \tag{1}$$

where, $T_{value,}$ is the coverage threshold value.

3.2 Nodes Deployment Optimization for Threshold Coverage Level

Sensor nodes lie in each virtual zone has precisely computed its location co-ordinates and coverage area in 2-D plane. Each node relay this information to base station. Base station then carries out computations for each virtual zone separately to analyze, whether coverage provided by these sensor nodes is greater than or equal to the coverage threshold value. To achieve accuracy in the computation of coverage area, base station isolates all the nodes, which lie completely outside the boundary of asymmetrical terrain as shown in Fig. 1.

1-Virtual Zone (1-VZ)

If the Euclidean distance between multiple sensor nodes is less than the sensing range $(d < 2\xi)$, then there is overlapping among the coverage area of those nodes. This category of deployed nodes is known as dense deployment. On the other hand, if the distance between multiple nodes is greater than or equal to the sensing range $(d \geq 2\xi)$, then this category of deployed nodes is known as sparse deployment. Therefore, the area covered by both categories of deployed nodes is different.

Theorem 2: *The total area covered by sparsely and densely deployed S_{VZ} sensor nodes in 1-virtual zone of any wireless sensor network is $CA_{1\text{-}VZ}$.*

Proof: Let us consider out of S_{VZ}, α sensor nodes, where $\alpha \subseteq S_{VZ}$ are sparsely deployed in 1-virtual zone. The total area covered by sparsely deployed sensor nodes A_{sparse} having ξ sensing range is given as

$$A_{sparse} = \alpha\pi\xi^2 \tag{2}$$

Suppose out of S_{VZ}, a set of β nodes, where, $\beta \subseteq S_{VZ}$ whose coverage area is overlapped with each other and β_i and β_j (where, i, j = 1, 2, 3 ... n and i $\neq$ j) are these two nodes. Due to overlapping, these nodes have some coverage area in common. Total area covered by both nodes is $\beta_i \cup \beta_j$ and computed as

$$A_{dense\_II} = \frac{\beta}{2}\left(2\pi\xi^2 - \xi^2\cos^{-1}\left(\frac{d_{i,j}}{2\xi}\right) + \frac{d_{i,j}}{2}\sqrt{(2\xi)^2 - (d_{i,j})^2}\right) \tag{3}$$

Suppose out of S_{VZ}, a set of γ sensor nodes, where $\gamma \subseteq S_{VZ}$ whose coverage area is overlapped with each other and γ_i, γ_j and γ_k (where, i, j, k = 1, 2, 3 ... n and $i \neq j \neq k$) are these three nodes. Total area covered by these three nodes is $\gamma_i \cup \gamma_j \cup \gamma_k$ and calculated as

A_{dense_III}

$$= \frac{\gamma}{3} \left(3\pi\xi^2 - \left(\sum_{1 \leq i < j \leq 3} \left(\xi^2 \cos^{-1}\left(\frac{d_{i,j}}{2\xi}\right) - \frac{d_{i,j}}{2}\sqrt{(2\xi)^2 - (d_{i,j})^2} \right) \right) + \sum_{n=1}^{3} \left(c_n^2 \sin^{-1}\left(\frac{a_n}{2c_n}\right) - \frac{a_n}{4}\sqrt{4c_n^2 - a_n^2} \right) + \sqrt{s\prod_{n=1}^{3}(s - a_n)} \right) \tag{4}$$

from (3) and (4) the total area covered by densely deployed sensor nodes is

$$A_{dense} = A_{dense\_II} + A_{dense\_III} \tag{5}$$

Hence, total coverage area CA_{1_VZ} provided by S_{VZ} sensor nodes in 1-virtual zone is calculated from Eqs. (2) and (5) as

$$CA_{1\_VZ} = (A_{sparse} + A_{dense}) \geq T_{value} \tag{6}$$

This equation represents that, if the total coverage area provided by a set of S_{VZ} sensor nodes in 1-virtual zone is equals to or greater than T_{value} then it is optimally covered otherwise deployment of more nodes, N_{more} given by (7) is required to achieve T_{value} and $N_{minimum} \leftarrow N_{minimum} + N_{more}$.

$$N_{more} \geq \left(\frac{T_{value} - CA_{1\_VZ}}{A_s} \right) \times A_T \tag{7}$$

Z-Virtual Zones (Z-VZ)

The coverage area for each virtual zone is computed with the help of Theorem 2 and then all the results are accumulated to compute overall coverage area. The total coverage area provided by $N_{minimum}$ sensor nodes deployed in given terrain of area A_T, divided into Z-virtual zones is given as

$$CA_{Z\_VZ} = \sum_{i=1}^{Z} (A_{sparse\_i} + A_{dense\_i}) \geq T_{value} \tag{8}$$

The probability P_{CA} in Eq. 9 represents the probability of total coverage area provided by $N_{minimum}$ sensor nodes

$$P_{CA} = \begin{cases} 1 & \text{if } CA_{Z\_VZ} \geq A_T \\ 1 - \prod_{i=1}^{z}(1 - p_i(CA_{i\_VZ})) & \text{if } CA_{Z\_VZ} < A_T \end{cases} \tag{9}$$

The whole procedure of OTCA is discussed in Algorithm 1. This algorithm computes total coverage area provided by $N_{minimum}$ nodes.

Algorithm 1: Algorithm for nodes deployment optimization of threshold coverage area (OTCA).

```
 1. Assign
    T_value   ← Coverage threshold value
    N_minimum ← Minimum number of sensor nodes
    C_A       ← Coverage area of sensor nodes
    total coverage area ← 0
 2. compute the minimum number of sensor nodes, N_minimum
    required for threshold coverage level by using
    equation 1.
 3. randomly deploy N_minimum sensor nodes in the given
    terrain.
 4. apply divide-and-conquer approach to the given ter-
    rain for Z virtual zones as shown in figure 1.
 5. for each virtual zone, V_zi, in Z-virtual zones
 6. begin
 7.     coverage area ← 0
 8.     S_vz ← set of sensors in V_zi
 9.     while (S_vz ≠ ϕ )
10. begin
11.         S_i ← take a sensor from S_vz
12.         check whether other sensors overlap the
               coverage area of S_i
13.         if there is no overlapping
14.             S_vz ← S_vz - S_i
15.             C_A = C_A + sensing area of S_i
16.         else
17.             S_vz ← S_vz - (S_i + sensors have been
                    overlapping with S_i)
18.             C_A = C_A +(area covered by S_i and
                        other overlapped sensors)
19. end
20. if coverage area is less than T_value
21.         compute the additional number of sensors,
               N_more using (7), required for achieving
               threshold coverage area.
22.         deploy N_more sensors in V_zi
23.         N_minimum ← N_minimum +N_more
24.         go to line 7
25.         compute total coverage area of terrain
               CA_z_vz
26.         total coverage area = total coverage area
                        + C_A
27.end
```

4 Performance Evaluation

This section represents the performance evaluation of our proposed protocol (OTCA). From (1), $N_{minimum}$ sensor nodes of 25 m sensing range are computed to achieve 80%, 90% and 100% coverage level for a fixed terrain size (3000×1000) m^2. According to [6], the network designer must maintain a proper trade-off between coverage level and network cost. To make WSN cost-effective the optimal threshold coverage level is 80% for random deployment.

If $N_{mimimum}$ nodes from (1) are not sufficient, to reach optimum threshold coverage level then N_{more} nodes are computed using (7). Figure 2 represents both total coverage area and overlapped area for both analytical and simulation results. Using Algorithm 1, the computed value for $N_{minimum}$ sensor nodes is 1305 after three iterations to cover 80% of terrain.

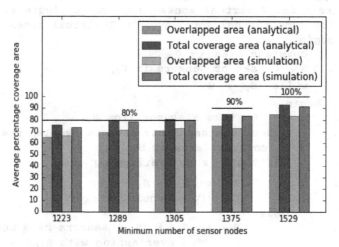

Fig. 2. Average coverage area in accordance to minimum number of sensor nodes for different coverage threshold

Figure 3 shows the optimum number of sensor nodes required for different terrain size to achieve threshold coverage level. We have analyzed that the required number of sensor nodes need to be incremented to the optimum number of nodes for a given terrain is in proportion to the percentage increment in the size of that terrain. The overlapped area is directly proportional to the increase in sensor count.

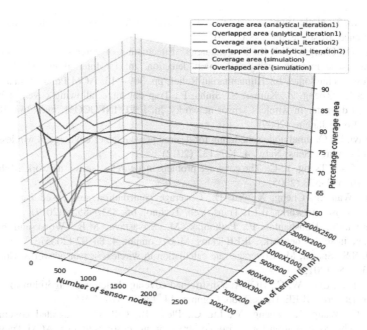

Fig. 3. Required number of sensor nodes for different terrain size to achieve 80% of threshold coverage threshold

5 Conclusion

One of the simplest way to deploy sensor nodes is random deployment, when the region is hostile. But this distribution impose many challenges such as: unbalanced deployment, coverage area overlapping and coverage holes in the given terrain. It requires a proper solution to mitigate these obstacles. Moreover, the network designers must have an approximate idea about number of nodes and average coverage level provided by these nodes for finite area size. In this paper we have computed the total number of sensor nodes that increase the probability in achieving optimum threshold coverage level. The actual coverage area computation is done, considering unbalanced deployment (sparse and dense deployment). This analysis of total number of sensor nodes is beneficial in designing a cost-effective WSN in hostile regions. Future scope of this paper is to schedule the sensor network by identifying the redundant nodes for prolonging the network's lifetime.

References

1. Wang, B.: Coverage problems in sensor networks. In: ACM Computing Surveys, CSUR, vol. 43, Article no. 32, pp. 1–53. ACM, New York (2011)
2. Sun, Z., Wang, P., Vuran, M.C., Al-Rodhaan, M.A., Al-Dhelaan, A.M., Akyildiz, I.F.: BorderSense: border patrol through advanced wireless sensor networks. Ad Hoc Netw. **9**, 468–477 (2011)

3. Bokareva, T., et al.: Wireless sensor networks for battlefield surveillance. In: Land Warfare Conference, Brisbane, pp. 1–8 (2006)
4. Sikdar, D., Bhargav, K.R.K., Dewangan, S.: Effectuation of wireless sensor networks for human rescue missions using RF signal detection. In: 1st International Conference on Wireless Technologies for Humanitarian Relief, pp. 309–313. ACM Press, Kerala (2011)
5. Balister, P., Zheng, Z., Kumar, S., Sinha, P.: Trap coverage: allowing coverage holes of bounded diameter in wireless sensor networks. In: IEEE INFOCOM, pp. 136–144. IEEE Press, Rio de Janeiro (2009)
6. Khosravi, H.: Optimal node scheduling for desired percentage of coverage in wireless sensor networks. Wirel. Sens. Netw. **4**, 127–132 (2012)
7. Huang, C.-F., Tseng, Y.-C.: The coverage problem in a wireless sensor network. Mob. Netw. Appl. **10**, 519–528 (2005)
8. Yu, J., Wan, S., Cheng, X., Yu, D.: Coverage contribution area based k-coverage for wireless sensor networks. IEEE Trans. Veh. Technol. **66**, 8510–8523 (2017)
9. Megerian, S., Koushanfar, F., Potkonjak, M., Srivastava, M.B.: Worst and best-case coverage in sensor networks. IEEE Trans. Mob. Comput. **4**, 84–92 (2005)
10. Kashi, S.S., Sharifi, M.: Coverage rate calculation in wireless sensor networks. Computing **94**, 833–856 (2012)
11. Sahoo, P.K., Liao, W.-C.: HORA: a distributed coverage hole repair algorithm for wireless sensor networks. IEEE Trans. Mob. Comput. **14**, 1397–1410 (2015)
12. Xing, G., Wang, X., Zhang, Y., Lu, C., Pless, R., Gill, C.: Integrated coverage and connectivity configuration for energy conservation in sensor networks. ACM Trans. Sens. Netw. **1**, 36–72 (2005)
13. Niculescu, D., Nath, B.: Ad hoc positioning system (APS). In: Global Telecommunications Conference, pp. 2926–2931. IEEE, San Antonio (2002)

Dataset Expansion and Accelerated Computation for Image Classification: A Practical Approach

Aditya Mohan and Nafisuddin Khan[✉]

Jaypee University of Information Technology, Waknaghat, Distt. Solan, India
adityamohanjuit@gmail.com, nafisuddin.khan@juit.ac.in

Abstract. The training dataset of many machine learning algorithms for various purposes mainly consists of images. The major hindrance and setback during the training of these datasets arises in the form of non-availability of the following three features - quantity of data, availability of GPUs (Graphic Processing Units) and high-rate computation catalysts. Many researchers have trouble independently training datasets and specifying features which can be in great quantity for images. In this paper, we present an approach for leveraging the power of "transfer learning" and easily accessible examples in the form of raw content from the internet not only to use already-prepared datasets made specifically for neural network training but also to bring into usage more training examples using the internet, sampling the average accuracy output rate of the images, along with reducing model training and execution time by parallel operations on different nodes.

Keywords: Machine learning · Transfer learning · Datasets · Neural networks Convolutional neural network (CNN)

1 Introduction

Neural network is an altogether different approach as compared to supervised machine learning algorithms with various reasons attributed, the most prominent one being the cost of running and processing algorithms over hardware.

The reasons for the above can be understood as follows. Random Access Memory (RAMs) on machines are cheap and are readily available. Hundreds of gigabytes of RAM is required to execute a complex supervised machine learning problem. This is can be easily afforded by users but on the other side, general access to Graphic Processing Units (GPUs) is not cheap. For instance, for gaining access to a hundred Gigabyte VRAM (Virtual RAM) on GPUs [1]. The procedure would be time consuming and would possibly involve significant costs.

A huge amount of machine learning approaches executed well only under a commonly accepted conjecture: the test data and training data are extracted from the same distribution and same feature regions.

When the distribution is amended (which mostly happens in the case of image-based datasets), maximum number of statistical models are required to be built-up from

© Springer Nature Singapore Pte Ltd. 2018
M. Singh et al. (Eds.): ICACDS 2018, CCIS 906, pp. 43–54, 2018.
https://doi.org/10.1007/978-981-13-1813-9_5

the beginning using freshly accumulated training data. In most real-life applications, it is expensive (as mentioned above) and becomes highly time-consuming and painstaking tore-gather the required data for training and then rebuild the models. So it would be of great help to reduce the efforts and time invested in re-collecting the data for training. And for these cases only transfer learning or knowledge transfer between domains of various tasks becomes highly appropriate. Therefore, "Transfer Learning" bestows upon us the ability to use pre-trained models from other sources (Google, independent researchers) by introducing small changes.

Throughout the entire process of implementing transfer learning, development of pre-trained models is a prerequisite. A pre-trained model is a model created by some other source for solving a problem in the same domain ex.: voice and image classification. General approach towards developing a pre-trained model involves usage of a model trained on another problem as a commencing point Instead of building a model from scratch.

For implementation of pre-trained models, various approaches are available for usage. But this requires, traditionally, handcrafting a bunch of features, for example – running edge detection for finding an individual's outlines or storing color histograms for any section of an individual (hair, teeth) which is not feasible accounting to a myriad of variations in the features belonging to the same category, which might be due to the robustness and image source variation(cameras from cell phones, surveillance cameras etc.; image rotation). Here it is worthwhile to note that [1] the faces here are representing various multidimensional, meaningful visual expressions and thus developing a computation based model for face recognition is strenuous. To cater to these discrepancies [2], neural networks are taken into consideration. A Neural network is a powerful technology for classifying visual (graphic) inputs arising from multiple sources of documents. From research and result comparison, it has been inferred that the most important practice is acquiring a training set with its size being as substantial as possible. Artificial neural networks can be interpreted as a linkage of separate neurons (or nodes) with the help of various linear or non-linear activation functions as shown in Fig. 1, but deep learning in simple terms attributes to multiple levels of these operations (number of layers and choice of the non-linear activation functions) without any restriction. Taking in view these points, we must consider the capability of deep learning VS traditional machine learning and why deep learning based approach has been taken in this paper. Figure 2 clearly shows the domain specific problem catering capability (of performance) or these algorithmic approaches. Taking a glimpse of history of neural networks is of paramount significance as it provides a unique and important perspective of how the development of this domain began, how it evolved and its relevance in incorporating it into various aspects of life- from manufacturing to health-care, from counter-terrorism system development to mindfulness applications, all also having one interesting question linked with them- how much relevance does this domain hold to them and to what extent is this domain going to improve/enhance the end products developed in all the sectors it touches. For getting this perspective based answer, we must see the major developments which took place from the day this domain came into existence. Development of artificial neural networks started in 1943 when researchers created a computational model for these networks based on mathematics and relevant algorithms which were called threshold logic. This resulted in the research of this domain to be bifurcated in two distinct approaches, one of them being more inclined towards working on the basis of functioning of the brain and in the other applying these networks in the area of artificial intelligence (AI). Further developments which go a long way from here added significant bits to evolve this domain, most important contributions being the developments of relevant algorithms in the year 1974 and 1986 by a group of researchers for performing proper optimization and output improvement. As analyzed by individual analysts and mentioned in Fig. 3, there is an approximate estimate being presented of the come-back of neural networks owing to the significant developments which were successfully deployed into large-scale or industry grade systems for developing breakthrough products, as mentioned above. In context of this paper, getting maximum number of closely related images for training. The next important practice is that convolutional neural networks (CNNs) are best fitted for operations on visual documents rather than on networks which are fully connected [1]. The convolutional neural networks are equipped with the ability to perform partial invariance for doing rotation, translation, deformation and scale. The convolutional neural network operates by extracting large features in a set of layers based on a neatly defined hierarchy.

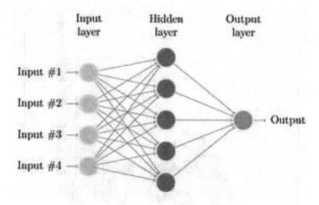

Fig. 1. Basic layout of an Artificial Neural Network (ANN).

Having mentioned the details, the most popular neural networks in use today include, but are not limited to Feed Forward Networks (FFN), Convolutional Neural Networks (CNN or ConvNet), Recurrent Neural Network (RNN), Autoencoders, whose popular application areas include (again- not limited to) image classification, Self Driving Cars, language driven image generation, value prediction spanning across various industries like marketing, retail and sales, banking and finance, medicine etc. With these in mind, we have chosen Convolutional Neural Networks for our purpose of image classification.

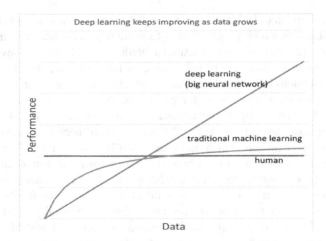

Fig. 2. Performance comparison of deep learning, traditional machine learning and human learning as compared to the rate of data growth.

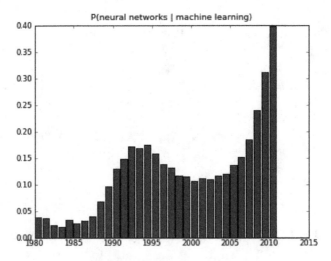

Fig. 3. Variation in popularity of artificial neural networks with time.

2 Convolutional Neural Networks

2.1 Functioning of CNN

A convolutional neural network consists of 3 types of layers [3]:-

Convolutional: These layers consist of a grid (rectangular in shape) of multiple neurons requiring that the previous layer *also* be consisting of neurons set-up in the same grid shape. Here, each neuron accepts inputs from a cuboidal segment of the previous layer; it is worthy to note that the weights for this grid section are the same for each neuron in that specific convolutional layer.

Max-Pooling: After each convolutional layer, there might be a pooling layer present. The pooling layer's task is to pick up small-sized rectangular blocks from the previous convolutional layer which is sub-sampled, thereby producing a single output from that block.

Fully-Connected: Finally, after operations done by several convolutional and max-pooling layers, the final, the high-level inference deduction in the neural network is performed by fully connected layers. A fully connected layer consumes all the neurons from the previous layer, connecting it to each and every single neuron it possesses.

Forward Propagation in Convolutional Layers
In an $N \times N$ *square neuron layer followed by a convolutional layer, if a* $m \times m$ *filter named* ω *is used*, the output of the convolutional layer shall have size $(N - m + 1)$ $(N - m + 1)$. Now, to compute the before-nonlinearity input to any unit x_{ij}^l on that layer, the contributions (with weights added to them by the filter components) from the previous layer cells have to be summed up using

$$x_{ij}^l = \sum_{a=0}^{m-1} \sum_{b=0}^{m-1} \omega_{ab} y_{(i+a)(j+b)}^{l-1} \tag{1}$$

Forward Propagation in Max-Pooling Layers
Here simply a $k \times k$ region is passed and the output is a single value, which itself is the maxima in that region.

Backward Propagation in Convolutional Layers
For some error function, E, and error values at the convolutional layer to our knowledge, the error required to be computed is the partial of E with respect to every neuron output $\frac{\partial E}{\partial y_{ij}^l}$. For computing gradient component for each weight, values of "deltas" are to be computed using

$$\frac{\partial E}{\partial x_{ij}^l} = \frac{\partial E}{\partial y_{ij}^l} \frac{\partial y_{ij}^l}{\partial x_{ij}^l} = \frac{\partial E}{\partial y_{ij}^l} \frac{\partial}{\partial x_{ij}^l} \left(\sigma \left(x_{ij}^l \right) \right) = \frac{\partial E}{\partial y_{ij}^l} \sigma' \left(x_{ij}^l \right) \tag{2}$$

Propagating errors back to the layers using chain rule-

$$\frac{\partial E}{\partial y_{ij}^{l-1}} = \sum_{a=0}^{m-1} \sum_{b=0}^{m-1} \frac{\partial E}{\partial x_{(i-a)(j-b)}^l} \frac{\partial x_{(i-a)(j-b)}^l}{\partial y_{ij}^{l-1}} = \sum_{a=0}^{m-1} \sum_{b=0}^{m-1} \frac{\partial E}{\partial x_{(i-a)(j-b)}^l} \omega_{ab} \tag{3}$$

Backward Propagation in Max-Pooling Layers
The back-propagated error(s) belonging to the max-pooling layers remain sparse, thus not doing any learning by themselves.

2.2   Integrating Pre-trained CNN Models [4]

Pre-trained CNN models are very time-efficient which require less computation power as well as are cheaper in implementation of transfer learning. The process includes re-training the last layer on features of the targeted image set to be used for classification training and this holds true for multiple classes. Deep learning libraries like Keras have provided five Convolutional Neural Networks that have been pre-trained on ImageNet dataset, namely - VGG19, VGG16, ResNet50, Inception V3 and Xception out of which this paper uses Inception V3 pre-trained CNN model. Inception was used due to the fact that it was trained by Google on 100,000 images with 1000 categories, making it highly preferable for achieving maximum training accuracy.

ImageNet

ImageNet is a project targeted at categorizing and labeling images into approx. 22000 distinct object categories for serving the purpose of computer vision research. ImageNet in context of deep learning and Convolutional Neural Networks, refers to ImageNet large scale visual recognition challenge (ILSVRC). Its primary goal is to train a model capable of correctly classifying an input image into 1000 distinct object categories.

Here models are trained on 1.2 million training images with 50,000 more pictures for validation purpose and 100000 pictures for testing. The mentioned 1000 image categories represent object classes encountered in our everyday happenings such as squirrel species, cat species, indoor and outdoor objects, vehicle types.

The Inception Model

The Inception micro-architecture was initially introduced and presented by Szegedy et al. in their 2014 paper, "*Going deeper with convolutions*" [5]. The primary goal of this module includes performing as a feature extractor (itself being multi-leveled) by computation of $1 \times 1, 3 \times 3$, and 5×5 convolutions within the *exactly same* module of that network and consequently the output of these filters are stacked along the channel dimensions before being passed onto the next layer of that network.

The original, initial version (presented) of this architecture was called *GoogLeNet*, with subsequent manifestations being simply called *Inception vM,* where *M* refers to the version set out by Google. The Inception VM (M = 3) architecture included in Keras deep learning library core comes from Szegedy et al's later publication named *Rethinking the Inception Architecture for Computer Vision* (2015) [6] which proposes various updates to inception module for further boosting the classification accuracy of ImageNet. The weights for Inception V3 are smaller than both ResNet and VGG close to 96 MegaBytes. Since ResNet boasts of using global average pooling rather than fully connected layers, its model size turns out to be *smaller* and this in turn reduces the model size down to 102 MB for ResNet50 (50 layers of weights). Owing to its depth and the count of fully connected nodes, VGG has size over 533 MegaBytes for VGG16 and 574 MegaBytes for VGG19 and this makes deploying VGG a time-consuming task (Figs. 4 and 5).

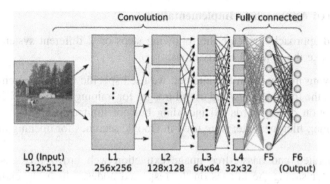

Fig. 4. General layout of a Convolutional Neural Network [7].

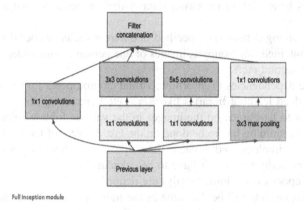

Fig. 5. Layout of inception module [4].

2.3 Training the Inception Model

On feeding images as the input on each layer, a series of operations on the data is performed until it outputs a label and classification percentage. Each layer has its own abstractions, for example, edge detection on one, shape detection on the other which keep on getting increasingly more abstract as layers proceed. The last 2 layers in the inception module comprise of the highest-level detectors for all objects and as per training specification, these last two layers are to be trained on the features of the desired classification parameters (image clusters in separate folders to be used for training the classifier etc. etc.).

2.4   Proposed Approach to Implementation

The proposed approach- Execute the following steps on 2 different systems simultaneously and take the required observations.

- For retrieving images from the internet, we used specific Google search keywords for getting the most relevant and useful images for training the model. For instance, a combination of keywords [8] including but not limited to allintext:, allintitle:, inurl:, intitle:, filetype:, site: were used in Google searches for opening the relevant images.
- For accelerated and hassle-free image extraction web browser extensions were deployed for saving the images on the respected nodes, which, depending on the system speed, extracted the image results directly in separate folders. This is a unique and easy-to-use method which when combined with the other steps can prove highly beneficial for increasing dataset size and reduction dataset preparation time.
- The entire training dataset was specified in different folders as per the classification data they contained (for example, images of one person in one folder, images of the other in the second etc.).
- After all the dependencies (Tensorflow, virtual environments for running the entire process in, deep learning libraries like Keras etc.) are set-up, the Inception model classifier has to be trained on the images in the various folders created above.
- Now since the training has to be done on the last 2 layers of the model. Therefore, commands are implemented to cache the outputs of the lower layer on the disk so they that repeatedly they don't have to be calculated.
- Number of epochs (iterations, mostly) are defined.
- Output labels (which will be the same as the training folder name) and graphs are defined for ease of reading and interpreting the outputs.
- The training is executed for training the classifier.
- After the training, scripts in Tensorflow are implemented to use the newly trained classifier for classifying images from the test dataset as being a part of the training dataset (images in folders, in this case).

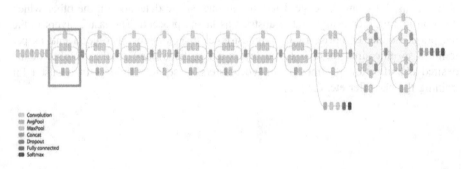

Convolution
AvgPool
MaxPool
Concat
Dropout
Fully connected
Softmax

Green box shows parallel region of GoogLeNet

Fig. 6. Training layers of Inception model.

- The scripts comprise of the trained model and test data images stored in variables and for the operation part it includes feeding the image-based data into the model (which is now retrained) to get the production output. Here Softmax function is used to map the input data into different probabilities of a positively anticipated (and mentioned) output.
- Same process is undertaken from different systems for accomplishing the same goal.
- IMPORTANT: The training accuracy, classification accuracy and processing time (model training and classification time) are observed and taken a note of on both the systems (Fig. 6).

3 Results

- The classifier was trained on training datasets comprising of photographs separated in 2 folders.
- The training of the classifier took place step-wise, displaying training accuracy, cross-entropy and validation accuracy for each training image as it was used to train the model.
- Commands were executed for implementation classification – target images used – images bearing resemblance to images in both the datasets.
- Applying the above step for testing various images, accuracy score for each image was brought up, graphs were plotted for understanding the execution time (Figs. 7, 8, 9, 10 and 11).

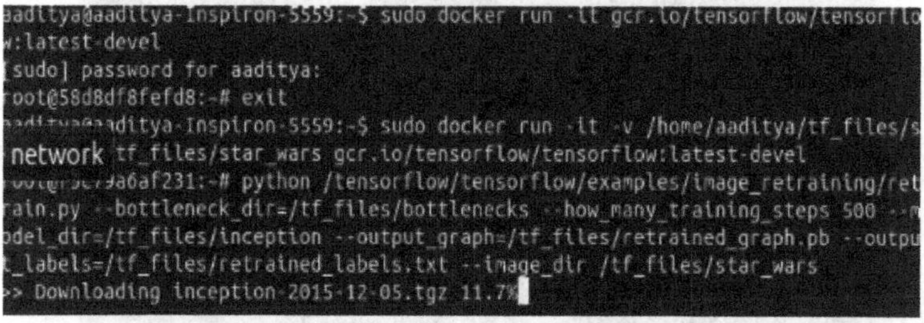

Fig. 7. Inception module preparation before training.

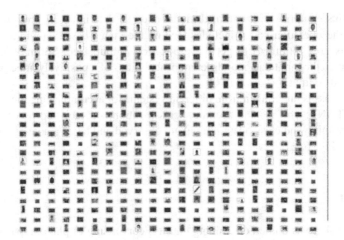

Fig. 8. Image dataset (zoomed out to 50%) of one folder (one type) of images for training the data.

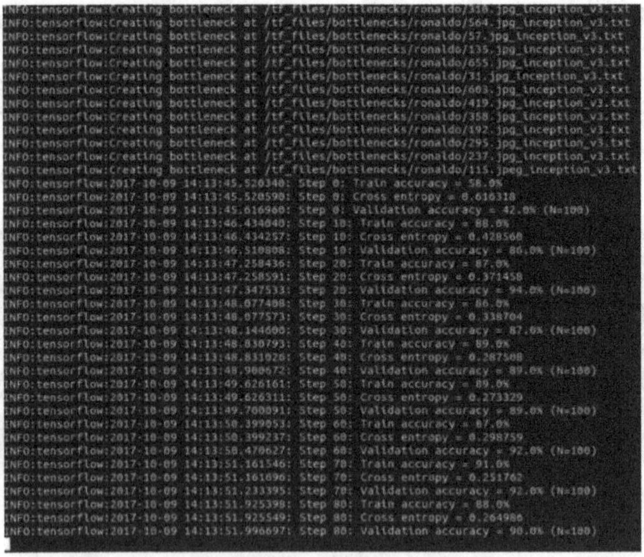

Fig. 9. Training, accuracy, cross-entropy and validation accuracy for each training image while being used to train the model.

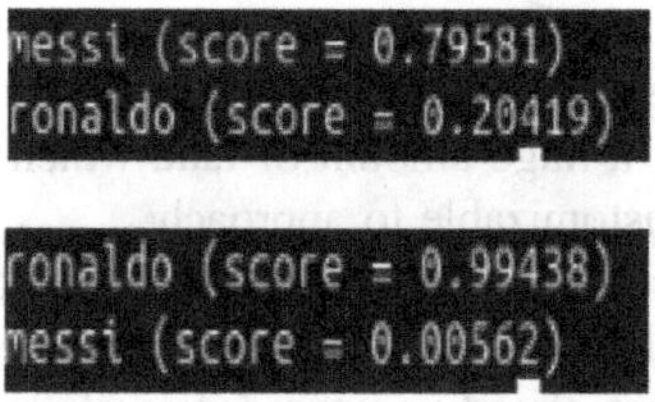

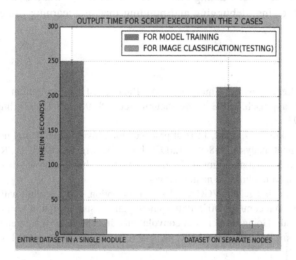

Fig. 10. Final result after training the model and testing it on individual target images bearing resemblance to each of the training dataset, one by one.

Fig. 11. Graphical comparison of time required for training the model and testing of images for classification with data concentrated on a single node and (ii) data distributed on 2 different nodes for simultaneous application.

4 Conclusion

The proposed training model is able to classify the test dataset images with high accuracy in lesser time when on distributed nodes as compared to when done on a single node (as is visible on the graph- the time difference in both the cases is significant) and this is one exhibition of the fact that as the dataset- containing both relevant and standard and unambiguous (as per their theme) increases in size, more the amount of accuracy or the accuracy rate increases for classification, also that all the costs associated with time required to train the model and predict target images can be significantly reduced if the task is distributed on different nodes and is performed simultaneously.

As mentioned above, we successfully dispatched the training work on different nodes and by combining their average output accuracy rate for specific test images, we were able to successfully map out high accuracy rate for classification of the test dataset images, thereby distributing the model training and classification time on different nodes speeded up model training and in-turn speeded up classification which itself demonstrates the fact that distribution of tasks to nodes has accelerated the process of training and classification of a huge amount of data which also benefits the users by being non-centralized and customizable to approach.

Thus, we have clearly justified the objective and the aim of the paper to leverage the power of "transfer learning" and easily accessible examples in the form of raw content on the internet not only to use already-prepared datasets made specifically for neural network training but to bring into usage more training examples using the same. We successfully sampled the average accuracy output rate of the images and also used distributed nodes for faster training and classification of the images, thereby boosting the efficiency of testing, debugging and building machine learning projects.

References

1. Lawrence, S., Lee Giles, C., Chung Tsoi, A., Back, A.: Face recognition: a convolutional neural network approach. IEEE Trans. Neural Netw. **8**, 98–113 (1997). https://doi.org/10.1109/72.554195
2. Simard, P., Steinkraus, D., Platt, J.: Best practices for convolutional neural networks applied to visual document analysis, 958–962 (2003). https://doi.org/10.1109/ICDAR.2003.1227801
3. Andrew Gibiansky: Convolutional Neural Networks. http://andrew.gibiansky.com/blog/machine-learning/convolutional-neural-networks
4. Adrian Rosebrock: ImageNet: VGGNet, ResNet, Inception, and Xception with Keras. https://www.pyimagesearch.com/2017/03/20/imagenet-vggnet-resnet-inception-xception-keras
5. Szegedy, C., et al.: Going deeper with convolutions. In: The IEEE Conference on Computer Vision and Pattern Recognition, CVPR, pp. 1–9 (2015). https://doi.org/10.1109/CVPR.2015.7298594
6. Szegedy, C., Vanhoucke, V., Ioffe, S., Shlens, J., Wojna, Z.: Rethinking the inception architecture for computer vision, 2818–2826 (2016). https://doi.org/10.1109/CVPR.2016.308
7. Algobeans.com: Convolutional Neural Networks (CNN) Introduction. https://algobeans.com/2016/01/26/introduction-to-convolutional-neural-network
8. Googleguide.com: Google search operators. http://www.googleguide.com/advanced_operators_reference.html

Resilient Algorithm Solution for MongoDB Applications

Ayush Jindal[1], Pavi Saraswat[1], Chandan Kapoor[1],
and Punit Gupta[2(✉)]

[1] Amity University, Noida, Uttar Pradesh 201313, India
ayushjindal15030@gmail.com, pavisaraswat@gmail.com,
chandan.kapoor72@gmail.com
[2] JUIT, Wakhnaghat, Shimla, India
punitg07@gmail.com

Abstract. Algorithms and applications for large systems have usually assumed a fairly basic failure model: The computer is a reliable digital machine, with unchanging execution times and rare failures. If failure occurs, recovery can be handled by checkpoint-restart. With the push toward exascale computing, the concern of preserving the reliable, digital machine model will become too costly has become even greater, and we must focus towards Resilient programming to improve algorithms. In this Paper we discuss a Strategy for programming resilience in MongoDB.

Keywords: Resilient · MongoDB · Idempotent · Algorithm · Queries
Non-idempotent

1 Introduction

Errors and random corruptions may affect the result computation of many modern machines. Resilient algorithms [1] and programming is a strategy that deals with network errors and outages and command errors. These are algorithms that are designed to perform in the presence of memory errors.

MongoDB is a leading NoSQL database, an open-source document and distributed database. MongoDB is a database that stores data in JSON-like documents. These documents can vary in structure. Through the MongoDB query language Related information is stored together for fast query access. MongoDB is written in C++ and features auto-sharding and is designed with scalability and high availability in mind.

MongoDB uses dynamic schemas, which allows us to not define the structure first and still being able to create records. You can change the structure of documents simply by deleting existing fields or adding new ones.

By supporting range queries and regular expression searches, MongoDB allows ad hoc queries. Documents in a collection do not need to have same type of information. MongoDB is designed around the principle that data isn't always the same.

© Springer Nature Singapore Pte Ltd. 2018
M. Singh et al. (Eds.): ICACDS 2018, CCIS 906, pp. 55–65, 2018.
https://doi.org/10.1007/978-981-13-1813-9_6

Example of insert, find and update queries in MongoDB.

```
db.users.insert({

  user_id: 'bcd001',

  weight: 85,

  status: 'C'
})
db.users.find()
db.users.update(
  { weight: { $gt: 65 } },
  { $set: { status: 'A' } },
  { multi: false }
)
```

2 Literature Survey

This section of the paper surveys many research papers that what are the problems that MongoDB faces and how resilient data structure can help for it.

[1] proposes the resilient SDN (Software Defined Network) based architecture for Industrial Control Networks and it portrays several SDN based fast technologies. In [2] a design theory is developed for resilient software intensive-systems because of which different communities having different technologies can share a common frame of reference and knowledge (Fig. 1).

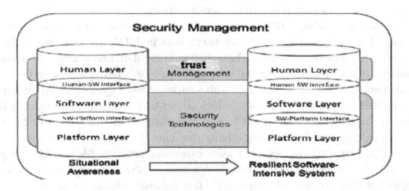

Fig. 1. Resilient software intensive-systems

In [3] Persistency-of-communication (PoC) is been introduced that deals with the communication failure problem of self triggered consensus network. [4] Provides jest of resilient software defined networks for technology related disasters. In [5] focus is mainly on the automatic load balancing of the MongoDB and proposes heat based load balancing at a very low cost (Fig. 2).

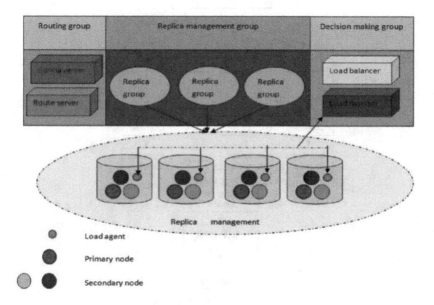

Fig. 2. Load balancing in MongoDB

In [6] modeling style of MongoDB or NoSql is discussed that if normalization is extended as it has less space for document or collection, then how it reduces the query execution time without using join operations. [7] Provides the modeling of the MongoDB with the relational algebra and also analyses the feasibility of moving from SQL database to NoSql. It does provide the optimization of the MongoDB.

[8] Proposes a method which can achieve robustness to transmission errors of Dirac which is an open source video codec (Fig. 3).

[9] Proposes an algorithm that detects fault tolerant termination based of Dijkstra that is previous fault sensitive scheme. [10] Proposes a monitor that can integrate any MongoDB deployment with the help of easy configuration changes results shows the it requires low overhead access. [11] Shows that a document based on NoSql (MongoDB) which uses JSON data and how it explores the merits of NoSql Databases (Fig. 4).

[12] Bhamra has presented a study on various type of distributed NoSql and has compared them based on various performance parameters like scalability, availability, consistency and partitioning tolerance named as CAP theory. Study shows various aspects to select a correct technology of NoSql for your application. The parameters are as follows (Fig. 5):

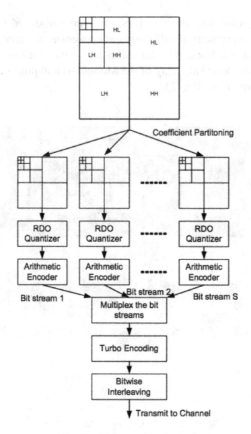

Fig. 3. Video codec method

Data model, Security, Consistency model, Ease of use, Available APIs, Platform dependency, CAP classification, Query model, Available resources such as documentation and community.

3 Proposed Work

This Paper will give you deep understanding on MongoDB concepts needed to deploy a resilient database.

We're going to do UpdateOne resiliently:

```
updateOne({'_id': '2016-06-28'},
          {'$inc': {'counter': 1}},
          upsert=True)
```

Fig. 4. MongoDB security model

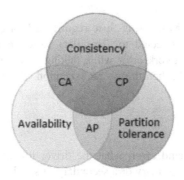

Fig. 5. CAP classification

The operation counts the number of times an event occurred, by incrementing a field named "counter" in a document whose id is today's date. Pass "upsert = True" to create the document if this is the first event in the day.

We identify two errors that could occur while sending our message to MongoDB. These are errors bring contradiction to the data. Resilient algorithms will allow us to eliminate these errors and bring atomicity to our program.

3.1   Transient Errors

When we send his updateOne message to MongoDB, the driver may see a transient error from the network layer, such as a TCP reset or a timeout. The driver cannot tell if the server received the message or not, so we don't know whether his counter was incremented. There are other transient errors that look the same as a network blip. If the primary server goes down, the driver gets a network error the next time it tries to send it a message. This error is brief, since the replica set elects a new primary in a couple seconds. Similarly, if the primary server steps down (it's still functioning but it has resigned its primary role) it closes all connections. The next time the driver sends a message to the server it thought was primary, it gets a network error or a "not master" reply from the server.

Persistent Errors

There might also be a lasting network outage. When the driver first detects this problem it looks like a blip: the driver sends a message and can't read the response. Again, we cannot tell whether the server received the message and incremented the counter or not.

3.2   Command Errors

When the driver sends a message, MongoDB might return a specific error, saying that the command was received but it could not be executed. Perhaps the command was misformatted, the server is out of disk space, or the application isn't authorized.

Handling the Errors

The Server Discovery and Monitoring Spec requires a MongoDB driver to track the state of each server it's connected to. This data structure is called the "topology description". If there's a network error while talking to a server, the driver sets that server's type to "Unknown", then throws an exception. The topology description is:

Server 1: Unknown
Server 2: Secondary
Server 3: Secondary

In the case of a command error, what the driver thinks about the server hasn't changed: if the server was a primary or a secondary, it still is. Thus the driver does not change the state of the server in its topology description, it just throws the exception.

Code that is about resilience tries 5 times or even 10 times.

```
i = 0

while True:

    try:

        do_operation()

        break

    except network error:

        i += 1

        if i == MAX_RETRY_COUNT:

            throw
```

In the case of a network blip, we no longer risks undercounting. Now we risk overcounting, because if the server read our first updateOne message before we got a network error, then the second updateOne message increments the counter a second time.

During a persistent outage, retrying more than once wastes time. After the first network error, the driver marks the primary server "unknown"; when we retry the operation, it blocks while the driver attempts to reconnect, checking twice per second for 30 s. If all that effort within the driver code hasn't succeeded, then trying again from his code, reentering the driver's retry loop, is fruitless.

These are errors bring contradiction to the data. Resilient algorithms will allow us to eliminate these errors and bring atomicity to our program.

4 Results

Idempotent operations are those which have the same outcome whether you do them once or multiple times. If we make all the operations idempotent, we can safely retry them without danger of over counting or any other kind of incorrect data from sending the message twice.

MongoDB has four kinds of operations: find, insert, delete, and update.

4.1   Find

Queries are naturally idempotent.

```
try:
  doc = findOne()
except network err:
  doc = findOne()
```

4.2   Insert

This insert is idempotent. The only warning is, we have assumed we have no unique index on the collection besides the one on _id that MongoDB automatically creates.

```
doc = {_id: ObjectId(), ...}
try:
   insertOne(doc)
except network err:
    try:
        insertOne(doc)
    except DuplicateKeyError:
        pass  # first try worked
    throw
```

4.3   Delete

If we delete one document using a unique value for the key, then doing it twice is just the same as doing it once.

```
try:
   deleteOne({'key': uniqueValue})
except network err:
   deleteOne({'key': uniqueValue})
```

4.4   Update

This Update is Naturally indempotent.

```
updateOne({ '_id': '2016-06-28'}, {'$set':{'sunny': True}},
upsert=True)
```

Dealing with the original non-idempotent updateOne:

```
updateOne({ '_id': '2016-06-28'},

          {'$inc': {'counter': 1}},

          upsert=True)
```

We're going to split it into two parts. Each will be idempotent, and by transforming this into a pair of idempotent operations we'll make it safe to retry.

In Part One, we leave N alone, we just add a token to a "pending" array. We need something unique to go here; an ObjectId does nicely:

```
oid = ObjectId()

try:

  updateOne({ '_id': '2016-06-28'},

            {'$addToSet': {'pending': oid}},

            upsert=True)

except network err:

    try again, then throw
```

For Part Two, with a single message we query for the document by its _id and its pending token, delete the pending token, and increment the counter.

```
try:

    # Search for the document by _id and pending token.
    updateOne({'_id': '2016-06-28',
              'pending': oid},
             {'$pull': {'pending': oid},
              '$inc': {'counter': 1}},
             upsert=False)
except network err:
    try again, then throw
```

So we can safely retry this updateOne. Whether it's executed once or twice, the document ends up the same:

```
{
    _id: '2016-06-28',
    counter: N + 1,
    pending: [ ]
}
```

The Results obtained after resiliently coding are algorithms which do not act redundantly due to error Sect. 3.1 and maintain atomicity by not being affected by error Sect. 3.2.

5   Conclusion

The Algorithm Solution introduced in this research paper, is a modified query that provides a network error reduction alternative. We presented an algorithm solution for using Resilient Programming. It does not use repetitions, which makes it more effective over a for loop error prevention method.

This superiority increases exponentially as the lengthquri of the code increases. In this paper we took queries and converted them into the proposed Resilient queries. Manually Coding for Resilience results in a zero Energy Model, which is desirable.

References

1. Vestin, J., Kassler, A., Akerberg, J.: Resilient software defined networking for industrial control networks. In: 2015 10th International Conference on Information, Communications and Signal Processing (ICICS), Singapore, pp. 1–5 (2015)
2. Rajamäki, J., Pirinen, R.: Critical infrastructure protection: towards a design theory for resilient software-intensive systems. In: 2015 European Intelligence and Security Informatics Conference, Manchester, p. 184 (2015)
3. Senejohnny, D., Tesi, P., De Persis, C.: A jamming-resilient algorithm for self-triggered network coordination. IEEE Trans. Control Netw. Syst. **PP**(99), 1 (2016)
4. Mas Machuca, C., et al.: Technology-related disasters: a survey towards disaster-resilient software defined networks. In: 2016 8th International Workshop on Resilient Networks Design and Modeling (RNDM), Halmstad, pp. 35–42 (2016)
5. Wang, X., Chen, H., Wang, Z.: Research on improvement of dynamic load balancing in MongoDB. In: 2013 IEEE 11th International Conference on Dependable, Autonomic and Secure Computing, Chengdu, pp. 124–130 (2013)
6. Kanade, A., Gopal, A., Kanade, S.: A study of normalization and embedding in MongoDB. In: 2014 IEEE International Advance Computing Conference (IACC), Gurgaon, pp. 416–421 (2014)
7. Zhao, G., Huang, W., Liang, S., Tang, Y.: Modeling MongoDB with relational model. In: 2013 Fourth International Conference on Emerging Intelligent Data and Web Technologies, Xi'an, pp. 115–121 (2013)
8. Myo, T., Fernando, W.A.C.: An error-resilient algorithm based on partitioning of the wavelet transform coefficients for a DIRAC video codec. In: Tenth International Conference on Information Visualisation (IV 2006), London, England, pp. 615–620 (2006)
9. Lai, T.-H., Wu, L.-F.: An (N-1)-resilient algorithm for distributed termination detection. IEEE Trans. Parallel Distrib. Syst. **6**(1), 63–78 (1995)
10. Colombo, P., Ferrari, E.: Enhancing MongoDB with purpose-based access control. IEEE Trans. Dependable Secur. Comput. **14**(6), 591–604 (2017)
11. Jose, B., Abraham, S.: Exploring the merits of NoSQL: a study based on MongoDB. In: 2017 International Conference on Networks and Advances in Computational Technologies (NetACT), Thiruvananthapuram, pp. 266–271 (2017)
12. Bhamra, K.: A comparative analysis of MongoDB and Cassandra. Master's thesis, The University of Bergen (2017)

An Automatic Annotation Scheme for Scene Text Archival Applications

Ayatullah Faruk Mollah[1(✉)], Subhadip Basu[2], and Mita Nasipuri[2]

[1] Department of Computer Science and Engineering,
Aliah University, IIA/27 New Town, Kolkata 700156, India
afmollah@aliah.ac.in
[2] Department of Computer Science and Engineering, Jadavpur University,
Kolkata 700032, India
{subhadip,mnasipuri}@cse.jdvu.ac.in

Abstract. Smart automated management and access to ever increasing number of scene text images is a pressing need to enable individuals and organizations save time and energy. Text embedded in such an image is an important descriptor of the image itself. In this paper, a novel scheme for automatic generation of annotations by OCRing scene text images is presented and the performance is demonstrated on a smart infobase, a knowledge base designed with *trie* data structure. A neuro-fuzzy approach is used for text detection and multi-layer perceptron is incorporated for character recognition. Appropriate post-processing has increased the classification performance from 90.73% to 96.86% (i.e. higher than Tesseract 3.01 that yields 93.51%). Q-gram based *index keys* are generated from the OCR'd text and indexed in the infobase enabling appropriate relevance scoring. Besides 'query text', the system also supports 'query image'. The retrieval engine returns scene images in order of relevance i.e. in decreasing order. The performance is successfully demonstrated on a set of 100 camera captured scene text images. The system works satisfactorily within the present scope of applications.

Keywords: Automatic annotation · Indexing and retrieval · Scene text
Smart access · MLP · TRIE

1 Introduction

Ubiquitous usage of digital camera has led to the pressing need of managing ever increasing number of images. Access to these images needs to be automated enabling the user save time and energy besides making it feasible to him/her. Conventional indexing and retrieval techniques can be categorized into three groups [1]. Firstly, text based annotation in which few key phrases describing the documents are indexed, requiring manual involvement. Secondly, content based image retrieval (CBIR) in which low level color, shape and texture features extracted from the images are indexed. Thirdly, automatic annotation that includes automatic key phrase generation from images. Unlike CBIR, automatic annotation approach does not essentially require an image for retrieval and hence it is considered to be the most preferred. Automatic

© Springer Nature Singapore Pte Ltd. 2018
M. Singh et al. (Eds.): ICACDS 2018, CCIS 906, pp. 66–76, 2018.
https://doi.org/10.1007/978-981-13-1813-9_7

key phrase generation task broadly targets for (i) image containing text and (ii) image without text. Text, being a very important descriptor of the image containing it, has a strong possibility in automatic key phrase generation from optically scanned images for the purpose of efficient access through indexing. Thus, managing scene/document images containing texts, acquired with digital cameras of handheld devices is an active area of research in this domain. Only a few works have been reported in this direction. Feng et al. [2] have reported automatic caption generation technique from news images in two stages. Firstly, they identify what the image and the corresponding article is all about and then they express the content in the form of some words to be used for annotation. Tahir et al. [3] have presented an architecture for paperless operation of an organization. It archives past documents into a secure cloud supporting interactive needs of users. More historical document archival have been reported in [4, 5]. Not only images but also video archival has also been attempted by Lu et al. [6]. They have reported a video summarization and archival system using various features.

Unlike, news images or text-heavy document images, scene images contain limited amount of texts. Besides that, these images suffer from a number of degradation and geometric distortion issues. Arbitrary nature of text and its background is another matter of consideration. As a result, text detection and recognition from such images is the most challenging task for smart access, indexing, retrieval and archival of these image items. It needs to be followed by keyword generation and indexing. This model may support both 'query text' and 'query image' unlike conventional CBIR systems. To the best of our knowledge, automatic annotation following this approach is not adequately studied, mainly due to the complexity of text localization and subsequent recognition. Mishra et al. [7] has followed this approach and presented techniques for text localization and recognition followed by indexing of scene text images. But, for real world scene texts, it is still an open problem. In this paper, a novel scheme towards automatic annotation generation and subsequent indexing with the annotations generated are presented. The paper is organized as follows. In Sect. 2.1, a neuro-fuzzy approach to text detection and recognition is discussed and in Sect. 2.2, post-processing is applied on the OCR'd outputs for necessary correction using context information and post-processing features. Finally, q-gram based keyword generation and indexing using *trie* data structure is discussed and a mechanism for retrieval of images from the knowledge base in order of relevance is presented in Sect. 2.3. An appropriate scoring mechanism is also reported in this section.

2 Current Work

The block diagram of the proposed system is shown in Fig. 1. In the training phase, scene text images are processed to obtain the textual content present inside them. After that, q-gram based *index keys* are generated using the textual contents and indexed in a knowledge base, herein referred to as infobase. In the test phase, either a 'query text' or a 'query image' can be passed. A 'query text' is directly used for generating keywords and related images from the infobase. If a 'query image' containing text is passed, textual content retrieved from the image using the same optical character recognition

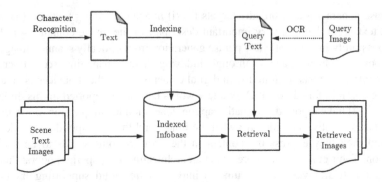

Fig. 1. Block diagram of proposed scene text archival system

(OCR) engine is treated as 'query text'. It may be stated that an archival application would require archival of images along with the infobase and active indexing/retrieval modules.

2.1   Textual Content Extraction

Text Components (TC) of an input image are, at first, localized for the purpose of segmentation and subsequent recognition. Text localization from given images is performed in two phases. In the first phase, the input image $I_{M \times N}$ is divided into some blocks B_i of equal size such that $B_i \cap B_j = \emptyset$ for all $i \neq j$ and $\cup B_i = I_{M \times N}$. Then, each block is classified as background block (BB) or information block (IB) based on an intensity variation based fuzzy block classification technique. In the second phase, connected IBs produce foreground components. These components are classified as Text or Non-text with a two class MLP classifier using various geometric, statistic and gradient features discussed in [8]. Non-text components are discarded and text components are taken to the next phase.

Some of the text components may be reverse text in which texts are written with light colors on relatively dark background. The segmentation module of the present work accepts normal text in which texts are written with dark colors over light background. So, reverse text correction i.e. reversal of reverse text is required. Reverse text detection and correction is carried out by our previously developed technique reported in [9]. After reverse text correction, all components turn to normal texts. These components are binarized with an adaptive method [10] and then segmented into lines, words and characters as described in one of our early works [11].

The present classifier employed for recognition of unknown alphabet patterns is an MLP classifier. Architecturally, the current MLP consists of one input layer, one output layer and one hidden or intermediate layer. The output from every neuron in a layer of the MLP is connected to an input of each neuron in the immediate next layer of the same. Neurons of the input layer of the MLP are all basically dummy neurons as they are used simply to pass on the inputs to the next layer just by computing an identity function. The classifier designed for the present work is trained with the Back Propagation (BP) algorithm. The number of neurons in a hidden layer is also adjusted during its training. According to a study [12], the number of symbols that usually occur in camera captured images is 73 (26 capital letters, 26 small letters, 10 numeric digits and 11 special characters). So, we designed a classifier for 73 classes. In the present case, the number of neurons at the output layer is 73 and the number of neurons at the input layer is the number of features adopted.

In order to recognize the segmented binarized characters, each character is bounded and normalized to a size of 48 × 48 pixels. Although, the shape of a character may be distorted after bounding and normalization, it contributes to objectivity of extracted feature values. So, these steps are essential in the present work. The size of a normalized character is empirically chosen. Some works have been reported to use 32 × 32 pixels [13, 14] and some have worked with 64 × 64 pixels [15]. It may be stated that 32 × 32 pixels size is preferred for numeral recognition and 64 × 64 pixels size is preferred for alphabet recognition. In the current work, both numerals and alphabets are present. So, we have chosen 48 × 48 pixels and obtained a reasonably good accuracy. It may be noted that for this work, we have considered a set of 60 features: (i) 16 octant centroid features [16], (ii) 24 shadow features [16] and (iii) 20 longest run features [17].

2.2 Post-processing for Improved Classification

Some characters are physically similar to each other viz. C(Capital)/c(Small)), 0(Zero)/ O(Capital)/o(Small), S(Capital)/s(Small), U(Capital)/u(Small), V(Capital)/ v(Small), W (Capital)/w(Small), Z(Capital)/z(Small) and I(Capital I)/l(Small L)/1(One). It is observed that majority of the misclassification occurs among these similar looking character classes. Therefore, a post-processing is essential to select the appropriate class.

The block diagram of the post-processing mechanism is shown in Fig. 2. It may be noted that the post-processing module requires the classified symbol and some additional information about the character image. The additional information is collected as post-processing features of the input character image.

As normalization of a character image reduces character image information, post-processing features are extracted from pre-normalized input character images. The features used for post-processing are as follows.

(i) *Vertical Position.* There are some symbols that are similar in shape and they are interpreted on the basis of their vertical position in the text line from which they are segmented as shown in Fig. 3(a-b). For example, 'V' is similar to 'v', 'S' is

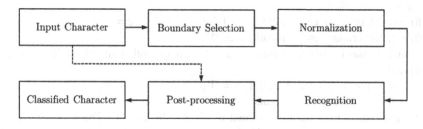

Fig. 2. Block diagram of character level post-processing

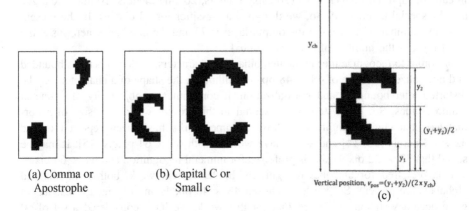

(a) Comma or Apostrophe　　(b) Capital C or Small c

Vertical position, $v_{pos}=(y_1+y_2)/(2 \times y_{ch})$

(c)

Fig. 3. (a–b) Similar shaped characters interpreted on the basis of their vertical position, (c) Illustration of vertical position feature of a character

similar to 's', 'C' is similar to 'c', 'O' is similar to 'o', etc. Vertical position v_{pos} is computed as illustrated in Fig. 3(c). It may be noted that $v_{pos} \in [0.0, 1.0]$. For lower case letters, the values of v_{pos} are smaller than those for upper case letters. Values of v_{pos} are significantly different for comma and apostrophe.

(ii) *Aspect Ratio.* Aspect ratio is one of the important character information. It is lost when a character is normalized to a standard dimension. After bounding the character image, aspect ratio is computed as the ratio of the width of the input character image (w_{ch}) to its height (h_{ch}) and denoted as r_a i.e. $r_a = w_{ch}/h_{ch}$.

(iii) *Coverage Ratio.* Coverage ratio is defined as the ratio of the number of foreground pixels (i.e. the number of black pixels in the present scenario) to the area of the character images computed in terms of the number of pixels. Coverage ratio is denoted as r_c. The character image must be minimally bounded before computing coverage ratio.

Using the above features, post-processing rules are applied for rectification of erroneous classification. The following post-processing rules are designed. Here, c denotes the obtained output class.

- *Rule 1*: Reverting misclassifications of '-'
  For '-', possible misclassified symbols are '.', 'I', and 'l'. The pseudo-code of the rule is given below.
  if((c=='.' || c=='I' || c=='l') && r_a > 1.5 && r_c > 0.7) c = '-';
- *Rule 2:* Reverting misclassifications of 'I'
  Capital 'I' may be misclassified as '.' and '-'. So, the following rule is designed and applied.
  if((c =='.' || c =='-') && r_a < 0.4) c = 'I';
- *Rule 3:* Reverting misclassifications of '.'
  The symbol '.' may be misclassified as 'I', '-', 'l' and '1'. The following comparison may revert the misclassified symbol to the true class.

if((c =='I' || c =='-' || c =='l' || c =='1')
&& fabs(r_a−1.0) < 0.35 && r_c > 0.75) c = '.';
Here, fabs returns the absolute value in floating point scale.

- *Rule 4:* Case conversion

  As the upper case and lower case letters of some symbols look similar, they are post-processed on the basis of vertical position, v_{pos} as shown below.

  float t = 0.33;
  if(c =='v' && v_{pos} > t) c = 'V';
  if(c =='c' && v_{pos} > t) c = 'C';
  if(c =='s' && v_{pos} > t) c = 'S';
  if(c =='o' && v_{pos} > t) c = 'O';
  if(c =='V' && v_{pos} <= t) c = 'v';
  if(c =='C' && v_{pos} <= t) c = 'c';
  if(c =='S' && v_{pos} <= t) c = 's';
  if(c =='O' && v_{pos} <= t) c = 'o';

2.3 Indexing and Retrieval

Classified symbols are reorganized in the form of words. Assume, a word has n number of symbols where $n \in N$, the set of natural numbers. Words with number of symbols less than 3 are rejected and the rest of the words are considered as *keywords*. These keywords are indexed with a q-gram based indexing technique. According to this technique, keys of various lengths are generated out of the keyword such that $q \leq L_{key} \leq n$ where L_{key} is the length of a key. Thus, we get a total of $\sum_{i=q}^{n} (n+1-i) = \frac{1}{2} \times (n+1-q) \times (n+2-q)$ number of keys. All such keys, referred to as *index key* are used for indexing. In Fig. 4, a keyword and the generated *index keys* are shown. It must be noted that *index keys* are made case invariant. Similar to indexing, *index keys* are generated from the search key(s) and for each *index key*, we get a score. These scores are added and thus the retrieved images are ranked with percentage of confidence.

When a 'query text' is passed to the retrieval system, *index keys* are generated from the 'query text' and for each key we get a score i.e. $1/(l - g + 1)$, where l is the length of 'query text' and g is the length of an *index key*. These scores are summed up and thus

J	A	D	A	V	P	U	R	n=8, q=3

L_{key}	Keys
8	JADAVPUR
7	JADAVPU ADAVPUR
6	JADAVP ADAVPU DAVPUR
5	JADAV ADAVP DAVPU AVPUR
4	JADA ADAV DAVP AVPU VPUR
3	JAD ADA DAV AVP VPU PUR

Fig. 4. Generation of *index keys* from a search key (L_{key} denotes the length of an index key)

the retrieved images are ranked with a confidence score in the range [0.0, 1.0]. Retrieved images are listed in the descending order of confidence scores. The main advantage of q-gram based indexing and retrieval system is: (i) Even when the recognition accuracy is not good enough, such technique works satisfactorily, and (ii) Scoring for measuring relevance becomes easy.

3   Experimental Results

As the current work is designed for scene text archival application framework, performance of the proposed system greatly depends upon the text detection and recognition performance. While performance of text detection [8] and segmentation [11] are reported previously, the performance of classification, post-processing and retrieval are analyzed and reported in this paper. To train our OCR engine, we have used a character dataset containing 16320 characters. These samples are randomly divided into training set and test set in 1:1 ratio (i.e. $\lceil n_s/2 \rceil$ and $\lfloor n_s/2 \rfloor$ where n_s is the no. of samples). Thus, we get 8178 training samples and 8142 test samples. The database contains wide variations of the symbols. Symbols are of various fonts and font-sizes. There are normal, bold, italic as well as their combinations. Some symbols have major variation in shape, e.g. {4, 4}, {ᵬ, ᵬ}, {ʼ, ʼ}, {ᵬ, ₵, ᵬ}, etc.

To ensure an optimal performance of the present MLP, several runs of BP algorithm with learning rate (η) = 0.8 and momentum term (α) = 0.7 are executed by varying the number of neurons in the hidden layer until the number giving an optimal recognition performance is identified. For this, a plot showing the variation of the recognition performance on the test set with increasing number of hidden layer neurons may be referred (Fig. 5).

Figure 5 shows the variation of the recognition performance of MLP with increase in the number of neurons in its hidden layer. It is required to fix up the number of neurons in the hidden layer of MLP so that it can show the optimal recognition performance on the test set. Recognition performances of the MLP, as observed from the curve initially rise as the number of neurons in the hidden layer is increased and fall

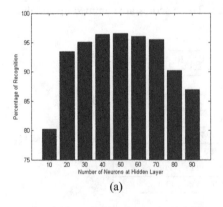
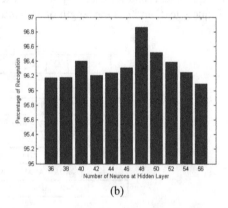

(a)   (b)

Fig. 5. Recognition performance with varying number of neurons at the hidden layer

after the same crosses some limiting value. It reflects the fact that for some fixed training and test sets, learning and generalization abilities of the MLP improve as the number of neurons in its hidden layer increases up to certain limiting value and any further increase in the number of neurons in the hidden layer thereafter degrades the abilities. It is called as over-fitting problem. A close observation on percentage of recognition is made between 36–56 neurons of the hidden layer in Fig. 5. The optimal recognition performance of the MLP is observed at a point, where the number of neurons in its hidden layer is set to 48. So, the number of neurons in the hidden layer of the MLP is finally fixed to 48.

It is found that post-processing drastically improves the recognition accuracy. Optimum recognition accuracy of 96.86% (shown in Fig. 5) is obtained with post-processing. If post-processing is disabled, it is found that the recognition accuracy drops to 90.73% only. A comparison of recognition performance obtained with Template matching [12], Tesseract [12] on a similar dataset is shown in Table 1. The number of classes considered here is 73. Percentage of recognition with template matching is comparatively less due to absence of post-processing whereas Tesseract is heavily post-processed.

Table 1. Comparison of recognition accuracy among template matching, tesseract and the present MLP based technique on the same character dataset

Classifier	Number of test patterns	Number of correct classification	% of recognition
Template matching [12] (without post-processing)	15807	13089	82.81
Tesseract 3.01 [12] (with post-processing)	15807	14781	93.51
MLP (with post-processing)	8142	7886	96.86

Some correctly classified samples from the test set are *(comma), 2(two), 3(three), C(capital c), a(a), a(a), s(small s) and r(r). Some misclassified samples are 5('s' misclassified as '5'), K('k' misclassified as 'x') and G('G' misclassified as 'C'). It may be stated that the shape of the samples that are misclassified is heavily deviated from the actual/expected shape. Number of some symbols, such as '#', 'q', 'z' etc. is very less. As a result, MLP is not properly trained for these symbols.

The retrieval engine produces highest score i.e. 1.0 if the entire 'query text' is found inside an image. It returns the lowest sore i.e. 0.0 when none of the *index keys* of q-grams are found in any image of the infobase. Selection of the value of q is an important issue. The higher the value of q, the lower the capacity of substring search and vice-versa. For instance, if n = q (i.e. when the length of a query and the *index key* are same), the entire query is searched into the infobase. When q = 1, it implies that search is performed at character level which may not be desirable. In case of *trie* data structure, a reasonably low value of q is suitable for this type of search from infobase. In the current work, q = 3 is taken and it is found that access to indexed images is quite acceptable. It is also observed that keywords obtained from OCR'd output greatly affect the performance of smart indexing and retrieval. Hence, OCR performance is a key factor of performance of the proposed system. The current performance of scene text OCR and indexing engine on a set of 100 camera captured scene text images is reasonably acceptable. Figure 6 shows the retrieved images for some given queries.

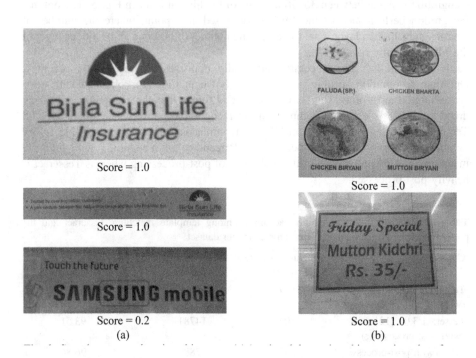

Fig. 6. Sample query and retrieved images. (a) 'sun' and the retrieved images in order of score of relevance, (b) 'mutton' and the retrieved images in order of score of relevance (only 3 and 2 occurrences are found respectively because there are no more occurrences of 3-gram index key in the infobase)

4   Conclusion

In this paper, a novel scheme for automatic generation of annotations from scene text images is presented for the purpose of smart access to such images through indexing and retrieval that in turn enables archival applications. As text is a powerful descriptor of text embedded images, the recognized texts have been used for indexing and retrieval of those images as well. Hence, emphasis is given for recognition of textual content from scene text images and the development of a knowledge base to efficiently index/retrieve the OCR'd output by implementing *trie* data structure. Appropriate post-processing followed by an MLP based classification engine has increased the OCR performance from 90.73% to 96.86%. This performance is higher than Tesseract 3.01 and Template matching that yield 82.81% and 93.51% respectively. Q-gram based *index keys* are generated and indexed in such a way that enables appropriate scoring indicating relevance to an image of infobase with the given 'query text'. Besides query by text, the present system also supports query by image. In that case, the query image will be recognized first and then the recognized information is considered as query text. The retrieval engine returns scene images in order of relevance i.e. in decreasing order. The performance is successfully demonstrated on a set of 100 camera captured scene text images. Although, our system works satisfactorily within the present scope of applications, there are scope of further improvements. More robust post-processing rules can be designed for improving the recognition accuracy. Scene text images having complex background and text artifacts should be taken into consideration.

References

1. Zhang, D., Islam, M.M., Lu, G.: A review on automatic image annotation techniques. Pattern Recogn. **45**(1), 346–362 (2012)
2. Feng, Y., Lapata, M.: Automatic caption generation for news images. IEEE Trans. Pattern Anal. Mach. Intell. **35**(4), 797–812 (2013)
3. Tahir, H., Tahir, R., McDonald-Maier, K.: A novel private cloud document archival system architecture based on ICmetrics. In: Fourth International Conference on Emerging Security Technologies (EST), pp. 102–106 (2013)
4. Baechler, M., Bloechle, J.L., Ingold, R.: Semi-automatic annotation tool for medieval manuscripts. In: International Conference on Frontiers in Handwriting Recognition, pp. 182–187 (2010)
5. Messaoud, I.B., Abed, H.E.: Automatic annotation for handwritten historical documents using markov models. In: International Conference on Frontiers in Handwriting Recognition (ICFHR), pp. 381–386. IEEE (2010)
6. Lu, S., King, I., Lyu, M.R.: A novel video summarization framework for document preparation and archival applications. In: IEEE Aerospace Conference, pp. 1–10 (2005)
7. Mishra, A., Karteek, A., Jawahar. C.V.: Image retrieval using textual cues. In: Proceedings of the IEEE International Conference on Computer Vision (ICCV), pp. 3040–3047 (2013)
8. Mollah, A.F., Basu, S., Nasipuri, M.: Text detection from camera captured images using a novel fuzzy-based technique. In: Proceedings of the Third International Conference on Emerging Applications of Information Technology (EAIT), pp. 291–294. IEEE (2012)
9. Mollah, A.F., Basu, S., Nasipuri, M.: Handheld device-based character recognition system for camera captured images. Int. J. Image Graph. **13**(4), 1350016 (2013)
10. Mollah, A.F., Basu, S., Nasipuri, M.: Handheld mobile device based text region extraction and binarization of image embedded text documents. J. Intell. Syst. **22**(1), 25–47 (2013)
11. Mollah, A.F., Basu, S., Nasipuri, M.: Segmentation of camera captured business card images for mobile devices. Int. J. Comput. Sci. Appl. **1**(1), 33–37 (2010)
12. Mollah, A.F., Majumder, N., Basu, S., Nasipuri, M.: Design of an optical character recognition system for camera-based handheld devices. Int. J. Comput. Sci. Issues **8**(4), 283–289 (2011)
13. Basu, S., Das, N., Sarkar, R., Kundu, M., Nasipuri, M., Basu, D.K.: An MLP based approach for recognition of handwritten Bangla numerals. In: Second Indian International Conference on Artificial Intelligence (IICAI), pp. 407–417 (2005)

14. Das, N., Mollah, A. F., Saha, S., Haque, S.S.: Handwritten arabic numeral recognition using a multi-layer perceptron. In: National Conference on Recent Trends in Information Systems (ReTIS-06), pp. 200–203 (2006)
15. Basu, S., Das, N., Sarkar, R., Kundu, M., Nasipuri, M., Basu, D.K.: Handwritten Bangla alphabet recognition using an MLP based classifier. In: 2nd National Conference on Computer Processing of Bangla, pp. 285–291 (2005)
16. Basu, S., Das, N., Sarkar, R., Kundu, M., Nasipuri, M., Basu, D.K.: A hierarchical approach to recognition of handwritten Bangla characters. Pattern Recogn. **42**(7), 1467–1484 (2009)
17. Basu, S., Das, N., Sarkar, R., Kundu, M., Nasipuri, M., Basu, D.K.: A novel framework for automatic sorting of postal documents with multi-script address blocks. Pattern Recogn. **43** (10), 3507–3521 (2010)

FDSS: Fuzzy Based Decision Support System for Aspect Based Sentiment Analysis in Big Data

A. Jenifer Jothi Mary$^{(\boxtimes)}$ and L. Arockiam

Department of Computer Science, St. Joseph's College (Autonomous),
Tiruchirappalli, Tamil Nadu, India
ajenifer.jothi@gmail.com

Abstract. Sentiment analysis (SA) is an pioneering computing technology to advance the decision making process. Social media is used to bind the people by sharing their opinions. Opinion is in the free form of reviews or comments on micro-blogging sites such as online discussion forums, Twitter, Facebook and other different types of social networking sites. Fuzzy logic is one of the multi-valued logic. It considers the reasoning which is closer to the actual in lieu with fixed and exact. This research integrates fuzzy system to make business decisions in the proposed Fuzzy based Decision Support System (FDSS). The FDSS system uses the results of the analysis of the online sentiments and makes decisions based on some fuzzy rules. The fuzzy rules are defined to aid in the decision making process by classifying the sentiments of the aspects of a product. The Twitter mobile product dataset is used for experimental analysis and results show that the proposed FDSS system produces better results for decision making.

Keywords: Sentiment analysis · Opinion · Fuzzy logic · Fuzzy rules
Non-opinionated sentences · Big data

1 Introduction

Online social media and web sites have added new dimensions in the production and propagation of information and news in the internet world. Social media sites proliferate the information by sharing the reviews and comments in the social interaction. It replaces the traditional way of communication with an interactive environment. These user generated contents help companies to perform analytics to determine people's opinion and moods. These commercial companies collect the online product reviews, use sentiment analysis to mine the opinions about a product or event and summarize the sentiments from the reviews using some summarization techniques. Based on the result of the opinion summarization, appropriate decision will be made out of it.

Normally, people make decisions based on a situation which are closer to logic is called as logical decisions. But fuzzy logic loosens this strictness of the condition by considering the most probable situation or condition. Fuzzy logic helps to manage the heterogeneous and vague information. It uses the rule based inference decision making process which will make the decision simpler as well as giving benefits to investors.

© Springer Nature Singapore Pte Ltd. 2018
M. Singh et al. (Eds.): ICACDS 2018, CCIS 906, pp. 77–87, 2018.
https://doi.org/10.1007/978-981-13-1813-9_8

2 Preliminaries

A list of terms related to fuzzy logic is defined in this chapter. Fuzzy Logic can be defined as follows. Let U be a set, called as Universe. It is defined by:

A fuzzy set λ on U is defined by its membership function $\lambda : U \rightarrow [0, 1]$ [1]. For any $k \in U$, the $\lambda(k)$ represents the extent to which the k belongs to the fuzzy set λ. The fuzzy set $\lambda(k)$ is defined as,

$$\lambda(k) = \{(k, \lambda(k)), k\varepsilon U\} \tag{1}$$

The fuzzy set U is discrete. For discrete fuzzy sets, $\lambda(k)$ can be written as,

$$\lambda(k) = \sum_{i=1}^{n} (\lambda(k_i))/k_i) \tag{2}$$

where n is the number of elements in U.

Let U be the universe set and S be the set of all possible parameters with respect to U. Usually, the parameters can be attributes, characteristics, or properties of aspects in U. In this research, it is taken as sentiments related to each aspect. (U, S) will be called a soft space. According to [2], a soft set can be defined as

A pair (F, X) is called as a soft set over U, where $X \subseteq S$ and F is a mapping given by $F : X \rightarrow P(U)$.

Suppose that, there are n aspects in the universe U given by $U = \{a_1, a_2, \ldots \ldots, a_n\}$ and m sentiments related with n aspects $S = \{s_1, s_2, \ldots \ldots, s_m\}$ is a set of parameters. The aspects taken for consideration are *Cost, Picture, Battery, Screen, Color and Sound* and the related sentiment words found are *awesome, not good, fantastic, really expensive, nice and not long*. In this case, defining a soft set means to point out nice color, awesome sound and so on. The soft set (F, S) may describe the 'attractiveness of the mobile phone' that Mr. A is going to buy. Suppose, $F(a_1) = \{s_4\}$, $F(a_5) = \{s_2, s_5\}$ $F(a_2) = \{s_1, s_2, s_3, s_5\}$, $F(a_3) = \{s_1, s_2, s_6\}$, $F(a_4) = \{s_1, s_2, s_3, s_5\}$ and $F(a_6) = \{\}$. Then, the soft set (F, S) is a parameterized family $\{F(s)\}$ for all the six subsets of U and give us a collection of approximate descriptions of an aspect. $F(a_1) = \{s_4\}$ means aspect a_1 is 'awesome' which is represented in Fig. 1.

Consider the set of sentiment words in the AFINN sentiment lexicon as the universal set U, a linguistic term $l_i \in \{l_i, l_2, \ldots l_n\}$ linguistically observed from the universal set U.

The inputs to the membership functions $\lambda_{FS}(k)$ are to be numeric values and should contain the real meanings of the linguistic terms. The initial sentiment value is for aspects of the Universe which has already enquired from the AFINN sentiment lexicon. In the proposed FDSS system, the fuzzy partitions are defined as [Strong Negative (SN), Negative (N), Medium (M), Positive (P), Strong Positive (SP)], which can be defined as the linguistic terms $\{l_1, l_2, \ldots, l_n\}$. By this way, the membership functions with crisp numerical values are defined and ascertained by using aforementioned fuzzy partitions.

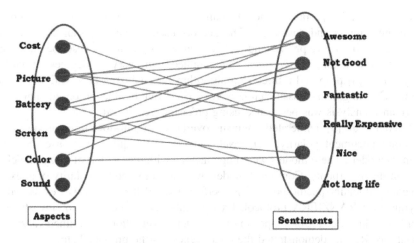

Fig. 1. Aspect and sentiment relationship

Since the type of the input data and the predefined linguistic terms would frequently create random sentiment combinations that fitted in a Gaussian distribution. The given Gaussian function is applied to define the membership functions [3].

$$Gaussian(k; \lambda, \sigma) = e^{-\frac{(k-\lambda)^2}{2\sigma^2}} \tag{3}$$

Where k is the aspect selected, σ is the standard deviation and λ is mean of the aspect k which can be defined as fixed values to be line with the theoretical average distribution of sentiment values. The parameter λ points the position of the center of the peak dynamically trained by the collected twitter textual data and the theoretical linguistic factors, thus to aid in decision making.

With the reference to the AFINN lexicon [4], the early sentiment values of a particular aspect are considered as the input for the defined membership functions, the parameters of the Gaussian function and different linguistic terms are defined based on the label of the selected AFINN lexicon.

3   Related Works

Suresh et al. [5] explained fuzzy clustering model for analyzing social media data related to the sentiments of a product. The authors collected the dataset for 12 months and a comparative analysis was performed with K Means and Expectation Maximization algorithms. The metrics execution time, precision, accuracy and recall were calculated. Indhuja et al. [6] proposed a new approach for extracting features from reviews. The authors classified the features using feature based method for sentiment classification. The proposed method was reviewed and the outcome proved that fuzzy logic performed well in SA.

Reshma et al. [7] proposed a novel technique to understand the aspects of products from manufacturers and customers. The authors used Naïve Bayesian classifier and fuzzy method to retrieve precise and realistic value of opinion. To describe vague and imprecise information, Fuzzy rules were applied with varying degrees of values. Supriya et al. [8] proposed a three step algorithm for analyzing tweets. Entity identification, Cleaning and Classification were carried out by the proposed algorithm. Performance analysis was performed using precision, recall and accuracy.

Dragoni et al. [9] deliberated linguistic overlaps in multi-domain environment for computing document polarity. SenticNet and General Inquirer were used to build sentiment models. These models were implemented with the support of fuzzy models to represent the uncertainty. Combined models were used to find the polarity of a text by aggregating domain-specific polity. The performance of the system was evaluated by applying the DRANZIERA protocol. Experiments laid foundations for investigating the enriched knowledge for supporting the model construction and refined fuzzy representations. Results demonstrated the effectiveness of the presented strategy.

Wu et al. [10] presented a fuzzy logic-based text classification applied on social media data. Hurricane Sandy 2012 related Twitter texts were used for experimentation. Authors also used manually labeled data subset and extract seven features for input. They processed Tweets used NLP techniques such as stemming, lemmatization for preprocessing. The proposed method was used to classify the Twitter text using fuzzy defuzzification methods. The centroid method was used in the fuzzy logic for comparing other defuzzification methods. Results showed that the proposed method was more suitable to classify the relevant and irrelevant text in Tweets.

Anuradha et at. [11] presented a feature based sentiment classification method. It had two phases namely, pre-processing phase and classification phases. In classification phase, Naïve bayes method was used for training the classifier and Fuzzy logic was used for evaluating each sentence in the test set. Classification was improved to provide the concise summary of the product. Fuzzy linguistic hedges and sentence ranking functions were incorporated into the sentiment classification tasks and for weighting the sentences respectively. The proposed system produced a high accuracy in both binary and fine grained sentiment classifications of user reviews.

Muhammad et al. [12] presented a fuzzy aspect based opinion classification system to extract aspects from user opinions. The fuzzy rules were built from frequent nouns using FURIA algorithm. A three-stage fuzzy aspect based opinion classification was used to classify the opinions of aspects. Experiments were conducted on real world datasets taken from restaurants and hotels reviews. FURIA algorithm achieved 90.12% accuracy on restaurants dataset as compared to other fuzzy classifiers. The same FLR algorithm achieved 86.02% accuracy on hotels dataset. Results proved that the proposed system was effective in aspect extraction as well as improved the classification accuracy.

Jefferson et al. [13] proposed a fuzzy rule based system for polarity classification. The proposed approach achieved the same level of performance compared with the accuracy of Naïve Bayes (NB) and Decision Trees (DT) machine learning algorithms. The experimental results indicated that the proposed approach performed marginally better than the NB and DT algorithms. The outputs reflected different intensities of sentiment without using a larger number of classes.

4   The Proposed System

The System architecture represents the framework in Fig. 2 and the Algorithm FDSS presents the procedure of the FDSS System. The workflow presents the flow and explain es the steps in the proposed system [9].

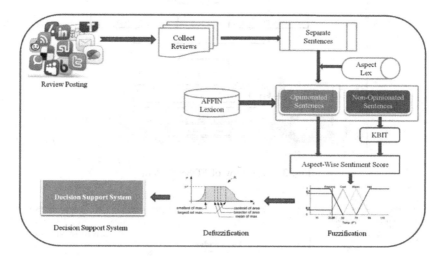

Fig. 2. The architecture of the FDSS

In this architecture, two lexicons namely, Aspect and AFINN lexicons are used for parsing an aspect and sentiment word identification. By using AFINN lexicon, the sentences are classified as opinionated and non- opinionated. The sentiment scores are calculated by adding these two types of sentences and passed as an input to the fuzzy inference system.

a. Workflow of FDSS

The workflow of the FDSS system is presented in Fig. 3. This working methodology combines the result of the aspect based parsing technique [10] KBIT. The fuzzy inference rules are designed for each aspect of the product. The given input is verified with these inference rules and if match occurs, the result is presented to aid in decision making process.

b. Methodology of the FDSS System

Fuzzy logic is a mapping technique to map the flow of information from an input space to an output space, with a list of fuzzy rules (if-then statements). The rules are evaluated in parallel. These rules express the set of conditions about any specific event. This section explains the input, output and fuzzy rules developed for the proposed System. The FDSS system consists of three linguistic variables, one output variable and 27 fuzzy rules as shown in the following Fig. 4.

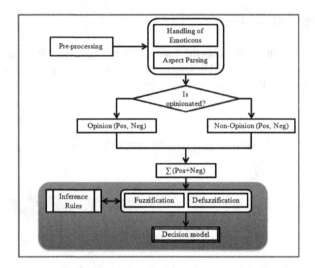

Fig. 3. Workflow of FDSS System

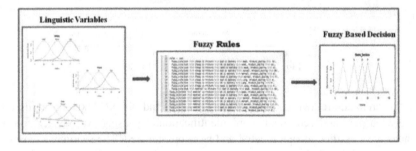

Fig. 4. Methodology of the Fuzzy based Decision Support System

The proposed FDSS system is working in five stages. They are:

   i. Setting up of the Universe
  ii. Defining the Linguistic variables
 iii. Deriving Fuzzy rules
 iv. Building the Model
  v. Creating Fuzzy inference and defuzzification.

i. Setting up the Universe

In the first stage, a range to the proposed system has to be defined for input. It acts as a boundary in which all values should fall. If the given input variables are in different ranges, normalization has to be performed. In the proposed system, the universe is set to 0 to 100. Though the sentiment scores of each aspect is high, normalization is carried out using the following equation,

$$FIP(a_i) = \left| \frac{SC(a_i)}{Count(s)} \right| \times 100 \qquad (4)$$

Where,

FIP (a_i) – Fuzzy input for aspect a_i

SC(a_i) - Sentiment Score of Each Aspect a_i

Count (s) - Total number of sentences in the data set.

ii. Defining Linguistic variables

A fuzzy set normally defines linguistic or membership variables based on the inherent intelligence of the human. Fuzzy rules are constructed based on the values of the linguistic variables. The membership value of the fuzzy set is defined between 0 and 1. The membership function maps an input value by relating to its appropriate membership value with the given fuzzy set. A linguistic variable has three information namely, name of the variable (N), term set of the variable (T(N)) and the universe of discourse (U).

The proposed FDSS system comprises of three linguistic variables namely, Battery, Picture and Cost. The term set of a linguistic variable 'Battery' is defined as

$$T(\text{Battery}) = \{\text{Weak, Normal, Long}\}$$

The range of the linguistic values of the variable **"Battery"** are [0–30], [30–70] and [70–100] respectively. This means that if the sentiment value of the aspect battery is less than or equal to 30 then, it is categorized as 'Weak', if it is between 30 to 70, it is 'Normal' and if it is 90, it is 'Long'.

Likewise, the linguistic variable **"Picture"** is categorized as 'Bad', if it is 60, it is 'Ok' and if it is 80, it is 'Good'. The other linguistic variable **"Cost"** is categorized as 'Cheap', if it is 60, it is 'Nominal' and if it is 80, it is 'Costly'.

The fourth linguistic variable **"Product_Rating"** is the fuzzy output variable that holds the five values as [0–15], [15–35], [35–55], [55–75] and [75–100] respectively (Figs. 5 and 6).

If (linguistic Variable 1 is Value 1) and

(linguistic Variable 1 is Value 1) and ... then

(Output Variable is OP1)

Fig. 5. Rule for FDSS system

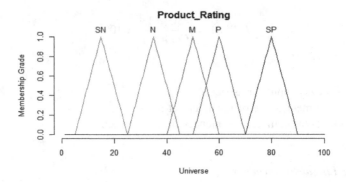

Fig. 6. Membership function for the linguistic variable "Product_Rating"

iii. Fuzzy Rules

Fuzzy rules are derived by defining fuzzy variables and their values. It is nothing but the conditional if-then structure to perform certain action. The fuzzy rules for the proposed FDSS system are in the following form as shown in Fig. 7.

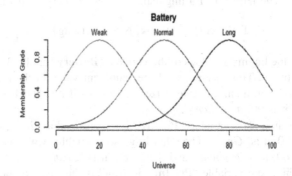

Fig. 7. Membership function for the linguistic variable "Battery"

In FDSS, the rules are designed in such way to help the decision making process of the production companies or individual users. For example, some rules are given below.

- If the Battery is 'Weak' and the Picture is 'Ok' and the Cost is 'Nominal', then the Product_Rating is 'Medium'.
- If the Battery is 'Normal' and the Picture is 'Bad' and the Cost is 'Costly, then the Product_Rating is 'Strong Negative'.
- If the Battery is 'Long' and the Picture is 'Ok' and the Cost is 'Costly', then the Product_Rating is 'Strong Positive'.

iv. Building the Fuzzy Model

If the fuzzy rules and the linguistic variables related to the fuzzy system are well-defined, then the fuzzy model can be built appropriately. The fuzzy model for Product_Rating linguistic variable is shown in Fig. 8.

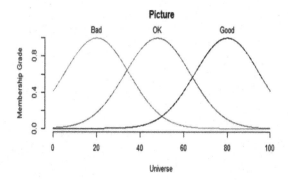

Fig. 8. Membership function for the linguistic variable "Picture"

The plot for the other linguistic variables "Battery", "Picture" and "Cost" are presented in Figs. 7, 8 and 9.

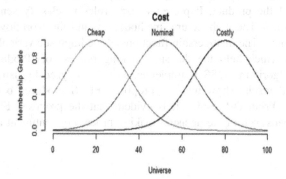

Fig. 9. Membership function for the linguistic variable "Cost"

v. FDSS based Decision Making

Fuzzy inference is a process of combining membership functions with the fuzzy rules to obtain a fuzzy output that helps in decision making. Using the proposed FDSS system, the linguistic variable 'Product_Rating' is inferred. Fuzzy inference process involves in specifying values for the linguistic variables 'Battery', 'Picutre' and 'cost' and inferring the linguistic variable 'Product_Rating'.

Case 1: Consider the sentiment score of the aspects Battery, Picture and Cost are 30 then the fuzzy inference system infers the linguistic variable 'Product_Rating' as *'Strong Negative'* which is shown in Fig. 10. The process of defuzzification produces the defuzzified Product_Rating as '15.02288' ≈ '15'.

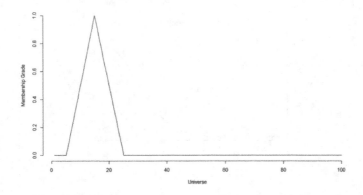

Fig. 10. Inferred membership for the linguistic variable 'Product_Rating'

5   Conclusion

A fuzzy based decision support system, FDSS is proposed for decision making based on the aspects of the product. It presents fuzzy rules to classify sentiments of the aspects of a product. The architecture, methodology and the workflow of the FDSS system are presented. The membership functions of the linguistic variables are defined. The fuzzy rules which help the decision making process of 'Product_Rating' are explained. The algorithm FDSS is implemented and analyzed by using the RStudio tool. The derived results show that the proposed FDSS produces better results for decision making. From the results, it is evident that the proposed FDSS system is simple but performs well in the decision making process of sentiment analysis in Big Data.

References

1. Molodtsov, D.: Soft set theory—first results. Comput. Math. Appl. **37**(4–5), 19–31 (1999)
2. Maji, P.K., Biswas, R., Roy, A.R.: Intuitionistic fuzzy soft sets. J. Fuzzy Math. **9**(3), 677–692 (2001)
3. Bing, L., Chan, K.C.: A fuzzy logic approach for opinion mining on large scale twitter data. In: IEEE/ACM 7th International Conference on Utility and Cloud Computing (UCC), pp. 652–657 (2014)
4. Nielsen, F.A.: A new ANEW: evaluation of a word list for sentiment analysis in microblogs, pp. 1–6 (2011)

5. Suresh, H.: An unsupervised fuzzy clustering method for twitter sentiment analysis. In: IEEE International Conference on Computation System and Information Technology for Sustainable Solutions (CSITSS), pp. 80–85 (2016)

6. Indhuja, K., Reghu, R.P.: Fuzzy logic based sentiment analysis of product review documents. In: IEEE First International Conference on Computational Systems and Communications (ICCSC), pp. 18–22 (2014)

7. Reshma, V., John, A.: Aspect based summarization of reviews using naïve Bayesian classifier and fuzzy logic. In: IEEE International Conference on Control Communication and Computing India (ICCC), pp. 617–621 (2015)

8. Supriya, B.N., Kallimani, V., Prakash, S., Akki, C.B.: Twitter sentiment analysis using binary classification technique. In: Vinh, P.C., Barolli, L. (eds.) ICTCC 2016. LNICST, vol. 168, pp. 391–396. Springer, Cham (2016). https://doi.org/10.1007/978-3-319-46909-6_36

9. Dragoni, M., Petrucci, G.: A fuzzy-based strategy for multi-domain sentiment analysis. Int. J. Approx. Reason. **93**, 59–73 (2018)

10. Wu, K.Y., Zhou, M.C., Lu, X.S., Huang, L.: A fuzzy logic-based text classification method for social media data. In: IEEE International Conference on Systems, Man, and Cybernetics (SMC), pp. 1942–1947 (2017)

11. Anuradha, G., Joel, D.J.: Fuzzy based summarization of product reviews for better analysis. Indian J. Sci. Technol. **9**(31), 1–9 (2016)

12. Afzaal, M., Usman, M., Fong, A.C.M., Fong, S., Zhuang, Y.: Fuzzy aspect based opinion classification system for mining tourist reviews. Adv. Fuzzy Syst. **2016**, 1–14 (2016)

13. Jefferson, C., Liu, H., Cocea, M.: Fuzzy approach for sentiment analysis. In: IEEE International Conference on Fuzzy Systems (FUZZ-IEEE), pp. 1–6 (2017)

14. Mary, A.J.J., Arockiam, L.: ASFuL: aspect based sentiment summarization using fuzzy logic. In: IEEE International Conference on Algorithms, Methodology, Models and Applications in Emerging Technologies (ICAMMAET), pp. 1–5 (2017)

15. Mary, A.J.J., Arockiam, L.: Aspect based parsing for sentiment analysis in big data. J. Comput. Sci. Mob. Appl. **5**(12), 1–7 (2017)

Load Adaptive and Priority Based MAC Protocol for Body Sensors and Consumer Electronic (CE) Devices

Deepshikha[(⊠)] and Siddhartha Chauhan

Computer Science and Engineering Department, NIT Hamirpur (H.P.),
Hamirpur, India
deepshikha@live.in, siddharthachauhan1@gmail.com

Abstract. Wireless body area network can potentially become the future of the
e-health applications with the advent of technological advancements in the
sensors devices and consumer electronic (CE) devices. The inclusion of CE
devices in a WBAN can equip them with the capability of determining the
geographical and environmental context. These contexts can then be used to
make informed decisions about the criticality of sensed physiological parameters
and also in carrying out data filtering and data compression. The first step
towards the inclusion of CE devices in WBAN is having a MAC protocol which
supports CE devices in addition to body sensors. In this paper, we have proposed a MAC protocol for WBAN, which supports body sensors devices and
CE applications for remote healthcare monitoring simultaneously. Performance
evaluation by simulation shows significant improvement in packet delivery
ratio, average latency and energy consumption, over existing protocols.

Keywords: Sensors · MAC protocols · WBAN · Remote health monitoring
CE devices

1 Introduction

Recent technological advancements in sensors devices have marked the beginning of a
new era in the field of remote health monitoring. The regular monitoring of a patient's
physiological parameters can now be performed remotely without the need of hospi-
talization which is helpful in saving valuable time and money [1]. The remote health
monitoring is made possible by the use of Wireless Body Area Networks (WBAN).
A WBAN is a network of sensor devices, actuators and consumer electronic (CE) devices which are applied in or around the human body. These devices sense and transmit
data to a special, resource rich node known as the coordinator node (PDA/
Smartphone), which in turn forwards the data to the main server through internet.

The sensors generate data packets with different constraints in a health monitoring
environment. In transportation of these data packets, a suitable MAC protocol can play
a vital role in efficient packet transmission and reducing energy consumption. In
addition to physiological parameters measured by various body sensors the contextual
data received from CE devices like location sensors, environmental sensors and fall

© Springer Nature Singapore Pte Ltd. 2018
M. Singh et al. (Eds.): ICACDS 2018, CCIS 906, pp. 88–97, 2018.
https://doi.org/10.1007/978-981-13-1813-9_9

detection system etc. can greatly aid in determination of patient's exact health condition. For example, a sudden rise in person's heart rate and body temperature is an alarming situation but for a person who is exercising in gymnasium, it is normal to have elevated heart rate and body temperature. This distinction can only be made if the geographical context is utilized while making the decision. Therefore, the addition of CE devices to the WBAN can offer better results for person's health detection in remote healthcare monitoring applications. The rate and type of data generated by body sensors and CE devices is different, for example the body sensors generate and send data periodically at low data rate whereas CE devices generate sporadic and bursty traffic [3, 12]. The use of CE devices has also been proposed in [2] but the non-availability of specialized MAC protocol has not been addressed. Most of the existing MAC protocols focus on the transmission of traffic generated by WBAN devices only. So there is need to design the MAC protocol which can handle traffic generated by body sensors as well as CE devices. The proposed protocol is variant of PLA-MAC [8] wherein, the super-frame structure of protocol is suitably modified to support WBAN devices and CE devices simultaneously. The inactive period of super-frame is used to accommodate traffic from CE devices and also to provide load adaption. The data packets are categorized as critical data packets, delay driven data packets, reliability driven data packets, ordinary data packets and CE data packets.

Rest of the paper is organized as follows. Section 2 describes the existing MAC protocols for WBAN. The proposed MAC protocol is described in Sect. 3 followed by performance evaluation in Sect. 4. The paper is concluded in Sect. 5.

2   Related Work

Multiple research efforts have been made to design MAC protocols which fulfill the WBAN MAC layer requirements such as Quality of service (QoS), energy efficiency. The IEEE 802.15.4 [4] and TDMA have been analyzed and tested for WBAN [7]. The investigation of the IEEE 802.15.4 for medical applications has found that the standard is limited to periodic and asymmetric traffic [5, 6]. The existing WSN MAC protocols have been tried for WBAN scenarios. A number for medium access protocols have been proposed for satisfying QoS provisioning, traffic prioritization and load adaptiveness. Most of the existing MAC protocols focus either on prioritization or on traffic load handling.

The lack of any traffic prioritization mechanism in IEEE 802.15.4 is addressed in [8] by converting the super-frame structure of IEEE 802.15.4 into dynamic super-frame structure. In the PLA-MAC [8] variation of IEEE 802.15.4, the super-frame structure depends upon traffic load. When traffic load is high, inactive period of super-frame structure is utilized by greater slot allocation whereas frame structure contains larger inactive period when traffic is low. Data is divided into four priority classes according to data type and generation rate, where high priority and emergency data is served first.

LDTA-MAC [9] has also done few improvements to overcome the limitations for IEEE 802.15.4. It focuses on handling of traffic load, where allocation of GTS (guaranteed time slots) happens dynamically according to traffic load. There is no consideration of data priority of medical applications.

ATLAS [10] is also a traffic load aware protocol where super-frame structure varies according to estimated traffic load and it follows the multi-hop communication patterns.

Another protocol PNP-MAC [11] has applied techniques like preemptive slot allocation, non-preemptive transmission and super-frame flexibility but duration of contention-free period (CFP) remains fixed in IEEE 802.15.4 frame structure. Moreover there is little balance between priority considerations and traffic load. As low priority sensors can generate high traffic data but they have higher back off time so most of the data could be lost which is not adequate for medical environments.

None of the above protocols consider the data generated by Consumer electronic (CE) applications/devices (which include environmental sensors and actuators too) which can potentially play a vital role in detecting the accurate health condition of the patients. Many CE applications such as GPS, CCTV cameras, fall detection systems, AC's etc. can be helpful in remote patient monitoring systems. For example, assume a patient enters into bathroom and we can monitor his physiological conditions using body sensors and can get the location by CE application (GPS). Patient's heartbeat can be increased by staying longer time in hot bath tub, which is not alarming situation but not easily distinguishable until we have the exact temperature, humidity, and location information. OCDP [3] is one protocol that is designed for WBAN and CE applications by introducing Opportunistic Contention Decision Period (OCDP). It supports CE burst data and emergency data by applying temporary switching between inactive period and opportunity period. The OCDP doesn't support the prioritization of data traffic.

A channel access algorithm based on IEEE 802.15.6 [13] to solve the contention complexity of WBAN has been proposed in [12]. It follows the categorization of packet levels, defining delay threshold for each level, partition of CEP into sub-phases and calculations of offset for deciding length of sub-phase. It considers both WBAN and CE applications but there is lack of support for traffic load.

We have proposed a MAC protocol which fulfills the requirements of traffic load adaptation and data priority consideration for both WBAN & CE generated traffic.

3 Proposed MAC Protocol

The system consists of a Body Area Network formed by body sensor nodes, one coordinator node and few consumer electronic devices (CE). The body sensor nodes have small processing, trans-receiving and battery capabilities. The coordinator node is equipped with larger capabilities in terms of processing, communication and energy. CE devices are assumed to have communication capabilities. The data generated by CE devices is sporadic and bursty [3].

The proposed WBAN MAC protocol divides the traffic in five different classes and also assigns priority to each class. First traffic class consists of ordinary data packets which include physiological parameters like temperature. These packets need not be prioritization high because they do not have any delay and reliability constraints.

Delay sensitive data packets: This type of data packets must be delivered before expiration of packet's maximum life time beyond which they are useless. These packets are time constrained so these are highly prioritized in our proposed protocol e.g. telemedicine video [1].

Reliability driven data packets are no loss tolerant packets having no delay constraint for example PH monitoring. Critical data packets [8] possess tight constraints both in delay and reliability for example ECG. Since the critical data packets are more important in diagnosis and treatment of patients so they have the highest priority, followed by delay sensitive, reliability driven and ordinary packets.

As CE applications generate sporadic and burst data so we have considered the priority of CE packets after that of ordinary packets.

Back-off Range. The Range for random back-off period is calculated using priority levels to ensure resource availability as shown in Table 1. The lower value of P means higher priority. Considering the back-off range, it is apparent from Table 1 that the critical data packets get highest chance of transmission in case of collision in contention access period (CAP).

Table 1. Traffic categorization

Priority (P)	Traffic class	Back off range $[0, 2^{P+1}-1]$
1	Critical Data Packets (CDP)	[0,3]
2	Delay-sensitive data packets (DSP)	[0,7]
3	Reliability-driven data packets (RDP)	[0,15]
4	Ordinary Data Packets (ODP)	[0,31]
5	CE data Packets (CEP)	[0,63]

Super-Frame Structure. The hybrid super-frame structure of our proposed scheme uses both contention based and time division based techniques to support both BAN traffic and CE traffic while ensuring the priority of patient's data. We have modified frame structure of PLA-MAC [8] to accommodate traffic from CE devices by utilizing its inactive period. As shown in Fig. 1 the super-fame structure consists of fixed length contention access period (CAP), dynamic length contention free period (CFP), emergency time slots (ETS) and data time slots (DTS).

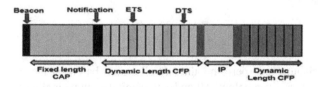

Fig. 1. Super frame structure of proposed protocol

The proposed protocol uses the priority of data packets to allocate slots to sensors or CE devices. The slots allocated to lower priority data are pre-empted and given to higher priority data. Since the CFP is dynamic in PLA-MAC, there is a possibility of some slots being occupied by CE devices when the sensor devices request more slots. Since the data from CE devices has lower priority our protocol pre-empts the slots allocated to CE data packets and allocates them to sensor data packets. The Frame structure includes beacon, Contention Access Period (CAP), notification, dynamic contention free period (DCFP) followed by inactive period which can be used as flexible CFP for CE data.

Every frame structure starts with beacon period informing all nodes about coordinator node. After the beacon period, CAP starts wherein all nodes having critical, reliability driven, ordinary packets and CE data packets request for slots from coordinator as per the program ReceiveNotification given below. The delay constrained data packets are allowed to be transmitted directly in CAP without slot requesting. The delay sensitive packets (DSP), can also contest for slot allocation in CAP if required by the application or, if the data size is too large to fit in CAP.

```
program ReceiveNotification(RxPacket)
  GtsStart, GtsEnd : integer;
  newGtsRequestPacket : MacPacket;
begin
  if selfId ε RxPacket.GtsList then
    GtsStart := RxPacket.GtsList[selfId].start;
    GtsEnd := RxPacket.GtsList[selfId].length;
    SetTimer(GtsStart) and
    transmit(dataPacketToSend) when timer expires;
  else
    newGtsRequestPacket := constructNewGtsRequest();
    performClearChannelAssessment();
    if isChannelFree then
      transmitInCap(newGtsRequestPacket);
    else
      backOffPeriod = {x:x ε random(0,2^{P+1}-1)};
      backOffTime = curentTime() + backOffPeriod;
      setTimer(backOffTime) and
      retry transmitInCap(newGtsRequestPacket)
      when timer expires;
    end
  end
end
```

The coordinator node performs the slot allocation based on the program HandleGtsRequest given below. All nodes transmit data in their allocated DTS slots in CFP and then enter sleep mode during inactive period after completion of their transmission period. Unexpected emergency data is handled by ETS (emergency transmission slots). These slots are fixed and whenever any node requires an ETS for transmission, it checks for specific reserved free slots by clear channel assessment (CCA) method and transmits data in ETS.

```
program HandleGtsRequests(requestorNode)
  freeSlotList,  GtsList : list;
  index : integer;
begin
  if(freeSlotList != Ø) then
    slot := getOneSlot(freeSlotList);
    add(slot,GtsList,requestorNode.Id);
  else if requestorNode.Type == SENSOR then
    preemptedSlot := Ø; index := 0;
    repeat
      if GtsList[index].Type == CE_DEVICE then
        GtsList[index].Id = requestorNode.Id;
        preemptedSlot := GtsList[index]
      end
      index := index + 1;
    until index < GtsList.length;
    if preemptedSlot == Ø then
      index := 0;
      repeat
        if (requestorNode.dataPriority <
            GtsList[index].dataPriority)then
          GtsList[index].Id = requestorNode.Id;
        end
      until index < GtsList.length
    end
  end
end
```

4   Performance Evaluation

The performance of the proposed protocol was evaluated by simulating it using OMNET++ network simulator based Castalia framework which is an object oriented discrete event network simulation framework. We have considered a Body Sensor Network considering of body sensors and CE devices. The network follows the single hop, star topology, while coordinator node has more computational capabilities. Table 2 below lists out the values of various simulation parameters used.

The Performance was compared with that of ZigBee MAC and PLA-MAC in terms of average latency, energy consumption and packet reception rate. Packet reception rate was taken as the ratio of total number of data packets received by the coordinator node to the total number of data packets transmitted by all nodes throughout the simulation. Average latency used was the mean of time taken for a packet to reach from source application layer to destination application layer. The Total energy spent for

Table 2. Simulation parameters

S. No	Parameter	Value
1.	Number of nodes	6
2.	Channel data rate	250 kbps
3.	Number of slots in super-frame	128
4.	Slot duration	60,480 symbols
5.	CAP length	20 slots
6.	Super-frame period	1 s
7.	Simulation time	500 s
8.	MAC header	8 bytes
9.	Payload size	100 bytes

transmission and reception of messages during entire simulation process was taken as energy consumption.

4.1 Simulation Results

Packet Reception Rate. As shown in Fig. 2 the proposed protocol has the highest packet reception rate as compared to Zigbee MAC & PLA-MAC because it caters to sensor as well as CE nodes. Although PLA-MAC has the dynamic size CFP period and same number of slots but there is no provision for handling CE devices, so data generated by CE devices will also be transmitted through same CFP period of frame structure. Zigbee MAC has fixed CFP period, so all data have to be transmitted through fixed GTS. Due to dynamic frame structure and specific provision for CE devices the proposed protocol outperforms the other two protocols.

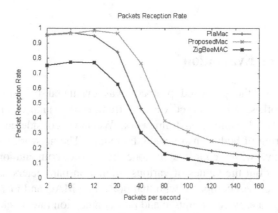

Fig. 2. Comparison of packet reception rate with variable packet rate

Average Latency. The Fig. 3 depicts that our proposed protocol has average latency less than PLA-MAC but little higher than Zigbee MAC. In Zigbee, there is no Classification for data generated by sensor node, so as soon as a sensor node makes request for slot allocation to the coordinator node, it allocates slots from GTS and transmission occurs with least delay. The proposed protocol however has to make allocations as per priorities of data traffic and node type (sensor or CE). This slot allocation process has some computation overhead which leads to increase in overall latency.

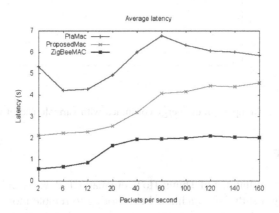

Fig. 3. Comparison of average latency (seconds) with variable packet rate

PLA-MAC has highest latency as compared to both protocols because every time when data needs to be transmitted, sensor nodes calculate priority of each and every packet which is dependent of traffic class and data generation rate. In proposed protocol, priority is calculated on the basis of traffic class only. For example, if sensor node is used to determine heart rate of a patient, then each and every time data sensed by acoustic sensor will be urgent or critical category. There is no need for calculating priority of each and every packet which adds extra delay in transmission.

Energy Consumption. Figure 4 shows the energy consumption of the three compared protocols. ZigBee MAC shows lowest energy consumption due to fixed inactive period and lesser computational overhead. Proposed MAC protocol and PLA-MAC consume more energy due to additional priority calculation and dynamic Contention free period. In the proposed protocol priority of every packet is not calculated every time, this leads to lesser energy consumption as compared to PLA-MAC.

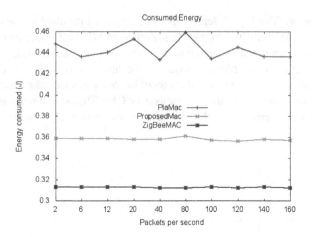

Fig. 4. Comparison of energy consumed with variable packet rate

5   Conclusion

The increasing use of Internet of Things (IoT) or smart CE devices and bio-sensors can result in a paradigm shift from traditional monitoring to remote monitoring. The data from CE devices can be used to determine environmental and geographical context of the patient. A WBAN can make use of such contexts for data filtering and data compression if the underlying MAC layer protocol caters to CE data in addition to sensor data. In this paper, we have proposed a variation of PLA-MAC protocol for WBAN, which supports body sensors devices and CE devices for remote healthcare monitoring simultaneously. We have accommodated higher WBAN traffic in case of continuous remote health monitoring by making use of the inactive period of super frame structure. The resource availability to the highest priority traffic is ensured by using the priority level in the computation of back-off period. We have evaluated the performance of proposed protocol in comparison with ZigBee and PLA-MAC proto-cols. The proposed protocol gives better packet delivery ratio than ZigBee. The lack of support for CE devices in Zigbee results in lesser average latency and energy con-sumption than the proposed protocol. The PLA-MAC is outperformed by the proposed protocol on all three compared metrics namely packet reception rate, average latency and energy consumption.

References

1. Pandit, S., Sarkar, K., Razzaque, M.A., Sarkar, A.J.: An energy efficient multiconstrained QoS aware MAC protocol for body sensor networks. Multimed. Tools Appl. **74**, 5353–5374 (2015)
2. Lee, H., Park, K., Lee, B., Choi, J., Elmasri, R.: Issues in data fusion for healthcare monitoring. In: ACM International Conference on Pervasive Technologies Related to Assistive Environments, PETRA 2008, pp. 86–90 (2008)

3. Seo, Y.-S., Kim, D.-Y., Cho, J., Lee, B.: OCDP: a WBAN MAC protocol for contention-based medical and CE applications. In: ICUIMC 2010, Suwon, Korea, 14–15 January 2010. ACM. 978-1-60558-893-3
4. IEEE 802.15.4 Standard-2003: Part 15.4: Wireless Medium Access Control (MAC) and Physical Layer(PHY) Specifications for Low-Rate Wireless Personal Area Networks (LR-WPANs) (2003)
5. IEEE, 802. 15. 4: Wireless Medium Access Control (MAC) and Physical Layer (PHY) Specifications for Wireless Personal Area Networks (WPANs) Used in or around a Body, IEEE, Piscataway, NJ, USA (2006)
6. Timmons, N.F., Scanlon, W.G.: Analysis of the performance of IEEE 802.15.4 for medical sensor body area networking. In: Proceedings of the 1st Annual IEEE Communications Society Conference on Sensor and Ad Hoc Communications and Networks (SECON 2004), Santa Clara, Calif, USA, pp. 16–24, October 2004
7. Omeni, O., Wong, A., Burdett, A.J., Toumazou, C.: Energy efficient medium access protocol for wireless medical body area sensor networks. IEEE Trans. Biomed. Circ. Syst. 2(4), 251–259 (2008)
8. Anjum, I., Alam, N., Razzaque, M.A., Mehedi Hassan, M., Alamri, A.: Traffic priority and load adaptive MAC protocol for QoS provisioning in body sensor networks. Int. J. Distrib. Sens. Netw. 9(3), 205192 (2013)
9. Min, C., Chenglin, P., Xingming, G., Jianmei, L.: A novel MAC protocol for wireless physiological information sensor network. In: 4th IEEE/EMBS International Summer School and Symposium on Medical Devices and Biosensors, pp. 79–81 (2007)
10. Rahman, OMd, Hong, C.S., Lee, S., Bang, Y.-C.: ATLAS: a traffic load aware sensor MAC design for collaborative body area sensor networks. Sensors 11(12), 11560–11580 (2011)
11. Yoon, J.S., Ahn, G.-S., Joo, S.-S., Lee, M.J.: PNP-MAC: preemptive slot allocation and non-preemptive transmission for providing QoS in body area networks. In: IEEE CCNC (2010)
12. Kim, B.S., Cho, J.: A novel priority-based channel access algorithm for contention-based MAC protocol in WBANs. In: ICUIMC 2012, 20–22 February 2012
13. IEEE Standards Association: 802.15. 6–2012 IEEE standards for local and metropolitan area networks–Part 15.6: wireless body area networks

ProRank-Product Ranking on the Basis
of Twitter Sentiment Analysis

Aysha Khan[(⊠)] and Rashid Ali

Department of Computer Engineering, Zakir Husain College of Engineering and
Technology, Aligarh Muslim University, Aligarh, Uttar Pradesh, India
aisha.khan9413@gmail.com, rashidaliamu@rediffmail.com

Abstract. Nowadays, social networking has become the most useful means by
which people share about the happenings of their lives. This has tremendously
increased the use of online social networking sites for varying purposes. People
have become very much comfortable about sharing their lives on these sites.
These social networking sites generate an enormous amount of data which is
generally used for research and other purposes. Whenever a customer wants to
buy a product, there are millions of millions of reviews about those products so
it becomes impossible for the customers to read and go through each and every
review. In this paper, we have tried to analyze the views of people on online
social networking sites and then provided the results. The main idea is to find the
best product according to the popularity of that product on that particular online
social networking site like Twitter or Facebook according to the tweets or
comments of the user.

Keywords: Recommendations · Tweets · Data preprocessing
Lexicon-based approach · Sentiment analysis

1 Introduction

In the past few years, the use of online social networking sites has shown an enormous
growth among the people. People love to share their lives, discuss events, share
opinions, and have suggestions on social networking sites. During earlier days, when
people used to buy anything, they used to discuss with their relatives, friends etc. about
the products. These nearby people used to provide their different point of opinions
according to their experiences. There were also shopkeepers who used to tell customers
about the reviews of the products and then the respective person used to buy these
products. But as the technology advanced, these methods become less feasible. With
the emergence of technology, there are systems developed which directly provides
customized recommendations to users according to their own specific interests. These
recommender systems are found everywhere whether it's about suggesting a product on
any e-commerce sites like Flipkart, Amazon or it's about suggesting friends on
Facebook, Twitter etc. Whenever we visit Amazon, we often come across various kind
of suggestions, like we want to buy a gel eyeliner of Maybelline, then Amazon will also
show us gel eyeliners of other brands also like Lakme, Mac, etc. and it will also show
us suggestions of pencil, liquid eyeliners also in the form of "people also bought these

products". So Amazon shows us all these suggestions. These are the results of recommender systems. These recommender systems generally utilize the click of a user and use collaborative filtering for it's recommendations. But these recommender systems don't utilize the social relationships of the users.

Online social networking sites like Facebook, Instagram, Twitter etc. has been in the boom now a days and Twitter has been very much popular out of these. Millions of users around the world tweet every day which is very useful for a variety of purposes.

In this paper, we have tried our best to analyze the tweets of the Twitter users about smartphones and then provide a ranking of those smartphones. We have used Twitter Public Search API to generate the tweets about popular smartphones. Since the tweets are generally in an unstructured format, so data pre-processing has been performed in order to bring them in structured form. Then sentiment analysis has been performed in order know about the sentiments of people about these products and then a ranking is provided.

The rest of the paper is organized as follows. Section 2 sets the background for recommendation systems. It discusses different systems developed for recommendations. In Sect. 3 the proposed scheme is described. This is followed by a discussion. Finally, the paper is concluded with the future work.

2 Related Work

There has been a lot of work done related to opinion mining of different online social networks using many techniques. In this section, we talk about the different studies conducted on finding sentiment of people using online social networks.

Fernandes et al. [1] focused on providing opinion on a particular product using Twitter data because Twitter generates millions of tweets just about a single product so it becomes impossible for any individual to go through each review and examine the quality of that product. Their work focuses on classifying the overall percentage of positive, negative, neutral tweets. Their main scheme is automatically suggesting products to a customer based on their previous tweets which helps the customer in effective decision making. They also provided criteria for product feedback which helps companies to improve.

Golukrishnan et al. [2] proposed an approach to demonstrate the switching trends in the purchase of products. Their work has focused on discovering the sentiments of individuals by collecting the tweets and classifying them as negative, positive, neutral. They also compared the performance of various algorithms like Naive Bayes, Random Forest, Support Vector Machines etc. based on their precision and recall.

Hu and Liu [3] have outlined a list of negative and positive words which are based on customer reviews. They generated a list of positive words which is comprised of 2006 words and then generated a list of negative words is comprised of 4783 words. In these lists, misspelled words are also included that are generally found in online social media data.

Barbosa et al. [4] suggested an approach for sentiment classification of Twitter data in which they have tagged 1000 tweets by using polarity predictions from multiple sites and then used some other tweets for testing. They have considered tweets features like meta-information like re-tweets, punctuations, hashtags, and exclamation marks. The accuracy obtained in their results was very high.

3   System Design

Figure 1 shows the generalized flow of the system. Initially the tweets are generated using the Twitter Public Search API. Since the data generated is in unstructured form and consist of unwanted noise so it has to be pre-processed in order to use it [5]. Then the words used for the description of a particular smartphone are calculated. After this positive and negative words along with their term frequency are calculated. Then score of the words is calculated and finally a ranking is provided.

3.1   Dataset Generation

Tweets are extracted on a large scale about smartphones using the Twitter public search API. These generated tweets are then saved into CSV files. CSV is a comma separated value in the form of table separated by a comma separator where each row is separated by a newline character. In this project, we collected tweets about some particular mobile phones like Iphone7, Redmi Note4, Vivo V7+, etc. Since Twitter provides a well-defined set of filtering parameters we collected the tweets with different hashtags like "Iphone7", "Vivo v7+" etc. Since Twitter users tend to use informal language so several other combinations are also tried for a particular smartphone in order to get the maximum results. Like "VivoV7+" is also searched as "Vivov7Plus". Similarly in this way for other smartphones also various combinations are also being tried. We also collected tweets about phones based on their features like primary camera, selfie camera, ram, etc. So we downloaded tweets with hashtags as "Iphone7 selfie", "Iphone7 camera", "Iphone7 battery" etc. Similarly, we collected tweets for other phones also.

Table 1 shows a sample of the tweets about the smartphone iPhone7 downloaded from Twitter. As can be observed from the above table that the dataset generated is consisting of many unwanted data like punctuations, URLS, etc. which are of no use to us.

3.2   Approach Used

We have started with text analytics initially in our work. Text Analytics is completely different from the conventional approaches. The conventional approaches fundamentally work only on structured data whereas this approach can be useful with the data that is multilingual, loosely structured, and often contains grammatical errors (tweets) which makes the task more demanding and interesting.

There are various techniques available for sentiment analysis namely supervised and unsupervised [9, 10]. Under supervised approaches there comes techniques which try to identify the sentiment on the class labels already provided to them. Under non-supervised approaches there is no prior labelling of data.

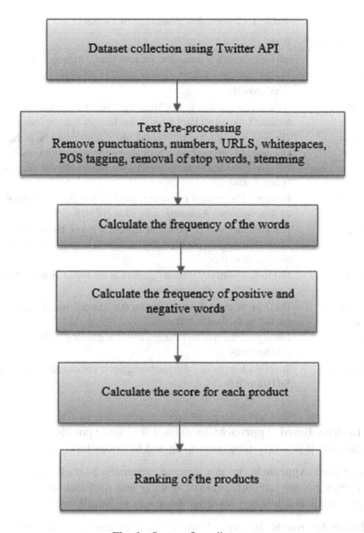

Fig. 1. System flow diagram

In our work, we have used the Lexicon-Based approach with a dictionary which is an unsupervised learning approach as it don't need any prior training. Basically, lexicon approach is based on semantic orientation to opinion mining in which sentiment polarity of features which is present in the given document is determined by comparing these features with semantic lexicons. Semantic lexicon generally contains lists of words whose sentiment orientation is determined in advance. Then the document is classified by aggregating the sentiment orientation of all opinion words present in the document, documents which have more positive word lexicons are classified as positive document and the documents which have more negative word lexicons are classified as negative document. It uses many approaches [6]:

Table 1. Tweets downloaded from Twitter

ID	Screenname	Text
Id1	User1	Iphone7 camera is awesome for low light…#Iphone7 #camera
Id2	User2	Testing out the Iphone7 camera and it is goooood https://t.co/1chSbmawIK
Id3	User3	"Few Evenings Are Better Than Rest For No Reason". Camera: #iPhone7 #mypixeldiary #goa #goaevenings #streetphotography
Id4	User4	The best camera is the usually the one you have on you at the time. In this case, an iPhone7 on a walk down the street from my home. #iPhone7 #bestcameraistheonewithyou #nicewalk #scenic #peaceful #pond #twinlakes
Id5	User5	#Instapic The #moon out of my window tonight. Love the #camera on this #iphone7 #iphonography ift.tt/2FCrfz8
Id6	User6	The #iPhone7 can be powerful camera – if you know how to use it. These little-known photography hacks will help you get the most of it on your next trip
Id7	User7	Just took it with my iPhone7 camera at the top of Hotel Indigo. What a view. #iPhone #Iphone7 #photography
Id8	User8	The 7 mega-pixel front camera on the iPhone7 you are guaranteed to get the perfect selfie.#iphone7
Id9	User9	Testing out the Iphone7 camera and it is goooood #iphone https://t.co/1chSbmawIK
Id10	User10	Street walk #iphone7 #streetphotography #blackandwhite https://t.co/XdTBfimOk0

Manual Lexicon Based Approach: In manual lexicon approach, the lexicons are created manually. It is a very time-consuming and laborious task.

Dictionary-Based Approach: In this scheme, generally a small set of sentiment words and their polarity are determined manually and then this set is widened by adding more words into it using WordNet dictionary or SentiWordNet.

Corpus-Based Approach: In corpus-based lexicon construction, syntactic patterns of the words are considered within the documents. It requires annotated training data to produces accurate semantic words.

4 Implementation

4.1 Data-Preprocessing

Once we get the tweets, we need to do pre-processing on them as they contain unstructured and noisy data. Data pre-processing is one of the most important and crucial tasks to be performed during sentiment analysis. Since we all are aware that Twitter is a social networking profile so users share an enormous amount of data in the way they like [7]. There are no formal rules of how you type your text and each and every person has a different style of expressing their views. So in this way the data becomes very much unstructured and difficult to use. In order to bring uniformity and have clean data, it is important to perform data pre-processing [8]. This data pre-processing involves replacing of emoticons, handling URL, hashtags, whitespaces, identifying punctuations and lower case conversion. These can be further looked upon:

- **Lower case:** The tweet data may consist of upper case, lower case or a combination of both as the users generally tend to use informal language. E.g. (IpHoNe7 IS AwESOME). So this contains a mixture of lower and upper case letters both, so for the purpose of uniformity all the tweets from upper cases are converted to lower case so that they can all be in the same format.
- **Identifying punctuations:** In microblogging sites it is common to use punctuations. Tweets contain different punctuation marks (like !. , ;) which is of no use for analyzing the sentiment so such symbols are removed.
- **Removal of URLs:** Since the URL analysis is a very tidy task and we are not aware whether the URL is a spam or not so we have also removed the URLs.
- **Whitespaces:** Tweets may have many whitespaces, so these whitespaces need to be stripped off so that text analysis can be performed better.
- **Stemming:** Stemming is the process of deducting the words into their root form. In this step, data is stemmed. E.g. words like loving, loved, lovable are all treated as single word love.
- **Stop Word Removal:** Many words appearing in the tweet actually have no importance in performing sentiment analysis. So such words must be removed from tweets. In this process we tried to remove the stop words like is, an, the, etc. that don't are not generally helpful.
- **Part-of-Speech Tagging:** This step identifies the different parts of speech present in a sentence. This basically helps in identifying the meaning that a sentence indicates and this technique terms to be useful in feature-specific analysis. In this step, each word is tagged by considering its position in grammatical context. It has been performed utilizing NLP.

The Table 2 shows the different parts-of-speech of a sentence "Iphone7 camera is awesome for low light". Here NN represents noun, VBZ represents verb, present tense, JJ represents adjective, IN represents conjunction or preposition.

4.2 Calculating Positive Term Frequency

In this step, the term frequency is calculated in order to identify the maximum words used for a particular mobile phone. Term frequency is an indication of how many times a particular world occurred in the document. It is generally defined as:

$$\text{Tf}(t, d) = F(t, d)$$

where $F(t, d)$ is defined as the number of occurrences of term "t" in a document "d".

Table 3 shows a sample of the positive words along with their frequency about iPhone7. As we can see that "best" is a positive word which has a term frequency of 21. Similarly in this way all the words along with their frequency are calculated. Once we

Table 2. POS tagging

Id	type	Start	end	Features
1	sentence	1	40	Constituents ≪integer, 8≫
2	word	1	6	POS = NN
3	word	8	8	POS = CD
4	word	10	10	POS = NN
5	word	17	17	POS = VBZ
6	word	20	20	POS = JJ
7	word	28	28	POS = IN
8	word	32	32	POS = JJ
9	word	36	40	POS = NN

Table 3. Term frequency of positive words

Text	Sentiment	Frequency
Best	Positive	21
Luck	Positive	9
Love	Positive	7
Main	Positive	16
Modern	Positive	1
Maximum	Positive	1
New	Positive	8

get all these positive term frequencies, then all the positive term frequencies are added in order to get the total sum of positive term frequencies.

4.3   Calculating Negative Term Frequency

Table 4 shows a sample of the negative words along with their frequency about iPhone7. It can be observed from the above table that "bad" is a negative word with a term frequency of 15. Similarly in this way all the words along with their frequencies

Table 4. Term frequency of negative words

Text	Sentiment	Frequency
Bad	Negative	15
Corrupt	Negative	10
Crash	Negative	3
Danger	Negative	2
Die	Negative	6
Delay	Negative	8
Death	Negative	6

are calculated. Once we get all the negative term frequencies, then all these frequencies are added up in order to get the total sum of negative term frequencies.

4.4 Score Calculation

In this step, the score of the mobile phones are calculated with the formula:

Score = sum of term frequency of positive words − sum of term frequency of negative words

The negative term frequencies that we calculated are subtracted from the positive term frequencies in order to get the score value (Table 5).

Table 5. Score computed using the proposed method for the three smart phones

Score	Mobile phone
2274	Redmi Note 4
1090	Iphone7
657	Vivov7plus

Similarly, in this way the score of all other mobile phones can also be calculated. The phone that gets the higher score is ranked at higher position as compared with the phone that gets a lower score and this way the ranking of the mobile phones is presented.

4.5 Generating Word Clouds

To know about what are the maximum words used in our tweets to describe any particular smartphone, word clouds are used. Word clouds shows us all the words used in our tweets with words having the maximum frequency being placed at the center surrounded by the words with lesser frequencies. Word clouds are a way of visualizing the results. Similarly some other visualizations can also be used.

The Fig. 2 shows the word cloud of the words used in the description of a smartphone.

The word cloud on the left shows the positive word cloud of a smartphone. Here it can be observed that 'love', 'relief', 'good', 'afford' are the maximum positive words used in the description of a smartphone whereas 'great', 'star' etc. are the minimum positive words used in the description of a smartphone.

The word cloud on the right is the negative word cloud of a smartphone. Here it can be observed that 'fear', 'corrupt', 'death' are the maximum negative words used in the description of the smartphone whereas 'hard', 'never', 'late', 'drop' are minimum negative words used in the description of the smartphone.

Since all the results are saved in CSV files so it is easier to use them into MYSQL database. An interactive GUI is made to display these results for use.

Fig. 2. Word cloud of tweets

5 Conclusion

People have become very much comfortable sharing their opinions with the rise of online social media like Twitter, Facebook. In this work, we collected and analysed the tweets about multiple smartphones on the basis of sentiment analysis. The ranking of the product is presented on the basis of the tweets of the users. This kind of work can be very helpful to a wide variety of audience ranging from normal customers to business companies who look forward to improve their products according to the need of the customers.

6 Future Work

In this section, we have listed the future scope of this work:

- In our future work, we can consider more products and can rank the products on a wider base.
- We have used a simple approach to sentiment analysis to rank the products. In future, we are looking forward to work upon some other machine learning approaches also.

References

1. Fernandes, R., D'Souza, R.: Analysis of product Twitter data though opinion mining. In: IEEE Annual India Conference (INDICON), Bangalore, pp. 1–5 (2016)
2. Gokulakrishnan, B., Priyanthan, P., Ragavan, T., Prasath, N., Perera, A.: Opinion mining and sentiment analysis on a Twitter data stream. In: International Conference on Advances in ICT for Emerging Regions (ICTer2012), Colombo, pp. 182–188 (2012)

3. Hu, M., Liu, B.: Mining and summarizing reviews. In: Proceeding of the 10th ACM SIGKDD International Conference on Knowledge Discovery and Data Mining, USA, pp. 168–177 (2004)

4. Barbosa, L., Feng, J.: Robust sentiment detection on twitter from biased and noisy data. In: 23rd International Conference on Computational Linguistics: Posters, pp. 36–44 (2010)

5. Bahrainian, S.A., Dengel, A.: Sentiment analysis and summarization of twitter data. In: IEEE 16th International Conference on Computational Science and Engineering, Sydney, NSW, pp. 227–234 (2013)

6. Pasarate, S., Shedge, R.: Comparative study of feature extraction techniques used in sentiment analysis. In: International Conference on Innovation and Challenges in Cyber Security (ICICCS-INBUSH), Noida, pp. 182–186 (2016)

7. Patil, H.P., Atique, M.: Sentiment analysis for social media: a survey. In: 2nd International Conference on Information Science and Security (ICISS), Seoul, pp. 1–4 (2015)

8. Hridoy, S.A.A., Ekram, M.T., Islam, M.S., Ahmed, F., Rahman, R.M.: Localized twitter opinion mining using sentiment analysis. Decis. Anal. **2**, 8 (2015)

9. Madhoushi, Z., Hamdan, A.R., Zainudin, S.: Sentiment analysis techniques in recent works. In: Science and Information Conference (SAI), London, pp. 288–291 (2015)

10. Abirami, M., Gayathri, V.: A survey on sentiment analysis methods and approach. In: 8th International Conference on Advanced Computing (ICoAC), Chennai, pp. 72–76 (2017)

Parallelization of Protein Clustering Algorithm Using OpenMP

Dhruv Dhar$^{(\boxtimes)}$, Lakshana Hegde, Mahesh S. Patil,
and Satyadhyan Chickerur

Department of Computer Science and Engineering, B.V.B College of
Engineering and Technology, Centre for High Performance Computing,
KLE Technological University, Hubballi 580031, Karnataka, India
dhruvdhar1@gmail.com, lakshanaghegde@gmail.com,
mahesh_patil@bvb.edu, chickerursr@kletech.ac.in

Abstract. Proteins are the building blocks of all living organisms and its analysis can help us to understand the bimolecular mechanics of living organisms.

Protein clustering attempts to group similar protein sequences and has diverse applications in bioinformatics. However, this operation faces various computational challenges because of dependency on complex data structures, high memory usage and irregular memory access patterns. In genome studies, the time consideration for alignment is also an important parameter and should be minimized.

Conventional solutions have rather been unsuccessful in achieving decent runtime performance because these algorithms are designed for serial computation which means that they use a single processor to perform computations. These algorithms can be improved upon by modifying them to use multiple processing elements.

The purpose of this research is to modify existing protein clustering algorithm and apply parallelization techniques on them in order to optimize protein sequencing operation for faster results without sacrificing accuracy.

Keywords: Proteins · Protein clustering · Bioinformatics · Protein sequences
Serial computation · Parallelization

1 Introduction

Clustering or cluster analysis is the process of grouping objects in such a way that the objects within a group have more similarities to each other than the objects in other groups. Each group is referred to as a cluster. Each cluster can have different size and the number of clusters that will be generated is not known at input. Clustering process can also be employed to find out the relationship between each cluster.

Clustering has numerous applications in the field of computational biology some of which include sequence analysis, clustering similar genes based on microarray data, gene expression analysis. In this paper, our focus will be on using cluster analysis for

© Springer Nature Singapore Pte Ltd. 2018
M. Singh et al. (Eds.): ICACDS 2018, CCIS 906, pp. 108–118, 2018.
https://doi.org/10.1007/978-981-13-1813-9_11

grouping similar protein sequences. Our work is based on the serial *pclust* algorithm by Ananth et al.

Though clustering may seem to be a powerful algorithm for bioinformatics, its use is limited and it cannot be applied to all projects. This is because clustering is a data-intensive process and can easily become compute-intensive as well [3, 4].

The performance of the serial implementation of these algorithms is generally limited. These algorithms also face scalability issues. That is why the serial pclust algorithm does not scale beyond 15K–20K sequences on a desktop computer with 2 GB of RAM due to memory requirements [3, 4].

Parallelization techniques can be used to improve these algorithms. Parallelization can not only help in improving the run-time performance but can also help in achieving higher scalability with better results. We have tried to leverage multi-core computing architecture to solve the problem of protein clustering in parallel. In this project, we use OpenMP which is a shared memory parallelization library. OpenMP allows the programmer to explicitly create multiple threads. A thread is a basic unit of execution and can be scheduled parallelly onto multiple cores for simultaneous execution of multiple tasks. We have chosen OpenMP because it is easy to use compared to some conventional multi-threading libraries like POSIX and MPI.

While writing parallel programs, it should be made sure that all the threads are properly synchronized. Improper or incorrect synchronization may cause race condition leading to the generation of incorrect results. OpenMP provides various synchronization constructs like barrier, atomic and critical. However, it should also be noted that there is a certain amount of overhead associated with these constructs so the use of synchronization constructs must be minimized within the code.

This modified pclust algorithm which we have named as "*pclust-v7*" stands out from the conventional pclust algorithm not only because it provides better performance and output but also it offers better output visualization by use of bar graphs and pie charts. We have deployed our code in the cloud which helps us to achieve better security and flexibility of use. The software can be accessed from any client device at any location.

2 Literature Survey

With the evolution of high-performance workstations, parallel computing has attracted a lot of interest. In parallel computing, an application is designed in such a way that it can run on multiple processing elements simultaneously. For example, consider a for loop with 8 iterations and each iteration requires 1 unit of processing time. If we run the for loop on a single processor, the for loop will consume 8 units of time. Now consider a computing system with 4 processing elements. The for loop iterations are divided among the 4 processing elements so each processor gets 2 iterations to compute. If each of these processors perform their computations parallelly, the system would require only 2 units of time for computation leading to 4 times performance gain. Under the practical scenario, this is not the case as there are many overheads associated with parallel programs including synchronization overheads, idling, and load imbalances. It is the responsibility of the developer to minimize these overheads.

Our survey showed us that parallel computing is one of the best ways that can be used to optimize computation. Parallel computing has been employed in various areas of computational research for a long time. We tried different kinds of parallelization techniques on different algorithms before applying them on the pclust algorithm and noticed that parallelization significantly improves application performance for large input.

In spite of the numerous applications of clustering in computational biology, it is considered a dampening computational task due to involved complexities. In computational biology, it is also difficult to find suitable datasets.

There are two major classes of clustering methods which are hierarchical clustering and partitioning. In hierarchical clustering, each cluster is subdivided into smaller clusters, leading to a tree-shaped structure or a Dendrogram [15]. In partitioning method, the data is divided into a predetermined number of subsets where there is no hierarchical relationship between clusters [15]. The quality of clusters can be evaluated based on how compact and well separated the clusters are.

In biological areas, graph algorithms are widely used in biology network field such as drug target test, sequencing analysis, and alignment in getting to know the functions of various proteins and genes, to find the relationship between diseases and determining the antidote for them.

Biological research areas involve large computations involved in the field of molecular biology such as molecular modelling and developing an algorithm for analysis. Computations are also utilized by biogenetics, neural sciences etc.

As they involve a large number of computations and network analysis along with large datasets required for accurate results, it is better and more efficient to use parallel programming, as it would assist to reduce the time taken and often scales with the increase in the dataset. It also helps in making the program independent of the physical constraint of operating on a single processor (memory constraints etc.).

Clustering is one of the first steps carried out while performing gene expression analysis. This program focusses solely on clustering of proteins i.e. grouping similar proteins together. It uses shingling approach developed by Gibson et al. to perform clustering of protein molecules. This clustering algorithm can be used in various biological research fields. It is very important in the field of gene clustering where clustering similar genes are grouped to infer a function for each group. The clustering algorithm used in pclust can be used for gene clustering also. Optimizing the clustering process can help us to significantly reduce the time for performing expression analysis and other methods that involve biological clustering as a major step.

Before Pclust, BLAST algorithm was used universally for sequence alignment. In spite of its widespread use, BLAST cannot guarantee optimal alignment of sequences. The serial Pclust program makes use of shingling algorithm which occurs in two stages. In shingling algorithm, denser subgraphs are created if the vertices share s of their out links as such vertices are grouped together. As the value of s grows the probability that two vertices share the same shingle decreases. The algorithm develops c random shingles at the beginning for vertex v. As the value of c increases, the density of sub graphs also increases. Pclust works in three stages:

1. Shingling Phase I
2. Shingling Phase II
3. Connected Component Detection.

All these stages involve different types of computation but the basic parallelization techniques remain the same.

Several previous attempts have also been made in the same field. These have been discussed below:

- **Pclust-sm:** A parallel approach was developed by Ananth et al., for his OpenMP based implementation for clustering of biological graphs [3]. In his paper, he discusses use of hash tables instead of quick sort algorithm in order to reduce time complexity of the algorithm and thus reduce the overall runtime. Hash table is used to group together all the vertices generating a given shingle, thus eliminating the need for a separate sorting algorithm.
- **Pclust-mr:** We also came across a multistage MapReduce based implementation of serial graph clustering heuristic also developed by Ananth et al. [11]. The underlying algorithm transforms the Shingling heuristic operation into a combination of standard MapReduce primitives such as map, reduce and group/sort [11]. The algorithm was implemented and tested on a Hadoop cluster with 64 cores which did not perform very well.

3 Proposed Solution

A solution has been proposed to improve the performance of pclust protein clustering algorithm. This solution makes use of OpenMP library and involves the following steps:

1. Identifying the contention spots in the algorithm.
2. Determining how parallelization can be used to reduce or eliminate contention.
3. Applying OpenMP constructs to the algorithm.
4. Testing the parallelized algorithm for errors such as race condition and comparing its performance to the serial algorithm.
5. Verifying the results produced by the parallelized algorithm.

The algorithm involves a 2-pass Shingling process. The main idea of the Shingling algorithm is as follows: Intuitively, two vertices sharing a shingle. The algorithm seeks to group such vertices together and use them as building blocks for dense sub graphs [3, 4, 11, 16]. The input to the algorithm is a FASTA file with n sequences, variables s and c. Variables s and c denote the size of shingle and the number of trials respectively. Larger the value of s, lesser the probability that two vertices share a shingle. The parameter c is intended to create the opposite effect [3].

We start the parallelization process by modifying the init_vars function which is used to allocate memory to different variables. In the following code, allocation of one variable is completely independent from the allocation of other variables so rather than executing these statements serially, they can be run parallelly on different processors using the section construct. Consider the following code:

```
#pragma omp parallel
#pragma omp sections
  #pragma omp section
    vidmap = emalloc(gN*(sizeof *vidmap));
  #pragma omp section
    gA = emalloc(gC*(sizeof *gA));
  #pragma omp section
    gB = emalloc(gC*(sizeof *gB));
  #pragma omp section
    mfSglCnt = gN*gC;
    gFSgl = ecalloc(mfSglCnt, sizeof *gFSgl);
  #pragma omp section
    n2gidHash = ecalloc(gN, sizeof(*n2gidHash));
//end of sections
```

Next, we parallelize the free_vars function which is used to deallocate the variables. Here we are using the same approach as init_vars. However, instead of using separate sections for each free (memory deallocation) statement, we put four free statements inside one section. This will schedule four free statements to a single processor. We do this because the deallocation process is relatively less time taking. So if we schedule each free statement to a single processor, the overhead increases which is undesirable. Consider the following code:

```
#pragma omp parallel
  #pragma omp sections
    #pragma omp section
      free(vidmap);
      free(gA);
      free(gB);
      free_union(uSet);
    #pragma omp section
      free_sgl(gFSgl, fSglCnt);
      free_sgl(gSSgl, msSglCnt);
      free_hash();
      free_gid_hash(n2gidHash, gNN);
  //end of sections
```

We are only adding OpenMP constructs to the code and not modifying the logic of the algorithm until required. It is also important to note that some parts of the algorithm cannot be parallelized due to presence of I/O bound statements.

Parallelization can only be performed on CPU bound statements. For example, consider the function shingle which adds a lot to the total overhead due to presence of many for loops which are highly dependent on I/O.

It is very evident that for loops are the major contention spots in a program. Optimizing these loops can help to improve the run-time performance of the code. One method of optimizing them can be by splitting the iterations and scheduling them on multiple processors.

Functions like free_hash(), free_gid_hash(), free_adjList(), free_sgl(), init_union(), init_vidmap() have for loops with CPU bound statements which can effectively be parallelized by using #pragma omp parallel for directive. Parallelizing these loops effectively reduce the time for which these loops run thus improving the overall performance. Consider the following for loops:

FREE_HASH ():

```
......
#pragma    omp    parallel    for schedule
(dynamic,500) num_threads(4) shared(i)
  for(i=0; i<HASH_SIZE; i++)
    if(hashTbl[i])
       for(p=hashTbl[i]; p!=NULL; p=q)
         q= p->next;
         free(p->key);
         free(p);
  //End of pragma for
```

INIT_UNION (SIZE):

```
......
#pragma omp parallel for schedule(dynamic,150)
shared(i) num_threads(2)
  for(i=0; i<size; i++)
    ufSet[i].parent = i;
    ufSet[i].rank = 0;
  //End of pragma for
return ufSet;
```

In both the code snippets, shared(i) has been used because variable i has to be shared among all the threads. Schedule(dynamic, n) means that n iterations will be dynamically allocated to any one of the available processors. Apart from the for construct, we also used constructs like task and other synchronization constructs like atomic and critical to making the algorithm more efficient and reliable.

A GUI interface was also created and attached with the algorithm for easy access to the algorithm. The GUI interfaces were created using Qt creator which produces '.ui' files as output. These '.ui' files were later converted to python files using piuic4 command. The graphs were created using python Matplotlib library. These python interfaces were attached to the c code. Following are some of the screenshots (Figs. 1, 2):

Figure 3 shows a bar graph which describes the number of members in each cluster having more than one member. This graph shows an overall trend that can be used to get quick insights.

```
ubuntu@ip-172-31-15-153:~/original_src_code/src_pclust$ ./kshingle -f tes
n 2230 -s 10 -c 1000
Initialization succeed...
#vertices:2230 => 1204
First level shingling succeed...
Second level shingling succeed...
Dumping clusters succeed...
time taken= 131.460232
```

Fig. 1. Shows the command line interface present in the original pclust algorithm. The command line arguments -f, -n, -s, -c denote the name of file, number of vertices, size of shingle and number of trials respectively.

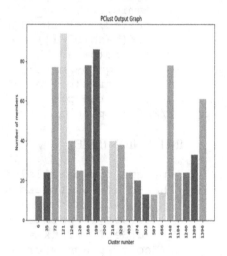

Fig. 2. Graphical user interface for the new program Pclust-v7.

Fig. 3. Graph of cluster number v/s number of members

4   Results

In order to evaluate performance, both the serial and the parallel algorithms were deployed on the same machine and were run one after the other and the results were compared. The machine used by us had a 16 thread Intel Xeon-E5 2.3 GHz processor coupled with 32 GB memory. The dataset used was a FASTA file with 2230 protein sequences. The protein sequences look like following:

```
>ENS_PEP_ENSAPMP00000000218:>ENS_PEP_ENSCAFP00000
005470;
>JCVI_PEP_1096131504461:>JCVI_PEP_1096131655745;
>JCVI_PEP_1096133581735:>NCBI_PEP_27924029;
>JCVI_PEP_1096134202821:>ENS_PEP_ENSCAFP00000002867;
>NCBI_PEP_24582285:>ENS_PEP_ENSAPMP00000012063; etc...
```

Figure 5 shows the side by side runtime performance comparison between both the algorithms for s = 15. Note that we have randomly chosen s value as 15 but other values can also be used. We have kept the number of processing elements constant here (16). The blue bars denote the time taken by the serial pclust algorithm whereas the green bars denote the time taken by the parallel pclust-v7 algorithm.

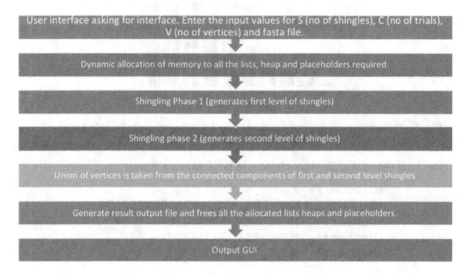

Fig. 4. Flow diagram listing all the processes involved in the algorithm.

We can infer from the graph that for large values of c, the performance gain is also higher. This happens because the total parallel overhead function, To is a function of both, problem size (W) and number of processing elements (p) used [1].

$$W = KT_o(W, p) \qquad (1)$$

In many cases, the overhead increases sub-linearly with respect to the problem size. In such cases, the efficiency increases if the problem size is increased keeping the number of processing elements constant (in this case: 16). So the performance gain will continue to increase with increasing input size (Fig. 5). The following table shows the time taken for both the algorithms to complete clustering for various values of c (Table 1):

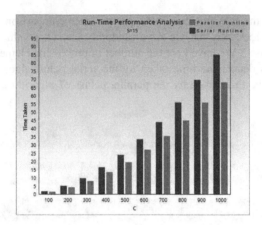

Fig. 5. Performance analysis of serial and parallel algorithms side by side for s = 15

The final output file displays clusters in the following format:

```
{Cluster#}  3
{Member#}   ENS_PEP_ENSCAFP00000029679
{Member#}   NCBI_PEP_33341450
{Member#}   NCBI_PEP_30354202
{Member#}   NCBI_PEP_28573069
......
{Cluster#}  18
{Member#}   ENS_PEP_ENSDARP00000050238
{Member#}   NCBI_PEP_862457
{Member#}   NCBI_PEP_57098165
{Member#}   NCBI_PEP_55777830
......
```

Table 1. The run-time (in seconds) of pclust and pclust-v7 on various input for s = 15. The variable t denotes the number of threads.

Number of trials	Pclust runtime (seconds)	Pclust-v7 runtime (s)	
		t = 4	t = 16
C = 200	6.23	5.89	4.6
C = 400	17.65	15.48	12.23
C = 600	33.84	30.87	27.56
C = 800	58.44	52.69	45.30
C = 1000	85.24	76.57	68.65

5   Conclusion and Future Scope

This paper describes a method to parallelize a protein clustering algorithm to make it more efficient. This algorithm performs better with large input as compared to the standard algorithm and also offers easy usage. The use of graphs also provides better output visualization. This algorithm is deployed on cloud, so hardware scaling can also be done flexibly when the need arises. The ability of pclust-v7 to cluster the proteins of hundreds of organisms on a desktop computer in a matter of minutes will allow scientists to conduct their research without the need to access expensive clustered computers.

Pclust algorithm has shown itself as a practical substitution for BLAST algorithm. In the future, we plan to extend the parallelization by use of libraries like CUDA which enables the algorithm to be executed on powerful GPUs instead of CPU. The scope of parallel computing is not just limited to bioinformatics but it can also be applied to other domains like Big Data, image processing, 3D-simulations, artificial intelligence etc.

The implementation discussed herein may not be highly precise and can still be improved further for higher accuracy.

Acknowledgements. The research was performed at Centre for High Performance Computing, KLE Technological University under the guidance of Prof. Mahesh S. Patil and Prof. Satyadhyan R Chickerur.

References

1. Grama, A.: Introduction to Parallel Computing, 2nd edn. Addison-Wesley, Boston (2003)
2. Bioinformatics and Computational Biology Group, School of Electrical Engineering and Computer Science, Washington State University (2015–2016). Pclust Manual
3. Chapman, T., Kalyanaraman, A.: An OpenMP algorithm and implementation for clustering biological graphs. In: Proceedings of the 1st Workshop on Irregular Applications: Architectures and Algorithm - IAAA 2011 (2011). https://doi.org/10.1145/2089142. 2089146
4. Rytsareva, I., Chapman, T., Kalyanaraman, A.: Parallel algorithms for clustering biological graphs on distributed and shared memory architectures. Int. J. High Perform. Comput. Netw. **7**(4), 241 (2014). https://doi.org/10.1504/ijhpcn.2014.062724
5. Rytsareva, I., Kalyanaraman, A., Konwar, K., Hallam, S.J.: Scalable heuristics for clustering biological graphs. In: IEEE 3rd International Conference on Computational Advances in Bio and Medical Sciences (ICCABS) (2013). https://doi.org/10.1109/iccabs.2013.6629214
6. Introduction to OpenMP - Tim Mattson (Intel) [Video file] (n.d.). Accessed. https://www. youtube.com/playlist?list=PLLX-Q6B8xqZ8n8bwjGdzBJ25X2utwnoEG
7. OpenMP Architecture Review Board.: OpenMP Application Program Interface version 4.0. (2013). Accessed. http://www.openmp.org/wp-content/uploads/OpenMP4.0.0.pdf
8. Lockwood, S., Brayton, K.A., Broschat, S.L.: Comparative genomics reveals multiple pathways to mutualism for tick-borne pathogens. BMC Genom. **17**(1), 481 (2016). https:// doi.org/10.1186/s12864-016-2744-9

9. Daily, J., Kalyanaraman, A., Krishnamoorthy, S., Vishnu, A.: A work stealing based approach for enabling scalable optimal sequence homology detection. J. Parallel Distrib. Comput. **79–80**, 132–142 (2015). https://doi.org/10.1016/j.jpdc.2014.08.009

10. Lu, H., Halappanavar, M., Kalyanaraman, A., Choudhury, S.: Parallel heuristics for scalable community detection. In: IEEE International Parallel and Distributed Processing Symposium Workshops (2014). https://doi.org/10.1109/ipdpsw.2014.155

11. Rytsareva, I., Kalyanaraman, A.: An efficient MapReduce algorithm for parallelizing large-scale graph clustering. In: Proceedings of the ParGraph' 2011 - Workshop on Parallel Algorithms and Software for Analysis of Massive Graphs, Held in Conjunction with HiPC 2011, Bengaluru, India (2011)

12. Computational Biology, 15 Jan 2015. Accessed. https://en.wikipedia.org/wiki/Computational_biology

13. Cluster analysis, 18 Jan 2018. Accessed. https://en.wikipedia.org/wiki/Cluster_analysis (2018)

14. D'haeseleer, P.: How does gene expression cluster work? Nat. Biotechnol. **23**, 1499–1501 (2006). https://doi.org/10.1038/nbt1205-1499

15. Gibson, D., Kumar, R., Tomkins, A.: Discovering large dense sub graphs in Massive graphs. In: Proceedings of the International Conference on Very Large Data Bases, pp. 721–732 (2005)

Intelligent Face Recognition System
for Visually Impaired

Riya Goyal[✉], Karan Kalra, Parteek Kumar, and Sanmeet Kaur

Computer Science and Engineering Department (CSED), Thapar Institute of
Engineering and Technology, Patiala 147001, Punjab, India
riyagoyal9328@gmail.com, karankalrall@gmail.com,
{parteek.bhatia,sanmeet.bhatia}@thapar.edu

Abstract. This paper presents a real-time system designed for visually impaired to aid them in social interactions. This system implemented a facial recognition algorithm which when embedded in a wearable device helps to detect the known and unknown faces at any crowded location or gathering. Our aim is to build a fully functional portable assistant that can recognize known faces, objects as well as the text from books. This system acts as the third eye for the blind. The facial recognition algorithm explained in this paper is the initial step towards this approach. Building such a prototype is a very challenging task as the portable camera is subjected to blur images due to the motion of the object and noise in uncertain lighting conditions. So, this paper presents an approach which is resilient to any change in illumination and is trained to detect the faces from the database with high accuracy. The two-tier architecture followed in this approach first identifies presence of a person and then applying face recognition to detect its identity. The object detection part helps in differentiating objects like photo frames and posters from a person and thus, proves more reliable than a standard face recognition framework. A dataset of 1000 images are taken for each face to train the model and system achieves a detection accuracy of 93.2% at a very high frame rate.

Keywords: Face recognition · Wearable computing
Assistive device for visually impaired · Social interaction aide

1   Introduction

The most challenging inability in a human is his vision and according to the statistics, India has the greatest number of visually impaired people [1]. Vision plays a vital role in our daily life as without this one cannot imagine the world around him. So is the case of the visually impaired people who live their life with this inability every single second. These people are unable to interact readily compared to their sighted counterparts which separate them from being the part of the society. Researches have shown that non-verbal communication is the major source of exchange of information between

---

R. Goyal and K. Kalra—Contributed equally to this work.

M. Singh et al. (Eds.): ICACDS 2018, CCIS 906, pp. 119–128, 2018.
https://doi.org/10.1007/978-981-13-1813-9_12

two persons. Without vision, a person feels inefficient to participate in such communications independently. An automated method proves effective in mitigating the vision loss through computation intensive tasks such as face recognition and object detection [2, 3]. These tasks require huge chunks of image data being processed which needs a significant amount of computational power [4, 5]. Today's technology enhancement is able to implement these tasks which increases the applicability of the portable devices in the field of assistive technologies [6] for disabled people. Static detection of objects and faces is generally considered as an easier task compared to the dynamic detection. Major difficulties encountered with the incorporation of motion in computer vision include location change, obstacles, constant movement, smudged images, lighting conditions [5]. The smart navigation prototype is an example of an assistive mobile-based system that helps the blind persons by providing them GPS based navigation. Another mobile based navigation system was presented by Willis et al. which uses RFID (Radio Frequency Identification) programmed tags. None of these technologies facilitate social interaction among disabled people.

In this paper, an indispensable facial recognition problem is discussed in the context of creating an assistive solution for people having visual impairments. There are many systems capable of recognizing faces with high accuracy but none of them are efficient enough for their usage in real-world scenarios. Our approach follows a two-tier architecture which is initially trained to recognize whether a person is present in a frame or not. If present, the frame is further evaluated for the presence of facial features. These facial features are then extracted and compared with the dataset for their recognition. The main challenges faced by the face detection algorithms are the changes in the angle of the face and intensity of light. Our approach uses different image enhancement techniques to improve the detection algorithm and make it resilient towards different illuminating conditions.

2 Related Work

Face recognition is a method of locating and identifying peoples' face using different algorithms [7, 8] in a real-time environment given an input image stream. Detection of faces is mainly done for a task such as verification of the identity of a person to be unknown or known and for validating whether a person is what he claims or not. This is done by extracting the facial features of a person and comparing it with the given database. A linearly approximated sparse representation-based classification algorithm (LASRC) is used by Ortiz et al. to recognize the face images from the social network. SRC algorithm proves to be slower than the LASRC [9] algorithm by a factor of 100–250. A modular face recognition system was proposed by Raghavendra et al. in which features of a face module are extracted by using the combination of PCA algorithm [10, 11] and the text independent speaker verification are used for the speech module [12].

Furthermore, a multi-resolution based feature fusion [13] technique was developed by Pong et al. for building an efficient face recognition system. This system improves the feature extraction process by using a combination of low and high-resolution facial images. These features were then combined by using genetic algorithms to form a single feature vector. A face authentication based access control system was proposed by Stallkamp et al. [14] for identifying the people entering to a laboratory door. The system was efficient in tackling challenges like the variation in facial expressions, lighting conditions, occlusion, and pose and an appearance based algorithm was used for recognition. Each individual frame contributed to the overall decision of classification by using three different measures and reported accuracy ranging from 91.8 to 92.5%.

Another system was proposed by Gorodnichy et al. [15] that focused on building a video stream based face recognition system. This system used a bilateral architecture for acquiring facial data by using static images for hard biometrics and video for soft biometrics. This shows the clear difference between the data obtained from images and videos and both are of two different modalities. The database consists of 11 persons from video and the image recognized by the computer is of 12 pixels which give a rate of 95%. There is a fixed location for the camera in a video-based detection system. A mobile input source has been used in autonomous driving and pedestrian detection system [16, 17]. The motion of objects increases the system complexity in recognizing and detection. A real-world autonomous driving system was introduced by Levinson et al. [16] in which the obstacles are classified automatically while driving cycle and vehicles. This system is unaffected by the lighting and weather conditions.

Gavrila et al. [17] made a system to detect and track the moving vehicle by using multicore vision system. The experiments have shown an accuracy of 62–100% in urban traffic conditions. Also, the labeled faces in the wild (LFW) approach obtained a high performance in face recognition and presented by Cox et al. [18]. This is achieved by using Brute-Force approach combining with machine learning algorithms. Ding et al. [19] introduced a robust approach to improve the illumination, pose and expressions and extracted the multi-directional multi-level dual-cross patterns (MDML-DCPs) features. This system was based on the textural structure of human faces and helps in reducing the lighting conditions.

3 Proposed Work

This section describes how the face is detected. The aim of this system is to find the economical solution for the visually impaired which provides an audio feedback to the user after recognizing the person in the field of view. System architecture for the system is depicted in Fig. 1. The application of the proposed architecture consists of three main modules: Face Detection, Image Preprocessing and Model Building.

3.1 Face Detection

3.1.1 Data Acquisition

It is the initial step towards building a face recognition system. A huge dataset of high-quality facial images is required to make our system efficient for recognizing faces with high accuracy. Our dataset comprises of 1000 images per person taken through a camera device. To achieve this objective a video stream is used rather than the static image from a camera source to capture the frames. These frames are further evaluated

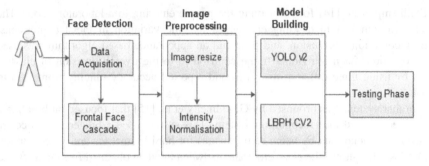

Fig. 1. System architecture of the proposed work.

for the presence of facial features through the use of frontal face cascade build on top of Haar cascade [20].

3.1.2 Frontal Face Haar Cascade

It is pre-trained cascade classifiers to detect the frontal facial features of a person as shown in Fig. 2. The idea behind this cascade is to feed the classifier with a large number of images having faces i.e. positive images and images that don't contain any face known as negative images.

Fig. 2. The output from the frontal face cascade with the face region marked.

Feature extraction is done using Edge feature, Line features, and four rectangle features and then Adaboost is applied for selecting top relevant features among them. To reduce the time consumption for detection, a technique is used where the grouping of a feature in multiple stages is done as shown in Fig. 3 and each stage is applied sequentially. If an image fails at one stage then the whole process is aborted and the image is rejected.

3.2 Image Preprocessing

Before training the model to detect faces, image preprocessing is implemented to enhance the image quality and remove the noise. First, the extraction of facial

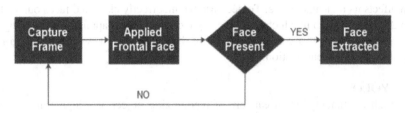

Fig. 3. Workflow to extract the region of the face.

coordinates from a given frame is done by applying frontal face Haar Cascade. These extracted coordinates are used to crop out the subject's face from a video stream. This cropped facial image then helps in removing the complexity of the background and in training the model by letting it focus only on the region of interest i.e. the face of the person as shown in Fig. 4.

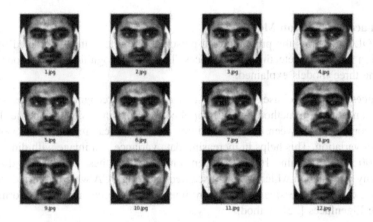

Fig. 4. Subsets of one face set taken from the database.

The next step is to increase the efficiency of the classifier in recognizing the known faces by implementing the intensity normalization function. This function removes the variation in skin color due to different lighting conditions and thus makes our system resilient towards recognizing faces in any illumination.

3.3   Model Building

After collecting dataset and applying image preprocessing the next requirement is to train a model for recognizing faces. Normal face recognition models have a major shortcoming of incorrectly classified faces. One approach to help remove this misdetection is by using eye cascade filter that searches for eyes in the ROI. If eye cascade returns a value greater than 2 or 0 that that ROI is rejected. The drawback of using this is that system is not able to recognize eyes if a person is wearing spectacles or goggles which effects its real-time usage. To decrease the incorrectly classified faces our system uses a 2 level approach in which first object detection model is applied for checking the presence of a person. If a person is present in the image than it is further sent to face recognition model identification.

3.3.1   YOLO

It is a highly efficient system capable of recognizing object at a high frame rate of 90 fps with an mAP of 78.6% on VOC 2007. Previous object detection systems apply classifiers on different scales and location of the image and consider region with the high matching score as detection. YOLO [21] in contrary to previous approaches used only one neural network on the whole image making globally informed predictions. The neural network divides an image into small parts and outputs probability of each region by applying bounding boxes. This Yolo model is applied by our system to detect whether a person is present in a scene or not. It is a pre-trained model to detect 20 different classes but we have downscaled it to detect only the person class in a given frame.

3.3.2   Face Recognition Models

When YOLO confirms the presence of a person that frame is then evaluated by face recognition model for detecting known faces. This face recognition can be done using any of the three models explained.

Eigen Faces. This model uses PCA as its core method for recognizing images. PCA is a dimension reduction method dermally applied to high dimensional numeric data. It uses the correlation between different features an discard feature having the very less amount of variation. This helps in increasing data variance. An image with dimensions 400×400 pixels contains 160,000 dimensions. Most of these dimensions does not contain any information which is then discarded by using PCA which in turn decreases the complexity and excessive computation time. The face recognition is performed by using the Eigenfaces [22] method.

- Importing all training data into PCA
- Importing testing image to PCA
- Comparing Testing Image and training data by finding the nearest neighbor.

Fisher Faces. In Eigen faces the total variance in data exceeds by the linear combination of features founded by PCA. Although being a robust way of presenting data, the limitation of Eigenfaces was the loss of discriminative information on throwing away the components [23]. Let's assume light be the variance in data. In PCA the discriminative information may lack out, so the classification becomes impossible by smearing all the samples together.

The great statistician, Sir R. A. Fisher invented LDA (Linear Discriminant Analysis) which reduces the dimensions of the specific classes. In 1936, he used this to classify the flowers in his paper named as the use of multiple measurements in taxonomic problems [Fisher36]. Instead of maximizing the overall scatter, LDA maximizes the ratio between the classes to within classes. The main idea was to cluster the same classes together and differentiate the lower dimensional classes as far as possible. This was also called by Hespanhaand Krieg man, Belhumeur as they applied LDA for face recognition [BHK97].

LBPH (Local Binary Patterns Histograms). Both the Eigenfaces and Fisherfaces try to reduce the High Dimensional data using a holistic approach. Eigen Face approach faces difficulty when variance originated in the image due to external sources. In this case, the maximum variance doesn't mean the information is present in these components. To preserve the discriminant information from being lost LDA is applied using Fisherface. This method works great in scenarios of the constrained environment but fails to provide the same amount of accuracy in a real-world scenario.

This shows that the exact light settings cannot be assured in only 10 images of a person. The question arises when there is only one image per person, in that case, the image recognized may be horribly wrong. To get good results one at least needs 9 ($\pm$1) images per person so fisherface method fails here. But there are other factors that affect the image like rotation, scaling etc. LBPH [24] helps tackle these difficulties by comparing the intensity of each pixel with its neighborhood to summarize the local structure of the image. If the given pixel's intensity is equal to or greater than its neighbor pixels than it is tagged with 1 otherwise 0. So if we take 8 neighbor pixels than each pixel is denoted by 8-bit local binary pattern as 11101111.

Algorithmic Description. The description of the LBP operator is shown in Eq. 1.

$$LBPH\ (a_x,\ bo_x) = \sum\nolimits_{q=0}^{q-1} 2^q S(jq - jx) \tag{1}$$

with (a_x, bo_x) as a central pixel with intensity j_q; and j_n being the intensity of the neighbor pixel. S is the sign function defined in Eq. 2.

$$s(x) = \begin{cases} 1 & \text{if } x \geq 0 \\ 0 & \text{else} \end{cases} \tag{2}$$

In these very minute, details of the image are obtained. During our evaluation, LBPH Model performs the best out of the three models so for further evaluations LBPH is selected as the base model. This model is highly robust towards grayscale monotonic transformations. Once the model is trained then the label that contains the name of the identified person is returned from the model that label is sent to the python text to speech library i.e. pyttsx. This library contains a function say () that takes the returned label as an input and sends the speech command to the speaker module.

4 Results

In this section, the experimental results are performed on 4 different face detection models to detect the best algorithm that can be used to recognize the faces in a real-world scenario to help the visually impaired. For an algorithm to be used in a real world, it is necessary to make it robust and flexible for every circumstance without affecting the performance and speed of the system. This system contains 1000 images each for 4 different subjects to train the classifier.

The experiments are performed on 3 pre-defined models along with the proposed model. This proposed model is two-tier architecture i.e. YOLO and LBPH which reduces the misdetection of faces by using object detection YOLO model. It acts as a screening process which identifies that a person exists in a frame or not and if the person is present then the frame is forwarded to the face detection LBPH module for detecting the label of the faces. This additional layer is embedded with the purpose of screening to make it a more efficient way of suppressing the model's inability to misinterpret different objects as the face of the person.

This method is more efficient with respect to the other feature selection cascade like eye cascade which uses the count of eyes to detect whether the region of interest is a face or not. The use of the eye cascade cannot be applied in a real world as the use of spectacles or goggles by the subject hinders the performance of the system. Therefore, our system experiments with a set of 50 images each for four different models as shown in Table 1.

Table 1. Comparison of different face recognition models.

Model	Total images (T)	Right prediction (R)	Wrong prediction (W)	W/T
Eigen face	50	39	11	0.22
Fisher face	50	42	8	0.16
LBPH	50	46	4	0.08
YOLO + LBPH	50	47	3	0.06

The experimental results show that the YOLO + LBPH performs the best by increasing the accuracy of the system as shown in Fig. 5 and at the same time suppressing the false detection of the faces.

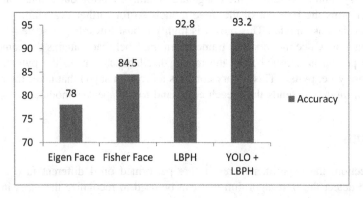

Fig. 5. Accuracy comparison of different models applied to the dataset.

This approach aims to create a real-time face detection system that is highly reliable to detect known faces. A threshold is applied to the system where only the detected faces having the confidence rate greater than 50% are considered and the rest of the detections are rejected. Figure 6 shows the label with its confidence score in the blue rectangle and the pink circle is representing the facial coordinates of the person.

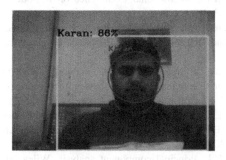

Fig. 6. Confidence score and image label.

5   Conclusion

In this paper, a face recognition system is presented and the algorithm is validated by comparing it with a different state of the art face detection models. This system is fully automated from data extraction to model implementation. This automation makes the system user-friendly and highly flexible to be implemented as an assistive device for visually impaired. Addition of object detection layer for detecting the presence of person increases the robustness of the system preventing it to give audio feedback from posters and photo frames.

This system performs equally well in different illuminations due to intensity normalization of the captured image. Experimental results show that the system is able to detect known faces at a high accuracy of 93.2%. In future, the aim is to build a portable and economical prototype by integrating the proposed system with IOT to aid the visually impaired during the social interactions. Further, this work can be extended by implementing object detection and object character recognition and thus creating a complete solution for the disabled people.

References

1. WHO.: Visual impairment and blindness (2014). http://www.webcitation.org/6YfcCRh9L
2. Jhonny, G.P., Carlos, V.A., Luis, S.A., Eduardo, P.V.: Special glasses for obstacle detection with location system in case of emergency and aid for recognition of dollar bills for visually impaired persons. In: Healthcare Innovations and Point of Care Technologies (HI-POCT), 2017 IEEE, pp. 68–71. IEEE (2017)

3. Ishikiriyama, J., Suzuki, K.: An interactive virtual mirror to support makeup for visually impaired persons. In: IEEE International Conference on Systems, Man, and Cybernetics (SMC), 2017, pp. 1393–1398. IEEE (2017)
4. Lu, C., Adluru, N., Ling, H., Zhu, G., Latecki, L.J.: Contour-based object detection using part bundles. Comput. Vis. Image Underst. **114**(7), 827–834 (2010)
5. Ess, A., Leibe, B., Schindler, K., Van Gool, L.: Moving obstacle detection in highly dynamic scenes. In: IEEE International Conference on Robotics and Automation, 2009, ICRA 2009, pp. 56–63. IEEE (2009)
6. Moreno, M., Shahrabadi, S., José, J., du Buf, J.H., Rodrigues, J.M.: Real-time local navigation for the blind: detection of lateral doors and sound interface. Proc. Comput. Sci. **14**, 74–82 (2012)
7. Sun, Y., Wang, X., Tang, X.: Deep convolutional network cascade for facial point detection. In: IEEE Conference on Computer Vision and Pattern Recognition (CVPR), 2013, pp. 3476–3483. IEEE (2013)
8. Zhang, C., Zhang, Z.: A survey of recent advances in face detection (2010)
9. Ortiz, E.G., Becker, B.C.: Face recognition for web-scale datasets. Comput. Vis. Image Underst. **118**, 153–170 (2014)
10. Abdi, H., Williams, L.J.: Principal component analysis. Wiley Interdiscip. Rev. Comput. Stat. **2**(4), 433–459 (2010)
11. Fisher, R.A.: The use of multiple measurements in taxonomic problems. Ann. Hum. Genet. **7**(2), 179–188 (1936)
12. Raghavendra, R., Rao, A., Kumar, G.H.: Multimodal person verification system using face and speech. Proc. Comput. Sci. **2**, 181–187 (2010)
13. Pong, K.H., Lam, K.M.: Multi-resolution feature fusion for face recognition. Pattern Recogn. **47**(2), 556–567 (2014)
14. Stallkamp, J., Ekenel, H.K., Stiefelhagen, R.: Video-based face recognition on real-world data. In: IEEE 11th International Conference on Computer Vision, ICCV 2007, pp. 1–8. IEEE (2007)
15. Gorodnichy, D.O.: Video-based framework for face recognition in video. In: Proceedings of the 2nd Canadian conference on computer and robot vision, pp. 330–338. IEEE (2005)
16. Levinson, J., Askeland, J., Becker, J., Dolson, J., Held, D., Kammel, S., Sokolsky, M.: Towards fully autonomous driving: systems and algorithms. In: Intelligent Vehicles Symposium (IV), 2011 IEEE, pp. 163–168. IEEE (2011)
17. Gavrila, D.M., Munder, S.: Multi-cue pedestrian detection and tracking from a moving vehicle. Int. J. Comput. Vision **73**(1), 41–59 (2007)
18. Huang, G.B., Ramesh, M., Berg, T., Learned-Miller, E.: Labeled faces in the wild: a database for studying face recognition in unconstrained environments, vol. 1, no. 2, p. 3. Technical Report 07-49, University of Massachusetts, Amherst (2007)
19. Ding, C., Choi, J., Tao, D., Davis, L.S.: Multi-directional multi-level dual-cross patterns for robust face recognition. IEEE Trans. Pattern Anal. Mach. Intell. **38**(3), 518–531 (2016)
20. Viola, P., Jones, M.: Rapid object detection using a boosted cascade of simple features. In: Proceedings of the 2001 IEEE Computer Society Conference on Computer Vision and Pattern Recognition 2001. CVPR 2001, vol. 1, p. 1. IEEE (2001)
21. Redmon, J., Farhadi, A.: YOLO9000: better, faster, stronger. arXiv preprint, 1612 (2016)
22. Turk, M., Pentland, A.: Eigenfaces for recognition. J. Cogn. Neurosci. **3**(1), 71–86 (1991)
23. Belhumeur, P.N., Hespanha, J.P., Kriegman, D.J.: Eigenfaces vs. fisherfaces: recognition using class specific linear projection. IEEE Trans. Pattern Anal. Mach. Intell. **19**(7), 711–720 (1997)
24. Shan, C., Gritti, T.: Learning discriminative LBP-histogram bins for facial expression recognition. In: BMVC, pp. 1–10, September 2008

Ranking of Cancer Mediating Genes: A Novel Approach Using Genetic Algorithm in DNA Microarray Gene Expression Dataset

Sujay Saha[1]($\boxtimes$), Priyojit Das[2], Anupam Ghosh[3], and Kashi Nath Dey[4]

[1] Department of CSE, Heritage Institute of Technology, Kolkata 700107,
West Bengal, India
`sujay.saha@heritageit.edu`
[2] Department of CSE, National Institute of Technology Calicut, Kattangal
673601, Kerala, India
`priyodas3@gmail.com`
[3] Department of CSE, Netaji Subhash Engineering College, Kolkata 700152,
West Bengal, India
`anupam.ghosh@rediffmail.com`
[4] Department of CSE, University of Calcutta, Kolkata 700073, West Bengal,
India
`kndey55@gmail.com`

Abstract. Genes need to be investigated either in Gene Interaction Network or in a DNA microarray gene expression data to understand the role they play in complex diseases like cancer. The prioritized genes can help us to know the molecular mechanism, as well as to discover the promising candidates of cancer. Several gene ranking algorithms already have been proposed that produces the top ranked genes according to their importance with respect to a particular disease. In this work, we have developed one Genetic Algorithm (GA) based algorithm, MicroarrayGA, to rank the genes responsible for a particular cancer to occur. The whole research works on six datasets like Colorectal Cancer, Diffuse Large B-Cell Lymphoma, Pediatric Immune Thrombocytopenia (ITP), Small Cell Lung Cancer (SCLC), Breast Cancer and Prostate Cancer, publicly available from NCBI (National Center for Biotechnology Information) online repository. We have validated the outcome of the proposed algorithm by classification step using Support Vector Machine (SVM) classifier and we have also compared the results of MicroarrayGA with three existing methods on the basis of percentage of accuracy, precision, recall, F1-Score and G-Mean metrics.

Keywords: Gene ranking · Gene interaction · Microarray · Genetic algorithm
SVM classifier

1 Introduction

Uncontrollable growth of cells in an unusual fashion is the primary basis of cancer, which is often classified as a group of diseases [1]. Thousands of several genes are responsible for a particular cancer to occur. But all those genes may not be equally

© Springer Nature Singapore Pte Ltd. 2018
M. Singh et al. (Eds.): ICACDS 2018, CCIS 906, pp. 129–137, 2018.
https://doi.org/10.1007/978-981-13-1813-9_13

significant in this case. Due to this reason, selection of genes based on their ranks for a specific cancer is highly important [2]. In this work, we try to find the significant mediating genes of six various human cancer datasets and to prioritize them as well.

The algorithm used in this paper to rank the genes is primarily constructed by analyzing the expression change of the genes between a diseased and a normal sample. The Genetic Algorithm (GA) based implementations, namely MicroarryGA is applied on microarray gene expression datasets of different cancers to rank genes. Genetic Algorithm can be considered as one of the popular evolutionary algorithms [3, 4]. Later, these ranks are validated by classification step using SVM classifiers [5, 6]. The workflow of the proposed MicroarrayGA method is given in Fig. 1.

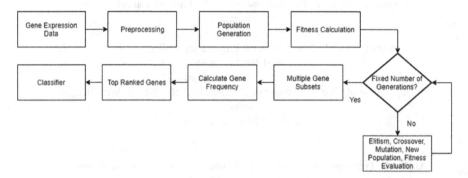

Fig. 1. Workflow of the proposed MicroarrayGA method

2   Related Earlier Works

Ranking genes based on the information from several DNA microarray gene expression data is of fundamental importance [7]. Since data sources contain thousands of several genes, so to determine the set of prioritized genes according to their significance order is an important task. Some of methods from current literature are mentioned briefly as follows:

A soft clustering based microarray expression analysis algorithm is proposed in [8] to analyze genes responsible for acute leukemia. Another method mentioned in [9] uses non-parametric statistical tests - Mann-Whitney U test and k-sample Kruskal-Wallis H test to rank genes. A statistical gene subset selection algorithm using Wilcoxon rank sum test is presented in [10].

Huerta et al. [13] analyzed Leukemia [12] and Colon cancer [14] datasets using their proposed genetic algorithm based gene selection method along with SVM classifier. Mondal et al. presented a multi-objective GA based gene ranking approach in [15]. Another method proposed in [16], selects significant features using genetic algorithms (GAs) and then uses Constructive Neural Networks (CNN) [17], C-Mantec [18] based classification methods to validate the results. A neuro-fuzzy approach is proposed in [19] to select those genes responsible for a particular type of cancers. Another method presented in [20] uses graph theory based approach to identify most significant as well as most non-redundant genes from a DNA gene expression dataset. Dragon Wrapper Feature Selection (DWFS), a web based tool, proposed in [21], is used to select significant features for a various types of problems efficiently.

Another new approach was proposed in [22] to rank the genes of microarray gene expression data using squared Pearson correlation coefficient. Another work presented in [23] developed a fuzzy set theory based index, named as Gaussian Fuzzy Index (GFI) to select a set of cancer mediating genes. GeneRank developed by Morrison et al. [24], is a straightforward generalization of PageRank [25] algorithm used by Google.

3   Methodology

We have developed following GA based approach named as MicroarrayGA. This method initially begins with pre-selection based on filtering, and then generates gene subset G_P of P genes, where P is problem dependent. A small set of the most important genes are selected from this reduced subset of genes, which give the highest accuracy when used with classification task. Detailed steps of this approach are given below:

1. In the first step, genes/features form the microarray are sorted using Fisher's Discriminant Criteria [26] in decreasing order. Then from the sorted genes, top P genes are selected for our calculation.
2. Then N different gene subsets are generated randomly from selected P genes and they are used as initial GA population. To encode each of the gene subsets of the population, binary chromosome representation is used, given in Fig. 2. If a particular gene is present in the gene subset, then the corresponding bit is set to 1, otherwise set to 0 in that chromosome representation.

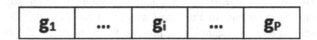

Fig. 2. Chromosome representation

3. After obtaining the initial population, a minimizing fitness function is applied on each of the chromosomes to find the individual fitness value. For each gene present in chromosome, p-value is calculated from Student's two-tailed t test between the two types of sample corresponding to that gene (normal and cancerous). After calculating the p-values of each of the genes present in the chromosome, the average p-value is calculated, which is the fitness value of the chromosome.
4. In this step, a temporary population N' is created which will be used as a population N in the next generation. The new population N', is filled up in three steps. In the first step, the top 40% individuals (based on fitness value; in this method from lower to higher) of N are copied to N' (elitism). In the next two steps, genetic operators: uniform crossover and binary mutation operators are applied respectively to obtain new chromosomes (child solutions).

5. A random pair of solutions are selected from N and uniform crossover operator is applied on these two individuals. The resulting new child solution is inserted in N'. This step is repeated for $0.4 * |N|$ times, where 0.4 is crossover probability (P_c).

6. In this step, mutation operator is applied on individual solution selected randomly from N. This step is repeated for $0.2 * |N|$ times, where 0.2 is mutation probability (P_m).

7. Replace N with N' and repeat the steps from 3 to 7 until fixed number of generations are completed.

8. After the completion of all the generations, each gene is assigned an importance value depending on the frequency of selection among all the N gene subsets. A gene having higher frequency of appearance gets high importance value and vice versa. Their significance is tested by the classification performance using SVM classifier.

4   Experimental Results

MicroarrayGA based approach is applied on microarray gene expression dataset of six various types of cancers, like Breast Cancer, Prostate Cancer, Pediatric Immune Thrombocytopenia (ITP), Small Cell Lung Cancer, Diffuse Large B-Cell Lymphoma (DLBCL) and Colorectal Cancer available at NCBI online repository.

4.1   Dataset Used

Colorectal Cancer tumor (GDS4382) [27, 32] dataset contains 17 samples are of type normal and 17 are of type diseased. Small Cell Lung Cancer (GDS4794) [28, 32] dataset is divided into diseased and normal sample subsets of size 23 and 42 respectively. For DLBCL-FL (GDS4236) [29, 32] dataset, 8 samples are rapamycin sensitive and 6 are rapamycin resistant. In Prostate Cancer (GDS4824) [30, 32] Dataset, 13 diseased samples and 8 normal samples are present. Breast Cancer (GDS4056) [11, 32] contains 32 diseased samples and 29 normal samples. Pediatric Immune Thrombocytopenia (ITP) [31, 32] dataset has total 13 samples out of which 7 are of type newly diagnosed immune thrombocytopenia samples and 6 are of type chronic immune thrombocytopenia samples.

4.2   Parameter Settings

The parameters of the GA applied on microarray gene expression dataset are represented in Table 1 below:

Table 1. GA parameters for MicroarrayGA

N	No. of generations	P	Genes selected	P_c	P_m
100	100	1000	490–500	0.4	0.2

4.3   Results and Comparison with Other Methods

Classification algorithm is used to validate the proposed GA based algorithm's effectiveness in gene ranking. The proposed method's efficiency is compared with some existing ranking methods on the basis of percentage of classification accuracy along with some other metrics.

We take top 20 genes from the ranked set of 1000 genes. These ranking is validated again by the classification process using SVM method with three kernels. Before the classification process starts, we divide the whole sample space into 60:40 ratio. Following Fig. 3 shows how the MicroarrayGA's performance varies on the basis of

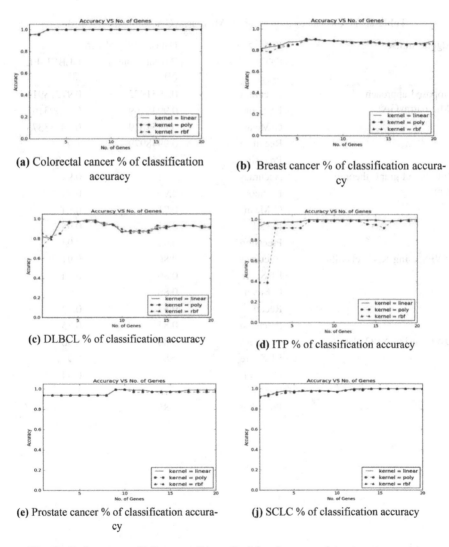

(a) Colorectal cancer % of classification accuracy

(b) Breast cancer % of classification accuracy

(c) DLBCL % of classification accuracy

(d) ITP % of classification accuracy

(e) Prostate cancer % of classification accuracy

(j) SCLC % of classification accuracy

Fig. 3. Performance of MicroarrayGA method for six cancer dataset on two metrics

percentage of accuracy using only top most 20 genes for six cancer datasets. From that figure it is clear that for which dataset what is the percentage of classification accuracy proposed algorithm achieves by using how many genes. Although we have done our experiment on six publicly available cancer datasets, but to compare our GA based method's performance with three state-of-the art methods, like Particle Swarm Optimization (PSO) based Graph Theoretic Approach [20], DWFS using K-Nearest Neighbor (KNN) classifier and DWFS using Naïve Bayes (NBC) classifier [21] only two datasets, Prostate Cancer and DLBCL-FL are used. Table 2 shows this comparative study on the basis of percentage of classification accuracy, F1 Score, G-Mean, Recall, Precision [33].

Table 2. Performance comparison of MicroarrayGA with existing works

| Algorithm used | Performance metrics | Dataset (No. of genes) | |
		Prostate cancer (9)	DLBCL-FL (3)
Proposed approach (MicroarrayGA)	Accuracy	0.9931972	0.97278911
	F1 Score	0.9948169	0.97993197
	G-Mean	0.9954079	0.98388373
	Recall	0.9948979	1.0
	Precision	0.9959183	0.96802721
PSO based graph theoretic approach	Accuracy	0.91	0.94
	F1 Score	0.91	0.89
	G-Mean	0.91	0.94
	Recall	0.91	0.95
	Precision	0.92	0.94
DWFS using KNN classifier	Accuracy	0.86	0.91
	F1 Score	0.86	0.94
	G-Mean	0.86	0.9
	Recall	0.87	0.97
	Precision	0.85	0.85
DWFS using NBC classifier	Accuracy	0.80	0.96
	F1 Score	0.8	0.9
	G-Mean	0.78	0.94
	Recall	0.76	1
	Precision	0.85	0.9

Following Table 3 shows top 15 genes returned by MicroarrayGA algorithm.

Table 3. Top-most 15 genes from all six cancer datasets

Rank	Colorectal cancer	DLBCL-FL	ITP	SCLC	Breast cancer	Prostate cancer
1	LPAR1	C16orf45	CHST2	FANCI	CRIP1	CALM3
2	FAM60A	AAK1	BE670797	SRSF1	C9orf116	SIN3A
3	ABCA8	OR7D4	NR1D2	SPAST	TSPAN13	PRKAA2
4	UTP23	CSPG4P5	KMT2A	HAUS1	MREG	ZNF697
5	BRWD3	SRR	MYBL2	SUMO1	MCCC2	LOC100287413
6	MYC	RFESD	SNX5	NUSAP1	GFRA1	GAL
7	AJUBA	PLPP2	SEC31B	BUB3	TPBG	TIMM8A
8	MGA	chr7:43234021-43234081	SFPQ	RSRC1	ARMT1	RAB17
9	FAM214A	RFC1	GOLGA1	NUP133	PNPLA4	CRISPLD2
10	MRE11A	RHOBTB3	ATPAF1	SRP9	FBP1	FNDC3A
11	SYNCRIP	NIPSNAP3B	OAS2	TMEM258	AGR2	MMGT1
12	GART	GALR1	SLC30A5	SUB1	TFF3	OR7E14P
13	CASZ1	AKR7A2P1	237398_at	UBE2V2	P2RX4	STARD4
14	PPM1H	HIVEP2	FBXO38	SNRPG	TBC1D9	PTRF
15	MMP28	TRPT1	DZIP3	DYNLT1	GATA3	MAGI2

5 Conclusion and Future Scope

In the proposed approach, a genetic algorithm based implementation, MicroarrayGA is used to rank the genes causing various cancers. Ranking is validated by SVM classifier method with three kernels. From Fig. 3 it is clear that for which dataset what is the percentage of classification accuracy proposed algorithm achieves by using how many genes. Three different existing methods from current literature are used in this paper along with MicroarrayGA method for the performance comparison purpose. From the performance scores given in Table 2, it can be concluded that our GA based approach surpasses the other methods. Since MicroarrayGA uses gene expression dataset, the results shows that this approach uses top most 3 genes to top most 9 genes for various cancer datasets to achieve percentage of classification accuracy close to 100%.

We have used only microarray dataset to rank genes. But it is quite possible that gene dataset is obtained in terms of gene interaction network. In that case we need to think about new ways to rank the genes involved in the network. Another modification that can be done is the generation of multiple gene subsets (non-dominated solutions) rather than a single gene subset, which can be used for further biological analysis. For that we can think about multi-objective genetic algorithm. That may improve our results further.

References

1. Defining Cancer: National Cancer Institute, June 2014
2. Zhang, C., Lu, X., Zhang, X.: Significance of gene ranking for classification of microarray samples. IEEE/ACM Trans. Comput. Biol. Bioinform. (TCBB) **3**(3), 312–320 (2006)
3. Goldberg, D.E.: Genetic Algorithms in Search, Optimization and Machine Learning. Addison-Wesley, Boston (1989)
4. Holland, J.H.: Adaptation in Natural and Artificial Systems, 2nd edn. MIT Press, Cambridge (1975)
5. Boser, B.E., Guyon, I., Vapnik, V.: A training algorithm for optimal margin classifiers. In: Proceedings of 5th Annual Workshop on Computational Learning Theory, pp. 144–152. ACM Press (1992)
6. Zisserman, A.: The SVM Classifier. Lecture Notes (2015)
7. Wang, Y., et al.: Gene selection from microarray data for cancer classification—a machine learning approach. Comput. Biol. Chem. **29**(1), 37–46 (2005)
8. Yoo, C.K., Leeb, I.B., Vanrolleghema, P.A.: Interpreting patterns and analysis of acute leukemia gene expression data by multivariate fuzzy statistical analysis. In: Proceedings of 14th European Symposium on Computer Aided Process Engineering. ESCAPE-14, vol. 29, no. 6, pp. 1345–1356 (2005)
9. Peterson, L.E., Coleman, M.A.: Comparison of gene identification based on artificial neural network pre-processing with k-means cluster and principal component analysis. In: Bloch, I., Petrosino, A., Tettamanzi, A.G.B. (eds.) WILF 2005. LNCS (LNAI), vol. 3849, pp. 267–276. Springer, Heidelberg (2006). https://doi.org/10.1007/11676935_33
10. Liao, C., Li, S., Luo, Z.: Gene selection using Wilcoxon rank sum test and support vector machine for cancer classification. In: Wang, Y., Cheung, Y.-M., Liu, H. (eds.) CIS 2006. LNCS (LNAI), vol. 4456, pp. 57–66. Springer, Heidelberg (2007). https://doi.org/10.1007/978-3-540-74377-4_7
11. West, M., Blanchette, C., Dressman, H., et al.: Predicting the clinical status of human breast cancer using gene expression profiles. Proc. Natl. Acad. Sci. **98**, 11462–11467 (2001)
12. Golub, T.R., Slonim, D.K., Tamayo, P., Huard, C., Gaasenbeek, M., et al.: Molecular classification of cancer: class discovery and class prediction by gene expression monitoring. Science **286**(1999), 531–537 (1999)
13. Huerta, E.B., Duval, B., Hao, J.-K.: A Hybrid GA/SVM approach for gene selection and classification of microarray data. In: Rothlauf, F., et al. (eds.) EvoWorkshops 2006. LNCS, vol. 3907, pp. 34–44. Springer, Heidelberg (2006). https://doi.org/10.1007/11732242_4
14. Alon, U., Barkai, N., Notterman, D.A., Gish, K., Ybarra, S., et al.: Broad patterns of gene expression revealed by clustering analysis of tumor and normal colon tissues probed by oligonucleotide arrays. Proc. Natl. Acad. Sci. USA **96**, 6745–6750 (1999)
15. Mondal, K.C., Mukhopadhyay, A., Maulik, U., Bandhyapadhyay, S., Pasquier, N.: MOSCFRA: a multi-objective genetic approach for simultaneous clustering and gene ranking. In: Rizzo, R., Lisboa, P.J.G. (eds.) CIBB 2010. LNCS, vol. 6685, pp. 174–187. Springer, Heidelberg (2011). https://doi.org/10.1007/978-3-642-21946-7_14
16. Luque-Baena, R.M., Urda, D., Subirats, J.L., Franco, L., Jerez, J.M.: Analysis of cancer microarray data using constructive neural networks and genetic algorithms. In: 1st International Work-Conference on Bioinformatics and Biomedical Engineering-IWBBIO, Granada, Spain (2013)
17. Parekh, R., Yang, J., Honavar, V.: Constructive neural-network learning algorithms for pattern classification. IEEE Trans. Neural Netw. **11**(2), 436–451 (2000)

18. Subirats, J.L., Franco, L., Jerez, J.M.: C-Mantec: a novel constructive neural network algorithm incorporating competition between neurons. Neural Netw. **26**, 130–140 (2012)
19. Ghosh, A., Dhara, B.C., De, R.K.: Selection of genes mediating certain cancers, using neuro-fuzzy approach. Neurocomputing **133**, 122–140 (2014)
20. Mandal, M., Mukhopadhyay, A.: A novel PSO-based graph-theoretic approach for identifying most relevant and non-redundant gene markers from gene expression data. Int. J. Parallel Emerg. Distrib. Syst. **30**(3), 175–192 (2015)
21. Soufan, O., Kleftogiannis, D., Kalnis, P., Bajic, V.B.: DWFS: a wrapper feature selection tool based on a parallel genetic algorithm. PLoS One (2015). https://doi.org/10.1371/journal. pone.0117988
22. Demidenko, E.: Microarray enriched gene rank. BioData Min. **8**, 2 (2015). https://doi.org/10. 1186/s13040-014-0033-1
23. Ghosh, A., De, R.K.: Identification of certain cancer mediating genes using Gaussian Fuzzy cluster validity index (GFI). J. Biosci. **40**, 741–754 (2015)
24. Morrison, J.L., Breitling, R., Higham, D.J., Gilbert, D.R.: GeneRank: using search-engine technology for the analysis of microarray experiments. BMC Bioinform. **6**(2015), 233–247 (2015)
25. Page, L., Brin, S., Motwani, R., Winograd, T.: The PageRank Citation Ranking: Bringing Order to the Web. Stanford InfoLab, Stanford (1999)
26. Iatan, I.F.: The fisher's linear discriminant. In: Borgelt, C., et al. (eds.) Combining Soft Computing and Statistical Methods in Data Analysis, vol. 77, pp. 345–352. Springer, Heidelberg (2010). https://doi.org/10.1007/978-3-642-14746-3_43
27. Khamas, A., Ishikawa, T., Shimokawa, K., Mogushi, K., et al.: Screening for epigenetically masked genes in colorectal cancer using 5-Aza-2'-deoxycytidine, microarray and gene expression profile. Cancer Genom. Proteom. **9**(2), 67–75 (2012)
28. Sato, T., Kaneda, A., Tsuji, S., Isagawa, T., et al.: PRC2 over-expression and PRC2-target gene repression relating to poorer prognosis in small cell lung cancer. Sci. Rep. **3**, 1911 (2013)
29. Singh, D., et al.: Gene expression correlates of clinical prostate cancer behavior. Cancer Cell **1**(2002), 203–209 (2002)
30. Hans, C.P., Weisenburger, D.D., Greiner, T.C., Gascoyne, R.D., Delabie, J., et al.: Confirmation of the molecular classification of diffuse large B-cell lymphoma by immune histo-chemistry using a tissue microarray. Blood **103**(2004), 275–282 (2004)
31. Shad, A.T., Gonzalez, C.E., Sandler, S.G.: Treatment of immune thrombocytopenic purpura in children: current concepts. Paediatr. Drugs **7**(5), 325–336 (2005)
32. Seal, D.B., Saha, S., Mukherjee, P., Chatterjee, M., Mukherjee, A., Dey, K.N.: Gene ranking: an entropy & decision tree based approach. In: IEEE 7th Annual Ubiquitous Computing, Electronics & Mobile Communication Conference (UEMCON), New York City, NY, USA, pp. 1–5 (2016). https://doi.org/10.1109/UEMCON.2016.7777837
33. Powers, D.M.W.: Evaluation: from precision, recall and F-measure to ROC, informedness, markedness & correlation. J. Mach. Learn. Technol. **2**(1), 37–63 (2011)

Hand Gesture Recognition Using Gaussian Threshold and Different SVM Kernels

Shifali Sharma[1(✉)], Shatrughan Modi[2], Prashant Singh Rana[2],
and Jhilik Bhattacharya[2]

[1] Chandigarh University, Gharuan Mohali, Punjab, India
shifali.cse@cumail.in
[2] Thapar Institute of Engineering and Technology, Patiala, Punjab, India
{shatrughan.modi,prashant.singh,jhilik}@thapar.edu

Abstract. Hands play an important part in expressing one's actions and ideas thus Hand Gesture Recognition (HGR) is very significant in computer vision based gesture recognition for Human Computer Interaction (HCI). In our work, the dataset has been generated for five hand gestures (Close Hand, Open Hand, Victory Hand, Thumb Down and Thumb Up), by making videos of 10 different users doing the gestures with all possible variations resulting in total 16,240 entries. Firstly we have used image processing algorithms like Bilateral Filter, Median Blur and Gaussian Threshold for smoothing the images and then compared the performance of different Support Vector Machine (SVM) kernels i.e. rbfdot, vanilladot, polydot, tanhdot, laplacedot and besseldot, for HGR. The accuracy achieved with different SVM kernels varied from 24.17% to 85.07% with training-testing ratio of 70–30% for 16,240 entries in the dataset. The 10-fold cross validation is performed to prove the robustness of the kernel with SVM.

Keywords: Hand gesture recognition · Image processing · Gaussian threshold
Machine learning · Support Vector Machine · Support vector machine kernels

1 Introduction

Mechanical devices such as keyboards, mice, joysticks etc. can be a hindrance to Human Computer Interaction (HCI). The more natural the interaction is, more easily the interaction can take place between the humans and the computers. In recent years, gesture recognition has gained popularity in many areas such as gaming, medical science, communication systems for deaf and dumb etc. Gestures can refer to a particular movement or a posture made using body parts (head, face, hands, arms etc.). Communication using hands has been the preferred method after verbal communication. Hand gesture recognition, in which gestures are made using hands, by a computer system, is an important research field.

There are two classes of hand gestures: static hand gesture and dynamic hand gesture. Static hand gesture can be represented using a single image with static configuration and location of hand, without any movements (for example a fist) whereas dynamic hand gesture is represented using a series of frames of static hand gestures connected by a continuous movement in some specified time-span (for example waving a hand).

© Springer Nature Singapore Pte Ltd. 2018
M. Singh et al. (Eds.): ICACDS 2018, CCIS 906, pp. 138–147, 2018.
https://doi.org/10.1007/978-981-13-1813-9_14

Gestures are considered the most natural way for communication and its applications are not limited to HCI. A real time algorithm which can be used to interact with video game using hand gestures is proposed by Manresa et al. [1]. The algorithm uses the color cue for hand segmentation and hand morphological features are extracted from the tracking process for which constant velocity is assumed and pixel labeling approach is followed. The finite state classifier takes the extracted features as input and classifies the gesture according to its hand configuration. Ionescu et al. [2] describes a dynamic hand gesture recognition algorithm which is based on 2D representation of the skeleton of hand. Dynamic gesture signatures are created by superposing the hand skeleton of different postures of the gesture to give a single image. These signatures are then used for gesture recognition to guide robot from a distance by comparing them with the gesture alphabet and the dissimilarities in model parameters are measured using Baddeley's distance.

Human hands have many connected parts and joints, thus making it an articulated complex structure with roughly 27 degree of freedom when in motion [3]. Also, different humans have different hand structures varying in shape and size. The problem with gesture recognition is how to make computer understand gestures. Extra hardware like sensors or glove based devices maybe used to transmit hand configuration and movement data to the computer. A gesture recognition system which uses 5DT Company's 5th Data Glove System as an input device is described by Kim et al. [4]. It combines the fuzzy max-min composition along with Relational Database Management System to be implemented on Post-PC platform. The combination can provide improved data acquisition efficiency. Plawiak et al. [5] have used a special glove with 10 embedded sensors for collecting the data. After preprocessing the data, three machine learning algorithms (SVM, Probabilistic neural network and k-nearest neighbors algorithm) were used for training and testing using 10-fold cross-validation method. These extra hardware units do make the process of gesture recognition easier but these devices can be expensive and cumbersome in nature.

Support Vector Machine (SVM) is a linear machine, which is popular supervised learning algorithm. Using SVM training model, the built model can predict the class in which the new example falls. SVM can handle unknown data very well because for each class its feature space is divided. The main objective of SVM is the construction of an optimal separating hyper plane, as the decision surface, and maximizing the separation margin between positive and negative examples. SVM is used to train the feature vector after extracting the Gradient Direction Histogram (HoG) feature which is mostly used pedestrian detection [6]. HOG feature can alleviate the impact of illumination variations and rotation of the hand for the recognition rate. The decision about the gesture is taken using previously learned SVMs. Results are compared for different lighting conditions. Gupta et al. [7] used one against one multi-class SVM for classification. Using 15 local Gabor filters instead of 40 Gabor filters reduces complexity with increased accuracy. After that combination of Principal Component Analysis (PCA) [8] and Linear Discriminant Analysis (LDA) [9] are used for feature extraction and feature reduction. Thang et al. [10] studies the effectiveness, feasibility and comparison of Simplification of Support Vector Machine (SimpSVM) and Relevance Vector Machine (RVM) classification methods for Hand Gesture Recognition problem. SimpSVM is better than RVM in gesture recognition. Also, SimpSVM re-quires fewer training time during training phase. Performance changes with amount of data and number of features. Singha et al. [11] have discussed about how self co-articulation can be used as a feature for improving the performance of hand gesture recognition system. The self co-articulation features were detected from the trajectory of the gestures by adding speed to the information and adding a pause when a gesture is spotted. Other features that were used are hand's position, distance and ratio features. The ANN and the SVM models were used to test the feature's accuracy and performance for the hand gesture recognition.

Most of the papers discussed above have used a small dataset of images for training and testing the methods. Also, different variations of the hand gesture which can be either given by a user or different users are not considered. Either extra hardware other than the normal camera or marker based techniques have been used for detection of the hand. Computationally complex algorithms have been used for either pre-processing the images or for feature extraction from the images. Contributions of this paper are:

- We have created our own dataset, with 16,240 images (minimum 3,190 images per gesture). We made videos with 10 different users doing 5 hand gestures and then extracted images from the videos. This covered all different variations of the hand gestures and also different shapes and sizes of the hands.
- We have used computationally non complex algorithms for pre-processing of images and feature extraction from the images like bilateral filter and median blur for smoothing the images, Gaussian threshold for obtaining a proper outline of the hand gesture and convex hull points.
- Different SVM kernels i.e. rbfdot, vanilladot, polydot, tanhdot, laplacedot and besseldot are compared for the accuracy of the HGR proposed method.
- We have used a simple camera for making of the videos. No extra hardware has been used for detecting the hand. The hand has been detected using image processing algorithms.

2 Proposed Method

In our proposed work we have considered five different static hand gestures shown in Fig. 1 which were displayed in front of the camera with different variations by 10 different users in normal lighting conditions. Figure 2 shows the important steps to be carried out in our proposed methodology.

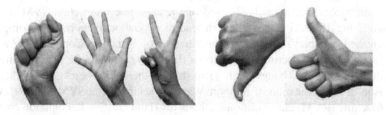

Fig. 1. Different types of hand gestures (Open Hand, Close Hand, Victory Hand, Thumb Down, Thumb Up (from left to right))

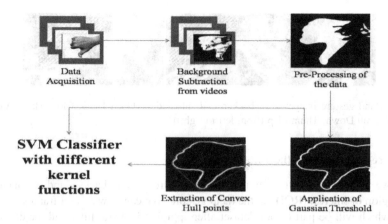

Fig. 2. Methodology used

2.1 Data Acquisition

We have made 10 videos of each of the 5 hand gestures using 10 different users. A Mobile Camera (13 Mega Pixels) for making videos of 720 × 1280 pixels at 30 fps has been used. The time range of each video is between 12 s to 22 s which entirely depends upon the user. The videos have been made in normal lighting conditions with following instructions to the users:

- User's hand should always be in the frame from beginning to the end of the video. Users are free to move the hand anywhere in the frame doing different variations of the hand gestures.
- There is no restriction on the speed of the hand movement while doing the hand gesture.
- The distance between the user and the camera is not restricted to a particular range.

2.2 Background Subtraction from the Videos

Background subtraction is used for extracting moving foreground from static background. It is an important preprocessing step. If image of the static background is available background subtraction can be done by just subtracting the background image from the new image to get foreground objects alone. Such images are not available in most of the cases and we have to adjust with the available images. Shadows can also complicate the process.

For background subtraction we have used BackgroundSubtractorMOG2 Gaussian mixture-based Background/Foreground Segmentation OpenCV algorithm [21, 22]. The essential feature of this algorithm is that for each pixel it selects an appropriate-ate number of Gaussian distribution and also in varying scenes due to illumination changes (etc.) it provides better adaptability. Figure 3 shows the images after background subtraction from video.

Fig. 3. Hand gesture images after background subtraction (Open Hand, Close Hand, Victory Hand, Thumb Down, Thumb Up (from left to right))

2.3 Pre-processing of the Data

Since we have extracted the moving foreground from static background, we have got our Region of Interest (ROI) i.e. the hand gesture. We can now extract frames from the video which will be part of our dataset after applying bilateral filter and median filter, image processing algorithms.

For smoothing the images, after extracting frames we apply bilateral filter and median filter on the frames. Image smoothing involves convolving the image using a low-pass filter kernel. It is helpful in removing high frequency content like noise, edges from the image which results in blurring of the edges too in the process.

Bilateral filter effectively keeps the edges sharp while removing noise. Bilateral filter takes two Gaussian filters, one a function of space which makes sure that during filtration, for blurring, only neighborhood pixels are considered and the other a function of pixel difference which makes sure that for blurring only the pixels with similar intensity to central pixel are considered.

Median filter is effective in removing salt and pepper noise. The median blur function always replaces the central element by some pixel in the image, calculated by taking median of all the pixels under kernel area. The size of the kernel should be odd and it must be a positive integer. Figure 4 shows the frame after applying firstly bilateral filter and then median blur on the extracted frame from video.

Fig. 4. Hand gesture images after pre-processing (Open Hand, Close Hand, Victory Hand, Thumb Down, Thumb Up (from left to right))

2.4 Application of Gaussian Threshold

Thresholding a grayscale image can create a binary image. In simple thresholding, if the pixel value is greater than the given threshold value the pixel value is set to one of the two values else it is set to the other value.

In adaptive thresholding, the threshold value is calculated for small regions in the image, such that the threshold value of the pixel is dependent on the pixel intensity of its neighboring pixels. In Gaussian threshold for threshold value, the weighted sum of the neighboring pixel values is calculated, where weights are a Gaussian window. Figure 5 shows the frames after applying Gaussian threshold. Noise is removed at a good rate after applying Gaussian threshold.

Fig. 5. Hand gesture images after applying Gaussian threshold (Open Hand, Close Hand, Victory Hand, Thumb Down, Thumb Up (from left to right))

The dataset is created by applying Gaussian threshold and resizing the images to 50×50 pixels.

2.5   Extraction of Convex Hull Points

After applying Gaussian threshold to the images, we calculated the convex hull of the hand and also the contour of the hand. A set, K, of points say k0, k1, k2, k3, k4,…, kn, is said to be convex if a line segment joining a pair of points in the set, should also be a part of the set. The convex hull of the set K will be the smallest convex polygon containing all the points in the set K [23]. Figure 6 shows the hand gestures with convex hull.

Fig. 6. Hand gesture images with convex hull (Open Hand, Close Hand, Victory Hand, Thumb Down, Thumb Up (from left to right))

2.6   Using SVM for Classification

Features extracted using Gaussian threshold and the convex hull points of each image are used to create a single Comma Separated Values (CSV) file f or the dataset. The data is then used to train and test the SVM classifier with different kernels in different ratios for HGR. SVM is one of the most used machine learning algorithm used for classification which builds a model and predicts in which class the new example falls into. The ability to generalize a problem is higher in SVM. SVMs are a set of related supervised learning methods used for classification, which means it is machine learning task of inferring the results from previously supervised trained data.

3 Experimental Results

This section analyzes the prediction results of SVM machine learning classification model with different kernels on the testing dataset. Total dataset has 16,240 entries which has five classes of different hand gestures with different variations collected from 10 users in different backgrounds. Each user has given different variations of the 5 gestures such that all possible ways to perform the gesture are covered.

The accuracy is calculated for the SVM model on 50–50, 60–40, 70–30 and 80–20 training-testing partitions and is shown in Table 1 for each SVM kernel. The accuracy has been calculated using the formula (R language):

Table 1. Performance comparison of SVM model with different kernels on diffrent training-testing data

SVM kernels	Accuracy with training – testing partition			
	50–50%	60–40%	70–30%	80–20%
Rbfdot	**79.32**	**82.09**	84.11	86.13
Vanilladot	75.00	80.35	**85.07**	**90.09**
Polydot	75.00	80.35	**85.07**	**90.09**
Tanhdot	24.18	24.12	24.17	24.28
Laplacedot	38.50	41.58	42.99	44.70
Besseldot	59.18	65.91	71.24	75.48

$$\% \, \text{Accuracy} = \frac{\text{Number of Hand Gestures Correctly Classified}}{\text{Total number of Hand Gestures}} \times 100 \qquad (1)$$

To determine the accuracy a confusion matrix is created which shows the information about actual and predicted classifications done by SVM. The diagonal elements of the confusion matrix represent the number of predicted entries whose values are equal to the actual values where as the off diagonal represent the number of predicted entries whose values are not equal to the actual values. The higher the value of the diagonal elements the higher is the accuracy. It is evident that the results obtained by using SVM kernels vanilladot and polydot with 70–30% and 80–20% training-testing partitions are satisfactory and as the training dataset increases the result tends to get better. For 50–50% and 60–40% training-testing partitions the results of SVM rbfdot kernel is satisfactory.

Cross validation is a predictive model evaluation technique to measure the robustness of the model in which some part of dataset is used to train the model and the other to evaluate it. In K-fold cross validation the original dataset is randomly partitioned into K equal size sub-datasets. From these sub-datasets one sub-dataset is used for the validation of the model and the other K-1 sub-datasets are used for the training of the model. The cross validation process is repeated K times (the folds) such that each of the K sub-dataset is used exactly once for validation of the model. The advantage of

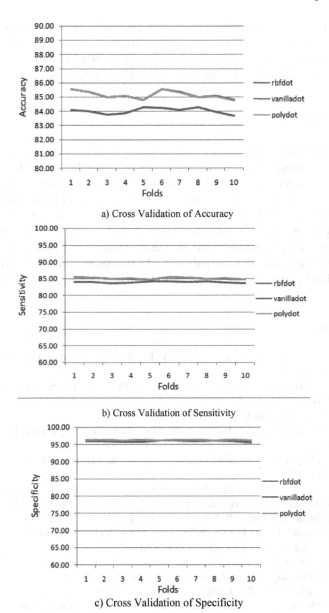

a) Cross Validation of Accuracy

b) Cross Validation of Sensitivity

c) Cross Validation of Specificity

Fig. 7. Results of 10-fold cross validation of the rbfdot, vanilladot and polydot SVM kernels and 70–30 training-testing data partition

cross-validation is that all the entries of the dataset are used for both training and testing of the model and each entry is used exactly once for testing the model. Here, we have used 10-fold cross validation to measure the robustness and performance of SVM model with rbfdot, vanilladot and polydot kernels on our dataset. Figure 7 shows the results of 10 fold Cross Validation for accuracy, sensitivity and specificity respectively calculated on training-testing dataset (70–30%). The results of cross-validation show a uniform performance in accuracy, sensitivity and specificity. Thus, validating the performance of SVM rbfdot, vanilladot and polydot kernels on our dataset.

4 Conclusion

In the proposed work, we have used various image processing algorithms along with Gaussian Threshold to pre-process the image before giving the data of these images to SVM for classification into 5 static hand gestures. The dataset used for this work has 16,240 entries used for training and testing of SVM model for HGR. The maximum accuracy is obtained by SVM kernels vanilladot and polydot with 70–30% and 80–20% training-testing partitions and SVM kernel rbfdot with 50–50% and 60–40% training-testing. Also, the results obtained from the 10-fold cross validation confirm the robustness of rbfdot, vanilladot and polydot SVM kernels. In future work, we will work on dynamic hand gesture recognition and also try to improve the accuracy of our work.

References

1. Manresa, C., Varona, J., Mas, R., Perales, F.J.: ELCVIA Electron. Lett. Comput. Vis. Image Anal. **5**(3), 96 (2005)
2. Ionescu, B., Coquin, D., Lambert, P., Buzuloiu, V.: EURASIP J. Adv. Sig. Proc. **2005**(13), 236190 (2005)
3. Wu, Y., Huang, T.S.: Studies **5**, 22 (2001)
4. Kim, J.H., Kim, D.G., Shin, J.H., Lee, S.W., Hong, K.S.: Fuzzy Syst. Knowl. Discov. 487–487 (2005)
5. Pławiak, P., Sośnicki, T., Niedźwiecki, M., Tabor, Z., Rzecki, K.: IEEE Trans. Ind. Inform. **12**(3), 1104 (2016)
6. Feng, K.P., Yuan, F.: In: 2013 2nd International Symposium on Instrumentation and Measurement, Sensor Network and Automation (IMSNA), pp. 936–938. IEEE (2013)
7. Gupta, S., Jaafar, J., Ahmad, W.F.W.: Proc. Eng. **41**, 827 (2012)
8. Pearson, K.: Lond. Edinb. Dublin Philos. Mag. J. Sci. **2**(11), 559 (1901)
9. Fisher, R.A.: Ann. Hum. Genet. **7**(2), 179 (1936)
10. Thang, P.Q., Dung, N.D., Thuy, N.T.: In: Proceedings of the 2017 International Conference on Machine Learning and Soft Computing, pp. 98–104. ACM (2017)
11. Singha, J., Laskar, R.H.: IET Comput. Vis. **10**(2), 143 (2016)
12. Ganapathyraju, S.: In: 2013 3rd International Conference on Instrumentation Control and Automation (ICA), pp. 63–67. IEEE (2013)
13. Temburwar, S., Jaiswal, P., Mande, S., Patil, S.: (2017)
14. Siby, J., Kader, H., Jose, J.: IJITR **3**(2), 1946 (2015)
15. Osimani, C., Piedra-Fernandez, J.A., Ojeda-Castelo, J.J., Iribarne, L.: Hand posture recognition with standard webcam for natural interaction. In: Rocha, Á., Correia, A.M., Adeli, H., Reis, L.P., Costanzo, S. (eds.) WorldCIST 2017. AISC, vol. 570, pp. 157–166. Springer, Cham (2017). https://doi.org/10.1007/978-3-319-56538-5_17
16. Shukla, J., Dwivedi, A.: In: 2014 Fourth International Conference on Communication Systems and Network Technologies (CSNT), pp. 919–923. IEEE (2014)

17. Oprisescu, S., Rasche, C., Su, B.: In: 2012 Proceedings of the 20th European Signal Processing Conference (EUSIPCO), pp. 2748–2751. IEEE (2012)
18. Igorevich, R.R., Park, P., Min, D., Park, Y., Choi, J., Choi, E.: In: 2010 4th International Conference on Application of Information and Communication Technologies (AICT), pp. 1–4. IEEE (2010)
19. Yeo, H.S., Lee, B.G., Lim, H.: Multimed. Tools Appl. **74**(8), 2687 (2015)
20. Shrivastava, R.: In: 2013 IEEE 3rd International on Advance Computing Conference (IACC), pp. 947–950. IEEE (2013)
21. Zivkovic, Z.: In: Proceedings of the 17th International Conference on Pattern Recognition, 2004. ICPR 2004, vol. 2, pp. 28–31. IEEE (2004)
22. Zivkovic, Z., Van Der Heijden, F.: Pattern Recog. Lett. **27**(7), 773 (2006)
23. De Berg, M., Cheong, O., Van Kreveld, M., Overmars, M.: Computational Geometry: Introduction. Springer, New York (2008). https://doi.org/10.1007/978-1-4612-1098-6
24. Chang, Y.W., Hsieh, C.J., Chang, K.W., Ringgaard, M., Lin, C.J.: J. Mach. Learn. Res. **11** (Apr), 1471 (2010)

Using Concept Map Network Based CLE for Teaching Learning and Evaluating the Knowledge Acquired by Learners

Sharma Minakshi$^{(\boxtimes)}$ and Chawla Sonal

Department of Computer Science and Applications,
Panjab University, Chandigarh, India
bminakshi@gmail.com, sonal_chawla@yahoo.com

Abstract. Constructivist learning has been an area of interest for researchers for past many years as it focuses on making the learner an active participant in the process of learning rather than merely being a passive recipient of knowledge. Tools like concept maps which are based on constructivist principles have been used very effectively to assist teachers in imparting knowledge. However, there is still a gap when it comes to the learning systems that allow learner to define his learning path. This paper presents one such tool for constructivist learning and assessment. A prototype of the tool was created to teach C programming and was tested with the students who were studying any programming language formally for the first time. Results show that there was a significant difference in level of knowledge acquired by the learners who used the tool as compared to those who were taught the same using classroom method.

Keywords: Concept maps · Concept map network · Conceptual assessment
Constructivist Learning Environments (CLE) · Learning stimulus
Skill based assessment

1 Introduction

Meaningful learning refers to the state where the concepts are understood completely and accurately by the learner and get completely integrated into his previously possessed knowledge structures [1]. Traditional methods of teaching learning focus on teacher centric approach for dissemination of knowledge. In such methods, learner is not actively participating in the learning process as teacher decides the structure of the learning path. Constructivist approach to learning advocates that knowledge has to be acquired by the learner, step by step, by becoming an active participant in the process rather than it being passively transmitted by the teacher [12]. This approach for learning has found acceptance among various learners and researchers alike and is an active area of research.

To gauge whether the learner has acquired right kind of knowledge, methods to assess the acquired knowledge are equally important. Mostly in traditional classroom methods, such assessment is done in the form of pen and paper test method which is not very effective and may encourage rote learning. Multiple choice questions based

© Springer Nature Singapore Pte Ltd. 2018
M. Singh et al. (Eds.): ICACDS 2018, CCIS 906, pp. 148–157, 2018.
https://doi.org/10.1007/978-981-13-1813-9_15

assessment can be more effective but has limitations in analyzing the learning outcomes in detail.

This paper focuses on using constructivist approach in creating a learning system that can facilitate meaningful learning and assess the acquired knowledge effectively. A tool based on constructivist approach was developed and its prototype was created to teach C programming which was then tested in real time to compare the learning outcomes with traditional classroom based teaching. Basic units for learning as well as assessment in the tool are the concept maps as technique of concept mapping is fundamentally based on the ideas of constructivism and meaningful learning [11] and has been successfully implemented in teaching different subjects.

2 Related Work

Theory of constructivism as a basis for new approach to teaching learning has been popular among educational researchers for the past few years. Use of concept maps in implementing constructivist approach to the process of teaching learning and assessment has also been an active area of research in subjects like physics, biology, history etc., where knowledge structures can be defined in hierarchical manner. In the field of computer science education also, researchers have used concept maps as teaching and learning tools and proved their effectiveness. Vural [15] studied the effectiveness of learner generated and expert generated concept mapping in computer based video learning and concluded that the group that used expert maps spent significantly less time while interacting with the instruction tool. Thain [13] studied the difference between recall ability among the students who used expert created concept maps as compared to the ones who used other visual organisers in the subject of animal psychology and concluded that students who used concept maps had enhanced recall ability. Similarly, Langford [6] studied importance of concept mapping to teach chemical equilibrium to grade 12 students. Vodovozov and Raud in [14] used concept mapping method to teach electronics engineering education and concluded that by the end of the course, most students acquired the conceptual knowledge. Kharatmal and Nagarjuna [5] presented refined concept maps (RCM) with a known finite set of relation names as a teaching aid in school students and showed that it was easy and feasible to use RCM by the school students as compared to other modes of knowledge representation. Pailai et al. in [3] presented a digital tool named kit-build concept map for supporting concept map strategy to represent instructor's expectations and to assess the understanding of learners in formative assessments.

Naeve in [10] presented a concept browser named Conzilla, a knowledge management tool that supports the construction, navigation, annotation and presentation of the information in a knowledge manifold. Mühling in [9] presented concept landscapes as means to investigate the state and development of knowledge structures using concept maps.

Although many researchers have used tools based on constructivist approach for teaching as well as assessment of knowledge, there is no integrated learning system that can be used independently by learners or teachers and that is completely learner-centric. This study proposes one such tool and tests its effectiveness in teaching 'C Programming'.

3 The Tool

A Constructivist Learning Environment (CLE) is defined as technology based space in which students explore, experiment, construct, converse and reflect on what they are doing so that they learn from their experiences [4]. In order to present an effective learning system based on constructivist theory, a CLE based tool was designed. This tool satisfies all the principles of constructivism and provides platform for acquiring conceptual knowledge as well as for the assessment of knowledge possessed by the learner. Moreover, it can be used for teaching-learning any subject where the content can be arranged hierarchically. The tool operates on two modes, the learner mode, used by the students for learning and submitting assignments and, the teacher mode, used by a teacher to create learning and assessment components.

3.1 Components of CLE

Figure 1 shows various components of the tool and brief introduction to these is given below:

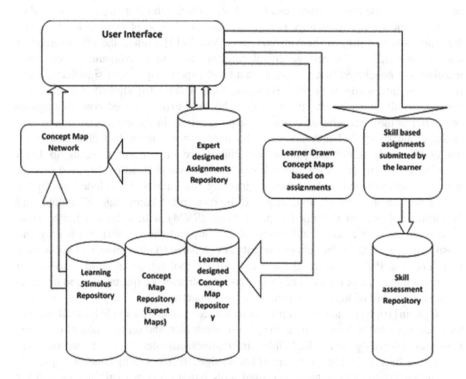

Fig. 1. Components of the CLE

User Interface. Same user interface (UI) can be used both by the teachers as well as students for interacting with other components of the tool. Students will use the CLE for learning as well as doing assignments and the teachers will use same interface for creating topic concept maps for learning as well as conceptual and skill based assignments.

Concept Map Network. Main learning component in this CLE is provided through concept map network, an interconnected network of concept maps combined through the common concepts. In addition to interlinking of concept maps, concept nodes also contain links to the learning objects stored in the learning stimulus repository. This gives learners a choice regarding their personal learning paths.

Learning Stimulus Repository. Learning stimulus repository contains the learning content in the form of presentations, videos, text files etc. In addition to this, it also contains activities for self-assessment by the learner. The learning stimulus is stored separately, independent of any concept or concept map, so that it could be shared among different concept maps.

Conceptual Assignments. Conceptual knowledge of the learner is evaluated using concept maps as well as through Multiple Choice Questions (MCQ) tests. For concept map based assessments, the learner is provided with a list of concepts and a focus question and is asked to draw a concept map using all the concepts given in the list. These assignments are scored automatically by the tool and the scores are available to students as well as the associated teacher. MCQ answers provided by the learner are also stored and scored automatically.

Skill Based Assignments. Skill based assignments are created as practical problems and stored by teachers under specific topics. The learner gives solution to the problem and submits it for further evaluation.

3.2 Scoring of Assignments

In order to quantify the assignments submitted by the learners, these have to assigned some scores. Various assignments are scored as follows:

Scoring of Concept Maps. Many researchers have proposed different methods for scoring of concept maps [2, 9]. In this research, two parameters have been selected for scoring the concept maps submitted by learners. The correct proposition count which indicates the number of correct concept-relation-concept representations and the sub-map count which represents the number of unlinked knowledge structures in the map. Of all the strategies available to assign correct proposition score, relation with master map proposed by McClure, Sonak and Suen [8] has been found to be the most reliable across various studies. Hence, score assignment for this parameter is based on relation with master map method. Scoring rubric for this method as given in [8] is shown in Table 1.

The system is provided with a master map (drawn by the teacher) and the learner's map and the learner's map is compared with the master map to assign appropriate scores. The tool did not assign score 2 to any of propositions as it was difficult to

Table 1. Relation with master map scoring scheme

Rule	Score
Link valid but not labelled correctly	1
Link valid and correctly labelled but does not represent a hierarchical, causal or sequential proposition	2
Link valid and correctly labelled and also represents a hierarchical, causal or sequential proposition	3

include all insignificant yet correct propositions in the expert map. Also, as it is difficult to automate label validity of a link, the tool assumes that if a link is correct and is labelled then the label is also correct.

Number of submaps indicate the number of concepts where a student could not find any relation. Higher score in this count indicates the scattered knowledge whereas fewer submaps indicate more coherent knowledge. Submap count score is also calculated automatically by the tool.

Scoring of Skill Based Assignments. Programs submitted as skill based assignments give insight into the level upto which a learner can use the concepts learnt in solving practical problems. The scoring does not consider the logic used and hence scores are given even if the program is using the concepts clearly but does not give the correct output. Scheme adopted to assign scores to practical assignments is given in Table 2.

Table 2. Scoring scheme for skill based assignments

Use of concepts	Score
Concept has been used where it should be and also follows correct syntax	2
Concept has been used where it should be but does not follow correct syntax	1
Concept is not used correctly	0

4   Methodology

A prototype of the tool was created for teaching 'C Programming' as programming is considered tough by many learners and quality of the acquired knowledge affects the problem solving skills of the learner [7]. Target group for testing consisted of the students of B.Sc. (CS) and B. Sc. (Bioinformatics) first year of Panjab University, Chandigarh, India, hence, the learning component was designed keeping in mind the syllabus of the above university for these students. Purpose of carrying out the study was to find out if there is any difference in learning outcomes of the students in terms of conceptual knowledge and skills acquired, when compared with traditional classroom methods.

4.1 Participants

The reason for selecting the above mentioned target group was that these students had C programming as one of their major subjects. Also, these students were studying any programming language for the first time in their course and hence it was easy to gauge the change in their knowledge of C programming after the study was over. At the end 106 students agreed to be part of the study. These students were randomly divided into two groups of 53 students each. One group called experiment group was taught using the CLE whereas the other group, the control group, was taught the same concepts using traditional classroom method.

4.2 The Study

The study was carried out for 40 lectures of one hour duration each. Learning objective to be achieved during the study was "Identifying components of a C program and writing a program to solve a given problem". Keeping in view the prescribed syllabus and learning objective, following topics were identified and subsequently covered:

Building blocks of C, Data and data types, Operators and Expressions, Compilation and execution of C program, Decision Control Statements, Loop Control Statements, Case control statements, Introduction to functions.

Pretest. In the first lecture, the idea of concept maps was explained to both the groups and they were made to practice with sample concept maps. Once they were familiar with concept mapping, they were asked to take pretest in order to gauge already existing knowledge. Pretest consisted of two tasks, one, drawing a concept map using the concepts from the list provided to them in answer to the focus question asked and second, a multiple choice question test which also consisted of the similar questions to assess the knowledge about same focus question.

Learning Phase. From third lecture onwards, the experiment group and the control group were taught separately. Experiment group used the CLE and each student followed his own learning path. Collaborative learning environment was provided as students could discuss among themselves and a teacher was also available, if any student needed help. Control group was taught using traditional classroom method and a teacher explained all the concepts to students along with examples and programs.

Posttest. After completion of learning phase, post-test was conducted with students of both the groups. Similar to pre-test, students were again asked to draw concept maps with the same concept list and same focus question along with multiple choice questions for testing same focus question. In addition to this, students were also assessed for the skills acquired to solve practical problems. For this, the students were asked to write a program in C for given problem and store it in the assessment repository.

Scoring. All the assignments submitted by the learners were scored according to the scheme described in Sect. 3.2. Scoring of skill based assignments was accomplished manually with the help of faculty, who have expertise in this field and have been teaching 'C Programming' for more than 10 years.

5   Results

5.1   Sample

Students were randomly divided into two groups, control group and experiment group and scores obtained in the pre-tests of both the groups were statistically analysed to ensure homogeneity of the groups. Result of independent samples t-test on pre-tests of both the groups resulted in p-value >.05 indicating no significant difference between the groups.

5.2   Reliability

Reliability for the concept map based scores assigned by the tool was established by following method. A total of 34 concept maps were rated manually by two experts who had more than 10 years of teaching and evaluating 'C Programming' university exam papers, on same parameters as that of the tool, i.e., correct proposition score and number of submaps. These raters were provided with the master map and relation with master map scoring rubric and were asked to assign scores according to these, however, they could add scores if they found some correct proposition not present in master map. Scores obtained from three raters, i.e., the tool, rater1 and rater2 were statistically analysed to find correlation between them. Pearson correlation coefficient values obtained were ($r = .988$, $n = 34$, $p < .05$) between the tool and rater1 and ($r = .882$, $n = 34$, $p < .05$) between the tool and rater2 in case of correct proposition score and perfect 1 with both the raters in case of submap score. As the results obtained were highly significant, the reliability of the scores assigned by the tool was highly reliable.

5.3   Validity

In order to check validity of the concept map based assessment method, scores obtained by the students in multiple choice assessment were compared with the concept map assessment scores to find if there is any correlation between them. Pearson correlation coefficient values obtained between MCQ score and Correct Proposition score were .614 ($p = .0001$) for pre-tests and .892 ($p = .0001$) for post-tests denoting significant correlation between both types of scores and hence validating the concept map assessment scores.

5.4   Research Questions

In order to study effectiveness of the CLE in comparison to the traditional teaching learning system, following research questions were framed and subsequently answered.

Research Question I. Can use of constructivist approach through concept maps change existing concepts of the students to more acceptable ones so that there is right knowledge accumulation?

Research Question II. Do Constructivist Learning Environments, designed using concept map network along with learning stimulus, help better to cater to the individual needs of the students in their own knowledge construction when compared to the traditional classroom method?

Research Question III. Is there any relation between the conceptual knowledge and the actual programming abilities of the students?

Results for all of these questions have been discussed below.

RQ I. Scores obtained from pre-test concept maps provided data about pre-existing conceptual knowledge and scores obtained from post-test concept maps provided data about newly acquired conceptual knowledge. Paired samples t-test on Cmap_pre(pre-test score) and Cmap_post(post-test scores) of experiment group (group 1) was conducted and the results are discussed below.

- There was a significant difference in the scores obtained in pre-test (M = 11.60, SD = 10.05) and post-test (M = 70, SD = 20.31) conditions; t(52) = 18.30, p = 0.005.
- As the p-value <.05, it indicates that there was significant difference between the pre-test and post-test scores and hence constructivist learning environment was able to change existing knowledge structures of the students to more acceptable ones.

RQ II. Concept map scores obtained by the students of both control group as well as experiment group were analysed in the following manner.

- Change in the knowledge acquired was calculated by finding the difference between post-test and pre-test scores for every student, in both the groups. Hence, the new score value was:
  difference = Cmap _post - Cmap _pre
- Both the groups (control group labeled as 2 and experiment group labeled as 1) were compared on the parameters Cmap_post and difference and results are given below:
- Comparison of Cmap_score_post between two groups gives M = 70 and SD = 20.31 for experiment group (group 1) and M = 37.43 and SD = 13.66 for control group (group 2) denoting highly significant difference between the scores.
- Similarly, for difference score, mean value M for experiment group was 58.39 and standard deviation SD was 23.22 and these values for control group were 23.92 and 14.36 respectively. These values again denote highly significant difference in scores between groups.

RQ III. For the purpose of answering this question, scores obtained by the students in conceptual assessment during post-test, i.e., Cmap_score_post was compared with the scores obtained in skill assessments to find if there is any correlation between them. Data of both the groups was taken together as the purpose was to find correlation between conceptual knowledge and programming skills irrespective of the teaching method used. There was a significant correlation (Pearson correlation value .496) between scores of students in conceptual assessment and scores obtained in correctness of the practical assignment.

6 Limitations

This research work was carried out to test the effectiveness of a concept map based CLE as an alternative method for teaching learning programming languages. Although the results obtained are quite encouraging, there are certain limitations to the study. These are listed below.

1. A prototype of the tool was created and implemented for teaching 'C Programming' and skill based assignment tasks were specifically related to programming only. While creating learning and assessment components for other subjects, subject specific constraints may be applied.
2. While scoring the concept maps for correct propositions, two assumptions were made. These assumptions made no significant difference while assessing conceptual knowledge in the subject of programming. However, these cannot be generalized for other subjects and while creating assignments in other subjects, these may have to be looked into.
3. Submap scores obtained by students are just treated as qualitative measure and have not been statistically analysed as a student can have less number of submaps but his maps contain wrong propositions. In this study, this score only helps a teacher in understanding the quality of solution provided by the student.

7 Conclusion

The constructivist learning environment designed using the concept map network for teaching C language concepts was proved to be more effective than the traditional classroom environment in this study. The CLE provided multiple learning paths to the students from which they could choose the path best suited to their style of learning. Also, as the learning stimulus repository contained different styles of learning stimulus, in the form of presentations, videos, activities etc., learners could select the one (or more) they find most attractive. Role of the teacher in this environment was also totally reversed as he is now not steering the students through his learning path, but is helping each of them in traversing their own learning paths.

However, effectiveness of the CLE depends upon various factors like selection of the concepts, designing the concept maps and navigation between various concept maps in addition to the quality of learning stimulus. Hence, the concepts should be selected carefully and the links between concepts and concept maps should be accurate. It should also be ensured that all the constructivist principles are followed by the learning model developed.

References

1. Ausubel, D.P.: Educational Psychology: A Cognitive View. Holt, Rinehart and Winston, Montreal (1968)
2. Butler, D.: Reliable measures of concept map examinations. Online J. Distance Educ. e-Learn. **2**, 27 (2014)
3. Pailai, J., Wunnasri, W., Yoshida, K., Hayashi, Y., Hirashima, T.: The practical use of Kit-Build concept map on formative assessment. Res. Pract. Technol. Enhanc. Learn. **12**, 20 (2017). https://doi.org/10.1186/s41039-017-0060-x
4. Jonassen, D.: Designing constructivist learning environments. In: Reigeluth, C.M. (ed.) Instructional Design Theories and Models, vol. 2, pp. 215–239. Lawrence Erlbaum Associates, Routledge (1991)
5. Kharatmal, M., Nagarjuna. G.: Representing change using concept maps. In: Nagarjuna, G., et.al. (eds.) Proceedings of epiSTEME 5 International Conference to Review Research on Science, Technology and Mathematics Education, pp. 124–131. Cinnamonteal, India (2013)
6. Langford, D.: The use of concept mapping to enhance the teaching of chemical equilibrium in a grade 12 physical science tutoring classroom. Masters' thesis, Cape Peninsula University of Technology (2014)
7. Malmi, L., et al.: Characterizing research in computing education: a preliminary analysis of the literature. In: Proceedings of the Sixth International Workshop on Computing Education Research, Aarhus, Denmark, 9–10 August 2010, pp. 3–12. ACM, New York (2010)
8. McClure, J.R., Sonak, B., Suen, H.K.: Concept map assessment of classroom learning: reliability, validity, and logistical practicality. J. Res. Sci. Teach. **36**(4), 475–492 (1999)
9. Mühling, A.: Investigating knowledge structures in computer science education. Doctoral dissertation, Technische Universität München (2014). https://mediatum.ub.tum.de/doc/1190967/1190967.pdf
10. Naeve, A.: The concept browser - a new form of knowledge management tool. In: Proceedings of the 2nd European Web-Based Learning Environments Conference. WBLE (2001)
11. Novak, J.D., Musonda, D.: A twelve-year longitudinal study of science concept learning. Am. Educ. Res. J. **28**(1), 117–153 (1991)
12. Piaget, J.: The Construction of Reality in the Child. Ballantine Books, New York City (1975)
13. Thain, D.: A study of semi-hierarchical organization in the construction of concept maps using the framework of cognitive load theory. Masters' thesis, Queen's University Kingston, Ontario, Canada (2012)
14. Vodovozov, V., Raud, Z.: Concept maps for teaching, learning and assessment in electronics. Educ. Res. Int. Article ID 849678 (2015). http://dx.doi.org/10.1155/2015/849678. Review article. Hindawi Publishing Corporation
15. Vural, O.F.: Effectiveness of concept maps in learning from a computer-based instructional video resource. Doctoral dissertation, Texas A&M University (2010)

Go-Park: A Parking Lot Allocation System in Smart Cities

Tanmoy Mukherjee[1]([✉]), Shayon Gupta[2], Poulomi Sen[3],
Vijay Pandey[1], and Kamalesh Karmakar[1]

[1] Meghnad Saha Institute of Technology, Kolkata, India
tanmoymukherjee02@gmail.com,
kumarvijay2510@gmail.com, kamalesh@msit.edu.in
[2] University of Colorado Boulder, Boulder, CO 80309, USA
Shayon.Gupta@colorado.edu
[3] University of Minnesota, Minneapolis, MN 55455, USA
sen00001@umn.edu

Abstract. Parking lot allocation in urban areas is a big challenge to the administrators of the cities, especially, in those cities where road traffic is very high. Spending time in finding a parking lot at nearest location of destination keeps the vehicle on road for a long time which in turn creates high traffic and increases pollution. Moreover, rapid growth in the number of private cars makes the situation worse enough. This research focuses on the reduction of the overall travel time of a car for finding a parking lot and allocating the cars at nearby parking location of the users' destination. In this research, a system is designed based on a mathematical model using Integer Linear Programming (ILP) and a heuristic algorithm is proposed to investigate the performance of the algorithms. To carry out this research work, an android application has been developed to run on users' cell-phone and a web application has been developed to run in a server where users' requests are processed for decision making.

Keywords: Car parking guidance system · Integer linear problem
Heuristic

1 Introduction

In an urban area, finding a parking lot in close proximity to a destination is a big challenge for the users. From administrator's perspective, parking lot allocation is a troublesome job as the number of private car users is increasing rapidly. In recent times, due to the exponential increase in the number of cars [1], finding a parking lot near one's destination has become a problem of great magnitude. As users are not aware of available spaces in nearby parking lots and location of parking spaces, at certain instances users often spend a long time in searching for parking spaces, although empty spaces may exist nearby.

The problem here is relatable to that of searching for charging stations for electric cars [11] and the parking spot management [19]. Moreover, the prices of vehicles are decreasing significantly day by day, which results in more car ownership, resulting in

© Springer Nature Singapore Pte Ltd. 2018
M. Singh et al. (Eds.): ICACDS 2018, CCIS 906, pp. 158–166, 2018.
https://doi.org/10.1007/978-981-13-1813-9_16

high traffic on the road and a large number of parking requests. In this context, the growing need of on-demand parking lot requires dynamic allocation system to assist users in the reduction of traveling time and cost [18].

In this context, rest of the paper is organized as follows. Section 2 covers related works. Section 3 provides the problem formulation, followed by our architecture in the next Sect. 4. Our proposed algorithms are provided in Sect. 5. Finally, results of this experiment are shown and analyzed in Sect. 6. Section 7 concludes the paper.

2 Related Work

In recent past, many research works have been published on parking lot allocation. The researchers have proposed different types of models to fit for different types of reservation systems, some of the related works are discussed below.

In 2011, IBM published a survey work on parking covering 20 international cities that shows 30% of the total traffic is caused by searching of parking lots resulting in congestion and high carbon emission [3]. In [2], Arnott *et al.* pointed out that average staying time of drivers on road is 7.8 more minutes in finding a parking space. This problem arises as a result of lack of proper parking lot allocation system [14]. In [17], authors proposed a parking guidance system to reduce travel time significantly.

There are some allocation models that are based on the availability of parking slots in real-time [7, 8, 12, 13, 16]. In [8], Inaba *et al.* proposed an RFID based allocation system provisioning for shared and real-time reservations. In shared time reservation the user has to exit the parking lot within the reservation time-frame and in real-time approach, the user can stay at the spot for an unlimited time. Wang *et al.* [16] proposed a distributed system model where vacant spaces are determined using WiFi and Bluetooth technology. In this model, all the requests are accumulated in a central server and decisions are redirected to local servers. An SMS (Short Message Service) based reservation system was presented in [4].

Authors of [6] proposed a model where users can reserve parking lots from the available parking slots provided by multiple service providers. But this work didn't focus on minimization of travel time and pollution. Another reservation based parking model is proposed in [15], which did not propose any algorithm for searching time optimization. An auction-based reservation system has been proposed in [5], where a parking lot is allocated to the highest bidder after waiting for a certain time. But, this approach doesn't give a fair chance to everyone. In another context, Ji *et al.* proposed an IoT based parking allocation model [9]. In this model, the authors developed a scalable Cloud-based middle-ware to run an algorithm.

IParker [10] proposed an algorithm where 50% of the parking lots are reserved as deadline constraint and remaining parking lots are reserved with flexible time. However, no explanation is given as proof of this ratio for optimality of the solution.

3 Problem Formulation

The objective of the current paper is designing a parking lot allocation algorithm, aiming reduction of average travel time. Here, the service providers register their parking lots along with locations, capacities, and availabilities. On the other hand, the users submit their requests to reserve parking slots at nearby parking areas of their destinations. Hence, parking lots need to be reserved for the users at their expected reach time, which can be determined based on their current and destination locations, and live-traffic information using *Google Traffic API*.

Though the reservation duration may vary in real-time scenario, in this experiment we have assumed that hard deadline is assigned to the reservation requests based on provided reservation duration. This duration cannot be expanded if the parking lot is not available for the extended duration. Moreover, if the user fails to release the parking lot at the mentioned time during peak hour, the user has to pay high penalty fees, by which the next user's parking fee will be waived.

4 Architecture

To carry out this experiment, three modules of the application have been developed as shown below:

(i)   *Client module:* runs on users' Android device by which request is submitted containing the current location, destination location and the maximum distance that the user may permit to walk in reaching his/her destination from the parking area,

(ii) *Service providers' module:* run on service providers device to manage location, capacity, and availability of the parking lots,

(iii) *Server module:* runs a centralized algorithm and coordinates users and service providers.

In this application, parking lot related information is stored in the server and the clients' requests are submitted to the server. Parking lot allocation algorithm runs on this server to process each and every parking request within feasible time.

Instead of triggering the algorithm to run immediately after receiving a request, the server application waits for a specific time interval and executes the algorithm taking all the received requests during the time interval, to determine best available parking lots for every user.

In solving this problem, a weight matrix is prepared based on the distance of each parking lot and the destination location of the requests. The distance between the destination of car C_i and parking lot P_j is represented by $W[i, j]$. Instead of calculating the distance between each parking lot (P_j) and desired destination location of the car (C_i), only the distance of those parking lots are considered for which the distance between parking lot and desired location is less than the maximum permissible walking distance (D_i) specified by the user at the time of booking.

Thus, W[i, j] is defined as follow:

$$W[i, j] = \begin{array}{ll} \text{dist}(\text{Dest}_i, \ P_j) & \text{if dist}(\text{Dest}_i, \ P_j) < D_i \\ \infty & \text{otherwise.} \end{array}$$

In this context, the next section discusses proposed polynomial time heuristics along with IPP based solution.

5 Proposed Algorithms

First, an ILP is formulated to allocate parking slots to the users which give an optimal solution at every clock. This ILP takes a long time to execute as it is NP-Hard problem; it may not be feasible to run in real-time. Hence, we have proposed a polynomial time algorithm to find near-optimal solution in reasonable time.

5.1 Optimal Cost Parking Lot Allocation (OCPLA)

Here, the allocation matrix A[i, j] represents the allocation of parking lots to the users, as shown below:

$$A[i,j] = \begin{array}{ll} 1 & \text{if } i^{th} \text{ car is placed in the jth parking lot} \\ 0 & \text{otherwise} \end{array}.$$

The availability of parking slots in the parking lot P_j at the current instance is represented by C[j]. Thus the objective function can be formulated as

$$Minimize \sum_{i=1}^{n} \sum_{j=1}^{m} W[i, j] * A[i, j];$$

subject to the following constraints

$$\sum_{i=1}^{n} A[i,j] \leq C[j] \quad \text{for all } j; \tag{1}$$

$$\sum_{j=1}^{m} A[i,j] \leq 1 \text{ for all } i; \tag{2}$$

Constraint-(1) ensures that the allocation of parking slots to the users never exceeds the capacity of the parking lots. Whereas, constraint-(2) ensures that only one parking lot is allocated for each car.

To compare the performance of the algorithms, a greedy parking lot allocation algorithm is presented in the following subsection.

5.2 Greedy Parking Lot Allocation (GPLA)

In this algorithm, reservation requests are processed according to their arrival time. This algorithm is triggered at the arrival of new reservation request or release of any previous allocation. At any clock, if more than one request is received, the requests are stored in a queue and processed one after another. Thus the closest available parking lot is allocated for the first requester followed by next requests based on availability. For every allocation or de-allocation, availability of the parking slots *is* updated accordingly.

5.3   Parking Lot Allocation Using Fine Tuning (PLAuFT)

This algorithm executes in every scheduling clock as defined in the scheduler, instead of being triggered at arrival or release of parking requests. Hence, in every scheduling clock, the release requests are processed first, followed by allocation of new requests. At the time of allocation or de-allocation, the availability of the parking lots are updated accordingly.

Algorithm 1: Parking Lot Allocation using Fine Tuning

```
input :  V = a set of reservation requests
         W = distance matrix
output :  R[1...m] = allocation vector
  begin
   R := GPLA(V, W)
   cost := calculateCost(R)
   for itr ∈ 1..noi do
     for i = 1..m do
       for j = 1..m do
         R' := swaping(v_i, v_j)
         cost' := calculateCost(R')
         if cost > cost' then
           cost := cost'
           R := R'
  end
```

In this Algorithm 1, first, a temporary allocation is made based on greedy approach. After this temporal allocation in every iteration, a parking request (v_i) is considered to be swapped with a request (v_j), if they are not allocated at the same parking lot and this swap contributes in the reduction of overall traveling cost. This swapping operation is performed for few rounds, where the number of rounds is defined based on the possibility of the arrival of number requests in a scheduling clock, to make this decision in feasible time.

6   Results and Discussion

To perform this simulation, all the presented algorithms have been implemented. Performance of the algorithms has been investigated preparing synthesized data-sets, due to unavailability of the required log files.

6.1 Simulation Setup

At the time of preparing the data-sets, the following parameters have been kept in mind.

1. $N_u^{lp} = 200$ number of location points, where from parking requests arrived.
2. $N_p^{lp} = 18$ number of parking lots.
3. N_{req} number of parking requests in a day.

In this experiment 200 real location points (actual GPS co-ordinates) are taken where from parking requests are initiated and 18 parking lots are considered. The geographical location of the parking lots is assumed to be in major areas of the city (Kolkata), where parking facilities are available. To investigate the performance of the algorithms with respect to varying parking requests, the data-sets are generated by varying the number of parking requests in a day.

To simulate this environment, parking requests are generated at random time interval, where multiple requests may arrive in a simulation clock. Every parking request contains current location of the user, desired destination and reservation time. The parking requests are generated by random selection of source and destination location from N_u^{lp}.

6.2 Result Analysis

To investigate the performance of the algorithms, a large number of parking requests have been taken to be allocated in the available parking lots. But, based on initial placement it cannot be concluded that an algorithm will perform well in long run with the change of availability. Thus, the performance of the algorithms has been investigated for continuously arrived parking requests for a whole day.

Initial Allocation: Performance of parking lot allocation algorithms are shown in Fig. 1 in terms of total traveling time of the users. The figure clearly depicts that the proposed algorithm, *PLAuFT*, performs very well compared greedy algorithm, though it performs very close to ILP based algorithm.

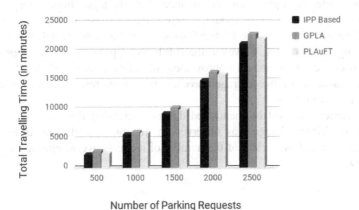

Fig. 1. Comparison of total travel time with respect to the number of parking requests

In this experiment, we have observed that the time consumption of the ILP based algorithm is very high as ILP is NP-Hard problem. Hence, ILP based algorithm cannot be used in real-time parking lot allocation for a large number of parking requests and a large number of parking lots. Thus, the proposed *PLAuFT* algorithm can be used which performs significantly better than the greedy algorithm. Moreover, the performance of the *PLAuFT* algorithm cannot be poorer than the greedy algorithm as it begins with the temporal greedy allocation and new allocation is accepted if reduces cost.

Continuous Allocation: In real-time scenario, a different number of parking requests arrives at every scheduling clock. Moreover, once a car is allocated to a parking lot, it cannot be reallocated. Hence, in every scheduling clock, the scheduler executes based on the available parking lots and newly arrived requests. In this context, the results are taken based on total traveling time, varying number of parking requests in a day as shown in Fig. 2.

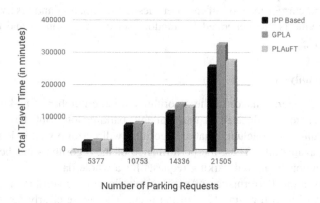

Fig. 2. Comparison of total travel time with respect to the different number of parking requests in a day

The Fig. 2 clearly depicts that performance of all the algorithms is very close for less number of parking requests, though a significant difference is observed for a large number of parking requests. The *PLAuFT* algorithm reduces the overall travel time by 15.24% compared to *GPLA*. However, the ILP based approach gives an improvement of 20.7% over the *GPLA* and an improvement of 6.43% over the *PLAuFT*. Figure 3 depicts the variation of the average traveling time with respect to the number of requests received in a day.

In this context, it must be mentioned that on increasing the number of requests further no significant change was observed in the total travel time as many cars remained unallocated as a result of the number of requests overwhelming the parking lot capacity.

Fig. 3. Comparison of average travel time with respect to the different number of parking requests in a day

7 Conclusion

In parking lot allocation, the necessity of efficient placement algorithm is to reduce average travel time of the users, which in turn reduces pollution by reducing carbon emission. Thus allocating users to nearby parking lots of the desired location is an important aspect in terms of user satisfaction and reduction of pollution. In this paper, the results depict that our proposed algorithm outperforms with respect to greedy approach and performance of the proposed algorithm is very close to the ILP based approach. Moreover, the proposed heuristic runs in polynomial time, resulting solution in very short time even for a large number of parking requests and parking lots.

References

1. National travel survey (2015). https://www.gov.uk/government/statistics/national-travel-survey-2015. Accessed 10 Sept 2017
2. Arnott, R., Rave, T., Schöb, R., et al.: Alleviating Urban Traffic Congestion, vol. 1. MIT Press, Cambridge (2005)
3. Gallivan, S.: IBM global parking survey: drivers share worldwide parking woes. Technical report, IBM (2011)
4. Hanif, N.H.H.M., Badiozaman, M.H., Daud, H.: Smart parking reservation system using short message services (SMS). In: 2010 International Conference on Intelligent and Advanced Systems (ICIAS), pp. 1–5. IEEE (2010)
5. Hashimoto, S., Kanamori, R., Ito, T.: Auction-based parking reservation system with electricity trading. In: 2013 IEEE 15th Conference on Business Informatics (CBI), pp. 33–40. IEEE (2013)
6. Hodel, T.B., Cong, S.: Parking space optimization services, a uniformed web application architecture. In: ITS World Congress Proceedings, pp. 16–20 (2003)
7. Idris, M., Leng, Y., Tamil, E., Noor, N., Razak, Z.: Park system: a review of smart parking system and its technology. Inf. Technol. J. **8**(2), 101–113 (2009)

8. Inaba, K., Shibui, M., Naganawa, T., Ogiwara, M., Yoshikai, N.: Intelligent parking reservation service on the internet. In: 2001 Proceedings of the Symposium on Applications and the Internet Workshops, pp. 159–164. IEEE (2001)
9. Ji, Z., Ganchev, I., O'Droma, M., Zhao, L., Zhang, X.: A cloud-based car parking middleware for iot-based smart cities: design and implementation. Sensors 14(12), 22372–22393 (2014)
10. Kotb, A.O., Shen, Y.C., Zhu, X., Huang, Y.: Iparkera new smart car-parking system based on dynamic resource allocation and pricing. IEEE Trans. Intell. Transp. Syst. 17(9), 2637–2647 (2016)
11. Lee, J., Park, G.L., Kim, H.J., Jeon, H.: Fast scheduling policy for electric vehicle charging stations in smart transportation. In: Proceedings of the 2011 ACM Symposium on Research in Applied Computation, pp. 110–112. ACM (2011)
12. Mathew, S.S., Atif, Y., Sheng, Q.Z., Maamar, Z.: Building sustainable parking lots with the web of things. Pers. Ubiquit. Comput. 18(4), 895–907 (2014)
13. Propst, J., Poole, K., Hallstrom, J.O.: An embedded sensing approach to monitoring parking lot occupancy. In: Proceedings of the 50th Annual Southeast Regional Conference, pp. 309–314. ACM (2012)
14. Shang, H., Wenji, L., Huang, H.: Empirical study of parking problem on university campus. J. Transp. Syst. Eng. Inf. Technol. 7(2), 135–140 (2007)
15. Tsai, M.T., Chu, C.P.: Evaluating parking reservation policy in urban areas: an environmental perspective. In: 2011 Proceedings of the 9th International Conference of Eastern Asia Society for Transportation Studies, pp. 272–272. Eastern Asia Society for Transportation Studies (2011)
16. Wang, H., He, W.: A reservation-based smart parking system. In: 2011 IEEE Conference on Computer Communications Workshops (INFOCOM WKSHPS), pp. 690–695. IEEE (2011)
17. Waterson, B., Hounsell, N., Chatterjee, K., et al.: Quantifying the potential savings in travel time resulting from parking guidance systems-a simulation case study. J. Oper. Res. Soc. 52(10), 1067–1077 (2001)
18. Pattanaik, V., Singh, M., Gupta, P.K., Singh, S.K.: Smart real-time traffic congestion estimation and clustering technique for urban vehicular roads. In: 2016 IEEE Region 10 Conference (TENCON), Singapore, pp. 3420–3423 (2016)
19. Xu, B., Ouksel, A., Wolfson, O.: Opportunistic resource exchange in inter-vehicle ad-hoc networks. In: Proceedings of the 2004 IEEE International Conference on Mobile Data Management, pp. 4–12. IEEE (2004)

A Question Answering Model Based on Semantic Matcher for Support Ticketing System

Suyog Trivedi, Gopichand Agnihotram$^{(\boxtimes)}$, Balaji Jagan,
and Pandurang Naik

Wipro Technology Limited, Wipro CTO Office, Wipro, Bangalore 560100, India
strivedi2505@gmail.com, {gopichand.agnihotram,
balaji.jagan,Pradeep.naik}@wipro.com

Abstract. In this paper, we propose an approach to search for the best semantic match of a user query for the question answering system. To achieve this, we make use of word embeddings with a help of trained model using the question answering corpus and its variations to detect the word senses of search queries by the user and show the top best matches which belongs to the same class of question answering pairs and retrieves the corresponding answer to the user. This solution is deployed in ticketing system in large IT industry to automate the user query to retrieve the answers. Word level to context level semantics are achieved through trained model of semantic knowledge with word embeddings.

Keywords: Question answering model · Feature vectors · SpaCy model
GloVe · Cosine similarity · Ticketing system

1 Introduction

Semantic matching is one of the important tasks in many natural language processing (NLP) applications, such as information retrieval [1], question answering [2], etc. Considering question answering system as an example, given a pair of question and answer, a matching function is required to determine the degree of matching between two sentences such as question and user query to match with the questions. Moreover, matching the user's query or question with the list of question answer pairs is a difficult task where the user queries are not always complete, grammatically, and syntactically correct. In addition, capturing the intent of the query involves finding the semantic information at a deeper level to capture all the variations of the user questions. Nowadays, deep neural network based models have been applied to overcome such issues. A lot of deep learning models follow a criterion to represent the question and answer in a single distributed representation, and then compute similarities between the query vectors and the question answer pair vectors to output the matching score.

To properly represent words in a continuous space, the idea of a neural model [3] is employed to enable jointly learn to embed of words into an n-dimensional vector space and to use these vectors to predict how likely a word is given its context. Skip-gram model [4] is a widely used approach to compute such an embedding. The skip-gram

© Springer Nature Singapore Pte Ltd. 2018
M. Singh et al. (Eds.): ICACDS 2018, CCIS 906, pp. 167–176, 2018.
https://doi.org/10.1007/978-981-13-1813-9_17

networks are optimized via gradient ascent, the derivatives modify the word embedding matrix $L \in R$ ($n \times |V|$), where $|V|$ is the size of the vocabulary. The word vectors inside the embedding matrix capture distributional syntactic and semantic information via the word co-occurrence statistics [3, 4]. Once this matrix is learned on an unlabeled corpus, it can be used for subsequent tasks by using each word's vector (a column in L) to represent that word.

In this paper, we propose an approach on semantic matcher for a user query where the top K results are obtained based on the neural embedding models. To achieve this, the unlabeled corpus is pre-processed by POS (parts of speech) tagging the words, lemmatization and then building the random word vectors for both questions answers of the corpus. The word embeddings/word feature vector is created with the help of pre-trained models (spaCy Model, [14]) and the words that are not present in the spaCy model are then given to the GloVe (Global vector representation) [5, 15] which creates the word co-occurrence form the corpus. In the same way, with the user query vectors/questions are created and matched with the reference corpus question answering model. The cosine similarity measure/Euclidean Distance is then applied on the matched vectors to compute the similarity and perform the ranking. The matched items with low ranking are filtered out and shows the top K results of matching question answering model and retrieve the user the corresponding answer. This solution is deployed in ticketing system in large Information Technology (IT) industry to automate the user query to retrieve the answers. For example, the system addresses the user queries related to leave policies, visa related queries, salary related queries etc.

The rest of the paper is organized as follows. Section 2 describes the related work. Section 3 discuss the proposed approach on how semantic matching is carried out using the distributed vector representation. Section 4 deals with the Results and discussion using distributed semantic models which discusses about building the word vectors using the pre-trained vectors based neural models and GloVe word vector representation. Section 5 describes the conclusions and future enhancements followed by References.

2   Related Work

In this section, we discuss the recent works carried out on semantic mapping of query with document, advertisements, passages, etc. using distributed vector representation.

Shen et al. [6] integrated the advantages of translation model and word embedding model to capture the word-to-word relation called a Word Embedding Correlation (WEC) model. The words in the query are mapped to vectors to identify the co-occurrence relationships between words. The word level relationship is extended to the sentence level to calculate the relevance between question and answers. Kutuzov and Kuzmenko [7] proposed an approach for identifying the senses of search queries and perform the semantic clustering on each search engine page results. The word sense disambiguation is performed with the use of distributed word vector representations with the help of prediction-based neural embedding models.

Wan et al. [8] tackled the problem of matching two sentences with multiple positional sentence representation using bidirectional LSTM (Long Short-Term

Memory) in which the contextual information is captured. The interaction between two representations is performed through k-max pooling and a multi-layer perceptron by which the matching score is generated. Using this positional independent matching procedure, any part of the queries can be matched. This type of approach is useful in handling the data of fully and/or partially free-word order languages.

Grbovic et al. [9] presented a search2vec model, a semantic embedding based approach, for queries and ads in which the embedding is learned using various components such as search queries, clicked ads, search links, dwell time and implicit negative signals. In case of the absence of information on new ads, the vector learns the context information from the textual content of the new ads including the bid term context vector. Guo et al. [10] introduced a novel semantic matching based retrieval model based on the Bag of Words Embedding (BoWE) representation. The semantic matching between queries and documents can be viewed as a non-linear word transportation (NWT) problem (based on document word capacity and transportation profit).

Molino and Aiello [11] proposed a semantic matching approach using skip gram model, a distributed representation learned with neural networks for matching questions and answers based on their semantic similarity. The question and answers are represented at different linguistic levels to extract various features that overlap each other. The overlapping features are then used to obtain the linguistic similarity. Giordani and Moschitti [12] proposed an approach to translate a natural language question into a SQL queries where the semantic mapping is carried out with the use of syntactic analyzer. The syntactic trees of questions and queries are represented as relational pairs and are encoded using the SVM based kernel functions.

3   Semantic Matching Approach

The proposed approach deals with the semantic matching of the user query/question/ utterances and produces top K questions for a search query. The semantic matching of a query is determined using the word embeddings/feature vectors created with the help of pre-trained models such as spaCy and GloVe vectors to detect the closest match of the user search query. The method proposed an idea of building query words based vector representation. The words and its context information are captured through these vectors where the similarity between the words are measured through the trained models using the domain specific corpus. In addition, words that are semantically similar and/or semantically related to the query but are not part of the vectors, are added to the word embedding vectors incrementally using GloVe of co-occurrence words. Therefore, two words are semantically similar and/or semantically related, if their distributional vector representation are similar based on some established collocation measure. The semantic similarity between the query word vectors and the document word vectors is computed using a traditional measure such as Cosine Similarity or Euclidian distance measure. The cosine distance between word vectors in the trained model is used as a feature determining whether the distance is closer to these words in the user query words.

The corpus is constructed using the question answers utterances (1) such as

$$C = \{(Q1, A1), (Q2, A2), (Q3, A3) \ldots, (Qn, An)\} \tag{1}$$

where Qi is the ith question and $i = 1, 2, \ldots, n$; Ai is the ith answer $i = 1, 2, \ldots, n$.

The following steps involves creating word embeddings using question answering utterances with the pre-trained models.

3.1 Preprocessing

The data under consideration provides a list of question answers utterances as given in (1). The preprocessing module consists of tokenizer, lemmatizer, and POS tagger. The tokenizer tokenizes all the words in the question and answers utterances after removing the stop words and special characters such as "is", "the", "are", "_", "%", etc. For all tokenized words, the nltk WordNet Lemmatization and Stemming is used to obtain the lemma of each word with the help of the nltk POS tagger for example: car, cars, car's, cars to the root word car "fishing", "fished", and "fisher" to the root word, "fish etc. If the word is not in the lemmatizer, then the actual word itself is returned as a lemma. To obtain the correct lemma of a word in a sentence, the POS tag of a word is also considered while finding out the lemma through WordNet lemmatizer. The question answer vector represented after preprocessing is as given in (2) below.

$$(Qi, Ai) = (Sq, Sa) = \{(w1q, w2q, \ldots wnq), (w1a, w2a, \ldots, wna)\} \tag{2}$$

where Sq is the sentence corresponding to question and Sa is the sentence corresponding to answer, wiq is the ith word corresponding to the question after preprocessing and similarly wia is the ith word corresponding to the answer, $i = 1, 2, \ldots, n$.

After preprocessing these words are given to the spaCy pre-trained model to create the word embeddings/feature vectors where the semantic matching criterion is accomplished along with the help of the GloVe vector representation and semantic similarity measure. The next step/subsection discusses the word embedding/feature vector creation using the corpus after preprocessing.

3.2　Word Embedding/Feature Vector Creation

In this method, we have adopted the pre-trained neural embedding model for building the feature vectors. Word vectors encode semantic meaning and capture many different degrees of similarity as explained in the paper [13]. There are a variety of computational models that implement the distributional hypothesis, including word2vec, GloVe, dependency-based word embeddings, spaCy and Random Indexing.

In this paper, we use the dependency-based word embeddings implemented in spaCy for troubleshooting data consists of a set of questions answers. This set is used as a training data to build the spaCy word embedding model with the help of the already built pre-trained model [14]. The pre-trained model is available in spaCy where the model uses huge corpus comprises of news articles, Wikipedia documents, weblogs, newsgroups, blogs etc. for building the model. The spaCy model has different features such POS tagger, NER (Named Entity Recognition), sentiment analysis, along with creating semantic word embeddings. The spaCy model builds semantic word embeddings/feature vectors and internally uses the GloVe vectors and computes the top list words matching with distance measures such as Cosine Similarity and Euclidian distance approach. The spaCy has trained for one million-word vectors. Here vectors ranging from −1 to 1 of each word represent feature vectors.

Along with the use of spaCy model, the question answer set is used to build the domain specific word vectors representation using the one million-word vectors. To build the word vector representation, the sentences in the corpus are preprocessed to derive the words and trained with the pre-trained spaCy model to build the feature vectors. The word embeddings are initialized to the 300-dimensional feature vectors. The word embeddings are given in (3)–(7) below for example sake,

From (2)

$$w1q = [0.145357, -0.227473, \ldots, -0.297674,]_{1 \times 300} \tag{3}$$
$$\ldots \ldots$$

$$wnq = [-0.545021, 0.064370, \ldots, 0.246844]_{1 \times 300} \tag{4}$$

$$\text{similarly,} \quad w1a = [0.167175, 0.287581, \ldots, -0.165552]_{1 \times 300} \tag{5}$$
$$\ldots \ldots$$

$$wna = [0.299463, 0.317821, \ldots, 0.026345]_{1 \times 300} \tag{6}$$

Finally,

$$(Sq, Sa) = [((1 \times 300), (1 \times 300), \ldots, (1 \times 300))_{n \times 300}, ((1 \times 300), \ldots, (1 \times 300))_{n \times 300}] \tag{7}$$

In case of the absence of the word in the pre-trained model, the natural language word searches for the vectors in the GloVe word vector representation as explained in the next section.

Once the word vectors are created from the data, the similar procedure is applied to the user query/user question to build the query word vectors representation using preprocessing steps and spaCy model. The GloVe word representation for the missing words are explained in the next step/section.

3.3 GloVe Vector Representation

GloVe is an unsupervised machine learning algorithm for obtaining vector representations for words. The GloVe builds the training model using the aggregated global word-word co-occurrence statistics from a corpus. The method uses semantic similarity words using Euclidian distance or cosine similarity measure to build the resulting word representation with the word vector space.

In the GloVe vector representation for question answering model uses question answering corpus and builds the co-occurrence of unigram, bigram and trigram words using the GloVe to compute the words of 300-dimential features vectors. Here we use the GloVe to the words of our corpus which are not find in spaCy model. From (2) the GloVe representation of the words are given from (8) – (9) below.

$$(Qi, Ai) = \{(w1q^1, w2q^1, \ldots wnq^1), (w1a^1, w2a^1, \ldots, wna^1)\} \tag{8}$$

$$\text{Finally,} \quad (Sq, Sa) = \{(w1q, w2q, \ldots wnq), (w1a, w2a, \ldots, wna)\}U$$
$$\{(w1q^1, w2q^1, \ldots wnq^1), (w1a^1, w2a^1, \ldots, wna^1)\} \tag{9}$$

where $w1q^1, w2q^1, \ldots wnq^1$ are the words form question, which are not part of spaCy model. $w1a^1, w1a^1, \ldots, w1a^1$ are the words from answers which are not part of spaCy model. The feature vector representation of the words in the question answering corpus are given from (10) – (12) below as example.

$$w1q^1 = [0.064101, -0.544901, \ldots, 0.364538]_{1 \times 300} \tag{10}$$
$$\ldots$$

$$\text{Similarly,} \quad w1a^1 = [0.167175, 0.287581, \ldots, -0.165552]_{1 \times 300} \tag{11}$$
$$\ldots\ldots$$

$$wna^1 = [0.299463, 0.317821, \ldots, 0.026345]_{1 \times 300} \tag{12}$$

The feature vectors of the question answering corpus will be created using spaCy and Glove vector as explained in the above steps (Subsects. 3.1, 3.2 and 3.3). The next subsection discusses the user query processing in above steps or Subsect. 3.1 to 3.3.

3.4   User Query Processing

The user query will be processed in the above steps and arrive 300-dimensional feature vectors using spaCy and GloVe vectors. Let the user query/utterance is Ut which comprises of sequence of sentences or unique sentence. The Ut is processes through preprocessing step and removes all stop words and special characters as explained in Subsect. 3.1. The user utterance is shown in (13) below

$$Ut = (S_1, S_2, \ldots, S_n) = (w_1, w_2, \ldots, w_n) \tag{13}$$

here $S_1, S_2, \ldots, S_n$ are the sentences from the utterance and it can be unique sentence and sequence of sentence. $w_1, w_2, \ldots, w_n$ are the words extracted after preprocessing step. The spaCy and GloVe feature vectors of the utterance is shown from (14) – (15) below as example.

The spaCy feature vector of words in the utterance (16) is given as

$$w1S = [0.356557, -0.348621, \ldots, -0.569231]_{1 \times 300} \tag{14}$$
$$\ldots\ldots$$

$$wnS = [-0.002453, 0.026352, \ldots, -0.0369124]_{1 \times 300} \tag{15}$$

Here $w1S$, $w2S$, ..., wnS are the feature vectors of the words representation using spaCy model. There may be few words in Ut where spaCy model is not able to address those words will be addressed using GloVe feature vector as explained in Subsect. 3.3. The GloVe feature vectors are shown in (16) – (17) below.

$$w1G = [-0.378294, \ 0.629482, \ldots, \ -0.72359]_{1 \times 300} \tag{16}$$

$$\ldots\ldots$$

$$wnG = [0.452625, \ 0.252418, \ldots, \ -0.0013528]_{1 \times 300} \tag{17}$$

Here $w1G, w2G, \ldots, wnG$ are the words represent GloVe feature vectors. The utterance Ut is rewritten as given below in (18)

$$Ut = (w_1, \ w_2, \ldots, w_n) = (w1S, \ w2S, \ldots, wnS)U(w1G, \ w2G, \ldots, wnG) \tag{18}$$

Once the user query/utterance is encoded into a feature vector representation, it is matched with the question answering corpus feature vectors created in Subsects. 3.1–3.3 using the pre-trained models of spaCy and GloVe vector representation. The next subsection discusses the matching of the feature vectors.

3.5   Semantic Similarity Matching

The distance between the feature vectors of user query/question/utterance vs question answering corpus is measured by computing the cosine similarity or Euclidian distance methods. Here we adapt cosine similarity measure to compute the distance and cosine similarity is as given below (19) and (20)

$$(\underline{a}, \underline{b}) = ||\underline{a}|| ||\underline{b}|| \cos(\theta) \tag{19}$$

$$\cos(\theta) = \frac{\underline{a} \cdot \underline{b}}{||\underline{a}|| ||\underline{b}||} \tag{20}$$

where $\underline{a}$ is the feature vectors derived from (Qi, Ai) for each $i = 1, 2, \ldots, n$ and $\underline{b}$ is the feature vectors derived from Ut. Based on the confidence of the similarity, the best describes the context information, the top K matched questions and corresponding answers are obtained.

The architecture diagram given Fig. 1 depicts entire flow of Semantic model and semantic matcher explained in Sect. 3.

4   Results and Discussions

The solution is deployed in support ticketing system for large IT services to automate the user queries/questions based on leave, attendance, salary, travel, finance related queries. We have captured all the question answers related to leave, salary, travel etc. in to the systems and performed steps given in Sect. 3. The system can predict the answer

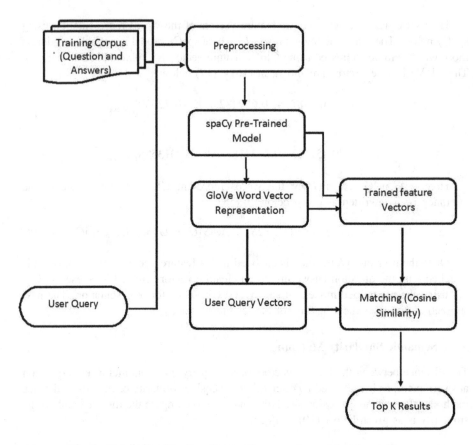

Fig. 1. Detailed architecture diagram for semantic model and matching

to the user query/question using question answering model. We can automate more than 80% of user queries using this solution and reduced to a large extent manual assistance. The current solution build on more than 10k question answering utterance and tested more than one lakh user utterances. We have achieved around 85% accuracy to address the right answer to the user queries using this solution.

The sample utterance for question answers and words which are used for feature vector computation are given in below tables as examples. Let the user utterance related to paternity leave is **"Is paternity leave subject to manager's approval,"** and users also asked the same user utterances in different way such as {**"paternity leaves require manager approval?", "any pointers on paternity approval related stuff", "after applying paternity leave whether It will go for any approval?", "what is the process to apply paternity leave"**}, these variations are processed through steps given in Sect. 3 and arrive the unique matching question 1 given in the Table 1 and corresponding answer is retrieved to the user.

For example, the question answers utterances are captured in the database and a few utterances are given in the Table 1. The utterances are preproceed and derive words

Table 1. Support ticketing system: question answers capture for training

Question	Answer
1. Is paternity leave subject to manager's approval	Paternity leave is an auto-approved leave however your manager gets an intimation of the same
2. What is the vertical level travel or FTR (Foreign Travel Request)	Dear user, you cannot raise the FTR/foreign travel request for vertical level. FTR is always project based
3. I am trying to raise the amendment but getting the error as "reservation is mandatory for raising amendment"	Employees must be reserved for an Onsite US (United States) indent before raising the Amendment, it's a valid message

Table 2. Words used for creating the feature vectors

Keywords separated by comma	
Question	Answer
Paternity leave, subject, manager, approval	Paternity, leave, auto, approve, leave, manager, intimation, same
Vertical, level, travel, FTR	User, cannot, raise, FTR, foreign, travel, request, vertical, level, FTR, project
Raise, amendment, get, error, reservation, mandatory, raise	Employee, reserve, Onsite, US, indent, before, raise, Amendment, valid, message

using preprocessed step explained in Sect. 3. The words which are shown in Table 2 are used to create the feature vectors with the help of spaCy and GloVe vectors.

5 Conclusions and Future Work

The solution proposed in this paper discusses the semantic model for question answering utterances. This model built based on pre-trained spaCy and GloVe vectors. The cosine similarity distance measure helps in matching the user query with the question answering utterances. The proposed solution is deployed in support ticketing system for large IT industry to automate user queries/utterances by in large. The solution able to capture more than 85% of accuracy on testing data sets of user queries.

In future, we want to extend this solution to multi-lingual support system such as Spanish, French, Dutch etc. to resolve user queries on support ticketing system or any other domains such as health care, finance, automobile etc.

References

1. Li, H., Xu, J.: Semantic matching in search. Found. Trends Inf. Retr. **7**, 343–469 (2013)
2. Berger, A., Caruana, R., Cohn, D., Freitag, D., Mittal, V.: Bridging the lexical chasm: statistical approaches to answer-finding. In: Proceedings of the 23rd Annual International ACM SIGIR Conference on Research and Development in Information Retrieval, pp. 192–199 (2000)
3. Bengio, Y., Ducharme, R., Vincent, P., Jauvin, C.: A neural probabilistic language model. J. Mach. Learn. Res. **3**(Feb), 1137–1155 (2003)
4. Mikolov, T., Sutskever, I., Chen, K., Corrado, G.S., Dean, J.: Distributed representations of words and phrases and their compositionality. In: Advances in Neural Information Processing Systems (NIPS), pp. 3111–3119 (2013)
5. Pennington, J., Socher, R., Manning, C.D.: GloVe: global vectors for word representation. In: Proceedings of the 2014 Conference on Empirical Methods in Natural Language Processing, pp. 1532–1543 (2014)
6. Shen, Y., Rong, W., Jiang, N., Peng, B., Tang, J., Xiong, Z.: Word embedding based correlation model for question/answer matching. In: Proceedings of the 31st AAAI Conference on Artificial Intelligence (AAAI-2017), pp. 3511–3517 (2017)
7. Kutuzov, A., Kuzmenko, E.: Neural embedding language models in semantic clustering of web search results. In: Proceedings of the 10th International Conference on Language Resources and Evaluation (LREC 2016), pp. 3044–3048 (2016)
8. Wan, S., Lan, Y., Guo, J., Xu, J, Pang, L., Cheng, X.: A deep architecture for semantic matching with multiple positional sentence representations. In: Proceedings of the 30th AAAI Conference on Artificial Intelligence, AAAI 2016, pp. 2835–2841 (2016)
9. Grbovic, M., Djuric, N., Feng, A., Ordentlich, E.: Scalable semantic matching of queries to ads in sponsored search advertising. In: Proceedings of the 39th International ACM SIGIR Conference on Research and Development in Information Retrieval, SIGIR 2016, pp. 375–384 (2016)
10. Guo, J., Fan, Y., Ai, Q., Croft, W.B.: Semantic matching by non-linear word transportation for information retrieval. In: Proceeding CIKM 2016 Proceedings of the 25th ACM International on Conference on Information and Knowledge Management, pp. 701–710 (2016)
11. Molino, P., Aiello, L.M.: Distributed representations for semantic matching in non-factoid question answering. In: Proceedings of Workshop on Semantic Matching in Information Retrieval Co-located with the 37th International {ACM} {SIGIR} Conference on Research and Development in Information Retrieval, SMIR@SIGIR 2014, pp. 38–45 (2014)
12. Giordani, A., Moschitti, A.: Semantic mapping between natural language questions and SQL queries via syntactic pairing. In: Horacek, H., Métais, E., Muñoz, R., Wolska, M. (eds.) NLDB 2009. LNCS, vol. 5723, pp. 207–221. Springer, Heidelberg (2010). https://doi.org/10.1007/978-3-642-12550-8_17
13. Levy, O., Goldberg, Y.: Dependency-based word embeddings. In: Proceedings of the 52nd Annual Meeting of the Association for Computational Linguistics (Volume 2: Short Papers), Baltimore, Maryland, pp. 302–308 (2014)
14. Models and Languages: spaCy Usage Documentation. https://spacy.io/. Accessed 08 Nov 2017
15. Pennington, J., Socher, R., Manning, C.: Glove: global vectors for word representation. In: Proceedings of the 2014 Conference on Empirical Methods in Natural Language Processing (EMNLP), pp. 1532–1543 (2014)

Multiple CAs Based Framework to Provide Remote Palliative Care for Patients Undergoing Chemotherapy

H. Lathashree[1(✉)], Niveditha J. Moka Katte[1], K. P. Pooja[1],
K. Bhargavi[1], and B. Sathish Babu[2]

[1] Department of Computer Science and Engineering,
Siddaganga Institute of Technology, Tumakuru 572 103, India
lathashreeharish01@gmail.com,
nivedithal0181@gmail.com, kppooja96@gmail.com,
bhargavi.tumkur@gmail.com
[2] Department of Computer Science and Engineering,
R.V. College of Engineering, Bengaluru 560059, India
bsbabu@rvce.edu.in

Abstract. Cancer is one of the deadly diseases in the world today. Cancer, also called as malignancy is the abnormal growth of cells in any part of the body that crowds out normal cells leading to tumours. Chemotherapy is one of the immensely used cancer treatment methods. It is accompanied by highly damaging side effects that need to be monitored with care in order to reduce the side effects. In this paper, a remote health palliative care framework that uses multiple cognitive agents is proposed for the patients undergoing chemotherapy. The objective of the paper is to provide palliative care to remotely located patients undergoing chemotherapy by identifying the side-effects of the treatment in early stages using cognitive agents as the agents possess self-instructing, self-learning ability while taking health critical decisions. The performance of the proposed framework is good in terms of delay, accuracy, and throughput.

Keywords: Chemotherapy · Cognitive agent · BOB model
Textual conversation · Facial analysis

1 Introduction

Cancer is a class of disease characterised by out-of-control cell growth which begins when genetic changes occur in the cell [1]. These cells form a mass called tumour which can be *cancerous* or *benign*. These affected cells, when multiplied to a greater extent, causes various symptoms indicating various forms of cancer-based on types of cell-targeted. Cancer can be treated in early stages using one of the or combinations of following methods: surgery, radiotherapy, bone marrow/Stem cell transplantation and chemotherapy [2].

Chemotherapy [3] is one of the widely used cancer treatments where powerful drugs are used to kill active cells, which grow quickly by dividing themselves. This treatment destroys both cancerous as well as healthy cells. Destruction of healthy cells causes many

© Springer Nature Singapore Pte Ltd. 2018
M. Singh et al. (Eds.): ICACDS 2018, CCIS 906, pp. 177–186, 2018.
https://doi.org/10.1007/978-981-13-1813-9_18

side effects which deteriorates the health condition of the patient. One of the solutions to this problem is to provide palliative or supportive care which includes continuous monitoring of the patient's health conditions after chemotherapy treatment [4].

Remotely monitoring the patient is a majorly sought requirement by doctors to make the given chemotherapy treatment effective while keeping the patient in comfort zone. Remote palliative care using Cognitive Agents (CAs) is one of the promising approaches [5] to provide long term care for patients suffering from life limiting disease like cancer and who are incapable to handle their daily chores. CAs have the relatable human intelligence to perceive the environment, make decisions, learn and stimulate reflexive actions [6]. These characteristics of the agent are exploited in the proposed framework to effectively monitor patients undergoing chemotherapy.

The organization of the paper is as follows: Sect. 2 documents the related works, Sect. 3 contains details on definitions of the medical terminologies used in further descriptions of the paper, Sect. 4 describes the proposed framework, Sect. 5 briefs on the results of the proposed framework and finally, Sect. 6 concludes the paper.

2   Related Works

A scalable, patient-centric, cloud-based social network styled platform i.e., Tiatros is proposed in [7] which provides collaborative services to cancer patients. The services are provided by care team members to the patients who upload medical data about their chemotherapy sessions through secure messaging, simple notification or email services. However, this platform does not notify the hospital team about the status of the patients during the emergency which minimizes the effectiveness of remote monitoring scheme.

In [8], a multi-layer remote mobile health monitoring system is proposed. It provides pervasive and continuous health-monitoring services to patients through mobile phone and web browser. The system consists of three parts, i.e., a portable terminal, smartphone and remote server. The portable terminal fetches input from the patients and the data flows to a remote server through the smartphone. The system provides stable monitoring of health in the indoor environment. But, the proposed system lacks in prior data analysis of the medical information obtained from the portable terminal which reduces the accuracy of health decisions taken.

The [9] proposes an autonomous health monitoring software framework consisting of multi-agents for remote patient monitoring. The framework consists of several Internet of Things (IoT) devices and software agents that are used to get the medical state of the patient using biometric sensors and internet-based microcontrollers. Although the framework proactively monitors the patient information using the cloud, the design is more generic and complex which reduces the performance and increases the cost of the multi-agent system.

A remote real-time telehealth monitoring system for blood cancer patients undergoing chemotherapy through a mobile phone application is proposed in [10]. The application requires data input to be given by the patient and this is sent to the real-time server where the data is analysed using static algorithms. Based on the results of the analysis, the nurse is notified about the status of the patient and the self-care module of the application gives appropriate advices. However, the transmission and communication of each and every input data from patients to server of the hospital increases the network traffic and the static algorithms used to analyse the medical data of the patient provides not so accurate status about the patients.

3 Definitions

In this section, the explanation for definitions and terminologies used in the paper are provided.

Vital Parameters: Vital parameters indicate important human body factors used to determine the condition of the patient.
Example: Blood Pressure (BP), blood glucose level, pulse rate, Body Mass Index (BMI), Red Blood Cells (RBC) count and White Blood Cells (WBC) count.

Textual Conversation: It is the process where caretaker of the patient is allowed to enter patient's symptoms in the textual form which will be synthesised and analysed to draw a conclusion that aids to determine the condition of the patient.
Example: Feeling uneasy, severe hair fall, drowsiness, imbalance in the sleep-wake cycle, and so on.

Facial Analysis: It is the process of capturing the facial image of the patient and performing analysis using neural visual model [11] by considering the important human facial factors.
Example: Hair density, size of the face and skin discoloration.

Patients Condition Storage (PCS): This database is located at Cognitive Agent-Patient (CA-P) for maintaining dataset about behaviours exhibited by patient's body. Each tuple in PCS contains attributes like blood pressure, pulse rate, blood glucose level, BMI, RBC count and WBC count.

Patients History Storage (PHS): This storage is located in hospital's private cloud that is directly linked to Cognitive Agent-Doctor (CA-D) and it stores beliefs and complete history of patients.
Example: Regular Condition (RC), Alarm Condition (AC) and Critical Condition (CC).

Behaviour-Observation-Belief (BOB) model [12]

Behaviour: Behaviour is derived from the vital parameters exhibited by the patient's body.

Example: A behaviour *'Normal BP'* is obtained when one of the vital parameters BP is in range of 120–139/80–89 mmHg.

Observation: An observation is the aggregation of various behaviours formulated over the patient's body.

Example: An observation *'Usual'* is deduced by using behaviours such as {Normal pulse rate, Normal weight, Normal RBC count and Normal WBC count}.

Belief: A belief is a collection of various observations formed over the patient's body. The working of BOB model is shown in Fig. 1.

Example: A belief *'Critical'* is derived when observations are {Attention, Alert}.

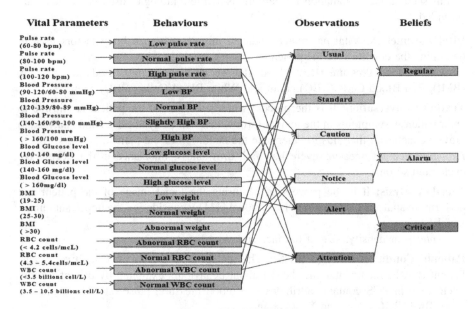

Fig. 1. The BOB model

4   Proposed Framework

The architecture of proposed multiple CAs based framework to provide remote palliative care for patients undergoing chemotherapy is shown in Fig. 2 [10]. The framework consists of three cognitive agents i.e., CA-Patient (CA-P), CA-Intermediate (CA-I) and CA-Doctor (CA-D). In this section, the functions of CAs are described with their corresponding algorithms.

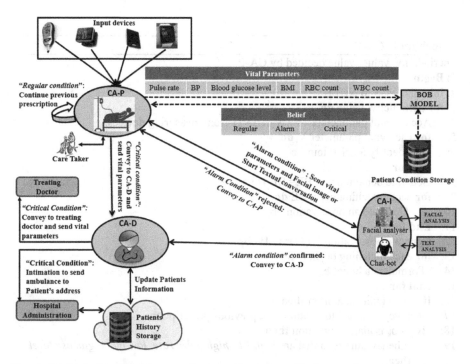

Fig. 2. Multiple CAs based framework to provide remote palliative care for patients undergoing chemotherapy

CA-P: The CA-P is deployed remotely in patient's environment whose role is to monitor the health condition of the patient periodically. Different devices like blood pressure monitor, blood glucose monitor, weighing device, RBC analyser and WBC analyser are used to obtain various vital parameters readings. These vital parameters are fed as input to CA-P by the caretaker.

BOB model in-turn uses these parameters and generates three beliefs i.e., RC, AC and CC. Based on the belief generated for a patient, the periodicity_value of collecting vital parameters is decided. The working of CA-P is given in Algorithm 1.

Algorithm 1: CA-P

//periodicity_value: value decided by CA-P

1: **Begin**
2: Initialize PCS to NULL
3: **for** periodicity_value **do**
4:    Accept vital parameters $\{V_1, V_2..., V_n\}$ from measuring devices.
5:    **for** each vital parameter V_i **do**
6:        Identify a behaviour be_i
7:    **end for**
8:    Generate behaviour set BE= BE **U** be_i
9:    **for** each matching be_i in BE **do**
10:        Generate an observation ob_j
11:    **End for**
12:    Generate observation set O = O **U** ob_j
13:    **for** each matching ob_j in O **do**
14:        Formulate a belief b_k
15:    **End for**
16:    **if** b_k is regular-condition **then**
17:        Convey to CA-P to continue the previous prescription
18:    **else if** b_k is alarm-condition **then**
19:        **if** behaviours recorded are *high BP, high pulse rate, low blood glucose level* **then**
20:            Choose facial analysis method and capture the facial image of the patient
21:            Send belief b_k and captured facial image to CA-I
22:        **else**
23:            Choose the chat-bot method
24:            Send belief b_k to CA-I and start the conversation with caretaker via chat-bot
25:            **for** each question asked by CA-I **do**
26:                Fetch care taker's response and send it to CA-I
27:            **End for**
28:        **End if**
29:    **else if** b_k is critical-condition **then**
30:        Send belief b_k to CA-D
31:    **End if**
32:    Periodically update PCS
33: **End for**
34: **End**

CA-I: CA-I is initiated when CA-P detects AC which conveys that the condition of the patient is in ambiguous range i.e., it is neither RC nor CC. Since there exists dilemma in deducing the condition, a double check is made by CA-I. It performs facial analysis or initiates textual conversations with the caretaker of the patient based on the method chosen by CA-P. The working of CA-I is given in Algorithm 2.

Algorithm 2: CA-I

1: **Begin**
2: **while** alarm condition is received **do**
3:    **if** method chosen for the double check is
    facial analysis **then**
4:        Perform facial analysis by fetching facial parameters
5:        Compare fetched data with recent data to confirm the alarm-condition of the patient
6:    **else if** method chosen for the double check is chat-bot **then**
7:        **do**
8:         Question caretaker about symptoms of the patient
9:         Perform text analysis on care taker's response
10:     **until** patient's health condition is determined
11:   **End if**
12: **End while**
13: **if** alarm-condition is confirmed **then**
14:   Convey the deduced condition to CA-D along with vital parameters
15: **else if** alarm-condition is rejected **then**
16:   Convey the condition to CA-P
17: **End if**
18: **End**

CA-D: The CA-D acts as a collaborating agent between all the CA-Ps situated at patient's remote environment and Hospital. CA-D informs the corresponding patient's treating doctor about the CC of the patient. Meanwhile, it also intimates the hospital administration to send an ambulance to patient's location. The working of CA-D is given in Algorithm 3.

Algorithm 3: CA-D

1: **Begin**
2: **for** each condition received **do**
3:    **if** condition received is critical or alarm condition is confirmed **then**
4:        Consult PHS to fetch case history, patient's details
5:        **if** CC is due to *abnormal WBC count, abnormal RBC count, high BP, high pulse rate* **then**
6:         Inform treating doctor about patient's condition along with vital parameters to re-look into prescription
7:        **else if** CC is due to *low weight, low glucose level, low pulse rate, low BP* **then**
8:         Intimate hospital administration to send an ambulance to patient's location
9:         Intimate treating doctor to provide emergency services
10:     **End if**
11:     Update PHS with patient's current health condition
12:   **End if**
13: **End for**
14: **End**

---

5 Results and Discussion

This section discusses the comparison between proposed framework and the existing work [10].

The number of varied vital parameters in patient's health condition versus throughput is represented in Fig. 3. Here, throughput is defined as the number of vital parameters handled per second. For every condition, the BOB model intelligently maps various vital parameters into a single belief. This combined knowledge of belief over a patient increases the throughput by 45%. Whereas in the existing work to arrive at a decision over patient's health condition various stages of parameter processing is done which decreases the rate of processing of vital parameters.

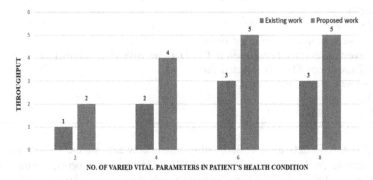

Fig. 3. Number of varied vital parameters in patient's health condition versus throughput

Figure 4 shows the graph of time versus delay. In the proposed framework, CAs are trained to handle all possible health conditions so that whenever similar condition appears the belief is chosen that avoids recurrent processes of belief generation thereby delay is reduced by 35%. Whereas in the existing work for every condition the patient's parameters are fetched and sent to the server at the hospital which consumes time.

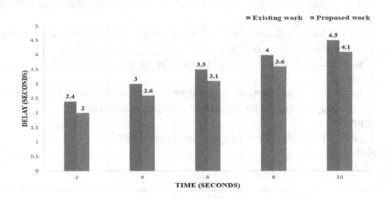

Fig. 4. Time (seconds) versus delay (seconds)

The graph of beliefs formulated versus decision accuracy is shown in Fig. 5. It is observed from the graph that the accuracy of the proposed CAs based framework is higher than the existing work because when the patient's vital parameters fall in the ambiguous range, the CA-I's suggestion is taken into consideration before arriving at the final decision. Whereas in the existing work ambiguous situation is not handled.

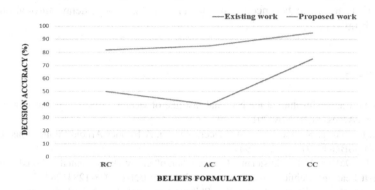

Fig. 5. Beliefs formulated vs. decision accuracy (%)

In Fig. 6, the graph of time versus the number of messages exchanged is shown. It can be observed that the number of messages exchanged is minimised compared to the existing work, as the CAs present in the proposed framework takes independent decisions and works autonomously. Whereas in the existing work the decision is taken by the hospital management with many interactions involved between the management and application that in-turn increases the number of messages exchanged.

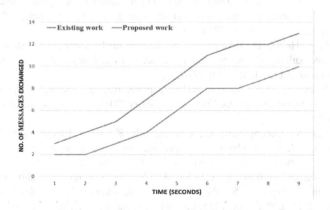

Fig. 6. Time (seconds) versus the number of messages exchanged

6 Conclusion

The proposed framework describes the remote health palliative care framework using multiple CAs for patients undergoing chemotherapy. The framework aims to provide effective treatment while keeping patients in comfort zone and tries to bridge the gap of communication and observation between doctor and patient. The performance of the framework is found to be encouraging in terms of accuracy, delay, throughput, and bandwidth utilization.

References

1. National Cancer Institute at the National Institute of Health. https://www.cancer.gov/about-cancer/. Accessed 10 Nov 2017
2. Price, P., Sikora, K.: Treatment of Cancer, 6th edn. A Hodder Arnold Publications, London (2008). ISBN-13 978-1482214949
3. Chu, E., DeVita, V.T.: Physicians' Cancer Chemotherapy Drug Manual, 17th edn. Jones & Bartlett Learning Publications, Burlington (2016). ISBN-13 978-1284124477
4. Kajal Singh, F., Divya Sharma, S., Shipra Aggarwal, T.: A real time patient health monitoring system based on artificial neural fuzzy inference system (ANFIS). In: Int. J. Comput. Appl. (2016). https://doi.org/10.5120/ijca2016910959
5. Baig, M.M., Gholamhosseini, H.: Smart health monitoring systems: an overview of design and modeling. J. Med. Syst. **37**(2), 9898 (2013). https://doi.org/10.1007/s10916-012-9898-z
6. Fernandes, C.O., De Lucena, C.J.P.: A software framework for remote monitoring by using multi-agent systems support. J. Med. Internet Res. Med. Inf. (2017). https://doi.org/10.2196/medinform.6693
7. Kim, K.K., Bell, J., Reed, S., Whitney, R.: A novel personal health network for patient-centered chemotherapy care coordination. In: International Conference on Collaboration Technologies and Systems (CTS), p. 81. IEEE (2016). ISBN 9780128021156
8. Zhang, Y., Liu, H., Su, X., Jiang, P., Wei, D.: Remote mobile health monitoring system based on smart phone and browser/server structure. J. Healthc. Eng. **6**(4), 717–738 (2015). https://doi.org/10.1260/2040-2295.6.4.717
9. Ghosh, A.M., Halder, D., Hossain, S.K.A.: Remote health monitoring system through IoT. In: 5th International Conference on Informatics, Electronics and Vision. IEEE (2016). https://doi.org/10.1109/ICIEV.2016.7760135
10. Sibilah Breen, F., et al.: Remote real-time monitoring for chemotherapy side-effects in patients with blood cancers. In: Collegian. Elsevier (2017). https://doi.org/10.1016/j.colegn.2016.10.009
11. Phimoltares, S., Lursinsapand, C., Chamnongth, K.: Face detection and facial feature localization without considering the appearance of image context. In: Image and vision computing. Elsevier (2007). https://doi.org/10.1016/j.imavis.2006.05.017
12. Bhargavi, K., Sathish Babu, B.: CAs-based QoS scheme for remote health monitoring over WMSN. In: Thilagam, P.S., Pais, A.R., Chandrasekaran, K., Balakrishnan, N. (eds.) ADCONS 2011. LNCS, vol. 7135, pp. 381–388. Springer, Heidelberg (2012). https://doi.org/10.1007/978-3-642-29280-4_45

A Collaborative Filtering Approach for Movies Recommendation Based on User Clustering and Item Clustering

Shristi[1(✉)], Alok Kumar Jagadev[1], and Sachi Nandan Mohanty[2]

[1] KIIT Deemed to be University, Bhubaneswar, India
shristi.shristi19@gmail.com,
alok.jagadevfcs@kiit.ac.in
[2] Gandhi Institute for Technology, Gramadiha, India
dr.sachinandan@gift.edu.in

Abstract. Recommender systems (RS) are software tools that have become increasingly popular in recent years. RS are utilized in a variety of areas including movies, music, news, books, research articles, etc. Typically, there are many items and many users present in these areas making the problem hard and expensive to solve. Collaborative filtering is a widely used approach to design of recommender systems. This method is based on collecting and analyzing a large amount of information on users' behaviors, activities or preferences and predicting what users will like based on their similarity to other users. A key advantage of the collaborative filtering approach is that it does not rely on machine analyzable content and therefore it is capable of accurately recommending complex items like movies without requiring an understanding of the item itself. We present a new approach based on user clustering and item clustering to recommendation for the active user. The K-means clustering algorithm is used to categorize users based on their interests. Our result shows that the proposed algorithm provides improved quality of clusters and also render a better recommendation to the users.

Keywords: Recommender system · Collaborative filtering · K-means
Clustering

1 Introduction

Recommender system uses the opinion of a group of users to help individuals in context to identify more effectively the contents of interest from a possibly overwhelming choices set [1]. It has changed the way inanimate websites communicate with their users. The goal of this paper is to provide affordable, personal and high quality recommendations according to users preferences on an item. Types:

1. Content-based Recommendation
2. Collaborative Recommendation
3. Knowledge-based Recommendation
4. Hybrid Recommendation

© Springer Nature Singapore Pte Ltd. 2018
M. Singh et al. (Eds.): ICACDS 2018, CCIS 906, pp. 187–196, 2018.
https://doi.org/10.1007/978-981-13-1813-9_19

Recommender system that is content-based, recommends items to the users on the basis of correlation in-between the user preferences and the content of items [2]. In this type of system, the user gets recommendation about items that matches the items the user favored in the past [3]. Text documents are widely used as the information source. For making recommendations, content-based structure mostly works by calculating how strongly an item that is not yet seen similar to the active user preferred items in the past.

Collaborative filtering systems are based on gathering and studying a huge volume of info on user's behavior, preferences or activities and then predicting what the user will prefer on the basis of their similarity to another user. Collaborative filtering methods are further categorized as model-based and memory-based collaborative filtering. An eminent case of a memory-based methods is user-based algorithm [4] and that of a model-based methods is kernel-mapping recommender [5].

Regarding the recommendation on the basis of knowledge of user specific tasks can address problem by a knowledge based model. A recommender that is based on knowledge, recommends items on the basis of suggestions about the user's choices and requirements. These knowledges at times hold explicit useful information about how features of a particular product meet users need [6, 7]. A more hybrid method, merging content-based filtering and collaborative filtering. Hybrid methodologies can also be applied in many ways: by making collaborative-based and content-based forecasts individually and then binding them; by adding collaborative-based approach to a content-based capabilities (and vice versa); or by combing the approaches into a single model [8] for an entire review of recommender system. A number of studies empirically match the performance of the content-based and pure collaborative methods with the hybrid and prove that the hybrid approach can offer more precise recommendations than the pure approach. These hybrid methods can be used to eradicate some of the most common issues in recommender systems such as the sparsity problem and cold start.

1.1   Collaborative Filtering

Similarities between users and items and manipulation of relationships between them is computed in the collaborative filtering system. The system manages the interaction of a user with the preferred items. Then the items are recommended in which the targeted user is likely to be interested. Collaborative filtering applies the ratings of the user's community. For this the system forecasts the aimed user's ratings for the items which are not rated till now, so the system has no straight knowledge to define if the user dislikes or likes them [9]. Then the items are ordered according to ranks and the items with top anticipated ratings as per the predicted ranking are recommended to the user.

1.2   Item and User Clustering

User clustering is done on the basis of classifying set of users who seem to have alike ratings. After that the cluster is made and then it becomes easier to make guesses for an aimed user by simply aligning other user's opinion in that cluster.

Item clustering is done on the basis of classifying set of items which seem to have alike ratings. After that the cluster is made and then it becomes easier to make guesses for an aimed user by simply aligning other user's opinion in that cluster.

2 Literature Survey

With the rising concepts in Recommender system approaches and methods, a few existing work discussed as follows:

Phongsavanh Phorasium et al. [10] discusses in this a recommendation method on the basis of user clustering where Euclidean distance is used to calculate two number of users to the clustered dataset. In this paper, recent strategies has been surveyed by grouping them into personalization and hybridization.

Elahi et al. presented the complete outline of interpretation methods that has been applied for testing active learning methods of collaborative filtering [11]. K-means clustering is a method of cluster analysis in which the initial k-centroids are picked up randomly and every item is allocated to the cluster which have the closest centroid. Genetic algorithm works on the candidate solution population; every solution's proximity for best solution of the issue is indicated by its fitness value.

Bhao et al. [12] suggested a new approach where k-means clustering was mapped with genetic algorithm for improving the value of clusters and provided better recommendation to the user. Complexity metrics helps to accelerate error identification and reconstruct task on the most complex parts of a knowledge base.

Felfernig et al. [13] presented knowledge sources to simplify the relationships between different recommendation techniques and outlined open research issues.

Herlocker et al. [14] showed the explanation to the automated collaborative systems has been addressed on the basis of user's conceptual model and experimental evidences has been provided that showed the improvement in the acceptance of automated collaborative systems.

Despite collaborative filtering being mostly used algorithm, it undergoes high running time. In this paper k-means algorithm along with collaborative filtering method enables the users to save time by providing choices to users in less time. Also this paper emphasizes on user and item clustering methods which provides better results than the existing methods on movies recommendations.

3 Problem Definition

We need to examine the application of k-means clustering and collaborative filtering techniques for better recommendations and develop a hybrid algorithm and compare it with the existing algorithm for getting better quality of clusters and less time consumption.

4 Methodology

The proposed framework is shown in Fig. 1. The system shows the work after active user gives a rating to the movie when you watched and requests a recommendation of other movies [13]. User clustering is performed with the k-means algorithm and find out user similarity with Pearson correlation in order to compare profile of active user to others which are under same cluster with active user. Then select closest N neigh-borhoods that bring profile to all who predict rating movies of current user that has not visited before and then ranked and rated the movies to the current users in order to recommend movies by applying collaborative filtering.

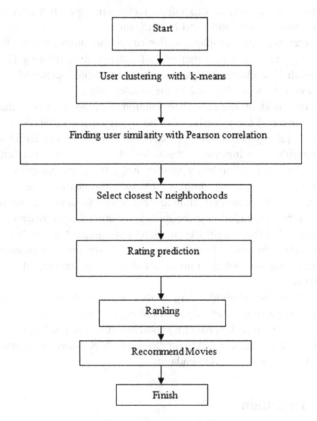

Fig. 1. Proposed model

4.1 Dataset Description

The above model displays the work after active 943 users gives 100000 rating to 1682 movies, when you watched and requests a recommendation system of other movies. The data has been considered from website movie lens project http://grouplens.org/ datasets/. Then, by with the help of k means the active user will be clustered by the system to the recommended group, then the active user will be compared by the system for getting the cluster which have same properties as the active user from the different users who are in the same cluster using Pearson correlation coefficient as the comparison tool. Collaborative filtering will compute the rating between users within the cluster, after that it will compare the similarity values in the user-user similarity matrix. It will select closest user similarity and pull data similarity values for neighbors that come out and compute the predicted rating and put in store to search highest predicted rating for relevant user and recommendation to the user.

4.2   Processing K-means and Collaborative Filtering

The system will search group for users by using k-means to find distance between the users, the group of users and clustering of users. The system performs clustering with the k-means algorithm by calculating the distance of each data point from the center of the 19 groups by using Euclidean distance and calculated information will be collected in the database as shown in Table 1.

Table 1. Initial non-rating values

1,20,	4,50,	7,32,	10,7
1,33,	4,260,	7,163,	10,16
1,61,	4,264,	7,382,	10,100
1,117,	4,288,	7,430,	10,175
1,155,	4,294,	7,455,	10,285
1,160,	4,303,	7,479,	10,461
1,171,	4,354,	7,492,	10,486
1,189,	4,356,	7,497,	10,488
1,202,	4,357,	7,648,	10,504
1,265,	4,361,	7,661,	10,611
2,13,	5,1,8,	22,	11,38
2,50,	5,2,8,	50,	11,110
2,251,	5,17,8,	79,	11,111
2,280,	5,98,8,	89,	11,227
2,281,	5,110,	8,182,	11,425
2,290,	5,225,	8,294,	11,558
2,292,	5,363,	8,338,	11,723
2,297,	5,424,	8,385,	11,725
2,312,	5,439,	8,457,	11,732
2,314,	5,454,	8,550,	11,740
3,245,	6,14,	9,6,	12,82
3,294,	6,23,	9,286,	12,96
3,323,	6,69,	9,298,	12,97
3,328,	6,86,	9,340,	12,132
3,331,	6,98,	9,479,	12,143
3,332,	6,258,	9,487,	12,172
3,334,	6,301,	9,507,	12,204
3,335,	6,463,	9,521,	12,300
3,337,	6,492,	9,527,	12,471
3,343,	6,517,	9,691,	12,735

After that, the system will search for a user similarity established on the definition and will create a matrix of data between users on the movies as shown in Table 2.

Table 2. Values from Pearson correlation

[1:2] = -0.027046	[1:3] = 0.366547	[1:4] = 0.375964	[1:5] = 0.030415
[1:8] = 0.025755	[1:9] = -0.061102	[1:10] = -0.209068	[1:11] = 0.225009
[1:14] = -0.210460	[1:15] = 0.154863	[1:16] = 0.169840	[1:17] = 0.102967
[1:20] = 0.059862	[1:21] = 0.340243	[1:22] = 0.525411	[1:23] = -0.025513
[1:26] = 0.063825	[1:27] = 0.077704	[1:28] = -0.249809	[1:29] = -0.136661
[1:32] = 0.026309	[1:33] = 0.005773	[1:34] = 0.060832	[1:35] = -0.095517
[1:38] = -0.066236	[1:39] = -0.196438	[1:40] = 0.066372	[1:41] = -0.160233
[1:44] = -0.220306	[1:45] = 0.544769	[1:46] = 0.095071	[1:47] = 0.204483
[1:50] = -0.208768	[1:51] = -0.004138	[1:52] = -0.183185	[1:53] = -0.115057
[1:56] = 0.221590	[1:57] = 0.365535	[1:58] = 0.226752	[1:59] = 0.386534
[1:62] = 0.178297	[1:63] = 0.434215	[1:64] = -0.150062	[1:65] = 0.448463
[1:68] = 0.111250	[1:69] = -0.089132	[1:70] = 0.038691	[1:71] = 0.663358
[1:74] = 0.118426	[1:75] = 0.133271	[1:76] = 0.255047	[1:77] = -0.144694
[1:80] = 0.266248	[1:81] = 0.304979	[1:82] = -0.155222	[1:83] = 0.162837
[1:86] = 0.339964	[1:87] = 0.144032	[1:88] = 0.001942	[1:89] = 0.044825
[1:92] = 0.431812	[1:93] = 0.264581	[1:94] = 0.526021	[1:95] = -0.093788
[1:98] = 0.196812	[1:99] = 0.025080	[1:100] = 0.039290	[1:101] = 0.002772
[1:104] = -0.096853	[1:105] = -0.011006	[1:106] = -0.025008	[1:107] = 0.043351
[1:110] = 0.420462	[1:111] = 0.011002	[1:112] = 0.060912	[1:113] = 0.120490
[1:116] = 0.007559	[1:117] = 0.168349	[1:118] = 0.118157	[1:119] = 0.088839
[1:122] = 0.012231	[1:123] = -0.221455	[1:124] = 0.282288	[1:125] = -0.593173
[1:128] = -0.144119	[1:129] = -0.193517	[1:130] = 0.126576	[1:131] = -0.363107
[1:134] = -0.051010	[1:135] = 0.157475	[1:136] = -0.086090	[1:137] = -0.119110
[1:140] = 0.121372	[1:141] = 0.100078	[1:142] = 0.113705	[1:143] = -0.085680
[1:146] = -0.133287	[1:147] = -0.475249	[1:148] = 0.003732	[1:149] = 0.000306
[1:152] = -0.141169	[1:153] = -0.039955	[1:154] = -0.210857	[1:155] = -0.120756
[1:158] = -0.054972	[1:159] = -0.024189	[1:160] = 0.283674	[1:161] = 0.532374
[1:164] = -0.058478	[1:165] = 0.226578	[1:166] = -0.120245	[1:167] = -0.137346
[1:170] = -0.255002	[1:171] = 0.295665	[1:172] = -0.316508	[1:173] = -0.100848
[1:176] = 0.261707	[1:177] = -0.219091	[1:178] = -0.057724	[1:179] = -0.019160
[1:182] = -0.040158	[1:183] = -0.001536	[1:184] = -0.068143	[1:185] = -0.365917
[1:188] = 0.195445	[1:189] = 0.050084	[1:190] = 0.196985	[1:191] = -0.028975
[1:194] = 0.057709	[1:195] = 0.114948	[1:196] = 0.330779	[1:197] = -0.145631
[1:200] = -0.273434	[1:201] = 0.262768	[1:202] = -0.118991	[1:203] = -0.101803
[1:206] = -0.029630	[1:207] = 0.079559	[1:208] = -0.145406	[1:209] = 0.340360
[1:212] = -0.195339	[1:213] = 0.059014	[1:214] = -0.089849	[1:215] = -0.232644

The system will be examined by users who are similar, and compare user 1 to all the others who have pieces of information rating include the user with other user, so at this stage to make a correlation between the User 1 and remaining other users respectively. Pearson correlation displays the similarity to the closeness of making comparisons. After that, the process of leading the user that looks for rating similar to the target the number of k to predict satisfaction as possible by weight sum equation as shown in Table 3.

4.3   Result Discussion

The goal of clustering is to know how many people in the groups and the centroid of the group are present. Then bring centroid to a cluster group for new user to the group by k-means algorithm. In this we use a WEKA software. It is used to cluster a group of users, the data downloaded from the website movie lens project data. It is so big to choose 943 users, 1682 movies records and 100000 ratings. First, we should convert

Table 3. Guessing values from Pearson correlation

1, 20, 3.6923	1, 33, 3.4737	1, 61, 4.2083
1, 155, 3.0000	1, 160, 4.2083	1, 171, 3.3878
1, 202, 3.8667	1, 265, 3.4737	2, 13, 3.6000
2, 251, 3.6000	2, 280, 4.3000	2, 281, 3.7500
2, 292, 3.7647	2, 297, 3.7647	2, 312, 5.0000
3, 245, 3.0000	3, 294, 2.8000	3, 323, 3.0000
3, 331, 2.0000	3, 332, 3.0000	3, 334, 1.0000
3, 337, 4.0000	3, 343, 2.7500	4, 50, 3.0000
4, 264, 5.0000	4, 288, 4.2170	4, 294, 5.0000
4, 354, 4.3418	4, 356, 5.0000	4, 357, 5.0000
5, 1, 3.2500	5, 2, 2.8571	5, 17, 2.8571
5, 110, 3.4167	5, 225, 3.0926	5, 363, 2.8000
5, 439, 2.2381	5, 454, 2.4615	6, 14, 3.6667
6, 69, 3.7333	6, 86, 3.6552	6, 98, 4.5000
6, 301, 3.3611	6, 463, 3.8889	6, 492, 3.6552
7, 32, 4.2500	7, 163, 3.8113	7, 382, 4.4444
7, 455, 3.1429	7, 479, 4.0714	7, 492, 4.1892
7, 648, 3.4167	7, 661, 4.0769	8, 22, 4.6667
8, 79, 4.0000	8, 89, 4.3750	8, 182, 4.1250
8, 338, 2.2857	8, 385, 3.7500	8, 457, 5.0000
9, 6, 4.0000	9, 286, 4.6667	9, 298, 3.9129
9, 479, 4.0552	9, 487, 4.0000	9, 507, 4.0000
9, 527, 4.0000	9, 691, 4.0000	10, 7, 4.2750
10, 100, 4.3333	10, 175, 4.4000	10, 285, 4.2750
10, 486, 3.9000	10, 488, 4.3750	10, 504, 4.2750
11, 38, 3.2747	11, 110, 2.8750	11, 111, 3.4118
11, 425, 3.2750	11, 558, 3.4286	11, 723, 3.7143
11, 732, 3.4118	11, 740, 3.8125	12, 82, 4.0000
12, 97, 4.3000	12, 132, 3.9890	12, 143, 3.0000
12, 204, 4.5000	12, 300, 4.5000	12, 471, 5.0000
13, 56, 3.6091	13, 98, 2.8667	13, 186, 2.8491
13, 215, 3.6091	13, 272, 3.6091	13, 344, 3.6091
13, 526, 2.6522	13, 836, 3.3171	14, 22, 4.4141
14, 111, 3.0000	14, 174, 4.6667	14, 213, 3.8571
14, 357, 4.1500	14, 474, 4.4141	14, 530, 4.3333
15, 25, 2.3077	15, 127, 3.3600	15, 222, 3.3333

data from excel to CSV because this file is supported by WEKA. We can delete something if irrelevant to our data.

In our case we only use user, movies name and rating shown in the Fig. 4. The data is selected and converted into a comma separated values (CSV) and formatted using the CSV converter and then cluster imported to WEKA program. It is the first open WEKA program, explorer, pre-process, and then open your file and click the cluster, after that you will see so many options and then click on the choose button to choose simple k-means. Next left click on the simple k-means N 2-A weka.core. Euclidean Distance R first-last then it will show function. On these pages we can set the number of clusters depending on how many groups do you want. In our paper, we use 10 clusters to get the results as shown in Tables 4 and 5.

Table 5 shows that group 1 includes 6387 people, group 2 includes 4847 people, group 3 includes 4198 people, group 4 includes 6557 people, group 5 includes 3494 people, group 6 includes 4957 people, group 7 includes 4121 people, group 8 includes 5169 people, group 9 includes 5172 people, group 10 includes 4032 people, group 11 includes 5182, group 12 includes 5714 people, group 13 includes 3340 people, group 14 includes 4102 people, group 15 includes 2521 people, group 16 includes 5404

Table 4. Number of group and member of group

```
Time taken to build model (full training data) : 9.52 seconds
=== Model and evaluation on training set ===
Clustered Instances

    0        6387 (   7%)
    1        4847 (   5%)
    2        4198 (   5%)
    3        3865 (   4%)
    4        6557 (   7%)
    5        3494 (   4%)
    6        4957 (   5%)
    7        4121 (   5%)
    8        5169 (   6%)
    9        5172 (   6%)
   10        4032 (   4%)
   11        5182 (   6%)
   12        5714 (   6%)
   13        3340 (   4%)
   14        4102 (   5%)
   15        2521 (   3%)
   16        5404 (   6%)
   17        4840 (   5%)
   18        6668 (   7%)
```

Table 5. Centroid of group

```
=== Run information ===

Scheme:weka.clusterers.SimpleKMeans -N 19 -A "weka.core.EuclideanDistance -R first-last" -I 500 -S 10
Relation:     database-weka.filters.unsupervised.attribute.Remove-R4
Instances:    90570
Attributes:   3
              userid
              movieid
              rating
Test mode:evaluate on training data

=== Model and evaluation on training set ===


kMeans
======

Number of iterations: 78
Within cluster sum of squared errors: 2438.9141903981917
Missing values globally replaced with mean/mode

Cluster centroids:
                   Cluster#
Attribute  Full Data      0        1        2        3        4        5        6        7        8        9
           (90570)    (6387)   (4847)   (4198)   (3865)   (6557)   (3494)   (4957)   (4121)   (5169)   (5172)
=================================================================================================================
userid      461.494   425.963  562.6872 822.7504 744.8533 556.0554 261.8074 783.3758  78.5404 318.5136  92.2769
movieid    428.1049   268.4555 283.5112 268.6198 869.8116 275.3576 963.2521 249.3609 314.7023 247.5222 303.8213
rating       3.5238         5        3        3   4.2753        4   1.5461        5   2.7607        3        4



Time taken to build model (full training data) : 9.52 seconds
```

people, group 17 includes 4840 people and the last group 18 includes 6868 people, on the same time we will see Fig. 6, that is centroids of all group for movies. Moreover, by considering this set of different groups, using the centroid method we figured out that while the group is increasing, members are getting enhanced in number too.

5   Conclusion and Future Work

This paper suggests an approach to recommendation system where collaborative filtering is used along with k-means algorithm for improving feature of clusters and thereby providing better recommendation to the users. Collaborative filtering provides predictions to users by identifying similar users with k-means. Although this algorithm is preferable it suffers low accuracy. Therefore in future a lot of work still needs to be done to propose a technique for identifying optimum number of clusters for the k-means algorithm. Also, instead of k-means algorithm other techniques like fuzzy c-means can be used to get more effective clusters.

References

1. Ricci, F., Rokach, L., Shapira, B.: Introduction to recommender systems handbook. In: Ricci, F., Rokach, L., Shapira, B., Kantor, P.B. (eds.) Recommender Systems Handbook, pp. 1–35. Springer, Boston, MA (2011). https://doi.org/10.1007/978-0-387-85820-3_1
2. Facebook, Pandora Lead Rise of Recommendation Engines—TIME, 27 May 2010. TIME. com. Accessed 1 June 2015
3. Pu, P., Chen, L.: A user-centric evaluation framework of recommender systems. In: Proceedings of the ACM RecSys 2010 Workshop on User-Centric Evaluation of Recommender Systems and Their Interfaces (UCERSTI), Barcelona, Spain, 30 September, pp. 14–21 (2010)
4. Shardanand, U., Maes, P.: Social information filtering: algorithms for automating "word of mouth". In: Proceedings of the SIGCHI Conference on Human Factors in Computing Systems, CHI 1995, pp. 210–217 (1995)
5. Balabanović, M., Shoham, Y.: Fab: content-based, collaborative recommendation. Commun. ACM CACM Homepage Arch. **40**(3), 66–72 (1997)
6. Breese, J.S., Heckerman, D., Kadie, C.: Empirical analysis of predictive algorithms for collaborative filtering. In: Proceedings of the Fourteenth Conference on Uncertainty in Artificial Intelligence, UAI 1998, pp. 43–52 (1998)
7. Kernel-mapping recommender system algorithms. Inf. Sci. pp. 81–104 (2015)
8. Zapata, B.C., et al: Revista Ib, Association Ib America de Sistemas e Technologias de Informa, pp. 35–50 (2014)
9. Felfernig, A., Burke, R.: Constraint-based recommender systems: technologies and research issues. In: Proceedings of the 10th International Conference on Electronic Commerce, ICEC 2008 (2008). Article no. 3
10. Adomavicius, G., Tuzhilin, A.: Toward the next generation of recommender systems: a survey of the state-of-the-art and possible extensions. IEEE Trans. Knowl. Data Eng. Arch. **17**(6), 734–749 (2005)
11. Elahia, M., Riccib, F., Rubensc, N.: A Survey of Active Learning in Collaborative Filtering Recommender Systems. Elsevier, London (2016)

12. Bhao, K., Kumar, D., Saroj.: An evolutionary k-means clustering approach to recommender systems. In: International Conference on Advanced Computing, Communication and Networks, pp. 851–855 (2011)
13. Phongsavanh, P., Yu, L.: Movies recommendation system using collaborative filtering and k-means. Int. J. Adv. Comput. Res. **7**(29), 52–59 (2018)
14. Herlocker, J.L., Konstan, J.A., Riedl, J.: Explaining collaborative filtering recommendations. In: Proceedings of the 2000 ACM Conference on Computer Supported Cooperative Work, pp. 241–250. ACM (2000)

Investigations of Optimized Optical Network Performance Under Different Traffic Models

Himanshi Saini[✉] and Amit Kumar Garg

ECE Department, Deenbandhu Chhotu Ram University of Science and
Technology, Murthal, Sonepat, Haryana 131027, India
himanshi.4887@gmail.com, garg_amit03@yahoo.co.in

Abstract. Network planning for existing as well as future high-speed networks
is important for extracting best performance of networks. Network planning
requires reliable traffic model which can serve constant as well as variable
ingress traffic. In this paper, network performance is investigated with uniform
and population-distance traffic models. Open Shortest Path First (OSPF) protocol is used for routing and link weight determination is a crucial task for this
routing. Link weights in networks of different densities are optimized with an
objective of minimizing network congestion. Ant Colony Optimization (ACO),
Genetic Algorithm (GA) and Simulated Annealing (SAN) optimization techniques are applied to examine link weights of National Science Foundation
NETwork (NSFNET) and standard COST 239 networks. The novelty of the
work lies in investigations of network performance with different optimization
techniques, traffic models and density. The outcome of this work can assist in
optimizing overall network planning. Maximum latency and congestion of both
networks are compared for each optimization and traffic model. It is observed
that population-distance traffic modeling has reduced network congestion for
both the networks but this traffic model has increased maximum latency of
NSFNET. Performance of COST 239 network which is denser than NSFNET,
has improved with population-distance traffic model w.r.t. congestion and
latency.

Keywords: Traffic model · ACO · GA · SAN · Link utilization
Latency

1 Introduction

The process of network planning for high speed optical networks has to take into
consideration requirements of existing network as well as expanding requirements of
future networks. The network planning tasks such as routing, traffic grooming, survivability and meeting all possible requirement driven Quality of Service (QoS) parameters, require traffic matrix as prime input. Traffic matrices define the traffic offered
between any two nodes in the network. A network with K nodes, has $K * K$ traffic
matrix with its diagonal elements null.

An example coordinate (i, j) of $K * K$ matrix implies the amount of traffic offered
by node, i and carried by node, j. Traffic matrices are prediction of network traffic and
the modeled matrices have to face errors because of stochastic variations, alterations in

© Springer Nature Singapore Pte Ltd. 2018
M. Singh et al. (Eds.): ICACDS 2018, CCIS 906, pp. 197–204, 2018.
https://doi.org/10.1007/978-981-13-1813-9_20

routing policies and modeling errors [1]. Modeling errors can be avoided with careful observation of past network data. Change of routing is one of the major reasons for large variations in network traffic, though this event is rare. In such cases, traffic predicted through traffic matrix will be different from actual traffic. Identifying the cause for large traffic variation and designing traffic matrix taking into account these variations are steps expected from network operator [2].

Traffic matrix can be internal or external to network [3]. Traffic demands associated with core network formulate internal traffic matrix and reflect the routing changes within the core network. In this paper, uniform and population-distance traffic models are used to investigate network performance. In uniform model, matrix is composed of random values in a specified range (0–10). One or multiple traffic matrices can be generated using population-distance traffic model. The input parameters for this model are number of nodes, position of nodes, population and node level. Traffic, T from 'a' to 'b' modeled as population-distance model [4] is shown in Eq. 1.

Parameters used for modeling the traffic are briefly explained in Table 1.

Table 1. Parameters of traffic equation

Parameter	Detail
$(1 - rf + 2 * rf * rand())$	Random factor
$rand()$	Sample of uniform distribution in range (0–1)
rf	Indicates level of randomness $rf = 0$: no randomness; $rf = 1$: maximum randomness
$Level(La, Lb)$	Matrix with multiplicative constants for traffic matrix
$\left(\frac{Pa*Pb}{Pmax^2} + Poff\right)^{powerP}$	Population factor
$Poff$	Population offset factor
Pa	Population at node a
Pb	Population at node b
$Pmax$	Maximum node population
$powerP$	Factor for controlling effect of Population on traffic matrix $powerP = 0$: traffic is not dependent on node population
$\left(\frac{Dab}{Dmax} + Doff\right)^{powerD}$	Distance factor: this factor models traffic in inverse proportionality to distance between nodes
Dab	Distance between nodes a and b
$Dmax$	Maximum distance between nodes in a network
$Doff$	Distance offset factor
$powerD$	Factor for controlling effect of distance on traffic matrix

$$T = (1 - rf + 2 * rf * rand()) * Level(La, Lb) * \frac{\left(\frac{Pa*Pb}{Pmax^2} + Poff\right)^{powerP}}{\left(\frac{Dab}{Dmax} + Doff\right)^{powerD}} \qquad (1)$$

In the present work, OSPF routing is optimized in NSFNET and COST 239 networks by ACO, GA and SAN optimization techniques.

The performance of these networks is investigated with uniform and population-distance traffic models. ACO, GA and SAN optimization techniques have been briefly described in Fig. 1.

```
ACO: In each iteration of loop

        Generate initial population of ants
        Evaluate the value of objective function by each ant by greedy randomized scheme based on pheromone
        Accumulate solutions by each ant
        Pheromone is assigned to each solution component
        Update the obtained solution
        if obtained solution == optimal solution; exit
        else
        Reinforcement: Increment pheromone of traversed solution components
        Evaporation: Decrement pheromone of all solution components
        Repeat till optimal solution obtained

GA: In each iteration of loop

        Initial population generated
        Evaluate the value of objective function using pure or greedy randomized procedure
        Accumulate problem solutions
        if obtained solution == optimal solution; exit
        else
        Pairs of solutions (x, y) from solutions are chosen as parents
        Crossover: Children created from each pair inherits characteristics of both x and y
        Mutation: Children carry random characteristics
        Apply solution selection process
        Repeat till optimal solution obtained

SAN: In each iteration of loop

        Initialize with high value of temperature
        Set an initial solution
        Decrease temperature in steps
                In each iteration of loop
                Decrement temperature
                        In each iteration
                        Equilibrium state is approached at that particular temperature
                        Update the initial solution
        if initial solution == optimal solution; exit
        else
        continue with next temperature decrement iteration
```

Fig. 1. Algorithm for AntColony, GA and SAN optimization [5]

2 Related Work

The mixed integer linear programming formulations for optimization of large sized networks are complex and complexity increases with size of the network, so the heuristic formulations which provide approximate solutions are implemented for large size networks [6]. Many contributions in the area of optical network planning involve application of heuristic or meta-heuristic approaches.

Risso et al. [7] utilized metaheuristics in design of multilayer optical networks. They have designed cost effective resilient IP over DWDM network. Their work also combines traffic and bandwidth constraints. Martins et al. [8] have investigated on applicability of metaheuristics in various telecommunication issues. They have presented a survey on common components and basic principles of various meta-heuristics. The main focus of their work is toward highlighting the applications of metaheuristics in communication networks.

Risso et al. [9] have proposed a survivable and cost effective network design approach with integrated traffic engineering features by implementing various meta-heurisic techniques. Evolutionary and GRASP (Greedy Randomized Adaptive Search Procedure) techniques are observed to offer best results.

Bhanja et al. [10] validated evolutionary optimization approach and proposed the evolutionary approach with problem specific inputs and suitable soft constraints. They have compared the proposal with existing optimization approaches and the proposed technique has proved an edge over existing techniques.

Kharroubi et al. [11] implemented random optimization, genetic and tabu search meta-heuristics for addressing RWA problem in optical networks. Meta-heuristics have been applied on randomly generated topologies and fixed topologies. In order to serve large number of demands, genetic approach outperforms the other approaches. Mohan et al. [12] have demonstrated the implementation of ant colony optimization to select restoration path after occurrence of single link failure. Attempt has been made to reduce the restoration delay as compared to conventional path based restoration method.

Applicability of meta-heuristics to determine the locations of hub placement in optical networks has been highlighted by Rabbani et al. [13]. They have targeted the meta-heuristic implementation for minimization of installation and wiring cost of optical fibers. Mata et al. [14] presented a comprehensive review of contributions focused on integration of artificial intelligence with optical networks and systems. They have given the scope where intelligent techniques can be further implemented to enhance the performance of optical networks. They have discussed meta-heuristic implementations for optical networks survivability, resource allocation, connection establishment, reconfiguration and fault detection.

In this paper, meta-heuristic optimization techniques on networks of different densities are compared and network performance is investigated under uniform and population-distance traffic models. Simulation environment and network topologies are discussed in Sect. 3. Maximum network latency and congestion plots are presented in Sect. 4. Section 4 covers explanation of results obtained for both the simulated topologies. Section 5 concludes the investigation and results obtained.

3 Simulation Environment

Investigations are carried out on network simulator for network planning, Net2Plan [15]. NSFNET (14 nodes and 21 links) and COST 239 (11 nodes and 26 links) network topologies are illustrated in Fig. 2. ACO, GA and SAN optimizations are implemented on both networks. These optimization techniques find link weights with objective to reduce network congestion. It is assumed that all the network nodes are configured with OSPF routing. GA is executed for maximum number of 100 iterations, 200 numbers of child in offspring and 1000 number of elements in population.

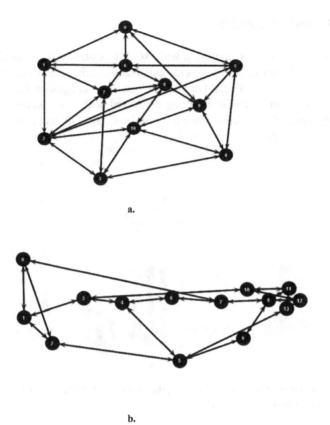

Fig. 2. (a) COST 239 (11 nodes, 26 links) network. (b) NSFNET (14 nodes, 21 links) network.

ACO is executed for maximum number of 100 iterations and 10 numbers of ants. SAN is executed for 50 outer loop iterations. OSPF link weights are constrained between 1 and 16 for ACO, GA and SAN. Minimizing network congestion is modeled as function of maximum and average link utilization. Uniform traffic considered in this analysis, models traffic matrix with random values in range (0–10). Population-distance traffic model is configured to take into consideration effect of distance on traffic matrix. Population factor has been ignored in this analysis. COST 239 is denser than NSFNET because it has more connectivity.

NSFNET has more traffic demands due to more number of nodes as compared to COST 239. Networks with different density are observed to attain different state after application of optimization technique. This subsequently results in different congestion and latency metrics for networks of different density. Network congestion is analyzed from bottleneck link utilization in a network which is calculated as ratio of load on most utilized link to capacity of most utilized link.

4   Results and Discussions

OSPF routing in networks is optimized with ACO, GA and SAN. Figure 3 illustrates network congestion metric with different optimization techniques under uniform and population-distance traffic models. For both the networks, congestion has reduced with population-distance traffic model. Routing optimized with SAN technique results in high network congestion whereas routing optimized with GA technique offers minimum network congestion.

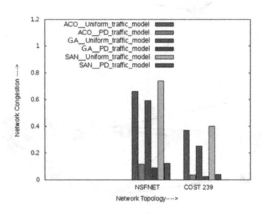

Fig. 3. Network congestion for different optimization and traffic models (Uniform and Population-Distance (PD) traffic models)

In COST 239 network which is denser than NSFNET, overall congestion is less than NSFNET for any traffic model. Figure 4 illustrates maximum End to End (E2E) latency metric with different optimization techniques under uniform and population-distance traffic models. In COST 239 network which is denser than NSFNET, E2E delay is less than NSFNET for any traffic model. Network latency has increased with population-distance traffic model in NSFNET as compared to latency with uniform traffic model. Similar latency increase is observed in SAN optimized COST 239.

For ACO and GA optimization, COST 239 experience reduction in network latency with population-distance traffic model.

Network congestion obtained with uniform traffic model is more as compared to population-distance traffic model. Population-distance model predicts the traffic between nodes taking into account the node population and distance between nodes which results into reduction of bottleneck link utilization in a network and hence reduction in network congestion. COST 239 network has 26 bidirectional links and 4.7 node out degree whereas NSFNET has 21 bidirectional links and 3 node out degree. Total traffic demands are less in COST 239 network. These factors make COST 239 network less congested than NSFNET for same network capacity.

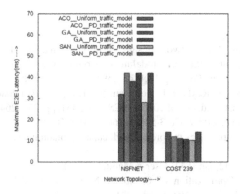

Fig. 4. Maximum E2E latency for different optimization and traffic models

E2E latency obtained with population-distance traffic model in NSFNET remains same for ACO, GA and SAN technique which is higher than latency obtained with uniform traffic model. Least latency in NSFNET is obtained when routing is optimized with SAN technique.

There are only 5 traffic demands with router hops greater than 1 in COST 239 network whereas there are 68 such traffic demands in NSFNET. Hence E2E latency is less in COST 239 network. SAN optimization and uniform traffic model has resulted in least E2E latency in COST 239 network.

5 Conclusion and Future Scope

Optimizing the routing and reliable traffic modeling are important aspects of high-speed network planning. The investigations performed in this paper covers implementation of various traffic models and optimization aspects in network design and planning. NSFNET and COST 239 networks have been considered to observe impact of traffic models and optimization on network performance. It has been observed that a population-distance traffic model reduces network congestion for both the networks optimized with ACO, GA and SAN. For NSFNET, network maximum E2E latency has increased with population-distance traffic model. 50% increase in E2E latency is observed with SAN optimized NSFNET and 37% increase in E2E latency is observed for COST 239 with population-distance traffic. In ACO and GA optimization of COST 239, E2E latency is less for population-distance as compared to uniform traffic. In denser network like COST 239, GA optimized network routing with link distance dependent traffic model like population-distance results in improved network performance as compared to other optimization techniques and uniform traffic model. Further, the investigation can be performed on number of topologies with variable demand set. In this work, network survivability can be incorporated for strengthening network planning.

References

1. Tune, P., Roughan, M.: Network-design sensitivity analysis. In: ACM International Conference on Measurement and Modeling of Computer Systems, SIGMETRICS 2014, pp. 449–461 (2014). https://doi.org/10.1145/2591971.2591979. ISBN 978-1-4503-2789-3
2. Teixeira, R., Duffield, N., Rexford, J., Roughan, M.: Traffic matrix reloaded: impact of routing changes. In: Dovrolis, C. (ed.) PAM 2005. LNCS, vol. 3431, pp. 251–264. Springer, Heidelberg (2005). https://doi.org/10.1007/978-3-540-31966-5_20. ISBN 978-3-540-31966-5
3. Cisco document: best practices in core network capacity planning, C11-728551-00, pp. 1–11 (2013)
4. Pavon-Mariño, P.: net2plan 0.4.0 User's Manual (2016)
5. Pavon-Mariño, P.: Optimization of Computer Networks—Modeling and Algorithms: A Hands-On Approach. Wiley, New York (2016)
6. Pavon-Mariño, P., Aparicio-Pardo, R., Moreno-Muñoz, G., Garcia-Haro, J., Veiga-Gontan, J.: MatPlanWDM: an educational tool for network planning in wavelength-routing networks. In: Tomkos, I., Neri, F., Solé Pareta, J., Masip Bruin, X., Sánchez Lopez, S. (eds.) ONDM 2007. LNCS, vol. 4534, pp. 58–67. Springer, Heidelberg (2007). https://doi.org/10.1007/978-3-540-72731-6_7
7. Risso, C., Canale, E., Robledo, F., Rubino, G.: Using metaheuristics for planning resilient and cost-effective multilayer networks. In: 5th International Congress on Ultra Modern Telecommunications and Control Systems and Workshops (ICUMT), Almaty, pp. 201–207 (2013)
8. Martins, S.L., Ribeiro, C.C.: Metaheuristics and applications to optimization problems in telecommunications. In: Resende, M.G.C., Pardalos, P.M. (eds.) Handbook of Optimization in Telecommunications, pp. 103–128. Springer, Boston (2006). https://doi.org/10.1007/978-0-387-30165-5_4
9. Risso, C., Nesmachnow, S., Robledo, F.: Metaheuristic approaches for IP/MPLS network design. Int. Trans. Oper. Res. **25**(2), 599–625 (2018)
10. Bhanja, U., Mahapatra, S.: A metaheuristic approach for optical network optimization problems. Appl. Soft Comput. **13**, 981–997 (2013)
11. Kharroubi, F., He, J., Chen, L.: Performance analysis of GA, ROA, and TSA for solving the Max-RWA problem in optical networks, OFC 2014, San Francisco, CA, pp. 1–3 (2014). https://doi.org/10.1364/OFC.2014.W2A.48
12. Mohan, N., Wason, A., Sandhu, P.S.: ACO based single link failure recovery in all optical networks. Optik **127**, 8469–8474 (2016)
13. Rabbani, M., Ravanbakhsh, M., Farrokhi-Asl, H., Taheri, M.: Using metaheuristic algorithms for solving a hub location problem: application in passive optical network planning. Int. J. Supply Oper. Manag. **4**(1), 15–32 (2017)
14. Mata, J., et al.: Artificial intelligence (AI) methods in Optical Networks: A Comprehensive Survey. https://arxiv.org/abs/1801.01704v2 [cs.AI], Optical Switching and Networking (2018)
15. Network Simulator: Net2Plan. http://www.net2plan.com/

Deployment Consideration on Secure Computation for Radix-16 Scalar Multiplication

Gautam Kumar[1($\boxtimes$)], Hemraj Saini[2], and U. M. Fernandes Dimlo[1]

[1] Department of Computer Science and Engineering, Narsimha Reddy
Engineering College, Maisammaguda, Secundarabad 500100, TS, India
gautam2lujrb@gmail.com, mariaprakashu2000@yahoo.com
[2] Department of Computer Science and Engineering, Jaypee University of
Information Technology, Waknaghat, Solan 173234, HP, India
hemraj1977@yahoo.co.in

Abstract. An Elliptic Curve Cryptography (ECC) algorithm is one of the most powerful with respect to better security and performance than RSA algorithm. Most of applications prefer to implement this approach due to the use of shorter key sizes, low computation costs and most probably the discrete logarithmic problem is hard to achieve. In addition to it, with the support of hardware most of computation costs have been reduced in the general observation and widely available the reduction of pre-computed operations using strategies is playing one of the concerns in research gap creation. In the manuscript, we analyzed the proposed Radix-16 scalar multiplications without pre-computation for ECC and considered to be one of advanced approach technique, which is counted in the form of reduced complexity costs, reliable and secure computing. It also consists in relation to the more appropriateness for low memory devices and reduced instruction set computing, therefore a possible deployment is considered.

Keywords: ECC · PKC · Scalar multiplication · Radix-16 · Complexity

1 Introduction

Cryptography is one of most important technique used to hide the original information when it hangs in between the medium. It is considered to be a science with respect to the secret information to be safe, where algorithms are playing crucial role responsiveness. In a modern day applications, cryptography is a mixed resultant of the three disciplines such as mathematical approach, make it programmable through the use of computer science and finally make it applicable to end users support on electronically implementable. In all these respects, the major attention to protect information from discloser, secure transmission in unsecured environment, authenticity, and integrity purposes [1].

Diffie and Hellman [2] were the first two authors who enlighten public key cryptography (PKC). After that variety of PKC algorithms are in propositions, but Elliptic Curve Cryptography (ECC) in all of them is attracting the most attention from the research community. A number of proposed algorithms have been showing the

© Springer Nature Singapore Pte Ltd. 2018
M. Singh et al. (Eds.): ICACDS 2018, CCIS 906, pp. 205–216, 2018.
https://doi.org/10.1007/978-981-13-1813-9_21

appropriate security need, but the major problem is the use of higher key lengths. Due its increased overhead for computation doesn't a suite for low memory containing devices in the fast growing world, where ECC is able to give the almost equal level of security strengths on comparatively shorter key sizes, as recommended by the National Institute of Standard Technology (NIST). According to the NIST-2012 guideline, the differences in key size ratio (in bits) between RSA & ECC algorithm and a comparative protection strength from attack on relative is presented in Table 1:

Table 1. Differences in security strength of RSA vs. ECC

RSA	ECC	Key size ratio	Protection from attack
1024	160–223	1:6	Until 2010
2048	224–255	1:9	Until 2031
3072	256–383	1:12	Beyond 2031
7680	384–511	1:20	...
15360	512+	1:30	...

The difference is an abstract idea to implement in manufacturing devices and acting as a key role makes. If RSA algorithm is in used on 1024 bits, for the same level of security and strength ECC works on minimum of 160 bits. The report available on NIST considered to be secured on the given subsequent periods. The major attraction appears in speedup enhancement on ratio of key sizes. The use of ECC is releasing so many benefits in terms of faster computation costs, bandwidth consumptions, most efficient key generations, almost be safe on little higher lengths of the key, etc. In general, the computation cost is reduced with the development of the new and/or modifications in the proposed approaches. What so ever is evolved for ECC, but from the research point of view it is still an excess been considered and improvements in the same is possible issue with respect to the current computations [3].

Discrete Logarithmic Problem (DLP) is playing important role responsiveness in establishing the secure computation and is one of the major concerns in ECC, for ECC named by ECC-DLP. ECC-DLP is working on two elliptic points as an assumptions (P and Q) on the standard cubic curve equation, to determine the secret key used as k, that follow $Q = kP$, which is the heart of ECC in PKC and its building block for security issues [4]. It is based on algorithms on repeated point doubling (DBL) and point addition (ADD) operations on used scalar. DLP is one of the hearts of cryptography, where secret keys are full responsible for the same. The big significance releasing here from the research point of view is to do the computations costs with the reduced DBLs and ADDs operations and it is showing a motivations. The algorithms are playing a pivotal role for security guarantees and determining for the same in effective implementation. A low mark has been observed on the used algorithms if it is not with the appropriate satisfaction and convincing. Where, in the other ways, performances with faster algorithms are leading with high performance and high-speed in the growing field of computing and communication systems. If the assumptions proceeds in the forward direction but behaves like negligible to revert back of used scalar k, is a major intention of the algorithms and scalar multiplication.

The three approaches are the basis for the smooth conduct of ECC operations. The first approach is its underlying operations on finite basis and either the operations based on binary field or prime fields arithmetic assumptions. The next approach is the used algorithm, the scalar representation, which decides their computational complexity costs. Here are some of the existing methods that are in the forms of Most Significant Bit (MSB) algorithm, Least Significant Bit (LSB) algorithm, Nonadjacent form (NAF), Window Method, Sliding Window Method, Width Nonadjacent Form, Frobenious Map and Radix-rNAF (r-NAF) [5–10]. Third approach uses both of the previous two approaches with the support of hardware utilizations that are effectively utilizing in reduction of pre-computation operations, and/or using in generalization of parallel operations [11–13] or/and pipelining approaches [14].

In this manuscript, the first and second approaches are combined to the third approach for dependability and likely safety measures are managed sufficiently in secure computing. The overall scenario is considered for an efficient scalar multiplication for the proposed ECC. The below following points are reflecting throughout in this presentation:

- An extended work from radix-8 to radix-16 scalar multiplication is available, that illustrates on how dependency varies from one existing platform to new platform and how measures of deployment varies.
- To analyze the security strength at various levels for its deployment i.e., power analysis, safe-error fault attacks, side channel attacks, computations costs, and in some generic considerations.

We have set the deployment of our proposed strategy is secure, stronger and efficient in comparisons to known approaches in reference to the ECC scalar multiplication algorithms. The difficult is on cryptanalysis for the cryptographers to find the used secret. In relation to the same our contribution is a deployment specification with respect to performance enhancement and security validity.

Our manuscript is organized as follows. Section 2 presents dependency on interrelated existing algorithms. In Sect. 3, the deployment perspective has been considered with the security related analysis that highlights the advantages of proposed strategy against the side channel attacks (SSCAs) and in general considered objective. Finally, we summarized our manuscript the same.

2 Dependency of Scalar Multiplication on Existing Algorithms

ECC is based on consistent operations, organized in hierarchy, and well designed on its interrelated four levels as like to be shown in Fig. 1. The top level keeps the used algorithms of ECC, which depends on scalar multiplication kP, where it depends on group operations, such as point doubling and point addition, and further these are considered in group operations based on arithmetic operations such as multiplication, subtraction, addition, inversion and squaring. Each level of operations consists in the form of costs, where reduction in costs using the proposed methodology is one of the research gaps. A reference from [15] is tested on Star core 41000 series processor reporting a cost for one doubling is 14,000 clock cycles and for one addition is 13,617 clock cycles.

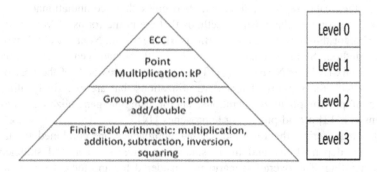

Fig. 1. Hierarchy of ECC

The most motivational concern in ECC is reduction in the computational costs. The architectural behavior of ECC is tested on the various algorithms for its better performance and is treated in the forms of advanced algorithms for end users applications. Further, these are treated in systems performance. Each algorithm consists a section of computations are in the form of pre-computation and or use of critical section. Precomputation is an act of operations before-or-in critical section midair. Here is highlighted of enormous thought of its existing algorithms with its relative costs. On secret key k, or in general it is scalar, is considered in m-bits. The Most-Significant-Bit (MSB) algorithm needs m doublings and on average m/2 bits of addition operations. Means any scalar of m = 128 bits based requires 128 * 14000 clock cycle of doubling and 64 * 13617 clock cycle of addition operations. In a similar fashion Least-Significant-Bit (LSB) algorithm needs on average m/2 bits of doublings and same bits of additions. But both algorithms are suffer from side channel attack is possible that try to abstract the original key used for the algorithm, which has been considered to an extra source of information gain from physical implementations such as electromagnetic leakages, power consumption and sound released from the systems. Electromagnetic leakage is alarming in a sense the signal passes through medium are decoding by the adversary through the use of auxiliary equipments, instead the signals are low signals but for the interested users vulnerabilities have been reported. In a similar sense on behalf of power consumption and sound leads as a extra source of vulnerabilities. One solution for eliminating the side channel attack is use of Montgomery algorithm; in this the complexity is higher in m doubling and m addition. Further, using non-adjacent form (NAF) is one of variation of algorithm use to avoid the side channel attack on reduced complexity on average m/2 additions and m/2 doublings, representation of algorithm is in $\{-1, 0, 1\}$ [16, 17]. Again a window (w-NAF) method has been proposed on reduced complexity $m/(w + 1)$ in additions only [18, 19]. One more variation in window method is available on escaping the series of zero on w-NAF, named by sliding w-NAF, also known by Frobenious operations, that has counted as an enhancement in scalar multiplication [20, 21]. For the complexity determination, hamming-weight is in general be used for scalar representation.

ECC is likely to be secure on shorter lengths keys, due this reason it is attracting a relatively more favorable attention in more appropriateness to end user applications, as well as most suit for short memory devices, higher performance achievers etc. The real life applications are widely available in the forms of smart-cards, internet banking, mobile banking, etc. for its efficient and secure implementation approach. The applications are considered in exceptionally good functionalities in addition that may not lead to any leakages [22]. Abdulrahman and Masoleh [23] proposed a methodology on Radix-8 scalar multiplication without pre-computations with resistance to side channel attack. The main advantage of this proposed approach is without using doubling and addition, they are directly switched to arithmetic operations. This has given a slightly a new path for scalar multiplication on the computation cost $\log_8(m + 1)$.

Therefore, in relation to above already proposed methodologies are representing a research gap to find a more efficient method to accelerate the scalar multiplication for ECC. Here we are going to extend the work of Radix-8 scalar multiplication without pre-computation to Radix-16 scalar multiplication. Also, we are going to elaborate the execution dependency from the hardware in Fig. 2, (here only its designed/comparison is available, interested author(s) refer the base paper) where the hardware implementation in its computation cost (basis (1/3 to 1/4) in %) = 8.33% accelerated, in Fig. 3. Further, the software execution and performance in presented in Fig. 4, where the major objective is in the relation to find the more efficient technique for accelerating the scalar multiplication in Elliptic Curve Cryptography (through the series of identified research gap), and established the same in more appropriateness with resistance to side channel attacks and safe-error fault attacks. Therefore, the novel contribution is based on the proposed algorithm of Radix-16 scalar multiplication, which is established on computation cost at $\log_{16}(k + 1)$. Compare to recently proposed Radix-8 scalar multiplication algorithm from the implementation point of view, the software performance gets an acceleration on proposed methodology with the basic difference's in its base or its computation cost on (1/8 to 1/16) in % = 6.25%, in Fig. 5.

3 Deployment Perspective of Radix-16 Scalar Multiplication

The Radix-16 scalar multiplication methodology is presented by Gautam and Hemraj [24] to records the Discrete Logarithmic Problem (DLP) for its assumed significance on finite basis. The DLP is computationally probable infeasible to get the used secret (scalar) key. In relation to these preferences the software and hardware performances are significantly improved. Interested author(s) can refer the dependency graph for the solution presented in 'Secure and Efficient ECC: Radix-16 Scalar Multiplication without Pre-Computation'. The proposed scalar multiplication technique is enriching its benefits on low computation costs. The new era's are mostly looking with stronger security in connection to advanced security approaches, where our objective is meeting with the same. The major attention is to deploy the same for application purposes. The applications are in online and offline services, such as in data processing, transactions

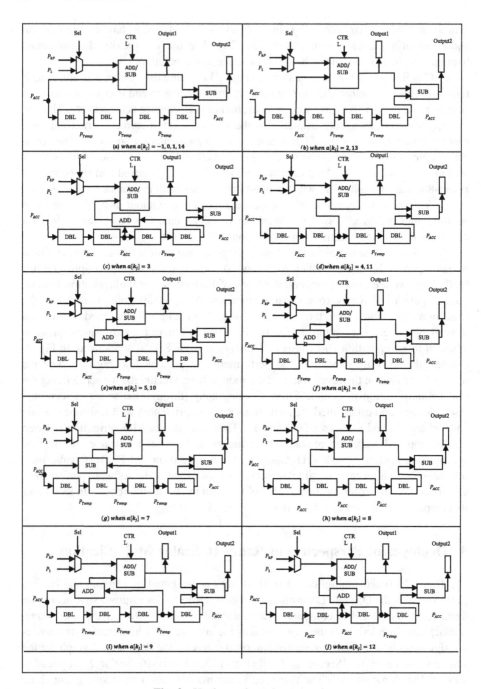

Fig. 2. Hardware dependency graph

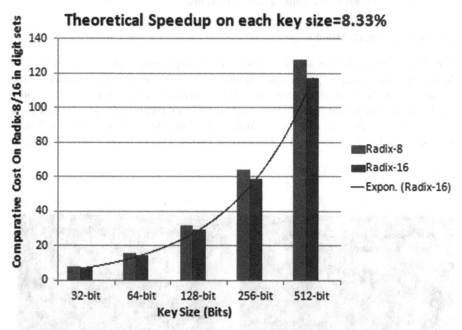

Fig. 3. Performance enhancement from hardware perspective

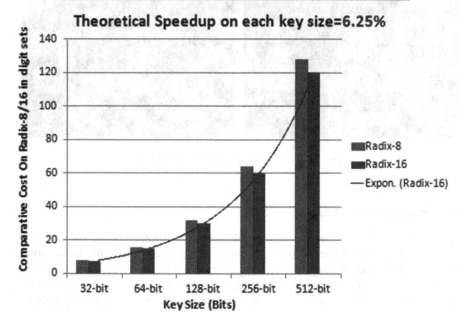

Fig. 4. Performance enhancement from hardware perspective

are most favorable cases. Implementing the same in firmware as a component of security points are also be a considerable situations.

3.1 Side Channel Attacks

Side channel attack defines an information gain from physical implementation such as electromagnetic leakages, power consumption, or sound that can give an extra source of information but it doesn't care about the theoretical computation or brute force attacks. It has considered independently outside the computation phase. This has been added to provide the various services against the following scenarios such as Power Analysis Attacks, Timing Attacks, Differential Faults Attacks, Data remanence etc.

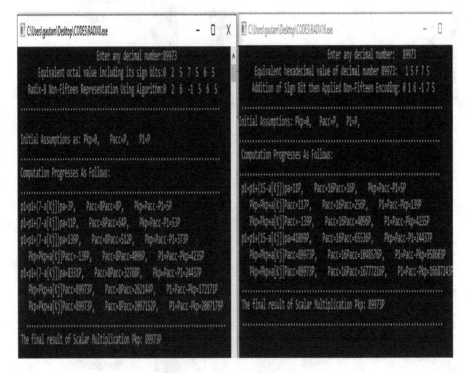

Fig. 5. Comparison in radix-8 and radix-16

3.2 Power Analysis Attacks

The power analysis provides the detailed information about the power consumption by the CPU or cryptographic circuits. The attacks are differentiated in simple power analysis (SPA) and differential power analysis (DPA). The SPA interprets power traces, or graphs generations on electrical activity shown over time. Whereas the DPA allows the attacker to compute intermediate cryptographic computations on statistical analysis collected from multiple operations. Using the newly introduced algorithm of radix-16 scalar multiplication in operation with the hardware support, power analysis attack can mostly be too sophisticated. In case of power analysis, the adversary(s) try to get secret key information either from internet, passing information through channel or from physical implementation. In a similar fashion its analysis is categorized on SPA and DPA. SPA observes the proposed scheme is fixed. The scheme is intrinsic confined against simple side channel attacks on each iterations in the main loop involment. It is observed from the adopted design principles, any dummy operations except in its domain brings an incorrect result on scalar. It is in favor to safe-error fault attacks if any inclusion.

3.3 Timing Attacks

The transmissions of signals release are the part of computer operations. But, due to interested adversary that try to abstract the pattern using the cryptographic algorithms and same pattern generations for its security appearances may lead to vulnerable issues. This is treated as a stunning that is alarming in the two senses: (i) a random interference comes first, which can be only be burglars, and (ii) these signals can be amplify through some auxiliary equipments for some useful purposes. A report is available that are suggesting on electromagnetic radiation interference with radio navigation devices, as (i) it is a general procedure and it is not a point to be considerable issue, but if (ii) applies who are interested in generating of such pattern of abstraction, then decoding and restoration can lead to vulnerable information safety, feedbacks and/or secret information leakage, where an adversary try to determine the private key by keeping track on how long a computer takes to decipher the secrets messages. In practice, proposed assumptions do lead to extreme timing variations. So in regards to the same enough variations to make the algorithms be a practical choice for applications.

3.4 Differential Fault Analysis

The differential fault analysis principle induces on faults due to unexpected conditions on environmental factors using the cryptographic algorithms design and implementations that steals to their internal working. Where, our proposed approach is meeting with the cryptographic function generations on fixed computations costs on multifold security properties. The real beauty of the algorithm lies on working nature in support of hardware perspective. Due this nature, the most level of confusion is applied to frustrate the adversaries.

3.5 Data Remanence

The data remanence is one of the important factor that represents the residual information that release or hide the information in likely intractable forms. The resultant residual may left intact information, or keeps nominal information even after deletion, or reformatting does not erase the data for verification purpose at later stage, or physical properties may be recoverable on previous used activity. It may make inadvertent in uncontrolled environment to sensitive information. Depending on the used algorithms, a vast amount of algorithms are available for data remanence. But, some specific methods are possible through which encryption, destruction, overwriting and disgusting is possible, where radix-16 releasing benefits low computations costs.

3.6 Brute-Force Attacks

Possibly finding all the secret key and making a defense attacks the proposed approach is suit here, and using the hardware support it adds the additional strengths. This type of approach considered to be the special case in Elliptic Curve Cryptography. Therefore the presented scenario is sufficiently works on the smaller keyed length. In relation to the same, the execution time takes a shorter time for execution and reflects a big impact on efficiency consideration. A sufficient number of reports are available in regard to the computational performance in comparison to ECC and RSA algorithms, where our approach in regards the speed, efficiency, and cryptanalysis are better in many ways.

3.7 Chosen-Ciphertext Attacks

This attack is a form of active attack, where adversaries try to find plaintext corresponding to its ciphertexts by its choice. The first choice may experience on decryption module on a random chosen ciphertexts, before the actual ciphertext sent for an interested use. The second choice involves the same module on input of one's choice at any time, where these all are recorded and try to gain the actual plaintexts. As the presented algorithm experience a blind feedbacks, where the Noncommutative cryptography is not a vulnerable one to chosen ciphertext attacks (CCA) especially for ring or semi-ring, group and Heisenberg elements; because in CCA an adversary chooses a number of ciphertext and try to decrypt with targeted private keys, where the chosen cipher text is hashed with the corresponding polynomial exponentials.

3.8 General Consideration

Radix-16 scalar multiplication is lowering feasibility parallel consideration on arithmetic operations. The abstract reason clears the fundamental principle on computation of hexadecimal on binary information conversion. To add a random delay in the proposed algorithm is one of the good way to more frustrate the adversaries, instead of the same blinding creation in modulus and/or exponential of the computational procedure. It offers relatively faster computation, less memory requirements, and smaller execution of memory area.

4 Conclusion

In this manuscript, a radix-16 scalar multiplication deployment scenario is presented. Using this approach, as assessment of digit set elements are identify uniquely by a single digit set of used Radix-16 algorithm, so this may be considered as one of the advanced way to do the computation and applicable for desired applications in the rapidly growing world. The scheme presentation is considered in software implementation point of view as well as hardware, where securities and performance are the most in demand and scarce resources use is the issue. In relation to same, reduced instruction set computing is one of the most suitable methods for widely applicable and use of short-memory devices are most attractive with resistant to simple-side channel attack and safe-error fault attack on deployment considerations.

References

1. Jirasek, V.: Practical application of information security models. Inf. Secur. Tech. Rep. **17** (1–2), 1–8 (2012)
2. Diffie, W., Hellman, M.E.: New directions in cryptography. IEEE Trans. Inf. Theory **22**(6), 644–654 (1976)
3. Jarvinen, K., Skytta, J.: Parallelization of high-speed processor for elliptic curve cryptography. IEEE Trans. VLSI **16**(9), 1162–1175 (2008)
4. Koblitz, N.: Elliptic curve cryptosystems. Math. Comput. **48**(177), 203–209 (1987)
5. Miller, V.S.: Use of elliptic curves in cryptography. Adv. Cryptol. **218**, 417–426 (1986)
6. Izu, T., Takagi, T.: Fast elliptic curve multiplications with SIMD operations. In: Deng, R., Bao, F., Zhou, J., Qing, S. (eds.) ICICS 2002. LNCS, vol. 2513, pp. 217–230. Springer, Heidelberg (2002). https://doi.org/10.1007/3-540-36159-6_19
7. Knudsen, E.W.: Elliptic scalar multiplication using point halving. In: Lam, K.-Y., Okamoto, E., Xing, C. (eds.) ASIACRYPT 1999. LNCS, vol. 1716, pp. 135–149. Springer, Heidelberg (1999). https://doi.org/10.1007/978-3-540-48000-6_12
8. Blake, I.F., Murty, V.K., Xu, G.: A note on window τ-adic NAF algorithm. Inf. Process. Lett. **95**, 496–502 (2005)
9. Hankerson, D., Vanstone, S., Menezes, A.: Guide to Elliptic Curve Cryptography. Springer Professional Computing. Springer, New York (2004). https://doi.org/10.1007/b97644
10. Arno, S., Wheeler, F.S.: Signed digit representations of minimal hamming weight. IEEE Trans. Comput. **2**(8), 1007–1010 (1993). https://doi.org/10.1109/12.238495
11. Longa, P., Miri, A.: Fast and flexible elliptic curve point arithmetic over prime fields. IEEE Trans. Comput. **57**(3), 289–302 (2008)
12. Faye, Y., Guyennet, H., Niang, I., Shou, Y.: Fast scalar multiplication on elliptic curve cryptography in selected intervals suitable for wireless sensor networks. In: Wang, G., Ray, I., Feng, D., Rajarajan, M. (eds.) CSS 2013. LNCS, vol. 8300, pp. 171–182. Springer, Cham (2013). https://doi.org/10.1007/978-3-319-03584-0_13
13. Fischer, W., Giraud, C., Knudsen, E.W., Seifert, J.P.: Parallel scalar multiplication on general elliptic curves over F(p) hedged against non-differential side-channel attacks. In: IACR (2002/007) Cryptology ePrint Archive (2002). http://eprint.iacr.org/2002/007
14. Mishra, P.K.: Pipelined computation of scalar multiplication in elliptic curve cryptosystems (extended version). IEEE Trans. Comput. **55**(8), 1000–1010 (2006)
15. Gebotys, C.H. (ed.): Security in Embedded Devices, pp. 75–109. Springer, New York (2010)
16. Heuberger, C., Pondinger, H.: Analysis of alternatives digits sets for non-adjacent representation. SIAM J. Discrete Math. **19**(1), 165–191 (2006)
17. Okeya, K., Takagi, T.: The width-w NAF method provides small memory and fast elliptic scalar multiplications secure against side channel attacks. In: Joye, M. (ed.) CT-RSA 2003. LNCS, vol. 2612, pp. 328–343. Springer, Heidelberg (2003). https://doi.org/10.1007/3-540-36563-X_23

18. Vuillaume, C., Okeya, K., Takagi, T.: Short-memory scalar multiplication for Koblitz curve. IEEE Trans. Comput. **57**(4), 481–489 (2008). https://doi.org/10.1109/TC.2007.70824
19. Okeya, K., Kurumatani, H., Sakurai, K.: Elliptic curves with the montgomery-form and their cryptographic applications. In: Imai, H., Zheng, Y. (eds.) PKC 2000. LNCS, vol. 1751, pp. 238–257. Springer, Heidelberg (2000). https://doi.org/10.1007/978-3-540-46588-1_17
20. Ciet, M., Lange, T., Sica, F., Quisquater, J.-J.: Improved algorithms for efficient arithmetic on elliptic curves using fast endomorphisms. In: Biham, E. (ed.) EUROCRYPT 2003. LNCS, vol. 2656, pp. 388–400. Springer, Heidelberg (2003). https://doi.org/10.1007/3-540-39200-9_24
21. Parhami, B. (ed.): Computer Arithmetic: Algorithms and Hardware Designs. Oxford University Press, New York (2010)
22. Avanzi, R.M., Heuberger, C., Prodinger, H.: On redundant τ-adic expansions and non-adjacent digit sets. In: Biham, E., Youssef, A.M. (eds.) SAC 2006. LNCS, vol. 4356, pp. 285–301. Springer, Heidelberg (2007). https://doi.org/10.1007/978-3-540-74462-7_20
23. Abdulrahman, E.A.H., Reyhani-Masoleh, A.: New regular radix-8 scheme for elliptic curve scalar multiplication without pre-computation. IEEE Trans. Comput. **64**(2), 438–451 (2015)
24. Kumar, G., Saini, H.: Secure and efficient ECC: radix-16 scalar multiplication without pre-computation. In: International Conference on Big Data and Advanced Wireless Technologies. ACM Digital Library, USA (2016). https://doi.org/10.1145/3010089.3010105

Clustering of Social Networking Data Using SparkR in Big Data

Navneet Kaur[(✉)] and Niranjan Lal

Mody University of Science and Technology, Lakshmangarh,
Sikar, Rajasthan, India
navneetsaini93.ns@gmail.com,
niranjan_verma51@yahoo.com

Abstract. Due to every day growing amount of data and changing the formats, the storing and management of these data is the challenging task for the organizations. Not long ago, datasets contained thousands of data items. Currently, different technologies can store, manage and process data with increasing volumes of unstructured and heterogeneous data, data of this type are known as Big Data. Big Data is the period for a group of such huge and complicated datasets that makes it problematic to store, manage and process with existing data processing tools. Now, in Big Data, maximum of the data created is not structured. Therefore, the new situations imposed by Big Data present grave challenges at multiple levels, together with clustering problem of these data. Clustering is one of the significant Big Data analysis problems, where very large amount of heterogeneous and unstructured data must be grouped together. Here we have describe the k-mean and hierarchical clustering methods; great attention to k-means method lends itself because it remains one of the most sought-after other approaches and it is also implemented in innovative technologies for analyzing Big Data. This paper describes different categories of data, the management of unstructured data in Big Data and the clustering analysis of social network data using SparkR.

Keywords: Information retrieval · Data mining · Heterogeneous data
Data mining technique · Big data · SparkR · Clustering

1 Introduction

Big data is the famous term used in the present-day to extract information from large datasets. Big data is the set of complex and large datasets. Volume, variety, and velocity are three main challenges in Big data [1]. Big data is mostly related to unstructured data. Nowadays everyone is speaking about unstructured data but actually, what does this unstructured data means? Where the unstructured data comes from, how they are analyzed, processes and also how the results are really used. More than 90% of Big data is unstructured data. In 2003, we are created almost 5 Exabyte of data that in the present time is believable in only two days. Going from 2003 to the following years, until 2012 the data expanded to almost 2.72 Zettabytes, and by 2017 they are expanded to 8 Zettabytes, which are doubled every two years. Twitter is a social site

© Springer Nature Singapore Pte Ltd. 2018
M. Singh et al. (Eds.): ICACDS 2018, CCIS 906, pp. 217–226, 2018.
https://doi.org/10.1007/978-981-13-1813-9_22

that allows the user to tweets as a form of unstructured textual data more than 140 characters. 6,000 tweets are uploading on Twitter in every second. More than 1 million servers, 6 billion mobile subscribers and 10 billion text messages sent every day from Google. Every minute more than 48 hours of video uploads on You-tube [2], internet traffic will rise to 80% by 2019, that will linked to the Internet, 50 billion mobile phones and computers by 2020 [8], Therefore, this information cannot be handled by the existing system. Big data is a phrase used to define structured (Data with some fixed format, like RDB) [4], unstructured (Data without any fixed format, do not conform to predefined data models like; PPT, PDF, containing text, document, images, videos and heterogeneous etc.) [3], and semi-structured (data with some fixed format like, XML, NoSQL etc.). These type of cannot be handled together by traditional software and database techniques. Now a days 20% data is in structured format and another 80% is in heterogeneous format [2, 4, 17], the growing amount of unstructured data size is shown in Fig. 1.

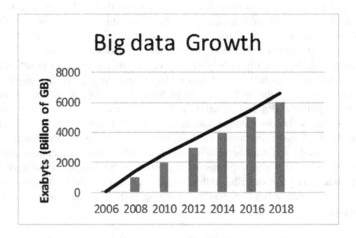

Fig. 1. Explosion in size of unstructured data

To analyze Big data various new technologies, algorithms for machine learning and data mining have been developed. Therefore, Big data generate new kinds of data storage mechanisms and different methods of analysis. When it comes to the huge amount of heterogeneous data, a problem of clustering data is one of the significant problems. Often datasets, mainly large data sets, are made up of some clusters and groups need to be found. Because Big data refers to Exabyte and Terabytes of data and clustering algorithms have high computing costs, the question is how to tackle this problem and how to implement Big data clustering techniques for unstructured and get outputs in near real-time with efficiency.

We have organized this paper as follows. Section 2, explains previous and related work in Big data mining and clustering, Sect. 3 defines the unstructured data management system in big data with its architecture, Sect. 4 explains the clustering of Big data with K-means and hierarchical clustering algorithm using Spark framework with R programming. In Sect. 5 implementation and results. Final Sect. 6 concludes the paper with future direction.

2 Related Works

We have studied several papers and articles on unstructured data in Big data and clustering algorithms for unstructured data, some research work is related our area using several clustering tools, some of which are described here.

Ahmed et al. [7], this paper describes techniques related analyze and process Big data like Hadoop, MapReduce, Spark, Hive. These techniques form the core of a frame of open source software that supports processing sets of the diverse and large size of data clustered systems. Software like Hadoop is an accomplished way to store unstructured data and analyze it. Also, introduce the well-formed way of handling big amount of unstructured data.

Siddaraju et al. [10], describe the MapReduce framework for large size data analysis and to solve complex data processing problems in large size data sets across multiple domains. An idea behind a MapReduce card provides an easy and effective way to resize your application. It easily scales from a singular machine to multiples, providing high performance.

Ajin et al. [11], discuss clustering algorithm for Big data and its different techniques. Mostly used, effective and simple algorithms are K-Means, BIRCH, FCM, CLIQUE algorithms. CLIQUE and BIRCH are appropriate clustering algorithms for dealing with bulky datasets.

Lal et al. [12], they perform K-means clustering on a social media data set and heterogeneous set of data using Euclidean distance. Discussing the K-means clustering algorithm for heterogeneous data sets is important in each file.

Kurasova et al. [13], they have introduced a clustering method based on neural networks and self-organizing map unattended.

Another recent work in this area is done by Davel and Gianey [14] has submitted a viewpoint to perform clustering at various resolutions, using k-means as a clustering algorithm.

3 Managing Unstructured Data in Big Data

Nowadays, managing unstructured data is the main problem in the technology industry; the main cause is that the techniques and tools that have proven so effective transform unstructured data into structured data. Unstructured data produced largely from email conversations, social networking sites as graphics and text. Heterogeneity and security problems with large Data hamper the progress at each stage of the process that can create huge value from data [6, 17]. Most of today's data is not basically in a structured layout, as blogs and tweets are in unstructured, while pictures and videos are not unstructured for storage and visualization, but not for semantic content and search. A view of data management in Big data is shown in Fig. 2.

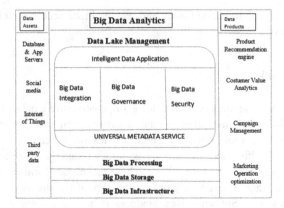

Fig. 2. A view of Big data management

Big data management contains the following components (1) Data Assets, that includes Database, different App servers, Social media data, some third party data and Internet of Things to store, manage and mapping of different types of data, (2) Data Lake management layer to handle stored Big data in terms of providing different rules of storing Big data, how these Big data will store in the form of clusters, providing the security policy for Big data, creating the meta data, Big data processing, (3) Third component is data product, that includes search engines for retrieval of data, data analysis for data comparison and marketing purpose. To manage Big data following tools may be used like; Hive, MapReduce, Spark and as well as NoSQL databases that help to analyze the data with clustering [7].

4 Proposed Approach for Clustering of Unstructured Data in Big Data

Big data text mining is the analysis of the data contained in the text in natural language. The use of text mining techniques (email, Facebook, Twitter, and Youtube) to solve business difficulties is called text analysis. In our proposed approach we have clustering that show the result analysis of unstructured data. Clustering is the job of grouping a group of objects so that objects in the same group are more linked than the object of other groups, clustering is shown in Fig. 3. It is a primary task of exploratory text mining and a usual technique for the analysis of data, which is used in various fields, image analysis, pattern recognition, machine learning, and information retrieval. Different data mining techniques are carried out taking into account the Big data criteria [13, 16].

The distinct types of clustering techniques are as follows:

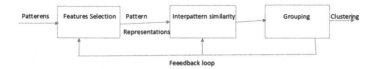

Fig. 3. Overview of clustering

4.1 Partitioning-based

Partitioning-based techniques divide the data elements into several small partitions that are obtained from the split data elements, where the separate separator characterizes a cluster and all the clusters are quickly determined in those techniques. The preliminary3 sets are established and the Reals are located towards a union. The requirements to be met are: one element must be present in each cluster and a cluster must have a set.

K-means is popular and most widely used clustering algorithm. At the beginning, you select the desired number k of clusters and are assigned the preliminary values of the cluster centroids. Therefore, each data points are allocated to the cluster with the nearest centers. In the second step, elements are allocated to the updated centers, and Centroids are updated again. The steps are repeated the same manner till the stopping criterion is reached or convergence [12].

4.2 Hierarchical-based

Hierarchical clustering is a technique that seeks to make a cluster hierarchy. The hierarchical clustering strategies are separated into two methods: (1) Merge the cluster pairs using agglomeration method [14], and (2) In the second method, all data elements are allocated to a group, so it is recursively divided known as divisive. The Dendrogram is a way to present the outputs of hierarchical clustering.

A proposed approach for comparing of two clustering algorithms, Partitioned based cluster and Hierarchical based is shown in Fig. 4. In our approach first we load the unstructured data from local directory or from specified web storage, after loading the unstructured data we preprocess the loaded data using our algorithm, after preprocessing find the frequent words from the unstructured data, and then after removing the frequent words we create cluster using two known algorithms K-means clustering and Hierarchical Clustering using SparkR programming on Big data.

5   Implementation and Results Analysis

For result analysis we have used the Windows operating system. On windows operating system first we have created a virtual machine using VMware and then we have installed the Haddop using Cloudera. A result of the clustering has been done on the spark framework using R language. To handle the large data sets Spark is used which are the major framework of the Big data technology, the Dataflow in SparkR is shown in Fig. 5. The number of the cluster into which the dataset is to be divided is 3 clusters in case of K-means algorithm and 3 clusters in case of the hierarchical algorithm. We

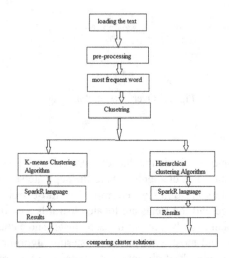

Fig. 4. Steps of our proposed approach

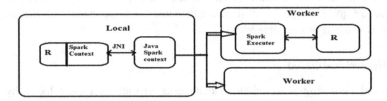

Fig. 5. Data flow in SparkR

have used K-means and hierarchical algorithm for comparison purpose. We have used Hadoop on Windows operating system with Cloudera. For result analysis we have used social media Youtube dataset, collected from UCI machine repository [15].

5.1 Steps of Proposed Approach

This paper used the K-means and Hierarchical clustering algorithms for comparison of the dataset, for comparison of these algorithms we have selected real-time data set of social media (Youtube) dataset from the following website 'https://archive.ics.uci.edu/ml/datasets.html' [15], that is stored in the local drive.

The steps for clustering procedure are as follows; (1) Firstly we have read files from the local drive using read.csv R function which is stored in CSV (comma-separated file) format. (2) In a second step we have pre-processed the stored data for removing of numbers, for removing special characters, for converting the unstructured data into lowercase, and removing of punctuations etc. the result is shown in Fig. 6 with document-term matrix that shows frequency of words available in dataset. (3) In the third we have found the most frequent word, In this step, we find out the word that is most frequently occurred in the documents and we also adjust the frequency of word like 100, the most frequent words available in our YouTube dataset is shown in Fig. 7.

```
> lords <- tm_map(lords, stripWhitespace)
> lords <- tm_map(lords, tolower)
> lords <- tm_map(lords, removeWords, stopwords("english"))
> lords <- tm_map(lords, stemDocument)
> dtm <- DocumentTermMatrix(docs)
> dtm
<<DocumentTermMatrix (documents: 350, terms: 251)>>
Non-/sparse entries: 1001/86849
Sparsity           : 99%
Maximal term length: 3
Weighting          : term frequency (tf)
> █
```

Fig. 6. A term-document matrix

```
> findFreqTerms(dtm, 100)
 [1] "2013"   "2014"    "2015"     "amp"    "can"    "channel"
 [7] "check"  "com"     "get"      "guy"    "http"   "https"
[13] "just"   "like"    "love"     "make"   "music"  "new"
[19] "plea"   "song"    "subscrib" "thank"  "video"  "watch"
[25] "will"   "www"     "youtube"  ""       "2viq"   "qnc6"
> █
```

Fig. 7. Word-frequencies

5.2   Big Data Text Mining of Social Media Data

Word cloud of resultant head terms of social media data is shown in Fig. 8. According to the word frequency, the WordCloud is plotted using SparkR programming.

Fig. 8. Word cloud

5.3   K-means Clustering

The K-means clustering technique will try to group words into a specific number of groups is shown in Fig. 9, such that the Euclidian distances between single words and one of the group midpoints. You can alter the number of groups seeking change within the specified k-means number.

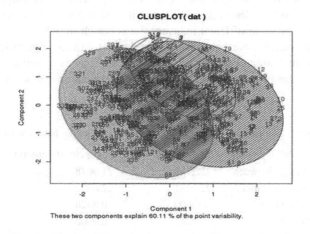

Fig. 9. Cluster of Youtube dataset using K-means clustering

5.4   Hierarchical Clustering

In K-means clustering we saw that there were 3 different specifics of flowers. Let see how well the Hierarchical clustering algorithm can do. We can use hclust for this hclust needs us to deliver the data in the form of distance matrix. We can do this by using dist (Fig. 10).

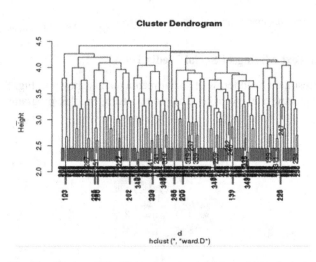

Fig. 10. Cluster of YouTube dataset using hierarchical clustering

6   Comparative Study of K-Means and Hierarchical Algorithms

Compute the clustering quality statistics for K-means and Hierarchical clustering look at Table 1 shows the results obtained by *K*-means and hierarchical clustering. The results showed Average between was higher than that with the Hierarchical and the average within lower, which is 22.6340 better than that obtained by the hierarchical algorithm. A higher value of Dunn indicates the better clustering.

For comparison purpose, we have selected the following parameters, Average between, Average within, Dunn index, Entropy. Entropy is a native measure, the lowest entropy is the best clustering. For the same unstructured and mixed data set, the

Table 1. Comparison table between K-means and hierarchical clustering

Validation measures	K-means clustering	Hierarchical clustering
Average between	22.2288	21.9078
Average within	22.2281	22.6340
Dunn index	0.9609	0.8528
Entropy	0.7243	0.9066

algorithm K-means and the hierarchical were obtained and the cluster was generated, the values indicated above show that K-means has a high value of the Dunn index and a low value of entropy. This indicates a good clustering. The hierarchical has a low Dunn value and a high entropy value as compared to the k-means algorithm. The K-means algorithm is more compliant for YouTube's unstructured data sets than the hierarchical.

For the mixed (YouTube) dataset, it is found that K-means is more efficient and accurate clustering for our dataset. The difference between K-mean and Hierarchical algorithms is shown in the Fig. 11.

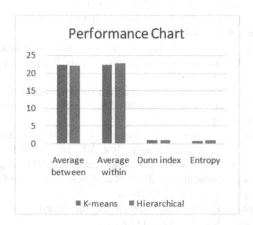

Fig. 11. Performance chart for K-means and hierarchical algorithm

7 Conclusion

In this research, we perform clustering on the unstructured dataset using different K-means and Hierarchical clustering algorithms. It can be seen from Table 1, that K-means clustering with three clusters performs the best in each case (Average between, Averages within, Dunn index, Entropy measures). K-means clustering algorithm for unstructured dataset has relevance in almost every field commercial, education and also in the medical sector. We analyze K-means clustering using distance measure is suitable for the unstructured type of data. The greatest attractive things of the k-means algorithm in data mining is its effectiveness in clustering bulky data sets.

Fast and high-quality document clustering algorithms play a significant role in providing intuitive navigation and browsing mechanisms by organizing big volumes of unstructured information into a small number of clusters. The main tentative result is to produce an improved clustering and reduce CPU utilization through the use of K-means. This paper was intended to a comparison between clustering approaches on same unstructured data.

Our main contribution in this paper, we have proposed an approach which can work on unstructured data using existing clustering technique which is effective for analysis of unstructured data.

In future, as we know data mining of heterogeneous data is a new area for latest research. So, we can apply clustering algorithm for mining of heterogeneous data like image, video, streams of data, big data analysis with appropriate data mining techniques with a new improved clustering algorithm.

References

1. Tekiner, F., Keane, J.A.: Big data framework. In: International Conference on Systems, Man, and Cybernetics, pp. 1494–1499. IEEE (2013)
2. Das, T.K., Mohan Kumar, P.: Big data analytics: a framework for unstructured data analysis. Int. J. Eng. Technol. 5(1), 154–156 (2013)
3. Subramaniyaswamy, V., Logesh, R., Indragandhi, V.: Unstructured data analysis on big data using map reduce. In: 2nd International Symposium on Big data and Cloud Computing (ISBCC 2015), pp. 456–465 (2015)
4. Saint, R., Schaffert, S., Stroka, S., Ferst, R.: Combining unstructured, fully structured and semi-structured information in semantic wikis. In 6th European Semantic Web Conference (ESWC), pp. 1–15 (2009)
5. Carlo, B., Daniele, B., Federico, C., Simone, G.: A data quality methodology for heterogeneous data. Int. J. Database Manag. Syst. 3(1), 60–79 (2011)
6. Blumberg, R., Atre, S.: The problem with unstructured data. DM Rev., 1–6 (2003)
7. Ahmed, Z.: Data management and big data text analytics. In: National Conference on Cloud Computing and Big data, pp. 140–144 (2013)
8. Griffin, G.K., Klemann, R.: Unlocking value in the fragmented world of big data analytics. Cisco Internet Business Solutions Group (2012)
9. Kaisler, S., Armour, F., Alberto Espinosa, J., Money, W.: Big data: issues and challenges moving forward. In: 46th Hawaii International Conference on System Science, pp. 995–1004. IEEE (2013)
10. Siddaraju, Sowmya, C.L., Rashmi, K., Rahul, M.: Efficient analysis of big data using mapreduce framework. Int. J. Rec. Dev. Eng. Technol. 2(6), 64–68 (2014)
11. Ajin, V.W., Kumar, L.D.: Big data and clustering algorithms. In: International Conference on Research Advances in Integrated Navigation Systems, pp. 1–5. IEEE (2016)
12. Kalra, M., Lal, N., Qamar, S.: K-mean clustering algorithm approach for data mining of heterogeneous data. In: Information and Communication Technology for Sustainable Development, pp. 61–70 (2017)
13. Kurasova, O., Marcinkevicius, V., Medvedev, V., Rapecka, A., Stefanovic, P.: Strategies for big data clustering. In: 26th International Conference on Tools with Artificial Intelligence, pp. 740–747. IEEE, Limassol (2014)
14. Davel, M., Gianey, R.: Different clustering algorithms for big data analytics: a review. In: 5th International Conference on System Modeling and Advancement in Research Trends. IEEE (2016)
15. Youtube Dataset for result analysis. 'https://archive.ics.uci.edu/ml/datasets.html
16. Srivastava, D.K.: Big challenges in big data research. Data Min. Knowl. Eng. 6(7), 282–286 (2014)
17. Lal, N., Qamar, S., Shiwani, S.: Search ranking for heterogeneous data over dataspace. Indian J. Sci. Technol. 9(36), 1–9 (2016)

Impact of Disruptive Technology on Juvenile Disruptive Behavior in Classroom

Vani Ramesh[(✉)]

Bangalore, India
sarada889@yahoo.in

Abstract. Bestowing to Christensen [1] (https://www.revolvy.com/main/index.php?s=Clayton+M.+Christensen&item_type), Disruptive Technology (DT) as an evolving technology which relocates the existing technology. Mobile computing, smart phones, cloud computing, social networking are some of the disruptive technologies that displaces conventional technologies. In near future the technology might transform the life style and there are 12 Disruptive Technologies (DT's) that are identified [2] (https://www.mckinsey.com/mgi/overview). Disruptive behaviour among juvenile in India, particularly in Bangalore (Karnataka) has become a great encounter for both parents and teachers. This study, first and foremost in this field of DT and intends to explore critically the influence of disruptive technology and disruptive behaviour among the school children. With the help of independent variables, such as demographic. Sociocultural, economic, political, environmental, infrastructural, and in addition the disruptive technological factors that are influencing the disruptive behaviour among school children are tested. The big five dimensions of personality, often referred to as "Big 5" personality traits J.M. Digman [3] (extraversion, agreeableness, openness, conscientiousness, and neuroticism) adopted to test the personality of the child. Primary data are to be used through a rigorous drop-off survey. The confirmatory factor analysis (CFA) approach is exploited to generate the results with the help of software IBM SPSS AMOS (Analysis of Moment Structures). Structural Equation Modelling (SEM) has been deployed to evaluate the original and modification indices of the model, which further establishes the improvement in SEM's effectiveness. The model establishes the significant impact of Disruptive Technology on class room behaviour. The targeted sample is 2000, includes high school children from 8th to 10th standard (both private and public), family members and teachers, and the response was 1679. Recommendation and policy implications are henceforth provided.

Keywords: Disruptive technology · Juvenile disruptive behaviour
Mobile computing

© Springer Nature Singapore Pte Ltd. 2018
M. Singh et al. (Eds.): ICACDS 2018, CCIS 906, pp. 227–238, 2018.
https://doi.org/10.1007/978-981-13-1813-9_23

1 Introduction

When advanced technological products are introduced into the market and replaced with the existing products or services, it is generally labelled as Disruptive Technology (**DT**) [4], and is generally introduced by unknown people out of enthusiasm. The other terms used are, 'new market disruption', 'serves the un served with existing players', and 'low-end disruption', enters the market when the customers capable of adopting the new performance. The systematic disruptive innovative software products that has been dynamic for 20 years are, 'nimble practice', 'fray', 'slender start-ups', which helped the industry to develop high quality product with low risk. 'Agile', the world's most popular disruptive innovative engine has really helped the industry to deliver faster than others. The competencies required for Disruptive Innovation are, 'leapfrogging mindset', 'boundary pushing', 'adaptive planning', 'break the rule and write new ones', 'open-minded', and 'decisive'.

This study is designed to examine the impact of these Disruptive Technology among high school children Disruptive Behaviour (**DB**) in the class room. Unruly conversation, lingering evasion of work, buffoonery, intrusive, niggling classmates, oral invectives, day dreaming, looking out of window, rudeness to teacher defiance and hostility are some of behaviours noticed, which are intensified with time and dropped academic performance and amplified delinquent behaviour. The prime objective of this study is to diagnose, categorise, understand and analyse weather these gadget usage and more access to technological advancement can be one of the main reasons for these disruptive behaviours in class room [5].

Also, the **Big 5** personality traits [3], which are believed as main drivers for the human behaviour are tested with the help of likert scale. Besides these disruptive behaviours, this study also aimed at identifying the common behaviours from the teacher's perspective. Contingent to teacher's idiosyncratic judgement and standards, proficient training and experience, these disruptive behaviours are empirically observed. Therefore, this study is eloquent in nature. The verdicts of this study expected to be a great contribution to the literature and have profound importance to council the students and chaperon them in a right direction.

The structure of the paper is designed as follows: The first part, introduces the title, statement and objectives of the study followed by tentative hypothesis. Part two research design, methodology and techniques, part three, literature review, part four analysis, findings, suggestions and conclusion.

1.1 Statement of the Problem

Sweeping spread in mobile computing devices and internet connectivity which are extensive range of areas with their disruptive technology and can influence the student disruptive behaviour in class room and has a negative impact on class room management. The present study aims to explore the impact on disruptive technology on disruptive class room behaviour of the students at school level.

1.2 Objective of the Study

As technology keeps on evolving and prohibition of physical reprimand in schools, it has become a quite challenging for the teachers to make the students to be determined with their studies, especially the behavioural, ethical and moral values, since the students are more well-versed with the law and technical environment. In possession of these challenges, the present study aims at the following objectives:

1. Examine the most recent disruptive technologies that are on stage in the market.
2. To access if Disruptive Technology (**DT**) influences the Disruptive Class Room Behaviour (**DCRB**) of the high school children in Bangalore.
3. Determine the dissimilar forms of Disruptive Behaviour (DB) as observed by the school teachers in Bangalore.
4. To advocate and endorse how to council and guide the students to realize the negative impact of disruptive technology on their behaviour.

2 Data Collection Technique and Methodology

A self-developed questionnaire on five-point likert scale Strongly Agree (**SA**), Agree (**A**), Neutral (**N**), Disagree (**DA**), and Strongly Agree (**SA**) was employed to explore the perceived observations of school children, teachers and parents regarding the extent of impact of disruptive technology on disruptive class room behaviour of school students through multistage random sampling. Questionnaire is administered with the help of drop-off survey [6]. Through multistage random sampling, 1000 respondents were selected from 20 schools (both public and private) in Bangalore. Respondents of 667 (66.7%) questionnaires were filled in and acknowledged.

3 Testing Framework

As exposed by the literature, the utmost communal investigational assessment methods in behavioural sciences today are experimental auctions [7]. Modelling consumer behaviour in the present context, the student disruptive behaviour may be problematic since the potential amount of zero values. A standard econometric procedure, ordinary least squares (OLS) will crop prejudiced and incompetent evaluations when the dependent variable includes zeros [8], while only counting students DT. Excluding observations can also root biased estimators due to a loss of valuable information [9].

The model can be expressed as follows:

(i) Exposure to DT

$$y_i = d \cdot y_i^{**} \tag{1a}$$

(ii) DT Adoption

$$w_i = \theta' z_i + u_i, \quad u_i \sim N(0, 1)$$
$$d = \begin{cases} 1 & \text{if } w_i > 0 \\ 0 & \text{otherwise} \end{cases} \tag{1b}$$

Both are assumed to be linear in their parameters (θ, β). The conditional probability of a value of u_i and v_i is excluded when these stochastic components are assumed to be uncorrelated.

The tentative Hypothesis set for this purpose is as below:

- **H1 (Demographic, Socio-economic characteristics):** Adoption of Disruptive Technology (**DT**) is a positive function of individual socio-demographic characteristics such as age, gender, economic status, residential area, parent's education. Their effects are undecided as several outcomes are stated in the literature.
- **H2 (Family Size):** Although family size and the presence of dependents are correlated, inclusion of both variables provided more information. Students with large family size are more likely to seek less expensive gadgets and adopt technology to economize [6].
- **H3 (Disruptive Technology adoption):** The additional amount that consumers will be willing to pay as compared to the conventional technology will depend upon certain factors; for instance, extraversion, agreeableness, openness, conscientiousness, neuroticism, reliability, appeal, accessibility and dependability are some of the landscapes that might have a constructive effect on the adoption of disruptive technology.
- **H4 (Disruptive Innovation Knowledge Index):** This particular component aims at analyzing the student knowledge about disruptive technology. Numerous questions are being asked in an attempt to capture students perception on disruptive technology adoption pros and cons.
- **H5 (Class room behaviour Index):** There is a positive relationship between impact of disruptive technology on school children and class room behaviour [8].

4 Literature Review

4.1 Disruptive Technology

The aspiration for the technology driven outside desktop, from smart phones and tablets to mobile apps and cloud computers has inspired a rapid growth of Big Data, high speed analytics, cloud computing and advanced cloud services (**Google or Apple's iCloud**), and more private clouds and hybrid clouds from businesses such as Flextronics, Siemens, Accenture, and manyothers. To highpoint few of them, **HaaS**, **SaaS**, Virtualization of Storage, Desktops Applications, and Networking, advanced simulations, Xbox and PlayStation, skill-based learning systemsare self-diagnostic and interactive, giving the user an immersive experience. Social Software for business has stretched a novel level of adoption to boost user friendly relationships, alliance, interacting and social validation.

For the purpose of this study, the following disruptive technologies are identified and observed:

Internet of Things (IoT): Which identifies objects and virtual representations in the internet, machine readable identifiers or minuscule identifying devices. These devices are generally used in health, mining manufacturing. etc. Though it is an interesting innovation, the danger of security risk is not ruled out.

Artificial Intelligence: A flexible agent that perceives its environment and takes the necessary action required, usually the cognitive functions of the human brainin learning and solving problems.

Space Colonization: NASA is the greatest example of space colonization with huge spacecrafts and with several space colonization projects such as the National Space Society and International Space Development Conference where students participate in contents.

3D Printing: 3D Printing is an advanced technology which is used to print settlements, space-stations and many others The Fig. 1 shows the statistics of worldwide 3D printing industry forecast.

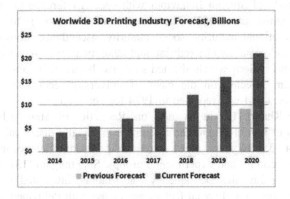

Fig. 1. World Wide 3D printing industry forecast. *Source:* https:i2.com

According to review, USA, Europe, and China are the top 3 places with the most 3D printer manufacturers in the world and will grow by 133% within three years, **from $9b in 2017 to $21b in 2020.**

Medical Innovations: Gene editing using CRISPR, cell-free fetal DNA testing, cancer screening through protein biomarker analysis, frictionless remote monitoring are some of the examples noted as Medical Innovations.

High-Speed Travel: Elon Musk, founder of the Hyperloop, intends to make Hyperloop One prototype propulsion system a reality before 2020 which can crack complex long distance matters, and has recently closed an $80 million funding round that includes investment from several other companies.

Robotics: Robotics with enhanced dexterity, senses, and intelligence which can accomplish errands that were formerly assumed affluent and tough are the exhilarating innovation disruptive technology, are becoming user friendly as days goes on among the most disruptive technologies of the 21st Century.

Autonomous Vehicles: Automated cars and drones that could operate and self-drive in many situations using advanced sensors such as LIDAR and other systems of communications from machines. These useful for farmers, architects, and even real estate agents [9][1].

Advanced Virtual Reality: Helps the users to enhance their memories or mental wellbeing, which is already at the commercial level. This is measured to be one of the significant DT.

4.2   Disruptive Behavior of School Children

Though there is no much literature available with reference to class room disruptive behaviour of the school children and influence of disruptive technology, the researcher tried to relate some of the social bond reasons [10] which can be related towards the advancement of the disruptive technology. Siddiqui [11], conducted a study on 'Social Psychological Study of Student Behaviour with special reference to indiscipline', at Aligarh Muslim University (**1962**). The objective of this study is to understand the psychological (emotional maturity, social maturity, ascendance-submission, security and aggression) and social factors (educational attainment, socio-economic status and rural or urban inhabitation) which affected students' behavior in general and indiscipline in particular, selected on the basis of university records, and opinions of authorities and peers and was repeated in **1974** for verification.

According to Khattri [12], in his study on 'Reduction of Abusive Behaviour as a function of types of reinforcement and awareness in socially disadvantaged children', with age group of 13 to 16 years, shows there is a significant difference in abusive word usage between the control and experimental groups. Shanmugam [13], 'Psychological Factors Underlying Juvenile Delinquency', at Madras, attempted to investigate a number of psychological and social factors associated with delinquency. Pareek [14–16], conducted a on Problematic Behaviour of Adolescents with special reference to their self and other acceptance and attitude towards freedom. The study identifies that the problematic adolescents have a distorted attitude towards their freedom and mostly depends on their home environment. Parwal [17], 'Disciplined Vs. In-disciplined Students: their personality and mental abilities', outlined disciplined and in disciplined students differ in introversion, extraversion, and mental abilities in terms of verbal reasoning, space relations, numerical ability, clerical speed and accuracy, and languageusage. Bhatt [18], in his study of 'A Comparative study of some Personality Traits of Problematic and Non-Problematic School-going Children'. Malhotra and Menon [19][2], 'Factors Contributing to Students' Indiscipline in the Polytechnics of

---

[1] https://books.google.co.in/books?isbn=0080516661.

[2] https://euacademic.org/UploadArticle/1247.pdf.

Haryana State'. independent study, attempts to identify the types of indiscipline, ragging, breaking furniture, wandering about the time the class was in progress, pulling out wire from switchboard and not bring the necessary material to the class, thus creating nuisance in the institution. Sharma and Pareek [20] looked into the managerial, disciplinary, financial, personal and academic problems faced by students. Dhondhyal [21], Personality Study of Victimised aggressors among Children', Singh, Meha [22][3], 'Effect of Family Violence on Adolescents Aggression and Reaction to Aggression', influential variable effecting reaction to aggression of the subjects. Poonam [23][4], 'The Effects of Parental Corporal Punishment on Self-esteem, Academic Achievement and Frustration Tolerance', Rajput, Sushil Kumar [24][5], 'Personal Determinant's of Mental Health among Sports Players', Shukla et al. [25][6], 'Violent Video Game: Gupta [26], 'Effect of Family Violence on Children's Cognitive Development and Social Responsibility. Pramod Kumar [27], 'A Study of Risk Taking Behaviour and Social Responsibility Among Sports Players', Pravin-Chandra [28], 'Peace Education Activity based Teaching', Edutracks, are some of the notable references.

5 Findings and Discussions

It is clearly evident that, the disruptive class room behaviour has created unrest among the teachers at school level. Based on this study observation, there is a positive correlation among the disruptive technology and disruptive behaviour among school children and seems indivisible. The teachers at schools are trying to identify and list out the students' problem behaviors in Bangalore. For this study, the author recognized the most common, disruptive and intolerable student class room behaviours, such as talking out of turn, verbal aggression, disrespecting teachers, non-attentiveness, daydreaming, idleness, sleeping, out of seat, habitual failure in submitting assignments, physical aggression, copying homework, nonverbal communication, clowning, playing, lateness to class, … etc. Other inimitable discoveries of this study are, "doing something in private", such as engaging more time on gadgets and electronic devices, than focusing on the academic affairs. Here would like to highlight on the recent threat the society had with online game "Blue Wale", Bangalore was listed one among the highest mobile users.

The other factors that are tested are personality traits, such as openness, conscientiousness, extraversion, agreeableness and neuroticism. Openness is considered as, a person who is open is people who considers himself as free and have unrestricted connection to awareness and information. Conscientiousness is the situation where a person cares for others, is discipline and very systematic in his work. A person is said to be extrovert when he is friendly, enjoy talk to people and cheerful. Agreeableness relates to warm, friendly and tactful. Finally, neuroticism is a stage is characterized by being anxious, moody and frustrated. The present study tries to relate these personality

---

[3] https://indiankanoon.org/doc/161538964/.

[4] journals.sagepub.com/doi/abs/https://doi.org/10.1177/0973184913411184.

[5] https://indiankanoon.org/doc/814655/.

[6] https://spst.up.nic.in/28-09-2017.pdf.

traits with the student's disruptive behavior along with other demographic, socioeconomic, political and environmental factors.

Table 1 shows, Disruptive Innovation Knowledge is 0.240 signifies the fractional outcome of Disruptive Technology adoption, holding the other path variables as constant. Unstandardized coefficient of Perception on Disruptive Innovation Knowledge is 0.392 represents the partial effect of Disruptive Technology adoption, holding the other path variables as constant. The estimated positive sign implies that such effect is positive that Satisfaction would increase by 0.392 for every unit increase in Perception and this coefficient value is significant at 1% level, 0.382 and 0.106. For the purpose of testing the model fit, null hypothesis and alternative hypothesis are framed Hypothesis X, Null hypothesis: The hypothesized model has a good fit.

Table 1. Table of descriptive analysis of variables

Variables	Mean	SD	Minimum	Maximum
Dependent variable				
Disruptive class room behaviour	3.06278	1.20712	1	5
Age	36.1629	12.8367	12	79
Gender				
Male	0.51719	0.50008	0	1
Female	0.48281	0.50008	0	1
Residential area				
Urban	0.63378	0.48213	0	1
Rural	0.36024	0.48043	0	1
Educational achievement				
8th std	0.27504	0.44687	0	1
9th std	0.22123	0.41538	0	1
10th std	0.32735	0.4696	0	1
Others (teachers and parents)	0.17788	0.3827	0	1
Family income				
Level 1: Below Rs 20000	0.14499	0.35236	0	1
Level 2: Rs 20000–Rs 30000	0.30344	0.46009	0	1
Level 3: Rs 30000–Rs 40000	0.30344	0.46009	0	14
Level 4: Above Rs 40000	3.97459	1.19164	1	5
Family size				
Disruptive innovation knowledge index	2.22721	1.19972	1	4
Disruptive technology adoption	2.49626	1.0477	1	4
Personality traits				
Openness	2.66368	1.09252	1	5
Conscientiousness	2.94519	0.79019	1	5
Extraversion	3.89586	0.82659	1	5
Agreeableness	3.44494	0.84325	1	5
Neuroticism	3.72496	0.73937	1	

Source: Computed. *Note:* N = 1679

Alternate hypothesis: The hypothesized model does not have a good fit.

The study also extended to test the coefficients using SEM (structural equation modeling) by creating a path diagram. The diagram 1 below shows Confirmatory Factor Analysis (CFA) of Impact of Disruptive Technology on Disruptive classroom behavior among school children (Fig. 2; Tables 2, 3).

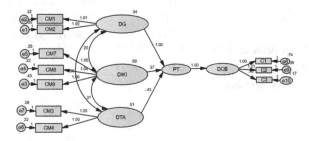

Fig. 2. Structural Equation Model (SEM) based on Standardised Coefficient Impact of Disruptive Technology on Disruptive classroom behavior among school children. *Source*: Authors computation. DG: Demographic indices; DIKI: Disruptive Innovation Knowledge; DTA: Disruptive Technology adoption, PT: PersonalityTraits; DCB: Disruptive Classroom Behaviour

Table 2. Variables in the structural equation model analysis

Variables			Unstandardised co-efficient (B)	S.E of B	Standardized coefficient (Beta)	t value	P value
Openness	←	Disruptive innovation knowledge	0.240	0.035	0.455	6.846	<0.001**
Conscientiousness	←	Perception	0.242	0.042	0.379	5.692	<0.001**
Extraversion	←	Perception	0.392	0.053	0.510	7.336	<0.001**
Agreeableness	←	Expectation	0.382	0.084	0.317	4.565	<0.001**
Neuroticism	←	Disruptive technology adoption	0.106	0.025	0.329	4.249	<0.001**

Note: ** Denotes significant at 1% level, *Source*: Authors computation

Table 3. Confirmatory Factor Analysis (CFA) of Impact of Disruptive Technology on Disruptive classroom behavior among school children

Indices	Enabler	Barrier	Suggested value
Number of statements before CFA	6	8	
Chi-square value	3.296	14.308	
DF			
Chi-square/Df			<5.00 (Hair et al. [29])
P value	0.655	0.112	>0.05 (Hair et al. [29])

(*continued*)

Table 3. (*continued*)

Indices	Enabler	Barrier	Suggested value
GFI	0.988		>0.90 (Hu and Bentler [31])
AGFI	0.963		>0.90 (Hair et al. [30])
NFI	0.977		>0.90 (Hu and Bentler [31])
CFI	1.000		>0.90 (Daire et al. [32])
RMR	0.011		<0.08 (Hair et al. [30])
RMSEA	0.000		<0.08 (Hair et al. [30])
Number of statements after CFA	5	6	
Cronbach Alpha	0.806	0.773	>0.6

Source: Authors computation

6   Conclusions and Recommendations

The study found from the empirical evidence that, the students class room disruptive behaviour is a big challenge and it is highly influential by their knowledge towards the disruptive technology, perception and level of adoption at schools of Bangalore. The teachers have unanimously reported the presence of disruptive behaviour among most of the school children and is evidenced strongly due to addiction to the gadgets and mobile devices.

These are some of the recommendations made from the findings of this study:

1. Teaching pedagogy and teaching methods need to be reviewed in the framework of student's disruptive behaviour to avoid or minimize the impacts of disruptive behaviour.
2. The well experienced professionals in juvenile domain need to be deployed to visit the secondary schools and deliver lectures periodically, keeping disruptive behaviour under consideration.
3. Frequent workshops, Seminars for parents, teachers and students may be arranged on the topic of disruptive behaviour to highlight the impacts, remedies and repercussions of student's disruptive behavior.
4. Some standing operating procedures may be introduced as remedy to disruptive behaviour on provinciallevel, preferably strict rule on no entry for gadgets at school premises and also control at un wanted exposure to disruptive technology at house.

References

1. King, A.A., Baatartogtokh, B.: Strategy, innovation, innovation strategy, developing strategy. How useful is the theory of disruptive innovation? (2015)
2. The McKinsey Global Institute (MGI): Global go to think tank index report published on January 31, 2018 by the Think Tank and Civil Society Program at the Lauder Institute, University of Pennsylvania (2017)

3. Tupes, E.C., Christal, R.E.: Recurrent personality factors based on trait ratings. Technical report ASD-TR-61-97, Personnel Laboratory, Air Force Systems Command, Lackland Air Force Base, TX (1961)

4. Digman, J.M.: Personality structure: emergence of the five-factormodel. Annu. Rev. Psychol. **41**, 417–440 (1990)

5. Burgelman, R.A., Maidique, M.A., Wheelwright, S.C.: Strategic Management of Technology and Innovation. McGraw-Hill, New York (2001)

6. Gebrezgabher, et al.: Evaluation of new farming technologies in Ethiopia using the Integrated Decision Support System (IDSS) (2017)

7. Corrigan, P.W., Larson, J.E., Ruesch, N.: Self-stigma and the "why try" effect: impact on life goals and evidence-based practices. World Psychiatry **8**(2), 75–81 (2009)

8. Tobler, M., et al.: An indigenous religious ritual selects for resistance to a toxicant in a level bearing fish (2011). https://www.researchgate.net/publication/236625781_Tobler_et_al_2011_Indigenous_ritural

9. Judge, G.G., Hill, R.C., Griffiths, W. E., Lutkepohl, H., Lee, T.-C.: Introduction to the Theory and Practice of Econometrics, 2nd edn. Wiley, New York (1988). TIME Magazine Cover: The ME MEME Generation

10. Hirschi's 1969, Causes of Delinquency, University of California Press, Social Science (1969)

11. Siddiqui, M.M.: On the inversion of the sample covariance matrix in a stationary autoregressive process. Ann. Math. Stat. (1976)

12. Khattri, P.K.: An optimized technique for determining stacking velocity from seismic reflection data, 1980 (1979). https://doi.org/10.1111/j.1365-2478.1980.tb01263.x

13. Shanmugam, T.E.: Psychological Factors Underlying Juvenile Delinquency. Madras University, Madras (1980)

14. Pareek, U.: Reliability of the Indian adaptation of Rosenzweig P-F study (children's form). J. Psychol. Res. **2**, 18–23 (1958)

15. Pareek, U.: Some preliminary data about the Indian adaptation of Resenzweg P-F study (children's form). Educ. Psychol. **5**, 105–113 (1958)

16. Pareek, U.: Studying cultural differences in personality development with the help of Rosenzweig P-F study (1958)

17. Parwal, S.: Development of EHV Cables. Institute of Electrical Engineers, Mumbai (1987)

18. Copel, S.L.: Behaviour Pathology of Childhood and Adolescence. Basic Books Inc., New York (Bhatt, D.B. 1990) (1973)

19. Malhotra, M.M., Menon, P.N.: Reviewing learner evaluation in india: an inside story (After Independence - 2000). European Academic Research, vol. II, Issue 10/January 2015 (1991)

20. Sharma, R., Mishra, M., Gupta, B., Parsania, C., Singla-Pareek, S.L., Pareek, A.: De novo assembly and characterization of stress transcriptome in a salinity-tolerant variety CS52 of Brassica juncea. PLoS ONE, e0126783 (2015). http://dx.doi.org/10.1371/journal.pone.0126783

21. Dhondhyal, S.: Personality study of victimised aggressors among children. Unpublished Doctoral thesis, Ch. Charan Singh University, Meerut (2007)

22. https://indiankanoon.org/doc/161538964/

23. TeacherEmpowerment, The Education Entitlement–Social Transformation Traverse, Poonam Batra, First Published January 1 (2009)

24. JUDGMENT Manmohan Sarin, J Page 3817, Sushil Kumar Rajput vs Director Of Education And Ors. on 24 November, 2006, Equivalent citations: 139 DLT 104 (2007)

25. http://www.spst.up.nic.in/28-09-2017.pdf
26. Ilgin, M.A., Gupta, S.M.: Environmentally conscious manufacturing and product recovery (ECMPRO): a review of the state of the art. J. Environ. Manag. **91**(3), 563–591 (2010)
27. Yadawa, P.K.: Computational study of ultrasonic parameters of HCP transition metals Fe, Co and Ni. Arab. J. Sci. Eng. **37**, 255–262 (2012)
28. Pravin-Chandra, K.R.: Occupational and environmental health: an integral part of community health. RGUHS J. Med. Sci. **12**(4), 34–38 (2011)
29. Hair, J., Anderson, R., Tatham, R.L., Black, W.C.: Multivariate data analysis (5th ed.). Prentice-Hall, Upper Saddle River, NJ (1998)
30. Hair, J.F., Black, W.C., Babin, B.J., Anderson, R.E., Tatham, R.L.: Multivariate Data Analysis (6th ed.). Prentice Hall (2006)
31. Hu, L., Bentler, P.M.: Evaluating model fit. In: Hoyle, R. (Ed.): Structural equation modeling: issues, concepts, and applications, pp. 76–99. Sage, Newbury Park, CA (1999)
32. Daire, et al.: Structural equation modelling: guidelines for determining model fit, p. 2. (2008). Articles

Learners' Satisfaction Analysis Using Machine Learning Approaches

Maksud Ahamad(✉) and Nesar Ahmad

Department of Computer Engineering, Aligarh Muslim University,
Aligarh, Uttar Pradesh, India
maksud.ahmad12@gmail.com, nesar.ahmad@gmail.com

Abstract. In this competitive world, the Universities have the challenge to genuinely analyze their performance with respect to teaching-learning process. The teacher and students should be answerable to each other. To analyze the teaching- learning performance, the feedback is very basic and essential tool. Here we present student feedback analysis concerning the instructor or educator using machine learning algorithms. In this paper, first, we grouped the feedback data from the University students to get a useful pattern with the help of clustering algorithms like K-means and EM (Expectation Maximization) and chosen the best one. After finding the clusters from feedback dataset, we have assigned three categories as, satisfactory, neutral, and dissatisfactory and used them as class labels for classification purpose. We have applied Naive Bayes, Multilayer Perceptron Neural Network, Random Forest (RF) and Support Vector Machine (SVM) classifier and found that Naïve Bayes got the highest accuracy, precision, and recall values as compare to the other classifiers. The results obtained here indicate the satisfaction level of students with a particular instructor is less positive as compared to other instructors.

Keywords: Machine learning · Clustering · Data mining algorithms
Classification

1 Introduction

In the educational environment, evaluating the performance, importance and value of learning process, are using to performance improvement. For the quality education at Institutions or Universities assessment of teaching quality and tracking the performance of students is very much important. As the role of a teacher in an educational Institution is very important to enhance student learning performance and the standard of education [3]. Universities collect the feedback from the students regarding subjects taught by the teachers. Now with this collected information, some opinion can be made by the administrators [1]. The collected data as feedback from students contains valuable data and with the help of artificial intelligence and machine learning, some patterns could be found. These patterns help educators to improve their performance.

Performance evaluation has long been involved in education system, mainly higher education to the success of educational programs and quality of education. One method of evaluating the effective teaching in higher education is teachers and students

© Springer Nature Singapore Pte Ltd. 2018
M. Singh et al. (Eds.): ICACDS 2018, CCIS 906, pp. 239–248, 2018.
https://doi.org/10.1007/978-981-13-1813-9_24

evaluation. The feedback of students may be used to provide some suggestions for an instructor.

The rest of the paper is structured as follows. In Sect. 2 related studies are discussed. In Sect. 3 preprocessing phase is included where indicators for performance measures are discussed. In Sect. 4 methodology used in this study is discussed. Result analysis and discussion are included in Sect. 5. Finally, Conclusion achieved from this study is described in Sect. 6.

2 Related Work

Kabakchieva [4], used K-nearest neighbor, decision tree, Bayesian classifiers, rule learners to find student's performance from the data collected. This study reported the best result from any algorithms or classifiers is 60–75% accurate, which is not remarkable to the importance of the work related to the performance evaluation.

Gunduzet et al. analyzed the data and found some interesting pattern with the help of supervised and unsupervised algorithms. Gunduz grouped the data with K-Means algorithm and hierarchical clustering algorithm, using R software. The clusters found here measured as an objective variable. The questions in spite of the other fields (difficulty level of course content, class, attendance, the frequency of repetition of a course) used as the input. With the help of decision tree technique, they found 93% of data accuracy for the classification [1].

The model presented here [6], with the help of clustering to improve the overall learning performance of educational institutions. They found some hidden patterns that could be helpful for curriculum planners, instructors, and others related to this [6]. Oyedotunn et al. predicted the success rate of students to pass the course. They used Radial Basis Function and propagation network. They mapped the features included in training to the frequency of repetition before clear the course. Result found in this study indicates that the propagation network gives better performance as compared to the radial function [5].

3 Preprocessing

Indicators: There are two different types of evaluating measures are recognized and compared to performance assessment outcome:

A. Visualization: With the help of ROC (Receiver Operating Curve) and Reject curves, the result of true values and false values for classifiers can be represented.

B. Statistical Analysis: mathematical formulae are used to evaluate the produced results of different classifiers like Confusion Matrix (accuracy), Recall, Precision, Sensitivity, F-Measure, and Specificity.

Confusion Matrix: It shows the share of errors along with all classes. Classifier accuracy is calculated as given below [8]:

$$\textbf{Accuracy} = (\text{TP(True Positive)} + \text{TN(True Negative)})/(\text{TP} + \text{TN} + \text{FP} + \text{FN}) * 100\%$$

Precision: It is a percentage of TP (true positive) and the values that are misclassified like positive *i.e. FP*. **Precision = TP/(TP + FP)**

Recall/Sensitivity and Specificity: Recall is a fraction of the correctly classified objects i.e. TP and the values that are classified incorrectly i.e. false negative. Results in true negative values are specified by Specificity.

$$\textbf{Recall/Sensitivity} = \text{TP}/(\text{TP} + \text{FN}) * 100\% \quad \textbf{Specificity} = \text{TN}/(\text{TN} + \text{FP}) * 100\%$$

F-Measure: It is another usual performance metrics that integrates recall and precision into a single value [9]. The formula is given below as:

$$\textbf{F--Measure} = 2 * (\text{precision} * \text{recall})/(\text{precision} + \text{recall})$$

ROC curve: Receiver Operating Curve (ROC) is linked with Error Type I and Error Type II. It represents the values of "False Positive" and "False Negative".

$$\text{Type I Error} = \frac{\text{FN}}{\text{TP} + \text{FN}} \quad \text{and Type II Error} = \frac{\text{FP}}{\text{TN} + \text{FP}}$$

4 Methodology

4.1 Data Set

Turkiye Student Evaluation dataset used in this paper is available at UCI repository of machine learning databases [2]. The data is collected with the help of 5820 students from a University. This dataset contains thirty-three attributes. All the attributes/questions are related to course content and instructor. Out of thirty-three attributes/questions, Q1 to Q12 are associated with course content and questions Q13 to Q28 are associated with the instructor [2, 6]. Rests of the five attributes are related to the difficulty level of course, class, attendance, no of times repeated the course and instructor identifier. The data set contains a category of the questions regarding the timing of course content, evaluating system and objective of the course. Another category of question is related educational material, evaluating scheme and satisfaction level of students with the course content.

The Questions related to the instructor are categorized as instructor level of knowledge, discipline, attitude towards students and evaluating perspective towards students. The summary of data set is available in Table 1.

Table 1. Summary of dataset

Total no of students	5820
Total no of attributes/questions	33
Course specific attributes (Q1 to Q28), possible values	28, {1, 2, 3, 4, 5}
Non-course specific attributes	05
Instructor identifier	{1, 2, 3}
Course code	{1–13}
No of times student repeating the course	{0, 1, 2, 3...}
Attendance level	{0, 1, 2, 3, 4}
Difficulty level of course perceived by student	{1, 2, 3, 4, 5}

4.2 Tool and Algorithms Used

In this study, we used Weka (Waikato Environment for Knowledge Analysis) software which is a well- known tool for machine learning software written in Java. It is developed at the University of Waikato, New Zealand. Weka is free software accessible under the GNU (General Public License) [7, 16].

The assessment and analysis of students or learners feedback data is a complex process. As there are so many issues, like the seriousness of students, parameters to evaluation are according to standard etc. To get any relation between given students feedback and the instructor, first we have to find, is there any information can be clustered or grouped? In different words, can we group student's feedback information that indicates some pattern to analysis the instructor performance? For analysis the cluster we are using two clustering algorithm. One is K-means and another one is Expectation maximization (EM). K-Means clustering algorithm, as the name suggests is based on the computation of averages that represent the centers of possible essential groups. We have used different classification techniques in this study as given below.

The **Naive Bayes (NB)** gives a straightforward approach, with learning probabilistic knowledge. It relies on two assumptions, the attributes using in prediction are independent given class and there are no suppressed attributes, control the prediction [12, 16].

MLP (Multilayer Perceptron) is normally used the neural network for classification purpose. The used architecture for the MLP throughout simulations with student's dataset includes three layers network: one input, one hidden, and one output layer. Parameters used for the model are: learning Rate = 0.3, momentum = 0.2, validation Threshold = 20, random Seed = 0, Number of Epochs = 500 [13].

RF (Random Forest) classifier is an ensemble of decision tree classifiers and developed to advance the classification accuracy [14, 15]. Each tree classifier in this, vote for the best class of any sample and the resultant class label is then identified via a majority voting method [16].

SVM (Support Vector Machines) also known as maximum margin classifiers, find out the optimal hyperplane that maximizes the distance between the hyperplane and support vectors [10]. These Support vectors are used as training vectors that are nearby from each class to the hyperplane. SVM can classify linear and non-linear separable data with the help of kernel function [11].

5 Result Analysis and Discussion

To evaluate the effectiveness of this work, we did some experiments using the performance measures indicators mentioned above. We are analyzing the dataset used in this study, separately for the instructors. We have analyzed the clusters with the help of centroid. Here we are using the Silhouette indices to find the better clustering [17]. With the Silhouette indicator, we found three clusters. Table 2, shows, the students who are highly satisfied with instructor 1, is 48% for K-means clustering and for EM (Expectation Maximization) is 47%. Another group has neutral views about the performance of instructor and the numbers are 33% and 35% for K-means and EM algorithms respectively. Lastly, the third group has the students who are not satisfied and the numbers are 19% and 18%. We can draw the same explanation for the rest of instructors included in the dataset from Table 2. As we can see from the Table 2, the percentages of students divided among different clusters are almost same for the K-means and EM algorithms. Here we have chosen EM algorithms to assign the class label because it is more significant as compared to K-means. It is undoubtedly would be more remarkable in the context of instructor's progress, to extract such clustering for each course and for the common course taught by instructors.

Table 2. Similar groups extracted from k-means and EM clustering algorithms

Instructor	K-means clustering			EM (expectation maximization) clustering		
	Cluster 1	Cluster 2	Cluster 3	Cluster 1	Cluster 2	Cluster 3
1	48%	33%	19%	47%	35%	18%
2	18%	42%	40%	46%	39%	15%
3	33%	43%	24%	32%	45%	23%
Proposed class label	Satisfactory	Neutral	Dissatisfactory	Satisfactory	Neutral	Dissatisfactory

With the help of clustering algorithms, we are assigning three labels as, {Satisfactory, Neutral, and Dissatisfactory} which are extracted from grouping the data. After labeling to the dataset, we have applied a variety of classification algorithms to analyze the feedback dataset to pattern recognition. Running different Machine learning algorithms on the selected dataset and came into the light that Naive Bayes (NB) got the highest classification accuracy (A), precision (P) and recall(R) for all the instructor as compare to multilayer perceptron neural network (NN), Random Forest (RF) and Support Vector Machine (SVM). As we can see from Table 3, for Naive Bayes the accuracies are 99.4%, 99.1%, 99.3% for instructor 1, instructor 2 and instructor 3 respectively.

Table 3. Performance comparisons of NB, NN, RF, and SVM

Instructor	NB			NN			RF			SVM		
	A	P	R	A	P	R	A	P	R	A	P	R
1	0.994	0.995	0.995	0.974	0.975	0.974	0.981	0.982	0.982	0.987	0.987	0.987
2	0.991	0.992	0.992	0.976	0.977	0.976	0.974	0.974	0.974	0.982	0.983	0.983
3	0.993	0.993	0.993	0.983	0.983	0.983	0.978	0.978	0.978	0.985	0.986	0.986

Based on the results which we found with different algorithm applied to the selected dataset, the graph is plotted which is in Fig. 1. Figure 1 shows the performance of different algorithms which we have applied.

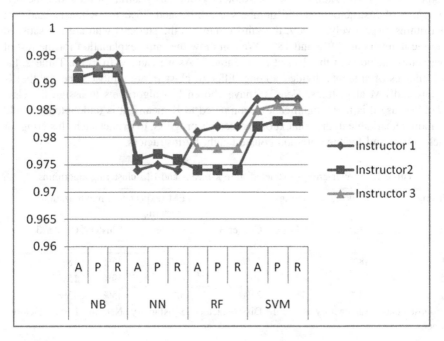

Fig. 1. Results comparisons of NB, NN, RF and SVM with Accuracy (A), Precision (P) and Recall(R)

Table 4 contains the results for the average accuracy of all the classifiers used in the study for an individual instructor. Here we found that instructor 2 got less accuracy as compare to instructor 1 and instructor 3. The average accuracy of all the algorithms for a particular instructor plotted in Fig. 2.

Table 4. Average accuracies for all the classifies.

Instructor	Average accuracy
Instructor 1	0.984
Instructor 2	0.981
Instructor 3	0.985

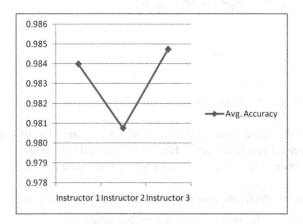

Fig. 2. Performance comparison of instructors with average accuracy

To evaluate the satisfactory level of students more significantly, we have reduced the class label to two (satisfactory and not satisfactory) from three (Satisfactory, Neutral, and Dissatisfactory) as above used. With different machine learning algorithms and cluster centroid analysis, we can see from Table 5 and Fig. 3, the satisfied students with instructor 2 are 55%, as compare to 76% and 70% for instructor 1 and instructor 3 respectively.

Table 5. Accuracies for instructors with two class label.

Instructor	Satisfactory	Not satisfactory
Instructor 1	76%	24%
Instructor 2	55%	45%
Instructor 3	70%	30%

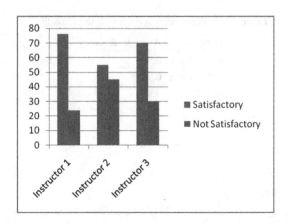

Fig. 3. Performance comparison with two class labels

Table 6 and Fig. 4 are showing the result which we found for the common course taught by instructor 2 and instructor 3. Here we found that 80% of the student showing satisfaction for instructor 2 as compared to 61% for the instructor 3.

Table 6. The results for the common course taught by instructor 2 and instructor 3.

Instructor	Satisfactory	Not satisfactory
Instructor 2	80%	20%
Instructor 3	61%	39%

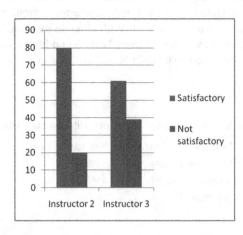

Fig. 4. Performance comparison for the common course

6 Conclusion

In this paper, we have analyzed the satisfaction level of the student with the course and instructor who taught a particular course. Here we used the supervised and unsupervised algorithm for the purpose of some useful pattern finding and classification. The algorithms used here are K-means and EM (Expectation Maximization) as clustering algorithm and Naive Bayes, Neural Network, Random Forest and Support Vector Machine (SVM) for classification purpose. We found that Naïve Bayes shows the highest accuracy, precision, and recall values as compared to other classifiers used. Naive Bayes's accuracies are 99.4%, 99.1% and 99.3% for instructor1, instructor 2 and instructor 3 respectively. For common subject taught by the instructor 2 and instructor 3, the instructor 2 had less positive feedback as compared to another. That means the instructor needs improvement in teaching-learning.

References

1. Gündüz N., Fokoue E.: Data Mining and Machine Learning Techniques for Extracting Patterns in Students' evaluations of Instructors. Rochester Institute of Technology, The John D. Hromi Center for Quality and Applied Statistics (KGCOE), pp. 1–28 (2013)
2. Gunduz, G., Fokoue, E.: UCI machine learning repository. The University of California, School of Information and Computer Science, Irvine (2013). http://archive.ics.uci.edu/ml/datasets/Turkiye+Student+Evaluation
3. Qu, H., Li, X.: Application of data mining the assessment of teaching quality. Front. Futur. Dev. Inf. Technol. Med. Educ. Lect. Notes Electr. Eng. **269**, 1813–1919 (2014)
4. Kabakchieva, D.: Predicting student performance by using data mining methods for classification. Cybern. Inf. Technol. **13**, 66–71 (2013)
5. Oyedotun, K., Tackie, N., Ebenezer, O.: Data mining of students' performance: Turkish students as a case study. Intell. Syst. Appl. **7**(9), 20 (2015)
6. Abaidullah, A.M., Ahmed, N., Ali, E.: Identifying hidden patterns in students' feedback through cluster analysis. Int. J. Comput. Theory Eng. **7**(1), 16–20 (2015)
7. Hall, M., Frank, E., Holmes, G., Pfahringer, G.B., Reutemann, P., Witten, I.H.: The WEKA, data mining software: an update. SIGKDD Explor. **11**(1), 10–18 (2009)
8. Sokolova, M., Lapalme, G.: A systematic analysis of performance measures for classification tasks. Inf. Proc. Manag. **45**, 427–437 (2009)
9. https://www.cs.cornell.edu/courses/cs578/2003fa/performance_measures.pdf
10. Chapelle, O., Haffner, P., Vapnik, V.N.: Support vector machines for histogram-based image classification. IEEE Trans. Neural Netw. **10**(5), 1055–1064 (1999)
11. Hofmann, T., Scholkopf, B., Smola, A.J.: Kernel methods in machine learning. Ann. Stat. Inst. Math. Stat. **36**(3), 1171–1220 (2008)
12. John, G.H., Langley, P.: Estimating continuous distributions in bayesian classifiers. In: Proceedings of the 11th Conference on Uncertainty in Artificial Intelligence, pp. 338–345. Morgan Kaufmann Publishers, San Francisco (1995)
13. Du, K.-L., Swamy, M.N.S.: Neural Networks and Statistical Learning. Springer, London (2014). https://doi.org/10.1007/978-1-4471-5571-3
14. Kuncheva, L.: Combining Pattern Classifiers: Methods and Algorithms. Wiley, Hoboken (2004)

15. Thanh Noi, P., Kappas, M.: Comparison of random forest, k-nearest neighbor, and support vector machine classifiers for land cover classification using sentinel-2 imagery. Sensors **18**, 18 (2017)
16. Witten, I.H., Frank, E., Mark, A.H.: Data Mining: Practical Machine Learning Tools and Techniques. Morgan Kaufmann, Burlington (2011)
17. Rousseeuw, P.: Silhouettes: a graphical aid to the interpretation and validation of cluster analysis. J. Comput. Appl. Math. **20**, 53–65 (1987)

Data Analysis: Opinion Mining and Sentiment Analysis of Opinionated Unstructured Data

Harshi Garg[✉] and Niranjan Lal

Mody University of Science and Technology, Lakshmangarh,
Sikar, Rajasthan, India
harshi123har@gmail.com, niranjan_verma51@yahoo.com

Abstract. With the evolution of technology, there is also a huge increase in unstructured data. Now a day's social media is an obvious source of current opinions and reviews and to extract the valuable suggestions on the basis of comments and opinions given on social network is very important. This paper includes data analysis and data mining with a special emphasis on Opinion mining and sentiment analysis. It is one of the most vigorous research areas in natural language processing and is also widely studied in areas like Web mining, and text mining. This paper tackles a comprehensive overview of last update in this field. For the very first time in human history, we now have a huge volume of opinionated data recorded in digital form for analysis. Users not only use the resources but also give their opinions and suggestions in the form of feedback for the improvement of the existing system. It is very important to analyze their opinions and to extract the valuable opinions and suggestions from the comments. This paper proposed algorithms of machine learning and lexicon based approaches to address the issue arised due to lack of analyzing tools.

Keywords: Opinion mining · Sentiment analysis · SVM · Naïve bayes
Lexicon-based · Machine learning

1 Introduction

In the present digital scenario, there is a vast progress and development of the web and online world wide technologies, due to this we aspect a huge volume of data and information present from many different resources services and sites which were not available to people just a few years ago. Data Analysis is the study of analyzing data and deriving business results from it and data mining discovers patterns in large data sets.

With the increase in questionnaire to get feedback about people's opinion in order to improve decision making, How to extract the valuable information from comments and suggestions, become the demand in many areas, and thus the opinion analysis for the data mining become a research focus in the field of data mining. Opinion Analysis and Sentiment Analysis is a method of automatic extraction of key knowledge from the opinion of others about some product review or problem. It is a computational mechanism that classifies the user's opinions either positive, negative or neutral comments and quotes underlying the text. This task is technically very challenging and practically very useful.

© Springer Nature Singapore Pte Ltd. 2018
M. Singh et al. (Eds.): ICACDS 2018, CCIS 906, pp. 249–258, 2018.
https://doi.org/10.1007/978-981-13-1813-9_25

Various algorithms in recent years are proposed to address the issue such as we can develop opinion classification system using Maximum Entropy (ME) and K-Means Clustering. Various data-driven techniques like Naïve Byes, HMM Pos Tagger and SVM can also be used [6]. To classify the sentiments we can use two approaches either machine learning or lexicon based approaches. A system is also proposed [9] which extracts opinions and aspects of products and it is a two stage process, the very first is knowledge extraction and sentiment analysis. In the first stage, NLP tools are used which extracts the syntactic knowledge and then opinions aspect relations are implied. Knowledge from the first stage is used to analyze new reviews and then summary is generated.

We have organized this paper as follows. Section 2 defines Opinion Mining and its synonyms used, Sect. 3 explains the previous work done in searching and ranking, Sect. 4 illustrates the classification approaches present, Sect. 5 explains the architecture of system, Sect. 6 explains the application areas, Sect. 7 explains the tools used in this field, Sect. 8 explains the research challenges arised, Sect. 9 conclude the paper with future directions.

2 Opinion Mining and Sentiment Analysis

Opinion Mining is a kind of natural language processing which helps in evaluating "What other people think"? Opinion mining deals with the opinion of the text while sentiment analysis score the opinions either positive, negative or neutral. It is well suited to various intelligence applications to improve their decision making process (Fig. 1).

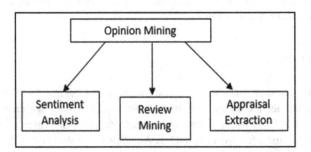

Fig. 1. Synonyms for opinion mining

3 Related Work

Pang and Lee [1] illustrated that availability of huge resources such as blogs, articles and information on web makes it necessary for us to deal with the computational usage of opinion, sentiments and subjectivity of words in text. They include wider issues related to manipulation, privacy and economic effect that the development of opinion-oriented information gives rise to access services based on review of people.

Haseena Rahmath [2] illustrated that people's opinion are very valuable for decision making. Due to the increased popularity of sites like FaceBook, twitter resulted huge collection of data in an unstructured manner. This give rise to emerging field opinion mining so that valuable opinions can be extracted from feedbacks. Various challenges and research applications like detection of fake reviews and arrogant words are discussed by author.

Kalarani et al. [3] illustrated that opinions reflect person's perspective, understanding, desires and attitudes. Several websites on web encourages users to express their feedbacks related to product, suggestions, comments related to product, policies and services. Extraction of useful opinions from these sources is a challenging task. Author discussed various challenges related to opinion mining.

Mago [4] illustrated that researchers aims to distinguish the opinions as positive or negative and summarize them in such a way which is easily understood by decision makers. Opinion Mining can be used for information retrieval and web data analysis. Author discussed various approaches which can be used to identify the sentiments and can be used for classify the polarity of opinions.

Songpan [7] illustrated that opinions can be open and close opinion. The open opinion refers the comment which shows emotions directly from consumer. But issue arises when customer give rating contrast along with comments. Author proposes the study and prediction rating related to customer reviews using probability's classifier model.

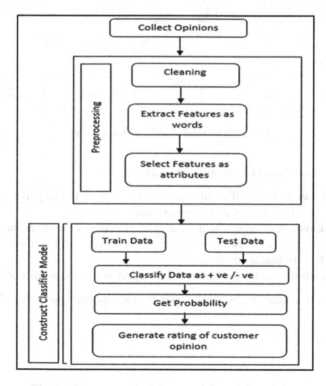

Fig. 2. Common methodology used for opinion mining

Guellil et al. [9] illustrated a survey in the form of table which includes all the research work done in the field of opinion mining and sentiment analysis. They considered 60 research papers and compare the work among various criterias.

Osimo et al. [10] presents the research challeneges arised in this field. GC1: Model based collaborative Governance and GC2: Data Powered Collective Intelligence and Action (Fig. 2).

4   Sentiment Analysis Classification Approaches

The goal of Sentiment Classification (SC) is to discover opinions, identify the sentiments and classify the polarity of opinions accordingly. Sentiment analysis classification is illustrated in the below Fig. 3.

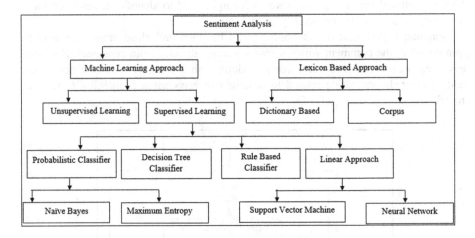

Fig. 3. Sentiment classification categories

There are three main classification levels exists:

- **Document-Level:** It classifies an opinion into positive and negative opinion and considers the whole text as an elementary information unit.
- **Sentence-Level:** It classifies sentiment in each sentence however there exist no fundamental difference between document and sentence level because sentences are just short text documents available.
- **Aspect Level:** It classifies sentiments with respect to specific aspects of entities [7].

Sentiment Classification (SC) techniques is based on two approaches (Fig. 4):

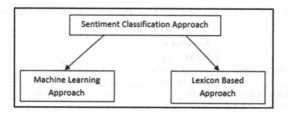

Fig. 4. Sentiment classification approach

4.1 Machine Learning Approach

In this mainly SVM which is used to classify text as either positive or negative and Naïve Bayes classifiers which is used to classify sentiment and this sentiment orientation performs well with more accuracy are used to classify sentiments and survey stated that SVM performs better than Naïve Bayes [6].

4.1.1 Naïve Bayes Classifier(NB)

This is the most frequently used classifier which computes the posterior probability of a class, this is based on the distribution of the words in the document. This classifier uses Bayes theorem to calculate the probability that a given feature set belongs to a particular label.

$$P(label|features) = \frac{P(label) * P(features|label)}{P(features)} \tag{1}$$

where P(label) is the prior probability of a label. P(features|label) is the prior probability that a given feature set is being classified as a label. P(features) is the prior probability that a given feature set is occurred.

4.1.2 Support Vector Machine Classifier (SVM)

It's principle is to determine linear separators in the search space which can best separate different classes. SVM can construct a nonlinear decision surface in the original feature space by mapping the data objects non-linearly to an inner product space where the classes can be separated linearly with a hyperplane. A separating hyper plane is written as:

$$W * X + b = 0 \tag{2}$$

where $W = \{w1, w2, w3, ..., wn\}$
wn is defined as weight vector of n attributes and b is defined as bias.

4.2 Lexicon Based Approach

In this Semantic orientation (SO) of expressions is determined as positive if it is more related to "best" and is considered to negative if it is more related to "poor". So SO values are dependent on calculation result which is calculated by taking average of SO value of all expressions which has been extracted (Table 1).

Table 1. Comparison between lexicon-based and machine learning

Parameters	Machine Learning	Lexicon-Based		
Classification Approach	Supervised	Unsupervised		
Domain	Dependent	Independent		
Statistical Significance	More	Less (Small Dataset)		
Require prior training of Dataset	Yes	No		
Adaptive Learning	Yes	No		
Accuracy	High	Low, Depends on Lexical Resources.		
		Resource	**Coverage**	
		SentiWordNet	117,659	
		WordNet Affect	200	
		SenticNet	14,000	
		MPQA	8,222	
Sensitive to quality and quantity of data	More	Little		
Time of Result Generation	Slow	Fast		
Maintenance	Not Required	Need maintenance of corpus		
Training Require	Yes	No		

5   Proposed Architecture of Opinion Mining

Proposed architecture is shown in Fig. 5 involves three key steps: the very first step is Opinion Retrieval then Opinion Classification and last Opinion Summarization. Opinions are retrieved from several review websites and many sources which can be

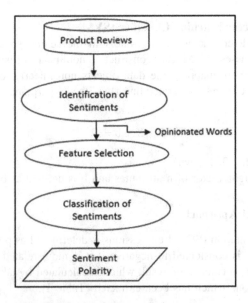

Fig. 5. Sentiment analysis process

either positive or negative review. At the end a summary is generated by considering it's frequent appearing features (Fig. 6).

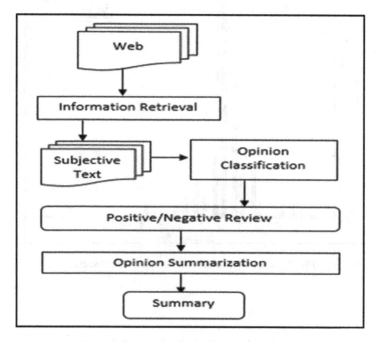

Fig. 6. Architecture of opinion mining

6 Applications of Opinion Mining

Different application are present in opinion mining:

- **Decision Making:** Opinion extraction plays a very important role in decision making. It gives an analyzed user's opinion which helps in improving the decision system.
- **Business Intelligence:** Manufacturers need to focus more on consumer reviews so that they can improve the product based on consumer feedback.
- **Junk-email Identification:** With the increase in amount of content, users intentionally upload junk contents or we can say spam contents so it is necessary to distinguish junk and authentic content.
- **Buying a Service or Commodity:** Valuable reviews extracted from opinions helps in taking right decision about the product that whether to buy it or not from a variety of options (Figs. 7, 8).

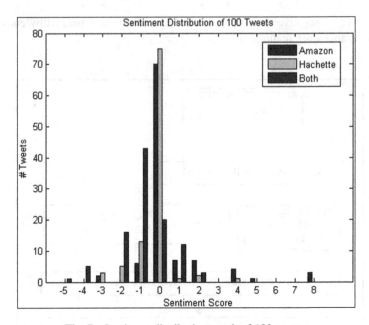

Fig. 7. Sentiment distribution graph of 100 tweets

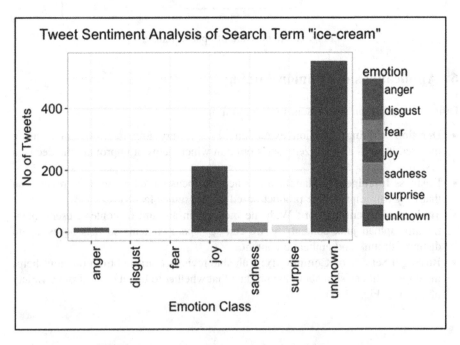

Fig. 8. Customer sentiments of search IceCream

7 Tools Used in Opinion Mining

Different tools can be used for opinion extraction and theses are:

- **Opinion Observer:** This tool analyze and compare opinions on the web using user generated contents and suggestions.
- **Social Mention:** This tool identify keywords in events, comments, news, blogs, videos and even audio media.
- **OpenNLP:** This tool perform NLP tasks such as POS tagging and entity extraction.
- **NTLK:** This tool is used for text processing, parsing, classification and tokenization.
- **Ling Pipe:** This tool is used for clustering classification and linguistic processing.

8 Research Challenges

There are many research challenges arises in this field, on the basis of our research study we analyze following issues:

- Major challenge arise in handling ambiguity in NLP as user may use correct semantics or may not use correct syntax [4].
- Some linguistic issue arise in opinion mining as language is not necessarily always English.
- Another challenge is the cost of tools which can only be afforded by large organizations and government funded groups.
- Another challenge is the domain dependency of words. One feature set may give good performance in one domain and poor in another.
- There is an asymmetry in the availability of opinion mining tools.

9 Conclusion

Opinion Mining is a vast research area and an emerging field of data mining which extract key knowledge from a huge volume of data available that may be about consumer reviews, feedbacks, suggestions, product review. It contains wide variety of tools and techniques to extract the data. Opinion mining is important for decision making, companies want to know what people think about their product so that they can improve the product based on their feedbacks and individuals also want to know about the summarized opinions of product when they want to buy it. This paper illustrates the algorithms used in the past to address the problem arises due to lack of analyzing opinionated data and also discuss two approaches used to extract valuable suggestions. Machine Learning approach is better as this approach have higher precision but slightly lacks in result generation as comparative to lexicon based approach.

This will establish a better customer relationship by providing them what they actually need. Several challenges are also exist in this field as the vocabulary of natural language is very large and these need to be tackled by using some solutions to improve the methods of sentiment analysis and classification.

References

1. Pang, B., Lee, L.: Opinion mining and sentiment analysis. Found. Trends Inf. Retr. **2**, 1–135 (2008)
2. Haseena Rahmath, P.: Opinion mining and sentiment analysis—challenges and applications. Int. J. Appl. Innov. Eng. Manag. **3**(5), 1–3 (2014)
3. Kalarani, P., Selva Brunda, S.: An overview on research challenges in opinion mining and sentiment analysis. Int. J. Innov. Res. Comput. Commun. Eng. **3**(10), 1–6 (2015)
4. Mago, N.: Opinion mining: applications, techniques, tools, challenges and future trends of sentiment analysis. Int. J. Comput. Eng. Appl. **10**(4), 1–10 (2016)
5. Vaghela, V.B., Jadav, B.M.: Analysis of various sentiment classification techniques. Int. J. Comput. Appl. **140**, 1–6 (2016)
6. Hamzah, A., Widyastuti, N.: Opinion classification using maximum entropy and K-means clustering. In: International Conference on Information, Communication Technology and System, IEEE International Conference, pp. 162–166 (2016)
7. Songpan, W.: The analysis and prediction of customer review rating using opinion mining. In: IEEE 15th International Conference on Software Engineering Research, Management and Applications (SERA), pp. 71–77 (2017)
8. Hailong, Z., Wenyan, G., Bo, J.: Machine learning and lexicon based methods for sentiment classification: a survey. In: IEEE International Conference on Web Information System and Application (WISA), pp. 262–265 (2014)
9. Guellil, I., Boukhalfa, K.: Social big data mining: a survey focused on opinion mining and sentiments analysis. In: 12th International Symposium on Programming and Systems (ISPS). IEEE (2015)
10. Osimo, D., Mureddu, F.: Research challenge on opinion mining and sentiment analysis. In: The CROSSROAD Roadmap on ICT for Governance and Policy Modeling (2010)
11. Vo, A.-D., Nguyen, Q.-P., Ock, C.-Y.: Opinion—aspect relations in cognizing customer feelings via reviews. In: IEEE, pp. 5415–5426 (2018)

Mobile Handset Selection Using Evolutionary Multi-objective Optimization Considering the Cost and Quality Parameters

Anurag Tiwari[1][(✉)], Vivek Kumar Singh[2],
and Praveen Kumar Shukla[3]

[1] Department of Computer Science and Engineering, Babu Banarasi Das
University, Lucknow, India
anuragrktiwari@gmail.com
[2] Department of Computer Science and Engineering, Babu Banarasi Das
Northern India Institute of Technology, Lucknow, India
viveksinghbbd@gmail.com
[3] Department of Information Technology, Babu Banarasi Das Northern India
Institute of Technology, Lucknow, India
drpraveenkumarshukla@gmail.com

Abstract. Multi-objective optimization is a mathematical framework to deal
with conflicting objectives simultaneously. Evolutionary algorithms are extremely useful in implementing multi-objective optimization problems resulting
into a new research area named Evolutionary Multi-objective Optimization
(EMO). This paper also implements the problem of mobile handset selection
considering two objectives which are conflicting, cost and quality of the handset
using EMO. The problem is implemented using 'gamultobj' solver available in
Matlab 'optimization' toolbox. The results are shown using Pareto Front at
different number of generations.

Keywords: Evolutionary Multi-objective Optimization (EMO)
Genetic algorithms · Pareto front · Non-dominated solutions

1 Introduction

The term 'Optimization' means "finding the best of something" [1]. In mathematical
sense, it is a technique to find a minimum or maximum value of a function having
different variables subjected to set of constraints. This was first time reported in 1940
by George Dantizig when he applied mathematical approach for generating "training
time tables and schedules" for military applications. The optimization is used in
multiple areas, like control systems, classification problems, medical applications,
economic applications etc. Multi objective and single objective optimization are the
two aspects of optimization techniques. In single objective optimization, there is only
one objective for which an optimal solution is derived whereas more than one
conflicting objective functions are considered simultaneously in a multi-objective
optimization [2]. The purpose of multi-objective optimization is to derive single or

© Springer Nature Singapore Pte Ltd. 2018
M. Singh et al. (Eds.): ICACDS 2018, CCIS 906, pp. 259–268, 2018.
https://doi.org/10.1007/978-981-13-1813-9_26

multiple optimal solutions for example, to find a car with minimum cost and maximum comfort.

Evolutionary approaches [3] like genetic algorithms are extremely applicable to deal with multi-objective optimization problems. First time in 1967, Rosenberg hinted the potential of genetic algorithms in multi objective optimization. Genetic procedures work on the principle of Darwinian's approach "Evolutions based on Natural Selection".

Evolutionary Multi-objective Optimization (EMO) techniques are also applied in fuzzy systems, specially dealing with interpretability and accuracy-tradeoff [4–7]. Interpretability [8, 9] is the property of a fuzzy system that deals with the capability of a fuzzy system to explain itself or it shows the understandability of the fuzzy system functioning. The precision and interpretability features are contradicting with each other that means the improvement in one can be done on the loss in other. This leads to a situation called "Interpretability-Accuracy Trade-off" which is further dealt with EMO approaches.

This paper proposes a specific problem which is proposed and implemented which deals with the selection of the mobile handset depending on the parameters cost and quality. The module is implemented using MATLAB (gamultobj) function in the form of a multi-objective optimization problem. The proposed approach derives multiple solutions with cost and quality values.

The paper is presented in five sections. Section 2 is the background of the proposed work. Section 3 discusses the proposed model. The implementation and data analysis has been done in Sect. 4. Section 5 presented the conclusion and future scope.

2　Related Work

2.1　Fundamentals of Evolutionary Multi-objective Optimization

The multi-objective optimization is concerned with mathematical optimization problem which has simultaneous optimization of many objectives. This is famous with several other titles like vector optimization, Pareto optimization etc. [5] The objectives may be contradictory with each other. One example is related with fuzzy systems. The fuzzy systems have two features interpretability and accuracy. The interpretability is subject to the understandability of the fuzzy system by inspecting its internal functionalities however accuracy is concerned with the closeness of implemented model and the real model [6]. With the reduction of system's complexity, we can enhance the interpretability of system that will lead to reduction of accuracy and vice versa. This situation is called 'interpretability-accuracy trade-off' which is well managed and solved by using evolutionary multi-objective optimization concepts.

The mathematical function of multi objective optimization is define as [10]

$$\text{minimize } (F_1(x), F_2(x), \ldots \ldots .F_k(x))$$

which is subject to inequality constraints 'm'

$$G_i(x) \leq x \quad for = 1, 2, \ldots\ldots, m$$

here the equality constraints is p

$$H_j(x) = 0 \quad for \ j = 1, 2, \ldots\ldots, p$$

and the number of objective functions is k.

$$F_i : R_n \rightarrow R$$

$$x = [x_1, x_2, \ldots\ldots x_n]^T$$

also the vector of decision variables is x.

The objective is to achieve the specific set of the value $(x_1^*, x_2^*, \ldots\ldots x_n^*)$ which produces the optimal values of all the objective functions.

The set of such solutions is called 'Pareto Optimal Solutions' which are alternatively known as 'Non-dominated Solutions' [10]. Also, the image of Pareto Optimal set under the objective function is called Pareto front.

Several MOEA algorithms are developed to deal with the multi-objective optimization problems. few of them are as follows.

1. NSGA-Non-dominated Sorting Genetic Algorithm: The NSGA has been developed on the concept given by Goldberg [19] concerned with the several layers of classification of individuals. Srinivas and Deb [20] developed the NSGA. The ranking of the population is done as per the non-domination concept which has been done before the selection.
2. NPGA-Niched-Pareto Genetic Algorithm: it is based on the tournament selection mechanism directly concerned with Pareto dominance [21].
3. MOGA-Multi-Objective Genetic Algorithm: it assigns maximum fitness value for all non-dominated individuals. The number of chromosomes is the rank of an individual in this algorithm [22].

All the above algorithms are treated as in the first generation, however in second generation several other MOEA are developed which are discussed below.

1. SPEA-Strength Pareto Evolutionary Algorithm: This algorithm is the consequence of merging many MOEAs. The algorithm uses external non-dominated set and computes a strength value [23, 24].
2. SPEA2- Strength Pareto Evolutionary Algorithm 2: This algorithm is different from SPEA with the following issues [25],
   a. SPEA2 has additional facility of fine-grained fitness assignment strategy
   b. SPEA2 uses nearest neighbor density estimation
   c. SPEA2 uses extended archive truncation technique.
3. PAES-Pareto Archived Evolution Strategy: This algorithms follows (1 + 1) evolution strategy and a historical archive that stores non-dominated solutions calculated before [26].

4. NSGA-II-Non-Dominated Sorting Genetic Algorithm II: This algorithm is the improved expansion of the NSGA [27, 28]. This uses the crowding distance concept.

The EMO is applicable in multiple areas; some of them are outlined in Table 1.

Table 1. Applications of MOEA

S. no.	Application area	References
1	Electrical and power system	[11–13]
2	Chemical engineering	[14]
3	Quantum computation	[15]
4	Ecological informatics and energy systems	[16–18]

3 Implementation Details

Cost of any mobile handset is proportional to the quality of the handset. The goal is to minimize the cost with a maximum quality of the handset. The quality of a handset is depending on the parameters; i.e. hardware, operating system, compatibility with other software apps, updation of existing software, connectivity issues and associated speeds etc.

The objective of the proposed and implemented model is to find a solution with minimum cost and maximum quality which further extends the satisfaction of the users. The data is collected using Google Forms from 500 users of a specific brand of the mobile handsets. From the data collected, the equations for the objectives are derived which are as follows,

$$function\ y = problem\ 2(x)$$

$$y(1) = -(778^*x - 22000)$$

$$y(2) = (0.838^*x - 0.991)$$

The multi-objective problem is formulated as a minimum function shown below

$$minimize\ (y(1),\ y(2))$$

where x represents the satisfaction level of the user and y(1) represents the cost of the handset whereas quality is represented by the function y(2).

4   Results and Findings

The proposed system is implemented using optimization toolbox in MATLAB. The 'gamultobj' is used to get Pareto solutions of the proposed problem. The Global Optimization Toolbox is designed to search for global solutions to the problems containing number of minima and maxima. Several computing facilities like Multi-Start, Global Search, Multi-Objective Genetic Algorithm (MOGA), Particle Swarm Optimization (PSO), Genetic Algorithms (GA), Simulated Annealing (SA) are the available in the toolbox. Figures 1, 2 and 3 shows the Pareto fronts of the proposed problem. The respective Pareto fronts are generated on the different number of generations noted along with the Figs. (4, 5).

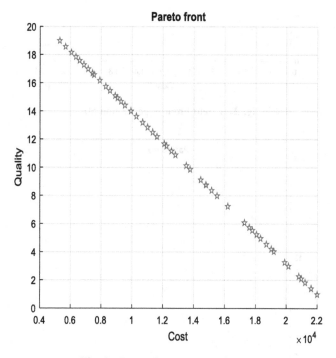

Fig. 1. Pareto front at generation 25

The details of the selection function are given in Fig. 6 and the relationship between individual and number of children is shown. In the experiment carried out, the Pareto front shows the results on the tradeoff line of cost and quality with different values.

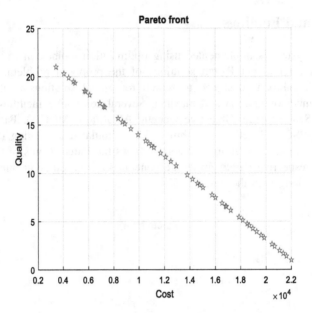

Fig. 2. Pareto Front at generation 50

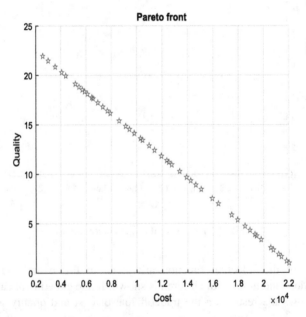

Fig. 3. Pareto Front at generation 75

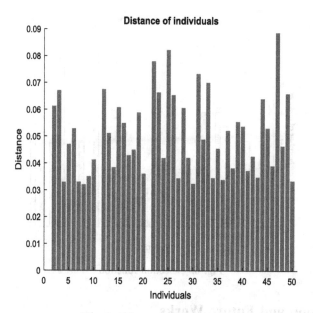

Fig. 4. Distance of individuals

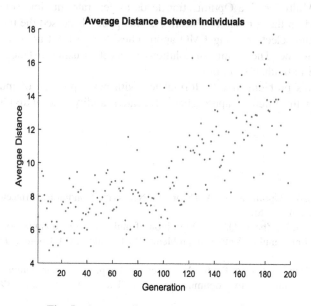

Fig. 5. Average distance between individuals

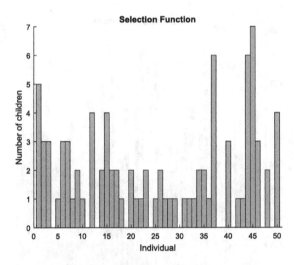

Fig. 6. Selection function

5 Conclusion and Future Works

Evolutionary Multiobjective Optimization leads to generate multiple solutions of the problems based on the conflicting objectives. This paper discussed the mobile handset classification and selection using EMO approaches. Pareto front are computed to get the desired outcome. The quality of solutions is checked using distance and average distance of the individual solutions.

In future this problem may be formulated with new approach of multi-objective optimization with different approaches of search ability and individual distance quantification.

References

1. Neustadt, L.W.: Optimization: A Theory of Necessary Conditions. Princeton University Press, Princeton (1976)
2. Liu, H.-L., Gu, F., Zhang, Q.: Decomposition of multi-objective optimization problem into number of simple multiobjective subproblems. IEEE Trans. Evol. Comput. **18**(3), 450–455 (2013)
3. Zhang, X., Tian, Y., Cheng, R., Jin, Y.: An efficient approach to non dominated sorting for evolutionary multi objective optimization. IEEE Trans. Evol. Comput. **19**(2), 201–213 (2014)
4. Shukla, P.K., Tripathi, S.P.: A survey on interpretability–accuracy (I–A) trade-off in evolutionary fuzzy Systems. In: IEEE International Conference on Genetic and Evolutionary Computation (ICGEC 2011), Japan, 29 August–1 September (2011)
5. Shukla, P.K., Tripathi, S.P.: A review on the interpretability-accuracy trade-off in evolutionary multi-objective fuzzy systems (EMOFS). Information **3**, 256–277 (2012)

6. Shukla, P.K., Tripathi, S.P.: Handling high dimensionality and interpretability accuracy trade-off issues in evolutionary multi-objective fuzzy classifiers. Int. J. Sci. Eng. Res. **5**(6), 665–671 (2014)
7. Shukla, P.K., Tripathi, S.P.: Interpretability and accuracy issues in evolutionary multi-objective fuzzy classifiers. Int. J. Soft Comput. Netw. **1**(1), 55–69 (2016)
8. Shukla, P.K., Tripathi, S.P.: On the design of interpretable evolutionary fuzzy system (I-EFS) with improved accuracy. In: International Conference on Computing Science, L. P. University, India (2012)
9. Shukla, P.K., Tripathi, S.P.: Interpretability issues evolutionary multi objective fuzzy knowledge base systems. In: 7th International Conference on Bio-Inspired Computing: Theories and Applications (BIC-7A2012), ABV-IIIT, Gwalior, India, 14–16 December (2012)
10. Abratiam, A., Jain, L., Goldberg, R. (eds.): Evolutionary Multi-objective Optimization: Theoretical Advances and Applications. Springer, Berlin (2005). https://doi.org/10.1007/1-84628-137-7
11. Burkart, R.M., Kolar, J.W.: Comparative life cycle cost analysis of Si and SiCPV converter systems based on advanced n-p-6 multi-objective optimization technique. IEEE Trans. Power Electron. **32**(6), 4344–4358 (2017)
12. G–Bediaga, A., Viller, I., Rujas, A., Nir, L., Rfurer, A.: Multi-objective optimization of medium frequency transformers for isolated soft-switching converters using a genetic algorithm. IEEE Trans. Power Electron. **32**(4), 2995–3006 (2017)
13. Shabestary, A.-R., Mohamed, I.: Analytical expressions for multi-objective optimization of converter-based DG operation under unbalanced grid conditions. IEEE Trans. Power Electron. **32**(9), 7284–7296 (2017)
14. Zaman, M., Rangaiah, G.P.: Multi-objective optimization application in chemical engineering. In: Multi-objective Optimization, pp. 29–62 (2017)
15. Wang, Y., Li, Y., Jiao, L.: Quantum-inspired multi-objective optimization evolutionary algorithm based on decomposition. Soft Comput. **20**(8), 3257–3272 (2016)
16. Perera, A.T.D., Sirinanna, M.P.G., Attalage, R.A., Perera, K.C.K., Dassanaake, V.P.C.: Multi objective optimization and multi criterion decision making in expanding existing standalone energy system combining renewable energy sources. In: Proceedings of Engineering and Applied Science (2012). https://doi.org/10.2316/P.2012.785-108
17. Esfe, M.H., Hajmohammad, H., Toghraie, D., Rostanian, H., Mahaian, O., Wongisses, S.: Multi-objective optimization of nanofluid flow in double tube heat exchangers for applications in energy systems. Energy **137**, 160–171 (2017)
18. Pastori, M., Udias, A., Bouraoui, F., Biodoglio, G.: A multi-objective approach to evaluate the economic and environmental impacts of alternative water and nutrient management strategies in Africa. J. Environ. Inform. **29**(1), 193–201 (2017)
19. Goldberg, D.E.: Genetic Algorithms in Search, Optimization and Machine Learning. Addison-Wesley Publishing Company, Reading, MA (1989)
20. Srinivas, N., Deb, K.: Multiobjective optimization using nondominated sorting in genetic algorithms. Evol. Comput. **2**(3), 221–248 (1994)
21. Horn, J., Nafpliotis, N., Goldberg, D.E.: A niched pareto genetic algorithm for multiobjective optimization. In: Proceedings of the First IEEE Conference on Evolutionary Computation, IEEE World Congress on Computational Intelligence, vol. 1, pp. 82–87, Piscataway, New Jersey, June 1994. IEEE Service Center (1994)
22. Fonseca, C.M., Fleming, P.J.: Genetic algorithms for multiobjective optimization: formulation, discussion and generalization. In: Forrest, S. (ed.), Proceedings of the Fifth International Conference on Genetic Algorithms, pp. 416–423, San Mateo, California. University of Illinois at Urbana-Champaign, Morgan Kauffman Publishers (1993)

23. Zitzler, E., Thiele, L.: Multiobjective optimization using evolutionary algorithms—a comparative study. In: Eiben, A.E. (ed.) Parallel Problem Solving from Nature V, pp. 292–301. Springer, Amsterdam (1998). https://doi.org/10.1007/BFb0056872
24. Zitzler, E., Thiele, L.: Multiobjective evolutionary algorithms: a comparative case study and the strength pareto approach. IEEE Trans. Evol. Comput. 3(4), 257–271 (1999)
25. Knowles, J.D., Corne, D.W.: Approximating the nondominated front using the pareto archived evolution strategy. Evol. Comput. 8(2), 149–172 (2000)
26. Zitzler, E., Laumanns, M., Thiele, L.: SPEA2: improving the strength pareto evolutionary algorithm. In: Giannakoglou, K., et al. (eds.) EUROGEN 2001. Evolutionary Methods for Design, Optimization and Control with Applications to Industrial Problems, pp. 95–100, Athens, Greece (2002)
27. Deb, K., Agrawal, S., Pratap, A., Meyarivan, T., et al.: A fast elitist non-dominated sorting genetic algorithm for multi-objective optimization: NSGA-II. In: Schoenauer, M. (ed.) PPSN 2000. LNCS, vol. 1917, pp. 849–858. Springer, Heidelberg (2000). https://doi.org/10.1007/3-540-45356-3_83
28. Deb, K., Pratap, A., Agarwal, S., Meyarivan, T.: A fast and elitist multiobjective genetic algorithm: NSGA–II. IEEE Trans. Evol. Comput. 6(2), 182–197 (2002)

An Adaptive Feature Dimensionality Reduction Technique Based on Random Forest on Employee Turnover Prediction Model

Md. Kabirul Islam[1]([⊠]), Mirza Mohtashim Alam[1],
Md. Baharul Islam[1,2], Karishma Mohiuddin[3], Amit Kishor Das[3],
and Md. Shamsul Kaonain[3]

[1] Department of Multimedia and Creative Technology,
Daffodil International University, Dhaka, Bangladesh
{kislam, baharul}@daffodilvarsity.edu.bd,
mirza.mct@diu.edu.bd
[2] School of Computing, Asia Pacific University of Technology and Innovation,
Kuala Lumpur, Malaysia
baharulislam.md@apu.edu.my
[3] Department of Computer Science and Engineering, BRAC University,
Dhaka, Bangladesh
natz.karishma@gmail.com, amitkishordas@gmail.com,
mkaonain@gmail.com

Abstract. This paper is based on the theme of employee attrition where the reasoning behind employee turnover has predicted with the help of machine learning approach. As employee turnover has become a vital issue these days due to heavy work pressure, less salary, less work satisfaction, poor working environment; it's high time to uphold a better solution on this term. Therefore, we have come up with a prediction model based on machine learning approach where we have used each feature's respective Random Forest importance weights while threshold based correlated feature merging into each of the single combined variable. Again, we scale specific features to get the correlated matrix of features matrix by defining threshold. Certainly, this newly developed technique has achieved good result for some algorithms compared to Principal Component Analysis (PCA) and Linear Discriminant Analysis (LDA) for the same dataset.

Keywords: Random forest · PCA · LDA · Dimensionality reduction
Classifier

1 Introduction

Employee turnover is the ratio between total departures of employees and the total number of employees within a specific period [1]. To carry out this research in this paper, we have used Scikit-Learn [2], Pandas, Matplotlib, Keras etc. for this research. Nowadays, attrition of employee has become a regular issue around the globe [3]. It has created a negative impact on well-reputed companies when their skilful employees resign their jobs to pursue higher goals [1]. Moreover, the status and dignity of a

© Springer Nature Singapore Pte Ltd. 2018
M. Singh et al. (Eds.): ICACDS 2018, CCIS 906, pp. 269–278, 2018.
https://doi.org/10.1007/978-981-13-1813-9_27

company also rely on the turnover of employee because the more employees left the job; it decreases the fame of that company [3]. It is necessary to look for proper solution to identify the main factors of employee turnover to hold a company's reputation and success [4].

Our main aim is to approach with a new model that keeps tracking of all the attributes whilst reducing the dimension to decrease over-fitting and to achieve higher accuracy for the dataset. This novel approach with the help of machine learning technique predicts the employee turnover rate with the cause of it and results in a higher accuracy.

2   Related Works

In paper [5], authors have uses Random Forest algorithm to achieve higher accuracy but in conventional way. Another group of author worked on PCA in their paper [6] and elaborately explained about the dimension reduction technique on Machine Learning algorithms. In our previous work [7], we have also attained k best features by Chi2 and Random Forest Importance before training our model. However, in this paper, Random Forest Importance has been used to determine the weight of each feature. Correlated features based on threshold value are taken and merged together with their importance weight. Afterwards, model training has been done using Random Forest. In paper [8], the authors had used Hybrid ANN and clustering analysis which is knows as self-organizing map (SOM) that showed the primary cause of employee turnover are lack of leadership, inner fidelity identification and management issue whereas in our approach we have figured out the actual cause of employee turnover are less satisfaction in job, poor working environment and less salary. As we have used dimension reduction technique with machine learning approach to only focus on the main criteria of employee turnover, our result only showed the best and most prominent reasons for employee attrition.

3   System Model

Our System model is consisted of several components. Firstly, from the raw data we pre-process the data. With the pre-processed data we try to get each feature's importance using Random Forest since not every feature is equally informative. On the other hand, we try to get the co-relation matrix from the dataset. From the co-relation matrix, we can find out criteria from which we can separate each group of variables based on their co-relation value. While putting each group of variables into a single feature set, we multiply them with their respective Random Forest Feature Importance values and add them together. Then, our data becomes ready to be classified using classification algorithms. We got best result using Random Forest Classifier with higher number of estimators (more trees in the forest) which can be seen in the results section. Our system model has been provided in the Fig. 1.

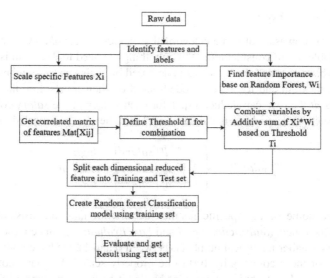

Fig. 1. System model

3.1 Raw Data

The dataset named "HR Analytics" which we have used has been taken from Kaggle [9]. It concerns to find out why valuable employees are leaving company prematurely. This dataset is consisted of 15000 employee's records where 3572 employees have left.

Since we are not concerned about the job type rather we will be focusing on the employee group as a whole we have taken the '*type*' column out of consideration. Then, we identify the features and labels. The label (dependent variable) is the 'left' column and the features (independent variable) are all the other columns except the '*type*' column (Table 1).

Table 1. Variable Description

Number	Variable	Brief description
1	Satisfaction_level	Employee satisfaction level
2	Last_evaluation	Employee last evaluation by the company
3	Number_project	Number of projects the employee have done
4	Average_montly_hours	Average monthly hours the employee have worked during till date
5	Time_spend_company	From when the employee is working for the company
6	Work_accident	Whether any of the employees have done accidents during his/her timeline
7	Left	The employee have left the job or not
8	Promotion_last_5years	The promotion factor of the employee during last 5 years
9	Type	The type of job
10	Salary	Employee salary payment level

3.2   Scale Specific Features

Our dataset was consisted of some categorical variables (*type, salary*). Since we have left type variable out of consideration, the only thing we need to deal with is the salary variable. We have encoded the salary variable based on their levels. The three levels of *salary* (high, medium and low) are encoded based on their levels. Let, the dataset be considered as *df* then we can deduce Eq. 1 for each values of the *salary* column. The high is indicated as 3, medium is indicated as 2 and the low is indicated as 1.

$$df['salary'] = \begin{cases} 3 & \text{if } df['salary'] = high \\ 2 & \text{if } df['salary'] = medium \\ 1 & \text{if } df['salary'] = low \end{cases} \tag{1}$$

We scaled some of the specific features because of their inconsistent range in compared to the others (*Satisfaction Level* and *Last Evaluation*). Since these values are ranged in very smaller numerical numbers (between 0 and 1), we have multiplied each of the values of these columns by 100 to be properly scaled. We have not used any standard feature scaling techniques provided by Scikit-Learn such Standard Scaler [10], Robust Scaler [11] and MinMax Scaler [12]. Let the Satisfaction Level be defined as *S*, Last evaluation be defined as *LE*, we can clearly deduce the scaling into Eqs. 2 and 3

$$df['S'] = df['S'] \times 100 \tag{2}$$

$$df['LE'] = df['LE'] \times 100 \tag{3}$$

3.3   Get Correlated Matrix of Features

To compute pairwise correlation of columns, we have used Panda's *corr()* function [13]. We have done this in order to grasp a sense how variables are correlated with each other since we want to merge *n* variables into a single one based on some threshold value. Let us consider Fig. 2 in order to demonstrate the correlation.

Based on these co-related values we have found *k* number of correlations based on unique column headers on some threshold values (here we took one combinational set based on the values which is equal or greater than 0.3, and for all other values we took

Index	satisfaction_level	last_evaluation	number_project	erage_montly_hoι	ne_spend_compa	Work_accident	ɔmotion_last_5yeι	salary
satisfaction_	1	0.105	-0.143	-0.02	-0.101	0.0587	0.0256	0.05
last_evaluat_	0.105	1	0.349	0.34	0.132	-0.0071	-0.00868	-0.013
number_proje_	-0.143	0.349	1	0.417	0.197	-0.00474	-0.00606	-0.0018
average_mont_	-0.02	0.34	0.417	1	0.128	-0.0101	-0.00354	-0.00224
time_spend_c_	-0.101	0.132	0.197	0.128	1	0.00212	0.0674	0.0487
Work_accident	0.0587	-0.0071	-0.00474	-0.0101	0.00212	1	0.0392	0.00925
promotion_la_	0.0256	-0.00868	-0.00606	-0.00354	0.0674	0.0392	1	0.0981
salary	0.05	-0.013	-0.0018	-0.00224	0.0487	0.00925	0.0981	1

Fig. 2. Correlation Matrix consists of correlation values

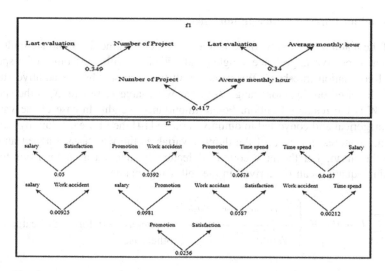

Fig. 3. Feature tuples of nearest correlation values based on threshold value

another combined variable set). We have taken the threshold value as 0.3 as an assumption because maximum values which are not highly correlated are below 0.3. Unique valued tuples are not repeated in other combined variable set. For a better understanding let us consider Fig. 3.

After getting the tuples we take each set of combined variables in such a way so that tuples of max correlation values remain in a single variable set and any member variable in a tuple does not remain in other combined features set, keeping in mind the threshold values. The work procedure of combining the correlated variables is stated in Algorithm 1.

Algorithm 1. Feature combining algorithm based on correlation:

```
threshold_value  ← Create threshold values based on
                    Matrix Specification
combination_fᵢ ←list; /*where each of the features for a
                    particular threshold value resides*/
for each threshold_value in range:
  for each column header in matrix:
      current_tuple ← Max (find_other _column_header
                          (max_correlation_value
                          (column header,other column
                          headers));
      If any header in current_tuple in combination:
          pass;
      else:
          combination_fᵢ ← combination_fᵢ ∪
                          current_tuple.members;
      i ←i+1;
```

3.4   Random Forest Feature Importance

Each of the features in the time of combination based on some threshold are multiplied with their respective importance weights and added up with each other of a specific range of correlation threshold. We combine all the variables by the additive sum of $X_i \times X_i$. W based on threshold range T_i to a new variable f_i. Where, X_i is the specific feature, W is the features Random Forest Importance weight. In case of the variable being categorical and converted to dummy variable [14] then for each dummy variable containing features, for each of the dummy variables the weights are added and calculated the mean. Let the new combined feature be defined as f, then our feature combining equation can be derived in the following manner,

$$f_k = \sum_{i=1}^{n} Feature_i \times \begin{cases} \dfrac{\sum_{j=1}^{m} Feature_i.Dummy_j.Weight}{m} & \text{if } dummy > 0 \text{ for each } Feature_i \\ Weight_i & \text{otherwise} \end{cases} \quad (4)$$

3.5   Build Classification Model with Random Forest

Random Forest became popular for their classification performance, scalability and ease of use. It has been built on ensemble of decision trees to combine weak learners to build more strong learner model. The main aim is to reduce overfitting. The algorithm creates bootstrap sample of n size, later creates decision trees from the bootstrap samples while randomly choosing features without any replacement and split the nodes in order to maximize the information gain. Finally, assign the class label by doing majority voting [15].

After combining each of the correlated features into a single variable, we get our dataset to be fitted into Random Forest classifier [16] with higher number of estimators. Estimators are the number of individual trees in the forest. Our main data is then consisting of combined features f_i and label '*left*' column, we split our dataset into training (80%) and test (20%) set by Scikit-learn's default test split [17] function. For model training we use the training set and the test set for model evaluation purpose. Training of the model has been provided in Algorithm 2.

Algorithm 2. Building Random Forest based classifier:
```
FeatureSet ← f₁, f₂,....., fk;
Label ← df['left'];
X_Train, Y_Train, X_Testset, Y_Testset ← Train_Test_Split
                                         (Feature,Label,
                                          Test set=0.20);
Model ← Build Random Forest Classifier(n estimator =
1000);
Model.Fit (X_Train, Y_Train);
Predicted_Value ← Model.Accuracy_Score (X_Test);
Create visualization plot of (Y_Test, Predicted_value);
```

4   Result and Analysis

To Carry out the research experiment we have used scikit learn's libraries of Random Forest Classifier, Random Forest Importance, Panda's Corr() function to carry out the pairwise correlation values. To Graph visualization we have used Matplotlib's graphical libraries. To apply PCA [18] and LDA [19] we have used Scikit Learn's libraries. We have fitted our model with various classifiers along with our Random Forest Classifier based model. After fitting into the classifiers, we have visualized the model performance using Receiver operating characteristic (ROC) curve [20]. Figure 4 shows the ROC curve of our model with adaptive weight based combined feature (here Random Forest shows better results) where most algorithms show the better results than LDA (most of the cases) and relatively similar results as PCA (for some cases better: SVM, GaussianNB).

Figure 5 shows the ROC curve after applying PCA and LDA respectively in several algorithms along with Random Forest Classifier. In most of the cases, our model has shown good results on this dataset since the area under the curve is larger. However, LDA shows relatively lower results in most of the cases than our adaptive dimensionality reduction model and PCA.

Finally, while visualizing the results of the test set we can clearly view which groups of employees under certain circumstance have the probability of leaving the company. Figure 6 shows the employees having possibility of leaving the company prematurely on a two-dimensional graph based on combined variables, $f1 = last$ $evaluation + Project$ $number + Average$ $Monthly$ $Hours$ where $f2 = satisfaction + Time$ $Spend$ in $Company + Salary + work$ $Accident + Promotion$ $last$ 5 $years$ (based on Random Forest Classifier). The Random Forest Classifier shows good results (accuracy 96%) after evaluating the model, which can easily be illustrated by comparing the test result against predicted results (Fig. 6). From the results we can deduce that there are three groups of employees who is leaving the company and they are: a. Higher f1 value and higher f2 value (not so dense population); b. High f1 but low f2 value (dense population); c. Average f2 but low f1 value (highly dense population). We have found the following hypothesis.

1. For low f1 value (combination of last evaluation, project number and average monthly hours), f2 value (combination of satisfaction, time spend in company, salary, work accident and promotion last five years) remains relatively low. That is why most people leave the organization as they do not get good number of projects, non-satisfactory evaluation, and they spend little amount of average hour in the company. This group (group c) has the most population.
2. People with high f1 value (combination of last evaluation, project number and average monthly hours) and low f2 value (combination of satisfaction, time spend in company, salary, work accident and promotion last five years) leaves the company. This group of people (group b) is so unsatisfied and gets less salary that they do not stay in the company for that long. Meanwhile, they do not get any promotion. In spite of having good evaluation score, large number of projects and having good average working hour per month; they prematurely leave.

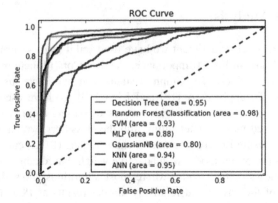

Fig. 4. ROC curve visualization after implementing our system model

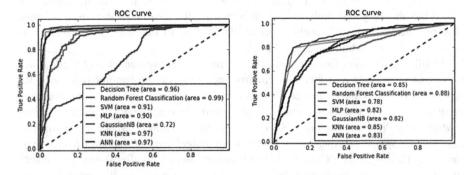

Fig. 5. ROC curve visualization after applying PCA (left) and LDA (Right)

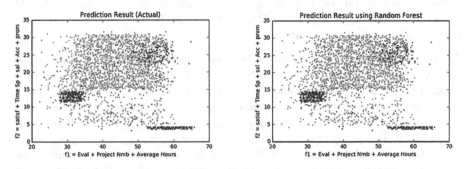

Fig. 6. Actual Result (left) and Prediction Result using Random Forest (Right)

3. In addition to these groups mentioned above, there are some people (group a) who leaves once they find better opportunity though they were provided with a better job environment (high f1 and f2 value). These people are less in number.

5   Conclusion and Future Work

In our model, we have used dimension-reduction technique by taking feature's weight from Random Forest Importance, which helps us to feature into a certain combination for further training and a better graph visualization. As per the scope, we may work on categorical data in combination with numerical data as features in near future because we have only used numerical data this time. Additionally, our plan is to implement our technique in corporate real world scenario to match our work with corporate world to boost a company's prosperity, predict their potential employee's turnover and aid HR management team to evaluate their employee's performances adequately.

References

1. Sikaroudi, E., Mohammad, A., Ghousi, R., Sikaroudi, A.: A data mining approach to employee turnover prediction (case study: Arak automotive parts manufacturing). J. Ind. Syst. Eng. **8**(4), 106–121 (2015)
2. Pedregosa, F., et al.: Scikit-learn: machine learning in python. J. Mach. Learn. Res. 12(Oct), 2825–2830 (2011)
3. Gao, Y.: Using decision tree to analyze the turnover of employees (2017)
4. Ajit, P.: Prediction of employee turnover in organizations using machine learning algorithms. Algorithms **4**(5), C5 (2016)
5. Howley, T., Madden, M.G., O'Connell, M.L., Ryder, A.G.: The effect of principal component analysis on machine learning accuracy with high-dimensional spectral data. Knowl. Based Syst. **19**(5), 363–370 (2006)
6. Maisuradze, M.: Predictive analysis on the example of employee turnover
7. Alam, M., Mohiuddin, K., Hassan, M.M., Islam, M., Allayear, S.: A machine learning approach to analyze and reduce features to a significant number for employee's turn over prediction model. In: IEEE Computing Conference 2018, London (2018)
8. Fan, C.Y., Fan, P.S., Chan, T.Y., Chang, S.H.: Using hybrid data mining and machine learning clustering analysis to predict the turnover rate for technology professionals. Expert Syst. Appl. **39**(10), 8844–8851 (2012)
9. L. (n.d.). HR Analytics. https://www.kaggle.com/ludobenistant/hr-analytics-1/notebook. Accessed 09 Dec 2017
10. Sklearn.preprocessing.StandardScaler   (n.d.).   http://scikit-learn.org/stable/modules/generated/sklearn.preprocessing.StandardScaler.html. Accessed 01 Oct 2017
11. Sklearn.preprocessing.RobustScaler (n.d.). http://scikit-learn.org/stable/modules/generated/sklearn.preprocessing.RobustScaler.html. Accessed 01 Oct 2017
12. Sklearn.preprocessing.MinMaxScaler (n.d.). http://scikit-learn.org/stable/modules/generated/sklearn.preprocessing.MinMaxScaler.html#sklearn.preprocessing.MinMaxScaler. Accessed 01 Oct 2017
13. Pandas.DataFrame.corr   (n.d.).   https://pandas.pydata.org/pandas-docs/stable/generated/pandas.DataFrame.corr.html. Accessed 09 Dec 2017
14. Pandas.get_dummies (n.d.). https://pandas.pydata.org/pandas-docs/stable/generated/pandas.get_dummies.html. Accessed
15. Raschka, S.: Python machine learning. Packt Publishing Ltd., Birmingham (2015)
16. Liaw, A., Wiener, M.: Classification and regression by randomForest. R News **2**(3), 18–22 (2002)

17. Sklearn.model_selection.train_test_split   (n.d.).   http://scikit-learn.org/stable/modules/generated/sklearn.model_selection.train_test_split.html. Accessed 10 Dec 2017
18. Wold, S., Esbensen, K., Geladi, P.: Principal component analysis. Chemometr. Intell. Lab. Syst. **2**(1–3), 37–52 (1987)
19. Izenman, A.J.: Linear discriminant analysis. In: Izenman, A.J. (ed.) Modern Multivariate Statistical Techniques. STS, pp. 237–280. Springer, New York (2013). https://doi.org/10.1007/978-0-387-78189-1_8
20. Hanley, J.A., McNeil, B.J.: The meaning and use of the area under a receiver operating characteristic (ROC) curve. Radiology **143**(1), 29–36 (1982)

A Comparative Evolution of Unsupervised Techniques for Effective Network Intrusion Detection in Hadoop

Priyanka Dahiya[1(✉)] and Devesh Kumar Srivastava[2]

[1] Mody University of Science and Technology, Laxmangarh, India
dahiyapriyanka814@gmail.com
[2] Manipal University Jaipur, Jaipur, India
devesh988@yahoo.com

Abstract. With the rising of enormous size in any field be in astronomy, health or education. Storage, analysis, and processing of big data are not only the big issue but security of these huge data is now big concern in the field of academia and industry. Network intrusion detection systems detect and stop network behaviors that interrupt or threaten network security. Supervised learning methods for intrusion detection are not so effective in detection of attacks of big data. Unsupervised models are mainly used for the detection of events or attributes that occur together. A new parallel K-medoid clustering method and k-nearest neighbor classification techniques are proposed for intrusion detection for huge amount of data. We have used NSL-KDD and UNSW-NB-15 datasets for experimental work. The results are compared with the proposed method. Experiments are performed in Hadoop environment and the performance is evaluated using accuracy, precision and confusion matrix.

Keywords: UNSW-NB15 dataset · NSL-KDD dataset · Hadoop

1 Introduction

The system which detects the intrusion in the system is known as IDS (Intrusion detection System). Intrusion detection is the technique of detecting the activities that are arising in the systems or networks and examining them for any type of mischievous activity or danger to computer security [1]. Big data is known as huge volume of data as structured, semi structured and unstructured, that inundates a business on a daily basis. Thus the big data creates large volumes of data in short periods of time and this data regularly comes from connected devices, such as cell phones, vehicle fleets or industrial machinery [2]. Processing of big data is very difficult as it contains the billions records of millions people which is unstructured form. Big data analytics analyze the huge amount of data to extract the hidden patterns and the other useful information for the use [3, 4].

Clustering is used to group the similar instances; the instances which are not grouped in any group are called outliers. This instance can be an intrusion to the network.

© Springer Nature Singapore Pte Ltd. 2018
M. Singh et al. (Eds.): ICACDS 2018, CCIS 906, pp. 279–287, 2018.
https://doi.org/10.1007/978-981-13-1813-9_28

Clustering is the groupings of examples that belong together are sought, when there is no specific class. Jianliang et al. [5] explained the K means clustering algorithm used for intrusion detection to detect unknown attack. A distributed intrusion detection framework is proposed in [6, 7]. The method is able to detect new attacks by using network traffic sensors fixed in key network points.

MapReduce [8], a parallel and distributed large-scale data processing paradigm widely adopted for big data applications [9]. MapReduce is a programming model which allows the processing of terabytes of data in parallel, on a large number of machines.

Hadoop [10] is a framework written in Java, distributed under Apache License, developed by Doug Cutting. Apache hadoop is a framework that allows for the distributed processing of large datasets, across clusters of commodity computers using a simple programming model.

Programmers and the system easy to use: hundreds of MapReduce programs have been implemented and upwards of one thousand MapReduce jobs are executed on Google's clusters every day.

There were many old datasets generated like KDD90 and KDDCUP99 inclusively reflect network traffic and modern low footprint attacks. The network benchmark data set is not available. For this reason, this paper uses a UNSW-NB15 dataset and compared the algorithms on NSLD- KDD dataset.

2 Datasets

The NSLKDD data set solve some inherent problem of KDDCUP 99, the classifier is not biased towards more frequent records and the numbers of records in train and test data is not unbalanced.

Based on literature review we have taken a UNSW-NB15 data set for classification.

2.1 Description of NSL-KDD Dataset

There are 41 attributes described in different features and label is assigned as an attack type or as normal in NSL-KDD dataset [11, 12].

2.2 Description of UNSW-NB 15 Dataset

UNSW-NB 15 dataset contains both real modern normal activities and synthetic contemporary attack behaviors [13].

UNSW-NB15 dataset is available in comma-separated values (CSV) file format. There are 49 attributes or features with 10 class values in this dataset. Attack types are Fuzzers, Analysis, Backdoors, DoS, Exploits, Generic, Reconnaissance, Shellcode and Worms. The attributes present in UNSW-NB dataset are shown in Table 1.

Table 1. List of attributes of UNSW- NB 15 dataset [13]

Attributes		
Srcip	ct_srv_dst	Dintpkt
ct_flw_http_mthd	Spkts	ct_src_ ltm
ct_state_ttl	Dpkts	synack
Dsport	swin	ackdat
ct_ftp_cmd	dwin	is_sm_ips_ports
State	stcpb	Dstip
Dur	dtcpb	Sport
Sbytes	smeansz	is_ftp_login
dbytes	dmeansz	Proto
tcprtt	trans_depth	service
ct_dst_sport_ltm	res_bdy_len	Dload
sloss	Sjit	ct_dst_ltm
dloss	Djit	sttl
ct_srv_src	Stime	ct_src_dport_ltm
Sload	Ltime	dttl
Sintpkt	attack_cat	ct_dst_src_ltm
		Label

3 Research Methodologies

Research methodology contains the below steps:

NSLDKDD dataset and UNSW-NB 15 datasets are selected due to network intrusion system.

- Implementation is done on big data framework Hadoop.
- K-mean clustering, k medoids and parallel K-medoids algorthms using mapreduce are applied for clustering the instances.
- Pre-processing is performed on training and testing data files.
- Classification and Clustering algorithms are implemented on both data sets and results are shown in tables.

3.1 MapReduce Programming Model

Hadoop framework process the data using the MapReduce programming model. This model is based on key-value pairs. Data is processed in Mapreduce concept in parallel an distributed way. All clustering methods distribute the data in different clusters using the mapreduce concept. The actual data is stored in slave nodes. Data is splits in 128 Mb block size in Hadoop 2x. One block size means one mapper. Depends on the size of data, blocks are created. No. of splits files is equal to no. of maps. Reducer can run in any of slave nodes.

3.2   K-mean Clustering Using MapReduce

The most famous non-hierarchical clustering algorithm is kmeans. It needs as input the number of clusters K. Firstly it computes some initial clustering, for example by random assignment into K clusters. Then we compute for each cluster current mean vector, also called centroid, and then for those centroids we again assign to them those points that are closest to them. And we continue this, we repeat this until the clusters do not stabilise. The most demanding part of kmeans is actually computing distances of each data point to all current centroids and detecting the closest centroid which yields new assignment. The map function therefore computes for each data point from the data block the distances to the current set of centroids and returns new assignment and the row sums of new clusters. The reduce function simply adds the key values over all keypairs and therefore contributes to new centroids. And we repeat this until the centroids or clusters stabilize.

K-Mean is a simple learning algorithm for clustering analysis. This algorithm is applied on NSLD-KDD and UNSW-NB15 dataset.

3.3   K-Medoids Clustering Using MapReduce

In the k-means algorithm, mean value of the object in a cluster is taken as reference point but the k-medoids algorithm can pick actual objects to signify the clusters, using one representative object per cluster. In order to improve the robustness, K-Medoids algorithm is proposed. It selects the center point as medoiod. It minimizes the cost between non medoids and medoids of the cluster. Parallel K-medoids algorithms use the Euclidean distance to find the similarity in the middle of data points.

3.4   Parallel K-Medoid Clustering Algorithm Based on Hadoop

The idea of parallel Medoids clustering algorithm is:

In Hadoop framework, sample data is stored in Hadoop Distributed File System (HDFS) and processing is handle by Map Reduce function. The Map function, assigns the initial cluster midpoint to all mappers by Euclidean method, the temporary mid-point for each cluster were calculated as intermediate key-value and this key-value is input to Reducer function to detect the last center. The output is in (key, value) pair. The result is used in next iteration.

4   Experiments and Results

In this section we discussed the different performance parameters used to evaluate the system. Then we discuss the results after applying intrusion detection using k-means clustering algorithm on NSLD-KDD dataset and on UNSW-dataset. We evaluated the performance of k-means clustering algorithm with different values of cluster size.

Then all other clustering methods with some fixed size of clusters are evaluated on both of these datasets.

4.1   Performance Parameters

There are many performance parameters are available for evaluating intrusion detection.

Confusion Matrix: It is the matrix which shows actual and predicted classifications shown in Table 2.

Table 2. Confusion matrix

Expected class		
Actual class	Normal	Attack
Normal	TP	FN
Attack	FP	TN

- True positive (TP): Normal instances which are predicted as Normal (Correct Prediction).
- True Negative (TN): Attack instances which are predicted as Attack (Correct Prediction).
- False positive (FP): Normal instances which are expected as Attacks (Wrong Prediction).
- False negative (FN): Attack instances which are expected as Normal (Wrong Prediction).

$$\text{Precision} = (\text{TP})/(\text{TP} + \text{FP}) \tag{1}$$

$$\text{Recall} = (\text{TP})/(\text{TP} + \text{FN}) \tag{2}$$

$$\text{Accuracy} = (\text{TP} + \text{TN})/(\text{TP} + \text{TN} + \text{FP} + \text{FN}) \tag{3}$$

4.2   Experimental Results

False positive rate, recall, precision and accuracy measures are used for evaluating system performance. These measures help in finding the ratio of intrusions detected as well as incorrect detection. We evaluated all three K-mean, K-medoids and parallel K-medoids clustering methods on NSLD-KDD dataset and UNSW-NB 15 datasets. We kept fixed cluster width as 5 clusters for all these clustering methods on one dataset. Compare the results with other dataset. Then second time cluster size is increased as 10 clusters and fixed these cluster for all three algorithms. Third time cluster width is increased as 20 clusters for all these clustering methods. We compare the results of accuracy, precision and recall values with all these cluster sizes.

The Table 3 and Fig. 1 shows that K-Medoids method on NSLD-KDD dataset with fixed 5 cluster size gives better accuracy compared with K-mean and Parallel K-medoids.

284   P. Dahiya and D. K. Srivastava

Table 3. Performance of Intrusion Detection System on NSLD-KDD dataset with 5 cluster size

Methods	TP	FP	TN	FN	Acc	Prec	Recall
K-mean	0.715	0.058	0.524	0.089	0.893	0.924	0.889
K-medoids	0.834	0.043	0.510	0.078	0.917	0.950	0.914
Parallel K-medoids	0.911	0.061	0.612	0.078	0.916	0.937	0.921

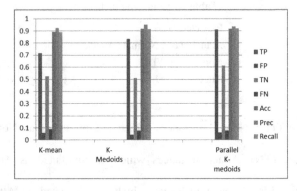

Fig. 1. Performance of Intrusion Detection System on NSLD-KDD dataset with 5 cluster size

The Table 4 and Fig. 2 shows that Parallel K-Medoids method on NSLD-KDD dataset with 10 cluster size gives better precision as compared to K-mean and K-medoids.

Table 4. Performance of Intrusion Detection System on NSLD-KDD dataset with 10 cluster size

Methods	TP	FP	TN	FN	Acc	Prec	Recall
K-mean	0.815	0.056	0.625	0.091	0.9073	0.935	0.899
K-medoids	0.838	0.050	0.615	0.081	0.917	0.943	0.911
Parallel K-medoids	0.914	0.062	0.634	0.078	0.917	0.936	0.921

The Table 5 and Fig. 3 shows that Parallel K-Medoids method on NSLD-KDD dataset with 20 cluster size gives better precision as compared to K-mean and K-medoids.

The Table 5 and Fig. 3 shows that Parallel K-Medoids method on UNSW NB 15 dataset with 5 cluster size gives better precision as compared to K-mean and K-medoids.

The Table 6 shows that Parallel K-Medoids method on UNSW NB 15 dataset with 10 cluster size gives better precision and accuracy as compared to K-mean and K-medoids.

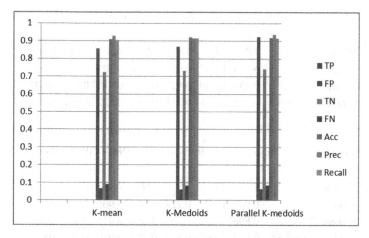

Fig. 2. Performance of Intrusion Detection System on NSLD-KDD dataset with 10 cluster size

Table 5. Performance of Intrusion Detection System on NSLD-KDD dataset with 20 cluster size

Methods	TP	FP	TN	FN	Acc	Prec	Recall
K-mean	0.856	0.067	0.723	0.091	0.909	0.927	0.903
K-medoids	0.867	0.060	0.731	0.081	0.919	0.914	0.914
Parallel K-medoids	0.922	0.064	0.742	0.085	0.917	0.935	0.915

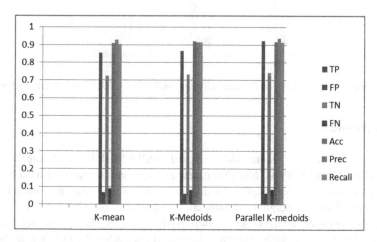

Fig. 3. Performance of Intrusion Detection System on NSLD-KDD dataset with 20 cluster size

The Table 7 shows that Parallel K-Medoids method on UNSW NB 15 dataset with 20 cluster size for all methods gives better precision and accuracy as compared to K-mean and K-medoids (Fig. 4).

Table 6. Performance of Intrusion Detection System on UNSW-NB15 dataset with 10 cluster size

Methods	TP	FP	TN	FN	Acc	Prec	Recall
K-mean	0.828	0.062	0.636	0.094	0.903	0.930	0.898
K-medoids	0.836	0.058	0.627	0.085	0.910	0.935	0.907
Parallel K-medoids	0.935	0.058	0.711	0.081	0.922	0.941	0.921

Table 7. Performance of Intrusion Detection System on UNSW-NB15 dataset with fixed 20 cluster size

Methods	TP	FP	TN	FN	Acc	Prec	Recall
K-mean	0.866	0.071	0.728	0.094	0.906	0.924	0.902
K-medoids	0.898	0.062	0.734	0.088	0.915	0.935	0.910
Parallel K-medoids	0.925	0.065	0.636	0.084	0.940	0.934	0.916

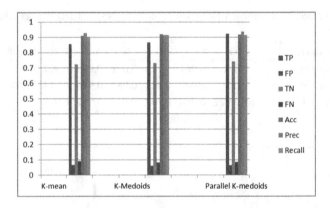

Fig. 4. Performance of Intrusion Detection System on UNSW- NB15 dataset with 5 cluster size

5 Conclusion

We have applied K-mean, K-medoid, proposed parallel Medoids clustering algorithms on NSLD-KDD and UNSW- NB 15 datasets and for classification we used k-nearest neighbor classification techniques. Evaluation results shows that that both *k*-means clustering and *k*-nearest neighbor classification outperforms over UNSW-NB 15 dataset in terms of confusion metrics. As we improved the no. of clusters the accuracy and precision of parallel Medoids method is improved than other, two clustering methods K-mean and k-medoids with different cluster values. The evaluation results show that accuracy is also improved in case of UNSW-NB 15 dataset. Hence UNSW-NB 15 dataset can be used for the evaluation of Anomaly based Network Intrusion Detection Systems.

References

1. Scarfone, K., Mell, P.: Guide to Intrusion Detection and Prevention Systems (IDPS). National Institute of Standards and Technology, Gaithersburg (2007)
2. Bilal, M., et al.: Big data in the construction industry: a review of present status, opportunities, and future trends. Adv. Eng. Inform. **30**(3), 500–521 (2016)
3. Ghemawat, S., Gobioff, H., Leung, S.: The Google file system. In: Proceedings of ACM Symposium on Operating Systems Principles, Lake George, pp. 29–43 (2003)
4. Lee, K.-H., Lee, Y.-J., Choi, H., Chung, Y.D., Moon, B.: Parallel data processing with mapreduce: a survey. ACM SIGMOD Rec. **40**(4), 11–20 (2012)
5. Marchal, S., Jiangz, X., State, R., Engel, T.: A big data architecture for large scale security monitoring. In: IEEE International Congress on Big Data, pp. 56–63 (2014)
6. Jianliang, M., Haikun, S., Ling, B.: The application on intrusion detection based on K-means cluster algorithm. In: International Forum on Information Technology and Application, vol. 1, pp. 150–152 (2009)
7. Wang, L., Jones, R.: Big data analytics for network intrusion detection: a survey. Int. J. Netw. Commun. **7**(1), 24–31 (2017)
8. Sekar, R., et al.: Specification-based anomaly detection: a new approach for detecting network intrusions. In Proceedings of 9th ACM Conference on Computer Communications Security (CCS), pp. 265–274 (2002)
9. Brown, Z.: Big data. 2nd edn. (2014). http://technologyadvice.com/category/big-data/
10. Siddiqui, M.K., Naahid, S.: Analysis of KDD CUP 99 dataset using clustering based data mining. Int. J. Database Theory Appl. **6**, 23–34 (2013)
11. NSL-KDD dataset. http://iscx.ca/NSL-KDD/(2006)
12. https://web.archive.org/web/20150205070216/http://nsl.cs.unb.ca/NSL-KDD/
13. Moustafa, N., Slay, J.: UNSW-NB15: a comprehensive data set for network intrusion detection systems. Inf. Secur. J. A Glob. Perspect. **25**(1), 1–6 (2015)

Effective Traffic Management to Avoid Traffic Congestion Using Recursive Re-routing Algorithm

K. Geetha$^{(\boxtimes)}$, N. Sasikaladevi, and G. T. Dhayaleni

School of Computing, SASTRA University, Thanjavur, Tamilnadu, India
geethavalavan@gmail.com

Abstract. The increase in population mobility due to the growing size of cities has determined a significant increase in the number of vehicles, which have resulted in many challenges for road traffic management authorities to control traffic congestion. The ultimate challenge lies in congestion detection and finding an alternate route for the vehicles to reach the destination on time. Several solutions for Traffic Management System (TMS) have been proposed to identify congestion and find alternate routes. In the present scenario, the system receives notifications about a traffic event from the vehicles that suffer from congestion, calculates new routes, and then notifies the drivers to follow new path by using inter-vehicle communication. When the server receives the alert message from the vehicle, it calculates new route and updates. In such systems, only on the event of congestion, the alternate route is processed by the server. To address this problem, we have proposed a new algorithm called Recursive Re-routing Algorithm (RRA). Here, the congestion information are pre-processed. The probability of expected congestion is calculated beforehand at every intermediate path from source to destination on the server side and it is returned to the vehicle. The shortest path between source and destination is calculated using DIJKSTRA. Traffic density and the threshold value are calculated from the traffic data available under different circumstances. Based on the congestion information inferred from the traffic density, and a threshold value fixed at every path, RRA re-routes to the new best path that can handle congestion intelligently and better than the existing systems.

Keywords: Traffic management · Congestion · VANET · Re-routing
Transportation

1 Introduction

Intelligent Transportation System (ITS) intends to provide various facilities to transportation system and also provide traffic management to ensure safe and smooth transport of people. The facilities provided include car navigation, controlling the traffic signs, giving information about weather and sometimes parking suggestions.

Traffic Management System (TMS) mentioned in [1] is the subfield of Intelligent Transportation System (ITS). It is the system which involves collection of traffic related information and providing the best possible solution based on the present scenario.

© Springer Nature Singapore Pte Ltd. 2018
M. Singh et al. (Eds.): ICACDS 2018, CCIS 906, pp. 288–297, 2018.
https://doi.org/10.1007/978-981-13-1813-9_29

Traffic Management System (TMS) helps in detecting traffic and providing means to reduce congestion effectively. It helps in reducing average trip time, fuel consumption, avoid accidents and also decrease the emission of harmful CO gases. TMS is achieved by Vehicular AdHoc Network (VANET) [2].

Congestion is a condition in road transport which is characterized by longer travel time, vehicles queuing and slower speeds. Congestion occurs because of various reasons. They may be created due to bad weather or may happen due to unexpected incidents like accidents or may be due to bad road condition. Congestion is the main reason which causes increase in emission of CO gases. VANETs [3] are decentralized network which consists of mobile vehicles coordinating with each other to form an Ad Hoc network. This contributes to establish communication among vehicles in the same geographical area.

2 Motivation

Mobility is the one of the basic needs of the world. This is accomplished by automobile vehicles. As population increases, number of vehicles also increases. But the road infrastructure does not increase simultaneously to accommodate the growing pace of vehicles. This leads to traffic congestion. Traffic management is the crucial problem in modern cities. Congestion increases the travel time, causes wastage of resources and may even lead to accidents. It is also a great threat to the cleanliness of the environment since it acts as a major reason for environmental pollution such as air pollution and noise pollution.

Increase in emission of CO_2 pollutes the atmosphere leading to many other problems like ozone layer depletion. Due to congestion, there is wastage of time and wastage of fuel. Wastage of fuel has a very large impact on the future generation and hence measure should be taken to reduce wastage of fuel on a large scale. Sometimes, it may even be very tiring and affects emotional characteristics of the driver. The driver may get frustrated due to long waiting time, delay for meetings, noise pollution and disruption in many other personal and official plans. This may in turn result in rage and violent road fights by the drivers.

Congestion can be caused by many events. It may be due to bad weather, road topography and sometimes due to variation in normal traffic due to occurrence of certain festive events. Unfortunately, topography cannot be changed all of sudden and controlling of weather is beyond our control. The lack in understanding of the public in choosing appropriate vehicles for different purposes of transportation also contribute a little to traffic congestion. It becomes very difficult to handle such situations and prevent congestion. Hence we are left with the only choice of developing new technologies to evade congestion and provide with most efficient solution to mitigate traffic congestion and to cope up with the increase in population especially in urban cities.

3 Literature Review

Traffic Management System (TMS) collects information from multiple sources through sensors and other devices and integrates them to gather a set of traffic related information and to avoid congestion. Improvement of traffic Condition through an Alerting and Re-routing System (ICARUS) [4] is a pro active system which detects the onset of congestion before- hand. Unlike other systems which detect congestion only after it has occurred. ICARUS works like it receives position information from vehicle, which then calculates new routes and suggests them through VANET. The suggestions are disseminated via various protocols.

One such technique is flooding. It simply re-transmits the packets among vehicles until information is reached out. This suffers with broad cast storm problem if the network is heavy. Another technique is Distance Based Relay Selection (DBRS) [5] which holds the information or packet for certain time interval without transmitting. This time interval is inversely proportional to the distance of the vehicle to this the information must be transmitted. It continuously hears the channel and when it senses the re-transmission of the same packet from some other node, it cancels its transmission. Data Dissemination Protocol in Vehicular Networks (DRIVE) [6] sends messages to only those vehicles which are in sweet spot.

Dynamic Shortest Path (DSP) [7] proposes shortest travel to destination with the purpose of reducing the travel time. But it does not really reduce congestion rather it shifts it to other spot. In order to overcome the drawback of DSP, Random K Shortest Path (RKSP) [8] was used. It selects a path taking care that the congestion does not shift to other spot. Entropy Balanced k Shortest Paths (EBkSP) improves RkSP while keeping the future density considerations in all those k paths.

Dijkstra uses length as cost function to calculate the route to destination and not suitable in case the traffic is heavy. A* uses traffic condition as heuristic to calculate route. It reduces the probability of occurrence of congestion in other selected route. Another approach is Probabilistic k-shortest Path (PkSP) [9] and it uses weight to calculate new route. The weight is calculated as traffic in whole route and it also represents the probability of a route to get selected as next alternative route.

Intelligent Transportation System (ITS) [10] measures traffic congestion by installing sensors along road side units. This technique is very expensive. Hence, a new system called cooperative technique based on vehicle to vehicle communication was introduced. This provided accurate real time traffic congestion information. This method is coupled with data dissemination protocols to warn the vehicles before- hand. Congestion must be handled by re-routing. The system collects information from sensors and supply different routes for each and every individual vehicle.

VANET integrates ad hoc network, wireless LAN and cellular technology to achieve inter vehicle communication. Evading congestion reduces travel time and fuel consumption. The system uses GPS to track the traffic data supplemented with peer to peer communication. It uses clustering and epidemic technique [11] to distribute traffic information. Vehicles are attached with processors, sensors and wireless communication devices so that they can communicate with other vehicles and Road Side Units (RSU) [12]. RSUs provide routing information only to those vehicles within its radius. The vehicles receive information from multiple RSUs and accordingly make travel decision.

4 Proposed RRA Model

The proposed RRA model is implemented in four phases. The first is Data Sensing and Gathering (DSG) which involves collecting traffic speed, density and road segregation and sends this to central server. The second phase is Data Fusion, Processing, and Aggregation (DFPA) involving gathering of useful information. The next phase is Data Exploitation (DE) which detect best route from the information extracted. The last phase is Service Delivery (SD) which deals with distributing this routing information to users through variety of devices.

Figure 1 shows the model of the proposed system which prevents congestion instead of handling it. When the vehicle travels from source to destination, traffic congestion information is updated to the vehicle at every intermediate node recursively which guarantees that the vehicle travels in the best route from source to destination. Hence, the vehicles travel in a route which has minimum possibilities for traffic events.

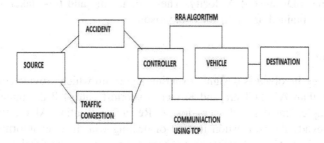

Fig. 1. RRA Model

Based on the information, the vehicle either travel in the same route or request for next shortest route with minimum distance which happens in the case of congestion. The transfer of congestion information, alert messages, new routes between the vehicle and the controller is done using TCP client-server protocol. This process is repeated until the destination is reached.

5 Methodology

5.1 Collection of Data

To identify the best path, distance between every intermediate node is measured. The shortest path need not be the optimal path in terms of travel time, so number of vehicles between the nodes and their speed is calculated for every one hour (used available dataset). The greater the number of vehicles below average speed, more the number of vehicles on road and a high probability for congestion. Initially the average speed in peak hour is found using the formula,

$$\text{Average speed} = \sum f_i x_i \div \sum f_i \tag{1}$$

x_i – speed of vehicle
f_i – number of vehicle

An assumption is made that congestion occurs when vehicles move lesser than the average speed. The speed of vehicles on congestion is calculated using the above Eq. (1), but the vehicles travelling below average speed alone are considered. The normal velocity and velocity at the time of congestion is obtained and are used to calculate the respective time of travel. Time is calculated using distance, velocity, time formula. Time = Distance ÷ Velocity. The normal time and time taken during congestion hence obtained are used for comparison.

5.2 Routing

Next major step involved is designing routing algorithm which provide comparatively better results than A*, Dijkstra and K means shortest path. All the three algorithms cannot be implemented in all scenarios. A Recursive Routing Algorithm (RRA) is designed to evade the congestion instead of dealing with it. User informs the server about his travel locations. Possible routes between source and destination is calculated using Dijkstra. RRA then checks for the probability of occurrence of congestion between any two points towards destination. It compares congestion information from several routes with a threshold. The threshold is a variable dependent on time. Based on the threshold, RRA suggests a path which involves comparatively less congestion among the other possible routes.

5.3 Recursive Routing Algorithm

```
1.    function RRA(src,dest);
2.    do
3.    call Dijkstra(G,src,dest)
4.    density <- 0
5.    adj [] <- adjacencies of each vertex v
6.    get l and n // l <- length of road, n<- number of cars
7.    density <- (n*1000)/l
8.    t <- threshold
9.    if density > t
10.   temp <- path[1]
11.   for i in 1 to length(temp.adj[])
12.       if temp.adj[] is not null and temp.adj[] is in G
13.           temp.adj[i] <- INFINITY
14.       else
15.           if  length(path) > 1
16.               src <- path[1]
17.           else
18.               src <-null
19.   while src not equal to dest
20.   return
```

```
1.    function Dijkstra(G, src, dest):
2.    dis[src] <- 0
3.    prv[src] <-UNDEFINED
4.    path[] <- NULL
5.    create vertex set S
6.    for each vertex v in G:
7.        if v is not src:
8.            dis[v] <- INFINITY
9.            prv[v] <- UNDEFINED
10.       add v to S
11.   while S is not empty:
12.       u <- vertex in S with min dis[u]
13.   remove u from S
14.   if src = dest:
15.           return dis[],prv[]
16.   for each neighbor v of u:
17.       alt <- dis[u] +length(u,v)
18.       if alt < dis[v]:
19.           dis[v] <- alt
20.           prv[v] <- u
21.   src1 <- src
22.   while src1 not equal to dest
23.       add src1 to path
24.       src1 <- src1.prv
25.   add dest to path
26.   reverse path
27.   return dis[],path[]
```

5.4 Performance Analysis

From the plot shown in Fig. 2, we observe there are comparatively many number of vehicles only during peak hours and hence there are greater chances for congestion at that time. Considering the source node as A and the destination node as F, the performance of the proposed algorithm has been analyzed.

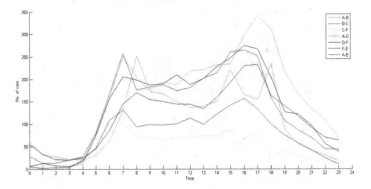

Fig. 2. Analysis of number of vehicles on every path at every interval

The distance from A to F through each route, namely ABCF, AEF, ACF, ACDF, ABCDF have been plotted. Similarly the normal travel times and time taken for travel during congestion through the respective routes to the destination have also been plotted in Figs. 3 and 4.

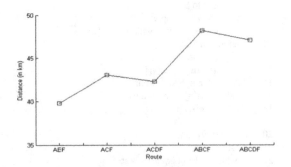

Fig. 3. Distances to reach F from A through all possible routes

5.5 Comparison with Dijkstra

In Dijkstra's algorithm, only the shortest distance is considered irrespective of congestion in that route. Hence, during congestion in the route AEF in the above figure it is seen that Dijkstra's algorithm chooses the path AEF while the proposed algorithm chooses ACF which is less congested as shown in the Fig. 5. Time taken through AEF

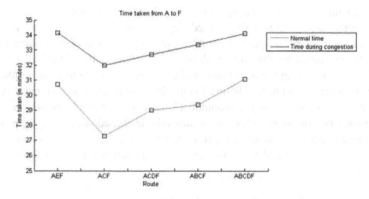

Fig. 4. Comparison of the time taken to reach the F from A using RRA algorithm under normal and congestion conditions

during congestion is 34.15 min while time taken through ACF which is less congested is 27.3 min. The difference in the time taken is 6.85 min. The path suggested by Dijkstra in this case has a higher travel time of 25.09% with respect to the path suggested by RRA. A* considers all nodes that are open irrespective of whether the node leads to the destination, thereby increasing the computation time. RRA on the other hand has an initial seed of routes to the destination which it uses at every node reached to reroute the path. This computation takes lesser time.

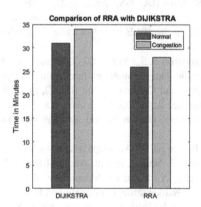

Fig. 5. Comparison of RRA with Dijkstra

6 Conclusion

The proposed RRA routing algorithm, aims to minimize the congestion of vehicles in urban centers using a vehicular network. The proposed solution aims to reduce the travel time, congestion time, and maximize the average speed of the vehicles during its trip. The percentage of travel time saved depends on the total distance, number of vehicles and their average speed. Congestion at every node between source and destination are considered for the travel path as it may influence travel time as well as fuel consumption. Optimizing the travel path will contribute to the reduction of emission of CO gases into the atmosphere. The inter-vehicular communication ensured that it does not suffer from broadcast storm problem. Communication happens between central server and any one of the vehicles and in turn vehicles broadcast the messages to other vehicles. Hence packets lost or network congestion is avoided. This ensured that the vehicles get timely alert and were able to reach destination on time and also ensured safe travel.

Acknowledgements. The part of this research work is supported by Department of Science and Technology (DST), Science and Engineering Board (SERB), Government of India under the ECR grant (ECR/2017/000679/ES).

References

1. Bauza, R., Gozalvez, J., Sanchez-Soriano, J.: Road traffic congestion detection through cooperative vehicle-to-vehicle communications. In: IEEE 35th Conference on Local Computer Networks (LCN), pp. 606–612. IEEE (2010)
2. Pan, J., Khan, M.A., Popa, I.S., Zeitouni, K., Borcea, C.: Proactive vehicle re-routing strategies for congestion avoidance. In: IEEE 8th International Conference on Distributed Computing in Sensor Systems (DCOSS), pp. 265–272. IEEE (2012)
3. Dornbush, S., Joshi, A.: StreetSmart traffic: discovering and disseminating automobile congestion using VANET's. In: IEEE 65th Vehicular Technology Conference. VTC2007-Spring, pp. 11–15. IEEE (2007)
4. de Souza, A.M., Yokoyama, R.S., Maia, G., Loureiro, A., Villas, L.: Real-time path planning to prevent traffic jam through an intelligent transportation system. In: IEEE Symposium on Computers and Communication (ISCC), pp. 726–731. IEEE (2016)
5. Da Cunha, F.D., Boukerche, A., Villas, L., Viana, A.C., Loureiro, A.A.: Data communication in VANETs: a survey, challenges and applications. Doctoral dissertation, INRIA Saclay, INRIA (2014)
6. Bakhouya, M., Gaber, J., Lorenz, P.: An adaptive approach for information dissemination in vehicular ad hoc networks. J. Netw. Comput. Appl. **34**(6), 1971–1978 (2011)
7. Souza, A.M.D., Boukerche, A., Maia, G., Meneguette, R.I., Loureiro, A.A., Villas, L.A.: Decreasing greenhouse emissions through an intelligent traffic information system based on inter-vehicle communication. In: Proceedings of the 12th ACM International Symposium on Mobility Management and Wireless Access, pp. 91–98. ACM (2014)
8. Li, F., Wang, Y.: Routing in vehicular ad hoc networks: a survey. IEEE Veh. Technol. Mag. **2**(2), 12–22 (2007)
9. Brennand, C.A., et al.: An intelligent transportation system for detection and control of congested roads in urban centers. In: IEEE Symposium on Computers and Communication (ISCC), pp. 663–668. IEEE (2015)
10. Pattanaik, V., Singh, M., Gupta, P.K., Singh, S.K.: Smart real-time traffic congestion estimation and clustering technique for urban vehicular roads. In: Region 10 Conference (TENCON), 22 November 2016, pp. 3420–3423. IEEE (2016)

11. Malekian, R., Kavishe, A.F., Maharaj, B.T., Gupta, P.K., Singh, G., Waschefort, H.: Smart vehicle navigation system using hidden Markov model and RFID technology. Wirel. Pers. Commun. **90**(4), 1717–1742 (2016)
12. Wang, X., Yuen, C., Hassan, N.U., An, N., Wu, W.: Electric vehicle charging station placement for urban public bus systems. IEEE Trans. Intell. Transp. Syst. **18**(1), 128–139 (2017)

A Normalized Cosine Distance Based Regression Model for Data Prediction in WSN

Arun Agarwal[1]($\boxtimes$) and Amita Dev[2]

[1] GGSIPU, Delhi, India
arun.261986@gmail.com
[2] BPIBS, Delhi, India
amita_dev@hotmail.com

Abstract. The growth of internet, technology, hardware and software devices has lead to many new inventions. Wireless Sensor Network is one among them which utilizes the attractive features of wireless communication along with the applications and capabilities of sensor nodes. The main constraint of WSN is limited energy resources. Several protocols have been developed to overcome this limitation. Also few methods have been suggested to reduce overall transmission cost. Data prediction becomes a popular technique to enhance performance by reducing data load on sensor node. It is observed that all data sensed by the SN is not necessary because the values received by the sink may contain duplicate, inappropriate and inconsistent values. So the new research design is focused on collecting and sending only that value which will be utilized by the sink. The transmission of irrelevant data is avoided to enhance the performance and lifetime of the network. This paper presents an approach to reduce transmission of data by establishing relationship between data values. The proposed approach is aimed to built a data prediction model which will be used to predict future values based upon the values received in past. The study suggested a normalized cosine method for distance calculation between data values. This distance is further utilized to establish relationship to predict future values. An enhanced regression prediction model is built based upon the normalized cosine distance.

The purpose of the proposed model is to exempt the sensor node for sending data for a specific duration in which BS will predict the data values based upon the model developed. The proposed model is compared with existing linear model. The results show that the proposed model works better as compared to linear model and it reduces mean square error. Another performance metric i.e. percentage reduction in energy dissipation is compared to prove that proposed solution is better than the existing method.

Keywords: WSN · Data prediction · Cosine distance · Regression analysis
Energy efficiency · Data management · Minimization

© Springer Nature Singapore Pte Ltd. 2018
M. Singh et al. (Eds.): ICACDS 2018, CCIS 906, pp. 298–308, 2018.
https://doi.org/10.1007/978-981-13-1813-9_30

1 Introduction

Wireless Sensor Network is a randomly deployed collection of sensor nodes with the aim to collect the information near its sensing area. The approach is to sense some event, record its respective data value and transmit it to a particular sink where this data value is utilized and thus become information [1]. A wireless Sensor Network is deployed in the area of interest to monitor the area and collect the desired information. The aim is to meet high information gain with minimum loss of energy. A Sensor Node is a smart device which consists of a sensing unit, a small inbuilt processor, memory, transmission and receiving unit and battery operated power source. The major task associated with each SN is sensing, transmission, aggregation and receiving and finally transmitting the collected information to base station. Sensor Nodes are the backbone of any WSN but in environment monitoring applications they are deployed with limited battery power. There are several applications of WSN. Environment monitoring, data logging, smart home monitoring, military applications, health monitoring area are few major applications [2]. The prime interest among all the above mentioned applications is environment monitoring and the major issue associated with this is energy. Due to these inherent limitations majority of research work is carried out to develop protocols which reduces total energy consumption and enhances overall network lifetime.

WSN is designed to collect information and several issues associated with design and implementations of WSN are routing, efficient energy dissipation, data and security. In the proposed approach prime focus is on management of data to provide an efficient solution. Data is an integral component of computation and it is the end result processed by the base station. Data is periodically sensed and transmitted by the SN and the aggregated data is routed to BS. Continuous sensing of data results in fast drain of energy which reduces overall lifetime. Also continuous sensing results in large amount of data which contains redundant and irrelevant information. So the aim is to develop a mechanism which filters out unnecessary data and only relevant and necessary information must be transmitted to base station. The management and optimization of this big data is essential in today's scenario to save the scarce energy resource.

In literature few methods have been proposed to reduce amount of data. Data prediction is one among the various techniques to reduce data. Other techniques may involve data compression or transmission of Meta data but the issue associated with each one of these technique is its complexity. The requirement is to establish a tradeoff between efficient energy dissipation and complexity. Taking the prediction techniques into consideration and minimizing the effort associated with data transmission there are several approaches available in literature which may differ in amount of data reduced and quantization error produced. The proposed approach is aimed to achieve small quantization error and high proportion of data minimization. Also this should be noted that a perceptible increase in lifetime must be observed while implementing any such strategy.

The main goal of applying prediction technique is to build a regression model that depicts relationship between past, present and future data values. The purpose is to design a relationship model between data values that minimizes the total data transmission by transmitting control packet instead of new data packet. The proposed prediction model is based on calculating cosine distance between the transmitted values. Also the sample of data values must be selected such that it represents the complete range of collected values. For this reason a vector of data values for each sensor node is chosen which consists of minimum, maximum, quartiles and average value. A data prediction model is established between total number of data values per sensor node and the vector corresponding to that sensor node. This paper proposes a technique to built regression model based upon the calculation of normalized cosine distance. The proposed technique is compared with simple regression model and mean square error is compared in both the cases. Simulation study reflects that the proposed approach reduces mean square error which signifies that the prediction accuracy is better in the proposed approach. Total energy dissipation is also measured in both the cases and the result reflects that proposed approach will give better results.

The remainder of this paper is organized as follows. Section 2 begins with the discussion of study of data prediction techniques. A brief explanation of several techniques that persists in literature is given. Section 3 discusses proposed approach and system model. Section 4 analyses the simulation process and tabulate the results obtained. Last section concludes the study and gives various future perspectives.

2 Literature Survey

Various protocols have been proposed to improve performance by managing the amount of data that is transmitted to base station. SPIN is negotiation based protocol [3] which efficiently disseminates data using some descriptors and converts it into Meta data. SPIN reduces transmission of redundant data to give reduced energy supply. A wide variety of work is carried out in field of data management using data prediction technique. Each technique uses different approach to reduce data and improve performance. Reducing data will result in reduced transmission costs. Samer Samarah proposes a prediction model [4] based upon integration of WSN and cloud computing that uses cloud system to reduce the overburden of data on SN thus reducing large data transfers and increases network lifetime. Somasekhar et al. [5] proposed a pre filtration method in which correlated data transmissions are identified to reduce redundant data. They proposed relative variation function to compare data values and to find similarity and correlation in data. They defined a data aggregative window function to find geographical and in data aggregation redundancy.

Haiying Shen [6] proposes an efficient data collection hybrid approach that integrates RFID and WSN data transmission. This paper proposed smart nodes that result in proactive data transmission, enhance efficiency and security. Halder and Ghosal [7] proposes a mobility based localization technique that reduces implementation and maintenance cost by reducing the number of nodes required for communication. In this paper an algorithm is designed to provide error free refinement mechanism for mobile anchor trajectories.

Rault et al. [8] presented a paper that lists the amount of energy consumption at different levels. In this survey few energy saving techniques have been discussed which includes data prediction and energy harvesting.

OSPF is Open Shortest Path First protocol [9] which periodically checks for any repetition of data and reduces communication overhead. It works on topology change where data must be filtered out from neighboring nodes to reduce redundancy and duplicity of data. Data prediction in WSN guesses upcoming values based on the values received in past. Regression models have build to predict continuous set of values. Some models like auto regressive model uses linear regression. Similar approach has been used by Tulone et al. [10] in which regression is implemented in addition with probabilistic query system that submit response to queries generated at base station where query is of the form of future values required by base station.

Dias, Bellalta and Oechsner [11] presented a brief survey about available prediction techniques. In this paper classification of prediction techniques have been listed. Explanation of Dual prediction and simple prediction techniques is given along with their pros and cons.

Mou et al. [12] in their paper monitors environmental parameters using WSN. They combine data prediction with compression and also suggested recovery of loss-less data at receiver end. They applied least mean square method for prediction of data values where CHs obtain an approximated value after stipulated time period given by optimal step size algorithm. In this aggregation schedule is focused to maintain synchronization.

Guiyi et al. [13] presents a different approach to handle data by removing temporal redundancy. The authors proposed a double queue mechanism to predict data values and to maintain synchronization between communicating nodes. In this study two different methods grey model and Kalman filter has been introduced for data aggregation and both were integrated to achieve better performance. It results in accuracy and reduced overhead.

Wang et al. [14] suggested a method to remove geographical redundancy. They find correlations between locations of sensor nodes and data transmitted by SNs associated with a given geographical coordinate.

3 Proposed Approach

The proposed model is build to reduce communication overhead and to prolong network lifetime. A data prediction technique is suggested based upon normalized cosine distance. The proposed method considers a random network composed of 25 sensor nodes which are uniformly distributed in 5 clusters. Base stationed is positioned in n-dimensional space and is placed in centre of the network. The proposed network structure is given in Fig. 1. Each cluster consists of 5 sensor nodes which are divided into two categories, Sensor node SN and Cluster Head CH. CH will collect data of current round from each sensor node, aggregate it and forward the same to base station. To accomplish equal dissipation of energy the CH is selected in round robin fashion, where each sensor node is allowed to become a CH in a predefined time slot which thereby termed as one round of communication. The proposed approach may also be analyzed in terms of total rounds of communication which defines checkpoints to measure the performance. These checkpoints may be given as first node die FND, half node alive HNA and last node alive. The proposed model uses two hop communications where first hop is transmission of data from SN to CH and next hop from CH to BS.

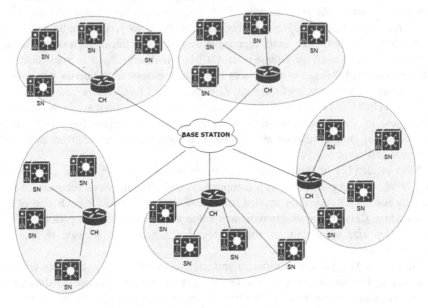

Fig. 1. Position of sensor nodes and base station

In transmission phase SN will collect its data value and will directly send the same to its own CH, CH upon receiving all SN's value aggregate these data values and transmit this aggregated value directly to base station. This process is termed as one round of computation and to set up the communication, data is being captured in rounds of equal time slots. The algorithm begins by analyzing one cluster and repeats the same process for remaining clusters. In each round a data value that is aggregated by the CH of the given cluster is transmitted directly to base station. All the sensor nodes are operated to sense data for a fixed duration and at the end of this duration it is switched to idle mode i.e. switch off the SN. Thousands of sensor readings were collected and transmitted to base station in the predefined time period. The variation of all the collected values is given in Fig. 2 which represents a sample of collected values for five sensor nodes in a cluster.

Sensor nodes are transmitting data values in a lock step manner where one data value is produced per round. These sensor readings were collected for a fixed duration in which a SN is directed to send its sensed data reading directly to respective CH. The above figure describe that there is a variation in data values collected by base station. The same variations are taken into consideration by operating the proposed model for longer durations. To encompass the complete range of values, sample data set is chosen such that it reflects all the sensed values.

Our proposed model allows random movement of sensor nodes. It results into completely dynamic approach. In each round sensor node coordinates is being

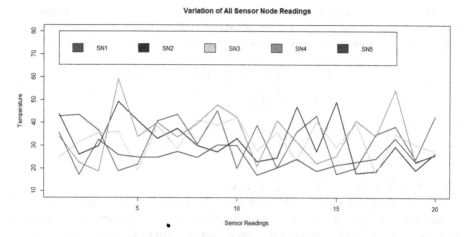

Fig. 2. Variation of sensor node data readings

determined and based upon the same clusters have been formed. Random network structure and cluster formation is done in the beginning of each round. The randomness is taken into consideration to closely resemble the real time scenario. Also random deployment of SN's encompasses wide domain of data values to be sensed in each round.

Upon receiving these values BS will compute a data vector of size n which consists of minimum, first quartile, second quartile, third quartile, maximum and average of all readings for each sensor. The computed vector will contain the following values as shown in Table 1:

Table 1. Description of data vector for calculation of normalized cosine distance

Sensor node	Minimum	1st Quartile	2nd Quartile	3rd Quartile	Maximum	Average
SN1	d11	d12	d13	d14	d15	d16
SN2	d21	d22	d23	d24	d25	d26
SN3	d31	d32	d33	d34	d35	d36
SN4	d41	d42	d43	d44	d45	d46
SN5	d51	d52	d53	d54	d55	d56

Proposed regression model is built by calculating cosine distance for the vectors defined above. The objective of the proposed model is to calculate regression line equation of the form:

$$\phi = \beta 1\chi + \beta 0 \tag{1}$$

Where ϕ is the predicted vector of each sensor node, χ is vector of number of sensor readings for each SN, $\beta1$ is normalised cosine distance and $\beta0$ is average weight vector value corresponding to every sensor node. $\beta1$ and $\beta0$ are calculated as:

$$\beta1 = \frac{|\prod di1| + |\prod di2| + |\prod di3|........+ |\prod dit|}{\sqrt{\sum(d1j)^2}.\sqrt{\sum(d2j)^2}.........\sqrt{\sum(dtj)}} \tag{2}$$

$$\beta0 = \sum_{k=1}^{5}\frac{di1}{n}, \sum_{k=1}^{5}\frac{di2}{n}, \sum_{k=1}^{5}\frac{di3}{n}, \sum_{k=1}^{5}\frac{di4}{n}, \sum_{k=1}^{5}\frac{di5}{n}, \sum_{k=1}^{5}\frac{di6}{n} \tag{3}$$

$\forall i = \{1, 2, 3, 4, 5\}$ and $\forall j = \{1, 2, 3, 4, 5, 6\}$.

The proposed regression model uses normalized cosine distance among vector of all computed values. By using different quartile values, minimum, maximum and average values the goal is to cover the entire range of data readings. These six sample values represent the complete data set consisting of thousand of values. Based upon these values a prediction equation is formulated. Using this equation BS will predict future values without actually receiving data values from SN in idle mode. In next time slot the sensor nodes are directed to keep them in idle mode to save energy. During this sleep period, base station will predict the data values based upon the proposed Regression Model. The sensor node will save its balance energy during this time period. This will enhance the overall lifetime to a greater instant. The analysis is carried out to determine total amount of energy saved during this period.

4   Simulation and Result Analysis

This section contains the simulation parameters. The results have been summarized and analyzed. The Intel Berkeley Research Lab Data [15] is used in this simulation. This data set consists of readings of Mica2Dot sensors which collect data values for temperature over a long period. We have taken temperature values to build our model and over 40000 data values for each sensor node is analyzed. All the temperature values are collected in degree Celsius. All the sensor nodes are connected to base station positioned in middle of network. Each sensor node is directed to transmit its data directly to cluster head of the current round which in turn aggregates and transmit the same to base station. All the sensor readings are collected by the base station and a vector is constructed for each SN which contains above defined six base values.

The performance is being measured in terms of mean square error which gives the degree of resemblance of predicted data value with respect to original data value. The expectation is to obtain zero mean square error so that the predicted value matches exactly with the actual value.

The proposed model is compared with simple regression model. Also to analyze the impact of random network change the proposed model is evaluated for three different network architectures. The network size is varied from 25 to 100 nodes. The comparison of simple regression model and proposed normalized cosine regression model is given in Table 2 along with the impact of change of network architecture.

Table 2. Comparison of simple regression and proposed prediction model in terms of mean square

Network size	Simple regression model mean squared error per sensor node	Proposed normalized cosine regression model mean squared error per sensor node
25 SN [5 × 5]	1.214191	0.095360
64 SN [8 × 8]	0.474294	0.037250
100 SN [10 × 10]	0.303548	0.023840

The proposed prediction model has been analyzed in terms of energy consumption, where total energy dissipation is measured in both cases. The experimental result shows that there is a significance improvement in network lifetime using the proposed approach. A total reduction in energy dissipation is computed and compared with actual energy dissipation. The results have been summarized in Table 3.

Table 3. Percentage reduction of energy for simple regression and proposed model

Network size	% Reduction of energy dissipation using simple regression model	% Reduction of energy dissipation using proposed normalized cosine regression model
25 SN [5 × 5]	12.5	21.6
64 SN [8 × 8]	18.0	33.5
100 SN [10 × 10]	32.5	54.6

Simulation is being carried out several times to test the randomness of network. Each time the performance is measured in terms of residuals which are the difference of actual value to the predicted value. The residuals are used to calculate prediction accuracy and the results have been compared with other prediction approaches.

5 Conclusion and Future Scope

This paper presented a normalized cosine distance based data prediction model to predict future sensor values based upon past values. The proposed model uses cosine distance which is widely used in data mining processes. The cosine distance is calculated to build relationship model. The proposed model is compared with linear regression model and the simulation results clearly states that the proposed model is better in terms of percentage reduction of energy dissipation and mean square error is also reduced. The reduction in residual value guarantees that proposed prediction model is more accurate in terms of predicting future values as compared to linear model. This paper opens up a wide domain of research techniques and will be benefitted by implementing various mathematical prediction techniques to design and develop different prediction models. In the upcoming paper the solution will be given to determine the actual time required to perform sensing and prediction. An energy efficient technique will be developed to correctly assess the operational and non operational timing boundaries of sensor nodes.

References

1. Akyildiz, I.F., Vuran, M.C.: Wireless Sensor Networks. Wiley, Hoboken (2010)
2. Wener-Allen, G., et al.: Deploying a wireless sensor network on an active volcano, data-driven applications in sensor networks. IEEE Internet Comput. (2006)
3. Kulik, J., Heinzelman, W., Balakrishnan, H.: Negotiation-based protocols for disseminating information in wireless sensor networks. Wirel. Netw. **8**, 169–185 (2002)
4. Samarah, S.: Data predication model for integrating wireless sensor networks and cloud computing. Procedia Comput. Sci. **52**, 1141–1146 (2015)
5. Kandukuri, S., Lebreton, J., Lorion, R., Murad, N., Lan-Sun-Luk, J.D.: Energy-efficient data aggregation techniques for exploiting spatio-temporal correlations in wireless sensor networks. IEEE (2016)
6. Shen, H., Li, Z., Yu, L., Qiu, C.: Efficient data collection for large-scale mobile monitoring applications. IEEE Trans. Parallel Distrib. Syst. **25**(6), 1424–1436 (2014)
7. Halder, S., Ghosal, A.: A survey on mobility-assisted localization techniques in wireless sensor networks. J. Netw. Comput. Appl. **60**, 82–94 (2016)
8. Rault, T., Bouabdallah, A., Challal, Y.: Energy efficiency in wireless sensor networks: a top-down survey. Comput. Netw. **67**, 104–122 (2014). https://doi.org/10.1016/j.comnet.2014.03.027
9. Moy, J.: OSPF Version 2, RFC 1583 (1991)
10. Tulone, D., Madden, S.: PAQ: Time series forecasting for approximate query answering in sensor networks. In: Römer, K., Karl, H., Mattern, F. (eds.) EWSN 2006. LNCS, vol. 3868, pp. 21–37. Springer, Heidelberg (2006). https://doi.org/10.1007/11669463_5
11. Dias, G.M., Bellalta, B., Oechsner, S.: A survey about prediction-based data reduction in wireless sensor networks. ACM Comput. Surv. **49**(3), Article 58 (2016)
12. Wu, M., Tan, L., Xiong, N.: Data prediction, compression, and recovery in clustered wireless sensor networks for environmental monitoring applications. Inf. Sci. **329**, 800–818 (2016)
13. Wei, G., Ling, Y., Guo, B., Xiao, B., Vasilakos, A.V.: Prediction-based data aggregation in wireless sensor networks: combining grey model and Kalman Filter. Comput. Commun. **34**, 793–802 (2011)
14. Wang, L., Deshpande, A.: Predictive modeling-based data collection in wireless sensor networks. In: Verdone, R. (ed.) EWSN 2008. LNCS, vol. 4913, pp. 34–51. Springer, Heidelberg (2008). https://doi.org/10.1007/978-3-540-77690-1_3
15. Bodik, P., Hong, W., Guestrin, C., Madden, S., Paskin, M., Thibaux, R.: Intel lab data (2004). http://db.csail.mit.edu/labdata/labdata.html
16. Anastasi, G., Conti, M., Di Francesco, M., Passarella, A.: Energy conservation in wireless sensor networks: a survey. Comput. Netw. 537–568 (2009)

17. Heinzelman, W.R., Chandrakasan, A., Balakrishnan, H.: Energy-efficient communication protocol for wireless microsensor networks. In: Proceedings of Hawaii International Conference on System Sciences (HICSS), pp. 1–10 (2000)
18. Yick, J., Mukherjee, B., Ghosal, D.: Wireless sensor network survey. Comput. Netw. **52**, 2292–2330 (2008)
19. Say, S., Inata, H., Liu, J., Shimamoto, S.: Priority-based data gathering framework in UAV-assisted wireless sensor networks. IEEE Sens. J. **16**(14), 5785–5794 (2016)
20. Chu, D., Deshpande, A., Hellerstein, J.M., Hong, W.: Approximate data collection in sensor networks using probabilistic models. In: Proceedings of the 22nd International Conference on Data Engineering (2006)
21. Szewczyk, R., Osterweil, E., Polastre, J., Hamilton, M., Mainwaring, A., Estrin, D.: Habitat monitoring with sensor networks. Commun. ACM **47**(6), 34–40 (2004)
22. Ingelrest, F., Barrenetxea, G., Schaefer, G., Vetterli, M., Couach, O., Parlange, M.: Sensorscope: application-specific sensor network for environmental monitoring. ACM Trans. Sens. Netw. **6**(2), 17 (2010)
23. Alippi, C., Camplani, R., Galperti, C., Roveri, M.: A robust, adaptive, solar-powered WSN framework for aquatic environmental monitoring. IEEE Sens. J. **11**(1), 45–55 (2011)
24. Liu, H., Meng, Z., Cui, S.: A wireless sensor network prototype for environmental monitoring in greenhouses. In: Proceedings of International Conference on Wireless Communications, Networking and Mobile Computing (WiCom), pp. 2344–2347 (2007)
25. Dargie, W., Poellabauer, C.: Fundamentals of Wireless Sensor Networks: Theory and Practice. Wiley, Hoboken (2010)
26. Yun, Y., Xia, Y.: Maximizing the lifetime of wireless sensor networks with mobile sink in delay-tolerant applications. IEEE Trans. Mob. Comput. **9**(9), 1308–1318 (2010)
27. Abdulla, A.E., Nishiyama, H., Kato, N.: Extending the lifetime of wireless sensor networks: a hybrid routing algorithm. Comput. Commun. **35**(9), 1056–1063 (2012)
28. Liu, A., Jin, X., Cui, G., Chen, Z.: Deployment guidelines for achieving maximum lifetime and avoiding energy holes in sensor network. Inf. Sci. **230**, 197–226 (2013)
29. Bicakci, K., Bagci, I.E., Tavli, B.: Communication/computation tradeoffs for prolonging network lifetime in wireless sensor networks: the case of digital signatures. Inf. Sci. **188**, 44–63 (2012)
30. Zhu, Y.-H., Wu, W.-D., Pan, J., Tang, Y.-P.: An energy-efficient data gathering algorithm to prolong lifetime of wireless sensor networks. Comput. Commun. **33**(5), 639–647 (2010)
31. Li, B.-Y., Chuang, P.-J.: Geographic energy-aware non-interfering multipath routing for multimedia transmission in wireless sensor networks. Inf. Sci. **249**, 24–37 (2013)
32. Guo, W., Xiong, N., Vasilakos, A.V., Chen, G., Cheng, H.: Multi-source temporal data aggregation in wireless sensor networks. Wirel. Pers. Commun. **56**, 359–370 (2011)
33. Zhao, J., Liu, H., Li, Z., Li, W.: Periodic data prediction algorithm in wireless sensor networks. In: Wang, R., Xiao, F. (eds.) CWSN 2012. CCIS, vol. 334, pp. 695–701. Springer, Heidelberg (2013). https://doi.org/10.1007/978-3-642-36252-1_65
34. Liu, Q., Zhang, Y.Y., Shen, J., Xiao, B., Linge, N.: A WSN-based prediction model of microclimate in a greenhouse using an extreme learning approach. In: Advanced Communication Technology, pp. 133–137 (2015)
35. Vuppala, S.K., Ghosh, A., Patil, K.A., Padmanabh, K.: A scalable WSN based data center monitoring solution with probabilistic event prediction. In: Advanced Information Networking and Applications (2012)
36. Zhang, Z., Deng, B., Chen, S., Li, L.: An improved HMM model for sensing data predicting in WSN. In: Cui, B., Zhang, N., Xu, J., Lian, X., Liu, D. (eds.) WAIM 2016. LNCS, vol. 9658, pp. 31–42. Springer, Cham (2016). https://doi.org/10.1007/978-3-319-39937-9_3

37. Sinha, A., Lobiyal, D.K.: Probabilistic data aggregation in information-based clustered sensor network. Wirel. Pers. Commun. **77**(2), 1287–1310 (2014)
38. Jiang, H., Jin, S., Wang, C.: Prediction or not? An energy-efficient framework for clustering-based data collection in wireless sensor networks. IEEE Trans. Parallel Distrib. Syst. **22**(6), 1064–1071 (2011)
39. Edara, P., Limaye, A., Ramamritham, K.: Asynchronous in-network prediction: Efficient aggregation in sensor networks. ACM Trans. Sens. Netw. **4**(4), 25–34 (2008)

Comparative Study of Regression Models Towards Performance Estimation in Soil Moisture Prediction

Amarendra Goap[1,2(✉)], Deepak Sharma[2], A. K. Shukla[2],
and C. Rama Krishna[1]

[1] National Institute of Technical Teachers Training and Research (NITTTR),
Chandigarh 160019, India
agoap@csio.res.in
[2] CSIR-Central Scientific Instruments Organization, Chandigarh 160030, India

Abstract. The global food demand is increasing with the increase in world population. The agriculture land and fresh water resources are limited and the water crisis is further enhanced due to the global warming and the shortfall of better water management systems. The precision agriculture can play a very important role in curtailing this crisis by improving irrigation management techniques. These techniques can efficiently utilize the natural rainwater and ground water. It is also beneficial for the energy saving and achieving the better growth of crop. Further, to maintain the proper growth with optimal pesticide, the soil moisture of crop is needed to be maintained during its whole life cycle. Moisture of soil is an essential aspect for hydrology system that represents the typical circumstances in a limited volume of soil. An effective prediction of soil moisture can save the water and energy and it is essential to develop effective irrigation management system for this purpose. Prediction of soil moisture is vital for better irrigation management system. This paper describes result of experimental scenario for different machine learning regression techniques to predict the soil moisture.

Keywords: Soil moisture prediction · Regression · Support Vector Regression
Ridge regression

1 Introduction

Water is an essential requirement of human life. The current human population is around 7.5 billion and a further increase of 2.6 billion is expected by 2050. Almost 80–90% of total available freshwater resources are used in irrigation around the globe [1]. To fulfill the future food demand, it is crucial to develop strategies based on advance technology for better utilization of freshwater with involvement of various stakeholders. Water is an essential requirement for agriculture yield in all aspects [2]. Good seeds and fertilizer will fail to provide maximum growth without the optimum use of water. Due to lack of cost-effective intelligent irrigation scheme, developing countries are using 2–3 times more water in contrast to developed countries for achieving same

© Springer Nature Singapore Pte Ltd. 2018
M. Singh et al. (Eds.): ICACDS 2018, CCIS 906, pp. 309–316, 2018.
https://doi.org/10.1007/978-981-13-1813-9_31

agricultural yield. India has approximately 4% of global fresh water resources to support 17% of the world population residing in the country [3].

Maintaining an optimum soil moisture for the field is the main aim for a smart irrigation system [4]. The accuracy of weather forecasting is improving due to the advancement of technology. Therefore, we can use the forecasted data like air Temperature, Humidity, and Ultraviolet (UV) radiation to predict the soil moisture. The precipitation and evaporation are most important factors, which affect soil moisture content. Daily soil moisture can be estimated by the ratio of daily evaporation to daily precipitation in the above context. The evaporation equation [5] is given by

$$E_T = x_0 + x_1 E_1 + x_2 E_2 \qquad (1)$$

where E_1 an be evaluated by relative humidity (air), temperature (air), radiation and the velocity of ground wind, and E_2 an be determined by latent heat of vaporization per unit mass and global radiation and x_0, x_1 and x_2 an be estimated by statistical regression.

The relation shows that air temperature, air relative humidity, and radiation are some important factors for dynamic evaporation of soil moisture. In this paper, we have collected the air temperature, air humidity, soil-moisture and UV from a field experimental setup using different sensors and stored the data on a server [6]. This data has been analyzed using different machine learning techniques (multiple regression, ridge regression, weighted regression, and support vector regression). The different regression models have been applied on the collected data and the results are analyzed to find the best approach for the scenario [12, 13].

Section 2 discusses the regression models in brief. Section 3 describes experiment setup followed by analysis of results.

2   Overview of Regression Techniques

For soil moisture prediction we have used supervised machine learning approaches. In supervised learning, a training data set is used to train the algorithm then testing and validation data set is used for testing the trained algorithm. This algorithm i.e. regression models involves targeted variable (or dependent variable) which is to be predicted from a known set of predictors (independent variables) [14].

2.1   Multiple Linear Regression (MLR)

Multiple Linear regression is a statistical analysis algorithm that allows to identify a relationship between a dependent variable and multiple independent variables. Once the relation between these independent and dependent variables is recognized, all information about the independent variables can be found and it can be used to provide considerable further influential and accurate predictions about the effects. The is mathematically represented as [7, 15]

$$P' = \alpha + \beta_1 X_1 + \beta_2 X_2 \tag{2}$$

P' = predicted value of P (dependent variable that is being predicted)
α = the P intercept
β_1 = the alteration in P for respectively 1 increment variation in X_1
β_2 = the alteration in P for respectively 1 increment variation in X_2
X_1, X_2, are an independent variable for which you are trying to predict a value of P.

2.2 Ridge Regression (RR)

Ridge Regression is a well-known technique for investigating multiple regression multi-collinearity data. Due to multi-collinearity, least squares variances are very far from the true value and value of variances are too large because of least squares estimation are unbiased. Ridge regression decreases the standard errors with adding a degree of bias to the regression estimation. By this, the total effect will provide a more reliable estimation.

The equation of RR model is described in the form of matrix as [8, 16]

$$Y = XB + e \tag{3}$$

where X is the independent variable, Y is the dependent variable, B is the regression coefficients to be predictable, and e denotes the errors are residuals.

2.3 Weighted Linear Regression (WLR)

In general, weighted regression is an observation technique for non-constant variances and non-zero correlations. Assuming zero correlation between the observations. Standard regression model [9, 12] is given by

$$Y = X\beta + eE(e) = 0, Cov(e) = \sigma^2 I \tag{4}$$

Weighted regression considers a relative model for data of non-similar variance. For this type of model, the variances themselves are unidentified but variances sizes are given. In this type of form, covariance equation will be modifying from $Cov(e) = \sigma^2 I$ to $Cov(e) = \sigma^2 ID(w)^{-1}$ and D(w) is the diagonal matrix (DM) with identified weights $w = (w_1 \ldots \ldots \ldots w_n)'$. The covariance matrix contains $D(w)^{-1}$, which is a DM with diagonal elements $1/w_1 \ldots \ldots \ldots 1/w_n$. The observation variance y_i is σ^2/w_i. If w_i is sizable as compared to other weights, the relative variance (y_i) will be small, so it contains more information in contrast of other observations and we should add further weight on it and vice versa [17, 19].

The noticeable point is the weights are relative, so we could multiply and divide them all by an invariable and obtain fundamentally with similar investigation. In standard regression case, all weights are equal to 1.

New model expression in matrix form will be

$$Y = X\beta + eE(e) = 0, \quad Cov(e) = \sigma^2 \tag{5}$$

In this weighted regression model, the covariance matrix is diagonal and due to this all the observations will be uncorrelated. The variance of any observation is unidentified because σ^2 is not known. However, the size of variance is known due to identified weights. Considerable point for this type of model is when this model is used for prediction, weights are an essential requirement for any future prediction [18].

2.4 Support Vector Regression (SVR)

Working principle of Support Vector Regression (SVR) is similar to Support Vector Machine (SVM) classification with minor differences, like dependent variables are numerical instead of categorical. SVR has many advantageous features like it allows creation of linear and nonlinear models without any change in the explanatory variables and it provides a better explanation of the resultant model. The SVR has many kernel functions for developing the models to get the required form. Some of the commonly used kernel methods in SVR are Linear, Nonlinear, Radial Basis function (RBF), Polynomial and Sigmodal. Selection of the appropriate kernel function is critical for the SVR technique. It depends on user requirement [19].

SVR model of Radial basis kernel [10]

$$Y_i = W.x_i + b \tag{6}$$

Where x_i notes a set of impendent variables, and b is the "bias" term.

SVR is a valuable and flexible practice for the geometry of the data and the common problem of model overfitting of distributional properties of underlying variables [20].

3 Experimental Results and Analysis

To capture actual parameters from the field, an open-source hardware platform (Raspberry-Pi and Arduino) based device has been designed and deployed at rose garden, CSIR-CSIO, Chandigarh. The sensors used in the experiment are Soil Moisture Sensor (VH-400), Temperature and Humidity Sensor (DHT22), and Ultraviolet (UV) Light Radiation Sensor (based on GUVA-S12SD and SGM8521 Op Amp).

The data received from these sensors via internet is stored in a database for analysis and decision-making. The regression analysis has been performed in R programming. To predict the soil-moisture values, for making irrigation decision, different regression methods have been applied and the results are compared. The regression models consider the average Soil-moisture, Humidity, Air temperature and UV on daily basis.

Based on the experimental data, the parameters, viz. Air relative humidity (H), Air temperature (T), UV and soil moisture difference (difference between soil moisture of previous day and next day) are shown in Fig. 1.

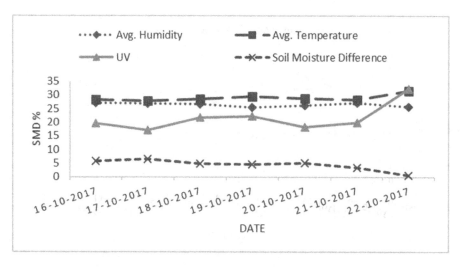

Fig. 1. Various parameters based on experimental data

The experimental results show increase in air temperature, and UV decreases soil moisture on day-to-day basis and the air temperature behaves in an inversely proportional manner to the air humidity. Further, when soil moisture reaches near 25% then the rate of decrement in soil moisture relatively less as previously [11]. Based on this observation, humidity (H), Air temperature (T) and UV are considered as independent variables and the Soil Moisture Difference (SMD) is considered as dependent variables for the analysis, where SMD is given by,

SMD = Average soil moisture for the previous day $(x - 1)$ – Average soil moisture for the current day (x).

Temperature, Humidity, and UV radiation are used in prediction of SMD. In Weighted Regression, the Temperature is considered as weighted parameter, In SVR we have used RBF kernel to predict the SMD.

Table 1 shows the analysis results based on different regression models. The result shows that the accuracy of Support Vector Regression is better than other discussed regression model.

Table 1. Analysis results based on different regression models

Regression method	R-squared	Standard error	Accuracy in %
Multiple linear regression	0.8555	0.66	85.55
Weighted linear regression	0.8554	0.65	85.54
Ridge regression	0.8374	0.64	83.74
Support vector regression	0.9383	0.66	93.83

Figure 2 shows the comparison of actual SMD recorded by sensor and prediction results of two models, Support Vector Regression (SVR) and Weighted Linear Regression (WLR). The values are further detailed in Table 2.

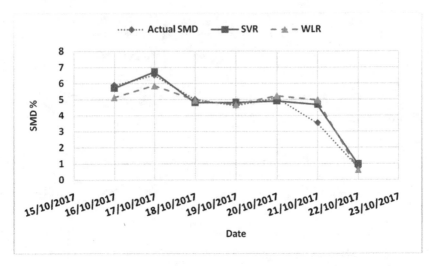

Fig. 2. Actual and predicted soil moisture difference

Table 2. A comparison of actual values and the predicted values of SMD

Date	Actual SMD (%)	Predicated SMD	
		SVR (%)	WLR (%)
16/10/2017	5.88815305	5.69878	5.13049
17/10/2017	6.523900124	6.713794	5.86132
18/10/2017	4.995666994	4.807244	4.95853
19/10/2017	4.627231611	4.815671	4.67789
20/10/2017	5.097155795	4.907146	5.2206
21/10/2017	3.534830317	4.679826	4.96598
22/10/2017	0.772429365	0.961912	0.62349

4   Conclusion

Prediction of soil moisture is vital for developing smart irrigation systems. The soil moisture is directly related to many environmental parameters like air temperature, air humidity, and UV. This paper analyzes different machine learning regression techniques to predict the soil moisture. The Support Vector Regression (SVR) performs better in terms of accuracy over the other three regression techniques. It has also observed that Support Vector Regression (SVR) performs better even if data has some nonlinearity. The accuracy of SVR in SMD prediction may vary depends upon the input data. In future, we can develop a tool that will automatically estimate which regression model is better for prediction of soil moisture.

Acknowledgements. Authors sincerely express thanks to The Director, CSIR-CSIO, and Chandigarh, India for support to this research work at CSIR-CSIO. Furthermore, authors acknowledge Sh. Suman Tewary for providing valuable suggestions.

References

1. Gutiérrez, J., Villa-medina, J.F., Nieto-Garibay, A., et al.: Automated irrigation system using a wireless sensor network and GPRS module. IEEE Trans. Instrum. Meas. **63**, 166–176 (2014). https://doi.org/10.1109/TIM.2013.2276487

2. Phillips, A.J., Newlands, N.K., Liang, S.H.L., Ellert, B.H.: Integrated sensing of soil moisture at the field-scale: measuring, modeling and sharing for improved agricultural decision support. Comput. Electron. Agric. **107**, 73–88 (2014). https://doi.org/10.1016/j.compag.2014.02.011

3. Government of India NITI Aayog: Raising agricultural productivity and making farming remunerative for farmers (2015). http://niti.gov.in/content/working_papers.php. Accessed 13 March 2016

4. Vellidis, G., Tucker, M., Perry, C., et al.: A real-time wireless smart sensor array for scheduling irrigation. Comput. Electron. Agric. **61**, 44–50 (2008). https://doi.org/10.1016/j.compag.2007.05.009

5. Adjei, S., Yankson, P.P.W.K., Principal, R.D., et al: Environment and globalizatio. Ph. D Proposal, pp. 1:1–1:40. (2012)https://doi.org/10.1017/cbo9781107415324.004

6. Shivling, V.D., Goap, A., Ghanshyam, C., et al.: A real time computational and statistical model (with high availability) of early warning for plant protection and pest control for crops (exp. kutki). In: 2015 IEEE International Conference on Computer Graphics, Vision and Information Security, CGVIS 2015, pp. 22–26 (2016)

7. Introduction to multiple regression. http://www.biddle.com/documents/bcg_comp_chapter4.pdf. Accessed 1 Feb 2018

8. Ridge regression. In: NCSS, LLC. https://ncss-wpengine.netdna-ssl.com/wp-content/themes/ncss/pdf/Procedures/NCSS/Ridge_Regression.pdf. Accessed 1 Feb 2018

9. Christensen, R.: Analysis of Variance, Design, and Regression: Applied Statistical Methods, 1st edn, pp. 451–452. CRC Press, Boca Raton (2006)

10. Sagar, C.: The advantage of support vector regression (SVR) over simple linear regression (SLR) models for predicting real values (2017). https://www.kdnuggets.com/2017/03/building-regression-models-support-vector-regression.html. Accessed 31 January 2018

11. Goddard, N., Entekhabi, D.: Assessing the relationship between surface temperature and soil moisture in southern Africa. In: 2000 Remote Sensing and Hydrology, Proceedings of a Symposium Held at Santa Fe, 2000, pp. 296–301 (2001)

12. Forkuor, G., Hounkpatin, O.K.L., Welp, G., Thiel, M.: High resolution mapping of soil properties using remote sensing variables in South-Western Burkina Faso: a comparison of machine learning and multiple linear regression models. PLoS ONE **12**(1), e0170478 (2017)

13. Were, K., Bui, D.T., Dick, Ø.B., Singh, B.R.: A comparative assessment of support vector regression, artificial neural networks, and random forests for predicting and mapping soil organic carbon stocks across an Afromontane landscape. Ecol. Ind. **52**, 394–403 (2015)

14. Lahmar, R., Bationo, B.A., Lamso, N.D., Guéro, Y., Tittonell, P.: Tailoring conservation agriculture technologies to West Africa semi-arid zones: building on traditional local practices for soil restoration. Field Crops Res. **132**, 158–167 (2012)

15. Niang, I., et al.: Africa. In: Barros, V.R., Field, C.B., Dokken, D.J., Mastrandrea, M.D., Mach, K.J., et al. (Eds.) Climate Change 2014: Impacts, Adaptation, and Vulnerability. Part B: Regional Aspects. Contribution of Working Group II to the Fifth Assessment Report of the Intergovernmental Panel of Climate Change, pp. 1199–1265. Cambridge University Press, Cambridge, United Kingdom and New York, NY, USA (2014)
16. Hengl, T., Heuvelink, G.B.M., Kempen, B., Leenaars, J.G.B., Walsh, M.G., Shepherd, K.D., et al.: Mapping soil properties of Africa at 250 m resolution: Random Forests significantly improve current predictions. PLoS ONE 10(6), 1–26 (2015)
17. Fabiyi, O.O., Ige-Olumide, O., Fabiyi, A.O.: Spatial analysis of soil fertility estimates and NDVI in South-Western Nigeria: a new paradigm for routine soil fertility mapping. Res. J. Agric. Environ. Manag. 2(12), 403–411 (2013)
18. Stevens, A., Miralles, I., van Wesemael, B.: Soil organic carbon predictions by airborne imaging spectroscopy: comparing cross-validation and validation. Soil Sci. Soc. Am. J. 76(6), 2174–2183 (2012)
19. Fujisada, H., Bailey, G.B., Kelly, G.G., Hara, S., Abrams, M.J.: Aster dem performance. IEEE Trans. Geosci. Remote Sens. 43(12), 2707–2714 (2005)
20. Ray, S., Singh, J., Das, G., Panigraphy, S.: Use of high resolution remote sensing data for generating site specific soil management plan. Int. Arch. Photogramm. Remote Sens. Spat. Inf. Sci. 35, 127–132 (2004)

Dynamics of Modified Leslie-Gower Model with Stochastic Influences

V. Nagaraju[1], B. R. Tapas Bapu[2], S. Pradeep[2],
and V. Madhusudanan[3(✉)]

[1] Department of Electronics and Communication Engineering,
RIT, Chennai, Tamilnadu, India
[2] Department of Electronics and Communication Engineering,
S.A. Engineering College, Chennai, Tamilnadu, India
[3] Department of Mathematics, S.A. Engineering College,
Chennai, Tamilnadu, India
mvms.maths@gmail.com

Abstract. The dynamics of modified Leslie-Gower prey-predator model exposed to stochastic influences are investigated in this paper. We inspect basic mathematical peculiarity of the proposed model such as positivity, boundedness of solution, Local stability of equilibrium point that exists in the system. The variation of population and the stability of the system about the positive equilibrium point controlled by the Gaussian white noise are computed. Finally, we effectuate the numerical simulation to illustrate the analytical findings.

Keywords: Local stability · Leslie-Gower model · Gaussian white noise

1 Introduction

In the studying of ecological interactions, the mathematical modeling act in a important role. Modeling the variations of an ecological system is the greatest advantageous approach to apprehend the intricacy of natural surroundings (i.e.) analyzing the interactions among species and growth of the species population. The inter relationship among the predators and its quarry is a powerful natural phenomenon and it helps researchers and biologists to deal with numerous interesting problems.

Deterministic models are stable with a cyclic behavior in the common period for the sizes of species population. Moreover these models may be inadequate for capturing the exact variability in nature. In predator-prey model, the oscillations arise from either environmental variability or internal species. In fact, biological systems are inherently random in nature and noise plays a major part to determine the structure and function of such system. These random fluctuations result in changing some degree of parameter in the deterministic environment.

Beddington-DeAngelis with Modified Leslie-Gower model functional reaction [3, 10, 12] and the model exhibited chaotic dynamics. Sokol and Howell [7] dedicated a basic Holling Type IV function of the form $\frac{dx}{d+x^2}$ and concluded that it is efficient and reliable than the original Holling Type IV functional response. The Holling type IV response [8, 9] signifies a state with high prey densities in which the predation rate

© Springer Nature Singapore Pte Ltd. 2018
M. Singh et al. (Eds.): ICACDS 2018, CCIS 906, pp. 317–326, 2018.
https://doi.org/10.1007/978-981-13-1813-9_32

decreases. Ruan [5] studied the bifurcation analysis of continuous time modified Holling type-IV. Analysis of Leslie-Gower type model [1, 2, 4, 11] and Sokol-Howell functional response [6] are comparatively lower than the other types like Lotka-Volterra and Beddington-DeAngelis useful retorts.

2 Mathematical Model

Mathematical model considered is based on the L-G predator-prey scheme with Sokel-Howell functional response.

$$
\begin{aligned}
\frac{dX}{dT} &= rX\left(1 - \left(\frac{X}{K}\right)\right) - \frac{\alpha XY}{\bar{m} + a_1 X^2} \\
\frac{dY}{dT} &= sY\left(1 - \frac{a_2 Y}{n + X}\right)
\end{aligned}
\tag{1}
$$

Here all parameters are assumed to be positive. Let $X(T)$ and $Y(T)$ represents the prey and predator population, r is the intrinsic growth rate of prey, K is the environmental carrying capacity of the prey, α and $\bar{m}$ represents capturing rate and half-saturation constant$s$ represents maximal per capita growth rate of predator, a_2 represents crowding effect of the predator.

To minimize the complexity, the number of parameters involved with the model system (1) is reduced and the system is written in non-dimensionalized form.

Consider X, Y and T as follow

$$
x \rightarrow \frac{X}{K}, y \rightarrow \frac{\alpha KY}{r} \text{ and } \quad t \rightarrow Tr
\tag{2}
$$

Using (2) in the system (1) becomes

$$
\begin{aligned}
\frac{dx}{dt} &= x(1 - (x)) - \frac{axy}{x^2 + m_1} \\
\frac{dy}{dt} &= y\left(c - \frac{by}{x + m_2}\right)
\end{aligned}
\tag{3}
$$

Where

$$
a = \frac{1}{a_1 K^3}, \quad m_1 = \frac{\bar{m}}{a_1 K^2}, \quad m_2 = \frac{n}{K}, \quad c = \frac{s}{r}, \quad b = \frac{sa_2}{\alpha K^2}
$$

With initial densities of system (2)

$$
x_0 > 0, y_0 > 0
\tag{4}
$$

The paper is organized as follows: we present some positive invariance and boundedness results in Sect. 3. We obtain the existence of the equilibrium points of model (3) in Sect. 4.

In Sect. 5, we investigate Local and Global behavior of the positive equilibrium point. In Sect. 6 analyses of the stochastic fluctuations of the model. At last Numerical simulations are illustrated to verify analytical finding of some of our result.

3 Positive Invariance and Boundedness

Biologically positive insures the population always positive and survive. The following theorems ensure that the positivity and boundedness of the system (3)

Theorem 1: System (3) with initial densities (4) is positive invariant.

Proof: From First equation of the system (3) it is observed that
$\frac{dx}{x} = \left[(1-x) - \frac{ay}{x^2 + m_1} \right] dt = \psi_1(x,y) dt$
Where $\psi_1(x,y) = (1-x) - \frac{ay}{x^2 + m_1}$

Integrating in the region $[0,t]$ we get $x(t) = x_0 e^{\left(\int \psi_1(x,y) dt \right)} > 0$ for all t.

From second equation of the system (3) it is observed that $\frac{dy}{y} = \left(c - \frac{by}{(x+m_2)} \right)$

Where $\psi_2(x,y) = \left(c - \frac{by}{x+m_2} \right)$

Integrating in the region $[0,t]$ we get $y(t) = y_0 e^{\left(\int \psi_2(x,y) dt \right)} > 0$ for all t

Hence, all solutions starting from interior of the first octant (In R^2_+) remain positive in it for future time.

Theorem 2: System (3) that initiate in R^2_+ are uniformly bounded.

Proof: Let $x(t), y(t)$ be any solution of the system (3), since, from first equation of model (3)

$\frac{dx}{dt} \le x(1-x)$, we have $\lim\limits_{t \to \infty} \sup x(t) \le 1$

Let $M = Max\{x(0), 1\}$, From second equation of (3) we have

$$\frac{dy}{dt} = y(c - \frac{by}{m_2 + M}) = y(c - Cy)$$

Where $C = \frac{b}{m_2 + M}$

By using standard comparison principle, $y(t) \le Max\left\{ y(0), \frac{c(m_2 + M)}{b} \right\}$

Hence positive solution of system (3) is uniformly bounded.

4 Existence of the Equilibrium Points

By simple computation, we can conclude that three non-negative fixed points are there.

(i) $E_0(0,0)$ is trivial equilibrium point exists always.

(ii) $E_1(1,0)$ is axial fixed point that lies on the boundary of the first octant.

(iii) $E_2(x^*, y^*)$ is the positive equilibrium point exists.

Where $y^* = \frac{c(x+m_2)}{b}$ and

x^* is positive root of the following cubic Equation

$$bx^3 - bx^2 + (bm_1 + ac)x + (acm_2 - bm_1) = 0 \tag{5}$$

$$\text{Provided with the condition } acm_2 < bm_1 \tag{6}$$

5   Stability Analysis

In order to examine the stability of the model (3), the jacobian matrix that corresponds to every steady state is computed. Based on the results we have

- The trivial equilibrium point E_0 is unstable in $x - y$ direction due to existence of positive eigenvalue.
- The axial free equilibrium point E_1 always is nodal source due to existence of one positive as well as one negative eigenvalue.

Theorem 3: The co-existence equilibrium point $E_2(x^*, y^*)$ asymptotically stable if $(x^{*2} + m_1)^2 > 2ax^*y^*$

Proof: The jacobian matrix at $E_2(x^*, y^*)$ is

$$J(E_2) = \begin{bmatrix} x^*\left(-1 + \frac{2x^*ay^*}{(x^{*2}+m_1)^2}\right) & \frac{-ax^*}{(x^{*2}+m_1)^2} \\ \frac{c^2}{b} & -c \end{bmatrix}$$

The corresponding characteristic equation of $E_2(x^*, y^*)$ is given by $f(\lambda) = \lambda^2 - Tr(E_2)\lambda + Det(E_2) = 0$

Where

$$Tr(E_2) = x^*\left(-1 + \frac{2x^*ay^*}{(x^{*2}+m_1)^2}\right) - c$$

$$Det\, J(E_2) = \left(\left(x^*(c - \frac{2cx^*ay^*}{(x^{*2}+m_1)^2})\right) + \frac{ax^*c^2}{b(x^{*2}+m_1)^2}\right) > 0$$

Hence $E_2(x^*, y^*)$ is asymptotically stable if the condition

$$(x^{*^2} + m_1)^2 > 2ax^*y^* \tag{7}$$

Theorem: 4: The positive equilibrium point E_2 of model system (3) is globally stable if $2ax^2y(x+m_2) < [x(x+m_2) + by].(x^2+m_1)^2$

Proof: consider the positive function $L(x,y) = \frac{1}{xy}$

Here $f(x,y) = x(1-x-\frac{ay}{x^2+m_1}); g(x,y) = y(c-\frac{by}{x+m_2})$

Now $\Delta(x,y) = \frac{\partial}{\partial x}(fL) + \frac{\partial}{\partial y}(gL)$

$$= \frac{-1}{y} + \frac{2ax}{(x^2+m_1)^2} - \frac{b}{x(x+m_2)}$$

$$= -[\frac{x(x+m_2)+by}{xy(x+m_2)} - \frac{2ax}{(x^2+m_1)^2}] < 0$$

clearly, it is evident that $\Delta(x, y)$ has no varying sign and is not identically zero in the interior of the positive quadrant. Hence the equilibrium point E_2 is globally stable.

6 Stochastic Analysis

In this section, we introduce stochastic disturbance of the variables x, y at the positive equilibrium E_2 when it is locally asymptotically stable. We consider the white noise stochastic perturbations which are equivalent to the distances of x, y from x^*, y^*. So the stochastically perturbed system (3) is given by

$$dx = \left(x(1-x) - \frac{axy}{x^2+m_1}\right)dt + \sigma_1(x-x^*)d\xi_t^1 \tag{8}$$

$$dy = \left(y(c - \frac{by}{x+m_2})\right)dt + \sigma_2(y-y^*)d\xi_t^2 \tag{9}$$

Where $\sigma_i, i = 1, 2$ are real constants, $\xi_t^i = \xi_t(t), i = 1, 2$ are independent from each other standard Wiener processes [12]. The dynamical behavior of model (3) is robust with respect to such a kind of stochasticity and the results are obtained for (3).

We will consider (8)–(9) as the Ito stochastic differential system. To explore the stochastic stability of E_2, we linearize the system of (8–9) around E_2 as follows:

Let $u_1 = x - x^*, u_2 = y - y^*$ then

$$du(t) = f(u(t))dt + g(u(t))d\xi(t) \tag{10}$$

Where $u(t) = Col(u_1(t), u_2(t)) : f(u(t)) = J(u(t)) :$

$$f(u(t)) = \begin{bmatrix} x^*\left(-1+\frac{2x^*ay^*}{(x^{*^2}+m_1)^2}\right) & \frac{-ax^*}{(x^{*^2}+m_1)^2} \\ \frac{c^2}{b} & -c \end{bmatrix}; \quad g(u) = \begin{bmatrix} \sigma_1 u_1 & 0 \\ 0 & \sigma_2 u_2 \end{bmatrix}$$

$$\therefore d\xi(t) = col\left(\xi_1(t), \xi_2(t)\right);$$

Let $U = \{(t \geq t_0) \times R^n, t_0 \in R^+\}$. Hence $V_2 \in C_2^0(U)$ is a continuous function with respect to t and a twice continuously differentiable function with respect to u. With reference to [12,13], we have.

$$LV(t,u) = \frac{\partial V(t,u)}{\partial t} + f^T(u)\frac{\partial V(t,u)}{\partial u} + \frac{1}{2}Tr\left(g^T(u)\frac{\partial V^2(t,u)}{\partial u^2}g(u)\right) \qquad (11)$$

Where $\frac{\partial V}{\partial u} = col\left(\frac{\partial V}{\partial u_1}, \frac{\partial V}{\partial u_2}\right); \frac{\partial V^2(t,u)}{\partial u^2} = \frac{\partial V^2}{\partial u_i \partial u_j}; i,j = 1,2$ and T means transposition

Theorem 5: If there exists a function $V_2 \in C_2^0(U)$ satisfying the following

$$K_1|u|^p \leq V(t,u) \leq K_2|u|^p; LV(t,u) \leq -K_3|u|^p \ K_i > 0, p > 0 \qquad (12)$$

Then the trivial solution of (8–9) is exponentially p-stable for $t \geq 0$.

Theorem 6: Suppose $\sigma_1^2 < 2\left[x^* - \frac{2x^*ay^*}{(x^{*^2}+m_1)^2} + \frac{ax^*}{(x^{*^2}+m_1)}\right], \sigma_2^2 < 2\left[\frac{c(b-c)}{b}\right]$ then the zero solution of (10) is asymptotically mean square stable

Proof: Let us consider the Lyapunov function

$$V(u) = \frac{1}{2}\left(w_1 u_1^2 + w_2 u_2^2\right), w_i > 0 \qquad (13)$$

Where w_i are real positive constants to be chosen. We easily verifying (12) be true with p = 2.
Then

$$LV(u) = w_1\left(x^*(-1 + \frac{2x^*ay^*}{(x^{*^2}+m_1)^2})u_1 + \frac{-ax^*}{(x^{*^2}+m_1)^2}u_2\right)u_1 + w_1\left(\frac{c^2}{b}u_1 - cu_2\right)u_2 + \frac{1}{2}Tr\left(g^T(u)\frac{\partial V^2(t,u)}{\partial u^2}g(u)\right)$$

$$(14)$$

We can easily observe that $\frac{\partial^2 V}{\partial u^2} = \begin{bmatrix} w_1 & 0 \\ 0 & w_2 \end{bmatrix}$ and hence $g^T(u)\frac{\partial V^2(t,u)}{\partial u^2}g(u) = \begin{bmatrix} w_1\sigma_1^2 u_1^2 & 0 \\ 0 & w_2\sigma_2^2 u_2^2 \end{bmatrix}$

With $\frac{1}{2}Tr\left(g^T(u)\frac{\partial V^2(t,u)}{\partial u^2}g(u)\right) = \frac{1}{2}\left(w_1\sigma_1^2 u_1^2 + w_2\sigma_2^2 u_2^2\right) \qquad (15)$

From (15), we have
If we choose $x_1^* w_1 = x_2^* w_2$ in (14) along (15) we get

$$LV(t,u) = -w_1 \left[x^* - \frac{2x^* a y^*}{(x^{*2} + m_1)^2} + \frac{a x^*}{(x^{*2} + m_1)} - \frac{1}{2}\sigma_1^2 \right] u_1^2 - w_2 \left[c - \frac{c^2}{b} - \frac{1}{2}\sigma_2^2 \right] u_2^2$$

Which is negative definite function. Hence the proof is completed based on theorem (5).

7 Numerical Simulation

In this segment, we validate and justify our mathematical findings by computer simulations with help of MATLAB software considering different sets of parameter values as follows:

Example 1: For the parameters $a = 2, b = 0.1, c = 0.03, m_1 = 1.5, m_2 = 0.8$ with densities $x_0 = 0.6, y_0 = 0.58$ having low strength of noise $\sigma_1 = 0.02, \sigma_2 = 0.02$. Figure 1 represents the numerical solution of system (3) and Fig. 2 represents phase portrait diagram among species.

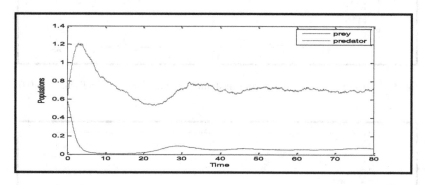

Fig. 1. Numerical solution of (3) with low strength of noise $\sigma_1 = 0.02, \sigma_2 = 0.02$

Example 2: For the parameters $a = 2, b = 0.1, c = 0.03, m_1 = 1.5, m_2 = 0.8$ with densities $x_0 = 0.6, y_0 = 0.58$ having Medium strength of noise with oscillations $\sigma_1 = 0.08, \sigma_2 = 0.08$. Figure 3 represents the variations of populations against time and Fig. 4 represents phase portrait diagram among species.

Example 3: For the parameters $a = 2, b = 0.1, c = 0.03, m_1 = 1.5, m_2 = 0.8$ having densities $x_0 = 0.6, y_0 = 0.58$ with High medium strength of noise $\sigma_1 = 0.2, \sigma_2 = 0.2$. Figure 5 represents the variations of populations against time and Fig. 6 represents phase portrait diagram among species.

Example 4: For the parameters $a = 2, b = 0.1, c = 0.03, m_1 = 1.5, m_2 = 0.8$ with densities $x_0 = 0.6, y_0 = 0.58$ having High strength of noise $\sigma_1 = 1.56, \sigma_2 = 1.56$. Figure 7 represents the variations of populations against time and Fig. 8 represents phase portrait diagram among species.

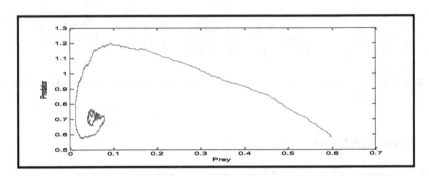

Fig. 2. Trajectories of system (3) of with low strength of noise $\sigma_1 = 0.02, \sigma_2 = 0.02$

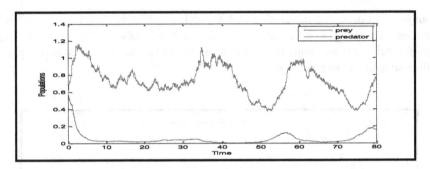

Fig. 3. Variations of populations with medium strength of noise $\sigma_1 = 0.08, \sigma_2 = 0.08$

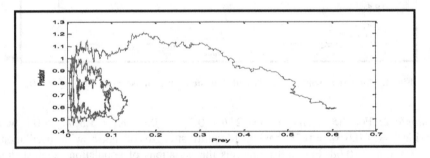

Fig. 4. Phase portrait of with medium strength of noise $\sigma_1 = 0.08, \sigma_2 = 0.08$

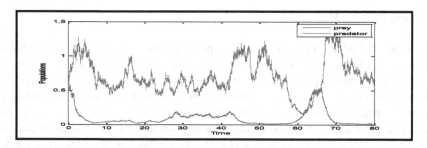

Fig. 5. Variations of populations with High medium strength of noise $\sigma_1 = 0.2, \sigma_2 = 0.2$

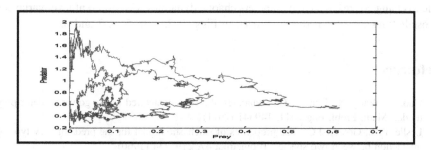

Fig. 6. Phase portrait of with High medium strength of noise $\sigma_1 = 0.2, \sigma_2 = 0.2$

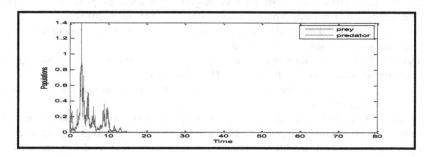

Fig. 7. Variations of populations High strength of noise $\sigma_1 = 1.56, \sigma_2 = 1.56$

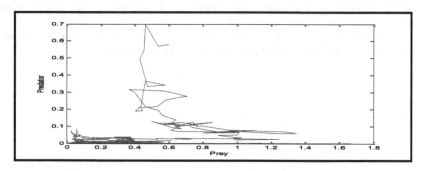

Fig. 8. Phase portrait of with High strength of noise $\sigma_1 = 1.56, \sigma_2 = 1.56$

8 Concluding Remarks

This paper studied the Leslie-Gower prey-predator model along with Sokel-Howell functional reaction around the interior steady state. We examined the system by introducing stochastic perturbations. By using Lyapunov function we proved the stochastic differential equation, of system is asymptotically mean square stable. In stochastic system, population variations have a prodigious role for the stochastic stability. The noise in the equation results in a big variance of fluctuations around the equilibrium point which suggests that our system oscillates with respect to the noisy environment. From the numerical simulation we conclude that the inclusion of stochastic perturbation creates a noteworthy variation in the intensity of populations. Due to change of responsive parameters chaotic dynamics with different level variances of oscillations are obtained and showed in Figs. 1, 2, 3, 4, 5, 6, 7 and 8.

References

1. Huo, H., Wang, X., Chavez, C.: Dynamics of a stage-structured Leslie-gower predator-prey model. Math. Probl. Eng **2011**, 149341 (2011)
2. Leslie, P.H., Gower, J.C.: The properties of stochastic model for the predator-prey type of interaction between two species. Biometrika **47**, 219–234 (1960)
3. Nindjin, A.F., Aziz-Alaoui, M.A.: Persistence and global stability in a delayed Leslie-Gower model with three species fochain. J. Math. Anal. Appl. **340**(1), 340 (2013)
4. Priyadarshi, A., Gakkar, S.: Dynamics of Leslie-gower type generalist predator in tri-trophic food web system. Commun. Nonlinear Sci. Simul. **18**, 3202–3218 (2013)
5. Ruan, S., Xiao, D.: Global analysis in a prey-predator system with non-monotonic function functional response. SIAM J. Appl. Math. **61**(4), 1445–1472 (2001)
6. Shen, C.: Permanence and global attractivity of food chain system with holling type IV functional response. Appl. Math. Comput. **215**, 179–185 (2009)
7. Sokol, W., Howell, J.A.: The kinetics of phenol oxidation by washed cells. Biotechnol. Bioeng. **30**, 921–927 (1987)
8. Upadhyay, R.K., Rsw, S.N.: Complex dynamics of a three species food chain model with holling type IV functional response. Nonlinear Anal. Model Control **16**(3), 353–374 (2011)
9. Upadhyay, R.K., Iyengar, S.R.K.: Introduction to Mathematical Modeling and Chaotic Dynamics. A Chapman and Hall Book. CRC Press, Boca Raton (2014)
10. Yu, S.: Global stability of a modified Leslie-Gower model with Beddington-DeAngelis functional response. Adv. Differ. Eqn. **2014**, 84 (2014)
11. Yue, Q.: Dynamics of a modified Leslie-Gower model with Holling Type II schemes and prey refuge. Springer Plus **5**, 461 (2016)
12. Yue, Q.: Permanence for a Leslie-gower model with beddington–DeAngelis functional response and feedback controls. Adv. Differ. Eq. **2015**, 81 (2015)

Electricity Consumption Forecasting Using Time Series Analysis

Praphula Kumar Jain$^{(\boxtimes)}$, Waris Quamer, and Rajendra Pamula

Department of Computer Science and Engineering,
Indian Institute of Technology (Indian School of Mines),
Dhanbad 826004, Jharkhand, India
praphulajnl@gmail.com, mr.warisquamer@gmail.com,
rajendrapamula@gmail.com

Abstract. The demand for electricity has been continuously increasing over the years. To understand the future consumption, a good predictive model is entailed. The ARIMA models have been extensively used for time series prediction showing encouraging results. In this paper, an attempt is made on forecasting the electricity consumption using the ARIMA model. Using the mean absolute percentage error (MAPE) to measure forecast accuracy, the model was able to forecast with an error of 6.63%. Results shows that the ARIMA model has a potential to compete with existing techniques for electricity consumption forecast.

Keywords: Electricity consumption · Forecast · ARIMA · Time series

1 Introduction

The demand for electricity has been continuously increasing in every sector [1]. The increased dependency on the electronic and electrical appliances necessitates the need for future demand forecast. Electricity consumption forecast plays an integral role in planning the future in terms of the size, location and type of the future generating plants as well as in deciding and planning for maintenance of the existing power systems [2].

The ARIMA model has been extensively used in forecasting economic, stock prices, marketing, social problems, industrial production etc. It is a statistical analysis model known to be efficient and robust for short-term forecast and requires at least 40 past data point's values.

In this paper, the electricity consumption in IIT(ISM) Dhanbad for the year 2008–09 is forecasted based on data from the year 2004 to 2008 using the ARIMA models, and then root mean square error (RMSE) and mean absolute percentage error (MAPE) is used to select the best model as the basis of model performance [24, 25].

Rest of the paper is organized as follows. In Sect. 2, the approaches used in the earlier research paper in the forecast of electricity consumption are reviewed and Sect. 3 presents a brief overview of ARIMA model. Section 4, then lays out the dataset used. Section 4 describes the methodology employed while in Sect. 5, the experimental results obtained are presented and analyzed. Last of all, Sect. 6 finalizes this paper with a conclusion and future research potentials.

© Springer Nature Singapore Pte Ltd. 2018
M. Singh et al. (Eds.): ICACDS 2018, CCIS 906, pp. 327–335, 2018.
https://doi.org/10.1007/978-981-13-1813-9_33

2   Related Work

For forecasting the electricity consumption, there are different methods deployed by researchers. Author [2] presented an integrated framework based on Artificial Neural Network, Multilayer Perceptron, conventional regression and design of experiment for forecasting household electricity consumption using five input variables viz. electricity price, urban house income, urban household size, refrigerator price index and TV price index.

Different variations are observed in the load profile of consumers depending on income level, residence type and locality as well as environmental factors [3, 4]. Author [5] adopted data mining techniques for analysis of electricity consumption in order to extract information using the K-means clustering algorithm.

Authors [6, 7] carried out an analysis of seasonal electricity consumption and made an attempt in recognizing environmental effects on the consumption.

Author [8] carried out a comparison of different models for electricity consumption forecasting, like regression, neural network, and least square support vector machine. Author [9] presented a approach for forecasting of daily electricity consumption in the administrating buildings. In the paper [10] author's indication is to a warning in the shortfall of electricity if the same situation exists.

3   ARIMA Model - an Overview

The ARIMA model, also known as Box-Jenkins has been widely used for short-term forecast. The Autoregressive (AR) part of the ARIMA indicates the regression of the time series over its own lagged values. Integrated (I) indicates that the values have undergone differencing and the Moving Average (MA) Indicates weighted moving average over regression errors [11]. A Non-seasonal ARIMA model is represented as ARIMA (p, d, q) where, p is the order (number of time lags) of AR model, d represents the degree of integration (differencing), and q is the order of the MA [12].

Seasonal ARIMA model is represented as ARIMA(p, d, q) $(P, D, Q)_m$, where the P, D, Q depict the autoregressive, differencing, and moving average terms for the seasonal part of the ARIMA model and m is the number of periods in each season [13, 14].

In order to estimate the values for the various terms of ARIMA model, the steps involving in finding autocorrelation and partial autocorrelation between the values of the data [15, 16]. Autocorrelation is the correlation of a time series with a delayed copy of itself and is defined as ACF = corr(X_t, X_{t+k}). Here X_t and X_{t+k} are the current observation and the observation after k period respectively.

Partial Auto-Correlation (PACF) [17] is the partial correlation of X_{t+k} with X_t i.e. it controls the values of the time series at all shorter lags which ACF does not. It is defined for positive lag only with values lying between −1 and +1. Table 1 gives the idea as how to make the estimation for initial values of ARIMA (p, d, q) [18].

Table 1. Characteristics of ACF and PACF graph for AR, MA and ARMA.

Characteristics	AR (p)	MA (q)	ARMA (p, q)
ACF	Decays	Cuts after q lags	Decays
PACF	Cuts after p lags	Decays	Decays

4 Dataset Description

Day by day demand of electricity is increasing because of uses of electrical and electronics instruments. To forecasting the electricity consumption, the electricity consumption data of Indian Institute of Technology (Indian School of Mines), Dhanbad, Jharkhand, India, collected from the electricity distribution unit of it. This data set contains the electricity consumption in unit (in kWh) from July 2004 to June 2009. The data specified the unit consumed every month between the mentioned periods [19–23].

5 Methodology Used

In order to build an ARIMA model, the steps used are as follow:

Step 1. Data Visualization
The data is visualized and it is determined whether the data shows any overall trend or seasonal trend. The time series data was decomposed into constituent's viz. Trend, Seasonality and Residual Values. The trend would represent the optional and often linear increasing or decreasing behavior of the series over time, whereas the seasonality would depict its optional repeating patterns or cycles of behavior over time. The residual values essentially take out the trend and seasonality of the data, making the values independent of time. The seasonal_decompose function in stats models was used for the same.

Step 2. Stationarity Testing
A time series is stationary if its statistical properties such as mean, variance are constant over time. In a time series, observations are dependent on time, but a linear regression assumes all the observations to be independent of each other. So stationarising the data could enable us to apply regression techniques to time dependent variables. The series is made stationary by estimating the trend and seasonality and eliminating them from the series. For this purpose the logarithmic transformation and differencing methods are applied.

In order to test the Stationarity of data following methods were used:

1. **Plotting Rolling Statistics:** A plot depicting moving average and moving standard deviation is drawn and it is observed if it varies with time. A moving average/standard deviation means that at any instant 't', the average/standard deviation of the last year, i.e. last 12 months is taken.
2. **Dickey-Fuller Test:** It is a statistical test for testing stationarity. Here, the null hypothesis is that the time series is non-stationary. The test results consists of a Test Statistic and some Critical Values for different confident levels. If the 'Test Statistic'

is less than the 'Critical Value', the null hypothesis can be rejected and it can be said that the series is stationary.

The two major reasons for the time series to be non-stationary is the trend and the seasonality. The series is made stationary by estimating the trend and seasonality and eliminating them from the series. For this purpose the logarithmic transformation and differencing methods are applied.

Step 3. Deduction of Optimal Parameters
ACF and PACF are used to determine the suitable model parameters.

Step 4. Model Validation
This step involved validating the model using statistics and confidence intervals and tracking of model performances.

Step 5. Forecast
The best model obtained is implemented on the series and used to forecast the future values. The values are reverted back to the original scale.

6   Result Analysis

The electricity consumption in IIT(ISM) during the period July 2004 to June 2009 is depicted in Figs. 1 and 2 represents the constituents of the time series viz. are trend, seasonality and residual values. It can be observed that the electricity consumption data contains both an overall upward trend and has a seasonality to it and thus, seasonal ARIMA was used for forecasting.

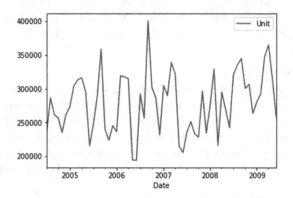

Fig. 1. Electricity consumption data for period 2004–09.

The presence of trend and seasonality makes the data non-stationary and the same can be confirmed by the rolling statistics and Dickey-Fuller test on the electricity consumption data as illustrated in Fig. 3 and Table 2 respectively. Although slight change in standard deviation is seen, but it can be clearly observed that the mean is varying with time. Also, the test statistics confirm the same since it is greater than the the critical values.

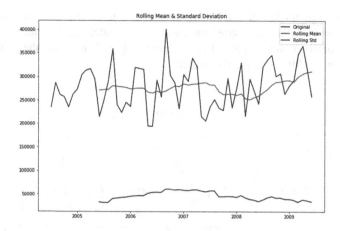

Fig. 2. Constituents of the electricity data.

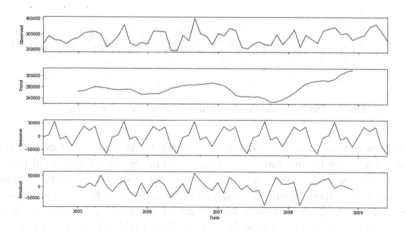

Fig. 3. Rolling statistics for the electricity data.

Table 2. Results of dickey-fuller test on the electricity data.

Statistics	Value
Test statistics	−2.144462
p-value	0.227016
#Lags used	7
Number of observations	52
Critical value (1%)	−3.562879
Critical value (5%)	−2.918973
Critical value (10%)	−2.597393

The series was made stationary using logarithmic transformation and differencing methods. It became stationary after the seasonal first difference was taken. The ACF and PACF correlogram was plotted as depicted in Fig. 4, to select the suitable AR, MA, SAR, and MAR terms for the model.

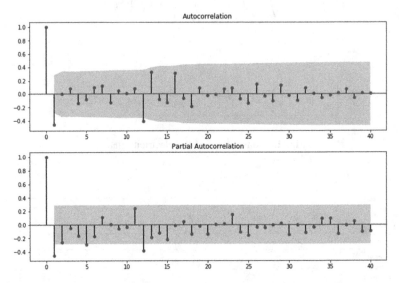

Fig. 4. The ACF and PACF graph for the first seasonal difference.

From the correlograms, it was observed that both the ACF and PACF cuts the upper confidence level for the first time at lag value 0 and hence, the coefficients of both AR and MA terms would zero i.e. p = 0 and q = 0. Since the ACF and PACF plot is negative at lag 12, there should be a SMA and SAR term to the model. A function was created using all possible combinations of parameters for fitting the models, the outcome was predicted using the models, and the model with the smallest MAPE was selected. The best model was found to be seasonal ARIMA(0, 1, 0)×(2, 0, 1, 12) model which was used to forecast the future electricity consumption.

Figure 5 shows the forecasted electricity consumption (yellow) for the academic year 2008–09 and the actual data (blue), also tabulated in Table 3. The best model was able to forecast the consumption with a MAPE of 6.63%.

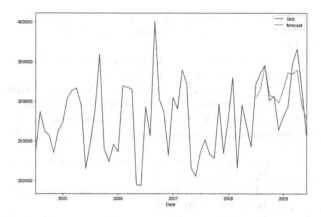

Fig. 5. Actual data Vs forecasted data.

Table 3. Actual data of electricity consumption Vs the forecasted data.

Month	JAN	FEB	MARCH	APRIL	MAY	JUNE	JULY	AUG	SEP	OCT	NOV	DEC
Actual	280572	292272	347604	365376	316116	258036	321408	335580	345156	300744	306600	263340
Predicted	314373	335838	334558	339294	295065	278028	304447	314965	345496	307510	305122	297856

7 Conclusions

Electricity demand forecasting plays an integral role in planning for the electricity production and determine the resources needed to operate the plants such as fuels. Furthermore, it helps in planning for future electricity needs and thus establishing new plants and networks.

The analysis of the electricity consumption in IIT(ISM) for the period 2004–2008 gave us a seasonal ARIMA $(0, 1, 0) \times (2, 0, 1, 12)$ model as the best model and it was able to forecast the consumption for year 2008–2009 with a MAPE of 6.63%.

References

1. Navani, J.P., Sharma, N.K., Sapra, S.: Technical and non-technical losses in power system and its economic consequence in Indian economy. Int. J. Electron. Comput. Sci. Eng. **1**(2), 757–761 (2016)
2. Azadeh, A., Faiz, Z.S.: A meta-heuristic framework for forecasting household electricity consumption. Appl. Soft Comput. **11**(1), 614–620 (2011)
3. Dzobo, O., et al.: Multi-dimensional customer segmentation model for power system reliability-worth analysis. Int. J. Electr. Power Energy Syst. **62**, 532–539 (2014)
4. Min, B., Golden, M.: Electoral cycles in electricity losses in India. Energy Policy **65**, 619–625 (2014)

5. Rathod, R.R., Garg, R.D.: Regional electricity consumption analysis for consumers using data mining techniques and consumer meter reading data. Int. J. Electr. Power Energy Syst. **78**, 368–374 (2016)
6. Chen, C.S., Hwang, J.C., Huang, C.W.: Application of load survey systems to proper tariff design. IEEE Trans. Power Syst. **12**(4), 1746–1751 (1997)
7. Benítez, I., et al.: Dynamic clustering segmentation applied to load profiles of energy consumption from Spanish customers. Int. J. Electr. Power Energy Syst. **55**, 437–448 (2014)
8. Kaytez, F., et al.: Forecasting electricity consumption: a comparison of regression analysis, neural networks and least squares support vector machines. Int. J. Electr. Power Energy Syst. **67**, 431–438 (2015)
9. Dong, B., et al.: A hybrid model approach for forecasting future residential electricity consumption. Energy Build. **117**, 341–351 (2016)
10. Hussain, A., Rahman, M., Memon, J.A.: Forecasting electricity consumption in Pakistan: the way forward. Energy Policy **90**, 73–80 (2016)
11. Nguyen, H., Hansen, C.K: Short-term electricity load forecasting with time series analysis. In: 2017 IEEE International Conference on Prognostics and Health Management (ICPHM), Dallas, TX, pp. 214–221 (2017)
12. Nichiforov, C., Stamatescu, I., Făgărăşan, I., Stamatescu, G.: Energy consumption forecasting using ARIMA and neural network models. In: 2017 5th International Symposium on Electrical and Electronics Engineering (ISEEE), Galati, pp. 1–4 (2017)
13. Mahalakshmi, G., Sridevi, S., Rajaram, S.: A survey on forecasting of time series data. In: 2016 International Conference on Computing Technologies and Intelligent Data Engineering (ICCTIDE 2016), Kovilpatti, pp. 1–8 (2016)
14. Papadopoulos, S., Karakatsanis, I.: Short-term electricity load forecasting using time series and ensemble learning methods. In: 2015 IEEE Power and Energy Conference at Illinois (PECI), Champaign, IL, pp. 1–6 (2015)
15. Zhou, R., Pan, Y., Huang, Z., Wang, Q.: Building energy use prediction using time series analysis. In: 2013 IEEE 6th International Conference on Service-oriented Computing and Applications, Koloa, HI, pp. 309–313 (2013)
16. Fahmi, F, Sofyan, H.: Forecasting household electricity consumption in the province of Aceh using combination time series model. In: 2017 International Conference on Electrical Engineering and Informatics (ICELTICs), Banda Aceh, pp. 97–102 (2017)
17. Deng, J., Jirutitijaroen, P.: Short-term load forecasting using time series analysis: a case study for Singapore. In: 2010 IEEE Conference on Cybernetics and Intelligent Systems, Singapore, pp. 231–236 (2010)
18. Haydari, Z., Kavehnia, F., Askari, M., Ganbariyan, M.: Time-series load modelling and load forecasting using neuro-fuzzy techniques. In: 2007 9th International Conference on Electrical Power Quality and Utilisation, Barcelona, pp. 1–6 (2007)
19. Jifri, M.H., Hassan, E.E., Miswan, N.H.: Forecasting performance of time series and regression in modeling electricity load demand. In: 2017 7th IEEE International Conference on System Engineering and Technology (ICSET), Shah Alam, pp. 12–16 (2017)
20. Ridzuan, M.R.M., Hassan, E.E., Abdullah, A.R., Bahaman, N., Kadir, A.F.A.: A new meta heuristic evolutionary programming (NMEP) in optimizing economic energy dispatch. J. Telecommun. Electron. Comput. Eng. **8**(2), 35–40 (2016)
21. Miswan, N.H., Said, R.M., Anuar, S.H.H.: ARIMA with regression model in modelling electricity load demand. J. Telecommun. Electron. Comput. Eng. **8**(12), 113–116 (2016)
22. Ferhatosmanoglu, N., Macit, B.: Incorporating explanatory effects of neighbour airports in forecasting models for airline passenger volumes. In: Proceedings of 5th the International Conference on Operations Research and Enterprise Systems, ICORES, pp. 178–185 (2016)

23. Miswan, N.H., Ping, P.Y., Ahmad, M.H.: On parameter estimation for malaysian gold prices modelling and forecasting. Int. J. Math. Anal. **7**(21–24), 1059–1068 (2013)
24. Usha, T., Balamurugan, S.: Seasonal based electricity demand forecasting using time series analysis. Circuits Syst. **7**, 3320–3328 (2016)
25. Espinoza, M., Joye, C., Belmans, R., Moor, B.D.: Short-term load forecasting profile identification and customer segmentation: a methodology based on periodic time series. IEEE Trans. Power Syst. **20**(3), 443 (2005)

A Comparative Analysis of Fuzzy Logic Based Query Expansion Approaches for Document Retrieval

Dilip Kumar Sharma[1,2(✉)], Rajendra Pamula[1], and D. S. Chauhan[2]

[1] IIT (ISM) Dhanbad, Dhanbad, India
rajendrapamula@gmail.com
[2] GLA University, Mathura, India
dilip.sharma@gla.ac.in, pdschauhan@gmail.com

Abstract. Query expansion is one of the techniques to find suitable terms for redefining the queries so that the document retrieval performance can be enhanced. This paper presents a comparative analysis of recently developed query expansion approaches using fuzzy logic to retrieve relevant documents from large datasets for a given user query. In this paper, two query expansion approaches are compared and analyzed in different manner for two benchmark datasets: CISI and CACM. Both the approaches are based on fuzzy logic and term selection methods. On the basis performance evaluating parameters such as precision, recall, MAP and precision-recall graph, it is found that the approach proposed in [13] improves document retrieval in comparison to the approach proposed in [32].

Keywords: Fuzzy logic · Query expansion · Term weighting
Term selection · Precision · Recall

1 Introduction

Document retrieval system retrieves the most relevant documents from a large data corpus according to user's queries. Document retrieval consists of various components like searching, querying, document indexing and ranking. It is used in many areas such as information filtering, digital libraries, media search, recommender system, news retrieval, blog search, search engines (mobile search, enterprise search, web search and federal search) and many others.

The main issue with document retrieval effectiveness is "term mismatch problem". This problem states that it is not necessarily the same words are used by users and indexers who (who performs indexing) for searching the documents. This problem is also known as the *"vocabulary problem"* [1]. Synonymy and polysemy make this problem more complex. Synonymy means that the same words have different meanings such as "apple". This word has two meanings: an organization and a fruit. Polysemy means that different words have the same meaning such as "television" and "tv". Synonymy decreases recall by not retrieving all for any word "television" and "tv". Similarly, Polysemy decreases precision by retrieving more non- relevant documents in comparison to relevant documents.

© Springer Nature Singapore Pte Ltd. 2018
M. Singh et al. (Eds.): ICACDS 2018, CCIS 906, pp. 336–345, 2018.
https://doi.org/10.1007/978-981-13-1813-9_34

One of the most successful and widely used techniques is query expansion to resolve term mismatch problem. Query expansion assists users in framing new queries from original queries. It has been observed in literature that the average length of query is 2.30 words [2], which were already reported by Lau and Horvitz [3]. Later, Lovins noticed a slight increment in query length for long queries in 1968 [3], but still most of the queries consist of one, two or three words at most. Such type of situation makes vocabulary problem more critical. This shows that there is a huge scope for optimized query expansion approaches.

An initial query given by user is always incomplete and inadequate to represent user's need. Therefore, query expansion technique is used, which helps to select most suitable terms to be added with original query and in this way, the document retrieval performance can be enhanced [3]. To overcome above mentioned problems to a certain extent, researchers have proposed may query expansion approaches to formulate better queries [4–8]. Conceptually, the performance must be improved after applying query expansion approaches, but this is not the case always. Adding a new term to query creates a risk of query drift (the original query is changed topically) and diverts the searching into another direction. Therefore, there is need of extensive research to explore query expansion approaches with respect to their efficiency in improving retrieval effectiveness.

In last few decades, researchers analyzed various aspects of automatic query expansion (AQE) and have done research in several domains. The first work was reported by Van Rijsbergen in 1979 [4]. The proposed work was based on relevance feedback. Yang and Korfaghe [9] used real coded Genetic algorithm (GA) with random mutation and two-point crossover operators for improving the performance of query expansion. Sanchez et al. proposed GA based query expansion approach using user relevance feedback. GA was used to determine weights of all possible expanded terms for Boolean queries [10]. They tested their approach on patent dataset consisting 479 documents. Robertson and Willet [11] used evolutionary algorithm to identify the upper bound of relevance feedback for automatic query expansion technique in vector space model based document retrieval systems. They compared their results with Robertson et al.'s retrospective relevance weighting technique [12]. The results were satisfactory.

In recent years, Pseudo Relevance Feedback (PRF) based AQE is used widely and improved query expansion performance and retrieval processes. PRF is a type of local query expansion technique. However there are a lot of limitations in PRF based QE in term of accuracy and computational complexity. To overcome these limitations, some other techniques were used with PRF i.e. semantic filtering such as WordNet etc. [13]. However it is also reported in literature that WordNet alone does not improve query expansion to large extent. Therefore, different variants were also introduced in recent years [13]. The use of concept and context of queries and documents is another way to enhance PRF based query expansion. Later on, some researchers also used soft computing technique to improve the performance of query expansion.

A new co-occurrence based query expansion techniques was proposed for improving document retrieval and tested on CACM, CISI datasets [14]. This approach successfully enhanced the performance of the system. Two different query expansion approaches using local collocation and global collocation were proposed [15]. These approaches were based on long span collocates. A new semantic similarity based query expansion approach using clusters was proposed to overcome the limitation of ambiguous and short queries [16]. This approach constructed various clusters of documents those are retrieved by the original query, and each cluster ranked on the basis of content similarity with the query. At last, this approach was suggesting terms from these ranked clusters to disambiguate the query.

A new query expansion technique using WordNet lexical chains was proposed by Gong et al. [17]. The proposed work was based on synonym and hypernym/hyponymy relations in WordNet. They used lexical chains as expansion rules. This approach improved query performance dramatically. Bendersky et al. [18] presented a new term reweighting method for query expansion to enhance the performance of document retrieval. They used GA to reweight a user's query vector in their approach. The proposed approach was based on the user's relevance feedback. Cooper et al. [19] proposed a GUI for users with graphical relations between different items by lexical neighborhoods for prompted query refinement. A novel term weighting based query expansion approach was proposed by Horng et al. [20]. They used GA to adapt the query term weights in order to get the closest query vector to the optimal one. Chen et al. [21] framed association rules to find out the degrees of similarity among terms and constructed a tree structure of these terms to select for query expansion. Chang et al. [22] proposed a new query expansion approach using fuzzy rules. The results were satisfactorily. Chang et al. [23] proposed a novel query expansion approach using weighting and re-weighting methods to enhance the performance of document retrieval. Chang et al. [24] framed fuzzy rules for user relevance based query expansion approach for document retrieval. Carlos et al. [25] proposed an approach to learn terms which actually helped to bridge the terminology gap existing between initial query and the relevant documents. Tayal et al. [26] used fuzzy logic to give weights to each query term using fuzzy triangular membership function. Gupta et al. [33] used fuzzy logic for constructing ranking function to enhance the performance of document retrieval process. Sharma et al. [34] presented the concepts of deep web and its analysis for web searching.

Rivas et al. [27] applied developed query expansion technique in biomedical document retrieval system. They combined text preprocessing with query expansion approach to improve the performance of document retrieval. They used one of the part of MEDLINE dataset, called Cystic Fibrosis for all the experiments. Li et al. [28] analyzed various query weighting approaches on L2R dataset for two transfer ranking frameworks: AdaRank and LambdaMART.

Singh et al. [29, 30] combined various term selection based query expansion approaches to improve document retrieval performance. They also used Word2vec for selecting query expansion terms semantically. They obtained satisfactorily results. Singh et al. [31] proposed PRF and corpus-based term co-occurrence approach to find suitable terms for query expansion. They tested their approach on two datasets: FIRE and TREC-3. Singh et al. [32] presented a novel query expansion approach based on fuzzy logic. Authors obtained better recall and precision for the proposed AQE approach. Gupta et al. [13] proposed a novel automatic query expansion approach based on term weighting to extract relevant documents from datasets. The proposed approaches was compared with existing approaches and found improvement in document retrieval process.

This paper presents a comparative analysis of recently proposed fuzzy logic based query expansion approaches [13, 32]. Both the query expansion approaches are compared in terms of adopted approaches, number of membership functions, framed fuzzy rules and results. The rest of the paper is presented as follows. The theoretical background of both the query expansion approaches is discussed in Sect. 2. In Sect. 3, the results and analysis of performance of both the approaches are discussed. Finally, in Sect. 4, the conclusion of the paper is presented.

2   Theoretical Foundation of Fuzzy Logic Based Query Expansion Approaches

This section describes the theoretical background of fuzzy logic based query expansion in terms of approaches adopted in these approaches, membership functions and fuzzy rule base used in both the approaches.

2.1   Adopted Approaches

In [32], a fuzzy logic based query expansion approach is proposed. This approach considers top-retrieved document as the most relevant documents to find suitable expanded terms. This approach includes various terms selection methods for query expansion approaches. These term selection methods determine the importance of all unique terms in terms of relevance score [35]. All unique are selected from top-retrieved documents. The proposed method combines these weights of each term by using fuzzy logic to determine the weights of possible expanded query terms. Then, a new query vector is created by combining additional query term weights and original query term weights.

In [32], firstly, authors used Okapi-BM25 ranking function to retrieve the relevant documents from the dataset against original query. Then top retrieved documents were selected as PRF documents and all unique terms were identified from these documents to form a candidate term pool. Further, three types of term weighting methods such as class based, statistics based and co-occurrence based methods are used to give the weights to all terms of the term pool. Fuzzy logic is used to combine these methods at two levels: at first level, three different fuzzy logic controllers are developed and at second level, another fuzzy logic controller is developed. After that, a semantic filter is used to remove noisy and redundant terms; those are obtained for query expansion. Then after, all the terms are ranked in decreasing order of relevance score and top ranked terms are selected for query expansion.

In [13], authors proposed two approaches to extract relevant documents from large datasets. First approach was a new query expansion approach, which was based on term weighting scheme and second approach was a new combined semantic filter. In first approach, they used Particle Swarm Optimization (PSO) to determine the optimal weights of information retrieval evidences for all terms. Further, fuzzy logic was used to make PSO dynamic by controlling its parameters such as acceleration coefficients and inertia during the optimization process. In second approach, noisy terms were removed using proposed combined semantic filtering method. Then after, Rocchio method [16] was used to reweight the terms. The proposed approach improved the performance of document retrieval process effectively.

2.2 Membership Functions Used in Approaches

In [32], triangular membership function is used for fuzzification process. The ranges of membership for all variables are represented by three linguistic terms as high, medium and low. In [13], authors also used three membership functions for input and output variables such as High, Medium and Low. In both the approaches, Triangular type of membership is used to express the membership functions in this approach.

2.3 Fuzzy Rule Base

Fuzzy rules are framed in both the approaches on the basis of domain knowledge. In [32], total 21 fuzzy rules are framed and domain knowledge is tabulated in Table 1.

Table 1. Domain Knowledge for framing fuzzy rules in [32].

S. no.	Domain knowledge base
1	If ("Wstatistical is High") and ("Wclass is High") and ("Wco-occurrence is High") then "Wcombine is High"
2	If ("Wstatistical is Medium") and ("Wclass is Low") and ("Wco-occurrence is High") then "Wcombine is Medium"
3	If ("TFIDF is Low") and ("Wcombine is Low") then "Wfinal is Low"
4	If ("TFIDF is High") and ("Wcombine is Medium") then "Wfinal is Medium"

Table 2. Domain Knowledge for framing fuzzy rules in [13].

S. no.	Domain knowledge base	Examples
1	If *"Normalized gbest* is *low"*, *"UN* is *low"* and "acceleration coefficients (c_1 and c_2) are also *low"* then "variation in c_1 (Δc_1)" and "variation in c_2 (Δc_2)" are likely to be *"medium"*	"If *Normalized gbest* is *Low* and *UN* is *Low* and c_1, c_2 are *Low* then Δc_1 and Δc_2 are *Medium"*
2	If *"Normalized gbest* is *low"* and *"UN* is *low"* and "acceleration coefficients (c_1 and c_2) are *High"* then "variation in c_1 (Δc_1) and variation in c_2 (Δc_2)" are likely to be *"high"*	"If *Normalized gbest* is *Low* and *UN* is *Low* and c_1, c_2 are *High* then Δc_1 and Δc_2 are *High"*
3	If *"Normalized gbest* is *low"* and *"UN* is *medium"* and "inertia (ω) is *medium"* then "variation in inertia ($\Delta\omega$)" is likely to be *"low"*	"If *Normalized gbest* is *Low* and *UN* is *Medium* and ω is *Medium* then $\Delta\omega$ is *Low"*
4	If *"Normalized gbest* is *high"* and *"UN* is *low"* and "inertia (ω) is *low"* then "variation in inertia ($\Delta\omega$) is likely to be *high"*	"If *Normalized gbest* is *High* and *UN* is *Low* and ω is *Low* then $\Delta\omega$ is *High"*

In [13], total 27 fuzzy rules are framed and the following domain knowledge is used to create these rules:

3 Experimental Results and Analysis

To analyze both the approaches, CACM and CISI datasets are used as benchmark datasets. Random fifty queries are selected from each dataset. The analysis is presented in two ways: analysis for overall effectiveness and query wise analysis.

3.1 Overall Effectiveness

The overall effectiveness of both the approaches is compared in terms of *MAP*, *P@rank* and precision-recall graph. Table 2 tabulates the comparison of MAP values of both query expansion approaches. It is clear from this table that query expansion approach proposed in [13] gives better MAP values in comparison to the approach which is proposed in [32] for both datasets. Tables 3 and 4 shows the results for both the approaches in terms of P@rank. These tables clearly show that query expansion approach proposed in [13] gives better results in comparison to the approach proposed in [32]. Precision-recall graphs are also plotted for CACM and CISI as shown in Figs. 1 and 2. These figures depict that approach proposed in [13] is better than the approach proposed in [32]. The approach proposed in [13] gets better precision values at all recall points in comparison to approach proposed in [32].

Table 3. Comparison of *MAP* for both query expansion approaches.

Dataset	Query expansion approach proposed in [32]	Query expansion approach proposed in [13]
CACM	0.2801	0.2842
CISI	0.2512	0.2553

Table 4. Comparison of *P@rank* for both query expansion approaches for *CACM* dataset.

	Query expansion approach proposed in [32]	Query expansion approach proposed in [13]
P@5	0.7847	0.8012
P@10	0.7351	0.7487
P@15	0.6895	0.7043
P@20	0.6519	0.6728
P@30	0.6051	0.6245
P@50	0.5104	0.5230

Table 5. Comparison of *P@rank* for both query expansion approaches for *CISI* dataset.

	Query expansion approach proposed in [32]	Query expansion approach proposed in [13]
P@5	0.6642	0.6756
P@10	0.6121	0.6308
P@15	0.5609	0.5771
P@20	0.5228	0.5398
P@30	0.4703	0.4814
P@50	0.3883	0.4087

3.2 Query Wise Analysis

To analyze the query wise performance of both the approaches, four queries are selected randomly and the values of recall and precision are computed. These results

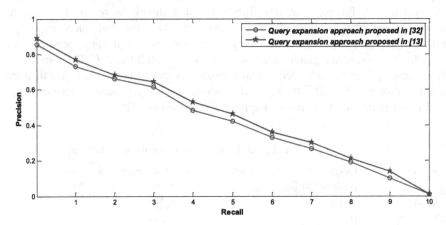

Fig. 1. Comparison of precision-recall graphs of approaches proposed in [13, 32] for CACM.

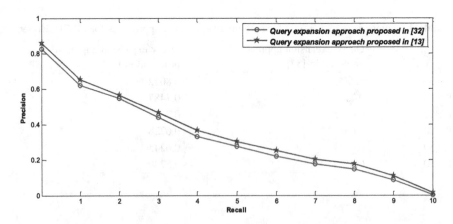

Fig. 2. Comparison of precision-recall graphs of approaches proposed in [13, 32] for CISI.

Table 6. *Recall* and *Precision* values in case of *CACM*.

Query no.	Query expansion approach proposed in [32]		Query expansion approach proposed in [13]	
	Recall	Precision	Recall	Precision
14	0.7954	0.3065	0.7954	0.3105
26	0.7667	0.3591	0.8000	0.3676
36	0.5172	0.3418	0.5172	0.3569
63	0.5000	0.4504	0.6250	0.4520

Table 7. *Recall* and *Precision* values in case of *CISI*.

Query no.	Query expansion approach proposed in [32]		Query expansion approach proposed in [13]	
	Recall	Precision	Recall	Precision
2	0.3207	0.2178	0.3461	0.2225
12	0.6154	0.1949	0.6423	0.2091
28	0.4333	0.3394	0.4500	0.3472
34	0.5789	0.2918	0.6052	0.3078

are tabulated in Tables 5 and 6 for CACM and CISI respectively. It is clear from these tables that the approach proposed in [13] is gets more precision and recall values in comparison to the approach proposed in [32] Table 7.

The following observations have been made during the comparison of results of both the approaches.

1. In [13], PSO optimizes the weights of used evidences which enable the approach to capture more features of queries and documents as well. Whereas in [32], only the weights of various term selection methods are optimized.
2. In [13], fuzzy logic is used to make PSO adaptive in nature, which enhances the capability of normal PSO. Whereas in [32], fuzzy logic is used to infer the weights of term selection methods.

Therefore, the approach presented in [13] gets better results in comparison to the approach proposed in [32].

4 Conclusion

A detailed comparison of recently developed fuzzy logic based query expansion approaches is presented in this paper. The performance of these query expansion approaches is compared in two ways: overall effectiveness of the approaches and query wise analysis of approaches. These approaches are also compared in terms of methodologies followed to develop in both approaches, membership functions and fuzzy rules framed to compute relevance score. CACM and CISI are used as benchmark dataset for performing all experiments. The comparison clearly shows that the approach proposed in [13] is better than the approach proposed in [32]. The query expansion approach proposed in [13] is superior in dealing with uncertainty, vagueness and impreciseness of queries and documents written in natural language in comparison to the approach proposed in [32]. As fuzzy logic is used in approach proposed in [32] for deciding the weights of various term selection methods whereas in [13], fuzzy logic and PSO are used to decide the weights of evidences.

References

1. Furnas, G., Landauer, T., Gomez, L., Dumais, S.: The vocabulary problem in human-system communication. ACM 30(11), 964–971 (1997)
2. www.hitwise.com/us/press-center/press-releases/2009/google-searches-oct-09/
3. Lovins, J.: Development of a stemming algorithm. Mech. Transl. Comput. Linguist. 11(1–2), 22–31 (1968)
4. Rijsbergen, C.: Information Retrieval, 2nd edn. Butterworth, Waltham (1979)
5. Sakai, T., Robertson, S.: Flexible pseudo relevance feedback using optimization tables. In: Louisiana, pp. 396–397 (2001)
6. Salton, G., Buckley, C.: Term-weighting approaches in automatic text retrieval. Inf. Process. Manag. 24(5), 513–523 (1988)
7. Witten, I., Moffat, A., Bell, T.: Managing Gigabytes: Compressing and Indexing Documents and Images. Morgan Kaufmann, Burlington (1999)
8. Molto, M., Svenonious, E.: Automatic recognition of title page names. Inf. Process. Manag. 27(1), 83–95 (1991)
9. Yang, J., Korfhage, R.: Query modifications using genetic algorithms in vector space models. Int. J. Expert Syst. 7(2), 165–191 (1994)
10. Sanchez, E., Miyano, H., Brachet, J.: Optimization of fuzzy queries with genetic algorithms. In: Proceedings of Applications to a Data Base of Patents in Biomedical Engineering, VI IFSA Congress, Sao-Paulo, pp. 293–296 (1995)
11. Robertson, A., Willet, P.: An upperbound to the performance for ranked-output searching: optimal weighting of query terms using a genetic algorithm. J. Doc. 52(4), 405–420 (1996)
12. Robertson, S., Jones, S.: Relevance weighting of search terms. J. Am. Soc. Inf. Sci. 27, 129–145 (1976)
13. Gupta, Y., Saini, A.: A novel Fuzzy-PSO term weighting automatic query expansion approach using semantic filtering. Knowl. Based Syst. 136, 97–120 (2017)
14. Xu, J., Croft, W.B.: Query expansion using local and global document analysis. In: ACM SIGIR Conference on Research and Development in Information Retrieval (1996)
15. Olga, V.: Query expansion with long-span collocates information retrieval. Am. Soc. Inf. Sci. Technol. 60(2), 251–273 (2009)
16. Barathi, M., Valli, S.: Query disambiguation using clustering and concept based semantic web search for efficient information retrieval. Life Sci. J. 10(2), 147–155 (2013)
17. Gong, Z., Cheang, C.W., Hou U, L.: Multi-term Web Query Expansion Using WordNet. In: Bressan, S., Küng, J., Wagner, R. (eds.) DEXA 2006. LNCS, vol. 4080, pp. 379–388. Springer, Heidelberg (2006). https://doi.org/10.1007/11827405_37

18. Bendersky, M., Metzler, D., Bruce, W.: Effective query expansion with multiple information sources. In: Fifth ACM International Conference on Web Search and Data Mining, ACM, USA (2012)
19. Cooper, J., Byrd, R.: BIWAN—a visual interface for prompted query refinement. In: Proceedings of the 31st Hawaii International Conference on System Sciences, Hawaii, vol. 2, pp. 277–285 (1998)
20. Horng, J., Yeh, C.: Applying genetic algorithms to query optimization in document retrieval. Inf. Process. Manag. **36**, 737–759 (2000)
21. Chen, H., Yu, J., Furuse, K., Ohbo, N.: Support IR query refinement by partial keyword set. In: Proceedings of the Second International Conference on Web Information Systems Engineering, vol. 11, pp. 245–253. Singapore (2001)
22. Chang, Y., Chen, S., Liau, C.: A new query expansion method based on fuzzy rules. In: Proceedings of the Seventh Joint Conference on AI, Fuzzy System, and Grey System, Taipei (2003)
23. Chang, Y., Chen, C.: A new query reweighting method for document retrieval based on genetic algorithms. IEEE Trans. Evolut. Comput. **10**(5), 617–622 (2006)
24. Chang, Y., Chen, S., Liau, C.: A new query expansion method for document retrieval based on the inference of fuzzy rules. J. Chin. Inst. Eng. **30**(3), 511–515 (2007)
25. Carlos, M., Maguitman, A.: A semi-supervised incremental algorithm to automatically formulate topical queries. Inf. Sci. **179**, 1881–1892 (2009)
26. Tayal, D., Sabharwal, S., Jain, A., Mittal, K.: Intelligent query expansion for the queries including numerical terms. In: National Conference on Communication Technologies and Its Impact on Next Generation Computing (2012)
27. Rivas, A., Iglesias, E., Borrajo, L.: Study of query expansion techniques and their application in the biomedical information retrieval. Sci. World J. **2014**, 1–10 (2014)
28. Li, P., Sanderson, S., Carman, M., Scholer, F.: On the effectiveness of query weighting for adapting rank learners to new unlabelled collections. In: CIKM, pp. 1413–1422 (2016)
29. Singh, J., Sharna, A.: Relevance feedback-based query expansion model using ranks combining and Word2Vec approach. J. IETE J. Res. **62**(5), 591–604 (2016)
30. Singh, J., Sharan, A.: Relevance feedback based query expansion model using borda count and semantic similarity approach. Comput. Intell. Neurosci. **2015**, 1–13 (2015). Article ID 568197
31. Singh, J., Sharan, A., Saini, M.: Term co-occurrence and context window-based combined approach for query expansion with the semantic notion of terms. Int. J. Web Sci. **3**(1), 32–57 (2017)
32. Singh, J., Sharan, A.: A new fuzzy logic-based query expansion model for efficient information retrieval using relevance feedback approach. J. Neural Comput. Appl. Arch. **28**(9), 2557–2580 (2017)
33. Gupta, Y., Saini, A., Saxena, A.: A new fuzzy logic based ranking function for efficient information retrieval system. Expert Syst. Appl. **42**, 1223–1234 (2015)
34. Sharma, D., Sharma, A.: Search engine: a backbone for information extraction in ICT scenario. Int. J. Inf. Commun. Technol. Hum. Dev. **3**(2), 38–51 (2011)
35. Singh, J., Prasad, M., Prasad, O., Joo, E., Saxena, A., Lin, C.: A novel fuzzy logic model for pseudo-relevance feedback-based query expansion. Int. J. Fuzzy Syst. **18**(6), 980–989 (2016)

Trends and Macro-economic Determinants of FDI Inflows to India

Jyoti Gupta[(⊠)]

Jaypee University of Engineering and Technology, Guna, India
guptajyoti78@gmail.com

Abstract. The study examines the trend in foreign direct investment (FDI) inflow to India for the period 1971 to 2016. The flow of FDI to world, developed countries, developing countries and India has been studied. Trend of FDI inflows to India along with its growth rate is also studied. This paper tries to come up with logic for variations in the flow and change in the macro-economic determinants of foreign direct investment (FDI) during the study period ranging from 1991–2016. After checking for stationarity, regression has been applied to estimate the various economic determinants that affect FDI inflows. Empirical results revealed that market size, external debt, exchange rate, reserves, total trade, and physical infrastructure are the vital macro-economic determinants of FDI inflows in India. Political and economic stability, infrastructure, law and order situation, curtailment of external debt, encouragement to domestic savings need to be ensured by the government to magnify the FDI inflows to India.

Keywords: Macro-economic · FDI · Infrastructure · Market size
Exchange rate

1 Introduction

Capital intensive projects around the world are being funded by Foreign Direct Investment (FDI). Insufficient domestic savings create a gap between the actual and the desired level of capital required for the development of a country, which is filled in by FDI inflows by pushing the actual capital stock to the desired level [1, 2]. Through its spillover effects FDI helps make the economy of the host country more competitive as it brings along better technology and management practices. Alongside, the risk of vulnerability to foreign exchange and international trade are surrogated through FDI. India has seen mammoth growth in FDI inflow since 1991 after it adapted the liberalization policy. Fixation of foreign investment in high priority industry, streamlining of the procedures, making the decision making process more transparent, doing away with bureaucratic controls were the significant changes that were made to the India's foreign policy to attract higher FDI inflows. Since then is India marching in the direction of amalgamation with the other economies of the world [3].

Various researchers view FDI flow from different theoretical perspectives. The earliest account for FDI was the theory of capital movement, which was later treated as a part of portfolio investment [4–6] innovative contribution was the first account of FDI. FDI was sought as a medium to transfer technical know-how and other assets to

© Springer Nature Singapore Pte Ltd. 2018
M. Singh et al. (Eds.): ICACDS 2018, CCIS 906, pp. 346–358, 2018.
https://doi.org/10.1007/978-981-13-1813-9_35

arrange manufacturing overseas. Then [7] gave a theory saying that firms set up manufacturing facility overseas for products that have already matured in the home country. This was given the name of product life cycle theory. [8, 9] treated FDI as a technique of utilizing ownership advantages available abroad, whereas [10] saw it as a method of risk diversification and was further seen as way of organizational assets and technical know-how transfer by [11]. Further, while [12, 13] explained the logic for internalizing transactions within the MNE, [14] posited that MNEs exhibit a band-wagon effect when they follow their rivals into new markets as a strategic response to oligopolistic rivalry [15].

Apart from above mentioned theories there are numerous other theories related to FDI inflow. But all of them have some limitations. The theory given by [8] was refined over period of time and came to be known as Eclectic Paradigm. The eclectic paradigm was further refined in 1988 which provides a theoretical and conceptual framework to analyze FDI determinants by specifying three conditions- ownership advantage, location advantage and internalization advantage (OLI) [16]. The theory states that a firm must possess-

(a) ownership advantage (O) to contend in the market it intends to invest with foreign and domestic firms;
(b) location advantage (L) to manufacture in a overseas market;
(c) internalization advantage (I) that it makes it desirable to capitalize on the owner-ship advantage within the firm, preferably than to license production [17].

[18] further specified that the location of FDI is ascertained by the investment rationale which could be classified into four categories: Market seeking (horizontal strategy to ingress the host country's local market), Resource seeking (to ingress raw material, labor force and physical infrastructure resources), Efficiency seeking (vertical strategy to take benefit of lower labor costs), and Strategic asset seeking (to ingress R&D, innovation and advanced technology). He further asserted that in the developing countries larger portion of FDI is fueled either by market seeking motives or by efficiency seeking and resource seeking motives.

2 Literature Review

The major theories on FDI include the product life cycle hypothesis [7], oligopolistic reactions hypothesis [14], industrial organization hypothesis [16], and eclectic theory. All the above mentioned theories mainly provide the explanation as to why the multinational corporations' select any one country over other countries to invest and also the choice of particular form of investment [19].

[20] worked on determinants of FDI inflows to transition economies (Central and Eastern Europe) taking into account host market size, labour cost, country risk and gravity factors from 1994 to 1998. The researchers found that country risk is influenced by industrial development, private sector development, government balance, reserves and corruption.

[21] found that openness, return on investment and GDP as proxy variable for market size, are significant variables for FDI fostering and infrastructure and political risk were found insignificant using Least Square technique.

[22] analyses the recent trends in FDI flows in India. This study found that inflows of FDI to India are not in tune with its economic potential. He further states that revised calculation method in tune with the international standards in calculation of FDI figures have led to a substantial improvement in the FDI figures.

[23] analyzed various determinants that influence FDI inflows to India. The study highlights that large pool of high quality labour force is one of the many competitive advantages with India to attract FDI inflows.

[24] enquired into the role of trade openness on FDI during 1980–2007. Trade openness was found to have a significant positive impact on FDI inflows. Social and political interplay among the organization at global level have also been promoted through globalization in addition to interdependence in economic relations through trade, investment, finance and the organization of manufacturing worldwide. Multivariate regression model has been used wherein FDI is treated as dependent variable and infrastructure investment, current account deficit as percentage of GDP, growth rate of real GDP, REER, Net term of trade and inflation are used as independent variables.

[25] took time series data for the period 1992–93 to 2008–09 and empirically examined the determinants of FDI in India. Applying regression he found that GDP, trade openness and inflation are important factors for attracting FDI inflows in India during post-reform period, whereas FOREX does play an important role in accounting for FDI inflow to India.

3 Objective of the Study

- To study FDI inflow trends over the period 1971 to 2016.
- To ascertain the macro-economic determinants of FDI inflow to India over the period of 1991 to 2016.

4 Research Methodology

To fulfill the afore-mentioned objectives the following research methodology has been adopted.

4.1 Nature and Source of Data

Secondary sources of data have been used for analysis in the present study. To that end, the required data has been collected from reports Department of Industrial Promotion and Policy (DIPP), Hand Book of Statistics on Indian Economy published by Reserve Bank of India, UNCTAD, World Bank.

4.2 Statistical Tools

- To study the trend of FDI flows in India along with its growth rate, exponential trend line has been fitted.
- To ascertain the macro-economic determinants of FDI flow to India, data for various variables was collected and Multi-variate regression using Ordinary Least Square has been applied.
- For applying regression, EVIEWS 9 has been used.

5 Trends of FDI Flows

In the recent years some varying trends have been observed in the flow of FDI by both the developed and developing economies as well as by the world economy at large. These trends have been discussed in this section.

World FDI flow was US $ 14241 million in the year 1971 which continued to increase year after year until the year 1982. The flow came down to US $ 58222 million in the year 1982 from US $ 69580 million in the previous year and further dropped to US $ 50393 million in 1983. From 1984 the FDI flows worldwide were on an increasing trend till 2001. In 2001 the FDI flow fell to US $ 772783 million from US $ 1360254 million in the previous year. FDI flows continued to decline badly worldwide till 2004, where the magnitude was a mere US $ 69710 million. Subsequently from 2005 the flows started improving, but once again in the year 2008 the flow declined to US $ 1499133 million and further to US $ 1190006 million in the next year. After that from 2010 the flow started improving and we can say that it is on an increasing trend with a slight decline in 2013 and 2014. Growing globalization is one of the dominant reasons for this enhanced FDI flow.

Developed countries constitute the countries of the European Union and Northern America. Their FDI inflow was US $ 10651 million in 1971; and dipped to US $ 16854 million in 1975 and further to US $ 15531 million in the subsequent year. From 1977 the flow to the developed countries started improving till 1982 in which the flow was US $ 31750 million in comparison to US $ 45734 million in the preceding year. 1983 saw an increase in the flow to developed countries till 1991 where the flow fell to US $ 114480 million and further to US $ 107868 in the next year. Subsequent years witnessed rising trend till 2001 with US $ 547918 million in comparison with US $ 1120510 million in the year 2000. The flow fell further in the coming years till 2004 which witnessed an increase in FDI inflow to the developed countries. 2008 being the year of global slowdown, witnessed a fall in the FDI flows also, which improved from the year 2011 to again fall in the year 2013 and further still in the year 2014. In the year 2015 the flow increased to US $ 984105 million to further US $ 1032373 million in 2016.

Developing Economies which constitutes Africa, Latin America and the Caribbean and Asia was with a FDI flow of US $ 3591 million in 1971, which witnessed oscillating trends till 1985. From 1986 the flow to the developing countries started increasing as the investing countries were able to capitalize on the large market size and availability of cheap labor. The investment in the developing countries were always on a rise with an exception in the year 2002 where the quantum of flow was less but again it improved from the very next year. Even in the years 2008 and 2009 which are considered as years of global slowdown the flow to the developing countries was on a rise.

Talking about India specifically the flow was always fluctuating and the quantum was very minute. It was only after the reforms of 1991 that the magnitude of flow increased to India. The government realized how important it was to receive FDI flow for the development of the country. It was during this time that the norms and formalities related to the foreign investment were relaxed, which encouraged the investors to invest in India. After 1991 major fall in the flow was in the year 2009 and 2010, the year of global slowdown. Since then the flow has been always on an rising trend with the exception of 2012. But if we see the flow to India in respect to share in the flow to the developing countries the magnitude is almost negligible. The reason for this is that our government has been following a restrictive policy as compared to other countries. Other major reason could be bureaucracy, corruption, weak infrastructure, complicated tax structure. The government still needs to work in these areas to improve the flow of FDI to India.

5.1   FDI Flows to India

This section examines the growth rate of FDI inflow from the year 1971 to 2016. Most of the studies till now have limited the study of growth of FDI to only after globalization, it becomes essential to check for the magnitude of FDI inflow for a long period of time to get a concrete view of the overall FDI inflow pattern.

Analysis of the growth rate indicates that from the year 1971 to 1980 the growth of FDI inflow was not considerably positive and highest amount of growth rate of 172% was recorded in the year 1979. In the year 1977 lowest growth rate to the tune of −170% was recorded. In the following ten year period starting from 1981 to 1990 highest amount of growth amounting to 458% was recorded in the year 1985. A lowest of −92% was recorded in year 1983. From 1991 to 2000 the inflow of FDI rose due to globalization. During this time period highest FDI inflow took place in the year 1997 amounting to US$ 3619 million and highest growth rate is recorded in the year 1992 to the tune of 236%. From 2001 to 2010 the growth rate fluctuated from as high as 167% in 2006 to as low as −24% in 2009. The time period from 2011 to 2016 saw a mediocre growth of around 25 to 35% with exception of a negative growth rate of 33% in the year 2012. In the year 2014 with coming up of the BJP government the FDI inflows rose up but in the year 2016 the growth rate was a mere 1%. The policies adopted by the government play a major role in the FDI position of any nation. As India is now in the race of attracting more FDI, it has made many policies related to FDI investment much user friendly, and the procedural formalities of entry of FDI have also been made simple.

6   Determinants of FDI Flow

A theoretical framework for examining FDI determinants is provided by Dunning's eclectic paradigm. Apart from Dunning, UNCTAD has been regularly publishing FDI Attraction and Potential Indices in its annual World Investment Report. The attractiveness of an economy towards inward FDI potential index is captured by four key economic determinants namely, attractiveness of the market, availability of low cost labour and skills, the presence of natural resources and the presence of FDI enabling infrastructure [27]. Based on the Eclectic paradigm and UNCTAD the following variables were studied.

6.1   Market Attractiveness

The most important factor of FDI location is considered to be the market size of the host country and also its growth prospects. Return on investment and profits are directly linked with the size of the market. Huge FDI flows are gravitated by countries with larger market size and higher growth rates.

H1: The GDP of host country is positively related to FDI inflows.

6.2   Inflation and Exchange Rate

Higher FDI flows are witnessed from countries with strong currency to the countries that have weak currency, as the investment enjoys higher purchasing power in the host economy. Similarly, FDI outflow would be discouraged by economies with higher inflation rates.

H2: Higher ratio of host to home country exchange rate yields larger FDI inflow.
H3: FDI outflows will be greatly hampered by higher inflation in the home country.

6.3   Total Trade

Higher volume of trade indicates a higher economic integration among countries, as MNEs are inclined to invest in the trade partner markets. Thus, greater bilateral trade will encourage more FDI flows to the host country.

H4: FDI inflow is directly related to the amount of trade.

6.4   Foreign Exchange Reserves

In India there is a gap between the imports and the exports so we are losing on the dollar reserves, which leads to depreciation of the rupee. Foreign investment is received in the form of either FPI or FDI, out of which FDI is a more reliable and a long term investment. FDI helps building the reserves which helps keep the value of rupee constant in terms of dollar.

H5: Higher foreign exchange reserves of the country higher the FDI inflows.

6.5   Population

The size of population also has an effect on the minds of the investor. Larger the size of population, larger the number of buyers in the market. India being the second largest populated country, attracts lot of FDI owing to its large potential in the market.

H6: Larger population attracts larger FDI inflows.

6.6   Infrastructure

Infrastructure is the backbone of any economy, this can be deduced from both Dunning's eclectic paradigm as well as proxy variables given by UNCTAD. Rail, road and telecom sector of the infrastructure are playing a vital role in a country like India.

H7: Larger number of telephone users attracts higher FDI flows.
H8: Greater the number of mobile subscribers larger the FDI flows.
H9: Larger number of internet subscribers attracts larger FDI inflows.
H10: Length of railway lines in the country help in attracting FDI inflows.
H11: Electric power consumption affects the FDI inflows to a country.

6.7   Natural Resources

Presence of natural resources in a country helps attract FDI inflows, as sometimes the production of some products may require the use of them. Investors do keep this in mind while investing (Figs. 1 and 2).

H12: Presence of natural resources attracts FDI inflows.

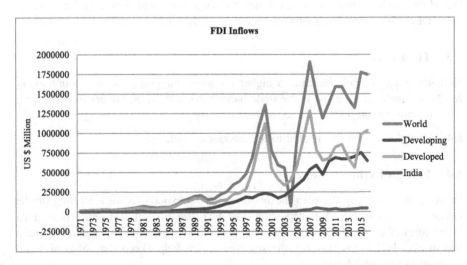

Fig. 1. FDI inflows to world, developed countries, developing countries and India (1971–2016). (Source: UNCTAD 2016) [26]

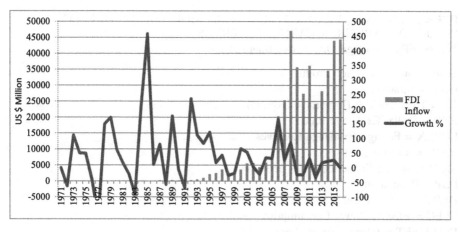

Fig. 2. FDI inflows to India (1971–2016) with its growth rate. (Source: UNCTAD, 2016) [26]

7   Analytical Models

To accomplish the objectives, the following models have been used.

7.1   Exponential Trend

A non-linear (exponential) trend has been proposed to estimate the trend of FDI inflow in to India during the period 1991 to 2016.

$$FDIt = Ae\alpha T + \varepsilon t$$

Where, FDIt = Foreign Direct Investment (in million Dollars)

A = Constant
e = Natural Logarithm
α = Coefficient
T = Time (Year)
εt = Error term

7.2   Multi-variate Linear Regression

In order to examine the relationships between FDI and the aforementioned macro-economic determinant variables, an empirical study has been conducted for the period 1991–2012. The functional relationship between FDI and its determinants is given as follows:

FDI = f(GDP, INFL, TT, EXR, FOREX, RAIL, MOB, POP, DEBT, ELEC, INTERNET, LABOUR, NATURAL, RESERVES, TEL)

Where, FDI = Foreign Direct Investment

GDP = Gross Domestic Product
INFL = Inflation
TT = Total Trade = (Imports + Exports)
EXR = Dollar Exchange Rate
FOREX = Foreign Exchange Reserves
RAIL = Rail Lines
MOB = Mobile Subscribers/100 persons
POP = Population
DEBT = External Debt
ELEC = Electric Power Consumption
INTERNET = Internet Subscribers
LABOUR = Labour Force
NATURAL = Natural Resources % of GDP
RESERVES = Total Reserves
TEL = Number of Fixed Telephone Lines

To estimate the relationship of the determinant variables with FDI and their direction, a multivariate linear regression model is used and is specified as

$$\begin{aligned} FDI_t = {} & \beta_0 + \beta_1 \, GDP_t + \beta_2 \, INFL_t + \beta_3 \, TT_t + \beta_4 \, EXR_t + \beta_5 \, FOREX_t + \beta_6 \, RAIL_t \\ & + \beta_7 MOB_t + \beta_8 POP_t + \beta_9 DEBT_t + \beta_{10} \, ELEC_t + \beta_{11} \, INTERNET_t + \beta_{12} \, LABOUR_t \\ & + \beta_{13} \, NATURAL_t + \beta_{14} \, RESERVES_t + \beta_{15} \, TEL_t + \varepsilon_t \end{aligned}$$

The explanatory variables and the ε_t (error term in the model) are assumed to follow the OLS properties.

8   Results and Discussions

8.1   Trend of FDI Inflows in to India During the Period 1991 to 2016

Figure 3 depicts the trend of FDI inflows (in Million Dollars) into India over the period 1991 to 2016.

During 1991, the FDI inflows was US $ 75 million and by 2016 it reached US $ 44486 million which is about 592 times higher than the FDI inflows compared to the 1991 value. A non-linear trend has been fitted to the data to see the pattern of the FDI inflow into the country over the years. The chart further suggests that there has been an exponential growth of FDI inflows in to India during the study period and a sharp rise is observed over 2006 to 2016. The high R2 value (0.869) suggests the exponential trend appearing to be a very good fit to the data on FDI inflows to India. The reason behind such a spurt in FDI inflows during the period may be attributed to easing of Foreign Direct Investment regulation by the Indian Government. The trend so observed is quite supportive of the fact that as and when the Indian government has taken initiatives to open up and liberalize the economy further; the foreign investors have reciprocated by infusing investments into the country.

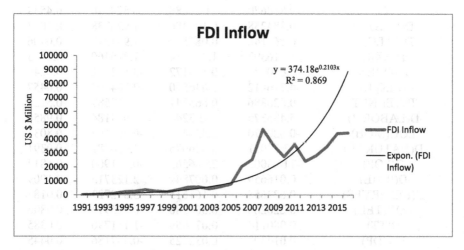

Fig. 3. Trend of FDI inflows to India (1991–2016) along with trend line. (Source: UNCTAD, 2016) [26]

8.2 Macro-economic Variables and the OLS Results

The data for all the variables selected for the study was collected from World Bank [28]. After collection of the data, first and foremost the data was checked for stability using ADF test. Some of the variables were found to be stationary at level, some at first difference and few at second difference. After that regression analysis was done using OLS technique using EVIEWS. The results for OLS are given in the table below.

Dependent Variable: D(FDI)
Method: Least Squares
Date: 03/11/18   Time: 20:10
Sample (adjusted): 1995 2014
Included observations: 20 after adjustments

Variable	Coefficient	Std. Error	t-Statistic	Prob.
C	-9.818670	11.85086	-0.828520	0.4539
D(DEBT,2)	0.384258	0.199486	1.926238	0.1064
D(ELEC,2)	0.261146	0.087509	2.984212	0.0406
D(EXR)	1.616393	1.317934	1.226460	0.2873
D(FOREX)	0.650643	0.185172	-3.513722	0.0246
D(INFL)	-4.716412	1.646560	-2.864403	0.0457
INTERNET	0.620886	0.865241	0.717587	0.5127
D(LABOR,2)	-5.435375	283.3244	-0.019184	0.9856
LOG(MOB)	-0.620170	2.327419	-0.266463	0.8031
D(NATURAL)	13.37021	4.426075	3.020781	0.0391
D(POP)	-114.3002	258.6565	-0.441900	0.6814
D(RAIL)	0.016659	0.007844	2.123715	0.1009
D(RESERVES)	0.622658	0.161615	3.852723	0.0183
LOG(TEL)	0.220268	8.500280	0.025913	0.9806
D(TT)	0.080114	0.072059	-1.111790	0.0385
D(GDP)	0.014307	0.032725	-0.437186	0.0445

R-squared	0.934763	Mean dependent var	1.680500
Adjusted R-squared	0.690126	S.D. dependent var	6.909593
S.E. of regression	3.846315	Akaike info criterion	5.522670
Sum squared resid	59.17657	Schwarz criterion	6.319256
Log likelihood	-39.22670	Hannan-Quinn criter.	5.678172
F-statistic	3.821019	Durbin-Watson stat	1.927394
Prob(F-statistic)	0.102080		

The linear regression model specified in the study is found to be a very good fit to the dataset and is evident from the high R-square value (0.934) of the model.

The regression equation is given below:

$$D(FDI) = -9.81866987458 + 0.261146025895 * D(ELEC,2)$$
$$+ 1.61639336274 * D(EXR) + 0.650643349979 * D(FOREX)$$
$$- 4.71641162645 * D(INFL) + 0.620885917198 * INTERNET$$
$$- 5.43537493275 * D(LABOR,2) - 0.6201703341 * LOG(MOB)$$
$$- 114.300210541 * D(POP) + 0.0166587374248 * D(RAIL)$$

$$+ \, 0.622658190329 * D(\text{RESERVES}) + 0.220268478285 * \text{LOG}(\text{TEL})$$
$$+ \, 0.0801141223971 * D(\text{TT}) + 0.014306781206 * D(\text{GDP})$$
$$+ \, 0.38425834412 * D(\text{DEBT},2) + 13.3702054477 * D(\text{NATURAL})$$

It is evident from the results that

External debt is significant and has a positive impact in determining the flow of FDI to India ($p < 0.10$). Electric power consumption has a positive and significant role ($p < 0.05$). Exchange rate has positive but insignificant role in the flow of FDI ($p > 0.10$). Foreign exchange reserves has significant and positive role in the flow of FDI ($p < 0.05$). Number of internet subscribers has positive but not significant role ($p > .10$). Presence of natural resources has positive and significant role ($p < .05$). Length of railway lines in the country has positive and significant role ($p < 0.10$). Total reserves has positive and significant role in the inflow of FDI ($p < 0.05$). Fixed telephone lines across the country has positive but not significant role ($p > 0.10$). Total trade in to country has positive and significant role ($p < 0.05$), GDP of the country has positive and significant role ($p < 0.05$). Inflation rate in the country has negative but significant role ($p < 0.05$). Labour cost has negative but insignificant role ($p > 0.10$). Population of the country has negative and insignificant role in the inflow of FDI to India ($p > 0.10$).

9 Conclusion

Ascertaining the determinants of FDI inflow to India is an impenetrable task. The study found that India's large market size which has been studied by GDP as proxy variable is a significant variable for FDI inflow. Whereas the huge population of India is having an insignificant role in the FDI flows. Inflation as predicted has a negative but significant impact which means the higher the inflation the lower the FDI flows. Exchange rate has an insignificant impact which means investors from other countries are not moved by the value of rupee as against dollar. Foreign exchange reserves do impact the flow of FDI which indicates that having surplus reserves of dollar attracts the foreign investors. Presence of natural resources also has an impact on the flow indicating how the investors are putting up facilities for consuming the natural resources found in India. Infrastructural facilities need to be improved upon further to facilitate the investors and hence multiply the FDI inflows to India. The government needs to work upon the policy framework regarding FDI, the ease of doing business aspect to improve the amount of FDI inflows to India.

References

1. Noorbaksh, F., Alberto, P., Ali, Y.: Human capital and FDI inflow in developing countries: new empirical evidences. World Dev. **29**(9), 1593–1610 (2001)
2. Hayami, Y.: Development Economics: From Poverty Alleviation to the Wealth of Nations, 2nd edn. Oxford University Press, New York (2001)

3. Singhania, M., Gupta, A.: Determinants of foreign direct investment in India. J. Int. Trade Law Policy **10**(1), 64–82 (2011)
4. Iversen, C.: Aspects of International Capital Movement. Levin and Munksgaard, London Copenhagen (1935)
5. Aliber, R.Z.: The multinational enterprise in a multi currency world. In: Dunning, J.H. (ed.) The Multinational Enterprise. Allen and Unwin, London (1971)
6. Hymer, S.H.: The international operations of national firms: a study of direct investment. Ph. D. thesis, MIT Press: Cambridge, MA (1960)
7. Vernon, R.: International investment and international trade in product cycle. Q. J. Econ. **80**, 190–207 (1966)
8. Dunning, J.H.: American Investment In British Manufacturing Industry. George Allen and Unwin, London (1958). Reprinted by Anno Press. New York (1971)
9. Caves, R.E.: Industrial corporations: the industrial economics of foreign investment. Economica **38**, 1–27 (1971)
10. Rugman, A.M.: International Diversification and the Multinational Enterprise. Lexington, MA (1979)
11. Kogut, B.: Foreign direct investment as a sequential process. In: Kindleberger, C.P., Audretsh, D.B. (eds.) The Multinational Corporation in the 1980s. MIT Press, Cambridge (1983)
12. Buckley, P.J., Casson, M.: The Future of the Multinational Enterprise. Macmillan, London (1976)
13. Hennart, J.F.: A Theory of Multinational Enterprise. University of Michigan Press, Ann Arbor (1982)
14. Knickerbocker, F.T.: Oligopolistic Reaction and the Multinational Enterprise. Harvard University Press, Cambridge (1973)
15. Sethi, D., Guisinger, S.E., Phelan, S.E., Berg, D.M.: Trends in foreign direct investment flows: a theoretical and empirical analysis. J. Int. Bus. Stud. **34**, 315–326 (2003)
16. Dunning, J.H.: Multinationals, Technology and Competitiveness. Unwin Hyman, London (1988)
17. Zheng, P.: A comparison of FDI determinants in China and India. Thunderbird Int. Bus. Rev. **51**(3), 263–279 (2009)
18. Dunning, J.H.: Location and the multinational enterprises: a neglected factor? J. Int. Bus. Stud. **29**(1), 45–66 (1998)
19. Moosa, I.A.: Foreign Direct Investment—Theory, Evidence and Practice. Palgrave Publications, New York (2002)
20. Bevan, A.A., Estrin, S.: Patterns of for Eign Direct Investment and Trade in Central and Eastern Europe. Mimeo, Budapest (2000)
21. Asiedu, E.: On the determinants of foreign direct investment to developing countries: Is Africa different? World Dept. **30**(1), 107–119 (2002)
22. Jha, R.: Recent trends in FDI flows and prospects for India. In: Jha, R. (ed.) Economic Growth, Economic Performance and Welfare in South Asia, pp. 305–322. Palgrave Macmillan UK, London (2005). https://doi.org/10.1057/9780230520318_15
23. Hu, P.: India's suitability for foreign direct investment. Working Paper No. 553, International Business with Special Reference to India, University of Arizona (2006)
24. Pradhan, R.P.: Trade openness and foreign direct investment in India: the globalization experience. IUP J. Appl. Finan. **16**(2), 26 (2010)
25. Sahni, P.: Trends and determinates of FDI in India: an empirical investigation. IJKR **2**(8), 144–161 (2012). ISSN:2249-1058
26. UNCTAD. http://unctadstat.unctad.org/wds/TableViewer/tableView.aspx?ReportId=96740
27. WIR 2012. http://unctad.org/en/PublicationsLibrary/wir2012_embargoed_en.pdf
28. World Bank. https://data.worldbank.org/country/india

A Technical Evaluation of Neo4j and Elasticsearch for Mining Twitter Data

Janet Zhu[1], Sreenivas Sremath Tirumala[1(✉)], and G. Anjan Babu[2]

[1] Unitec Institute of Technology, Auckland, New Zealand
stirumala@unitec.ac.nz
[2] Sri Venkateswara University, Tirupati, India

Abstract. Knowledge mining on social media datasets especially twitter has been widely acknowledge due to recent prospects of intelligent systems for various purposes. It has been the most reliable indicator of the wider pulse of the world and whats happening around the globe. witter being one of the largest social media network has an average of 317 active monthly users as on January 2017. Considering the real-time activities of these users like tweets, the data to mine constitute the characteristics of Big Data. The process to handle this Big Data requires an efficient storage and retrial mechanism which the current implementation Redis lacks in some aspects.

Considering the technical requirements of social media data in general and twitter in particular, we present an evaluation of two big data technologies Elasticsearch and Neo4j. Initially we present a suitability analysis followed by experimental evaluation of these two implementations.

With the experimental results, it is concluded that Neo4j, a graph database has overthrown Elasticsearch in both aspects of storage and operations. The storage mechanism of Neo4j has proven to be efficient constituting only 45% of what required for Elasticsearch. In operational which is considered to be the strength of Elasticsearch, Neo4j was able to perform better in terms of data load and retrieval operations.

Keywords: Elasticsearch · Neo4j · NoSQL · Redis · Twitter dataset

1 Introduction

Knowledge mining on social media datasets especially twitter has been widely acknowledge due to recent prospects of intelligent systems for various purposes like sentimental analysis [1], population estimation [2], location inferring [3], suicidal tendencies [4], understanding disaster resilience [5] etc. It has been the most reliable indicator of the wider pulse of the world and what happening around the globe [6]. Recent advances in machine learning, the scope of data analytics is widened with regular [7] as well as spatio-temporal data [8].

© Springer Nature Singapore Pte Ltd. 2018
M. Singh et al. (Eds.): ICACDS 2018, CCIS 906, pp. 359–369, 2018.
https://doi.org/10.1007/978-981-13-1813-9_36

Twitter being one of the largest social media network has an average of 317 active monthly users as on January 2017. Considering the real-time activities of these users like tweets, the data to mine constitute the characteristics of Big Data. The process to handle this Big Data requires an efficient storage and retrial mechanism particularly for availability.

Currently Twitter Inc. uses a memory-based database called Redis which is a Big Data key value store to handle user generated data [9]. The operations in Redis are atomic which makes it the first choice for social media systems. However, the strength of the Redis is some times is a huge drawback especially considering the hardware costs in particular, RAM. Another key drawback is Redis is not cluster friendly which is a basic requirement for Big data implementations [10]. Further, lack of relationship based data structures and complex server configuration producers makes it make it less user friendly technically and operationally [11]. Moreover, it is very significant to understand the influence of type of data [12] and possible purpose of implementation before choosing a type of data engineering technologies [13].

Another important aspect which inspired us to look for a alternate for Redis is its failure for principle requirement of availability, a principle requirement for Twitter. The CAP theorem ensures the fulfillment of requirements when choosing a distributed database system in this case Big data solution [14]. CAP refers to consistency, availability, and partition tolerance. Every distributed database fall under any two of the three categories of CAP [15]. As a key-value store, Redis falls into the CP realm. However, availability is equally important to a fast message delivery medium like Twitter which form the basis of this paper. Furthermore, recent popularity of graph based Big Data solutions (GraphDB) inspired us to explore and expose the potentiality of using GraphDB solutions for Twitter data [16].

Evaluation of technologies for data analysis and implementation is in fore front particular with recent advances in different types of implementation for the same problem [17]. Neo4j and Elasticsearch are the most popular and efficient big data solutions in terms of quality and speed. For social media data, Neo4j is designated as top and most widely used GraphDB [18] whereas Elasticsearch is credited with most efficient search solution [19]. In this paper, we present a technical evaluation of Neo4j and Elasticsearch for twitter datasets and analyze the feasibility of its implementation as a big data solution for twitter.

The paper is presented as follows. We have explained the relevance of selected Big Data technologies for the defined problem in Sect. 2. This is followed by the Sect. 3 in which we presented by experimental design. Section 4 consists of experimental results and discussion followed by conclusion and future work as Sect. 5.

2   Relevance of Big Data Solutions

In this section we present a brief literature review on Elasticsearch and Neo4j. We also present the suitability of these two Big Data solutions for social media datasets and present the rationale for choosing these solutions. The selection of the technologies is based on earlier implementations, current trend in research and development and relevance to the dataset.

2.1   Elasticsearch

According to db-engines.com, a knowledge base of relational and NoSQL database management systems, Elasticsearch was ranked as the number one in search category and eleven for overall functionality out of 372 database systems in May 2017 [20]. Elasticsearch is a distributed, schema-less database which falls under the category of Big Data document store. Elasticsearch has most powerful, effective and full-text search capabilities accessible through open API. Elasticsearch is build on the top of Apache Lucene with simple REST and JSON interface which is functionally open source [21]. Elasticsearch is capable of handling and processing massive volume of data and identify key words in near real time. This feature makes Elasticsearch potentially suitable for social media implementation like Twitter which is a fast medium to deliver breaking news and messages worldwide.

As mentioned in the previous sections, the drawbacks of Redis can also addressed using Elasticsearch as it is highly scalable and reliable. Network partitions can be easily created by shards, which are used to automatically divide a huge chunk of an index into multiple nodes. This way of splitting large volume of data greatly increases scalability. As a cluster-friendly system, Elasticsearch enables clusters with multiple nodes to work effortlessly.

Recent implementations show that similar social networking service like Facebook has successfully implemented Elasticsearch to build clusters and applications. A massive over 4 TB data and 3 indexing frameworks were established with Elasticsearch by Facebook [22]. As a search-intensive application, Elasticsearch is a suitable tool for Twitter to search through billions of tweets to get useful insights about what happening all over the world. Twitter can take full advantage of this tool to quickly identify trends and pulses on a global scale. Given the text nature of Twitter posts, a full-text search tool like Elasticsearch is ideal for providing advanced search functionality and respond quickly to comments and questions posted on Twitter.

Further, Elasticsearch data visualization interface Kibana is leading open source visualization tool which is extensively popular and widely used. Kibana is capable of presenting interactive visualization for instance popular tweets by users or topic which can be modeling with simple user interface.

2.2   Neo4j

Neo4j is a native GraphDB, designed to store and manage interrelated data especially which can be represented hierarchically. As social media data is high interrelated as well as hierarchical, neo4j presents an efficient way storing data using graph based notations as well as visual representation in presentable and easily understandable visual representation. Since Twitter data is densely connected and also requires a fast and efficient way to store, identify and process relationships GraphDB like Neo4j become a strong contender especially for optimized approach for handling relationships at speed and quality.

Another salient feature of Noe4j is high scalability. Its native graph processing engine called index-free adjacency, supports faster transactions and processing with real-time performance irrespective of the depth (levels) of relationship hierarchies [23].

Neo4j uses ACID consistency model to ensure data integrity which is crucial for text data [24]. Causal Cluster setup of Neo4j enabled it to be configured for eventual consistency, a key requirement for social media data [20].

Lack of availability feature in Redis is overcome by Neo4j with its high-availability features which makes it possible to replicate a complete relationship graph to each instance of the cluster, ensuring the application continues to operate in spite of missing externally related instances [23]. Neo4j also supports cache-based shading, which achieves horizontal scaling across large datasets can accommodate fast-growing Twitter social network [23].

Though Neo4j is native GraphDB, it uses human readable query language called Cypher for traverse, update and insert data relationships efficiently without complex or deep queries. Compare to the data retrieval processes in other Big Data solutions, Cypher is simple, easy yet powerful. LinkedIn China uses Neo4j whose processing speed allowed an effective way to handle rapidly increasing social network platform [25].

3   Experiment Design

The design idea was to create a single Twitter index for 1 million JSON records. They were split across 20 equally-sized types in Elasticsearch. Each type contains 50,000 documents. Each JSON document has 4 nested objects places, entities, tweets, and users. Only one server was used in this research and all the Twitter data were stored across 5 shards. To begin the ingestion, it is necessary to start Elasticsearch and Kibana in terminals first. After importing all the modules needed in Python, we started connecting with Elasticsearch server at local-host 9200. Despite the complexity of our Twitter data structure, Elasticsearch made the indexing and bulk mapping very easy. As mentioned above, all the JSON documents were ingested to Elasticsearch under one single index: Twitter. To avoid heap memory or HTTP error, each JSON file with 50000 documents was an individual type and was loaded to Elasticsearch separately. The date-time module made sure that the variable created at in JSON was mapped as a time-based field. After less than one minute of loading, by typing local-host 5601 in the browser, we could see that the Twitter records were gradually ingested to Kibana interface. By doing a simple search, it showed that there was one running instance of Elasticsearch stored across 5 shards.

The Discover tab in Kibana is an interactive tool for engaging with the Twitter data. By clicking on our Twitter index, we could see the first 10000 records were presented in either table or JSON format. Since we mapped the created at field as a time-based variable during index pattern configuration stage, we could see from the graph that all the data were collected on 1 May 2017. If we click on the list of fields on the left, we get the chance to freely explore the data structures and interact with various information. As data engineers, the design idea behind the five questions is a balanced combination of insights extracted from numerical and string fields, as well as different API features and the aggregation framework. For example, we were curious about questions such as which tweet was re-tweeted the most, and which hash-tags were the most popular during the time-frame available. Other questions such as users language and countries, and the utility they tweeted from also caught our attention.

The Dev Tools tab serves as a console to write and run interactive queries. As a REST based database, Elasticsearch takes full advantage of various APIs. The querying process naturally involved a large amount of interaction with different APIs. For instance, the five analytical questions designed all took advantage of both the get and search APIs to return JSON documents matched. Besides, the field stats API is used to answer the first question which tweet was re-tweeted the most. This API enables us to check the statistical properties of a field re-tweeted status. re-tweet count in this case. Before designing the queries for the other 4 questions, it is important to examine the twitter index under ManagementIndex Patterns. From the list of fields, we could see that the keywords concerned for answering the questions are both search-able and agreeable. This makes it possible to use the aggregations framework based on a search query. In the Visualize tab, there are eleven visualization types available. To simply show what the max re-tweet count is, one big number is enough to catch users attention. Thus, a single metric was used to present the visual for the first question. Column chart and pie chart were used to compare values for fields such as country, language, and utility. Different colors and tool-tips gave people a vivid visual of which one stood out at the top. The tag cloud tool was perfect for text data visualization where the word count and the importance of words were reflected by the font size. Overall, the flow chart for the system and application involved in the design and development process. The Twitter data was extracted from Twitter API, ingested into Elasticsearch and ran on 5 shards, and eventually presented visually in Kibana for better insights.

The implementation of Noe4j was based on version 3.1.3. In terms of the configuration of Neo4j, Page Cache Sizing memory was set to 4G which enabled the data to cache in memory and prevented costly disk access. In data modeling, nodes were mainly identified by twitter objects (User, Twitter, Entity, Place). The only difference is Entity object because property value in Neo4j can only support primitive types of arrays. Therefore, The Entity object was split into 3 nodes, including Source, Hashtag, and Link. Within different notes, there are nine types of relationships exist.

Before importing data, unique property constraints on each node were created, ensuring that database has no duplicated records. By adding a unique constraint on a property, an index on that property will also be added automatically, which makes the execution of Cypher query more effectively. To import data into neo4j, py2neo package was used to execute cypher query language in Python to create nodes and relationships. Neo4j Browser was used to answer the five analysis questions, where cypher can be executed directly to match the patterns of nodes and relationships, and the query process and the number of database hits were available simply by using profile prefix in cypher, thus the query performance can be tuned easily.

One of the key database technologies used for this project are current versions of Elasticsearch-5.3.0 and kibana-5.3.0 installed on Windows computer in Java Runtime Environment (java version 1.8.0121). Jupiter notebook from the Anaconda distribution was used to run Python 2.7.12 for importing data to Elasticsearch. The python modules involved in the implementation phase include JSON, requests, datetime and Elasticsearch. The JSON library was used to encode and decode JSON objects in Python [26]. The datetime module was used to manipulate date and time variables [27]. The requests module is a library for Python to make HTTP requests. The Elasticsearch library is a low-level client for Elasticsearch to make connections to the Elasticsearch server and run related queries. To get a clear idea of how the fields and objects are nested in complex JSON document, an online JSON viewer is used.

4   Experiment Results and Discussion

This section consists of experiment details and discussion. The performance given by Elasticsearch and Neo4j are compared and analyzed using the YCSB framework. All the experiments are carried out using Intel Core i7-4500U CPU @1.80GHz 2.40 GHz with 8 GB RAM on window 10 Pro operating system.

We used Elasticsearch version 5.3.0 and Neo4j version 3.1.3 which are most recent versions available online. We used 1 million Twitter records for the experiment. The size of the databases after data integration and upload on Elasticsearch and Neo4j is 5.88GB and 2.65GB respectively. Neo4j occupied less disk space compared to Elasticsearch. This difference may be attributed to the data compression feature of Neo4j. In Neo4j, the storage of property values can be compressed, which reduces the disk usage.

To have an apples-to-apples performance comparison, this paper took advantage of the popular Yahoo! Cloud Serving Benchmark (YCSB) framework. This bench-mark contains a series of workloads that support a mix of write, read and update operations. YCSB also allows specification of the number of records, client threads and target throughout per second. For the typical workload of Twitter, the read and write operations share equal importance. In order to test these mix operations, we implemented workloads A and C, and an update-only workload G, which is created by us.

To evaluate these databases, we first created 100000 test records. Each workload was executed in a defined range of target throughout (1000, 2000, 4000, 8000, 16000, 32000, 64000, 128000, 256000, 512000) and in 100 client threads. Corresponding number of test results were generated. Latency (milliseconds) was then recorded.

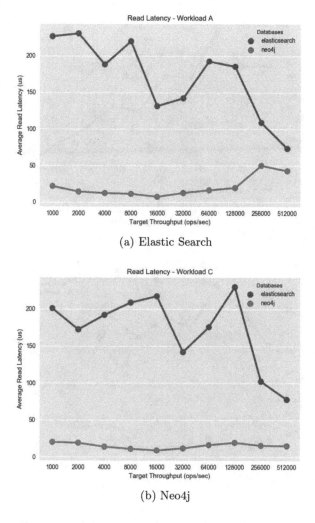

(a) Elastic Search

(b) Neo4j

Fig. 1. Comparison of read performance for Elasticsearch and Neo4j

The latency performance for Elasticsearch and Neo4j are shown in Figs. 1(a) and (b) for read and 2(a) and (b) for write (upload). In every workload, Neo4j delivered better overall latency performance, with slightly increase in overall latency as the number of target throughput increased in workload A and G, and roughly constant in workload C. For Elasticsearch, its performance was erratic within the specified throughput range. At the end of readupdate latency charts, the data points all showed a downward trend. This means that Elasticsearch gets better when handling massive updates.

In workload A, the read/update latency shown by Elasticsearch seems to decrease as the system scales. At the target throughout of 512000, its performance was almost on a par with that of Neo4j. This example illustrates the

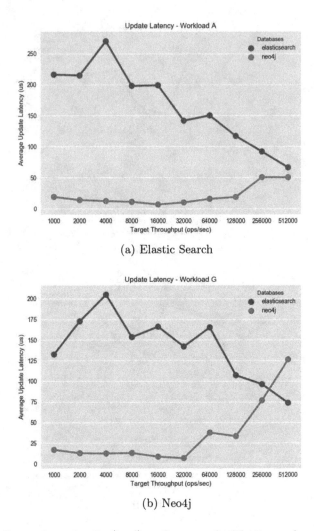

(a) Elastic Search

(b) Neo4j

Fig. 2. Comparison of write (load) performance for Elasticsearch and Neo4j

scalability of Elasticsearch as the volume of workload increased proportionally. In workload G, the update performance given by Elasticsearch overtook Neo4j after 256000 target throughput.

Summarizing, Neo4j outperformed Elasticsearch in two aspects. Firstly, in terms of storage space, Neo4j size was only 45% of Elasticsearch. Secondly, the Neo4j database achieved better overall latency for all workloads tested in this study. Comparatively speaking, Elasticsearch had higher latency. This may be due to the reason that the index was not cached. If we had more time to run the test multiple times, we would expect lower latency because of caching. What's more, we should not over-look Elasticsearch potential to scale well as the number of workload increases (Table 1).

Table 1. Workloads for read and update for Elasticsearch and Neo4j

Workload	Read%	Update %
A	50	50
C	100	
G		100

During the implementation and evaluation stages of this big data project for Twitter, the are some considerations that are needed to be adopted. For instance, aggregating 1 million records from Twitter's API on a non-stop basis was not easy. High computer specification is needed to store big datasets on a local computer. After lots of trial and error, we eventually incorporated the while loop to reconnect the Twitter API with AWS. At the evaluation stage, the testing process was often interrupted due to heap memory exception and computer hardware limits. Thus, we had to resume the tests multiple times to get the outputs. Due to the same reason, we were not able to rerun the test datasets and get the average output.

5   Conclusion and Future Work

In this paper, we exposed major drawbacks of Redis with respect to handling Twitter dataset and presented a technical feasibility of two Redis alternates Elasticsearch and Neo4j. The experiment results prove that Neo4j is efficient in both storage and data retrieval. The storage mechanism of Neo4j has proven to be efficient constituting only 45% of what required for Elasticsearch. In operational which is considered to be the strength of Elasticsearch, Neo4j was able to perform better in terms of data load and retrieval operations.

This research presents a new direction for implementing graph based database systems for Twitter which is explored for the first time. As this is an initial research with a subset of 1 millions records, we understand the limitations of this study and in future we plan to implement a full datasets in real world environment. Another direction is to explore the possible implementation of graph Database structure for storage using Titan. With Titan we can implement Elasticsearch together using Titan to build on top of Cassandra a NoSQL database.

Further, study only used 100 client threads due to time constraint, but this could also be tuned to 200, 500, 800, or even 1000. Because of Elasticsearch high scalability, it may pick up even better with increasing workloads. Another issue worth noticing is that, Elasticsearch made its latest release of Elasticsearch-5.4.0 after the project started. Some bugs were fixed and new features were added. This may potentially boost the testing performance too.

References

1. Kapase, H., Galande, K., Sonna, T., Pawar, D., Salunke, D.: A review on: sentiment polarity analysis on twitter data from different events (2018)
2. Yildiz, D., Munson, J., Vitali, A., Tinati, R., Holland, J.: Using Twitter data for population estimates (2017)
3. Lin, J., Cromley, R.G.: Inferring the home locations of Twitter users based on the spatiotemporal clustering of Twitter data. Trans. GIS **22**(1), 82–97 (2018)
4. Vioulès, M.J., Moulahi, B., Azé, J., Bringay, S.: Detection of suicide-related posts in Twitter data streams. IBM J. Res. Dev. **62**(1), 1–7 (2018)
5. Zou, L., Lam, N.S., Cai, H., Qiang, Y.: Mining Twitter data for improved understanding of disaster resilience. Ann. Am. Assoc. Geogr., 1–20 (2018)
6. Jones, A.S., Georgakis, P., Petalas, Y., Suresh, R.: Real-time traffic event detection using Twitter data. Infrastruct. Asset Manag., 1–33 (2018)
7. Tirumala, S.S., Shahamiri, S.R., Garhwal, A.S., Wang, R.: Speaker identification features extraction methods: a systematic review. Expert Syst. Appl. **90**, 250–271 (2017)
8. Ali, S., Tirumala, S.S., Sarrafzadeh, A.: SVM aggregation modelling for spatiotemporal air pollution analysis. In: IEEE 17th International Multi-Topic Conference (INMIC), pp. 249–254. IEEE (2014)
9. Ahuja, R., Malik, J., Tyagi, R., Brinda, R.: Role of open source software in big data storage. In: Handbook of Research on Big Data Storage and Visualization Techniques, pp. 123–150. IGI Global (2018)
10. Huang, K., Zhou, J., Huang, L., Shen, Y.: NVHT: an efficient key-value storage library for non-volatile memory. J. Parallel Distrib. Comput. **120**, 339–354 (2018)
11. Swami, D., Sahoo, S., Sahoo, B.: Storing and analyzing streaming data: a big data challenge. In: Big Data Analytics: Tools and Technology for Effective Planning, pp. 229–246 (2018)
12. Tirumala, S.S., Narayanan, A.: Hierarchical data classification using deep neural networks. In: Arik, S., Huang, T., Lai, W.K., Liu, Q. (eds.) ICONIP 2015. LNCS, vol. 9489, pp. 492–500. Springer, Cham (2015). https://doi.org/10.1007/978-3-319-26532-2_54
13. Roland, A., Tirumala, S.S., Babu, G.A.: Evaluating big data technologies for statistical homicide dataset. In: Second International Conference on Computing and Communications (IC3), India. Springer (2018)
14. Shapiro, M., Bieniusa, A., Preguiça, N., Balegas, V., Meiklejohn, C.: Just-right consistency: reconciling availability and safety. arXiv preprint arXiv:1801.06340 (2018)
15. Brewer, E.: Pushing the cap: strategies for consistency and availability. Computer **45**(2), 23–29 (2012)
16. Reniers, V., Rafique, A., Van Landuyt, D., Joosen, W.: Object-NoSQL database mappers: a benchmark study on the performance overhead. J. Internet Serv. Appl. **8**(1), 1 (2017)
17. Katragadda, R., Tirumala, S.S., Nandigam, D.: ETL tools for Data Warehousing: an empirical study of Open Source Talend Studio versus Microsoft SSIS (2015)
18. Drakopoulos, G., Kanavos, A., Tsakalidis, A.K.: Evaluating Twitter influence ranking with system theory. In: WEBIST, vol. 1, pp. 113–120 (2016)
19. Langi, P.P., Najib, W., Aji, T.B., et al.: An evaluation of Twitter river and Logstash performances as elasticsearch inputs for social media analysis of Twitter. In: 2015 International Conference on Information & Communication Technology and Systems (ICTS), pp. 181–186. IEEE (2015)

20. DBEngine. System properties comparison Elasticsearch vs. Neo4j (1999). https:// dbengines.com/en/system/Elasticsearch%3BNeo4j
21. Shahi, D.: Apache Solr: an introduction. Apache Solr, pp. 1–9. Apress, Berkeley (2015). https://doi.org/10.1007/978-1-4842-1070-3_1
22. Kononenko, O., Baysal, O., Holmes, R., Godfrey, M.W.: Mining modern repositories with elasticsearch. In: Proceedings of the 11th Working Conference on Mining Software Repositories, pp. 328–331. ACM (2014)
23. Gupta, S., Rani, R.: A comparative study of elasticsearch and CouchDB document oriented databases. In: International Conference on Inventive Computation Technologies (ICICT), vol. 1, pp. 1–4. IEEE (2016)
24. Montag, D.: Understanding Neo4j scalability. White Paper, Neotechnology (2013)
25. Sasaki, B.M.: Graph databases for beginners: acid vs. base explained (2015). https://neo4j.com/blog/acid-vs-baseconsistency-models-explained
26. Marinescu, P., Parry, C., Pomarole, M., Tian, Y., Tague, P., Papagiannis, I.: IVD: automatic learning and enforcement of authorization rules in online social networks. In: IEEE Symposium on Security and Privacy (SP), pp. 1094–1109. IEEE (2017)
27. Crockford, D.: The application/json Media Type for JavaScript Object Notation (JSON) (2006). [Online]. Available: https://tools.ietf.org/html/rfc4627

Visibility Prediction in Urban Localities Using Clustering

Apeksha Aggarwal$^{(\boxtimes)}$ and Durga Toshniwal

Department of CSE, Indian Institute of Technology Roorkee, Roorkee, India
apeksha.aggarwal785@gmail.com, durgafec@iitr.ac.in

Abstract. Various research works in computer science utilize data generated from cities, to make it smart and intelligent. Some of these works make use of data mining, sensor networks, internet of things, web of things, cloud computing techniques and machine learning techniques. In this work, smart mobility using data mining is mainly focused upon. Smart mobility is one of the crucial aspects of smart city addressing efficient movement of people and goods from one place to another. In the present work, several literature works on smart mobility have been discussed along with suggested improvement in mobility for several locations in India. This work focuses upon the issue of reduction in visibility in environment, which is caused by presence of certain atmospheric conditions. Reduction in visibility hinders traffic and causes accidents, thus affecting smooth movement of people and goods. The present work examines the humidity content of several locations in India, specifically metropolitan city of Bangalore have been considered in this research. Furthermore, clustering have been performed to investigate the humidity trends at these locations and results are found to be promising.

Keywords: Smart mobility · Visibility · Humidity

1 Introduction and Motivation

Smart mobility deploys intelligent transportation techniques to ensure faster, safer and environment friendly solution for movement of people and goods in urban space. There are different types of problems addressed in smart mobility such as finding long term traffic patterns in the city, prediction of driver behavior, saving time of drivers on roads, better and faster parking schemes, classification of transport etc. Detailed discussion is given in Sect. 2. Problem we are addressing in our work is reduction in visibility, which may hinder the smooth transportation services in the city.

Presence of aerosols i.e. solid or liquid particles suspended in air, example fog, dust, mist, humidity etc. suspended in already polluted areas can lead to haze in atmosphere [2,18]. This can cause reduction in visibility in the atmosphere which in turn hinders smooth traffic movement and causes accidents. Motivation of our work comes from the amount of accidents in previous years. Statistics

© Springer Nature Singapore Pte Ltd. 2018
M. Singh et al. (Eds.): ICACDS 2018, CCIS 906, pp. 370–379, 2018.
https://doi.org/10.1007/978-981-13-1813-9_37

shows that out of 1.25 million deaths every year due to road accidents, rain or humidity is among the top 10 causes of road accidents [3]. Prior information about humidity concentration can be advantageous for people suffering from slight visual impairment and allowed for driving. Further it can help people with normal visions too in case of high amount of haze in the environment for a particular location in future.

In this work, main focus is analyzing data of areas with high humidity concentration leading to increased probability of formation of aerosols in the environment. Thus, identification of localites which hinders smooth traffic movement due to reduced visibility in the environment is the ultimate goal of this work. Case study of efficient traffic mobility for one of the developing countries i.e. India is examined in this work. Several popular data mining techniques are used to analyze the data of relative humidity concentration for several locations of India.

This paper is organized as follows. Section 1 introduces the paper about smart mobility along with the motivation for the work. Section 2 discusses extensively the literature work done in the field of smart mobility using data mining techniques as well as other few traditional techniques. Section 3 presents our proposed data mining approach for visibility prediction which leads to efficient traffic movement. Experiments and results are given in Sect. 4. Section 5 concludes the paper with future scope and some research challenges.

2   Literature Survey

In this section manifold works on smart mobility are discussed. Different types of problems are identified from the literature like identifying best routes from long term traffic patterns in the city, passenger recommendation systems, detecting transportation modes in the city, taxi ride sharing systems, bike sharing etc. A few of them are discussed in detail in this section. Most of the works discussed in this section are taken from our work Aggarwal et al. [4].

For route prediction, various shortest path algorithms [5–7], are given in early research works. These methods took advantages of various shortest path algorithms like Dijkstra algorithm to find the shortest route at a given time. Later approaches such as Sing-Yiu et al. [8] and Gonzalez et al. [7] utilized the deployment of Sensor networks to identify traffic patterns in the city. Ge et al. [14] further suggested a taxi recommender system using skyline computing algorithms [25].

With the availability of huge platforms on sharing social media data voluntarily, participatory sensing emerged as a very powerful tool to sense the data from social networks such as instagram, flickr, twitter etc. [11]. Yuan et al. [9] proposed T-Drive, an extension over [10] in which data is collected from GPS points of moving vehicles. T-Drive finds quick routes from traffic flows on the roads and historical GPS trajectories data utilizing a novel concept of landmark graphs. Yuan et al. [12] proposed an extension of T-Drive [9] whereby along with recommendation of fastest path, future traffic conditions on a road segment is also predicted using Hidden Markov Model [13] along with prediction of best routes. In Yuan et al. [15] a recommender system for both taxi drivers and the passengers is proposed.

Other valuable contribution to reduce traffic and pollution emissions and a very popular method these days are taxi ride sharing or carpooling. In Shuo et al. [16] a real time taxi ride sharing service with efficient updating of route schedules and hence reduction in total average travel distance is introduced. Other works included in smart railway transportation systems are given by Van et al. [17].

Most of the previous works for mobility used traffic conditions and vehicular movement over the roads as primary focus. However, much less work is done depicting the effect of environmental conditions over mobility. Lee et al. [19] suggested traffic prediction model using variables of weather including temperature, humidity etc. Koesdwiady et al. [20] suggested deep neural network based framework for traffic and weather prediction. In various works, [21,22] visibility is predicted using videos and images. Other data mining methods such as regression [23] and fuzzy logic [24] etc. had also been used in the past for visibility forecasting.

Our proposed research tries to address the issue in brief, by analyzing humidity concentrations of several localities of India. Clustering is used to find out days which behave similarly. Our approach is different from previous approaches as a very few work is done in the past to analyze concentrations of atmosphere for smart mobility, discussed in Sect. 3 in detail. Further, as far as author's concern, data is not much used in previous works.

3   Proposed Methodology

Data are preprocessed in a form relevant for applying data mining methods, posterior to acquisition of heterogeneous data generated from urban localities. Data preprocessing includes, removal of missing values, noisy data and others. Subsequently, traditional data mining approaches like clustering are applied in order to extract knowledge from the data.

Figure 1 shows the basic steps of data mining as knowledge extracting process which includes data mining from urban data and using this knowledge for smart city applications.

In our work, aim is to identify locations with high humidity trends for each month. These trends can be of high rise type, in which all the points in the time sequence are above than mean value. Similarly, mid rise and low rise type of time series trends of humidity concentrations are identified.

Proposed research work uses clustering of similar trajectories, based upon Euclidean distances. This work identified three types of time clusters. High value clusters (HVC), Average value clusters (AVC) and Low value clusters (LVC). HVC, MVC and LVC are the clusters having high rise, mid rise and low rise type of time series respectively. Finally, knowledge acquired from this methodological process is applied to identify locations which are at a greater risk of reduced visibility. Thus, the identification of localites where traffic is hindered and are more prone to accidents.

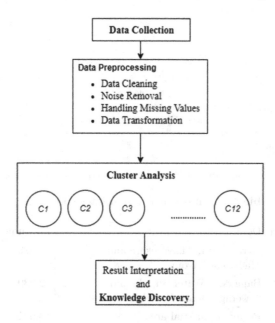

Fig. 1. Data mining approach to visibility prediction

4   Experiments and Results

This section provides the detailed explanation of experiments done and results.

4.1   Data Preprocessing

Data analyzed in our work consists of relative humidity concentration for time interval of every hour over a period of 1 year i.e. 2016 for five locations over the metropolitan city of Bangalore, Karnataka in India. Table 1 shows the locations of Bangalore analyzed in this work. Map in Fig. 2 depicts the five locations visualized on Google maps. Data preprocessing includes handling of missing values by simply ignoring the tuple because missing values were very less in amount as compared to the original data.

Min-max normalization method is used in this work to shift the original range of each of the time series between 0 and 1. Consider a variable x, the new normalized value x' is given by Eq. 1.

$$x' = \frac{x - min(x)}{max(x) - min(x)} \tag{1}$$

Where, $min(x)$ and $max(x)$ denotes the minimum and maximum values of variable x respectively.

Fig. 2. Locations of Bangalore marked on Google map

Table 1. Locations analyzed in Bangalore. India

S. no	Location	Description	Latitude	Longitude
1	BTM	Byrasandra, Thavarekere and Madiwala Layout	12.913	77.609
2	BWSSB	Bangalore Water Supply and Sewerage Board Kadabesanahalli	12.939	77.697
3	Peenya	Peenya industrial area	13.031	77.522
4	Seeghalli	Saneguruvanahalli	12.992	77.546
5	CRS	City Railway Station	12.977	77.571

4.2   Clustering of Time Series

Our further analysis depends upon the fact that there is existing similarity in daily trends of humidity concentrations analyzed monthwise. Figure 3 depicts the time series of any randomly selected 5 days for a particular month. Figure 3 shows the similarity of time series of several days of a month, formed from 24 h of a day. Hence, it would be useful to find the days which behave similarly for every month. For this, we have used Euclidean distances to calculate the distance between each of these time series. Note that we have used Euclidean distances because L2 norm perform better than L1 norm in low dimensions. Distance between i_{th} and j_{th} time series is given as per Eq. 2, where x'_{ik} and x'_{jk} are the ith and j^{th} sequences each of length k. $Dist_{(x''_{ij})}$ depicts the distance value.

$$Dist_{(x''_{ij})} = \sqrt{\sum_k (x'_{ik} - x'_{jk})^2} \qquad (2)$$

To find out the similarity between time series, the series are clustered using k-means algorithm [13]. Optimal value of k is identified using elbow curve [1]. Example elbow curve for data of month of several months for location of BTM in Bangalore is shown in Fig. 4. Figure 4 shows the knee or the optimal number of clusters is 3, with optimum value of within cluster sum square error [13] for most of the cases.

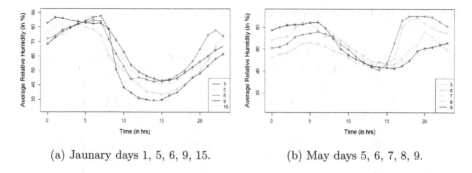

(a) Jaunary days 1, 5, 6, 9, 15.   (b) May days 5, 6, 7, 8, 9.

Fig. 3. Sampled time sequences for several days depicting hourly humidity concentration for BTM.

4.3 Knowledge Discovery

It is well known that Bangalore is a metropolitan city of India having high urban population. Bangalore has a tropical climate with distinct rainy season from May to October and dry season for the rest of the months of a year, with limited amounts of rainfall. From our work, it has been found that the 3rd cluster, LVC is highly sparse in nature and most of the time series belongs to HVC and AVC clusters. Bangalore is surrounded by lakes from all the major sides, hence humidity concentration is high for most of the times of year, thus the reason for such results is justified.

Figure 5 shows the general difference between three types of time series formed from clusters HVC, AVC and LVC. High rise time series are the time series having most of the data points in the sequence above the average mean for humidity concentration. Similarly, mid rise are those time series where most of the data points in the sequence are near to the average mean of the humidity concentration values. However, in our data we have found very few low rise time series, where data points' values lie below the average humidity concentration for most of the points in the sequence.

HVC cluster contains mostly week 1 and week 2 time series and type 2 contains mostly week 3 time series. Several days of week 4 belongs to HVC and a few days belong to AVC, which varies in different cases. As an example, Table 2(a) and (b) depicts the number of time series depicting number of sequences, that belong to clusters 1, 2 and 3 respectively for the stations of BTM and BWSSB. Similarly, clusters for all other stations have been formed from the dataset.

Results from these tables suggests that most of the time series belong to HVC and AVC type of clusters. Since, Bangalore is generally humid for most of the months of a year, all the stations have mostly high and mid rise type of time series for most of the months in a year. Figure 6 shows the locations of the five stations analyzed in this work with the results. Stations marked with red color depicts the stations with high rise type i,e. most of the series in these stations belongs to HVC cluster. While, for other stations depicted by blue color, it is identified that locations are of mid rise type, i.e. AVC cluster is the general trend for most of the time series in these stations.

Table 2. (a) Number of days in each clusters in BTM, Bangalore. (b) Number of days in each clusters in BWSSB, Bangalore.

Location	BTM			Location	BWSSB		
Month	HVC	AVC	LVC	Month	HVC	AVC	LVC
January	19	8	4	January	18	12	1
February	12	15	1	February	1	27	1
March	26	1	4	March	25	2	4
April	25	3	2	April	25	3	2
May	3	19	9	May	20	2	2
June	3	9	3	June	2	2	7
July	17	11	1	July	3	1	3
August	28	1	1	August	1	19	1
September	16	12	2	September	23	6	1
October	14	12	5	October	16	7	1
November	11	18	1	November	28	1	1
December	17	4	9	December	18	6	4

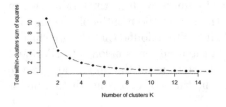
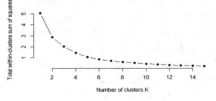

(a) Elbow curve for Jaunary.   (b) Elbow curve for May.

Fig. 4. Elbow curves for BTM for the sampled months.

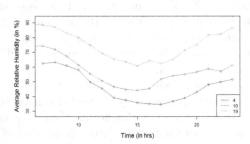

Fig. 5. Example time series of type high rise, mid rise and low rise respectively for days 19, 10 and 4 for the month of May, 2016.

4.4   Discussion

Validation for the analysis have been found out from the print and electronic media for Bangalore, over the period of January to December, 2016. Figure 7 shows snapshots of several news articles, depicting accidents of the time and locations where humidity concentration was high for the year 2016, i.e. where

Fig. 6. Locations of Bengluru, Bangalore depicting two types of time series for the month of January

clusters we have found are of high rise type. For example Fig. 7a shows news of accident in the month of February, 2016, at Chikkagollarahatti which is located near BTM. From our study, we have already identified that the month of February BTM is of high rise type, with high humidity concentration. Similarly, other results can be justified.

(a) Accident news report in February, 2016.

(b) Accident news report in June, 2016.

Fig. 7. News Reports of accidents in areas with high humidity.

5   Conclusion

There are several dimensions to make a city smart, one of these is smart mobility. Smart mobility ensures faster and safer commutation between places. In this work we have discussed literature survey on smart mobility, alongwith a case study related to visibility in environment, which hinders transportation. Presence of certain conditions in atmosphere can lead to decrease in visibility to the driver. This work studies the humidity concentration for several locations of Bangalore state in India. Main aim is to identify the humidity trends for each day, analyzed monthly over the year 2016. Euclidean distances between time series is used to identify the similarity and dissimilarities between them. Henceforth, clusters are formed to find the similar time series for each month. Thus, for any location the general trend of time series is known for the year 2016. In the given research work we have provided a brief study of the existing trends for each of the five locations. In future, we plan to evaluate the given study using statistical approaches and present the results based upon accuracies and errors metrices. Further, different types of analyses can be done like forecasting of humidity concentration trends and their evaluation etc. for the given data.

References

1. Northeast States for Coordinated Air Use Management (NESCAUM). https://www.hazecam.net/poor-vis.aspx. Accessed 1 Feb 2018
2. University of Maryland. https://www.sciencedaily.com/releases/2009/03/090312140850.htm. Accessed 1 Feb 2018
3. Michael Pines, APC. https://seriousaccidents.com/legal-advice/top-causes-of-car-accidents/. Accessed 1 Feb 2018
4. Aggarwal, A., Toshniwal, D.: Data mining techniques for smart mobility - a survey. In: Proceedings of the 5th International Conference on Advanced Computing, Networking, and Informatics (2017)
5. Cooke, K.L., Halsey, E.: The shortest route through a network with time-dependent internodal transit times. J. Math. Anal. Appl. **14**, 493–498 (1966)
6. Dean, B.C.: Continuous-time dynamic shortest path algorithms. Doctoral dissertation, Massachusetts Institute of Technology (1999)
7. Gonzalez, H., Han, J., Li, X., Myslinska, M., Sondag, J.P.: Adaptive fastest path computation on a road network: a traffic mining approach. In: Proceedings of the 33rd International Conference on Very Large Data Bases (2007)
8. Sing-Yiu, C., Varaiya, P.P.: Traffic surveillance by wireless sensor network. Final report, University of California, Berkeley (2007)
9. Yuan, J., Zheng, Y., Xie, X., Sun, G.: T-drive: enhancing driving directions with taxi driver's intelligence. IEEE Trans. Knowl. Data Eng. **25**, 220–233 (2010)
10. Yuan, J., Zheng, Y., Zhang, C., Xie, X., Sun, G.: An interactive-voting based map matching algorithm. In: Proceedings of the 2010 Eleventh International Conference on Mobile Data Management (2010)
11. Pan, B., Zheng, Y., Wilkie, D., Shahabi, C.: Crowd sensing of traffic anomalies based on human mobility and social media. In: Proceedings of the 21st ACM SIGSPATIAL International Conference on Advances in Geographic Information Systems (2013)
12. Yuan, J., Zheng, Y., Xie, X., Sun, G.: Driving with knowledge from the physical world. In: Proceedings of the 17th ACM SIGKDD International Conference on Knowledge Discovery and Data Mining (2011)
13. Han, J., Pei, J., Kamber, M.: Data Mining: Concepts and Techniques. Morgan Kaufmann Publishers, Burlington (2011)
14. Ge, Y., Xiong, Y., Tuzhilin, A., Xiao, K., Ruteser, M., Pazzani, M.: An energy-efficient mobile recommender system. In: Proceedings of the 16th ACM SIGKDD International Conference on Knowledge Discovery and Data Mining (2010)
15. Yuan, J., Zheng, Y., Zhang, L., Xie, X.: T-finder: recommender system for finding passengers and vacant taxis. IEEE Trans. Knowl. Data Eng. **25**, 2390–2404 (2013)
16. Shuo, M., Zheng, Y., Wolfson, O.: T-share: a large-scale dynamic taxi ridesharing service. In: IEEE 29th International Conference on Data Engineering (ICDE) (2013)

17. Van, E., Hurk, D., Kroon, L., Maróti, G., Vervest, P.: Deduction of passengers' route choices from smart card data. IEEE Trans. Intell. Transp. Syst. **16**, 430–440 (2015)
18. Kodinariya, T.M., Makwana, P.R.: Review on determining number of cluster in k-means clustering. Int. J. **1**, 90–95 (2013)
19. Lee, J., Hong, B., Lee, K., Jang, Y.J.: A prediction model of traffic congestion using weather data. In: IEEE International Conference on Data Science and Data Intensive Systems (DSDIS) (2015)
20. Koesdwiady, A., Soua, R., Karray, F.: Improving traffic flow prediction with weather information in connected cars: a deep learning approach. IEEE Trans. Veh. Technol. **65**, 9508–9517 (2016)
21. Choi, L.K., Cormack, L.K., Bovik, A.C.: Visibility prediction of flicker distortions on naturalistic videos. IEEE Trans. Image Process. **24**, 3888–3901 (2015)
22. Narwaria, M., Mantiuk, R., Da Silva, M.P., Le Callet, P.: HDR-VDP-2.2: a calibrated method for objective quality prediction of high-dynamic range and standard images. J. Electron. Imaging **24**, 010501 (2015)
23. Cornejo-Bueno, L., Casanova-Mateo, C., Sanz-Justo, J., Cerro-Prada, E., Salcedo-Sanz, S.: Efficient prediction of low-visibility events at airports using machine-learning regression. Bound.-Layer Meteorol. **165**, 349–370 (2017)
24. Tuba, Z., Bottyán, Z.: Fuzzy logic-based analogue forecasting and hybrid modelling of horizontal visibility. Meteorol. Atmos. Phys. **130**, 265–277 (2018)
25. Agarwal, A., Aggarwal, A., Agarwal, A.: An approach for augmenting selection operators of SQL queries using skyline and fuzzy-logic operators. Procedia Comput. Sci. **115**, 14–21 (2017)

Handling Web Spamming Using Logic Approach

Laxmi Ahuja[✉]

Amity Institute of Information Technology, Amity University Uttar Pradesh,
Noida, India
lahuja@amity.edu

Abstract. In the current years, we've seen a sensational addition within the volume of spam email. Other connected types of spam are increasingly uncovering as an issue of significance, extraordinarily the spam on Instant electronic messaging administrations, and Short Message Service (SMS) or portable spam. Like email spam, the SMS spam issue is drawn nearer with lawful, monetary or specialized measures. Among the extensive variety of specialized measures. There are two types of messages, first one is wanted messages from those people whom we know and other is unsolicited or unwanted messages, these unsolicited messages are called spams. Over the last 1.5 decade it has become a very big problem. Every day a very huge amount of spam messages is received by the users. This paper introduces an approach to classify the messages into spam/legitimate categories using the Rapid miner tool. In this Paper we have used Stop-word Removal in initial stages to filter spam of a Spam SMS Dataset on the basis of Content Based Filtering Technique. Then after getting the desired result that is when we have filtered the Messages. After that we have applied Nave-Bayes Classification with the Help of Rapid-Miner Tool which will help us in getting the desired out-come that is These messages will get categorized into Spam (bad) messages and Ham (Good) messages. This paper endeavors to order the predominant famous procedures for arranging messages as spam or ham and recommend the possible techniques

Keywords: Spam · Spam filters · Content based spam · Filtering
Stop-word removal · Nave-Bayes classifier · Rapid miner

1 Introduction

Messages are a strategy for trading advanced messages from a creator to at least one beneficiaries. Current messaging works over the Internet or other PC systems. As the web is turning into an essential piece of day by day lives of business clients as well as of individuals from each area with this the utilization of messages is likewise expanding. Likewise, the quantity of spam messages is expanding step by step. We have numerous answers for spam filtering in spite of that the spam sends are expanding quickly. For each sort of client, the spam is turns out to be expensive and baffling as well as a major security issue. What is spam to a person may not be a spam to another. This issue is to be tended to at various levels at sender, at system and furthermore at recipient's level.

© Springer Nature Singapore Pte Ltd. 2018
M. Singh et al. (Eds.): ICACDS 2018, CCIS 906, pp. 380–387, 2018.
https://doi.org/10.1007/978-981-13-1813-9_38

Undesired, spontaneous messages are disappointing to its beneficiaries as well as it is turning into a major security danger. We never realize that if we got message contains some treat grapping codes, to know our get to certifications (phishing) or it might be connected to a site that introduces malevolent programming to your machine and so forth.

There are extreme issues with spam messages e.g. wastage of time, harm to our systems of mobile devices, spam messages promoting unscrupulous substance, and a noteworthy one wastage of system assets particularly data transfer capacity.

In this paper, we tend to concentrate the chance of applying Nave Bayes Classifier systems to the problem of SMS spam Filtering. In this paper we've got taken Data set which has spam SMSs we filter those messages using the Stopword Removal Then, we tend to review variety of technical measures against spam email, specializing in Nave Thomas Bayes Classifier using the rapid miner Tool.

1.1 Spam Filtering

The Spam Filtering Techniques are of two types:

1. Machine Learning
2. Non Machine Learning

Machine Learning Approach: This approach requires delineating the undertakings that pick up as a matter of fact and endeavor to perceive outlines from data and perform gathering. Machine Learning techniques are broadly assembled into overseen and unsupervised learning. The fundamental refinement between the two is that Supervised learning tallies re-quire a covered up prepare set for help with demand while it is not required in Non-Supervised computations. Distinctive techniques used under Machine Learning philosophy are Bayesian request, neural frameworks, Markov-based models, and illustration discovery. These machine learning strategies have been used to fight against spam. Non Machine Learning includes Blacklist/white list, Content Based Filtering, Address Management, Digital Signatures, Mail Header Analysis etc. [2].

White List/Black List: These both methodologies basically produce a listing. In a white list there's a list which contains the e-mail id's or the entire domain that the user knows. In this type of list, it specifies which senders are allowed to send us email or a message. These addresses are placed on a trusted users list. In a Black-list, It is opposite of the whitelist in this list we tend to add id's that are harmful for users. In this technique, it attempts to stop the unwanted messages or emails by block messages from a pre-set list of senders that we or our organization's system administrator create [3].

Digital signatures Messages, which don't have a digital signature are spam. These Signatures may be given by the sender or the administration provider. This approach is fundamentally in view of generating a signature that encompasses a distinctive hash-value for every spam message. Address management comprises on the utilization of fleeting, machine delivered addresses, which are regulated naturally by the system, and discarded when they begin tolerating spam. E.g. the Channels framework.

1.2   Content Based Spam Filtering

This type of filter essentially evaluates the words or phrases that are found in every individual message to see whether or not an email is spam or ham. These sort of filters checks for Text within the body of Email, then computer address and It conjointly considers the mail header like subject for classification of text. It performs Text classification task by using preprocessing on TEXT in terms of hypertext mark-up language tag removal, Stopword Removal, Tokenizing and Word frequency calculation for deciding word chance to seek out whether a given mail is spam or [5].

1.3   Stop-Word Removal

Is a critical preprocessing system utilized as a part of Natural Language preparing applications to enhance the execution of the data Retrieval System, Analytics and process System, Text report, Question and Answer framework, stemming and so forth [6]. Usually, Articles and pronouns are classified as stop words.

1.4   Naive-Bayes Classifier

There are specific words utilized as a part of spam messages and non spam messages which have specific likeli-hood of happening in both messages. Every specific word or simply the foremost attention-grabbing words raise email's spam probability. This contribution is understood because the posterior likelihood and is calculated using the Bayes theorem. At that time, the spam messages chances are calculated all over throughout the word within the messages. If this total worth exceed over bound threshold then the filters can mark emails as spam. Ascertain the probability of a message being spam in view of its substance. Bayesian spam filtering gains from spam and from Ham mail, bringing about associate degree exceptionally vigorous, adjusting and productive hostile to spam approach that, better of all, profits barely any false positives. Naive-Bayes Classifier are otherwise referred to as Bayesian Spam Filter [7].

2   Literature Survey

Jose et al. [1] have analyzed to what extent Bayesian filtering techniques are accustomed to block the spam. They have taken two data sets one in English and other in Spanish language. They have tested the Data-set on various machine learning algorithms in terms of their effectiveness. Kanchan et al. [2] have given a comprehensive survey of techniques for detection of spam and mentioned their relevancy and performance in numerous situations wherever they outperformed the others. Zhu [3] have introduced the development and basic concept of the spam, they have classified the spam filtering techniques. Sunil [5] in his used Bayesian classification to check the performance in terms of Time, Precision, Exactness, Error and Recall. Jatinder et al. [6] have used Stopword removal algorithm to remove words from Sanskrit.

Chuan et al. [8] have exhibited an application to Hostile Spam Email utilizing another enhanced Bayesian-based email channel. They have utilized vector weights for speaking to word recurrence and embraced property choice in view of word entropy and conclude its relating recipe. It is demonstrated that their channel enhances add up to exhibitions clearly. Ranganayakulu et al. [9] considered Age of the domain area, Host based elements, Lexical components and Page rank for examination of URL to arrange into malevolent URL and Legitimate URL. They have utilized Bayesian classifier to enhance the precision by lessened component sets and considered phishtank dataset, the work was limited to URL in Email only.

Sahami et al. [10] has given a spam arrangement technique utilizing a Bayesian approach. A Bayesian classifier is statistical classifier works on independence computation of probability. They have considered of email with components of area of domain, and demonstrated that exactness can be expanded. Christina et al. [11] had demonstrated that the need of compelling spam channels increments. He talked about spam and spam filtering techniques and their associated issues. Sadeghian et al. [12] had exhibited spam identification in view of interval type-2 fuzzy sets. Georgios et al. [13] have investigated the performance of two machine learning algorithms in the context of anti-spam filtering. They have chosen the execution on openly available corpus for blameless bayes.

Qi et al. [14] have investigated two fundamental semantic methods: Bayesian algorithm and Sup-port Vector Machine (SVM). Recent spam channels are examined in this paper for deciding spam messages which use semantic examination data. Chuan et al. [15] have exhibited. An application to Hostile to Spam Email utilizing another enhanced Bayesian-based email channel. They have utilized vector weights for speaking to word recurrence and embraced property choice in view of word entropy and conclude its relating recipe. It is demonstrated that their channel enhances add up to exhibitions clearly.

Geerthik et al. [16] they have given an overview on the latest pattern and techniques in spam filtering. In there paper, it usually focuses on automatic, non-intelligent channels, with a large review going from business executions to contemplations sure to current raise regarding papers.

3 Proposed Work

3.1 Algorithm and Naive-Bayes Classifier

We have taken a random Data-sets of messages and then we have used Stopword Algorithm for filtering those messages which are to be content filtered. After those messages are content filtered we will use Naive-Bayes using the Rapid Miner Tool. In Rapid Miner we will Load our Data-Set which is content filtered on the tool. Then, we will use Naive Bayes as operator and apply some predictive operations which will let us know that in our Data-Set, how many messages where spam and how many messages where Ham.

Algorithm

Step 1: Choose a Dataset.
Step 2: Use Stop-Word Removal algorithmic rule to Content Filter the data Set.

Step 3: Use the rapid miner Tool and therefore the Naive-Bayes Classifier as the Operator to classify the spam and Ham Messages.

4 Implementation

Stop Word is a list of some common words that may be available in most of the message or emails which are not spam. These words include am, i, are, they'd, they'll, they're, they've etc. These words are removed initially to increase the effectiveness and efficiency of the process.

Algorithm

Step 1: The Message is tokenized and individual words are Kept within the array
Step 2: One stop word is perused from stopword list.
Step 3: The stop word is contrasted with target message in style of exhibit utilizing ordered inquiry procedure.
Step 4: If it coordinates, the word in array is removed, and therefore the examination is proceeded until length of the array
Step 5: once removal of stopword utterly, another stopword is perused from stopword list and once more the algorithmic rule follows step two.

The algorithmic rule runs systematically till all the stop-words area unit compared.

Step 6: Resultant text without stopwords is shown, likewise needed measurements like stopword removed, no. of stopwords aloof from target, add up to incorporate of words target, embody of words resultant, singular stop word embody discovered target text is shown

PSEUDO CODE FOR STOP-WORD

Define: List Of Stop-Word Removal
For i = 1 to Number Of words in the Data-Set
For j = 1 to Number Of words in the Stop-Word List
If Words(i) ==stopwords(j) then
Remove Word (i)
End If
End For

As in Fig. 1 we have shown that we will be using Naive Bayes Algorithm which will refine the Spam and the Ham which is in our Data-set after Applying the Stop-word Removal Algorithm.

Here we will be using the Rapid Miner Tool to which will train and Test and then classify whether the Message was a spam or Ham.

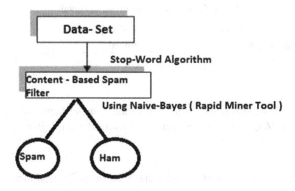

Fig. 1. Content based spam detection using stop word

5 Results

Using Stopword Removal we found that in the data-set there were 92484 words in the document and 45003 words where removed using the Algorithm (Tables 1 and 2).

Table 1. Result of stopword removal

Size of the file	Total words in the document	No of stop-words removed	Percentage removed
466 KB	92484	45003	25.98

Table 2. Result of bayesian classification using rapid miner

Name of technique	Spam	Ham
Naïve-Bayes	269	1766

Table 3. Result of stopword removal

Size of the file	Total words in the document	No of stopwords removed	Percentage removed
342 KB	68010	9871	13.90

Using Stopword Removal we found that in the data set there were 680101 words in the document and 9871 words where removed using the Algorithm (Tables 3 and 4).

Table 4. Result of stopword removal

Name of technique	Spam	Ham
Naïve-Bayes	3507	531

Table 5. Result of stopword removal

Size of the file	Total words in the document	No of stopwords removed	Percentage removed
172 KB	34254	5652	11.12

Using Stopword Removal we found that in the data-set there were 34254 words in the document and 5652 words where removed using the Algorithm (Tables 5 and 6).

Table 6. Result of Bayesian classification using rapid miner

Name of technique	Spam	Ham
Naïve-Bayes	736	4741

6 Conclusion

We have emphasized Bayesian approach for classifying Spam and legitimate mails using Stopword Removal algorithm. Applying the Bayesian classifier, we experimentally demonstrated that spam mails can be detected easily and accurately. We are working to find an efficient method to get the training dataset of keywords to get automatically updated so as to get better performance in the system.

References

1. Hidalgo, G., Mara, J., et al.: Content based SMS spam filtering. In: Proceedings of the 2006 ACM Symposium on Document Engineering, pp. 107–114. ACM (2006)
2. Kanchan, H., Laxmi, A., Mutto, S.K.: Approaches for web spam detection. Int. J. Comput. Appl. **101**(1), 38–44 (2014)
3. Zhu, Z.: Research on spam filtering techniques and trend analysis. IPASJ Int. J. Manag. (IIJM) **3**(8), 16–19 (2015)
4. Hall, R.J.: How to avoid unwanted email. Commun. ACM **41**, 88–95 (1998)
5. Rathod, S.B., Pattewar, T.M.: Content based spam detection in email using Bayesian classifier. In: IEEE ICCSP 2015 Conference, pp. 1257–1261 (2015)
6. Sain, J.R., Raulji, J.K.: Stop-word removal algorithm and its implementation for Sanskrit language. Int. J. Comput. Appl. **150**(2), 15–17 (2016)
7. Rekha, S.N.: A review on different spam detection approaches. Int. J. Eng. Trends Technol. (IJETT) **11**(6), 315–318 (2014)
8. Chuan, Z., Lu, X.-I., Zhou, X., Hou, M.: An improved Bayesian with application to anti-spam email. J. Electron. Sci. Technol. China **3**(1), 30–33 (2005)
9. Ranganayakulu, D., Chellappan, C.: Detecting malicious URLs in E-Mail: an implementation. In: AASRI Conference on Intelligent Systems and Control, vol. 4, pp. 125–131 (2013)
10. Sahami, M., Dumais, S., Heckerman, D., Horvitz, E.: A Bayesian approach to filtering junk e-mail. AAAi Technical report, WS-98-05, pp. 55–62

11. Christina, V.: A study on email spam filtering techniques. Int. J. Comput. Appl. **12**(1), 7–9 (2010)
12. Ariaeinejad, R., Sadeghian, A.: Spam detection system: a new approach based on interval type-2 fuzzy sets. In: 2011 24th Canadian Conference on Electrical and Computer Engineering (CCECE), pp. 000379–000384. IEEE (2011)
13. Androutsopoulos, I., Paliouras, G., Karkaletsis, V., Sakkis, G., Spy-ropoulos, C.D., Stamatopoulos, P.: Learning to filter spam e-mail: a comparison of a naive bayesian and a memory based approach. In: Proceedings of the Workshop on Machine Learning and Textual information Access, 4th European Conference on Principles and Practice of Knowledge Discovery in Databases (PKDD 2000), pp. 1–13 (2000)
14. Qi, M., Mousoli, R.: Semantic analysis for spam filtering. In: International Conference on Fuzzy Systems and Knowledge Discovery, vol. 6, pp. 2914–2917 (2010)
15. Chuan, Z., Lu, X.-I., Zhou, X., Hou, M.: An improved Bayesian with application to anti-spam email. J. Electron. Sci. Technol. China **3**(1) (2005)
16. Geerthik, S., Anish, T.P.: Filtering spam: current trends and techniques. Int. J. Mechatron. Electr. Comput. Technol. **3**(8), 208–223 (2013)

Spider Monkey Optimization Algorithm with Enhanced Learning

Bhagwanti[✉], Harish Sharma, and Nirmala Sharma

Rajasthan Technical University, Kota, India
Bhagwanti.verma15@gmail.com

Abstract. Spider Monkey Optimisation (SMO) is a new addition within the arena of nature-inspired algorithms. It is a recent Swarm Intelligence (SI) based algorithm, that models the food foraging behavior of a group of spider monkeys that mimic the Fission-Fusion Social System ($FFSS$) behavior. The SMO has been proven to be competitory and it balances the capabilities; exploitation and exploration efficiently. This article presents a significant variant of SMO, namely Spider Monkey Optimization with Enhanced Learning ($SMOEL$). In the proposed strategy, to increase the exploitation capability of SMO, an enhanced learning mechanism is introduced in the local leader stage that is based on the fitness of the solution. Reliability and accuracy of the intended algorithm are tested over 14 benchmarks functions and the comparison showed against various state of art algorithms available in the literature. The obtained outcomes prove the superiority of the intended algorithm.

Keywords: Swarm intelligence
Meta-heuristic optimization techniques
Spider monkey optimization algorithm · Learning method

1 Introduction

Swarm Intelligence (SI) is a discipline which deals with artificial and natural systems. These systems are composed of swarms of homogeneous individuals. In swarm behaviour of individuals, instead of everyone depending on a single central unit, all units are self-organized and they cooperate and share information to carry out their necessary tasks. A Meta-heuristic refers to a high-level problem independent framework which helps to develop heuristic optimization algorithms [14]. The recent advancements in SI have shown its tremendous capability in solving complex problems which otherwise is impossible to solve with other naive approaches. A number of SI algorithms like Bacterial Foraging Optimization (BFO) [9], Particle Swarm Optimization (PSO) [7], Artificial Bee Colony Optimization (ABC) [6], Gravitational Search Algorithm (GSA) [10], Shuffled Frog Leaping Algorithm ($SFLA$) [4] etc. has been proposed.

Bansal et al. [3] presented an algorithm based on fission-fusion social structure. This algorithm is known as Spider Monkey Optimization (SMO), mimics

© Springer Nature Singapore Pte Ltd. 2018
M. Singh et al. (Eds.): ICACDS 2018, CCIS 906, pp. 388–401, 2018.
https://doi.org/10.1007/978-981-13-1813-9_39

the social behavior of a South American species of monkeys called spider monkeys, those belong to the class of SI. While searching for an optimum solution the algorithm maintains the balance between deviation and selection processes which ensure exploration and exploitation, respectively. Being a latest addition in SI, SMO is attracting researchers for experimenting SMO capability in different real-world problems. Recently some significant variants of SMO have been developed and shown improvement in its performance. In 2015, Kumar et al. given a new way to update the position of solutions, hence the variant called Fitness Based Position Update in SMO ($FPSMO$) [8]. In 2016 Hazrati et al. presented a variant of SMO, named as "Modified Spider Monkey Optimization ($MSMO$) [5]". In proposed work, the metropolis principle of simulated annealing and probability were used. In 2017 Sharma et al. presented another variant in SMO called as Power Law-based Local search in Spider Monkey Optimization (PLSMO). In their work, they employ novel local search, specified as power low based local search [13]. In 2017 Agarwal et al. proposed another variant of SMO in light of acceleration coefficient, termed as Fast Convergent Spider Monkey Optimization Algorithm ($FCSMO$) [1].

In the above context, this paper also presents an efficient variant of SMO, named as Spider Monkey Optimization with Enhance Learning ($SMOEL$). In the proposed technique, an enhanced learning mechanism is introduced in the local leader phase of SMO. It improves the rate of convergence and exploration capability. Further, this strategy is being tested over 14 benchmark issues and the outcomes are being compared with the initial SMO and four other metaheuristic based algorithms, PSO, GSA, SFLA, Differential Evaluation (DE), and also compared with four significant variants of SMO namely, PLSMO, MSMO, Self-adaptive Spider Monkey Optimization Algorithm (SaSMO), Levy Flight Spider Monkey Optimization (LFSMO). It has been examined that the proposed algorithm perform well over various existing well-known algorithms.

This article is organised in the given way: The initial version of SMO algorithm is described in Sect. 2. Section 3 outlines the intended $SMOEL$ algorithm and Sect. 4 contains the experimental outcomes. Finally, Sect. 5 encompasses the surmised work.

2   Spider Monkey Optimization (SMO) Algorithm

There are six steps in SMO algorithm namely, Local Leader step, Global Leader step, Global Leader Learning step, Local Leader Learning step, Local Leader Decision step, and Global Leader Decision step [3].

Firstly, the population is initialized and then these steps are executed one by one respectively. The SMO spawn a smoothly scattered initial population of N spider monkeys each of dimension D in the pursuit space. Each dimension j of SM_i is initialized as follows:

$$SM_{ij} = SM_{minj} + U(0,1) \times (SM_{maxj} - SM_{minj}) \qquad (1)$$

where SM_{ij} is the ith spider monkey in j^{th} dimension, SM_{minj} and SM_{maxj} are the initial limits and final limits. U(0,1) is an evenly scattered random function in the scope $[0, 1]$.

2.1   Local Leader Step

This is the first step in which the spider monkeys update their positions according to the Local Leader position as well as from the randomly selected monkey of the group. So the position update equation for i^{th} spider monkey will be:

$$SMnew_{ij} = SM_{ij} + U(0,1) \times (LL_{kj} - SM_{ij}) + U(-1,1) \times (SM_{rj} - SM_{ij}) \quad (2)$$

where $SMnew_{ij}$ is the updated solution, LL_{kj} is the Local Leader in j^{th} dimension of kth group and SM_{rj} is the randomly selected spider monkey of jth dimension.

2.2   Global Leader Step

Now in the Global Leader step, the solutions update according to the position of the Global Leader as well as according to the position of any randomly selected monkey of the whole group. So, for i^{th} spider monkey the position update equation for this step will be:

$$SMnew_{ij} = SM_{ij} + U(0,1) \times (GL_j - SM_{ij}) + U(-1,1) \times (SM_{rj} - SM_{ij}) \quad (3)$$

where GL_j is the global leader in j^{th} dimension.

2.3   Global Leader Learning Step

The Global Leader Learning step helps to select the Global Leader in the swarm by employing the greedy choice based upon the fitness values. There is a counter namely, $GlobalLimitCount$ which is raised by one, if the position of Global Leader is not updating in each iteration.

2.4   Local Leader Learning Step

Same as the Global Leader Learning step, the Local Leader position is modified by employing greedy selection strategy, means a solution which have the best fitness in particular local group is elected as new local leader. If that position of the Local Leader is not updated in each iteration, then the associated counter namely, $LocalLimitCount$ is raised by one.

2.5   Local Leader Decision Step

In the given step, Local Leader position update process is examined. If Local Leader position is not renewed until predefined threshold counter namely $LocalLimitCount$, then the local group members are updated either by random initialization or by the following equation as per the perturbation rate (pr). Here, pr controls the amount of perturbation in the ongoing position.

$$SMnew_{ij} = SM_{ij} + U(0,1) \times (GL_j - SM_{ij}) + U(0,1) \times (SM_{ij} - LL_{ij}) \quad (4)$$

2.6   Global Leader Decision Step:

Here, in the Global Leader Decision step position of global leader is examined. If the counter associated with global leader limit namely, $GlobalLimitCount$ is crossed or regulated over the threshold value $GlobalLeaderLimit$ then global leader split the population into little groups. Here, the number of maximum groups (MG) should not exceed MG limit (MG = $N/10$ here N represent the total number of solutions). Every time when the new group is created then local leader learning step is performed for newly formed groups.

3   Spider Monkey Optimization Algorithm with Enhanced Learning ($SMOEL$)

To enhance the exploitation ability of the local swarm members, the position update process of local leader phase is modified as follows:

The Enhanced Learning Method: The position update process of the local leader phase of SMO is described below in Eq. 5. In Eq. 5 it is obvious that the social learning component of the position update process is a combination of two components: learning from the local leader and learning from the randomly selected neighbouring solution as shown in Eq. 5.

$$\overbrace{}^{\text{Local leader learning}} \qquad \overbrace{}^{\text{Neighbour Learning}}$$

$$SMnew_{ij} = SM_{ij} + w_1 \times \overbrace{(LL_{kj} - SM_{ij})} \quad + w2 \times \overbrace{(SM_{rj} - SM_{ij})} \quad (5)$$

In Eq. 5, w_1 and w_2 are the weights to the local leader component and the learning from neighbouring solution component. In the basic version of SMO, w_1, and w_2 are the randomly selected weights in the range $(0, 1)$ and $(-1, 1)$ respectively. It is clear from Eq. 5 that the weights play significant role to determine the directions and the step size of the solutions. High weight to the local leader component will enhance the convergence ability within the local search space i.e. the exploitation capability will improve while the high weight of the neighbour learning component will improve the diversification (exploration) ability of the solution. Therefore, the position update process of the local leader step is modified as shown in Eq. 6.

$$SMnew_{ij} = SM_{ij} + U(0,1) \times prob_i \times (LL_{kj} - SM_{ij}) + U(-1,1) \times (GL_j - SM_{ij})$$
$$(6)$$

As shown in Eq. 6, two modifications are done. First, the weight assigned to the local leader learning component is $w_1 = U(0, 1) \times prob_i$, earlier the weight was $w_1 = U(0, 1)$. Here, the $prob_i$ is a function of fitness and computed as given in Eq. 7 below.

$$prob_i = \frac{fitness_i}{\sum_{i=1}^{N} fitness_i} \qquad (7)$$

where $fitness_i$ is the fitness value of the ith SM.

So, it can be easily observed from Eq. 6 that the weight w_1 for the high fit solutions will be high while for the low fit solutions will be low, so high fit solutions will attract towards the local leader with high intensity and this will improve the convergence ability of the good solutions. Further, in the second modification, the global leader learning component is incorporated instead of the randomly selected neighbour learning component. Therefore, for the low fit solutions, the weight w_1 will be low, hence the attraction towards the local leader, so these solutions will be updated while taking inspiration from the global leader with large step sizes as the step size depends on the distance between the solution and the global leader current position. So that the low fit solution will take inspiration from the global leader and explore the search space. Therefore, the proposed modification will balance the position update process in terms of diversification and convergence abilities. Symbolic code of proposed $SMOEL$ is depicted in Algorithm 1 for the local leader step.

Algorithm 1. Enhanced learning mechanism in Local Leader step:

for each $k \in \{1, ..., MG\}$ do
   for each member $SM_i \in k^{th}$ group do
      for each $j \in \{1, ..., D\}$ do
         if $U(0, 1) \geq pr$ then
            $SMnew_{ij} = SM_{ij} + U(0,1) \times prob_i \times (LL_{kj} - SM_{ij}) + U(-1,1) \times (GL_j - SM_{ij})$.
         else
            $SMnew_{ij} = SM_{ij}$.
         end if
      end for
   end for
end for

Here, pr is varied from [0.1, 0.5] (Explained in Section 2.5).

---

4   Experimental Outcomes

The intended $SMOEL$ algorithm is being analysed on 14 different global optimization problems (f_1 to f_{14}) [2,17] which are shown in Table 1 with their offset values.

To examine the superiority of the intended algorithm $SMOEL$, a correlative comparison is also taken among $SMOEL$, SMO, and four of its significant variants, namely $PLSMO$, $LFSMO$, $SaSMO$, $MSMO$, and also with four other algorithms available in literature are PSO, DE, GSA, and $SFLA$. The Experimental settings which is taken into consideration to test $SMOEL$, SMO, $PLSMO$, $LFSMO$, $SaSMO$, and $MSMO$ over the regarded test problems are as follows:

– Number of simulations/run = 100,
– Swarm size $N = 50$ and Maximum Group $MG = N/10$,

– Rest of the parameter settings for the algorithms SMO, $PLSMO$, $LFSMO$, $SaSMO$, and $MSMO$ are taken same as their basic research papers.
– Range of pr is varied from $[0.1, 0.5]$.

The Parameter settings, which are considered to test [16] DE, PSO, GSA, and $SFLA$ are simulated from their primary research papers.

Termination boundary is the greatest number of function evaluation which is decided 200000 for all the considered algorithms.

Table 2 shows the comparison among $SMOEL$, SMO, $PLSMO$, $LFSMO$, $SaSMO$, $MSMO$, PSO, DE, GSA, and $SFLA$ in the form of standard deviation (SD), mean error (ME), average number of function evaluations (AFE), and success rate (SR). It is very much obvious from the outcomes that are displayed in Table 2 that $SMOEL$ performs better in form of authenticity, capability, and veracity as contrasted to the other considered algorithms. Moreover, the convergence rates of the studied algorithms are contrasted by means of $AFEs$ (lesser the AFE, faster the convergence speed). Here, SR denotes the number of times, algorithm achieved the optima with acceptable error.

Additionally, an efficient and graphical comparison is shown by boxplots [11] for average number of function evaluations is carried out for every one of the algorithms $SMOEL$, SMO, $PLSMO$, $LFSMO$, $SaSMO$, $MSMO$, PSO, DE, GSA, and $SFLA$ to show the empirical distribution of data pictorially. The boxplots diagram is shown in Fig. 1. Therefore, it is easily concluded from boxplots diagram (Fig. 1) that $SMOEL$ is cost efficient than SMO, $PLSMO$, $LFSMO$, $SaSMO$, $MSMO$, PSO, DE, GSA, and $SFLA$.

To suppress the impact of stochastic behaviour of the algorithms, function evaluations for every problem are taken as average over 100 runs. Also, the acceleration rate (AR) [15] is estimated in order to contrast the convergence speeds, which basically depends upon the $AFEs$ of the algorithms as shown below:

$$AR = \frac{AFE_{ALGO}}{AFE_{SMOEL}} \tag{8}$$

Here, $ALGO \in \{SMO, PLSMO, LFSMO, SaSMO, MSMO, PSO, DE, GSA,$ and $SFLA \}$.

Using Eq. 8, AR is calculated betwixt $SMOEL$ and SMO, $SMOEL$ and $PLSMO$, $SMOEL$ and $LFSMO$, $SMOEL$ and $SaSMO$, $SMOEL$ and $MSMO$, $SMOEL$ and PSO, $SMOEL$ and DE, $SMOEL$ and GSA, $SMOEL$ and $SFLA$. This comparison is tabulated in Table 3 and AR is greater than 1 clarifies that $SMOEL$ is fastest among all the considered algorithms for mojority of the test functions. Here, $AR > 1$, depicts that $SMOEL$ is comparatively fast shown in Table 3.

Apart from this, a non-parametric analysis namely, Mann-Whitney U rank sum [12] test is also performed on function evaluations in order to examine that whether these results are with a considerable difference or not. The comparison betwixt $SMOEL - SMO$, $SMOEL - PLSMO$, $SMOEL - LFSMO$, $SMOEL - SaSMO$, $SMOEL - MSMO$, $SMOEL - PSO$, $SMOEL - DE$, $SMOEL - GSA$, and $SMOEL - SFLA$.

Table 1. Test problems (Here; D: Dimension, AE: Acceptable Error)

S.No.	Test Problem	Objective function	Search Range	D	AE
1	Sphere	$f_1(x) = \sum_{i=1}^{D} x_i^2$	[-5.12, 5.12]	30	1.0E − 05
2	Griewank	$f_2(x) = 1 + \frac{1}{4000}\sum_{i=1}^{D} x_i^2 - \prod_{i=1}^{D}\cos(\frac{x_i}{\sqrt{i}})$	[-600, 600]	30	1.0E − 05
3	Rosenbrock	$f_3(x) = \sum_{i=1}^{D}(100(x_{i+1} - x_i^2)^2 + (x_i - 1)^2)$	[-30, 30]	30	1.0E − 02
4	Ackley	$f_4(x) = -20 + e + exp(-\frac{0.2}{D}\sqrt{\sum_{i=1}^{D} x_i^3}) - exp(\frac{1}{D}\sum_{i=1}^{D}\cos(2\pi.x_i)x_i)$	[-1, 1]	30	1.0E − 05
5	Cosine Mixture	$f_5(x) = \sum_{i=1}^{D} x_i^2 - 0.1(\sum_{i=1}^{D}\cos 5\pi x_i) + 0.1D$	[-1, 1]	30	1.0E − 05
6	Exponential	$f_6(x) = -(exp(-0.5\sum_{i=1}^{D} x_i^2)) + 1$	[-1, 1]	30	1.0E − 05
7	Zakharov	$f_7(x) = \sum_{i=1}^{D} x_i^2 + (\sum_{i=1}^{D}\frac{ix_i}{2})^2 + (\sum_{i=1}^{D}\frac{ix_i}{2})^4$	[-5.12, 5.12]	30	1.0E − 02
8	Salomon Problem	$f_8(x) = 1 - \cos(2\pi\sqrt{\sum_{i=1}^{D} x_i^2}) + 0.1(\sqrt{\sum_{i=1}^{D} x_i^2})$	[-100, 100]	30	1.0E − 01
9	Step Function	$f_9(x) = \sum_{i=1}^{D}(\lfloor x_i + 0.5\rfloor)^2$	[-100, 100]	30	1.0E − 05
10	Levy Montalvo 1	$f_{10}(x) = \frac{\pi}{D}(10\sin^2(\pi y_1) + \sum_{i=1}^{D-1}(y_i - 1)^2 \times (1 + 10\sin^2(\pi y_{i+1})) + (y_D - 1)^2)$, where $y_i = 1 + \frac{1}{4}(x_i + 1)$	[-10, 10]	30	1.0E − 05
11	Levy Montalvo 2	$f_{11}(x) = 0.1(\sin^2(3\pi x_1) + \sum_{i=1}^{D-1}(x_i - 1)^2 \times (1 + \sin^2(3\pi x_{i+1})) + (x_D - 1)^2(1 + \sin^2(2\pi x_D)))$	[-5, 5]	30	1.0E − 05
12	Branins's Function	$f_{12}(x) = a(x_2 - bx_1^2 + cx_1 - d)^2 + e(1 - f)\cos x_1 + e$	$x_1 \in [-5, 10], x_2 \in [0, 15]$	2	1.0E − 05
13	Easom's Function	$f_{13}(x) = -\cos x_1 \cos x_2 e^{((-(x_1-\Pi)^2 - (x_2-\Pi)^2))}$	[-10, 10]	2	1.0E − 13
14	Moved Axis Parallel Hyper-ellipsoid	$f_{14}(x) = \sum_{i=1}^{D} 5i \times x_i^2$	[-5.12, 5.12]	30	1.0E − 15

Table 2. Test problems comparison of the results (Here; Algo: Algorithm, TP: Test Problems)

TP	Algo	ME	SD	AFE	SR
f_1	SMOEL	1.13E−06	8.35E−06	7496.28	100
	SMO	8.37E−07	8.87E−06	13642.3	100
	PLSMO	8.15E−07	8.96E−06	13174.79	100
	LFSMO	9.02E−07	9.00E−06	15882.96	100
	SaSMO	1.72E−06	8.35E−06	44654.49	100
	MSMO	7.75E−07	9.02E−06	12696.75	100
	PSO	6.10E−07	9.33E−06	38101.5	100
	DE	8.24E−07	9.06E−06	22444	100
	GSA	9.42E−07	8.77E−06	95093.33	100
	SFLA	9.05E−07	8.89E−06	13973.13	100
f_2	SMOEL	1.21E−06	8.44E−06	12119.58	100
	SMO	5.48E−03	2.96E−03	77028.55	72
	PLSMO	4.25E−03	2.13E−03	74710.82	77
	LFSMO	4.65E−03	2.45E−03	85957.91	73
	SaSMO	7.35E−04	8.09E−05	90758.18	99
	MSMO	9.63E−03	6.00E−03	100121.73	58
	PSO	7.12E−03	3.87E−03	113502.5	69
	DE	5.00E−03	1.71E−03	55540	86
	GSA	3.21E−03	7.60E−01	200000	0
	SFLA	2.19E−02	8.25E−01	200000	0
f_3	SMOEL	1.15E+01	7.64E+00	144513.94	53
	SMO	4.53E+01	4.40E+01	199919.49	0
	PLSMO	4.30E+01	4.60E+01	199152.52	2
	LFSMO	4.36E+01	4.39E+01	200004.77	1
	SaSMO	1.08E+01	6.63E+00	193992.93	13
	MSMO	4.21E+01	4.12E+01	199630.27	1
	PSO	3.35E+01	3.97E+01	199663.5	1
	DE	4.29E+02	8.97E+01	200000	0
	GSA	3.42E+01	3.07E+01	200000	0
	SFLA	1.23E+01	5.18E+00	192758.47	30
f_4	SMOEL	6.41E−07	9.13E−06	13647.15	100
	SMO	7.09E−07	9.37E−06	28005.03	100
	PLSMO	4.93E−07	9.40E−06	31217.67	100
	LFSMO	1.30E−01	1.86E−02	35000.8	98
	SaSMO	1.07E−06	9.05E−06	107669.68	100
	MSMO	8.99E−07	9.39E−06	30869.71	100
	PSO	3.92E−07	9.60E−06	76295	100
	DE	4.42E−07	9.46E−06	43100.5	100
	GSA	5.84E−07	9.37E−06	161030	100
	SFLA	5.62E−01	2.69E−01	61437.8	80

(*continued*)

Table 2. (*continued*)

TP	Algo	ME	SD	AFE	SR
f_5	SMOEL	1.28E−06	8.36E−06	6869.61	100
	SMO	7.35E−02	2.66E−02	57513.35	86
	PLSMO	1.02E−01	5.76E−02	109755.83	72
	LFSMO	1.33E−01	8.13E−02	84869.53	66
	SaSMO	1.98E−06	8.25E−06	49805.37	100
	MSMO	7.02E−02	3.10E−02	56351.14	82
	PSO	6.73E−02	2.66E−02	64353	85
	DE	4.72E−02	1.33E−02	37386	92
	GSA	8.13E−07	8.66E−06	111176.67	100
	SFLA	2.47E−01	5.52E−01	193757.9	3
f_6	SMOEL	1.22E−06	8.31E−06	5457.87	100
	SMO	7.85E−07	8.80E−06	9708.93	100
	PLSMO	8.56E−07	8.87E−06	10172.3	100
	LFSMO	6.94E−07	9.06E−06	12203.88	100
	SaSMO	1.57E−06	8.42E−06	42773.67	100
	MSMO	1.00E−06	8.79E−06	9692.1	100
	PSO	6.28E−07	9.39E−06	28332.5	100
	DE	9.15E−07	8.98E−06	17269	100
	GSA	7.56E−07	8.86E−06	91298.33	100
	SFLA	7.73E−07	8.92E−06	10541.43	100
f_7	SMOEL	9.57E−04	8.88E−03	73538.94	100
	SMO	6.18E−04	9.41E−03	141818.34	100
	PLSMO	4.95E−04	9.65E−03	121187.1	100
	LFSMO	1.11E−03	9.44E−03	172136.9	99
	SaSMO	2.40E+01	1.29E+02	200053.48	0
	MSMO	6.85E−04	9.22E−03	128122.5	100
	PSO	1.62E−02	1.98E−02	196207.5	31
	DE	5.10E−04	9.43E−03	69828.5	100
	GSA	1.98E+00	3.61E+00	200000	0
	SFLA	3.75E−04	9.52E−03	46337.27	100
f_8	SMOEL	2.38E−02	1.06E−01	57205.29	94
	SMO	3.13E−02	1.89E−01	190609.68	11
	PLSMO	2.82E−02	1.98E−01	197091.37	5
	LFSMO	1.71E−02	1.97E−01	195537.39	3
	SaSMO	7.69E−02	9.57E−01	180945.2	63
	MSMO	3.57E−02	1.85E−01	188332.61	15
	PSO	3.20E−02	9.26E−01	42144.5	100
	DE	4.05E−02	9.22E−01	18000	100
	GSA	5.82E−02	8.00E−01	200000	0
	SFLA	1.47E−01	3.60E−01	167215.3	23

(*continued*)

Table 2. (*continued*)

TP	Algo	ME	SD	AFE	SR
f_9	SMOEL	0.00E+00	0.00E+00	5560.83	100
	SMO	9.95E−02	1.00E−02	13986.92	99
	PLSMO	0.00E+00	0.00E+00	17812.3	100
	LFSMO	2.18E−01	5.00E−02	23305.71	95
	SaSMO	0.00E+00	0.00E+00	22143.97	100
	MSMO	9.95E−02	1.00E−02	21184.41	99
	PSO	0.00E+00	0.00E+00	38897	100
	DE	1.96E−01	4.00E−02	22845.5	96
	GSA	0.00E+00	0.00E+00	11583.33	100
	SFLA	0.00E+00	0.00E+00	9004.93	100
f_{10}	SMOEL	1.29E−06	8.25E−06	6297.39	100
	SMO	1.03E−02	1.05E−03	19015.94	99
	PLSMO	2.03E−02	4.16E−03	25242.39	96
	LFSMO	3.17E−02	8.31E−03	28448.49	93
	SaSMO	1.54E−06	8.21E−06	39119.96	100
	MSMO	1.45E−02	2.09E−03	20695.69	98
	PSO	1.03E−02	1.05E−03	36135	99
	DE	8.91E−07	9.01E−06	19779	100
	GSA	8.82E−07	8.81E−06	90630	100
	SFLA	3.15E+00	4.85E+00	194013.27	3
f_{11}	SMOEL	1.19E−06	8.34E−06	6809.22	100
	SMO	1.54E−03	2.29E−04	17375.14	98
	PLSMO	1.87E−03	3.38E−04	27828.94	97
	LFSMO	1.87E−03	3.38E−04	20472.56	97
	SaSMO	2.02E−06	7.74E−06	44866.95	100
	MSMO	1.53E−03	2.28E−04	19148.28	98
	PSO	3.44E−03	1.22E−03	54985	89
	DE	2.15E−03	4.48E−04	27755.5	96
	GSA	6.13E−07	9.00E−06	95498.33	100
	SFLA	1.79E−02	3.32E−03	20893.87	97
f_{12}	SMOEL	6.46E−06	5.61E−06	23985.06	89
	SMO	6.70E−06	5.83E−06	25103.06	88
	PLSMO	7.18E−06	6.48E−06	36953.89	82
	LFSMO	6.69E−06	5.82E−06	14844.79	93
	SaSMO	6.69E−06	6.19E−06	24108.53	89
	MSMO	7.29E−06	6.69E−06	29024.18	86
	PSO	3.52E−06	6.12E−06	26572.5	88
	DE	7.46E−06	6.50E−06	35696.5	83
	GSA	3.29E−05	4.93E−05	37113.33	100
	SFLA	0.00E+00	0.00E+00	200000	0

(*continued*)

Table 2. (*continued*)

TP	Algo	ME	SD	AFE	SR
f_{13}	SMOEL	2.94E−14	4.74E−14	4185.72	100
	SMO	2.76E−14	4.56E−14	12240.36	100
	PLSMO	2.85E−14	4.77E−14	12395.83	100
	LFSMO	4.80E−14	4.88E−14	97658.37	52
	SaSMO	2.75E−14	4.21E−14	42216.27	100
	MSMO	3.18E−14	4.94E−14	23063.92	100
	PSO	2.93E−14	5.24E−14	9702.5	100
	DE	2.70E−14	4.55E−14	4810	100
	GSA	1.16E−05	1.17E−05	49801.67	100
	SFLA	0.00E+00	0.00E+00	200000	0
f_{14}	SMOEL	1.21E−16	8.30E−16	20635.56	100
	SMO	8.52E−17	8.91E−16	34288.65	100
	PLSMO	8.78E−17	9.03E−16	35662.74	100
	LFSMO	5.73E−06	5.12E−06	2504.88	100
	SaSMO	6.28E−17	9.43E−16	155466.96	100
	MSMO	8.27E−17	8.97E−16	33913.44	100
	PSO	6.30E−17	9.37E−16	105573.5	100
	DE	8.29E−17	8.97E−16	59413.5	100
	GSA	1.34E−12	1.34E−11	200000	0
	SFLA	4.86E−17	9.30E−16	37419.8	100

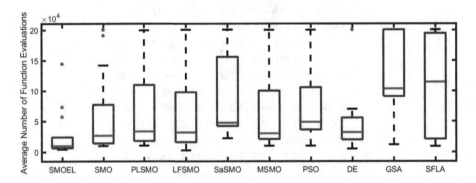

Fig. 1. Boxplots charts for average number of function evaluation

The consequences of the Mann-Whitney U rank sum test for mean function evaluations at $\alpha = 0.05$ (100 simulations) is shown in Table 4. Furthermore, for the conditions where *SMOEL* is performed better than other algorithms, '+' sign is used otherwise referred by '−' sign. As all shown in Table 4, which contains 120 '+' signs out of 126 comparisons. Thus, it can be inferred that the outcomes of *SMOEL* are cost-effective than *SMO, PLSMO, LFSMO, SaSMO, MSMO, PSO, DE, GSA*, and *SFLA* over considered test problems.

Table 3. Comparison of the basic $SMO, PLSMO, LFSMO, SaSMO, MSMO, PSO,$ DE, GSA and $SFLA$ based on Acceleration Rate (AR) of $SMOEL$

Test problems	SMO	PLSMO	LFSMO	SaSMO	MSMO	PSO	DE	GSA	SFLA
f_1	1.82	1.76	2.12	5.96	1.69	5.08	2.99	12.69	1.86
f_2	6.36	6.16	7.09	7.49	8.26	9.37	4.58	16.50	16.50
f_3	1.38	1.38	1.38	1.34	1.38	1.38	1.38	1.38	1.33
f_4	2.05	2.29	2.56	7.89	2.26	5.59	3.16	11.80	4.50
f_5	8.37	15.98	12.35	7.25	8.20	9.37	5.44	16.18	28.21
f_6	1.78	1.86	2.24	7.84	1.78	5.19	3.16	16.73	1.93
f_7	1.93	1.65	2.34	2.72	1.74	2.67	0.95	2.72	0.63
f_8	3.33	3.45	3.42	3.16	3.29	0.74	0.31	3.50	2.92
f_9	2.52	3.20	4.19	3.98	3.81	6.99	4.11	2.08	1.62
f_{10}	3.02	4.01	4.52	6.21	3.29	5.74	3.14	14.39	30.81
f_{11}	2.55	4.09	3.01	6.59	2.81	8.08	4.08	14.02	3.07
f_{12}	1.05	1.54	0.62	1.01	1.21	1.11	1.49	1.55	8.34
f_{13}	2.92	2.96	23.33	10.09	5.51	2.32	1.15	11.90	47.78
f_{14}	1.66	1.73	0.12	7.53	1.64	5.12	2.88	9.69	1.81

Table 4. Depending upon the mean function evaluations and the Mann-Whitney U rank sum test, comparison is done by taking $\alpha = 0.05$. at noteworthy level ('+' shows $SMOEL$ is consequently better, '−' shows $SMOEL$ is not better and '=' if no significant difference)

Test problems	SMOEL vs SMO	SMOEL vs PLSMO	SMOEL vs LFSMO	SMOEL vs SaSMO	SMOEL vs MSMO	SMOEL vs PSO	SMOEL vs DE	SMOEL vs GSA	SMOEL vs SFLA
f_1	+	+	+	+	+	+	+	+	+
f_2	+	+	+	+	+	+	+	+	+
f_3	+	+	+	+	+	+	+	+	+
f_4	+	+	+	+	+	+	+	+	+
f_5	+	+	+	+	+	+	+	+	+
f_6	+	+	+	+	+	+	+	+	+
f_7	+	+	+	+	+	+	−	+	−
f_8	+	+	+	+	+	−	−	+	+
f_9	+	+	+	+	+	+	+	+	+
f_{10}	+	+	+	+	+	+	+	+	+
f_{11}	+	+	+	+	+	+	+	+	+
f_{12}	+	+	−	+	+	+	+	+	+
f_{13}	+	+	+	+	+	+	+	+	+
f_{14}	+	+	−	+	+	+	+	+	+

5   Conclusion

This paper introduces an efficient variant of Spider Monkey Optimization (SMO) algorithm, namely SMO with Enhanced Learning $(SMOEL)$. In the proposed SMOEL, the position update procedure of local leader phase is altered by incorporating the fitness based weighted factor and global leader inspiration phenomenon. To validate the authenticity of the proposed SMOEL, it is applied on 14 complex optimization problems. This intended strategy is experimentally evaluated through several statistical test while comparing with the existing SMO and popular state of art algorithms. In future, the modified variant may be applied to resolve some real-world optimization problems.

References

1. Agarwal, N., Jain, S.C.: Fast convergent spider monkey optimization algorithm. In: Deep, K., et al. (eds.) Proceedings of Sixth International Conference on Soft Computing for Problem Solving. AISC, vol. 546, pp. 42–51. Springer, Singapore (2017). https://doi.org/10.1007/978-981-10-3322-3_5
2. Ali, M.M., Khompatraporn, C., Zabinsky, Z.B.: A numerical evaluation of several stochastic algorithms on selected continuous global optimization test problems. J. Glob. Optim. **31**(4), 635–672 (2005)
3. Bansal, J.C., Sharma, H., Jadon, S.S., Clerc, M.: Spider monkey optimization algorithm for numerical optimization. Memet. Comput. **6**(1), 31–47 (2014)
4. Eusuff, M., Lansey, K., Pasha, F.: Shuffled frog-leaping algorithm: a memetic meta-heuristic for discrete optimization. Eng. Optim. **38**(2), 129–154 (2006)
5. Hazrati, G., Sharma, H., Sharma, N., Bansal, J.C.: Modified spider monkey optimization. In: International Workshop on Computational Intelligence (IWCI), pp. 209–214. IEEE (2016)
6. Karaboga, D., Akay, B.: A comparative study of artificial Bee colony algorithm. Appl. Math. Comput. **214**(1), 108–132 (2009)
7. Kennedy, J.: Particle swarm optimization. In: Gass, S.I., Fu, M.C. (eds.) Encyclopedia of machine learning, pp. 760–766. Springer, Heidelberg (2011). https://doi.org/10.1007/978-1-4419-1153-7
8. Kumar, S., Kumari, R., Sharma, V.K.: Fitness based position update in spider monkey optimization algorithm. Procedia Comput. Sci. **62**, 442–449 (2015)
9. Passino, K.M.: Biomimicry of bacterial foraging for distributed optimization and control. IEEE Control Syst. **22**(3), 52–67 (2002)
10. Rashedi, E., Nezamabadi-Pour, H., Saryazdi, S.: GSA: a gravitational search algorithm. Inf. Sci. **179**(13), 2232–2248 (2009)
11. Sharma, A., Sharma, H., Bhargava, A., Sharma, N.: Optimal design of PIDA controller for induction motor using spider monkey optimization algorithm. Int. J. Metaheuristics **5**(3–4), 278–290 (2016)
12. Sharma, A., Sharma, H., Bhargava, A., Sharma, N.: Power law-based local search in spider monkey optimisation for lower order system modelling. Int. J. Syst. Sci. 1–11 (2016)
13. Sharma, A., Sharma, H., Bhargava, A., Sharma, N.: Power law-based local search in spider monkey optimisation for lower order system modelling. Int. J. Syst. Sci. **48**(1), 150–160 (2017)
14. Sharma, A., Sharma, A., Panigrahi, B.K., Kiran, D., Kumar, R.: Ageist spider monkey optimization algorithm. Swarm Evol. Comput. **28**, 58–77 (2016)
15. Sharma, N., Sharma, H., Sharma, A., Bansal, J.C.: Modified artificial bee colony algorithm based on disruption operator. In: Pant, M., Deep, K., Bansal, J., Nagar, A., Das, K. (eds.) Proceedings of Fifth International Conference on Soft Computing for Problem Solving. AISC, vol. 437, pp. 889–900. Springer, Singapore (2016). https://doi.org/10.1007/978-981-10-0451-3_79

16. Storn, R., Price, K.: Differential evolution-a simple and efficient heuristic for global optimization over continuous spaces. J. Glob. Optim. **11**(4), 341–359 (1997)
17. Suganthan, P.N., Hansen, N., Liang, J.J., Deb, K., Chen, Y.P., Auger, A., Tiwari, S.: Problem definitions and evaluation criteria for the CEC 2005: special session on real-parameter optimization. In: CEC 2005 (2005)

Performance Evaluation of Wavelet Based Image Compression for Wireless Multimedia Sensor Network

Addisalem Genta[(⊠)] and D. K. Lobiyal

School of Computer and System Sciences, Jawaharlal Nehru University,
New Delhi 110067, India
addisalemgenta@yahoo.com, lobiyal@gmail.com

Abstract. The advancement in the development of sensor nodes interms of acquiring multimedia data has fostered the applicability of Wireless Multimedia Sensor Network (WMSN) into various domains like surveillance and area monitoring. The energy consumption of such network is much higher than the conventional WSN due to the introduction of multimedia data to the network. Thus image compression, as energy optimized multimedia data processing and transmission technique, is critical required to prolong the life time of the network. In this paper, we evaluated the performance of three image compression algorithms (SPIHT, EZW, and WDR) with wavelet transforms (Haar, Daubechies, and biorthogonal) using three standard images. The compression techniques performance is measured by CR, PSNR, and MSE. The experiment is carried out in MATLAB. The experimental results i.e., visual and quantitative, show the supremacy of SPIHT algorithm over the rest of compression techniques explained.

Keywords: Image compression · Wavelet transforms · WMSN
PSNR · MSE · CR

1 Introduction

Wireless Multimedia Sensor Networks (WMSNs) consists of tiny embedded image and video motes capable of acquiring, compressing and transmitting multimedia information from the deployed area of interest to the sink node. Its main potential application areas include transportation and agriculture, biological and chemical detection, traffic surveillance, military, health care, security, monitoring, and plant monitoring. Unlike the classical wireless sensor network (WSN), WMSN experiences more challenges mainly due to their resource constraints on energy, bandwidth and memory [1] (Fig. 1).

Most of WMSNs make use of image in their applications. In fact, high resolution images usually occupy much memory space in the sensor node which rapidly drains the energy stored in their battery while transmitting to the sink. It is here that the role of image compression comes into picture since it can highly minimize the amount of the data either stored or transmitted. Compressing the volume of information transmitted over the network can enormously lowers the energy consumption of the nodes in particular and maximizes the life time of the network in general. Thus, it is imperative

© Springer Nature Singapore Pte Ltd. 2018
M. Singh et al. (Eds.): ICACDS 2018, CCIS 906, pp. 402–412, 2018.
https://doi.org/10.1007/978-981-13-1813-9_40

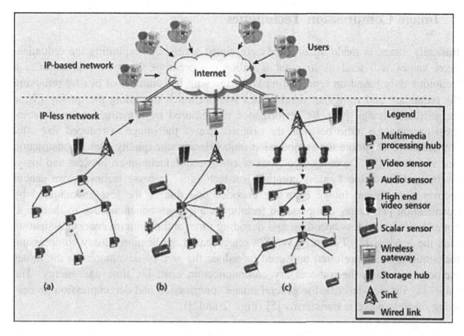

Fig. 1. WMSN architecture [12]

that image compression is an evident solution for efficient utilization of the finite energy resource of the wireless sensor network [2].

1.1 Motivation and Justification

The type of transform techniques employed for the compression algorithm can make a significant difference in the network performance. Wavelet transform is powerful and much superior than other transform techniques due to its multi-resolution analysis (MRA) and the transform operation is also done on the whole image than sub-images at a time which will eliminates the issue of 'blocking artifact'. For image compression, 2D DWT analysis will be used since images are 2D signals [3]. In this paper, we used wavelet transform (Haar, Daubechies and biorthogonal) coupled with encoding methods (EZW, SPIHT and WDR). We compared their performance using three different standard test images to identify the best compression technique for WMSN. The performance of the proposed techniques were measured by PSNR, MSE and CR [1, 4].

The rest of the paper is organized as follows. Basics of image compression are briefly presented in Sect. 2. In Sect. 3, wavelet transform is explained briefly. Section 4 describes the performance metrics used in analyzing image compression techniques. The result of the experiment conducted and the performance analysis of the algorithms is discussed in Sect. 5. Finally, conclusion is discussed in Sect. 6.

2   Image Compression Techniques

Basically image is made up of highly correlated pixels and exploiting the redundant pixel values will lead us to what is called compression. Image compression is a technique duly based on representing an image with less number of bits by removing the redundant and irrelevant pixel values without much degrading the quality of the reconstructed image [11]. Its performance is measured by a metric known us compression ratio, i.e. ratio between the original size of the image to reduced size after compression. The more the compression ratio is less image quality after reconstruction and vice versa [6]. There are two types of compression techniques, lossless and lossy.

In contrast to the lossless compression technique, in lossy technique we cannot recover the original image from the encoded one due to the loss encountered by quantization [7]. Lossy compression techniques are more beneficial due to their high compression ratio, less encoding and decoding time, and minimum energy dissipation than the lossless [2]. For most WMSN image based applications, lossy compression technique is more preferred and used to reduce the size of data stored in the motes memory and save the unnecessary communication cost, i.e. time and energy. The following Figures describe the general image compression and decompression process using discrete wavelet transforms [5] (Figs. 2 and 3).

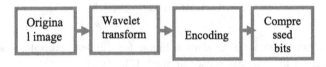

Fig. 2. Wavelet based image compression system

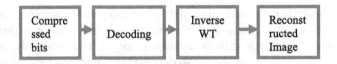

Fig. 3. Wavelet based image reconstruction system

In our study we employed the lossy and transform based image compression techniques SPIHT, EZW and WDR which are recent algorithms and have the highest perceptual quality and lowest errors per compression rate so far reported. Next we will briefly describe the compression techniques in detail.

2.1   EZW

EZW is an effective scheme for encoding compressed image bits according to their importance. This scheme results in embedded coding and progressive transmission where the encoder and decoder can cease the bit sending and receiving process at any point where the minimum quality is achieved [8].

EZW encoding

Step1: Initialization: Initialize the threshold value T as in the equation below.

$$T = 2^{\lfloor \log_2 |max(C_{i,j})| \rfloor} \tag{1}$$

where $C_{i,j}$ is the value of wavelet coefficient at location (i,j).

Step2: Significance Pass
- Identify the significant wavelet coefficient, $C_{i,j}$ by comparing its magnitude with threshold value, T.
- If $C_{i,j}$ is greater than T, then $C_{i,j}$ is significant.
- Output a symbol

Step3: Refinement Pass
- send one more bit of $C_{i,j}$'s binary representation

Step4: Quantization: Reduce the threshold value, T_n by half and go back to significance pass step if more iteration is needed, i.e, $T_n = T_{n-1}/2$.

In EZW, the scanning order is in such a way that children are scanned after their parents.

2.2 SPIHT

Set Partitioning In Hierarchical Tree (SPIHT) is an efficient coding mechanism for power constrained networks like WMSN. It achieves lower power consumption, higher compression ratio, less computational complexity, and less complex implementation [9].

- For every pass in the encoding process, all wavelet coefficients are encoded and transmitted as bit stream provided that their magnitudes should be greater than the threshold T as in Eq. 1.
- The significance test in every single iteration is made by using the equation below.

$$\text{Significance of}(C(i,j)) = \begin{cases} 1, & \max|C(i,j)| \geq T \\ 0, & \text{otherwise} \end{cases} \tag{2}$$

- It makes use of three lists for the encoding of the wavelet coefficients.

  (i)   LSP contains significant coefficients $C_{i,j}$ in every pass
  (ii) LIP contains insignificant coefficients $C_{i,j}$
  (iii) LIS is a set which contains coordinates of D(i, j) and L(i, j), where D(i, j) denotes set of all offspring's coordinates of the wavelet coefficient at position (i j), and L(i, j) = D(i, j) − O(i, j), where O(i, j) is set of $C_{i,j}$'s offspring coordinate.

The algorithm performs the encoding process in four steps.

SPIHT encoding
Step1: Initialization:
- ✓ computes the initial threshold, T_0 as in (1)
- ✓ set LSP =∅,
- ✓ add all the roots to LIP and
- ✓ add D(i,j)'s coordinate to LIS which is the descendant of the root

Step2: Sorting pass: In this step after performing the significance test on LIP and LIS, those coefficients which are found to be significant will shift to LSP and the remaining will move either to LIS or LIP.

Step3: Refinement pass: In this step the encoder outputs the MSB of the significant coefficients in LSP

Step4: Quantization update: In this pass, n is decremented by 1 and the steps (2) – (4) are repeated until n= 0 where $n = \lfloor log_2 |max(C_{i,j})| \rfloor$.

2.3   WDR

WDR is one of the wavelet based image compression techniques. In this method, the image will undergo bit-plane based WDR encoding after performing a wavelet transform [10].

WDR encoding
Step1: Initialization: Assign a zigzag scan order from higher to lower level sub-bands.
- ✓ Apply *row-based scanning* for wavelet coefficients in horizontal sub-bands; *column based scanning* for vertical sub bands, *zigzag scanning* for low-pass sub-bands.

During the scanning order, choose T_0 i.e. an initial threshold such that all the wavelet transform coefficients fulfil the two conditions below.
- ✓ all coefficients $|w_m|$ must not exceed T_0 and
- ✓ at least one coefficient value $|w_m|$ should exceed $T_0/2$

Step 2: Updating the threshold: Let $T_k = T_{k-1}/2$.

Step 3: Significance passes:
- • Identify the significant coefficient which is greater than or equal to the threshold value, T
- • The indexes values of the significant coefficients will be are encoded using the difference reduction method which basically comprises of a binary encoding from the index of the last to the current significant value.
- • The output from this step will be the signs of significant values with sequences of bits which describe its accurate location.

Step 4: Refinement passes: Using bit-plane quantization procedure generates the refined bits which are a better approximation of an exact transform coefficient value.

Step 5: Repeat steps (2) through (4) until the required number of bit is reached.

In the next section, we will briefly explain the various types of wavelet family used in digital image compression.

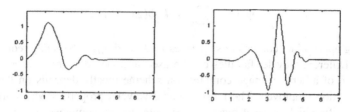

Fig. 4. Scaling, phi and wavelet function, psi

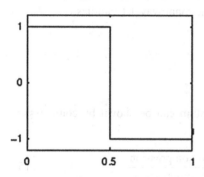

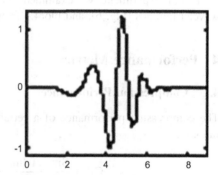

Fig. 5. Haar wavelet   **Fig. 6.** Db5 wavelet

3 Wavelet Transform

Image which undergoes a wavelet transform (WT) can be represented as a sum of series of functions called wavelets with various scales and locations [8]. And the proportion of the values of the wavelet transformed coefficients which are zero, or near zero, are many so that it helps in achieving high compression rate. As depicted in Fig. 4 the process of wavelet image decomposition consists of two functions, i.e. scaling function which represents low frequencies (approximation) and wavelet function which represents the detailed parts or the high frequency components of an image.

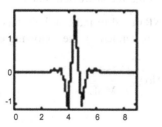

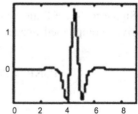

Fig. 7. Bior4.4 wavelet

The equation for the above two waveforms are shown in (3) and (4).

$$\Phi(x) = \sum_k a_L(k)\Phi(2x - k) \tag{3}$$

$$\psi(x) = \sum_k a_H(k)\Phi(2x - k) \tag{4}$$

Finding appropriate coefficient sequences $a_L(k)$ and $a_H(k)$ basically requires some effort [8]. Different wavelet families can be used in image compression process. The performance of a certain image compression scheme mostly depends on the type of wavelet function employed. The most essential wavelet properties which are mainly used to identify which wavelet function best suites to any compression are symmetry, compact support, degree of smoothness, orthogonality and regularity [9].

In our experiment, we examined Haar wavelet (Fig. 5), db-5 from daubechies wavelet families (Fig. 6), and bior4.4 from biorthogonal wavelet families (Fig. 7).

4 Performance Metrics

4.1 Compression Performance

The compression performance of a certain algorithm can be shown by compression ratio.

$$CR = \frac{\text{Size of Image before compression}}{\text{Size of image after compression}} \tag{5}$$

4.2 Perceptual Quality

To indicate the perception level of a reconstructed image, the following two metrics are used.

(a) The Mean Square Error (MSE) indicates the amount of error that existed between the uncompressed and reconstructed image.

$$MSE = \frac{1}{MN} \sum_{Y=1}^{M} \sum_{X=1}^{N} [I(X, Y) - I'(X', Y')]^2 \tag{6}$$

If MSE value is lower, then the error in the reconstructed image is also less.

(b) The Peak Signal to Noise Ratio (PSNR) used to indicate how much is the peak error in a given compressed image. It is defined by the following equation.

$$PSNR = 20 \log_{10} \frac{255}{\sqrt{MSE}} \tag{7}$$

If a certain compression technique comes with higher PSNR value, then the reconstructed image will have better quality. PSNR values between 30 and 50 db show better quality but if it goes beyond 40 db then it will be difficult to separate the original with the compressed one.

5   Result and Discussion

5.1   Experimental Results

The experiments were carried out in MATLAB-2016a on three standard grey scale images to compare the compression techniques described above. The test images are downloaded from *Public-Domain Test Images for Homework and Projects*. Five-level wavelet decomposition is performed and then simulation was carried out using SPIHT, EZW, and WDR coders (Figs. 8, 9, 10 and 11).

Fig. 8. Original test images

Fig. 9. EZW with Haar

Fig. 10. SPIHT with bior4.4

Fig. 11. WDR with db5

5.2   Performance Analysis

The results of the algorithms under investigation are compared in Figs. 12, 13 and 14. SPIHT algorithm has higher MSE than EZW and WDR with all the three wavelets and higher compression ratio. When we see the result of PSNR, EZW has higher PSNR values using all the three wavelets.

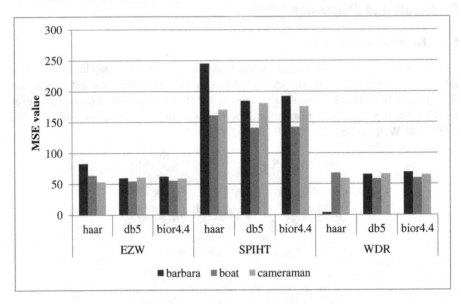

Fig. 12. Comparison of EZW, SPIHT and WDR with different wavelet codecs and images using MSE

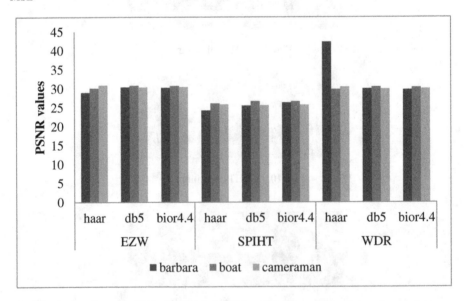

Fig. 13. Comparison of EZW, SPIHT and WDR with different Wavelet codecs and images using PSNR

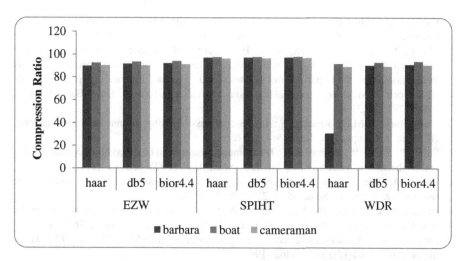

Fig. 14. Comparison of EZW, SPIHT and WDR with different wavelet codecs and images using Compression ratio

6 Conclusion

In this paper, the experimental results were analysed for the wavelet-based image compression techniques EZW, SPIHT and WDR. The effects of the wavelet functions Haar, db5 and bior4.4 were also examined to see which performed well in the compression process. All compression techniques were successfully tested with the three images. Compression ratio (CR), PSNR, and MSE values were calculated for the three techniques to identify the best performer in each metric. According to the experimental finding, Daubechies algorithm is more efficient for MSE with EZW and WDR while it achieves better compression ratio. It also shows that the MSE values from the reconstructed images by using SPIHT technique are higher than EZW and WDR. When MSE value is higher it means the reconstructed image's quality is poor. However, in various WMSN based applications like habitat monitoring where less quality of image is not big issue, SPIHT conserves energy of the overall network.

Finally, SPIHT algorithm performs well in resource constrained systems like WMSN since it helps to reduce the amount of energy wasted during transmission and computation due to its high compression result and its low computational complexity. In future, it is possible to come up with different methodological ways like changing the wavelet families, threshold values and scale parameters to further investigate and obtain the better outcome.

References

1. Ang, L., Seng, K.P., Chew, L.W, Yeong, L.S, Chia, W.C.: Wireless Multimedia Sensor Networks on Reconfigurable Hardwares, XXI 283, p. 73. Springer, Heidelberg (2013). https://doi.org/10.1007/978-3-642-38203-1

2. Eldin, H.Z., Elhosseini, M.A., Ali, H.A.: Image compression algorithms in wireless multimedia sensor networks: a survey. Ain Shams Eng. J. 6(2), 481–490 (2015)
3. Ma, T., Michael, H., Peng, D., Sharif, H.: A survey of energy-efficient compression and communication techniques for multimedia in resource constrained systems. Faculty Publications from the Department of Electrical and Computer Engineering, p. 293 (2013)
4. Al-Shereefi, N.M.: Image compression using wavelet transform. J. Univ. Babylon 21(5), 1784–1793 (2013)
5. Chowdhury, M.M.H., Khatun, A.: Image compression using discrete wavelet transform. IJCSI Int. J. Comput. Sci. Issues 9(4) (2012)
6. Singh, P., Singh, P., Sharma, R.K.: JPEG image compression based on biorthogonal, coiflets and daubechies wavelet families. Int. J. Comput. Appl. (0975–8887) 13(1) (2011)
7. Zabala, A., Pons, X.: Impact of lossy compression on mapping crop areas from remote sensing. Int. J. Remote Sens. 34(8), 2796–2813 (2013)
8. Mammeri, A., Hadjou, B., Khoumsi, A.: A survey of image compression algorithms for visual sensor networks. Int. Sch. Res. Netw. ISRN Sens. Netw. Article ID 760320 (2012)
9. Shapiro, J.M.: Embedded image coding using zero trees of wavelet coefficients. IEEE Trans. Signal Process. 41(12), 3445–3462 (1993)
10. Jai, A., Potnis, A.: Wavelet based video compression using STW, 3D-SPIHT and ASWDR techniques: a comparative study. Int. J. Adv. Eng. Technol. 3(2), 224–234 (2012)
11. Gupta, D., Choubey, S.: Discrete wavelet transform for image processing. Int. J. Emerg. Technol. Adv. Eng. 4(3), 598–602 (2015)
12. Bavarva, A.A., Jani, P.: Introduction to wireless multimedia sensor network. Electronics For You (2015)

NavIC Relative Positioning with Smoothing Filter and Comparison with Standalone NavIC

Ashish K. Shukla[1]($\boxtimes$), Pooja K. Thakkar[2], and Saurabh Bhalla[1]

[1] Space Applications Centre, ISRO, Ahmedabad, India
ashishs@sac.isro.gov.in
[2] C.S. Patel Institute of Technology, Changa, India

Abstract. Centimeter level positioning accuracy can be achieved from GNSS receivers using carrier phase based differential positioning technique. However, even in the absence of absolute carrier phase measurements, cm-level horizontal and vertical positioning accuracy can be achieved in differential mode using code phase based measurements (Pseudoranges) and delta Pseudorange measurements. Therefore, in this paper, a variant of Hatch Filter is proposed on single differenced Pseudorange and delta-Pseudorange measurements. Estimation of rover position in real time mode was done by transmitting the corrections from NavIC base receiver to rover receiver and analysis was done for 13 consecutive days at SAC, Ahmedabad. The baseline considered for analysis was 9.69 m with rover receiver in static condition. Proposed method gives consistent results with horizontal position accuracy of 49.5 cm and vertical position accuracy of 95.5 cm with atleast 50% improved standard deviation in comparison to standalone NavIC.

Keywords: NavIC · Differential positioning · Hatch filter · SVD

1 Introduction

India has its own regional satellite navigation system priory named as IRNSS (Indian Regional Navigational Satellite System). Indian Space Research Organization (ISRO) is developing this satellite system. After the successful launch of last satellite in the constellation in April 2016, IRNSS was renamed as NAVIC (Navigation with Indian Constellation). The requirement of NavIC is to develop a navigation system which works independently and may provide position, velocity and time services over the Indian region and beyond [4].

NavIC satellites transmit dual frequency signals on L5 (1176.45 MHz) and S (2492.028 MHz) band and is a promising system for its all-time and all weather coverage all over India [1]. It covers India and a region extending 1,500 km around it, with plans for further extension. The system at present consists of a constellation of seven satellites. NavIC receivers provide code and carrier-phase measurements using which position of a user can be obtained using appropriate navigation algorithms [5]. Generally, a user receiver computes its position in standalone mode using code phase or pseudorange measurements [4]. However, due to residual errors in pseudorange such

© Springer Nature Singapore Pte Ltd. 2018
M. Singh et al. (Eds.): ICACDS 2018, CCIS 906, pp. 413–422, 2018.
https://doi.org/10.1007/978-981-13-1813-9_41

as ephemeris and clock error, ionospheric errors, tropospheric errors, code noise and multipath, 5–10 m position accuracy can be achieved.

A more elegant and popular way to further reduce the residual errors is differential positioning method as shown in Fig. 1. The basic idea behind the Differential Positioning using IRNSS is to take advantage of the fact that the errors at two receivers due to satellite clock, ephemeris, and atmospheric propagation are similar if the receivers are separated by a short distance [16]. This technique works with atleast two receivers, one receiver designated as base or reference receiver and other one designated as rover or user receiver.

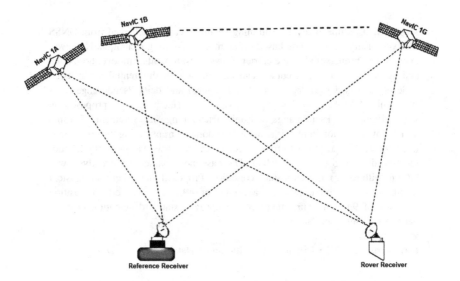

Fig. 1. Geometry of the differential positioning system

Position of base receiver is very accurately (mm level) known and rover receiver may be a fixed (static) or moving [9]. The distance between the base and rover receiver is known as the baseline. Under the assumption that both reference and rover receivers must see same set of satellite at their respective locations, common errors such as ephemeris and clock, ionosphere and troposphere gets cancelled out after differencing the data twice (be-tween receivers and between the satellites).

This method is applicable for short baseline and is able to provide cm-level accuracy of rover receiver using very precise carrier phase measurements. The positioning accuracy majorly depends on the baseline, the distance between the reference and rover receiver. In case of short baseline, ionosphere and tropospheric errors would be small in comparison with receiver noise and multipath. If the ionosphere is not active, then 100 km baseline may be qualified as a short baseline. However, if ionosphere is active, then even 20 km baseline may not be a short baseline.

However, in the absence of absolute carrier phase measurements, absolute pseudorange measurements and relative delta-pseudorange measurements can be used to smooth the noisy pseudorange measurements to obtain a more accurate and precise user position [2].

As we know that code (or pseudorange) measurements are unambiguous in nature but noisy whereas carrier-phase measurements are smooth in nature but ambiguous. Typical Measurement accuracy of code phase measurements is around 0.5 m whereas for carrier phase measurements it is 0.025 cycles (5 mm). Hence Combining carrier-phase measurements with raw code phase measurements, advantage of the precision of carrier phase measurements can be incorporated in code phase measurements to make them very accurate. This technique is known as carrier-based code smoothing and was first proposed by Ron Hatch in 1982 [13]. Using such combination effect of code noise and multipath in raw code phase based pseudo-ranges may be reduced up to a significant level. Therefore, carrier smoothed code (CSC) algorithm actually acts as a low pass filter or smoother that filters out the high frequency con-tent of the code phase measurements. This filtering leads to the improved user position accuracy and precision.

1.1   Mathematical Model of Code and Carrier Phase Measurements

Conventional stand-alone NavIC receivers mostly depend on code measurements, referred to as pseudo-ranges, to derive a positioning solution. Precise estimation of the pseudo-range from a satellite to the receiver is crucial for a NavIC receiver. The distance (r) is computed by measuring the propagation time required for a satellite generated ranging code to transit from the satellite to the user receiver antenna [17]. The receiver has to estimate exactly when the start of a frame arrives at the receiver. If the satellite clock and the receiver clock were perfectly synchronized, the correlation process would yield the true propagation time. By multiplying this propagation time, Δt by the speed of light, the true (i.e. geometric) satellite-to-user distance can be computed.

However, the satellite and receiver clocks are generally not synchronized. Therefore, the ranges measured by the receiver are corrupted and thus are called pseudo-ranges [12]. A mathematical model describing code and carrier-phase measurements (in units of meters) is as follows [11]:

$$\rho(t) = r(t) + c[\delta t_u(t) - \delta t^s(t - \tau)] + I(t) + T(t) + \varepsilon_\rho(t) \tag{1}$$

$$\Phi(t) = r(t) + c[\delta t_u(t) - \delta t^s(t - \tau)] - I(t) + T(t) + \lambda N + \varepsilon_\Phi(t) \tag{2}$$

Here, ρ is pseudo-range, δt_u is the receiver clock bias, δt^s is the bias in the satellite clock, I is the ionospheric delay in case of Eq. (1) and in carrier phase it is advancement as shown in Eq. (2), T is the tropospheric delay, λ is the carrier wavelength, N is the integer ambiguity term in carrier phase measurements and ε_ρ and ε_Φ are terms used to denote un-modeled effects, modeling errors and measurement errors in code and carrier phase measurements respectively. Code and carrier phase measurements can be combined to take advantage of both the measurements to work in an effective manner [14, 15].

1.2   Carrier-Smoothed Code Measurements: Basic Filter Description

Hatch Filter, a smoothing algorithm developed by Ron Hatch is used to smooth the code based pseudo-range measurements using accumulated delta-range measurements [10]. An efficient implementation of the Hatch filter is a recursive filter of length 'M' that only needs the smoothed pseudo-ranges from the previous epoch and the current epoch pseudo-range and time differenced delta-ranges [8]. The recursive filter is defined as,

$$\bar{\rho}(t_i) = \frac{1}{M}\rho(t_i) + \frac{(M-1)}{M}[\bar{\rho}(t_{i-1}) + (\Delta\Phi(t_i) - \Delta\Phi(t_{i-1}))] \tag{3}$$

$$\bar{\rho}(t_1) = \rho(t_1) \tag{4}$$

Here, $\Delta\Phi$ is Delta-Range (DR) measurements. Pseudo-range and DR measurements have been obtained from in-house developed NavIC receiver and are used for the present analysis.

The filter ascertains more weight to very precise carrier phase measurements than the code phase measurements. One should be careful enough to choose a suitable filter length for smoothing the code phase measurements. This filter assumes that for sufficiently manageable filter length, such as 100 s which is used here, code-carrier divergence due to the ionosphere is negligible, however, this effect may vary depending upon user location [7]. Since, the ionosphere varies with time so it introduces a bias in the single frequency smoothed code measurements due to the fact that the ionosphere introduces equal and opposite delays in code and carrier phase measurements when signal propagates through it, which is known as code-carrier divergence.

It should be noted here that different filter lengths will have different impact on smoothing process. For example, if filter length is more say 900 s, it will remove noise more efficiently due to the multipath but may introduce larger code-carrier divergence, whereas, if filter length is less say 30 s, it will be less effective in filtering the noise due to multipath in comparison to the 900 s filter but will introduce less or negligible code-carrier divergence. Therefore, depending upon the application, length of the filter must be chosen suitably in order to optimize effect of both the phenomenon: code-carrier divergence due to the ionosphere and multipath effect [3, 6].

2   Proposed Filter Description

The code phase measurements from NavIC receivers are used in differential mode (between reference and rover receivers) for the proposed algorithm. Single Difference is obtained by taking difference between the pseudo ranges of reference and rover receiver for kth satellite at same epoch. Hence the satellite clock and ephemeris errors are removed as they are common for both the reference and rover. Ionospheric and tropospheric errors are also removed for short baselines.

Same way single difference between the Delta-ranges has been taken. This gives an extra advantage in terms of removal of code carrier divergence as well which is a problem in applying Hatch Filter on raw code and carrier measurements for single frequency users. The resulting equation between code phase measurements and delta-ranges will be,

$$\rho_{ur}^{k} = \rho_{u}^{k} - \rho_{r}^{k} = r_{ur}^{k} + c * \delta t_{ur} + \varepsilon_{\rho,ur}^{k} \tag{5}$$

$$\Delta\Phi_{ur}^{k} = \Delta\Phi_{u}^{k} - \Delta\Phi_{r}^{k} \tag{6}$$

Hatch filter has been applied for single differenced pseudo ranges as mentioned above using single differenced code and carrier measurements. The equations for Single Differenced Hatch Filter, an efficient implementation of Basic Hatch Filter, will be,

$$\overline{\rho_{ur}^{k}}(t_i) = \frac{1}{M}\rho_{ur}^{k}(t_i) + \frac{(M-1)}{M}\left[\overline{\rho_{ur}^{k}}(t_{i-1}) + \Delta\Phi_{ur}^{k}\right] \tag{7}$$

$$\overline{\rho_{ur}^{k}}(t_1) = \rho_{ur}^{k}(t_1) \tag{8}$$

Similar procedure was done for satellite 'l' to get another set of smooth single differences. Between-satellite double difference measurements were derived from smoothed single differences for kth and lth satellites. Relative receiver clock bias will be removed after double difference. Equations for the double differences are given as,

$$\rho_{ur}^{kl} = \overline{\rho_{ur}^{k}} - \overline{\rho_{ur}^{l}} = r_{ur}^{kl} + \varepsilon \tag{9}$$

Flowchart in Fig. 2 shows the whole algorithmic procedure for the implementation of the methodology where it shows the step by step procedure for achieving the cm level accuracy using smoothing filter with differential positioning. This algorithmic procedure was used in the software implementation process to implement the proposed algorithm.

3   Software Implementation

Software implementation is a process of writing the source code, but in a broader sense, it includes all that is involved between the conception of the algorithm to the final working of the code, sometimes in a planned and structured process. For the testing purpose first the simulations were done in matlab and then The C code was developed for proposed algorithm for precise positioning and was optimized to process the data to make pseudo ranges smooth using delta-ranges for getting better position accuracy. C code for Singular Value Decomposition (SVD) was implemented to calculate inverse of the matrix. SVD can calculate inverse of any singular matrix with any dimensions, not necessarily square matrix, very efficiently. Because it's better performance and faster execution C language was chosen for coding. End to end software with GUI was made using C# language.

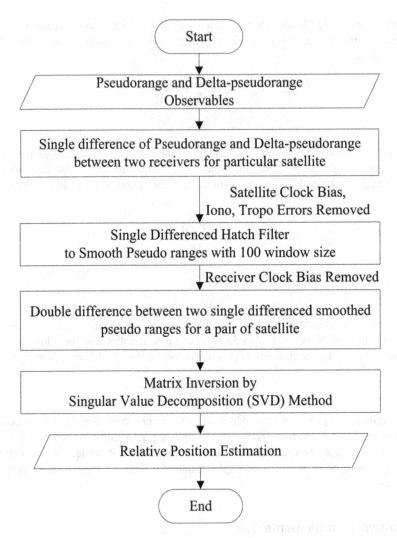

Fig. 2. Flow chart of the methodology.

4   Data Processing and Results

Data processing for the proposed approach was done for Live data of 24 h with 1 s time interval on 23rd January 2018 and results were collected for the same. Only single frequency pseudorange measurements and delta Pseudoranges on L5 (1176.45 MHz) frequency were used for the analysis as a cost effective solution which also suits well for short baselines.

Validation of the results was done by comparing the obtained position vector magnitude with accurately known position vector (accurate up to mm-level) between reference and rover stations. Table 1 shows the true Earth Centered Earth Fixed (ECEF) of reference and rover receiver positions in meters.

Table 1. True ECEF positions for reference and rover receivers

	X (m)	Y (m)	Z (m)
Reference receiver	1764534.623	5601756.403	2479140.498
Rover receiver	1764541.021	5601751.848	2479146.176

The horizontal, vertical and RMS 3D position errors in absolute position of the rover for 9.69 m baseline with smoothing filter on single differenced measurements were observed as 49.57, 95.52 and 1.07 m. Figure 3 shows the Scatter Plot of calculated rover positions using proposed filter with reference to original position of rover receiver. In Fig. 3, Horizontal axis represents Longitude, whereas Latitude is shown by vertical axis. It is observed from the figure that the estimated rover positions are scattered almost uniformly around the true rover position with standard deviation in cm level.

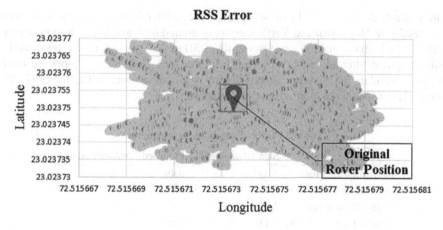

Fig. 3. Scatter Plot of RSS Error by Code Phase Differential Algorithm with smoothed pseudo ranges.

A comparison of rover position RSS errors was done between standalone NavIC and differential mode NavIC with smoothing. RSS position errors were estimated using raw code phase measurements in standalone iterative mode and single differenced carrier smoothed code pseudo ranges in differential mode as shown in Fig. 4. In Fig. 4, Horizontal axis represents Time epochs in seconds, whereas RSS error in position (in meters) is shown by vertical axis.

It can be observed from the figure that with standalone NavIC, RSS errors are very noisy due to larger code noise and multipath components in pseudo ranges. Standalone NavIC shows Horizontal and Vertical errors of around 1.44 and 3.32 m respectively

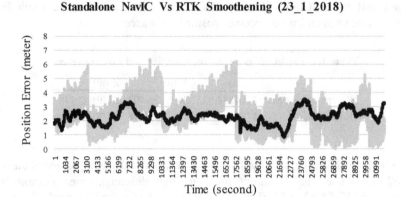

Fig. 4. RSS Error of Standalone NavIC with Iterative Algorithm vs. Code Phase Differential with smoothing on single differenced measurements.

with standard deviation of 1.11 m. Whereas proposed filter derived RSS errors are very smoothed with Horizontal and Vertical errors of around 49.5 and 95.5 cm respectively with standard deviation of 58 cm. Overall RMS-3D error is also improved significantly using proposed filter ass can be observed from the Table 2. Therefore, proposed filter can be a candidate for more precise positioning requirements such as landing of UAVs where very stringent position accuracy is required.

Table 2. Error statistics of position error

	Standalone NavIC	Proposed filter with NavIC
Horizontal error (m)	1.44	0.49
Vertical error (m)	3.32	0.95
RMS 3D error (m)	3.62	1.07
Standard deviation (m)	1.11	0.58

5   Conclusion

A smoothening filter algorithm in differential mode on single differenced pseudorange and delta-range NavIC measurements was implemented in real time. Advantage of this filter over basic hatch filter is that code-carrier divergence is minimized due to elimination of common errors with single differenced pseudoranges and delta pseudoranges. Proposed Algorithm was tested for a baseline of 9.69 m at Space Applications Center, ISRO, Ahmedabad. A comparison of performance was done between standalone NavIC and single differenced smoothing filter based on obtained RSS errors. It is found from the results that proposed filter provides cm-level horizontal and vertical position accuracy and standard deviation in real time as given in Table 2. Appropriateness of the proposed filter has to be assessed in future for longer baselines.

Acknowledgments. Authors are highly grateful to Shri Tapan Misra, Director, Space Applications Centre, Ahmedabad for his continuous support and guidance. Authors also express their sincere gratitude to Associate Director Shri D K Das and support of Group Director SNGG, Shri S N Satasia, Division Head, SNTD, Ms Saumi De and HOD of CE department of CSPIT, Changa, Dr. Amit Ganatra. Authors also acknowledge SNTD, SNGG and SNAA engineers who have provided their support in this activity.

References

1. Shukla, A., Thakkar, P., Ganatra, A.: NavIC carrier-phase based relative positioning using L5 single frequency measurements. In: 4th International Conference on Science, Technology and Management (ICSTM), vol. 4, no. 11, pp. 134–139. International Journal of Engineering Technology Science and Research (IJETSR), (2017)
2. Mark, P.: Can You List All the Properties of the Carrier-Smoothing Filter? Inside GNSS, pp. 32–37 (2015)
3. Zhang, X., Huang, P.: Optimal Hatch filter with an adaptive smoothing time based on SBAS. In: International Conference on Soft Computing in Information Communication Technology (SCICT), pp. 34–38 (2014)
4. Saini, M., Gupta, U.: Indian GPS satellite navigation system: an overview. Int. J. Enhanc. Res. Manag. Comput. Appl. **3**, 32–37 (2014)
5. Saikiran, B., Vikram, V.: IRNSS architecture and applications. KIET Int. J. Commun. Electron. **1**, 21–27 (2013)
6. Zhu, Z.: C/A code cross correlation error with carrier smoothing—the choice of time constant: 30 s vs. 100 s. In: International Technical Meeting of the Institute of Navigation, pp. 464–472 (2011)
7. Gunther, C., Henkel, P.: Reduced-noise ionosphere-free carrier smoothed code. IEEE Trans. Aerosp. Electron. Syst. **46**(1), 323–334 (2010)
8. Byungwoon, P., Changdon, K.: Optimal Hatch filter with a flexible smoothing window width. In: ION GNSS 18th International Technical Meeting of the Satellite Division, Long Beach, CA, pp. 592–602 (2005)
9. Thipparthi, S.: Improving Positional Accuracy Using Carrier Smoothing Techniques in Inexpensive GPS Receivers (2004)
10. Misra, P., Enge, P.: Gloabal Positioning System, Signals, Measurements and Performance, 2nd edn. Ganga-Jamuna Press, Lincoln (2001)
11. Tsui, J.: Fundamentals of Global Positioning System Receivers—A Software Approach. Wiley, Hoboken (2000)
12. Kaplan, E.D.: Understanding GPS: Principles and Applications. Artech House, Norwood (1996)
13. Hatch, R.: The Synergism of GPS code and carrier measurements. In: 3rd International Symposium on Satellite Doppler Positioning, DMA, Las Cruces, pp. 1213–1232 (1982)
14. Meyerhoff, S., Evans E.: Demonstration of the combined use of GPS pseudorange and Doppler measurements for improved dynamic positioning. In: Proceedings of 4th International Geodetic Symposium Satellite Positioning, Austin, TX, vol. 2, pp. 1397–1409, April–May 1986

15. Hofmann-Wellenhof, B., Lichtenegger, H., Collins, J.: Global Positioning System Theory and Practice. Springer, Viena (2001). https://doi.org/10.1007/978-3-7091-6199-9
16. Kang, C.: A differential dynamic positioning algorithm based on GPS/Beidou. In: Procedia Engineering, pp. 590–598 (2016)
17. Chang, X.-W., Paige, C.C., Yin, L.: Code and Carrier Based Short Baseline GPS Positioning: Computational Aspects

Extended Kalman Filter Based User Position Algorithm for Terrestrial Navigation System

Ashish K. Shukla[1]([⊠]), Komal G. Bansal[2], and Saurabh Bhalla[1]

[1] Space Applications Centre, ISRO, Ahmedabad, India
ashishs@sac.isro.gov.in
[2] C.S. Patel Institute of Technology, Changa, India

Abstract. An Extended Kalman Filter (EKF) based exact user position algorithm for the terrestrial navigation system is developed. The major advantage of such algorithm is that it does not require any initial guess since terrestrial systems are very sensitive to the initial guess for convergence to the true solution. Furthermore, a comparison of the iterative exact algorithm without EKF and with EKF was done on the data collected from an experiment with four terrestrial transmitters. It is observed that after applying EKF, the algorithm outperforms iterative exact solution in terms of accuracy and precision both. Horizontal, vertical position accuracies and RSS errors obtained using iterative exact solution are 9.09, 24.23 and 25.88 m whereas EKF based solution are 66 cm, 1.5 m and 1.69 m respectively with standard deviation (SD) of position errors significantly reduced to 33 cm.

Keywords: Terrestrial navigation · Ground-based transmitter
Iterative algorithm · SVD · Extended Kalman Filter

1 Introduction

Global Navigation Satellite Systems (GNSS) are satellite-based navigation systems which are being utilized worldwide for various services requiring position, navigation and time (PNT). Yet, there is a requirement for alternate positioning systems which are ground-based and that can work efficiently in limited coverage areas such as indoors or urban canyons and other areas where GNSS signals cannot reach [1].

Terrestrial navigation systems are being developed as an alternative to Global Navigation Satellite Systems (GNSS). Such Alternate Position Navigation and Timing Systems (APNT) are capable of providing standalone navigation services independent of satellite systems. Using signals received from ground-based transmitters, a user receiver can estimate its position co-ordinates very accurately. Terrestrial navigation systems are basically ground-based systems which transmit the signals from a very short range; therefore, user position algorithms used in GNSS systems which are based on linearization of pseudorange equations are no longer applicable.

The idea of ground-based navigation system seems promising in providing better position accuracy than GNSS due to many reasons. In terrestrial systems, the complete system is deployed on the ground itself and hence the signals do not travel through earth's dense and complex atmosphere which comprises of the ionosphere, one of the

M. Singh et al. (Eds.): ICACDS 2018, CCIS 906, pp. 423–432, 2018.
https://doi.org/10.1007/978-981-13-1813-9_42

major sources of error in GNSS for single frequency users [7]. In addition to that, mm level accurate positions of the transmitters can be known a priori by surveying or other methods and thus there will be no orbit/ephemeris errors, unlike GNSS where the position of satellites keeps on changing due to the relative motions of the earth and the satellites.

There are certain applications where even more availability, reliability, integrity and accuracy are needed such as projects wherein life-safety is crucially important. For such applications, a highly secure and precise navigation system is required. Following are few applications of the terrestrial navigation system,

- Testing the accuracy of unmanned vehicles,
- Mining in GNSS shadow regions,
- Accurate and safe landing of aerial vehicles,
- A backup navigation system in crucial times of war,
- Increasing the integrity of harbor loading/unloading applications etc. [6].

Such systems can be developed by using code phase as well as carrier-phase measurements depending upon the desired accuracy and robustness of the application. Carrier phase can be used in scenarios where centimeter level of accuracy is desired but it is less robust than code phase as handling the large integer ambiguities in real time is quite difficult [2, 4].

GNSS works on the iterative algorithm that works on the Taylor series linearization of the pseudo-ranges which is nothing but the approximate distance measured by the receiver to the satellites based on the time of arrival concept. This algorithm takes the center of earth as an initial guess and iteratively converge it to the actual user position by eliminating the errors in the initial value. For GNSS, this algorithm converges to the true position merely in 3 to 4 iterations and works efficiently [11]. The disadvantages of the standard iterative algorithm are:

- Requires initial guess.
- Sensitive to Initial Position Error.
- Doesn't guarantee convergence.
- May not handle non-linearity fine.
- Computational cost is high.

In, terrestrial navigation systems, the dimensions of the ranges between the transmitter and the user receiver is too small when compared to the satellite-based navigation systems which results into strong non-linearity for the algorithm [3] as shown in Fig. 1. Thus even a minor order of error in the pseudoranges can degrade the accuracy of the navigation solutions significantly [5, 8]. Due to this difference, the iterative algorithm fails to work for terrestrial systems and is vulnerable to converge to the accurate position.

In the case where transmitters are closely located, there will be significantly more error in the directional cosine matrix due to initial position error than for distant GNSS satellite in GEO/MEO orbits. A couple of meters on account of transmitters will cause a much more error in the network than a huge number of kilometers for GNSS. The conventional positioning method is critical in relation to an initial position error because linearization of nonlinear pseudo range equations is required in the true

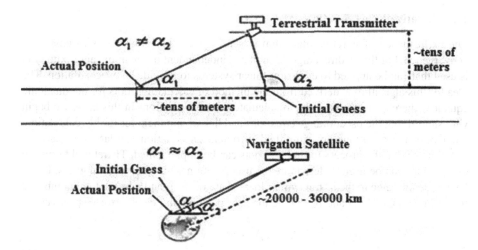

Fig. 1. Comparison of the change in linearity for GNSS and terrestrial navigation systems.

position vicinity. Thus, the simplest way to handle such problem is to start from a position which is priory known, but this is not always possible for real-time applications.

Dilution of Precision is another factor affecting the accuracy of navigation system. DOP is the overall impact of geometric distribution of the multiple transmitters with respect to the position of the receiver plays a crucial role over the position error. It may be noted that smaller the DOP, better will be the accuracy of the estimated user position. In case of satellite-based navigation systems, there is no equilibrium between the horizontal DOP (HDOP) and the vertical DOP (VDOP). When the overall distribution is even around the receiver in the horizontal plane, it leads to a good Horizontal DOP, however, this distribution cannot be so good in the vertical plane since the satellites which are in LOS are visible. Thus, the VDOP is usually poor than the HDOP. On the contrary, for ground-based navigation systems, things are completely different and the positions for the transmitters can be decided in a way that is in the favor of better results.

2 Methodology

In order to solve this problem of non-linearization and develop a new terrestrial navigation algorithm, direct solutions can be applied for closed regions which are not dependent on the initial guess. In [10, 13, 14] various closed form algorithms are explained. But the solutions of direct algorithms are directly vulnerable to the noises present in the input parameters. To overcome this issue, noise reduction filters such as Kalman Filter, Particle Filter, etc. can be helpful. Here, the authors have used Extended Kalman Filter for smoothing the input parameters in form of pseudoranges since it works well for non-linear systems.

2.1   Iterative Exact Solution

The performance of iterative algorithm is sensitive on the initial guess to ensure its convergence. For this, a direct algorithm that is independent of the initial approximation is used that can be applied to even non-linear systems to provide an exact solution. The idea for this algorithm is derived from the method of calculating roots for the quadratic equation, thereby using the roots to calculate the user position. In this case, we begin with simplifying the pseudorange equations and linearizing them for further calculation. Afterward, the equations are simplified to obtain an equation similar to a quadratic equation, so that the process to find the roots can be implemented. Thereby, this system of equations can be used to determine the user position without any initial guess. Let ρ_i be the pseudorange to the ith transmitter located at (x_i, y_i, z_i) and n be the total number of transmitters. (x_u, y_u, z_u) and b_u denote the user position and clock error respectively.

$$(\rho_i - b_u)^2 = (x_i - x_u)^2 + (y_i - y_u)^2 + (z_i - z_u)^2$$
$$\vdots$$
$$(\rho_n - b_u)^2 = (x_n - x_u)^2 + (y_n - y_u)^2 + (z_n - z_u)^2$$

$$(1)$$

$$2\underbrace{\begin{bmatrix} x_i & y_i & z_i & \rho_i \\ \vdots & \vdots & \vdots & \vdots \\ x_n & y_n & z_n & \rho_n \end{bmatrix}}_{A} \underbrace{\begin{bmatrix} x_u \\ y_u \\ z_u \\ b_u \end{bmatrix}}_{X} = \underbrace{\begin{bmatrix} 1 \\ 1 \\ 1 \\ 1 \end{bmatrix}}_{1} \underbrace{(x_u^2 + y_u^2 + z_u^2 + b_u^2)}_{\|X\|^2} + \underbrace{\begin{bmatrix} (x_i^2 + y_i^2 + z_i^2) - \rho_i \\ \vdots \\ (x_n^2 + y_n^2 + z_n^2) - \rho_n \end{bmatrix}}_{B}$$

$$(2)$$

On simplifying the above system of equations, the user position can be obtained by,

$$X = A^{-1}1\|X\|^2 + A^{-1}B$$

$$(3)$$

Solving the above quadratic equation, the user position can be estimated using one of the real roots [12]. A novel approach was introduced in this paper where the pseudorange measurements are iteratively refined by correcting the clock bias generated in each iteration. A new user position is estimated following the same procedure until the current iteration clock bias exceeds the previous iteration clock bias. The performance of the algorithm mostly depends on the accuracy of pseudo range measurements, since it solves another minimization problem. Also this algorithm considerably solves the convergence problem.

2.2   Extended Kalman Filter (EKF) Approach

In order to further enhance the performance of the system, where the receiver and the transmitters are located in a close region, the Extended Kalman Filter (EKF) is applied to the final solutions obtained from the iterative exact solution using methodology described in the previous section. These non-linear methods are implemented to refine the pseudorange measurements of the user receiver. EKF is a widely-known approach used in navigation which utilizes the historical information of previous measurements so as to provide the potential of a higher performance if a proper user dynamic model is employed [3, 9, 11, 15]. Generally, EKF linearizes the measurement model with the help of the first order Taylor expansion to handle the non-linearity because of short user-to-transmitter distance [6]. But, the crucial problem of nonlinear filtering is parameter estimation since the system matrices are dependent on the unknown parameter explicitly. Following are the state vector and the state transition equations for the user system for EKF,

Prediction

$$P_{k_{predicted}} = \emptyset P_{k_{prev}} \emptyset^T + Q_k \tag{4}$$

$$X_{k_{predicted}} = \emptyset X_{k_{prev}} \tag{5}$$

Innovation

$$\widehat{Z_k} = h\left(X_{k_{predicted}}\right) \tag{6}$$

$$V_k = Z_k - \widehat{Z_k} \tag{7}$$

Gain

$$K_{gain} = P_{k_{predicted}} H_k^T \left(H_k P_{k_{predicted}} H_k^T + R\right)^{-1} \tag{8}$$

Update

$$X_{k_{current}} = X_{k_{predicted}} + K_{gain} V_k \tag{9}$$

$$P_{k_{current}} = \left(I - K_{gain} H_k\right) P_{k_{predicted}} \tag{10}$$

Where I: Identity matrix, $\emptyset$: State transition matrix, R: Measurement noise matrix, Q_k: Process noise matrix, V_k: Measurement residual, K_{gain}: Kalman gain matrix, $X_{k_{current}}$: Updated state vector, $P_{k_{current}}$: Updated covariance matrix, $X_{k_{predicted}}$: Projected state vector and $P_{k_{predicted}}$: Projected covariance matrix. The entire algorithm is stated below.

Step 1.   Input transmitter coordinates and pseudoranges.
Step 2.   Perform Exact Solution Algorithm.
Step 3.   if current iteration clock bias <previous iteration clock bias
                 repeat step 2.
            else
                 intermediate user position ← last iteration solution
Step 4.   Refine the pseudoranges with clock bias in intermediate user position.
Step 5.   Apply Extended Kalman Filter to obtain final user position $(x_w y_w z_u)$.

3   Software Implementation

The proposed algorithm was implemented in C with modules for the iterative exact solution, EKF and Singular Value Decomposition (SVD) to perform matrix inversion. SVD can calculate the inverse of any singular matrix with any dimensions, not necessarily square matrix, very efficiently. Because it's better performance and faster execution C language was chosen for coding.

4   Data Processing and Results

The proposed EKF based algorithm was tested on the live data collected for a period of around 1 h on 28th of December, 2017 in static mode. Position solutions were obtained using iterative exact solution and EKF at every one second interval. Matrix inversions were done using Singular Value Decomposition (SVD). Optimal EKF solution was obtained after performing 100 iterations. It should be noted that 100 iterations take the only fraction of second and will not pose any difficulty in real time implementation as well.

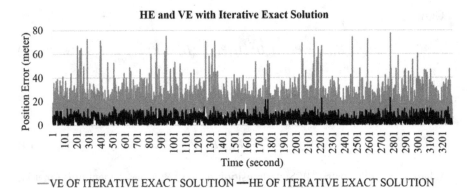

Fig. 2. Horizontal and vertical error of solutions obtained by iterative exact solution

The horizontal and vertical errors in the user positions derived every second from iterative exact solution are shown in Fig. 2. It can be seen that the algorithm is not that accurate in vertical plane and also the overall performance is quite noisy.

Horizontal and vertical errors in the user positions derived every second after applying Extended Kalman Filter to the solutions obtained from iterative exact solution are shown in Fig. 3. It can be seen that the results are improved drastically with RMS-3D error reduced from 25.89 to 1.69 m. The performance of the algorithm can be evaluated by comparing the errors in the horizontal and vertical plane of the solutions given by both the methods for every second. This comparison has been shown in Figs. 4 and 5 respectively.

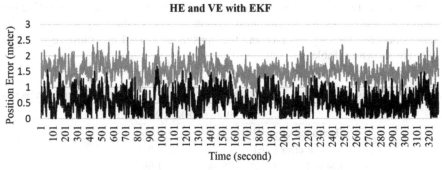

Fig. 3. Horizontal and vertical error after applying Extended Kalman Filter to the solutions of iterative exact solution

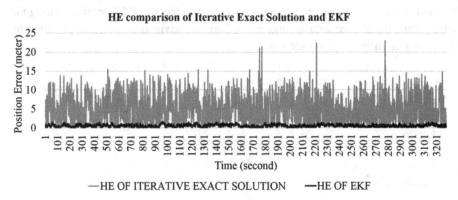

Fig. 4. Comparison between the horizontal errors of the solutions obtained by iterative exact solution and Extended Kalman Filter

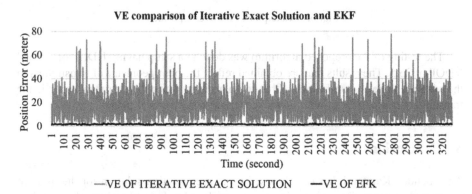

Fig. 5. Comparison between the vertical errors of the solutions obtained by iterative exact solution and Extended Kalman Filter

Based on the results from Figs. 4 and 5, it can be seen that on effectively tuning the Extended Kalman Filter for a non-linear system, it works efficiently for short pseudoranges between the user receiver and the transmitter located in a close region. The results are shown in Table 1.

Table 1. Comparison of errors before and after applying EKF to exact user solutions in meters

	Without EKF	With EKF
Horizontal error (HE)	9.09	0.66
Vertical error (VE)	24.23	1.55
RMS-3D	25.88	1.69
Standard deviation	16.86	0.33

A scatterplot of the entire receiver's position obtained at each instance on 28th of December, 2017 in static mode is shown in Fig. 6. The symbol '📍' denotes the actual location of the receiver which was measured using Septentrio RTK receiver during the setup, while the shaded area around the '📍' are the navigation solutions provided by the algorithm in live at each second.

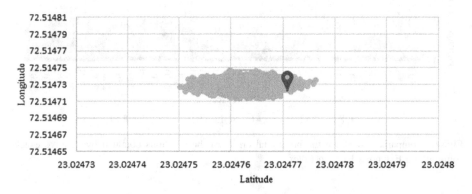

Fig. 6. Scatterplot of receiver's positions

The testing of the proposed algorithm was done in a setup having HDOP of 1.5 and VDOP of 23.5. The results that are obtained reflect the poor geometry of transmitters in the vertical plane. It can be noted that the algorithm can perform much better if the transmitters can be placed with better scattering in the vertical plane.

5 Conclusion

An Extended Kalman Filter (EKF) based exact user position solution for the users of the terrestrial navigation system is implemented which is independent of any initial guess. The overall performance of the algorithm is very high and it is observed that

EKF based solution outperforms iterative exact solution as shown in the Table 1. Currently, 4 states EKF for static positioning is implemented considering position and clock bias which can be further extended to 8 states to provide position, velocity, clock bias and clock drift. The major challenge lies in tuning the initial parameters in form of process and measurement noise for EKF which is very tedious and complex task. Also, a rigorous testing has to be performed in multiple environments to assure the correct tuning of the filter which is again very challenging task.

Acknowledgments. Authors are highly grateful to Mr. Tapan Misra, Director, Space Applications Centre, Ahmedabad for his support and guidance. Authors express their sincere gratitude to Associate Director Shri D K Das and support of Group Director SNGG, Shri S N Satasia and Division Head, SNTD, Ms Saumi De and HOD of CE Department of CSPIT (Changa), Dr. Amit Ganatra.

References

1. Shukla, A., Bansal, K., Ganatra, A.: Development of user position algorithm for terrestrial navigation system. In: 4th International Conference on Science, Technology and Management (ICSTM2017), vol. 4, no. 11, pp. 140–144. International Journal of Engineering Technology Science and Research (IJETSR) (2017)
2. Mazher, K., Tahir, M., Ali, K.: GNSS pseudorange smoothing: linear vs non-linear filtering paradigm. In: IEEE Aerospace Conference (2016)
3. Zhao, S., Yao, Z., Yin, J., Lu, M.: Application of extended and unscented kalman filtering for non-linear positioning in nearby region of navigation sources. In: Proceedings of the International Technical Meeting (ITM), 26–28 January, pp. 640–650. ION, Dana Point, California (2015)
4. Zhao, S., Cui, X., Guan, F.: A Kalman filter-based short baseline RTK algorithm for single-frequency combination of GPS and BDS. Sensors **14**, 15415–15433 (2014)
5. Wan, X., Zhan, X.: The research of indoor navigation system using pseudolites. In: Procedia Engineering, vol. 15, pp. 1446–1450. Elsevier (2011)
6. So, H., Lee, T., Jeon, S., Kim, C., Kee, C., Kim, T., Lee, S.: Implementation of a vector-based tracking loop receiver in a pseudolite navigation system. Sensors **10**, 6324–6346 (2010)
7. Pachter, J., Amt, J., Raquet, J.: Accurate positioning using a planar pseudolite array. IEEE, pp. 433–440 (2008)
8. Shockley, J., Raquet, J.: Estimation and mitigation of unmodeled errors for a pseudolite based reference system. In: 19th International Technical Meeting of the Satellite Division, 26–29 September, pp. 853–862. ION GNSS, Fort Worth (2006)
9. Bouska, T., Raquet, J., Maybeck, P.: The use of optimal smoothing and nonlinear filtering in pseudolite-based positioning systems. In: 59th Annual Meeting, 23–25 June, pp. 435–443. ION, Albuquerque (2003)
10. Sirola, N.: Closed-form algorithms in mobile positioning: myths and misconceptions. In: Positioning Navigation and Communication (WPNC) 7th Workshop, pp. 38–44 (2010)
11. Grewal, M., Weill, L., Andrews, A.: Global Positioning Systems, Inertial Navigation, and Integration. Wiley, New York (2001)
12. Bancroft, S.: An algebraic solution of the GPS equations. IEEE Trans. Aerosp. Electron. Syst. **21**(7), 56–59 (1986)

13. Sirola, N.: A versatile algorithm for local positioning in closed form. In: Proceedings of the 8th European Navigation Conference GNSS, 16–19 May, Rotterdam (2004)
14. Cheung, K., So, H., Chan, Y.: A constrained least squares approach to mobile positioning: algorithms and optimality. EURASIP J. Appl. Signal Process. **2006**, 1–23 (2006)
15. Ballet, R., Santos, D. A., and Zoran, S.: Position, velocity and heading estimation for unmanned aerial vehicles using camera and inertial sensors. In: Congresso Brasileiro de Engenharia Mecânica (CONEM) (2016)

Investigation of Iterative and Direct Strategies with Recurrent Neural Networks for Short-Term Traffic Flow Forecasting

Armando Fandango[1](✉) and Amita Kapoor[2]

[1] Institute for Simulation and Training, University of Central Florida,
Orlando, FL, USA
armando@ucf.edu
[2] Shaheed Rajguru College of Applied Sciences for Women,
University of Delhi, Delhi, India
dr.amita.kapoor@ieee.org

Abstract. For more than 40 years, various statistical time series forecasting, and machine learning methods have been applied to predict the short-term traffic flow. More recently, deep learning methods have emerged to show better results for short-term traffic flow prediction. For multi-step-ahead prediction, researchers have used iterative (also known as recursive) and direct (also known as independent) strategies with statistical methods for preparing input data, building models and creating forecasts. However, the iterative and direct strategies are not combined with the recurrent neural network architectures. Hence, we present the impact of these two strategies on accuracy of the Recurrent Neural Network models for short-term traffic flow forecasting.

Keywords: Short-term traffic flow forecasting · Recurrent neural networks
Long short-term memory networks · Gated recurrent unit networks

1 Introduction

The smart cities of modern nations rely on the smooth flow of transportation that depends on the predictions of the traffic flow patterns. Short-term traffic flow prediction enables the transportation officials to prevent traffic congestion, major accidents, reduce travel time, and assists in the planning and operations of traffic systems.

The traffic flow exhibits a high degree of uncertainty and stochasticity because of being influenced by various factors such as weather, special events, holidays, and placement of vacation, residential and commercial centers. On top of that, the traffic departments have access to large amounts of data from various sources such as traffic signals, cameras, sensors, IoT devices, connected vehicles, toll systems, social media, blogs, print and web news, and weather forecasts. Thus, the availability of large amounts of data and its influence on traffic flow, make the problem of short traffic flow prediction very complex in nature.

For more than 40 years, various statistical time series forecasting methods have been applied to predict the short-term traffic flow. Recently, deep learning based

M. Singh et al. (Eds.): ICACDS 2018, CCIS 906, pp. 433–441, 2018.
https://doi.org/10.1007/978-981-13-1813-9_43

methods, specifically Recurrent Neural Network (RNN) architectures have emerged to show better results for short-term traffic flow prediction [1–8]. While the above-mentioned research has reported that using RNN models improved predictions for short-term traffic flow, but the impact of combining iterative and direct strategies with the RNN model was not studied. On the other hand, the researchers have combined the direct and iterative strategies with other statistical methods to obtain better predictive model performance [9, 10].

Thus, in this paper, we present our investigation of the following question: Does combining the iterative or direct strategies with RNN models for short-term traffic flow prediction produce better accuracy as compared to not combining them? This paper extends our earlier work accepted for presentation in international conference on information system and data mining [11].

2   Methods

In this section we present the iterative and direct strategies for multi-step-ahead prediction and the recurrent neural network architectures that we implemented in our experiments.

2.1   Iterative or Recursive Strategy

In this strategy, a single model is trained to forecast one-step-ahead, formally depicted as follows:

$$x_{t+1} = f_\theta(\{x_t, \ldots, x_{t-w+1}; t \in \{w, \ldots, N-1\}\}; \theta) \qquad (1)$$

where:

- w is the window size, i.e. number of time steps to use as input for training the model.
- x is the traffic characteristic such as average speed, x_{t+1} is the value for next time step and $\{x_t, \ldots, x_{t-w+1}; t \in \{w, \ldots, N-1\}\}$ are the values for the previous w time steps.
- θ represents the set of parameters for the model.

The trained model f_θ is then used to predict the value at next time step $N+1$ and the predicted value is used as input to predict the value at next time step $N+2$ and so on until the values for the timesteps $N+H$ are predicted.

Algorithm for multi-step-ahead prediction with iterative or recursive strategy

Function: train $f_\theta(w)$

  For $t \in \{N,..., N + H - 1\}$

    Find θ such that

$$x_{t+1} = f_\theta\left(\{x_t,..., x_{t-w+1} \; ; t \in \{w,..., N-1\}\} \; ; \theta\right)$$

Function: predict(H,w)

  For $h \in \{1,..., H\}$

$$x_{N+h} = f_\theta\left(\{x_{N+h-1},..., x_{N+h-w}\}\right)$$

In the iterative strategy, if the window size is small as compared to the number of time steps to be forecasted then the future forecasts start having only forecasted values as input. Thus, the error in forecasts accumulates.

2.2 Direct or Independent Strategy

In this strategy, multiple models are trained to forecast one-step-ahead. One model is trained for each time step h in forecast horizon $\{1,..., H\}$, depicted as follows:

$$x_{t+h} = f_{h,\theta}(\{x_t,..., x_{t-w+1}; t \in \{w,..., N-1\}\}; \theta_h) \tag{2}$$

where:

- w is the window size, i.e. number of input time steps for training the model.
- x is the traffic characteristic such as average speed, x_{t+1} is the value for next time step and $\{x_t,..., x_{t-w+1} \; ; t \in \{w,..., N-1\}\}$ is the set of values for the previous w time steps.
- θ_h represents the set of parameters for the model at forecast horizon step h.

The trained models $f_{h,\theta}$ are then used to predict the values at time steps in forecast horizon $\{1,..., H\}$ with only the last w historical values as input.

Algorithm for multi-step-ahead prediction with direct or independent strategy

Function: train $f_{h,\theta}(w,h)$

  For $h \in \{1,..., H\}$

    Train $f_{h,\theta}$ such that

      For $t \in \{N,..., N + H - 1\}$

        Find θ such that

$$x_{t+h} = f_{h,\theta}\left(\{x_t,..., x_{t-w+1} \; ; t \in \{w,..., N-1\}\} \; ; \theta\right)$$

Function: predict(H,w)

  For $h \in \{1,..., H\}$

$$x_{N+h} = f_{h,\theta}\left(\{x_N,..., x_{N-w+1}\}\right)$$

2.3   Recurrent Neural Network Architectures

Recurrent Neural Network (RNN) architectures [12, 13] build on top of Feed Forward Neural Network (FFNN) by providing a mechanism for using the output from current state as input to the next state. This is different from the hidden layers in FFNN such that each state is a cell in the hidden layer to which it belongs. This kind of architecture suits well to time series datasets since in such datasets the inputs at next time step often depend on the previous time steps. Let us say we have data for ten time-steps, $x_t \in \{x_1, \ldots, x_{10}\}$. Here, each x_t is input to a cell in the first layer. In the RNN architecture, each cell also has an input h_{t-1} that is an output from the cell representing the previous time step. In the sections below, we describe the three kinds of RNN Architectures that we have implemented in our experiments.

2.4   Simple Recurrent Neural Network (SRNN)

An SRNN can be considered as a FFNN with loops as shown in Fig. 1.

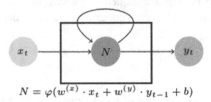

$$N = \varphi(w^{(x)} \cdot x_t + w^{(y)} \cdot y_{t-1} + b)$$

Fig. 1. Simple RNN

In Fig. 1, the x_t refers to the input, N refers to the RNN cell that produces output y_t and memory h_t. The memory becomes input for the next time step $t + 1$. SRNN cell N is formally depicted as follows:

$$N = \varphi(w^{(x)} \cdot x_t + w^{(y)} \cdot h_{t-1} + b) \tag{3}$$

Thus, one layer of an SRNN has several cells; each cell takes the value at time step t and the memory output from the previous step $t - 1$. SRNN can have multiple layers just like other neural network architectures. Each cell in the subsequent hidden layers takes two inputs: the memory output from the previous cell in the same layer and the output from the corresponding cell in the previous layer. In a way it is still a FFNN architecture with each layer feeding next layer, but with loops within the same layer. The RNN architecture suffers from vanishing and exploding gradients when more cells and layers are added to the model. The gradients become either too small that they become zero, or they become too large that they tend to approach ∞ (infinity). Hence, many variants of RNN have been proposed to handle the shortcomings of RNN architectures.

2.5   Long Short-Term Memory Network (LSTM)

LSTM network extends the RNN by adding long-term and short-term memories [14]. The LSTM cell (Fig. 2) takes three inputs: input x at time t, working memory h at time $t-1$, and long term memory c at time $t-1$. The output of an LSTM cell is long-term memory c and working memory h at time t. The gates of LSTM are listed below:

- Forget gate $f(\cdot) = \sigma(w^{(fx)} \cdot x_t + w^{(fh)} \cdot h_{t-1} + b^{(f)})$
- Input gate $i(\cdot) = \sigma(w^{(ix)} \cdot x_t + w^{(ih)} \cdot h_{t-1} + b^{(i)})$
- Candidate long term memory $\tilde{c}(\cdot) = tanh(w^{(\tilde{c}x)} \cdot x_t + w^{(\tilde{c}h)} \cdot h_{t-1} + b^{(\tilde{c})})$
- long term memory $c_t = c_{t-1} \times f(\cdot) + i(\cdot) \times \tilde{c}(\cdot)$
- Output gate $o(\cdot) = \sigma(w^{(ox)} \cdot x_t + w^{(oh)} \cdot h_{t-1} + b^{(o)})$
- new value of working memory $h_t = \varphi(c_t) \times o(\cdot)$

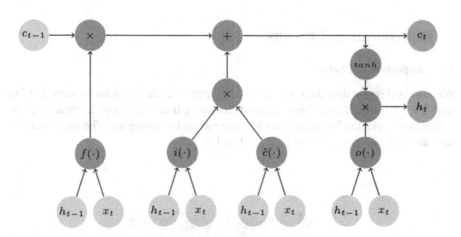

Fig. 2. Long Short-Term Memory (LSTM) cell

2.6   Gated Recurrent Unit Network (GRU)

GRU is a simplified architecture as compared to LSTM [15]. In GRU, fewer gates are used with only the concept of working memory h, thus making it computationally less expensive. The GRU cell has two inputs: input x at time t and memory h from time $t-1$ (Fig. 3). The gates of GRU are described below.

- Update gate $u(\cdot) = \sigma(w^{(ux)} \cdot x_t + w^{(uh)} \cdot h_{t-1} + b^{(u)})$
- Reset gate $r(\cdot) = \sigma(w^{(rx)} \cdot x_t + w^{(rh)} \cdot h_{t-1} + b^{(r)})$
- The candidate memory $\tilde{h}(\cdot) = tanh(w^{(\tilde{h}x)} \cdot x_t + w^{(\tilde{h}h)} \cdot (r_t \cdot h_{t-1}) + b^{(\tilde{h})})$
- The working memory for current time step $h_t = (u_t \cdot \tilde{h}_t) + ((1 - u_t) \cdot h_{t-1})$

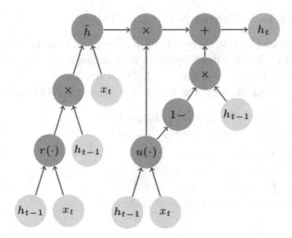

Fig. 3. Gated Recurrent Unit (GRU) cell.

3   Experiments and Results

3.1   Experimental Setup

We extracted traffic flow data consisting of average vehicle speed for January 2017 to June 2017 from California Department of Transportation. The 5-min interval data was split into five months for training set and one month for testing set. The data from two road segments is shown below in Figs. 4 and 5.

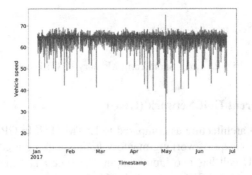

Fig. 4. Vehicle speed data from road segment 500010012.

The RNN, GRU and LSTM models were created using TensorFlow and Keras [16], the popular deep learning libraries from Google. A total of 16,000 combinations of hyper-parameters were tried to find the best hyper-parameters. The hyper-parameters values that we tried are listed in Table 1 below. The predictions were obtained with the iterative and direct strategies as well as without applying any strategy.

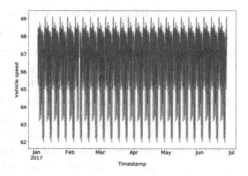

Fig. 5. Vehicle speed data from road segment 500010022.

Table 1. Hyper-parameter values

Hyper-parameters	Values
Number of layers	2, 6, 10
Number of cells	10, 20, 30, 40, 50
Number of epochs	10, 20
Batch size	1, 10
Dropout	0, 0.1, 0.5

3.2 Evaluation Metrics

We use the following metrics for evaluating the results by comparing the prediction error, i.e. the difference between the predicted value and actual value [17] of traffic speed.

- Mean Square Error: $MSE = \frac{1}{N} \sum_{t=1}^{N} (\widehat{y_t} - y_t)^2$

- Mean Absolute Error: $MAE = \frac{1}{N} \sum_{t=1}^{N} |\widehat{y_t} - y_t|$

- Mean Absolute Percentage Error: $MAPE = \frac{100}{N} \sum_{t=1}^{N} \left| \frac{\widehat{y_t} - y_t}{y_t} \right|$

- Symmetric MAPE: $SMAPE = \frac{100}{N} \sum_{t=1}^{N} \left| \frac{(\widehat{y_t} - y_t) \times 2}{\widehat{y_t} + y_t} \right|$

3.3 Results

We ran the experiment 10 times with each hyper-parameter combinations and averaged the results. Table 2 shows the results for two road segments.

For all the three architectures, the additional load of applying the strategies made the models slower by 1–20% at the time of training and 30–40% slower at the time of

Table 2. Evaluation metrics for different RNN architectures and strategies.

Highway segment	Neural network	Strategies	MSE	MAE	MAPE	SMAPE
s500010012	GRU	Iterative	0.0005	0.02	0.50	0.49
		Direct	0.049	0.19	4.85	5.0
		None	0.0003	0.016	0.41	0.41
	LSTM	Iterative	0.000002	0.004	0.09	0.09
		Direct	0.035	0.17	4.25	4.38
		None	0.001	0.03	0.75	0.75
	SRNN	Iterative	0.03	0.16	4.07	4.17
		Direct	0.0765	0.26	6.57	6.8
		None	0.01	0.08	1.95	1.98
s500010022	GRU	Iterative	0.00005	0.006	0.15	0.15
		Direct	0.042	0.187	4.68	4.8
		None	0.003	0.04	1.08	1.09
	LSTM	Iterative	0.000004	0.002	0.045	0.04
		Direct	0.029	0.156	3.9	4.03
		None	0.006	0.06	1.52	1.51
	SRNN	Iterative	0.017	0.12	2.97	2.92
		Direct	0.0749	0.248	6.2	6.45
		None	0.006	0.08	1.92	1.94

prediction, as compared to not having any strategy at all. The cost of additional time did not justify since the RNN models produced almost same or slightly better accuracy for all the four metrics without using the strategies. For LSTM, the error values were slightly lower with the iterative strategy, but this small benefit does not justify the cost of additional time. Direct strategy performed the worse by producing much larger MAPE errors.

Although the strategies performed better when combined with the traditional statistical models by other researchers, but since neural networks are 'end-to-end' models, hence the strategies did not add any advantages in terms of accuracy and instead added cost in terms of execution time and memory.

4   Conclusions and Future Work

In this paper, we presented our results from the investigation of implementing the iterative and direct strategies in the short-term traffic flow prediction with the recurrent neural network architectures. From our experiments we found that although the strategies benefit the traditional statistical models in some experiments done by other researchers, but for RNN based models the strategies did not add any advantages in terms of accuracy and instead added cost in terms of execution time and memory. The models for our experiments were built with SRNN, GRU and LSTM architecture and trained with 5 months of data from the California Transportation Department.

In the future we plan to continue investigating other strategies and extend our work by incorporating sequence to sequence networks. We also plan to extend our work by including more variables such as traffic density, lane type, flow direction and location of the transponder.

References

1. Koesdwiady, A., Soua, R., Karray, F.: Improving traffic flow prediction with weather information in connected cars: a deep learning approach. IEEE Trans. Veh. Technol. **65**, 9508–9517 (2016)
2. Polson, N.G., Sokolov, V.O.: Deep learning for short-term traffic flow prediction. Transp. Res. C Emerg. Technol. **79**, 1–17 (2017)
3. Siripanpornchana, C., Panichpapiboon, S., Chaovalit, P.: Travel-time prediction with deep learning. In: Proceedings of the IEE Region 10 Conference (TENCON), pp. 8–11. IEEE Press (2016)
4. Yang, H.-F., Dillon, T.S., Chen, Y.P.: Optimized structure of the traffic flow forecasting model with a deep learning approach. IEEE Trans. Neural Netw. Learn. Syst. **28**, 2371–2381 (2017)
5. Yi, H., Jung, H., Bae, S.: Deep neural networks for traffic flow prediction. In: IEEE International Conference on Big Data and Smart Computing, pp. 328–331. IEEE (2017)
6. Yu, B., Yin, H., Zhu, Z.: Spatio-temporal graph convolutional neural network: a deep learning framework for traffic forecasting. arXiv (2017)
7. Yuan, Z., Tu, C.: Short-term traffic flow forecasting based on feature selection with mutual information. AIP Conf. Proc. **1839**, 20179 (2017)
8. Zhou, T., Han, G., Xu, X., Lin, Z., Han, C., Huang, Y., Qin, J.: δ-agree AdaBoost stacked autoencoder for short-term traffic flow forecasting. Neurocomputing **247**, 31–38 (2017)
9. Taieb, S.B., Bontempi, G., Atiya, A.F., Sorjamaa, A.: A review and comparison of strategies for multi-step ahead time series forecasting based on the NN5 forecasting competition. Expert Syst. Appl. **39**, 7067–7083 (2012)
10. An, N.H., Anh, D.T.: Comparison of strategies for multi-step-ahead prediction of time series using neural network. In: Proceedings of the International Conference on Advanced Computing and Applications (ACOMP) 2015, pp. 142–149. IEEE Press (2015)
11. Fandango, A.: Towards investigation of iterative strategy for data mining of short-term traffic flow with recurrent neural networks. In: 2nd International Conference on Information System and Data Mining (2018, accepted for publication)
12. Lipton, Z.C., Berkowitz, J., Elkan, C.: A critical review of recurrent neural networks for sequence learning. arXiv (2015)
13. Elman, J.L.: Finding structure in time. Cogn. Sci. **14**, 179–211 (1990)
14. Hochreiter, S., Schmidhuber, J.: Long short-term memory. Neural Comput. **9**, 1735–1780 (1997)
15. Cho, K., van Merrienboer, B., Bahdanau, D., Bengio, Y.: On the properties of neural machine translation: encoder–decoder approaches. arXiv (2014)
16. Fandango, A.: Mastering TensorFlow 1.x. Packt Publishing, Birmingham (2018)
17. Barros, J., Araujo, M., Rossetti, R.J.F.: Short-term real-time traffic prediction methods: a survey. In: Proceedings of the International Conference on Models and Technologies for Intelligent Transportation Systems (MT-ITS), pp. 132–139. IEEE (2015)

Comparative Analysis of Pre- and Post-Classification Ensemble Methods for Android Malware Detection

Shikha Badhani[1(✉)] and Sunil K. Muttoo[2]

[1] Maitreyi College, University of Delhi, Delhi, India
sbadhani@maitreyi.du.ac.in
[2] Department of Computer Science, University of Delhi, Delhi, India
skmuttoo@cs.du.ac.in

Abstract. The influence of portable devices in our day-to-day activities is of a concern due to possibilities of a security breach. A large number of malwares are concealed inside Android apps which requires high-performance Android malware detection systems. To increase the performance, we have applied ensemble learning at feature selection level (pre-classification) and at prediction level (post-classification). The features extracted are the API classes and for generating the model, extreme learning machine (ELM) has been used. The filter feature selection methods employed are Chi-Square, OneR, and Relief. The experimental results on a corpus of 14762 Android apps show that ensemble learning is promising and results in high performance as compared to the individual classifier. We also present a comparison of the pre- and post-classification ensemble approaches for the Android malware detection problem.

Keywords: Android malware · Extreme learning machine · Static analysis
Feature selection · Ensemble

1 Introduction

Android has become the fastest-growing mobile OS. According to Web analytics firm StatCounter [1], in March 2017, Android dominated the worldwide OS internet usage market share with 37.93% shooting ahead of even Windows. The esteem of Android OS also reminds us of the influence of portable devices in our lives. These devices have become the storehouse of the details that we provide to the various apps that manage our day-to-day activities such as scheduling events, online shopping, chatting, etc. Virginia Tech researchers [2] have recently discovered that various apps which we use in our mobiles have been collaborating to trade information secretly. This may result in a security breach. Even the latest initiative for enhancing Android security, Google Play Protect [3], a new built-in antivirus program, failed in the Android antivirus tests conducted by independent German lab AV-TEST [4]. It detected only 65.8% of the latest malware and just 79.2% of month-old malware. Such weak detection rates themselves highlight the need for more robust Android malware detection tools. According to internal AV-TEST statistics [4], over 18 million malware

© Springer Nature Singapore Pte Ltd. 2018
M. Singh et al. (Eds.): ICACDS 2018, CCIS 906, pp. 442–453, 2018.
https://doi.org/10.1007/978-981-13-1813-9_44

samples are concealing in Android apps. Also, many third-party application stores provide more space for spreading malware.

The above-mentioned reasons were enough to motivate us to experiment and explore new methods for detecting Android malware. Most of the Android malware detection systems depend on three methods - static analysis, dynamic analysis, and their hybrid variants. Static analysis has an edge of over dynamic analysis because it is performed in a non-runtime environment and its ability to detect issues early before the app is executed. However, dynamic analysis may reveal the concerns that could not be detected during static analysis.

Various machine learning algorithms have been applied to detect Android malware using static features [5–7]. ELM has been explored in the past for Android malware detection [8–10]. However, in our study, we explore the effect of filter feature selection methods and their ensembles on the performance of ELM. Also, the features used in our study are API classes which differ from the ones used earlier (permissions, API calls, binder, memory, battery, CPU, network, Dalvik instructions) along with ELM.

The API classes as per Android API level 26 [11] are in thousands which constitute the features used in our study. It has been shown that insignificant features may be removed without affecting the performance of the neural network based Intrusion Detection Systems [12]. Thus, feature selection is an important step which not only eliminates useless features but also results in faster execution and simplification of the machine learning model [13]. Feature selection methods are categorized as filter methods, wrapper methods and embedded methods. We use the filter methods for selecting relevant features as they execute directly on the dataset and are not affected by the biases of any classifier. Also, they are fast as compared to other methods.

As compared to single machine learning model, combining the output of multiple prediction models known as ensemble learning, has been observed to achieve better performance [14]. Apart from classification, ensemble approach has also been applied to feature selection. In [15], five different filters were used to select a different subset of features which were used to train and test different classifiers and their outputs were combined using simple voting. In another study [16], three feature selection methods were combined based on union, intersection and multi-intersection techniques. In our work, we have compared the effect of performing ensemble at feature selection level and at prediction level. Our aim is to achieve better accuracy. We experiment with various filter feature selection methods and their ensembles and present a comparative study of their effect on the accuracy of ELM on a corpus of 14762 Android apps.

The rest of the paper is organized as follows. Section 2 describes filter feature selection methods. Section 3 introduces ELM. In Sect. 4, we present the research design. Section 5 presents the experimental results and analysis. Finally, we conclude in Sect. 6 along with possible future work.

2 Filter Feature Selection Methods

The essence of filter feature selection methods is that they rely on a statistical measure and use a feature ranking technique as the core criteria for feature selection by ordering. Filter methods are applied prior to the classification process to filter out less important features. The relevance of a feature is measured in terms of its usefulness in differentiating between classes. Then, a ranking is generated based on the relevance and subsets of features are selected according to a threshold value. Of the wide range of filter feature selection methods available, we use the following three methods which can be applied to categorical/binary data as the features extracted in our study are binary.

- Chi-Square [17] measures the extent of independence between a feature and a class and can be compared to the chi-square distribution with one degree of freedom to judge extremeness. The initial assumption is that the feature and class are independent of each other. A high score of chi-square signifies the dependence between feature and the class and thus, the relevance of the feature.
- OneR [18] builds one rule for each feature in the dataset i.e., it learns from a one-level decision tree and then ranks features based on the fact that features which result in more accurate trees are considered to be more relevant.
- Relief [19] algorithm works by repeated random sampling of an instance from the dataset, computing its nearest neighbor from the same class as well as from different class and then calculating the worth of a feature based on its ability to discriminate between instances from different classes.

3   Extreme Learning Machine

In this section, we describe the ELM concept. Feedforward neural networks have been used extensively in the past decade due to their capability of approximating complex nonlinear mappings directly from input samples and providing models for various artificial and natural events [20]. However, one of the major bottlenecks in using feedforward neural networks is their learning speed which is slower due to the slow gradient-based learning algorithms that are used to train neural networks and the iterative tuning required for all the parameters of the networks [21]. ELM [21, 22] was originally proposed for training single hidden layer feedforward neural networks (SLFNs). The core concept of ELM is: the hidden layers of SLFNs need not be tuned but can be randomly assigned independently and a simple generalized inverse operation of the hidden layer output matrix can be used to determine the output weights of the network [21]. Since there is no iterative tuning involved like in gradient descent based learning algorithms, ELM is fast and easy to implement. ELM also intends to reach smallest training error and smallest norm of output weights [21, 22]. Apart from the above advantages, studies have shown that it has less computational complexity, nominal optimization constraints, better scalability, and generalization performance.

Given N unique samples of input data, the SLFN with L hidden nodes (additive or RBF nodes) is represented as:

$$f_L(x) = \sum_{i=1}^{L} \beta_i G(c_i, a_i, x) \tag{1}$$

where (c_i, a_i) are the learning parameters of the ith hidden node, β_i is the weight vector linking i^{th} hidden node to the output node, $G(c_i, a_i, x)$ is the output of the ith hidden node w.r.t the input x.

The fact that standard SLFNs with L hidden nodes can approximate the N input samples $(x_j, t_j) \in R^n \times R^m$ with zero error implies that there exist β_i, c_i, and a_i such that

$$\sum_{i=1}^{L} \beta_i G(c_i, a_i, x) = t_j, \quad j = 1, 2, \ldots, N \tag{2}$$

The above equation can be compactly written as

$$H\beta = T \tag{3}$$

where,

$$H(c_1, \ldots c_L, a_1, \ldots a_L, x_1, \ldots x_N) = \begin{bmatrix} G(c_1, a_1, x_1) & \cdots & G(c_L, a_L, x_1) \\ \vdots & \ddots & \vdots \\ G(c_1, a_1, x_N) & \cdots & G(c_L, a_L, x_N) \end{bmatrix}_{N \times L}$$

$$\beta = \begin{bmatrix} \beta_1^T \\ \vdots \\ \beta_L^T \end{bmatrix}_{L \times m}, \quad T = \begin{bmatrix} t_1^T \\ \vdots \\ t_N^T \end{bmatrix}_{N \times m}.$$

β^T is the transpose of vector β. H is called as the hidden layer output matrix [23]. The ith row of H is the output vector of the hidden layer w.r.t input x_i and the jth column of H is the jth hidden node's output vector w.r.t inputs $x_1, x_2, \ldots, x_N$. Now the hidden node parameters c_i and a_i need not be tuned and may be assigned randomly. It has been proved in theory [22, 24, 25] that SLFNs with randomly chosen additive or RBF hidden nodes have the potential of universal approximation. Thus, independent of the training data, the hidden nodes can be generated randomly, i.e., for N unique samples of training data, randomly generated L ($\leq N$) hidden nodes, the output vector T and output matrix of the hidden layer H comprise a linear system and the output weights β are estimated as:

$$\hat{\beta} = H^+ T \tag{4}$$

where H^+ is the Moore-Penrose generalized inverse [26] of H. Thus, the output weights can be calculated in a single step without any iterative tuning of any control parameters.

The ELM algorithm can be summarized as follows [21]:

Given a training set $\{(x_i, t_i)\}_{i=1}^{N} \subset R^n \times R^m$, the hidden node output function $G(c_i, a_i, x)$ and L hidden nodes:

1. Randomly assign hidden node parameters (c_i, a_i), i = 1,2,......, L;
2. Calculate output weight vector β: $\beta = H^+T$.

4 Research Design

The research framework of this study is shown in Fig. 1. Our work uses static features (API classes). Three filter feature selection methods (Chi-Square, OneR, and Relief) are used to generate three subsets of features which were combined by taking the union of them for the simple reason of using the maximum possible relevant features and then classification is performed on this combined subset. This is referred to as pre-classification ensemble approach and the rationale behind this approach is to take advantage of the strengths of individual selectors and release the burden of deciding which feature selection would work for a domain [27]. In another experiment, the feature subsets generated by the three filter feature selection methods are used to train and test three classifiers whose outputs are aggregated using ensemble technique of majority vote which is referred to as the post-classification ensemble approach and the concept behind this approach is that combining multiple classifiers results in more robust solutions [28] and if the features selected by each feature selection methods are diverse, so will be their classifications and hence, the better the ensemble would be. In the majority voting, every classifier makes a prediction (votes) for each instance of the test set and the final prediction is the one that receives maximum votes. The classifier used in all experiments must be unique in order to make comparisons and we use the ELM classifier for the same. Ensemble learning has been used earlier for Android malware detection [6, 8, 29, 30] to improve the performance of the model since it is based on the concept of diversity and generalization. In our study, we compare the introduction of diversity at the feature selection level vs prediction level.

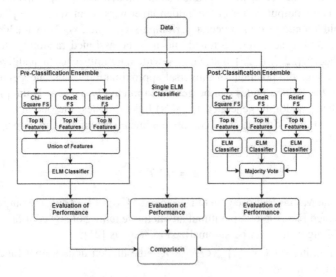

Fig. 1. Research framework

4.1   Dataset Preparation

Dataset is prepared using 7381 benign and 7381 malicious Android apps. The benign dataset is downloaded from Google play store [31] and the malicious dataset is constituted from samples collected from various sources (AndroTracker [32], Drebin database [33], Virus Total [34]). The dataset is partitioned into the training set (70%) and the test set (30%). To generalize the performance, 10-fold cross-validation was performed while generating classifier models in our experiment.

4.2   Feature Extraction

The Android API level 26 consists of 4140 API classes. Thus, we set the corresponding API class feature to 1 if an API belonging to that class is used in an app. For reverse engineering the Android app, Androguard tool [35] is used. Thus, a total of 4140 binary features are extracted.

4.3   Implementation Details

Firstly, features having zero variance are removed from the dataset as they contribute nothing to classification. After removal, we were left with 2392 features. Now, three filter feature selection methods (Chi-Square, OneR, and Relief) are applied on these 2392 features to generate three feature rankings. Most works in the previous research use several thresholds that hold different percentages of most relevant features [36]. However, the thresholds are dependent on the dataset being used. For our study, we use six different threshold values to reduce the dimension of data, including $\log_2(n)$ threshold, where n is the total number of features, following recommendations from literature to select $\log_2(n)$ metrics for software quality prediction [37]. The other five are the top 1%, 5%, 25%, 50%, and 75% of the most relevant features of the final ordered ranking obtained from each filter feature selection method. The classifier used in all the experiments is ELM.

In the pre-classification ensemble approach, we take union of the feature subsets for each of the six thresholds, generated by the three filter feature selection methods, which is then used for classification.

In the post-classification ensemble approach, each feature subset generated is used separately for classification thus resulting in three individual classifiers. Then, the output of each classifier is combined by using the majority vote.

R statistical software [38] is used to perform the experiments. For feature selection, we used the FSelector package [39] and for performing classification using ELM, we used the elmNN package [40].

4.4   Evaluation Measures

In this research, to assess the effectiveness of our proposed system, we analyzed the following measures: Accuracy (percentage of correctly identified applications); precision (percentage of actual malicious apps amongst the predicted malicious apps); recall (percentage of actual malicious apps predicted amongst the total malicious apps); F-measure (harmonic mean of precision and recall); and area under Receiver Operating Characteristic (ROC) curve. ROC curve is a graphical plot that illustrates how a diagnostic ability of a classifier change as the internal threshold changes. The area under ROC curve summarizes the performance of a classifier in a single number. It varies between 0 and 1. As it reaches 1, the classifier has better performance.

5   Experimental Results and Analysis

In our experiments, we apply the proposed framework to predict Android malware. In this section, we present the performance measure scores achieved by 10-fold cross-validation criterion of the following experiments - single ELM classifier, three individual feature selection based ELM classifiers (Chi-Square ranked features+ELM, OneR ranked features+ELM, Relief ranked features+ELM), pre-classification ensemble and lastly, post-classification ensemble. The accuracy, precision, recall, F-measure, and area under ROC curve for six different thresholds values of selected features are shown in Tables 1, 2, 3, 4 and 5 respectively.

Table 1. Comparison of prediction accuracy

Feature threshold	Chi-Square +ELM	OneR +ELM	Relief +ELM	Pre-classification ensemble	Post-classification ensemble
Log_2 (n = 2392)	0.9332	0.9338	0.8598	0.9438	0.9338
1%	0.9377	0.9363	0.9097	0.9496	0.9379
5%	0.9399	0.9298	0.9404	0.9429	0.9417
25%	0.9352	0.9246	0.937	0.9402	0.9388
50%	0.9379	0.9189	0.9404	0.9313	0.9415
75%	0.9336	0.9329	0.9343	0.9205	0.9404
100%	0.9264				

As shown in Table 1, for all the thresholds, the accuracy of the post-classification ensemble is on a higher side than the accuracies achieved by each individual feature selection method, but it is less than the accuracy achieved by the pre-classification ensemble for low threshold values. Also, the pre-classification ensemble outperforms the individual feature selection methods only for the low value of thresholds, and as the number of features increases, the accuracies show no improvement. The highest accuracy (0.9496) is achieved by the pre-classification ensemble for the top 1% of features. The prediction accuracy of single ELM classifier using all the features is 0.9264. Thus, the introduction of ensemble increased the accuracy by 2.32%. Due to the fact that there may be a lot of irrelevant features introduced in the union combination when the threshold increases, the accuracy of the pre-classification ensemble degrades. However, as we can see that the post-classification ensemble is more immune to the introduction of irrelevant features, irrespective of the threshold, it results in the increase in accuracy as compared to the individual feature selection methods.

Table 2. Comparison of precision

Feature threshold	Chi-Square +ELM	OneR +ELM	Relief +ELM	Pre-classification ensemble	Post-classification ensemble
Log$_2$ (n = 2392)	0.9255	0.9252	0.8752	0.9349	0.9256
1%	0.928	0.9274	0.8978	0.9426	0.928
5%	0.9395	0.9355	0.9333	0.9371	0.9386
25%	0.9303	0.92	0.9279	0.9269	0.9282
50%	0.9195	0.9106	0.9206	0.9081	0.9252
75%	0.9163	0.9158	0.9111	0.9009	0.9258
100%	0.9129				

Table 3. Comparison of recall

Feature threshold	Chi-Square +ELM	OneR +ELM	Relief +ELM	Pre-classification ensemble	Post-classification ensemble
Log$_2$ (n = 2392)	0.9422	0.944	0.8392	0.9539	0.9435
1%	0.949	0.9467	0.9246	0.9575	0.9494
5%	0.9404	0.9232	0.9485	0.9494	0.9453
25%	0.9408	0.93	0.9476	0.9557	0.9684
50%	0.9598	0.9291	0.9639	0.9598	0.9607
75%	0.9544	0.9535	0.9625	0.9449	0.9575
100%	0.9426				

Table 4. Comparison of F-measure

Feature threshold	Chi-Square +ELM	OneR +ELM	Relief +ELM	Pre-classification ensemble	Post-classification ensemble
Log$_2$ (n = 2392)	0.9338	0.9345	0.8568	0.9443	0.9345
1%	0.9384	0.937	0.911	0.95	0.9386
5%	0.94	0.9293	0.9409	0.9432	0.9419
25%	0.9355	0.925	0.9377	0.9411	0.9395
50%	0.9392	0.9197	0.9417	0.9332	0.9426
75%	0.935	0.9343	0.9361	0.9224	0.9414
100%	0.9276				

As shown in Tables 2 and 3, highest precision (0.9426) is again achieved by the pre-classification ensemble with top 1% of features but the post-classification ensemble exhibits the highest recall (0.9684) for the top 25% of features. Although the precision and recall values fluctuate for the pre- and post-classification ensembles, but the F-measure follows the same pattern as the accuracy as shown in Table 4, with the post-

Table 5. Comparison of area under ROC curve

Feature threshold	Chi-Square +ELM	OneR +ELM	Relief +ELM	Pre-classification ensemble	Post-classification ensemble
Log_2 (n = 2392)	0.9602	0.9572	0.9321	0.9792	0.9697
1%	0.9633	0.9664	0.9618	0.9864	0.9746
5%	0.9695	0.9663	0.9777	0.9805	0.9802
25%	0.9669	0.9649	0.9798	0.9788	0.9830
50%	0.9733	0.9602	0.9768	0.9723	0.9795
75%	0.9673	0.9679	0.9737	0.9665	0.9784
100%	0.974				

classification ensemble resulting in higher F-measure as compared to the individual feature selection methods for all thresholds and the pre-classification ensemble resulting in higher F-measure values for lower thresholds (highest F-measure of 0.95 for the top 1% of features) and then degrading as the threshold increases. As compared to the single ELM classifier results, the introduction of ensemble increases the precision by 2.97%, recall by 2.58% and F-measure by 2.24%. Table 5 illustrates that even area under the ROC curve increased by 1.24% for the ensemble in comparison to the single ELM classifier. The area under the ROC curve also complies with the accuracy and F-measure results with the highest area value of 0.9864 for the pre-classifier ensemble with top 1% of the features.

6   Conclusion

Android malware detection systems require classifiers with high accuracies. One of the ways of improving the accuracy has been the use of ensemble learning. In this paper, we employ ensemble learning at the feature selection level and at the prediction level to address the problem of Android malware detection. API classes are extracted from Android apps that constitute our binary feature set. At the feature selection level, we used three filter feature selection methods and combined their feature subsets by using the union combination where all the features selected by each of the three feature selection methods are used. Thus, ensemble learning is performed prior to classification and hence the name pre-classification ensemble. At the prediction level, ensemble learning is performed by taking the majority vote of the predictions of three individual classifiers trained on each of the feature subsets generated by the three filter feature selection methods. This approach is referred to as post-classification ensemble since ensemble learning is performed after classification. The significance of ensemble not only lies in the improved performance of the models as confirmed by the experimental results but it also relieves from the burden of selecting an appropriate feature selection method or classification algorithm for a specific dataset. The results indicate that the pre-classification ensemble performs good for low values of the threshold of feature subsets and then starts degrading as the threshold increases, the reason being introduction of irrelevant features. However, the post-classification ensemble is not affected by the thresholds as the predictions are now based on majority vote of three individual feature selection methods based classifiers.

As future work, we propose to compare the pre- and post-classification ensemble strategies for other machine learning algorithms. Also, we used only those filter methods that can be applied to binary data. The same can be explored with numeric features and other filter feature selection methods.

References

1. Simpson, R.: Android overtakes Windows for first time. http://gs.statcounter.com/press/android-overtakes-windows-for-first-time
2. Loeffler, A.: Virginia Tech researchers: Android apps can conspire to mine information from your smartphone. https://vtnews.vt.edu/articles/2017/03/eng-compsci-androidapps.html
3. Google Play Protect. https://www.android.com/play-protect
4. AV-TEST: Android Security Apps Provide Better Protection than Google Play Protect. https://www.av-test.org/en/news/news-single-view/android-security-apps-provide-better-protection-than-google-play-protect/
5. Yerima, S.Y., Sezer, S., McWilliams, G., Muttik, I.: A new android malware detection approach using Bayesian classification. In: 2013 IEEE 27th International Conference on Advanced Information Networking and Applications, pp. 121–128 (2013)
6. Idrees, F., Rajarajan, M., Conti, M., Chen, T.M., Rahulamathavan, Y.: PIndroid: a novel Android malware detection system using ensemble learning methods. Comput. Secur. **68**, 36–46 (2017)
7. Zhu, H.J., You, Z.H., Zhu, Z.X., Shi, W.L., Chen, X., Cheng, L.: DroidDet: effective and robust detection of android malware using static analysis along with rotation forest model. Neurocomputing **272**, 638–646 (2018)
8. Zhang, W., Ren, H., Jiang, Q., Zhang, K.: Exploring feature extraction and ELM in malware detection for android devices. In: Hu, X., Xia, Y., Zhang, Y., Zhao, D. (eds.) ISNN 2015. LNCS, vol. 9377, pp. 489–498. Springer, Cham (2015). https://doi.org/10.1007/978-3-319-25393-0_54
9. Demertzis, K., Iliadis, L.: Bio-inspired hybrid intelligent method for detecting android malware. Adv. Intell. Syst. Comput. **416**, 289–304 (2016)
10. Sun, Y., Xie, Y., Qiu, Z., Pan, Y., Weng, J., Guo, S.: Detecting android malware based on extreme learning machine. In: 2017 IEEE 15th International Conference on Dependable, Autonomic and Secure Computing, 15th International Conference on Pervasive Intelligence and Computing, 3rd International Conference on Big Data Intelligence and Computing and Cyber Science and Technology Congress (DASC/PiCom/DataCom/CyberSciTech), pp. 47–53 (2017)
11. Class Index. https://developer.android.com/reference/classes.html
12. Sung, A., Mukkamala, S.: Identifying important features for intrusion detection using support vector machines and neural networks. In: Proceedings of the 2003 Symposium on Applications and the Internet, pp. 3–10 (2003)
13. Guyon, I., Elisseeff, A.: An introduction to variable and feature selection. J. Mach. Learn. Res. **3**, 1157–1182 (2003)
14. Kuncheva, L.I., Whitaker, C.J.: Measures of diversity in classifier ensembles and their relationship with the ensemble accuracy. Mach. Learn. **51**, 181–207 (2003)

15. Bolón-Canedo, V., Sánchez-Maroño, N., Alonso-Betanzos, A.: An ensemble of filters and classifiers for microarray data classification. Pattern Recogn. **45**, 531–539 (2012)
16. Tsai, C.F., Hsiao, Y.C.: Combining multiple feature selection methods for stock prediction: union, intersection, and multi-intersection approaches. Decis. Support Syst. **50**, 258–269 (2010)
17. Imam, I.F., Michalski, R.S., Kerschberg, L.: Discovering attribute dependence in databases by integrating symbolic learning and statistical analysis techniques. In: Proceedings of the 1st International Workshop on Knowledge Discovery in Databases, Washington, DC, pp. 1–13 (1993)
18. Holte, R.C.: Very simple classification rules perform well on most commonly used datasets. Mach. Learn. **11**, 63–90 (1993)
19. Kira, K., Rendell, L.A.: The feature selection problem: traditional methods and a new algorithm. In: Proceedings of AAAI 1992, pp. 129–134 (1992)
20. Ding, S.F., Xu, X.Z., Nie, R.: Extreme learning machine and its applications. Neural Comput. Appl. **25**, 549–556 (2014)
21. Huang, G.-B., Zhu, Q.-Y., Siew, C.-K.: Extreme learning machine: a new learning scheme of feedforward neural networks. In: Proceedings of the IEEE International Joint Conference on Neural Networks, pp. 985–990 (2004)
22. Huang, G.-B.B., Zhu, Q.-Y.Y., Siew, C.-K.K.: Extreme learning machine: theory and applications. Neurocomputing **70**, 489–501 (2006)
23. Huang, G.B.: Learning capability and storage capacity of two-hidden-layer feedforward networks. IEEE Trans. Neural Netw. **14**, 274–281 (2003)
24. Huang, G.B., Chen, L.: Convex incremental extreme learning machine. Neurocomputing **70**, 3056–3062 (2007)
25. Huang, G.B., Chen, L., Siew, C.K.: Universal approximation using incremental constructive feedforward networks with random hidden nodes. IEEE Trans. Neural Netw. **17**, 879–892 (2006)
26. Rao, C.R., Mitra, S.K.: Generalized Inverse of Matrices and Its Applications, vol. 7. Wiley, New York (1971)
27. Petrakova, A., Affenzeller, M., Merkurjeva, G.: Heterogeneous versus homogeneous machine learning ensembles. Inf. Technol. Manag. Sci. **18**, 135–140 (2015)
28. Dietterich, T.G.: Ensemble methods in machine learning. In: International Workshop on Multiple Classifier Systems, pp. 1–15 (2000)
29. Aswini, A.M., Vinod, P.: Android malware analysis using ensemble features. In: Chakraborty, R.S., Matyas, V., Schaumont, P. (eds.) SPACE 2014. LNCS, vol. 8804, pp. 303–318. Springer, Cham (2014). https://doi.org/10.1007/978-3-319-12060-7_20
30. Sheen, S., Anitha, R., Natarajan, V.: Android based malware detection using a multifeature collaborative decision fusion approach. Neurocomputing **151**, 905–912 (2015)
31. Google Play. https://play.google.com
32. Kang, H., Jang, J.W., Mohaisen, A., Kim, H.K.: Detecting and classifying android malware using static analysis along with creator information. Int. J. Distrib. Sens. Netw. **2015** (2015)
33. Arp, D., Spreitzenbarth, M., Malte, H., Gascon, H., Rieck, K.: DREBIN: effective and explainable detection of android malware in your pocket. In: Symposium on Network and Distributed System Security, pp. 23–26 (2014)
34. Virus Total. https://www.virustotal.com/
35. Androguard. https://github.com/androguard/androguard
36. Bolon-Canedo, V., Sanchez-Marono, N., Alonso-Betanzos, A.: A review of feature selection methods on synthetic data. Knowl. Inf. Syst. **34**, 483–519 (2013)
37. Wang, H.: A comparative study of ensemble feature selection techniques for software defect prediction. Mach. Learn. Appl. 135–140 (2010)

38. R Development Core Team: R: a language and environment for statistical computing. The R Foundation for Statistical Computing, Vienna, Austria (2005)
39. Romanski, P., Kotthoff, L.: FSelector: Selecting Attributes. https://cran.r-project.org/package=FSelector
40. Gosso, A.: elmNN: implementation of ELM (Extreme Learning Machine) algorithm for SLFN (Single Hidden Layer Feedforward Neural Networks). https://cran.r-project.org/package=elmNN

Design and Implementation of a New Model for Privacy Preserving Classification of Data Streams

Aradhana Nyati[1], Shashi Kant Dargar[1]($\boxtimes$), and Sandeep Sharda[2]

[1] Sir Padampat Singhania University,
Bhatewar, Udaipur, Rajasthan 313601, India
aradhananyatisharda@gmail.com,
drshashikant.dargar@gmail.com
[2] DELL EMC, Bangalore 562130, India
sandeepsharda@gmail.com

Abstract. The rapid development in current information explosion has led to huge growth in data over time. Increase in internet and communication technology has resulted into generation of data streams. Due to its dynamic nature, the traditional techniques are not sufficient for privacy preservation of data streams. Researchers have been exploring alternative algorithms to achieve improved privacy of data streams. This paper proposes a novel approach to achieve reliable privacy preservation along with an efficient method for reverse engineering. The hashing based privacy preservation proposed in this paper optimizes the use of memory, reduces response time and shows high privacy level. Further the classification of the secured data obtained from this technique has also been analysed for the future behaviour of the data stream using appropriate tools.

Keywords: Data stream · Privacy preservation · Hashing · Classification
Reverse engineering

1 Introduction

In daily life almost all application areas viz. stock market, weather forecasting, social networking, banking, education, online marketing, medical, call center records, internet traffic etc. generate massive amount of data related to the services they offer. Such continuous, unbounded generated data stream mining can be achieved by classification, for the prediction of future data behavior For the future use of data it is utmost require to make the data stream private for protecting the privacy of individual data or sensitive knowledge without sacrificing the utility of the data.

In the past decade several techniques have been proposed i.e. anonymization [1], perturbation [2], randomization [3], condensation [4], cryptography [5] and its various sub-variants. Which resulted in some or other advantages and limitations in terms of privacy evaluation parameters. In this paper, a new efficient and reliable technique of

© Springer Nature Singapore Pte Ltd. 2018
M. Singh et al. (Eds.): ICACDS 2018, CCIS 906, pp. 454–462, 2018.
https://doi.org/10.1007/978-981-13-1813-9_45

privacy preservation based on hashing is proposed. Hashing is the procedure of mapping enormous volume of data item to a smaller fixed length with the help of a hashing function.

2   Background and Related Work

For the purpose of understanding past researches related to the development of techniques and achieved performances, a detailed literature review had been carried out. The review of literature revealed that researchers have been trying to obtain a better performing privacy preservation method, hence several algorithms are already available.

Fung et al. [1] proposed k-anonymization solution for classification and conducted intensive experiments to evaluate the impact of anonymization on the classification on future data. Ringne et al. [6] suggested the concept of moments to preserve the privacy of data streams along with compression of data but then the technique was suitable for univariate data stream only.

Chhinkaniwala et al. [2] introduced perturbation technique. The classification result of perturbed data set using proposed algorithms showed data privacy with minimal information loss. Disadvantage of proposed algorithms is that it can perturb sensitive attributes with numerical values only.

Bertino et al. [7] explained the aim of privacy preserving data mining algorithms to mine relevant knowledge from large amounts of data with protection of sensitive information. Jena et al. [8] focused to protect the private information and preserve the data utility as much as possible with an objective to find an optimal balance between privacy and utility.

Trambadiya and Bhanodia proposed a heuristic approach to preserve privacy with classification for stream data where the window approach algorithm is applied to perturb the data and Hoeffding tree algorithm is applied on perturbed data [9].

3   Framework

The framework proposed for the implementation of hashing based privacy preserving classification is illustrated in Fig. 1. This is proposed that the generated data stream or a collection of data stream should be applied to data stream mining system in two ways simultaneously. One in which original data stream (D) is fed to the data stream mining system and another when data stream mining system is fed after preserving privacy through hashing. The classification results of original data stream (R) and privacy preserved DS (R') is then compared. The comparison of two different results observed in this way will finally provide the performance parameters of the data stream.

4 Methodology

4.1 Data Collection

The framework proposed for the implementation of hashing based privacy preserving classification is as illustrated in Fig. 1. It is proposed that the generated data stream or a collection of data stream should be applied to data stream mining system in two ways simultaneously. One in which original data stream (D) is fed to the data stream mining system and another when data stream mining system is fed after preserving privacy through hashing based technique.

The experiment has been carried out on the standard adult data stream obtained from UCI repository with total 32,564 records. The preserved data stream through the designed hashing technique is subsequently classified using massive online analysis tool.

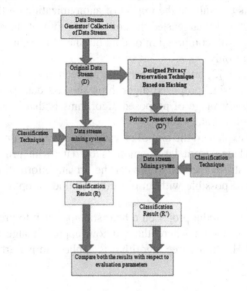

Fig. 1. Framework for privacy preserving classification of data stream.

The classification results of original data stream (R) and privacy preserved DS (R') is then compared. The comparison of two different results observed in this way will finally provide the performance parameters of the data stream.

4.2 Data Basics of Hashing

Hashing is the conversion of a string of character in short fixed length key which represent original character. The values returned by a hash function are called hash values or hash codes. Hashing uses map data structure to store the data set in key-value. Hashing has two main operations, one is data insertion and the other is data retrieval. It is logical algorithm has been designed and tested on JAVA SE 8. The procedure of data insertion in hashing is accomplished by using put (key, value) method. The algorithm representing the put (key, value) method is as follows:The operation i.e. data retrieval is performed using get (key) method. The algorithm of get (key) method is as follows:

Algorithm for put (key, value) method in hashing

```
Input: String of characters
Output: Data item insertion
Method:
inthashValue = key.hashCode();
int index = hashValue& (n-1);
if: bucket[index] == null;
  a) bucket [index] = put(key, value);
else:
inti = 0;
while (i<bucket.list.size()) {
        a) if: hashValue != bucket.list.[i].hashValue; // move to next 'key
                                                      - value' pair.
        b) else if: hashValue == bucket.list.[i].hashValue&&
key.equals(bucket.list.[i].key);
bucket.list.[i] = put(key, value); //over write value for
existing key.
c) else: i++;
bucket.list.[i] = put(key, value); //adding new pair
    }
```

Algorithm for get (key) method in hashing

```
Input: Key value
Output: Data item
Method:
inthashValue = key.hashCode();
int index = hashValue& (n-1);
Object value = null;
if: bucket[index] == null;
  a) return value; //no key value pair so returned value would be null.
else:
inti = 0;
while(i<bucket.list.size()) {
        a) if: hashValue != bucket.list.[i].hashValue; // move to next 'key -
value' pair.
        b) else if: hashValue == bucket.list.[i].hashValue&&
key.equals(bucket.list.[i].key);
value = get(key); // value will be assigned from existing
key.
break; //breaking while loop.
        c) else: i++;
    }
return value; //If no match found value would be null else returned the
assigned value in step (b)
```

4.3   Hashing Implementation in Preserving Privacy

Hashing based privacy preservation provide simple and easy user interface. It uses fast and robust hashing for preservation which can lookup data association with best O(1) and average O(n) time complexity. A new hash based privacy preservation technique designed as shown Fig. 2.

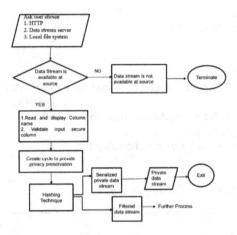

Fig. 2. Privacy preservation technique using hashing

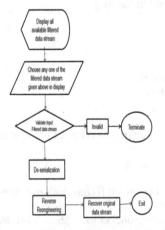

Fig. 3. Recuperate of original data

Reverse reengineering is applied to recover the original data streams. Reverse engineering help to recover original data stream from secured and filtered stream. The process of reverse reengineering is shown in Fig. 3. The filtered data stream obtained in the output of hashing based privacy preservation serve as a input in reverse reengineering process.

4.4   Hashing Recuperate the Original Data Stream

Reverse engineering help to recover original data stream from secured and filtered stream. The process of reverse reengineering is shown in Fig. 3.

5   Result and Discussions

5.1   Classification of Original Data Stream

Classification algorithms were applied on original data set with massive online analysis tool. Outputs are tabulated in Table 1.

5.2   Privacy Preservation Through Hashing

The parameters achieved on applying privacy preservation technique using hashing are as listed in Table 2. Privacy through hashing can be calculated as below.

Privacy quantity (%)

$$= \frac{\text{No. of private attributes for privacy preservation} * 100}{(\text{No. of total attributes in original data stream} - \text{No. of attributes in filtered Data stream})}$$

$$= \frac{5 * 100}{9} = 55.5\%$$

Privacy achieved (%)

$$= \frac{\text{No. of private attributes} * 100}{\{(\text{No. of total attributes in original data stream} - (\text{No. of attributes in filtered Data stream} - 1)\}}$$

$$= \frac{5 * 100}{9 - (5 - 1)} = 100\%.$$

Table 1. Classification of adult data stream

Classifiers	Adult data stream		
	Accuracy	Kappa statistics	Time (s)
NB	86.89	57.45	0.2
AWE	72.68	67.96	1.81
AUE	78.32	45.43	1.09
OCBOOST	89.98	86.8	1.05
OZABAG	95.89	88.4	0.8
OZABAGASHT	97.1	90.31	0.4
HT	87.34	77.29	0.2

5.3 Classification on Privacy Preserved Data Stream Using Hashing

The preserved data from hashing technique is further applied to classification algorithms so as to perform the learning on labeled data for prediction. In this work classification is done on the preserved data stream by using single and ensemble classifiers for the performance estimation.

Table 2. Classification of privacy preserved data stream

	Classifiers	Adult data stream		
		Accuracy	Kappa statistics	Time (s)
Privacy preserved data stream with hashing technique	NB	72.94	49.4	0.34
	AWE	68.31	18.3	1.29
	AUE	71.85	30.23	1.64
	OCBOOST	87.4	47.45	1.11
	OZABAG	86.32	57.47	1.42
	OZABAGASHT	91.89	89.42	1.76
	HT	81.58	67.97	0.48

Figure 4 shows the comparison of different classifiers based on accuracy obtained from original data stream and privacy preserved data stream. Accuracy of the data stream reduces after applying privacy preservation.

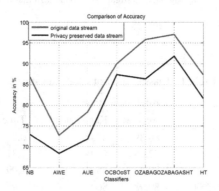

Fig. 4. Comparison of accuracy

The comparison of classifiers with the value of kappa statistics obtained from original data and hashed data stream is shown in Fig. 5. The comparison of classifiers with the value of kappa statistics obtained from original data and hashing technique data stream is shown in Fig. 6.

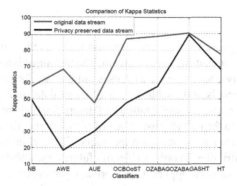

Fig. 5. Comparison of kappa statistics

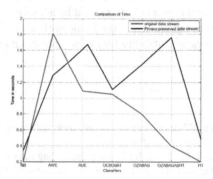

Fig. 6. Comparison of time in seconds

5.4   Comparison of Privacy Preservation Using Hashing with Anonymization Privacy Preservation Technique

The privacy quantity achieved using privacy preservation using hashing is 55.5% of comparison to 41% privacy quantity achieved using anonymization. The parameter values i.e. accuracy, kappa statistics and time in case of classification without applying privacy and after privacy preservation is depicted in Table 3.

Table 3. Parameter values after classification

Classifier applying OZABAGASHT	Kappa statistics	Accuracy	Speed (s)
Original data stream	90.31	97.1%	0.4
Hashing based privacy preserved data stream	89.42	91.89%	1.76
Anonymized data stream	64.9	83.54%	0.02

6 Conclusion

The proposed hashing based privacy preservation technique is found appropriate with upright level of privacy and utility of data stream. The technique is advantageous in terms of reliability, flexibility and efficiency as it uses unique key for hashing, compatibility with servers and protocols and usable for all types of data (numeric, alpha numeric, categorical). This technique use serialization and deserialization process, hence does not find limitation related to the memory use. The privacy quantity is obtained using hashing shows its superiority over anonymization technique. The technique provides complete privacy on sensitive attributes. In order to identify future predictability of data stream and utility, classification has been applied to the privacy preserved data stream and to the original data stream. Further the preserved data stream using proposed technique and anonymization technique is also compared for performance evaluation. This has been found that computed accuracy, kappa statistics and time for privacy preserved classification is 91.89%, 89.42 and 1.76 s respectively. Though the time is comparatively high but remarkable accuracy and kappa statistics could be achieved.

Overall, the methodology proposed in the framework results in immensely efficient parameter values and shows its suitability for privacy preservation classification of data streams.

References

1. Fung, B., Wang, K., Yu, P.: Anonymizing classification data for privacy preservation. IEEE Trans. Knowl. Data **19**, 711–725 (2007)
2. Chhinkaniwala, H., Patel, K., Garg, S.: Privacy preserving data stream classification using data perturbation techniques. In: Proceedings of International Conference on Emerging Trends in Electrical, Electronics and Communication Technologies, pp. 1–8 (2012)
3. Evfimievski, A., Gehrke, J., Srikant, R.: Limiting privacy breaches in privacy preserving data mining. In: Proceedings of ACM SIGMOD/PODS Conference, pp. 211–222 (2003)
4. Aggarwal, Charu C., Yu, Philip S.: A condensation approach to privacy preserving data mining. In: Bertino, E., Christodoulakis, S., Plexousakis, D., Christophides, V., Koubarakis, M., Böhm, K., Ferrari, E. (eds.) EDBT 2004. LNCS, vol. 2992, pp. 183–199. Springer, Heidelberg (2004). https://doi.org/10.1007/978-3-540-24741-8_12
5. Denning, D.: Cryptography and Data Security. Addison-Wesley, Boston (1982)
6. Ringne, A.G., Sood, D., Toshniwal, D.: Compression and privacy preservation of data streams using moments. Int. J. Mach. Learn. Comput. **1**, 473–478 (2011)
7. Bertino, E., Lin, D., Jiang, W.: A survey of quantification of privacy preserving data mining algorithms. In: Aggarwal, C.C., Yu, P.S. (eds.) Privacy-Preserving Data Mining, pp. 183–205. Springer, Boston (2008)
8. Jena, L., Kamila, N., Mishra, S.: Optimizing the convergence of data utility and privacy in data mining. Int. J. Appl. Innov. Eng. Manag. **2**(1), 155–165 (2013)
9. Trambadiya, J., Bhanodia, P.: A heuristic approach to preserve privacy in stream data with classification. Int. J. Eng. Res. Appl. **3**, 1096–1103 (2013)
10. Patel, M., Richariya, P., Shrivastava, A.: Privacy preserving using randomization and encryption methods. Sch. J. Eng. Tech. **1**, 117–121 (2013)
11. Brijlal, P., Shah, A.: An overview of privacy preserving techniques and data accuracy. Int. J. Adv. Res. Comput. Sci. Manag. Stud. **3**, 135–140 (2015)

Partial Confirmatory Factor Analysis for E-Service Delivery Outcomes Using E-Tools Provided by the Government

Seema Sahai[✉] and Gurinder Singh

Amity International Business School, Amity University, Noida, India
{ssahai,gsingh}@amity.edu

Abstract. The accomplishment of Good Governance through the medium of e-Tools for e-Governance, in the era of technological revolution is what every Government has been striving for. In an effort to study the achievement, this study is verifying the underlying model that can be used for assessing the service delivery outputs by the e-Tools provided by the Government of India. The Partial Confirmatory Factor Analysis done on the model has to a great extent justified the fact that the e-Tools service delivery outcomes can be measured using the factors of Standard of Service, Accessibility, Transparency, Affordability, Choice and Courtesy and the underlying structure of these factors. The study was conducted in the National Capital Region.

Keywords: e-Tools · e-Governance · Partial confirmatory factor analysis
Good governance

1 Introduction

Governments have been trying to increase their transparency, efficiency, increased performance and accountability amongst other aspects with the use of Information and Communication Technology. To enable this, the Government has provided a number of ways by which the citizens can directly participate in the process of governance. Some of these are the websites available at the government portal. To further ease the process of interaction and participation, the Government has developed Apps that are compatible with various handsets or mobile phones that people use. All the electronic tools provided by the Government for interaction and participation of citizens in the governing process has been termed as 'e-Tools' in my study.

The Government since the early 1990s in India has initiated e-Tools for its citizens. However, in the early days the focus was on increasing the use of technology, whereas, today the focus is on increasing participation of citizens in the governing process". Keeping this in mind the government planned to establish a more connected government through the use of various e-Tools" [4].

For the Government to reach its goal of Good Governance through e-Governance, it has to ensure the e-Tools that are available to citizens provide or deliver all the services essential for Good Governance. "The potential benefits of e-government are not easily manifested due to the initial implementation failures" [5] (Fig. 1).

© Springer Nature Singapore Pte Ltd. 2018
M. Singh et al. (Eds.): ICACDS 2018, CCIS 906, pp. 463–470, 2018.
https://doi.org/10.1007/978-981-13-1813-9_46

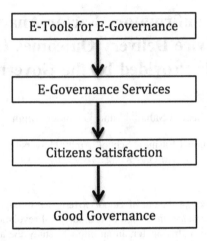

Fig. 1. Structure of good governance through e-tools

A similar service delivery outcome was conducted in the Batho Pele Principle in South Africa during the Nelson Mandela regime. The factors used in that study was taken for improving service delivery in the Educational System in South Africa.

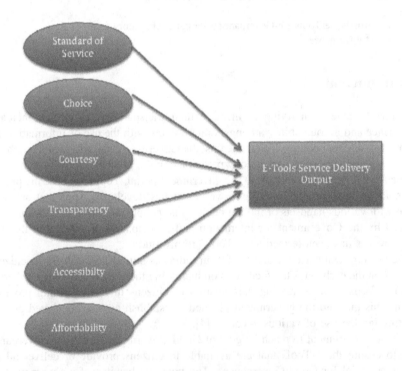

Fig. 2. Model for service delivery

This paper uses Partial Confirmatory Factor Analysis to test whether the factor structure taken from earlier studies can be taken for assessing the service delivery outcomes of the e-Tools provided by the Government for good governance in India.

With a little modification, the factors considered for assessing the service delivery of e-Tools in India are standard of service, choice, courtesy, transparency, accessibility and affordability (Fig. 2).

R. Heeks has described in his working paper, the initiatives of e-governance as follows: (Fig. 3).

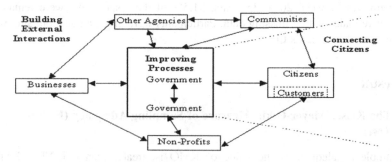

Fig. 3. Source: Heeks [3]

2 Review of Literature

Suhr, D. D (2006), "Confirmatory factor analysis (CFA) is a statistical tool used on a set of observed variables to verify its factor structure. CFA confirms the hypothesis that there is a relationship between observed variables and their underlying latent constructs" [6]. Exploratory Factor Analysis (EFA) is to identify underlying relationship between the measured variables.

Partial Confirmatory Factor Analysis is somewhere between CFA and EFA.

Hof, M. (2012), According to her the questionnaire cannot be told to be valid only based on results of Factor Analysis. It just tells that the items measure the same underlying construct. As per Hof, it is very difficult to develop a method, which can actually measure the validity of a Questionnaire.

Fricker, Ronald D, Kulzy, Walter W, Appleget, Jeffrey A (2012), "Population attitudes, perceptions, and beliefs often manifest as latent traits that can be only indirectly, incompletely, and sometimes imperfectly measured via single survey questions. Factor analysis is a method for estimating these latent traits from question-level survey data. One of the major challenges with large surveys is reducing the mass of data into useful information. Another challenge with surveys aimed at understanding the human terrain, particularly when applied to irregular warfare, is that the population charac-teristics of interest may not be directly measured via single questions. Factor analysis helps address both of these issues" [2].

3   Methods

The population of the study was the residents of NCR who had a minimum education of class 12. The sample taken was of 654 people residing in Delhi/Noida. The average age group was between 26 to 35 years. 51.5% of the respondents were female and 48.2% were males with 2 missing data. Participants were given a questionnaire, which they submitted in a day's time.

4   Result

4.1   The Kaiser-Meyer-Olkin Measure of Sampling Adequacy (KMO-Test)

The sample is adequate if the value of KMO is greater than 0.5. "The KMO is calculated for individual and multiple variables. It represents the ratio of the squared correlation between variables to the squared partial correlation between variables and its value lies between 0 and 1. A value of 0 indicates that the sum of partial correlations is large, as compared to the sum of correlations; this means that there is diffusion in the pattern of correlations (and therefore, factor analysis is likely to be inappropriate). A value close to 1 means that patterns of correlations are relatively close and so factor analysis should result in distinct and reliable factors. Kaiser (1974) recommends accepting values greater than 0.5 as barely acceptable" [1] (Fig. 4).

KMO and Bartlett's Test		
Kaiser-Meyer-Olkin Measure of Sampling Adequacy.		.765
Bartlett's Test of Sphericity	Approx. Chi-Square	7418.863
	df	351
	Sig.	.000

Fig. 4. KMO Bartlett's test

Here we see that the KMO measure is .765. This means that our sample is enough or else more data would have been needed.

The result of Bartlett's Test of Sphericity indicates that there were significantly sufficient correlations between the items to perform factor analysis. The approximate Chi-square being 7418.863 and highly significant $p < .05$.

4.2 Scree Plot

The scree plot showed that six factors had a larger proportion of variance apportioned to them than the remaining factors. A Direct Oblimin (oblique) rotation was used and six factors were highly correlated.

The factor analysis resulted in a 27-item scale, which loaded on six factors (Fig. 5).

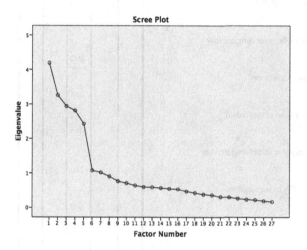

Fig. 5. Scree plot

4.3 Pattern Matrix

The factor pattern matrix contains the coefficients for the linear combination of the variables (Fig. 6).

Pattern Matrix[a]

	Factor					
	1	2	3	4	5	6
expectation of e-tools	.692					
standard as stated	.868					
timely addressal of queries	.606					
email available	.745					
server availability	.608					
software/browser compatibility			.800			
prompt assistance			.845			
service time as prescribed			.627			
flexibility in completion timings			.710			
flexibility in language			.689			
Courtesy						-.559
prompt addressal to complaints						
service charges if any are clearly stated				.532		
procedures are clearly informed				.729		
delay in service clearly informed				.560		
reasons for delay conveyed				.756		
policy updation intimated immediately				.755		

Fig. 6. Pattern matrix

easy availability of services through e-Tools	-.686				
accurate information	-.731				
changes in rules & regulation intimated	-.850				
unavailability of service conveyed timely	-.822				
downtime is as stipulated	-.791				
cost if any is best available				.328	
quality of service is as per cost				.483	
segregation of total cost conveyed				.717	
changes in cost of service intimated in advance				.742	
No discrimination of fees amongst citizen				.874	

Extraction Method: Principal Axis Factoring.

Rotation Method: Oblimin with Kaiser Normalization.a

a. Rotation converged in 7 iterations.

Fig. 6. (*continued*)

5 Conclusion

From the factor pattern matrix it was noted that 6 factors had certain underlying constructs as follows:

1. Factor 1 (Standard of Service): This factor had the following items defining it:
   (i)   expectation of e-tools
   (ii) standard as stated
   (iii) timely addressal of queries
   (iv) email available
   (v)   server availability.
2. Factor 2 (Accessibility):
   (i)   easy availability of services through e-Tools
   (ii) accurate information
   (iii) changes in rules & regulation intimated
   (iv) unavailability of service conveyed timely
   (v)   downtime is as stipulated

This factor has the above 5 items defining it

3. Factor 3 (Choice):
    (i)   software/browser compatibility
    (ii) prompt assistance
    (iii) service time as prescribed
    (iv) flexibility in completion timings
    (v)   flexibility in language

This factor has the above 5 items defining it

4. Factor 4 (Transparency):
    (i)   service charges if any are clearly stated
    (ii) procedures are clearly informed
    (iii) delay in service clearly informed
    (iv) reasons for delay conveyed
    (v)   policy updation intimated immediately

This factor has the above 5 items defining it

5. Factor 5 (Affordability):
    (i)   cost if any is best available
    (ii) quality of service is as per cost
    (iii) segregation of total cost conveyed
    (iv) changes in cost of service intimated in advance,
    (v)   No discrimination of fees amongst citizens

This factor has the above 5 items defining it

6. Factor 6 (Courtesy):
    (i)   Courtesy

This factor has only one item and therefore could either be eliminated in further study or more questions could be added to represent the factor.

This shows that there is a linear combination of variables and the underlying structure can be used for assessing service delivery outcomes of the e-Tools and that the model is appropriate if we remove Factor 6.

References

1. Field, A.: Discovering Statistics Using SPSS (Introducing Statistical Method) (2009). http://fac.ksu.edu.sa/sites/default/files/ktb_lktrwny_shml_fy_lhs.pdf
2. Fricker, R.D., Kulzy, W.W., Appleget, J.A.: From Data to Information: Using Factor Analysis with Survey Data, pp. 1–12 (2012). https://vtechworks.lib.vt.edu/bitstream/handle/10919/73891/Fricker-Kulzy-ApplegetPhalanxArticle.pdf?sequence=1
3. Heeks, R.: Working Paper Series eGovernment in Africa: Promise and Practice (2000). http://www.comnet.mt
4. Sahai, S., Singh, G.: Assessment of societal e-readiness for good governance through e-governance. Int. J. Res. Manag. **384**(07), 24–28 (2017). http://indusedu.org
5. Seema Lall Sahai, G.S.: Effectiveness of e-government implementations in india. Int. J. Emerg. Technol. Comput. Appl. Sci. (IJETCAS) 1(18), 30–32 (2016). http://iasir.net/IJETCASpapers/IJETCAS16-310.pdf
6. Suhr, D.: Exploratory or confirmatory factor analysis? Stat. Data Anal. (2006). https://doi.org/10.1002/da.20406

Finding Association Between Genes by Applying Filtering Mechanism on Microarray Dataset

Gauri Bhanegaonkar[1(✉)], Rakhi Wajgi[1], and Dipak Wajg[2]

[1] Department Computer Science and Engineering,
Yeshwantrao College of Engineering, Nagpur, India
Gauri24bhanegaonkar@gmail.com
[2] Computer Science and Engineering, SVPCE, Nagpur, India
wajgi.rakhi@gmail.com

Abstract. Data mining is a new powerful technology for extracting hidden predictive information from large databases. Considering severity of diseases like cancer, a systematic approach for learning and extracting rule-based knowledge from biological database is needed. Genes are playing important part in the understanding etiology of cancer. Ample amount of gene expressions are available in terms of microarray to carry out research in this area. In data mining, association rules are useful for analyzing and predicting gene expressions. The aim of this paper is to find strong association between genes as a part of preprocessing technique for classification. The resulting association between genes help to classify them into cancer and non-cancer class. The outcomes of this work is helpful in early diagnosis of disease and to plan proper therapeutic strategy.

Keywords: Microarray · Data mining · Gene expressions · Filtering
Discretization

1 Introduction

The 20th Century is frequently referred as the Century of Biology. There has been a great explosion of genomic data in recent years. This is due to the advances in various high-throughput biotechnologies such as gene expression microarrays. The gene expression dataset is fetched from National Centre for Bioinformatics (NCBI) online biological database. Breast cancer dataset has been used for this methodology, and the series used is GSE1379. These large genomic data sets are information-rich. The original dataset consists of 60 samples, out of which 32 samples are cancerous and 28 samples are normal. The proposed methodology targets on Associative Classification methodology that merge association rule mining and classification approach. The gene expression data in microarray are presented in M × N matrix. where the row represents genes g1, g2, g3..., gn and the column represents distinct samples s1, s2, s3... sn. every element as D [i, j] interprets the level of the gene expression gi in the sample sj (Table 1).

© Springer Nature Singapore Pte Ltd. 2018
M. Singh et al. (Eds.): ICACDS 2018, CCIS 906, pp. 471–478, 2018.
https://doi.org/10.1007/978-981-13-1813-9_47

Table 1. Gene expression data

Samples	Attributes(genes)				Category
	S 1	S 2	...	S m	
G1	G(1,1)	G(1,2)	...	G(1,m)	Normal
G2	G(2,1)	G(2,2)	...	G(2,m)	Cancer
...	...	...	...		...
Gn	G(3,1)	G(3,2)	...	G(3,m)	Normal

The prospective algorithm accommodates four stages known as filtering of gene, the discretization, the Class Association Rules and the assignment of class. Gene filtering is the process of finding out differentially expressed genes. Discretization is the process of converting or partitioning continuous values to discretized values and reserve values of gene into intervals. An act having class association rule stage is to discover a small rules set in the database that forms an accurate classifier.

2 Related Work

In order to do the analysis, numerous algorithms have been considered. For the diseases, searching the genes that are over expressed and then categorizes the gene expression by using gene intervals and association rules. For that we have to know the key learning of filtering methods, the discretization methods, Algorithms of association classification, and methods of validation.

Rama Sreepada, Swati Vipsita, Puspanjali Mohapatra, In this proposed system emphasis is given for significant feature extraction as well as efficient design of classifier. GA has efficiently search the huge eigen space to derive the optimal number of features. In phase2, GA has efficiently optimized the structure of PNN [1]. The disadvantage of GA is time taken for convergence.

Girija Chetty, Madhu Chetty, In this paper, the problem with a optimal feature selection technique using analysis based on statistical techniques to model the complex interactions between genes. The two different types of correlation modelling techniques based on the cross modal factor analysis (CFA) and canonical correlation analysis (CCA) were examined. A disadvantage of CFA is that it has ignored the supervision information [2].

Gerald Schaefer, Yasuyuki Yokota, In this paper, they show how fuzzy rule based classification can be applied successfully to analyze gene expression data. The generated classifier consists of an esnsemble of fuzzy if-then rules which together provide a reliable classification of the data. The main defect of classification which is based on fuzzy rule when they are practiced in problems of big data is the shortcoming of scalability [3].

Ranjita Das, Sriparna Saha, A new clustering technique using fuzzy point symmetric concept has been proposed which utilizes particle swarm optimization as the underline optimization strategy. This paper has deployed the clustering of microarray data as a single objective optimization problem [4].

Ranjita Das, Sriparna Saha, The proposed Fuzzy-MODEPS uses the search capability of differential evolution technique. The different parameter combinations which have been used for experimental analysis purpose [5].

Benny Y.M. Fung, Vincent T.Y. Ng, In this paper, they propose the "impact factors" (IFs) to measure the variations between individual classes in training samples and heterogeneous testing samples, and integrate the IFs to classifiers for classification of heterogeneous samples. If irrelevant attributes are present then vector distance is not necessarily well suited [6].

Xi Hang Cao and Zoran Obradovic, The paper mainly studies the key issues of time series data and proposes DTSP-V method that incorporates temporal information into the TSP framework. A data scaling algorithm to transform the data uniformly to an appropriate interval by learning a generalized logistic function to fit the empirical cumulative density function of the data [7].

Kaimin Wu, Xiaofei Nan, Yumei Chai, Liming Wang, Kun Li, The paper presents a transductive local Fisher discriminant analysis technique that handles the assessable unlabeled data in the training process. On the one hand, the label information is exploit to enlarge the inter-class gap in the embedding area. On the other hand, the local structural information of all samples is taken into attention to preserve the smoothness property [8].

3 Proposed Methodology

The recent advent in microarray technology produces large amount of data to the analyst. At that instance, from data it is very difficult to trace accurate as well as intelligible knowledge. So computer program can unpreventably classify gene expression as well as finds affected genes.

In order to enhance the data quality and mining results, raw data is preprocessed and also enhance the efficiency of mining process. Data preprocessing includes preparation and transformation of the initial dataset. The series of data processing includes two phases:

A. Gene Filtering
B. Discretization.

3.1   Gene Filter

The filtering of gene is to catch the genes which are expressed differentially and catch the genes which are significant in the gene expression. To distort the subsequent phenotype of the cells, it is sufficient to change in the patterns of expression of minor genes, for that sense the hypothesis testing is recycled to know the genetic variation among the cells. Hypothesis testing is a testing whether gene expressions are valid by finding out the odds gene expressions happened by chance. Gene filtering phase uses a t-test method. The t-statistic applies according to the following formula

$$T = \frac{(\bar{X} - \bar{Y})/\hat{\sigma}_{pool}}{\sqrt{\frac{1}{n} + \frac{1}{m}}} \tag{1}$$

$$\sigma_{pool} = \frac{\sum_1^n X_i^2 - nX^{-2} + \sum_1^m Y_i^2 - mY^{-2}}{n + m - 2} \tag{2}$$

Where $\bar{X} - \bar{Y}$ signifies sample means and for standard deviation, σ_{pool} be an unbiased estimator. The dissimilarity between normal as well as cancer cell is calculated using p value. In this paper, first the means and standard deviation for both groups are determined. Then t-statistic value and p value be calculated by using t-statistic formula. Finally, if $p < 0.5$ then that gene is significant having degree of freedom $n - 2$ and p is less than 0.5. The end phase of filtering gene discard that genes which are uninformative. Following figure shows the names of few filtered genes out of 22575 (Table 2).

The formula used for calculating entropy value is (3)

$$H(X) = -\sum_{i=0}^{n} p_i * \log_2(p_i) \tag{3}$$

Where $H(X)$ is the entropy information, and p_i express the probabilities of information X. ID3 is an algorithm for building a decision tree classifier based on maximizing information gain at each level of splitting across all available attributes. The way to find split points by using formula (4)

$$\text{Info}(S, T) = -p_{left} \sum_{j=1}^{m} p_{j,left} \log_2 p_{j,left}$$
$$- p_{left} \sum_{j=1}^{m} p_{j,right} \log_2 p_{j,right} \tag{4}$$

m be the number of classes in X, $p_{j,left}$ and $p_{j,right}$ are probabilities.

For each and every attributes of gene in the gene expression, the entropy and the split values are determined. Consequently, the values of gene expression are restored as the unique period or interval. The information gain are sorted in descending order. After discretization, the transaction table is created for generating rules. The transaction table having cancer and normal transaction.

Table 2. Some names of filtered genes

'(+)Pro25G_onG3PDH5 70_1(60)'	'(−)GD11'	'AF322641'	'AI885190'
'(−)GD11'	'(+)Pro25G'	'NM_01338 5'	'K01884'
'(−)3xSLv1'	'(−)3xSLv1'	'AA765792'	'AL117489'
'(+)Pro25G_onG3PDH5 70_1(60)'	'(+)Pro25G_onG3P DH570_1(60)'	'AI732890'	'BC000623'
'(−)GD11'	'(+)Pro25G'	'AI366784'	'AI308920'
'(+)Pro25G'	'(−)3xSLv1'	'AW613315'	'BF223871'
'(+)Pro25G'	'(−)GD11'	'AI745404'	'NM_017701'
'(−)3xSLv1'	'(−)3xSLv1'	'AL136867'	'NM_000303'
'(+)Pro25G'	'(+)Pro25G'	'AI865556'	'(+)Pro25G'
(−)3xSLv1	AI239743	AF247820	AK025402
AI701698	AI686631	AB009675	AF349446
BC012383	AI810341	AI142128	AK000449
NM_013385	BC012505	BC015308	BC001867
BC013166	BC008191	BC000623	AI308920
AA761767	N26480	AK025297	AW069477
AF143740	AF073518	NM_016815	AW237662
AI912097	AA600363	AL049346	T81325
AI918033	AI732890	AI815152	BF223871
AA765792	AI239743	AF247820	AL360202
AI890920	AI890920	AI890920	AI890920
...	....	...	.....

4 Result and Discussion

The preprocessing on microarray dataset helps in reducing volume of dataset. In filtering, there are total 22,275 genes out of which 2339 genes are filtered, that genes are used for discretization. After applying discretization 19 genes are filtered out which are listed in Table 3.

Table 3. Discretized genes

Sr. no.	Row no.	Gene name
1	17955	AK054839
2	20242	AI637899
3	21597	BC016056
4	22559	(+)Pro25G_onG3PDH570_1(60)
5	22518	(+)Pro25G
6	22556	(−)GD11

(continued)

Table 3. (*continued*)

Sr. no.	Row no.	Gene name
7	22306	AW612727
8	22449	(−)3xSLv1
9	20565	AI879768
10	22465	(−)3xSLv1
11	22548	(−)GD11
12	22349	BC017407
13	22543	(+)Pro25G_onG3PDH570_1(60)
14	22439	(+)Pro25G_onG3PDH570_1(60)
15	22508	(−)GD11
16	22344	AW068919
17	21532	AW071705
18	19324	AL080216
19	22222	AK022645

The above table represents the discretized genes and their associated feature number. There are 19 genes are discretized out of 2275 by sorting and merging.

Table 4. Discretized dataset

Gain	Accuracy	Threshold	Feature name	NC	CC
−0.5065	78.5714	0.1277	AK054839	22	23
−0.6226	75	−1.3661	AI637899	21	21
−0.6580	71.4286	0.4183	BC016056	20	21
−0.6909	67.8571	0.0712	(+)Pro25G_on G3PDH570_1(60)	19	21
−0.7565	64.2857	−0.2322	(+)Pro25G	20	18
−0.7838	60.7143	0.1326	(−)GD11	17	20
−0.6073	57.1429	−0.3617	AW612727	16	25
−0.9437	53.5714	−0.1372	(−)3xSLv1	15	16
−0.8467	50	0.0746	AI879768	14	20
−1.0278	46.4386	0.0897	(−)3xSLv1	13	13
−1.0378	42.8571	0.1425	(−)GD11	12	13
−1.0534	39.2857	1.6643	BC017407	11	12
−1.0129	35.7143	−1.6021	(+)Pro25G_on G3PDH570_1(60)	10	15
−1.0526	32.1429	3.9386	(+)Pro25G_on G3PDH570_1(60)	9	9
−1.0427	28.5714	0.1686	(−)GD11	8	9
−1.0305	25	0.4191	AW068919	7	10
−1.0067	21.4286	0.4979	AW071705	6	10

(*continued*)

Table 4. (*continued*)

Gain	Accuracy	Threshold	Feature name	NC	CC
−0.9743	17.8571	0.9065	AL080216	5	10
−0.7123	14.2827	0.0701	AK022645	4	21

The above Table 4 represents the 19 selected features and their associated attributes. For each feature, gain is calculated. Column NC represents count of normal samples for each feature and Column CC represents count of cancer samples for each feature

Table 5. Cancer transactions

Gain	Combinations	Thresholds	TC	Index
59.3750	[AK054839, AI637899]	[0.1277027, −1.3660733]	19	[1, 2]
56.250	[AK054839, BC016056]	[0.1277027,0.4183 027]	18	[1, 3]
62.500	[AK054839, (+)Pro25G_onG3PDH570_1 (60)]	[0.12770,0.071242 70]	20	[1, 4]
53.1250	[AI637899, BC016056]	[−1.3660,0.41830]	17	[2, 3]
50	[AI637899, (+)Pro25G_onG3PDH570_1 (60)]	[−1.3660,0.0712427 0]	16	[2, 4]
56.2500	[BC016056, (+)Pro25G_onG3PDH570_1 (60)]	[0.41830,0.071242]	18	[3, 4]
43.7500	[AK054839, AI637899, BC016056]	[0.12770,- 1.3660,0.41830]	14	[1–3]
46.8750	[AK054839, AI637899, (+)Pro25G_onG3PDH570_1 (60)]	[0.12770,1.3660,0. 0712427]	15	[1, 2, 4]
50	[AK054839, BC016056, (+)Pro25G_onG3PDH570_1 (60)]	[0.12770,0.4183,0. 0712427]	16	[1, 3, 4]
43.7500	[AI637899, BC016056, (+)Pro25G_onG3PDH570_1 (60)]	[−1.3661,0.41830,0. 07124]	14	[2–4]

Table 6. Normal transactions

Gain	Combinations	Thresholds	T C	Index
67.857142	[AK054839, AI637899]	[0.1277027,−1.3660733]	19	[1, 2]
57.142857	[AK054839, BC016056]	[0.1277027,0.41830270]	16	[1, 3]
57.142857	[AK054839, (+)Pro25G_onG3PDH570_1(6 0)]	[0.12770270,0.07124270]	16	[1, 4]
53.571428	[AI637899, BC016056]	[−1.36607330,0.41830270]	15	[2, 3]
50	[AI637899,	[−1.36607330,0.07124270]	14	[2, 4]

The above Table 5 represents the transactional cancer data and Table 6 represents transactional normal data. Table shows the combinations of genes and for each combination, gain is calculated. The number of samples having threshold between range of genes combination threshold are placed in TC column.

References

1. Sreepada, R., Vipsita, S., Mohapatra, P.: An efficient approach for classification of gene expression microarray. In: Fourth International Conference of Emerging Applications of Information Technology (2014)
2. Chetty, G., Chetty, M.: Multiclass microarray gene expression classification based on fusion of correlation features. In: IEEE Trans
3. Schaefer, G., Yokota, Y.: Fuzzy classification of gene expression data. In: IEEE (2007)
4. Das, R., Saha, S.: Gene expression classification using a fuzzy points symmetry based PSO clustering technique. In: Second International Conference on Soft Computing and Machine Intelligence (2015)
5. Das, R., Saha, S.: Microarray gene expression data classification using modified differential evolution based algorithm. In: IEEE INDICON (2015)
6. Fung, B.Y.M., Ng, V.T.Y.: Classification of heterogeneous gene expression data. ACM SIGKDD Explor. Newsl. 2, 69–78 (2003)
7. Cao, X.H., Obradovic, Z.: A robust data scaling algorithm for gene expression classification. In: 2015 IEEE (2015)
8. Wu, K., Nan, X., Chai, Y., Wang, L., Li, K.: DTSP-V: a trend-based top scoring pairs method for classification of time series gene expression data. In: 2016 IEEE International Conference on Bioinformatics and Biomedicine (BIBM)
9. Josserand, T.M.: Classification of gene expression data using pca-based fault detection and identification. In: 2008 IEEE (2008)
10. Liangliang, S., Nian, W., Jun, T., Le, C., Ruiping, W.: The classification of gene expression profile based on the adjacency matrix spectral decomposition. In: 2010 International Conference on Computer Application and System Modeling (ICCASM 2010)
11. García, S., Luengo, J., Sáez, J.A., Lopez, V., Herrera, F.: A survey of discretization techniques: taxonomy and empirical analysis in supervised learning. IEEE Trans. Knowl. Data Eng. 25(4), 734–750 (2013)
12. Raza, M., Gondal, I., Green, D., Coppel, R.L.: Feature selection and classification of gene expression profile in hereditary Breast cancer. In: Proceedings of the Fourth International Conference on Hybrid Intelligent Systems (HIS 2004) IEEE
13. Han, J., Kamber, M.: Data mining: concepts and techniques. Morgan Kaufmann Publishers, Elsevier (2002)
14. Nagata, K., Washio, T., Kawahara, Y., Unami, A.: Toxicity prediction from toxicogenomic data based on class association rule mining. Toxicol. Rep. Elsevier 1, 1133–1142 (2014)

Comparitive Study of Bergman and Augmented Minimal Model with Conventional Controller for Type 1 Diabetes

Surekha Kamath[(✉)], Cifha Crecil Dias, K. Pawan Kumar,
and Meenal Budhiraja

Manipal Institute of Technology, Manipal, Karnataka, India
surekha.kamath@manipal.edu,
cifhasaldanha@yahoo.in, pawankumar9656@gmail.com,
budhiraja.meenal13@gmail.com

Abstract. Diabetes - a global disease is spreading worldwide at an alarming rate. According to World Health Organization (WHO), the number of people suffering from diabetes has become four times in the last three decades. Therefore, monitoring and controlling diabetes has become of major concern lately. This paper focuses on the comparison of Diabetic minimal model (Bergman model) and Augmented minimal model for patients suffering from Type 1 diabetes. The focus will be on developing both the models on Simulink and comparing them to find the best results for regulation of insulin and glucose levels inside the body. Further, we also aim to develop a controller for both the models and tune the parameters for effective output. It is then observed that augmented minimal model shows better response.

Keywords: Diabetes · Bergman model · Augmented minimal model
PID controller

1 Introduction

At present, diabetes is one of the most life threatening diseases in the world. As per the statistics of 2017, around 422 million people worldwide suffer from type 1 diabetes. India was ranked at the top of the list of countries with highest number of diabetic patients in the country in 2017. Currently diabetes is affecting almost 62 million Indians which is more than 7% of the population and this number is expected to cross 100 million people by 2035 [1].

Diabetes mellitus refers to a group of diseases that affect how the body uses glucose (blood sugar). When a person suffers from diabetes, the blood glucose level inside the body becomes very high. The basal value (optimum value) of glucose concentration inside the human body is 80–90 mg/dl. The main source of glucose is food consumption. There is usually a sudden increase with ingesting a meal, especially one high in carbohydrates. The plasma glucose levels of a healthy person hardly go over about 120–140 mg/dl, but if the plasma levels are higher than these levels, the excess glucose

© Springer Nature Singapore Pte Ltd. 2018
M. Singh et al. (Eds.): ICACDS 2018, CCIS 906, pp. 479–488, 2018.
https://doi.org/10.1007/978-981-13-1813-9_48

is taken into liver and muscle cells and stored as glycogen. There is a maximum of glycogen that the body can store and the excess beyond this is converted into fat. And when the glucose concentration is very low compared to the basal level, the liver produces glucose endogenously through either glycogenolysis (stored glycogen in the liver is catabolized into glucose) or gluconeogenesis (fatty and amino acids in the liver are converted to glucose) [2].

Few of the symptoms of diabetes are frequent hunger, increased thirst and frequent urination.

Diabetes can be classified into 2 categories:

Type1 - It is referred to as insulin dependent diabetes. In this case the body produces none or very low insulin inside the body. At this available insulin level the blood glucose does not decrease fast enough when carbohydrates or fats are taken in. A type 1 patient is treated using insulin injections because nothing is secreted and the body cannot handle such high levels of glucose.

Two complications that occur due to type 1 diabetes are-hypoglycemia (blood glucose is too low-60 mg/dl) and hyperglycemia (blood glucose is too high-270 mg/dl).

Type2 - In this case the body is able to produce enough insulin for a healthy individual but it is not able to affect the cells, therefore the insulin inside the body is ineffective.

Over time, researchers have modeled the behavior of the glucose–insulin system in diabetes patients by using compartment modelling equations. These models are referred to as the patient models.

2 Bergman Model (Diabetic Minimal Model)

Bergman proposed this model in 1981, which came to be known as the minimal diabetic model later. The model aims to show the response of the blood glucose concentration inside the body. It consists of three compartments and the model describes the behavior of glucose concentration in plasma G(t) and insulin concentration in plasma I(t) which are connected by an insulin-effect remote compartment X(t) [3] (Fig. 1).

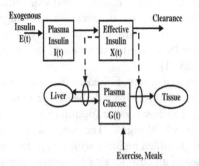

Fig. 1. Schematic of minimal model

The minimal model is described using the following compartment equations [3]:

$$\frac{dG(t)}{dt} = -(p_1 + X(t))G(t) + p_1 G_b \tag{1}$$

$$\frac{dX(t)}{dt} = -p_2 X(t) + p_3(I(t) - I_b) \tag{2}$$

$$\frac{dI(t)}{dt} = -n(I(t) + \gamma(G(t) - h)t \tag{3}$$

From Eq. (1), we can see that the plasma glucose decays at the rate p_1, and is proportional to the difference between the plasma glucose level G(t) and the basal glucose value G_b.

The term X(t)G(t) in Eq. (1), represents the mechanism by which glucose disappears from plasma by clearance effect of insulin.

X(t) represents the insulin remote compartment and it decays at the rate of p_2, and is proportional to the difference between plasma insulin level I(t) and the basal value of insulin I_b.

The plasma insulin concentration I(t) is proportional to the fractional disappearance rate of insulin and also to the difference between the plasma glucose concentration and the target glucose level to achieve [4].

The parameters used in these equations are described in the table below:

Parameter	Value	Unit	Description
G(t)	–	mg/dL	Glucose level in plasma
I(t)	–	mU/L	Blood insulin concentration
X(t)	–	1/min	Effect of active insulin
G_b	92	mg/dL	Basal glucose value
I_b	11	mU/L	Basal insulin value
n	0.287	mU/L	Fractional disappearance rate of insulin
γ	0.0041	$\frac{mU*dL}{L*mg*min}$	Rate of pancreatic release after glucose bolus
h	83.6	mg/dL	Target glucose level
t	Clock	min	Time interval from glucose injection
p_1	0.026	1/min	Glucose clearance rate independent of insulin
p_2	0.025	1/min	Clearance rate of active insulin
p_3	0.0000125	L/min^2 mU	Increase in uptake ability cause by insulin

The simulation on Simulink demonstrates the relationship between the plasma glucose concentration G(t) with time. The glucose value starts at a peak as this model is a patient specific model and the initial value of glucose concentration is given to be 279 (g_0) for a single patient and settles near basal value within 60–70 min.

Two major limitations were reported in this model that the disposal of glucose cannot separate from its production and there is poor precision of parameters used (Fig. 2).

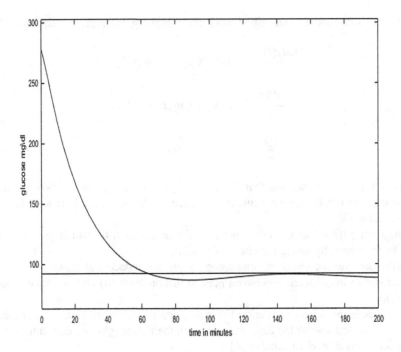

Fig. 2. Simulation result of Bergman model

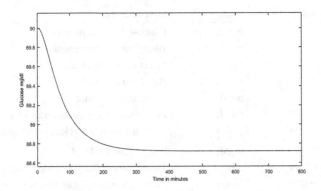

Fig. 3. Simulation result of augmented minimal model

3   Augmented Minimal Model

The purpose of introducing the augmented minimal model for type 1 diabetes is that, it takes into consideration the effects of both insulin and glucagon on the blood glucose concentration inside the body.

It includes time-independent sections for both endogenous insulin and glucagon production.

It also takes care of the external disturbance factors affecting blood glucose and plasma insulin.

The following equations represent this model [3]:

$$\frac{dI_{ex}}{dt} = -p_4 I_{ex}(t) + \frac{U(t)}{v_1} \tag{4}$$

$$\frac{dI_{en}}{dt} = \alpha I_{en}(t) + \beta \max[G_b + G(t) - \theta, 0] \tag{5}$$

$$\frac{dX}{dt} = -p_2 X(t) + p_3 [I_{ex}(t) + I_{en}(t)] \tag{6}$$

$$\frac{dG}{dt} = -p_1 G(t) - X(t)[G_b(t) + G(t)] + D(t) \tag{7}$$

$$Y(t) = G_b(t) + G(t) + N(t) \tag{8}$$

Here the variables imply:

$G(t)$: variation of blood sugar with respect to its basal value (90 mg/dL)
$X(t)$: variable of insulin action (1/min)
$D(t)$: disturbance in glucose rate caused by internal and external factors (mg/dL/min)
$U(t)$: rate of endovenously infused insulin (mg/dL/min)
$I_{ex}(t)$: concentration of plasma insulin due to exogenous infusion
$I_{en}(t)$: concentration of plasma insulin due to endogenous infusion
$N(t)$: noise (mg/dL)
$Y(t)$: glucose measurements (mg/dL)-output.

The constants used in the equations are given below (Table 1):

Table 1. Parameters of augmented minimal model

Parameter	Value	Unit	Description
G_b	90	mg/dL	Basal glucose value
V_1	3.1	L	
α	0.16	1/min	
β	0.0085	(mU/L)(1/(mg/dL))(1/min)	
Θ	90	mg/dL	Set point of blood glucose
P_1	0.016	1/min	Glucose clearance rate independent of insulin
P_2	0.06	1/min	Clearance rate of active insulin
P_3	$1.2 \times 10^{(-5)}$	L/(min^2)mU	Increase in uptake ability cause by insulin
P_4	0.26	1/min	Glucagon clearance rate

The simulation on Simulink demonstrates the relationship between blood glucose concentration and time. This is not a patient specific model but is general in its nature. The value settles in around 200 min. If any external disturbance (meals or exercise) is given the graph starts at a higher value of G(t) and takes for time to settle near the basal value (Fig. 3).

4   PID Controller Setup for Both Patient Models

A PID controller is a combination of proportional, integral and derivative actions. These three values are altered in every PID controller for different applications to obtain a specific response [5]. The values of P, I and D for this controller are (Table 2):

Table 2. Values of PID

Parameter	Value
P	−0.3387
I	−0.006161
D	−2.088

Generally, a set point is the desired response of the process. For example, some process needs to be maintained at 90 mg/dL and that is the set point. Assume that the measured blood glucose level is 140 mg/dL from the sensor (which is a process variable) set point is 90 mg/dL. The deviation of actual value from the required value in the PID algorithm produces an output and sends to an actuator (here it is an insulin injection) according to the values of proportional, integral and derivative responses. Therefore, the PID controller constantly varies the output, until the process variable

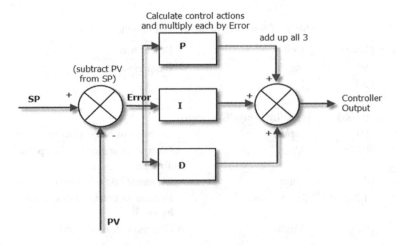

Fig. 4. Block diagram of a PID controller

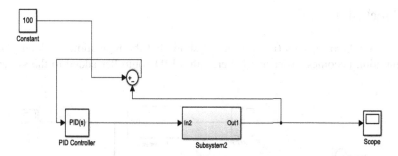

Fig. 5. Block diagram of Bergman model with PID controller

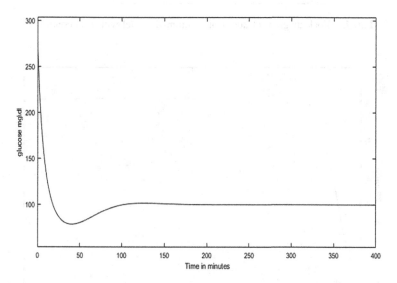

Fig. 6. Simulation result of Bergman model with PID controller

settles down near the set point. The **proportional controller** yields the output proportional to the error. The **integral controller**s main aim in the system is to reduce the steady state error. The **derivative controller** shows the rate of change of process variable and then give the output proportional to this rate [6] (Figs. 4 and 5).

Bergman Model

Augmented Minimal Model

The values of P, I and D for this controller are (Table 3):

Table 3. Values of PID

Parameter	Value
P	−1.25
I	−0.02482
D	−4.391

5 Conclusion

The two simulation results (Figs. 7 and 8) show that the regulation of blood glucose concentration becomes easier and better with a PID controller added to the system.

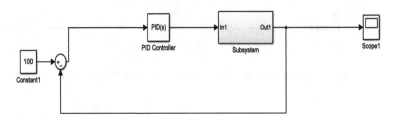

Fig. 7. Block diagram of augmented minimal model with PID controller

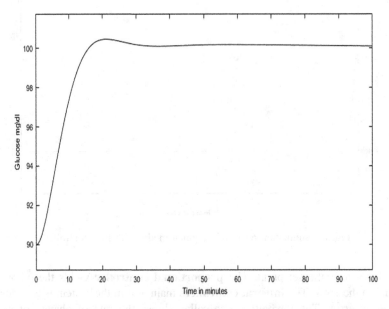

Fig. 8. Simulation result of augmented minimal model with PID controller

In Bergman model, by comparing Figs. 2 and 6 we can see the difference that the PID controller adds to our setup. The controller adds stability and quick response to our output. In Fig. 2, at time = 0 the value of glucose is 279 mg/dL given by us as the initial condition of the function G(t). The value of glucose decreases with time and reaches the required basal value at around 65 min which represents good timing but does not settle at this value. The output keeps oscillating around the basal value which when realized practically is not suitable for the human body. When compared to Fig. 6 (Bergman output with PID controller), we can see the same starting value of 279 but the decrease from 279 to required settling value of 100 is very fast which can be attributed to the controller action. The curve from time = 0 to 100 depicts the non-linearity of the human body processes which explains why the value goes below our set point of 100. Beyond time = 100 min, the glucose level stays at 100 only for further time. This stabilization is added by the controller which helps us to maintain the value inside the human body. For Bergman model, adding the controller and tuning the parameters lowered the settling point (where glucose reaches basal value) but the change is not very prominent. Therefore the controller does not help much to regulate blood glucose in Bergman model.

In Augmented minimal model, by comparing Figs. 3 and 8 the change that the PID controller adds is also clearly seen. The controller adds stability and quick response to the output. In Fig. 3, at time = 0 the value of glucose is 90 mg/dL which is given by us as initial glucose level inside the human body. This value decreases gradually and takes about 250–300 min to settle down at a particular value. The time it takes is more than our requirement but it does not have any oscillations and displays a very stable output. The settling time is altered by adding a PID controller to the augmented minimal model setup. In Fig. 8, the starting value of glucose is at 90 mg/dL as given by us. As the controller starts acting its aim is to settle the value of glucose at 100 mg/dL. Initial 30 min can be attributed to the non-linearity of the human body process which is why the glucose value goes beyond 100 mg/dL in that time. The controller shows very effective results as output settles at the required set point within 50 min. For augmented minimal model, adding the controller and tuning the parameters lowered the settling point (where glucose reaches its basal value) to around 40–50 min which shows a difference of almost 180 min as compared to the setup without the controller [7–9].

These results show that adding the controller to the augmented setup increases the rate at which the glucose value settles near the basal value and how the augmented setup is better than the minimal setup. Further the controller can be modified and improved to show patient specific results.

References

1. Wild, S.H., Roglic, G., Green, A., Sicree, R., King, H.: Global prevalence of diabetes: estimates for the year 2000 and projections for 2030: response to Rathman and Giani. Diabetes Care **27**(10), 2569 (2004)
2. Sorensen, J.T.: A physiologic model of glucose metabolism in man and its use to design and assess improved insulin therapies for diabetes. Ph.D. thesis, Massachusetts Institute of Technology (1985)
3. Torres, N.V., Santos, G.: The (mathematical) modeling process in biosciences. Front. Genet. **6**, 354 (2015)
4. Bolie, V.W.: Coefficients of normal blood glucose regulation. J. Appl. Physiol. **16**(5), 783–788 (1961)
5. Ramprasad, Y.: Model based controllers for blood glucose regulation in type I diabetics. Ph. D. thesis (2005)
6. Wai, H.Y., Audrey, Y.: Patient-specific controller for an implantable artificial pancreas. Ph.D. thesis (2016)

7. Markakis, M.G., Mitsis, G.D., Marmarelis, V.Z.: Computational study of an augmented minimal model for glycaemia control. In: 30th Annual International Conference of the IEEE on Engineering in Medicine and Biology Society, EMBS 2008, pp. 5445–5448. IEEE (2008)
8. Marchetti, G., Barolo, M., Jovanovič, L., Zisser, H., Seborg, D.E.: A feedforward–feedback glucose control strategy for type 1 diabetes mellitus. J. Process Control **18**(2), 149–162 (2008)
9. Farmer Jr., T.G., Edgar, T.F., Peppas, N.A.: Effectiveness of intravenous infusion algorithms for glucose control in diabetic patients using different simulation models. NIH Public Access, March 2009

Performance Comparison of Machine Learning Classification Algorithms

K. M. Veena$^{(\boxtimes)}$, K. Manjula Shenoy, and K. B. Ajitha Shenoy

Manipal Institute of Technology, Manipal Academy of Higher Education,
Manipal 576104, India
{veena.gv,manju.shenoy,ajith.shenoy}@manipal.edu

Abstract. Classification of binary and multi-class datasets to draw meaningful decisions is the key in today's scientific world. Machine learning algorithms are known to effectively classify complex datasets. This paper attempts to study and compare the classification performance if four supervised machine learning classification algorithms, viz., "Classification And Regression Trees, k-Nearest Neighbor, Support Vector Machines and Naive Bayes" to five different types of data sets, viz., mushrooms, page-block, satimage, thyroid and wine. The classification accuracy of each algorithm is evaluated using the 10-fold cross-validation technique. "The Classification And Regression Tree" algorithm is found to give the best classification accuracy.

Keywords: Machine learning · Classification · Datasets · Cross-validation

1 Introduction

The Machine Learning (ML) is the process of preparing systems to perform a specific task automatically. Various ML algorithms have been designed that can learn the characteristics of a specific system, based on experience, and render useful services later on. Machine learning algorithms used to train and test the machines on various data sets. The input data for machine learning algorithms include a set of features and the output is the grouping or ranking of data based on their features. The available data may be classified as training data and testing data. The training data makes the machine learn the task and testing data is used to test the performance of the machine in performing the task. Machine learning tasks include ranking, classification, regression, dimensionality reduction, feature selection, and clustering. The machine learning algorithms may be classified as supervised, unsupervised or semi-supervised. The training data includes target class labels in supervised learning, whereas target class label is not provided in unsupervised learning. Target class label for few input data is available in case of semi-supervised learning.

The classification techniques of ML help in labeling the data sets based on its various distinguishing features or characteristics. Diverse machine learning based classification algorithms exist such as "Classification And Regression Trees (CART), k-Nearest Neighbor (KNN), Support Vector Machines (SVM) Naive Bayes (NB), Neural Networks (NN)", etc. The input features for classification may be binary, continuous or categorical.

© Springer Nature Singapore Pte Ltd. 2018
M. Singh et al. (Eds.): ICACDS 2018, CCIS 906, pp. 489–497, 2018.
https://doi.org/10.1007/978-981-13-1813-9_49

In this paper, the machine learning classification algorithms namely KNN, CART, NB, and SVM are executed on five different datasets. The performance of each algorithm is evaluated using 10-fold cross-validation procedure.

2   Background

The background focuses on the various machine learning algorithms implemented in this paper. A classification model adjusts its parameters to match its output with the targets. To adjust the model's parameters, a learning algorithm is applied, this occurs in a training phase when the model is being constructed. Many algorithms exist to construct a classification model. Such few algorithms are KNN, CART, NB, and SVM.

The most basic yet effective and efficient non-parametric technique for classification is Nearest Neighbor (NN). NN classifies the unknown data instance based on the known neighboring data points class. In 1967, the k-nearest neighbor technique was proposed [1]. KNN works on the assumption that samples with similar input values are likely to belong to the same class. The class labels of neighboring samples are used to determine label of the new sample. The value of k determines the number of closest neighbors to consider. If k is nine, then nine nearest neighbors of the new sample are considered, in deciding the class label of a new sample using the majority voting method. The new sample will be labeled with that of most of its neighbors. An odd number is chosen as the value of k to break the tie in majority voting. If k value is even number, then an equal number of neighbors may belong to same class. The measure of similarity is found by calculating the distance between samples. Distance measure such as Euclidean distance, Manhattan distance, Hamming distance could be used. KNN can be slow as the distance between the new sample and all samples must be computed to classify new sample [2].

CART is discovered by Breiman et al. [3] in the year 1984. CART technique is used to construct prediction models. The data space is recursively partitioned to obtain the model, the obtained partition can be represented as a decision tree. Whenever the target variable is categorical, binary or nominal, the classification decision tree can be constructed. Whereas when the target variable is continuous the regression decision tree can be constructed. Both the regression and classification binary decision trees can be built using CART algorithm. CART uses Gini index as impurity index, which is a generalization of binomial variance. A sequence of if else bi-division is carried out on the training data [4]. A binary tree is built by making the internal node to hold condition, denoting decision in branches and leaf node to hold class label. The test data is checked against the decision tree branches to decide it's class. Advantages of CART include simple to understand, interpret and visualize. It can handle both numerical and categorical data. Data preparation is easy. Non-linear relationships between parameters do not effect it's performance [5].

Disadvantages of CART are decision tree may create over complex trees that don't generalize the data well. This is known as over-fitting. Decision trees can become unstable because small variations in the data may result in complete different tree generated, known as variance, which needs to be lowered by using methods of bagging and boosting. Greedy algorithms can't guarantee to return the globally optimal decision tree [6, 7].

NB classification model uses a probabilistic approach for classification. Relationships between input features and class is expressed as probabilities. So, given the input features for a sample the probability for each class is estimated. The class with the highest probability then determines the label for the sample. In addition to using a probabilistic framework for classification the NB classifier also uses the bayes theorem. The application of bayes theorem makes the estimating the probability easier [8]. NB assumes that the input features are statistically independent of one another. For a given class, the value of one feature does not affect the value of any other feature. This independence is over simplified and does not always hold true and so is considered a 'naive' assumption. Naive independence assumption and the use of bayes theorem gives this classification model it's name [9].

NB algorithm works by calculating probabilities and performing some multiplication. So, very simple to implement and probabilities that are needed can be calculated with a single scan of the dataset and stored in a table. Iterative processing of the data is not necessary as with many other machine learning algorithms. So, model building and testing are very fast. Due to independent assumption, the probability of each feature can be independently estimated. This means that feature probabilities can be calculated in parallel. This also means data set size does not have to grow exponentially with the number of features. This avoids many problems associated with higher dimensionality. Nb algorithm does not need lot of data to build the model. The number of parameters scale linearly with the number of features [8].

The independence assumption of NB does not hold true for many cases. However, the NB classifier still tends to perform very well. This is because, even though NB doesn't provide good estimation of correct class, it is sufficient as long as correct class is more probable then any other incorrect class, the correct classification will be reached. The independence assumption also prevents the NB classifier to model the interaction between features which limits it's classification power. The NB classifier has been applied to many real world problems including spam filtering, document classification and sentiment analysis [10].

SVM finds the extreme data points in each class to form a decision boundary, which is also referred as hyper-plane. SVM is a frontier which best segregates two classes using hyper-plane. Unoptimized decision boundary could result in greater misclassifications on new data. Support vectors are vectors which define hyper-planes. The algorithm basically implies that only support vectors are important whereas other training examples are ignorable. The linearly separable classes could be separated using LSVM (linear SVM). For, linearly not separable data non-linear SVM should be used. Non-linear data should be transformed to high-dimensional space to make them linearly separable. The problem with such transformation is that it is computationally expensive. To reduce the transformation's computational cost kernel trick or kernel functions could be used. Kernel function accepts the vectors in original space as input and returns the dot product of the vectors in the feature space. Using a kernel function we can apply a dot product between two vectors so that every point is mapped into high dimensional space through transformation. Some popular kernel functions include polynomial kernel, radial basis function kernel, sigmoid kernel. Choosing a correct kernel is tricky and it's choice may depend on the task in hand. For any kernel chosen, the kernel parameters need to be decided to achieve good performance [11].

Advantages of SVM include effective in high dimensional space, memory efficient as the subset of training set could be used for testing. Kernel functions could be combined together to achieve complex hyper-plane. Disadvantages of SVM are poor performance when number of features is more than number of samples. SVMs do not directly provide probability estimates. Even though SVM is designed to perform binary classification, it could perform multi-class classification using 1VR [12], 1V1 [13], SimMSVM [14] and other techniques.

3 Methodology

Supervised learning algorithms viz., KNN, CART, NB, SVM are implemented using Python scripting. Their performances are compared using five different data sets available at KEEL dataset repository [15], namely mushrooms, page-block, satimage, thyroid and wine. The characteristics of these data sets are given in Table 1.

Table 1. Properties of input data sets

Data set name	No. of instances	No. of features	Number of classes
Mushrooms	8124	22	2
Page-block	5473	10	5
Satimage	6435	36	7
Thyroid	7200	21	3
Wine	4898	11	11

The mushroom spices dataset is categorized as eatable or deadly. The page-block dataset determines the page block content as graphic, text, picture, horizontal line or vertical line. The satimage dataset use satellite image to identify the soil type.

The thyroid dataset contains people's detail and classifies them as normal, suffering from hyperthyroidism or hypothyroidism. The wine dataset includes the features of white wine and class label quality whose value range from 0 to 10.

The value of k used in KNN is 5. CART uses gini index for impurity calculation and entropy for information gain. The NB uses Gaussian method to find the probability of input features, which uses the following probability density function which is given in Eq. 1.

$$f(x/\mu, \sigma^2) = \frac{1}{\sqrt{2\pi\sigma^2}} exp\left(-\frac{(x-\mu^2)}{2\sigma^2}\right) \tag{1}$$

SVM implementation uses libsvm. The multiclass classification is achieved using the one-vs-one technique. RBF kernel function is used. Polynomial kernel function degree used is 3.

3.1 Validation

Each of the algorithm's performance is evaluated using 10-fold cross validation procedure. The same random seed is used to ensure that the same splits are used to train
and test each of the models. Thus, the models are evaluated in a similar manner.

3.1.1 K-Fold Cross Validation

The problems associated with splitting the dataset into fixed training and testing set is
the dilemma in deciding the split ratio giving raise to less accurate results. K-fold cross
validation overcomes these problems. It partitions the data set into k bins of equal size.
For example, if the data set size is 200 and k is ten then each of the k bins holds 20 data
points. Then k number of passes are used to validate the algorithm's performance. In
each pass, data points in a single bin are used for testing and data points in remaining
$(k - 1)$ bins are used for training. The average performance of k runs is used as the
performance validation score. K-cross validation takes more time to compute the
performance validation score, but it uses all the data points for training as well as for
testing and thus improves the accuracy of validation.

4 Results and Discussion

The performance of the supervised machine learning algorithms is measured using the
k-fold cross validation technique, where k is set to 10. The ten different validation
measures obtained from 10-fold cross validation technique for each model is depicted
using a box and whisker plot. The plot shows the spread of the accuracy scores across
each cross-validation fold for each algorithm. The performance accuracy measure of
supervised algorithms on five different data sets is shown in the Figs. 1, 2, 3, 4 and 5.
The average accuracy of the supervised machine learning algorithms is shown in
Table 2.

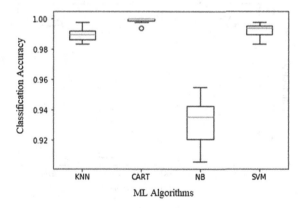

Fig. 1. Performance of machine learning algorithms on mushroom data set

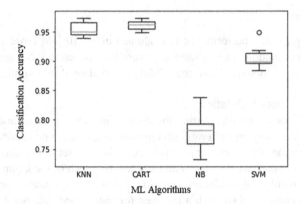

Fig. 2. Performance of machine learning algorithms on page-block data set

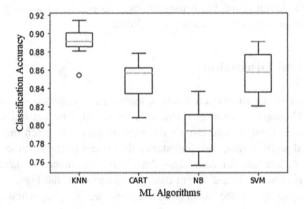

Fig. 3. Performance of machine learning algorithms on a satimage dataset

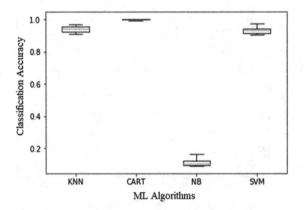

Fig. 4. Performance of machine learning algorithms on thyroid data set

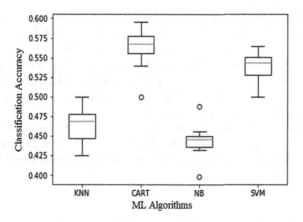

Fig. 5. Performance of machine learning algorithms on wine data set

Table 2. Performance of supervised learning algorithms

Algorithm/data set	Mushroom	Page-block	Satimage	Thyroid	Wine
KNN	98.9%	95.3%	89%	94%	46.5%
CART	99.8%	96.1%	84.7%	99.6%	56.2%
NB	93.2%	77.9%	79.2%	11.1%	44.3%
SVM	99.2%	90.5%	85.5%	93%	53.6%

Figure 6 shows the performance comparison of supervised learning algorithms. CART showed best results on mushroom, page-block, thyroid and wine datasets. KNN has performed best classification on satimage dataset. Mushroom dataset is best

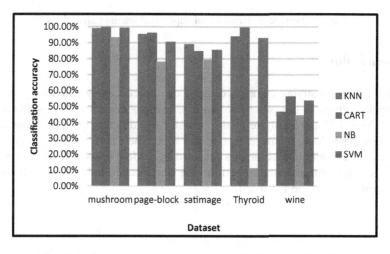

Fig. 6. Performance comparison of supervised learning algorithms

classified by all the classifiers as it has binary class label and class features are distinct across it's classes. Wine dataset is not classified well by any of the used classifiers as most of data values are repeated across its various classes. Thyroid dataset has 15 binary values features which makes NB to misclassify it by achieving only 11.1% classification accuracy. NB after removing 15 binary valued features of thyroid dataset achieved the 94.8% classification accuracy, which shows the ill effect of binary valued features on the NB classifier's performance.

Figure 7 shows the average performance accuracy of classification algorithms. CART has achieved the best results, NB has achieved the worst results. The performance of KNN and SVM are similar. KNN has well performed than SVM on all the datasets except only on wine dataset.

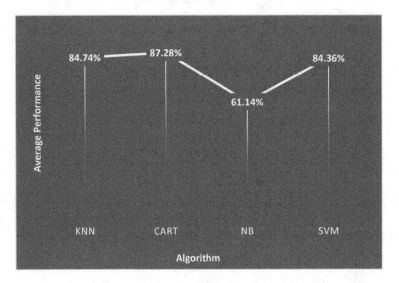

Fig. 7. Average performance of supervised learning algorithms

5 Conclusions

The process of classifying complex datasets can be effectively handled by machine learning algorithms. In this paper four machine learning classification algorithms, viz., KNN, CART, NB and SVM are used to classify five different types of datasets, viz., mushroom, page-block, satimage, thyroid and wine. There performances are compared through their classification accuracies obtained by 10-fold cross validation technique. The CART algorithm is found to perform the classification task the best whereas the NB algorithm performed the worst.

References

1. Cover, T., Hart, P.: Nearest neighbor pattern classification. IEEE Trans. Inf. Theory **13**(1), 21–27 (1967)
2. Mucherino, A., Papajorgji, P.J., Pardalos, P.M.: k-nearest neighbor classification. In: Mucherino, A., Papajorgji, P.J., Pardalos, P.M. (eds.) Data Mining in Agriculture, pp. 83–106. Springer, New York (2009). https://doi.org/10.1007/978-0-387-88615-2_4
3. Breiman, L., Friedman, J., Olshen, R., Stone, C.: Classification and Regression Trees. Wadsworth and Brooks, Monterey (1984)
4. Unda-Trillas, E., Rivera-Rovelo, J.: A Method to Build Classification and Regression Trees. In: Bayro-Corrochano, E., Hancock, E. (eds.) CIARP 2014. LNCS, vol. 8827, pp. 448–453. Springer, Cham (2014). https://doi.org/10.1007/978-3-319-12568-8_55
5. Trendowicz, A., Jeffery, R.: Classification and Regression Trees, pp. 295–304. Springer, Cham (2014)
6. Berk, R.A.: Classification and regression trees (CART). In: Berk, R.A. (ed.) Statistical Learning from a Regression Perspective, 129–186. Springer, Cham (2016). https://doi.org/10.1007/978-3-319-44048-4_3
7. Duda, R.O., Hart, P.E., Stork, D.G.: Pattern Classification, 2nd edn. Wiley, London (2001)
8. Webb, G.I.: Naïve Bayes. In: Sammut, C., Webb, G.I. (eds.) Encyclopedia of Machine Learning, pp. 713–714. Springer, Boston (2011). https://doi.org/10.1007/978-0-387-30164-8_576
9. Kotsiantis, S.B., Zaharakis, I., Pintelas, P.: Supervised machine learning: a review of classification techniques (2007)
10. Kirk, M.: Thoughtful Machine Learning: A Test-Driven Approach. O'Reilly Media, Inc., Newton (2014)
11. Ben-Hur, A., Weston, J.: A User's Guide to Support Vector Machines, pp. 223–239. Humana Press, Totowa (2010)
12. Vapnik, V.N., Vapnik, V.: Statistical Learning Theory, vol. 1. Wiley, New York (1998)
13. Kreßel, U.H.-G.: Pairwise classification and support vector machines. In: Schölkopf, B., Burges, C.J.C., Smola, A.J. (eds.) Advances in Kernel Methods, pp. 255–268. MIT Press, Cambridge (1999)
14. Wang, Z., Xue, X.: Multi-class support vector machine. In: Ma, Y., Guo, G. (eds.) Support Vector Machines Applications, pp. 23–48. Springer, Cham (2014). https://doi.org/10.1007/978-3-319-02300-7_2
15. KEEL dataset repository. http://sci2s.ugr.es/keel/category.php?cat=clas&order=clas#sub2. Accessed 25 Jan 2018

Deep Learning and GPU Based Approaches to Protein Secondary Structure Prediction

Maulika S. Patel[(✉)]

G H Patel College of Engineering and Technology,
Vallabh Vidyanagar, Gujarat, India
maulika.sandip@gmail.com

Abstract. Characterization of proteins remains a problem of significant importance in analysis of disease progression, drug identification, phylogenetic analysis etc. The popular methods include use of Hidden Markov Models, Support Vector Machines, Neural Networks, hybrid methods and other machine learning methods. However, Deep learning has come out as the most trending approach for a variety of problems including protein characterization. We explore some of the most successful deep learning architectures and the variations there in. Deep learning has also shown promising results in other domains such as speech analysis, natural language processing, bio medical image and signal analysis and human computer interactive systems. GPUs have been extensively used for compute intensive tasks including bioinformatics and deep learning. An effort has been made to highlight the contributions involving deep learning, protein secondary structure prediction and GPU based computing.

Keywords: Deep learning · Graphics processing units
Convolutional neural networks · Recurrent neural networks · Bioinformatics

1 Introduction

No field is left uninfluenced from computer based methods and so is biology. A major paradigm shift is observed in this domain in last 20 years. The wet world of biology is quickly coinciding with the logic driven approaches of computer science. This has given birth to the altogether new area of computational biology. Broadly, computational biology covers research in genomics, proteomics, and bioinformatics. Statisticians, mathematicians, computer scientists, pharmacists, biologists, etc. are working in synergy all over the world to address the unsolved issues of biology. It is well established that DNA, RNA and Proteins can be represented as a string of alphabets [5]. This makes it convenient and possible for computer scientists to apply string based algorithms on these data for sequence similarity, structure identification and phylogenetic analysis. The wet world of biology cannot keep pace with the increasing demand of analyzing the exponentially increasing genomic and proteomic data.

Computational tools and techniques are in demand to complement the experimental methods for the solving the problems in molecular biology. "Biology itself has over 500 years of problems to solve". This is quoted by famous algorithmic personality, Donald Knuth. Following are the major problems of concern in molecular biology [4, 7].

© Springer Nature Singapore Pte Ltd. 2018
M. Singh et al. (Eds.): ICACDS 2018, CCIS 906, pp. 498–506, 2018.
https://doi.org/10.1007/978-981-13-1813-9_50

1. Gene finding
2. Drug design
3. Motif identification
4. Molecular docking
5. Protein structure prediction
6. Phylogenetic analysis
7. Personalized medicine

In this paper, the problem of Protein secondary structure prediction (PSSP) and the most recent deep learning based approaches to address PSSP are discussed. The paper is structured as follows. Section 2 presents the necessary introduction to biological concepts. Section 3 explains the protein secondary structure problem. Section 4 presents various algorithms using deep learning and Graphics processing units (GPUs) for PSSP. Conclusion is given in Sect. 5.

2 Biology Basics

All cells are bounded by a plasma membrane; contain several macromolecules including DNA and Proteins. DNA (a set of genes) is a polymer of nucleotides and is contained within a nucleoid (prokaryotes) or nucleus (eukaryotes). It is responsible for transfer of genetic information from one generation to the other. It is a double helix structure discovered by Watson and Crick in 1953 (Fig. 2 and 3) [2].

The four nucleotide bases present in the DNA are Adenine (A), Thymine (T), Cytosine (C), and Guanine (G). Due to the chemical bonding, if there is an A in one strand pair, the corresponding location on the complementary strand must contain a T, and vice versa. Similarly, C pairs with G. It is possible to generate another strand from a given strand of DNA. RNA is transcribed from DNA with G being replaced with Uracil (U). The process of synthesizing Proteins from RNA is known as translation (Figs. 1 and 4). Different genes code for different proteins. These proteins carry out various functions in the living organisms such as oxygen transfer, regulatory information and also act enzymes in accelerating certain biological processes. Therefore, it is rightly said that DNA contains the genetic code of a living organism.

DNA<=====> RNA =====> Protein
Transcription   Translation

Fig. 1. Central dogma of molecular biology

Protein is a polypeptide chain of monomer units called amino acids. A protein can be represented as a sequence of alphabets, each alphabet representing one of the 20 amino acids. Proteins acquire a 3-dimensional shape and structure from a 1-dimensional amino acid sequence. This process is known as protein folding [8].

The underlying phenomenon behind folding is not yet fully understood. Based on the structure, the protein performs specific function. For example, Hemoglobin is a

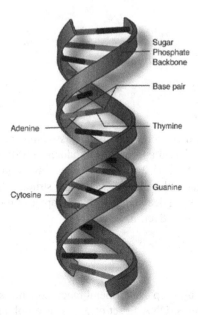

Fig. 2. DNA double helix structure

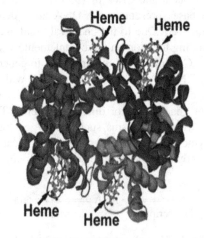

Fig. 3. 3-Dimensional structure of Hemoglobin: a protein capable of oxygen transfer in human beings

protein complex containing 4 polypeptide chains. It assumes a disc like structure (Fig. 3) which makes it capable of binding 4 oxygen molecules and then transferring and releasing the oxygen molecules to the destination. Therefore it is utmost necessary to understand the structure of a protein and thereby its function.

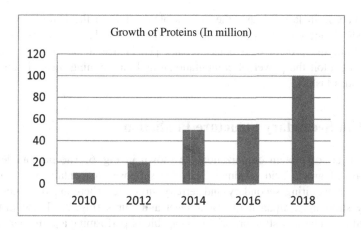

Fig. 4. Growth of protein database in last 7 years [3]

A protein comprised of a polypeptide chain of amino acids folds into a stable structure. It has been also experimented that even if the structure is unfolded, it again folds back. It can be said that the information for folding is embedded in the amino acid sequence. In some cases refolding may not happen and the protein is said to have been denatured and lost its function. Structure prediction using experimental methods includes techniques such as X-ray crystallography or Nuclear Magnetic Resonance (NMR) techniques. But these methods are time consuming, require expertise and are costly in terms of labor as well [19].

The gap between the known proteins and known structures is very wide to be filled up the experimental methods of structure determination. Figure 4 shows the growth of

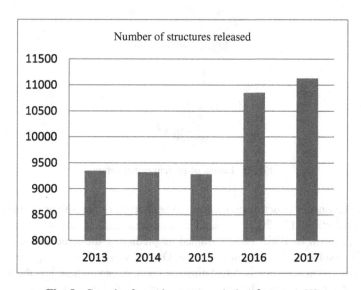

Fig. 5. Growth of protein structures in last five years [1]

protein database in last 5 years (the data is obtained from the Uniprot website [3]. Figure 5 shows the growth of protein structure database in last five years (The data is obtained from the protein data bank website [1]. Hence it has become absolutely essential to exploit the power of computational and data mining methods for various bioinformatics tasks.

3   Protein Secondary Structure Prediction

The four levels of protein organization are shown in Fig. 6. The primary level is a linear chain of amino acid residues. They are supposed to contain the information necessary for acquiring secondary and tertiary structure. There are basically 3 main secondary structures. Alpha helix, Beta sheet and Turns (Fig. 7). These further get compacted into a tertiary structure which is capable of performing a particular function. Multiple tertiary structures bind and form a quaternary structure.

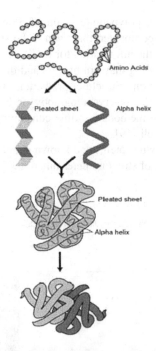

Fig. 6. Levels of protein organization

Protein secondary structure prediction can be thought of as a sub problem of tertiary structure prediction. The 20 amino acid residues can assume any of the three states [20]. The problem of PSSP can be framed as predicting the structure state for each amino acid residue in the protein sequence. One of ways of assessing the secondary structure prediction accuracy is calculating the Qk accuracy, where k is the number of secondary structure classes. The per-residue accuracy, Qk, can be defined as the ratio of

Fig. 7. Types of secondary structures

number of residues (Ci) for which the predicted secondary structure is correct, relative to the total number of residues(L) present in the chain.

$$Qk = 100 * Ci/L \tag{1}$$

It is known that several combinations of secondary structures are possible for a particular tertiary structure. This sets the theoretical upper limit of PSSP to 88% [6]. A portion of the database containing the PDB ID, the sequence and its secondary structure is given in Fig. 8.

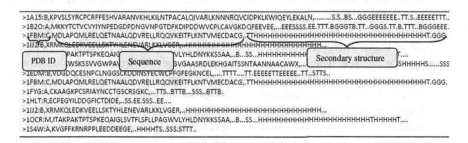

Fig. 8. Database of protein sequence and secondary structure pair

4 Deep Learning and PSSP Based on Deep Learning

Deep learning is a machine learning algorithm inspired from Artificial neural networks. It is difficult to train an ANN with many layers. A lot of applications have been built that use ANN with 1 or 2 hidden layers. Increased accuracy may be obtained by increasing the number of nodes at the hidden layers. This causes the widening of the network. However, the entire network becomes inefficient with the increase in the number of hidden layers and also introduces the problem of vanishing gradient descent.

A neural network is deep if there are more than 3 hidden layers and if the parameters of each and every layer are trainable [11].

Patel and Mazumdar have used neural network to refine the predictions generated in the first phase using a knowledge base obtained by processing the input sequence-structure data. The method is called KB-PROSSP-NN. The Q3 accuracy of 90.16% and 82.28% achieved on the RS126 and CB396 test sets respectively [17].

Convolutional neural networks and recurrent neural networks can be called deep neural networks. In the subsequent section, the recent works using DNN for PSSP are discussed.

i. Deep convolutional and recurrent neural network (DCRNN) for protein secondary structure prediction consists of a feature embedding layer, multiscale CNN layers for local context extraction, stacked bidirectional RNN layers for global context extraction, fully connected and softmax layers for final joint secondary structure and solvent accessibility classification. 69.7% Q8 accuracy on the CB513 dataset, 76.9% Q8 accuracy on CASP10 and 73.1% Q8 accuracy on CASP11 is achieved [10].

ii. Deep convolution neural network is used to directly classify a protein sequence into one of all 1,195 folds defined in SCOP 1.75. The network accepts the features of proteins of variable sequence length (L) as input. datasets curated from SCOP1.75 are used and a classification accuracy of 80.4% is achieved while the classification accuracy of 77.0% is obtained on the independent testing dataset curated from SCOP2.06 [9].

iii. DNCON2, is an improved protein contact map predictor based on two-level deep convolutional neural networks. It consists of six convolutional neural networks and a two level approach to prediction [12].

iv. SSpro5 uses 100 bi-directional recurrent NNs and a 10 fold cross-validation on each of them. These networks can parse information of an arbitrarily large input sequence at once. The number of 100 networks results from the double cross-validation procedure which first splits the training set into 10 folds and then performs 10-fold cross-validation on each of them [18].

v. Wang et al. proposed to use deep convolutional neural fields that combines the advantages of deep convolutional neural networks and convolutional neural field and captures long range sequence information. DeepCNF method gives a Q3 accuracy of 84.7 on the standard CB513 dataset [16].

GPU GeForce 8800 is used by Byran et al. [14] for classification problems on various datasets and speedup of 132 + is achieved. The genomic and proteomic data required for training the deep neural networks are growing exponentially and there is a fair level of maturity in GPU enabled computing. However, the application of GPU enabled computing in the area of bioinformatics is slowly gaining momentum.

It is obvious that the combination of deep learning tools and power of GPUs will accelerate the research in the field of computational biology. In the subsequent section, GPU enabled algorithms for PSSP are discussed.

  i. GOR method is one of the earliest methods for PSSP. The GOR algorithm for prediction of secondary structure is implemented on CUDA enabled GPU and the speedup of 172 is achieved by Gan et al. [13]. The GPU used is GeForce GTX280.

  ii. To improve the secondary structure predictions, Spencer and Cheng used a system of three deep networks called DNSS. Two independently trained deep networks predicted the secondary structure of a protein while the third deep network used these predictions as input and generated a refined prediction. Spencer and Cheng also used a CUDA based GPU implementation to achieve efficient training of the deep networks. The Q3 accuracy reported by DNSS on a set of 198 proteins was 80.7% [15].

  iii. The DCRNN method discussed above is implemented in Theano, a publicly available deep learning software using Keras, a machine learning library to train the entire deep network on a single NVIDIA GeForce GTX TITAN X GPU.

5   Conclusion and Future Work

Deep learning has emerged as a rapidly growing field used to build models for complex input output pairs of data. This paper brings forward few of the recent works in the area where DNNs are used for protein structure prediction problem. The enormous genomic and proteomic data has triggered the use of machine learning methods for these problems. GPUs along with the efficient deep learning methods have made it possible to use these huge data resources for training and testing. The combination of deep learning techniques and power of GPUs will certainly contribute to efficient and accurate prediction of the secondary structures of proteins and thereby, the functions of the proteins.

Acknowledgement. This ongoing work is supported by a Minor Research Project Grant from Gujarat Council on Science and Technology (GUJCOST), DST, India.

References

1. Berman, H.M., et al.: The protein data bank. Nucleic Acids Res. **28**, 235–242 (2000)
2. Watson, J.D., Crick, F.C.: Molecular structures of nucleic acids. Nature **171**, 737–738 (1953)
3. Suzek, B.E., Huang, H., McGarvey, P., Mazumder, R., Wu, C.H.: UniRef: comprehensive and non-redundant UniProt reference clusters. Bioinf. Adv. Access **23**, 1282–1288 (2007)
4. Setubal, C., Meidanis, J.: Introduction to Computational Molecular Biology. Cengage Learning, Delhi (1997)
5. Cheng, J., Tegge, A., Baldi, P.: Machine learning methods for protein structure prediction. IEEE Rev. Biomed. Eng. **1**, 41–49 (2008)
6. Pedersen, C.N.S.: Algorithms in computational biology. Ph.D. dissertation, Presented to the Faculty of Science of the University of Aarhus, Denmark (1999)

7. Rost, B.: Rising accuracy of protein secondary structure prediction. In: Chasman, D. (ed.) Protein Structure Determination, Analysis, and Modeling for Drug Discovery, pp. 207–249. Marcel Dekker, New York (2003)

8. Ray, S.S., Bandyopadhyay, S., Mitra, P., Pal, S.K.: Bioinformatics in neurocomputing framework. IEE Proc.-Circuits Dev. Syst. **152**(5), 556–564 (2005)

9. Hou, J., Adhikari, B., Cheng, J.: DeepSF: deep convolutional neural network for mapping protein sequences to folds. Bioinformatics **34**, 1295–1303 (2017)

10. Li, Z., Yizhou, Y.: Protein secondary structure prediction using cascaded convolutional and recurrent neural networks. In: Proceedings of the Twenty-Fifth International Joint Conference on Artificial Intelligence (IJCAI 2016) (2016)

11. Cho, K.: Foundations of advances in deep learning. Doctoral dissertation, Aalto University, School of Science (2014)

12. Adhikari, B., Hou, J., Cheng, J.: DNCON2: improved protein contact prediction using two-level deep convolutional neural networks. Bioinformatics (2017). https://doi.org/10.1093/bioinformatics/btx781

13. Gan, X., et al.: Accelerating GOR algorithm using CUDA. Appl. Math. Inf. Sci. **7**(21), 563–567 (2013)

14. Catanzaro, B., et al.: Fast Support Vector Machine Training and Classification on Graphics Processors. University of California, Berkeley (2008)

15. Spencer, A., et al.: A deep learning network approach to ab initio protein secondary structure prediction. IEEE/ACM Trans. Comput. Biol. Bioinf. **12**, 103–112 (2015)

16. Wang, S., Peng, J., Ma, J., Jinbo, X.: Protein secondary structure prediction using deep convolutional neural fields. Sci Rep. **6**, 18962 (2016). https://doi.org/10.1038/srep18962

17. Patel, M.S., Mazumdar, H.S.: Knowledge base and neural network approach for protein secondary structure prediction. Int. J. Theor. Biol. **361**, 182–189 (2014)

18. Magnan, C.N., Baldi, P.: SSpro/ACCpro 5: almost perfect prediction of protein secondary structure and relative solvent accessibility using profiles, machine learning and structural similarity. Bioinformatics **30**, 2592–2597 (2014)

19. Aydin, Z., Altunbasak, Y., Borodovsky, M.: Protein secondary structure prediction for a single-sequence using hidden semi-Markov models. BMC Bioinf. **7**, 178 (2006)

20. Gkioxari, G., Toshev, A., Jaitly, N.: Chained predictions using convolutional neural networks. In: Leibe, B., Matas, J., Sebe, N., Welling, M. (eds.) ECCV 2016. LNCS, vol. 9908, pp. 728–743. Springer, Cham (2016). https://doi.org/10.1007/978-3-319-46493-0_44

J-PAKE and ECC Based Authentication Protocol for Smart Grid Network

Aarti Agarkar[1]([✉]) and Himanshu Agrawal[2]

[1] Symbiosis International (Deemed) University, Pune 412 115, India
Pratibha26@gmail.com
[2] Symbiosis Institute of Technology, Symbiosis International (Deemed) University, Pune 412 115, India
himanshu.agrawal@sitpune.edu.in

Abstract. Traditional utility network is gradually transforming into Smart Grid (SG) network to better address the challenges in energy supply and demand gap. SG offers bidirectional communication and bidirectional energy flow. Authenticated access of customers' information is one of the research challenge in SG. Some attempts have been made by various research groups in the direction of password based authentication protocols to address the security challenges in SG. This paper presents a multilayer protocol using Password Authenticated Key Exchange by Juggling (J-PAKE) combined with Elliptic Curve Cryptography (ECC). Performance is compared with previous Password Authenticated Key Exchange based solutions. Theoretical analysis suggests that the proposed protocol is more secure than previous attempts and offers reduced communication and computation cost as compared to J-PAKE.

Keywords: Authentication · Elliptic curve cryptography
Password authenticated key exchange · Security · Smart grid network
Internet of Things

1 Introduction

In the last two decades, Information and Communication Technology (ICT) has witnessed a phenomenal growth. Various devices are supported by short range smart communication interfaces and are part of Internet of Things (IoT). Smart Grid is one such domain where ICT is integrated with traditional power grid. Smart grid supports bidirectional flow of communication and bidirectional flow of energy. Energy flow from utility to consumer and from consumer to other consumer or utility [1].

As shown in Fig. 1, smart grid is a hierarchical network. Sensors mounted at appliances communicates with the smart meter which is considered as a Home area network (HAN) and provides the electricity usage information. Building Area Network (BAN) consists of various HANs and communicates the detailing of information to next layer i.e. Neighborhood Area Network (NAN). Finally, data is collected at the Control Center (CC) for further analytics [2].

Despite obvious benefits, there are some issues like security and privacy concern. Last mile in SG is wireless, therefore it is most susceptible to security threats. The

© Springer Nature Singapore Pte Ltd. 2018
M. Singh et al. (Eds.): ICACDS 2018, CCIS 906, pp. 507–522, 2018.
https://doi.org/10.1007/978-981-13-1813-9_51

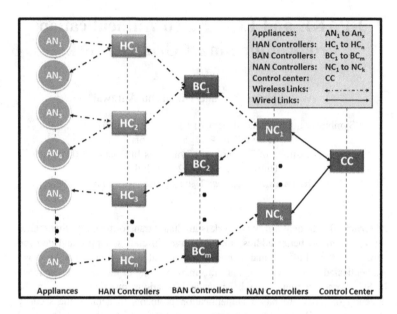

Fig. 1. Smart grid network

proposed work presents the password authenticated key exchange protocol, which is based on Password Authenticated Key Exchange by Juggling (J-PAKE) and Elliptic Curve Cryptography (ECC). The protocol provides mutual authentication and generates session keys between appliances and all upstream controllers and keys between adjacent controllers. The contribution of the research work is as follows:

- To design multilayer authentication protocol which combines benefits of both, J-PAKE and ECC protocol for smart grid environment.
- Theoretical analysis suggests that proposed protocol provides authentication without requiring Public Key Infrastructure (PKI) and offers reduced computation cost as compared to J-PAKE.

Organization of the paper is as follows. Section 2 provides related work. Section 3 presents details of proposed SG-EJPAK protocol. Section 4 discuss about security and performance analysis. Conclusion is presented in Sect. 5.

2   Related Work

This section describes about the previous work related to PAKE protocols used in smart grid followed by details of the J-PAKE protocol.

2.1   Password Authenticated Key Exchange Protocols

Authentication systems are based on Group theory. Diffie–Hellman key exchange (D–H) protocol is group based protocol introduced in 1976 [3]. In this protocol two parties,

Alice and Bob, share a secret key for secure communication. Both parties use multiplicative group of integers mod p and agree on prime p and primitive root mod p which is g. Alice chooses random number from group i.e. x and send g^x mod p to Bob. In same fashion, Bob chooses random number from group y and sends g^y mod p to Alice. Now both parties are able to find secret shared key which is $K = g^{xy}$ mod p.

Concept of D–H protocol is further extended with the help of shared password. Password authenticated key exchange (PAKE) [4] is based on D–H protocol, whose main aim is to establish secure communication between two parties like Alice and Bob using shared password. The first PAKE protocol is EKE [5] followed by SPEKE which has proved that PAKE is solvable. The main advantage of these protocols is they do not assume any third party for calculation of key.

Hasen Nicanfar and Victor C.M. Leung introduced the idea to use PAKE protocol for smart grid environment [6]. It assumes that the network contains appliances, various controllers like HAN controller, BAN controller, NAN controller and control center. For making key exchange process stronger, all controllers in the path are involved for calculation of secret parameters on which basis keys are generated. Appliance and all upstream controllers calculate session keys for communication with the appliance. These keys can be further used for authentication purpose for actual data transmission. The work is extended in [7] with Elliptic Curve Cryptography. These protocols are resilient for various attacks as well as improve security process data delivery time by 50% to 75% as compared to PAKE protocol.

2.2 Password Authenticated Key Exchange by Juggling (J-PAKE) Protocol

In 1996, Jaspan [8] proved that a straightforward implementation of PAKE is insecure. Attacker can detect the password using dictionary attack. To overcome the disadvantage of PAKE, Feng Hao and Peter Ryan designed Password Authenticated Key Exchange by Juggling (J-PAKE) protocol in 2008 [9, 10]. In this scheme two communication parties have secret information, such as password, based on which session key can be defined. J-PAKE consists of two rounds of message exchange where each party sends message to other party. Hao has published a draft where a three-pass variant of J-PAKE is designed [11, 12]. Advantages of J-PAKE are it is more secure than PAKE and is zero knowledge proof (ZKP) [13, 14]. ZKP is an interactive protocol where there is communication between two parties which already shares some secret information. PROVER party tries to convince VERIFIER that it knows some facts without actually sending the secret information. VERIFIER verifies the message sent by PROVER and can define validity of PROVER. Thus the secret information cannot be compromised.

J-PAKE defines communication between two parties Alice and Bob. Following are the parameters.

- G_q is a subgroup of Z_p^* with prime order q, in which the Decisional Diffie–Hellman problem (DDH) is intractable.
- p and q are large primes and q divides $p - 1$.
- g be a generator in G_q. Any non-identity element in G_q can be a generator.

Alice and Bob agree on (p, q, g), as defined by NIST.

Three pass variant J-PAKE has three passes. Figure 2 shows the communication between two parties Alice and Bob share a secret key information s.

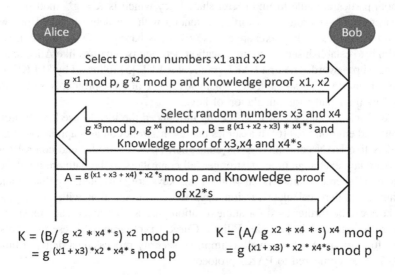

$$K = (B/g^{\,x2\,*\,x4\,*\,s})^{\,x2} \bmod p$$
$$= g^{\,(x1+x3)\,*x2\,*\,x4\,*\,s} \bmod p$$

$$K = (A/g^{\,x2\,*\,x4\,*\,s})^{\,x4} \bmod p$$
$$= g^{\,(x1+x3)\,*\,x2\,*\,x4\,*s} \bmod p$$

Fig. 2. J-PAKE protocol with three pass variant

Pass 1: Alice selects two random numbers $x1 \in [0, p-1]$ and $x2 \in [1, p-1]$. It calculates $g^{x1} \bmod p$, $g^{x2} \bmod p$ and forwards it to Bob with the knowledge proof of $x1$ and $x2$.

Pass 2: Bob verifies the received knowledge proofs and also checks secret s. Bob selects two random numbers $x3 \in [0, p-1]$ and $x4 \in [1, p-1]$. It calculates $g^{x3} \bmod p$, $g^{x4} \bmod p$, and as it knows values forwarded from Alice it also calculates $B = g^{(x1+x2+x3)*x4*s} \bmod p$. Then Bob forwards $g^{x3} \bmod p$, $g^{x4} \bmod p$, and B along with knowledge proof of $x3$, $x4$, and $(x4*s)$.

Pass 3: Alice verifies the received knowledge proofs and also checks that $gx4^! = 1 \bmod p$. Now as the last step of communication, Alice calculates $A = g^{(x1+x3+x4)*x2*s} \bmod p$ and sends to Bob along with a knowledge proof for $x2*s$.

At the end of three passes, Alice calculates

$$K = \left(B/g^{(x2*x4*s)}\right)^{x2} \bmod p = g^{(x1+x3)*x2*x4*s} \bmod p \tag{1}$$

And Bob calculates

$$K = \left(A/g^{(x2*x4*s)}\right)^{x4} \bmod p = g^{(x1+x3)*x2*x4*s} \bmod p \tag{2}$$

Now both parties have session key K for further communication. It is proved that under the Discrete Logarithm (DL) assumption, Bob cannot compute $(x1 + x3 + x4)$ and under the Decision Diffie–Hellman (DDH) assumption, Bob cannot distinguish Alice's ciphertext $A = g^{(x1+x3+x4)*x2*s}$ mod p from a random element in the group.

In our previous work [15], we have provided the study of related protocol. This is the extension of our work.

3 ECC Based Password Authentication Key Exchange by Juggling Protocol for Smart Grid (SG-EJPAK)

The SG-EJPAK protocol is designed to take advantage of J-PAKE and ECC. This section provides the detailed implementation of the SG-EJPAK protocol.

Table 1 shows the parameter list used in the protocol. In SG-EJPAK, session keys between appliance and all other controllers are generated with the help of random values generated by all parties. The communication takes place in three phases. Figure 3 shows the messaging between all parties. Design of SG-EJPAK is based on the following assumptions.

1. The hash function H, H' and D–H values g and p are known to all parties.
2. Appliance and HAN has shared password PW_{AH}. All remaining passwords are generated using PW_{AH}.
3. Symmetric keys k_{HB}, k_{BN} and k_{NC} are shared between HAN-BAN, BAN-NAN and NAN-CC respectively.
4. Appliance knows the ID of HAN.
5. Identity vector ID_J collects IDs of all controllers during communication.

Table 1. List of parameters for SG-EJPAK protocol

Parameter	Description
PW_{XY}	Password shared between two controllers
p	Large prime number
q	A large prime divisor of $p - 1$
Zp^*	A multiplicative group of integers modulo p
G_q	Subgroup of Zp^* with prime order q
g	Generator in Gq
g^x	g raised to the power of x
x mod y	x modulo y
x*y	x multiplied by y
k_{XY}	Symmetric keys between controllers X and Y
ID_J	Array of IDs of controller
H, H'	Hash functions
d_{x1}, d_{x2}	Random numbers of x controller
Q_{1x}, Q_{2x}	Elliptic curve points of x controller

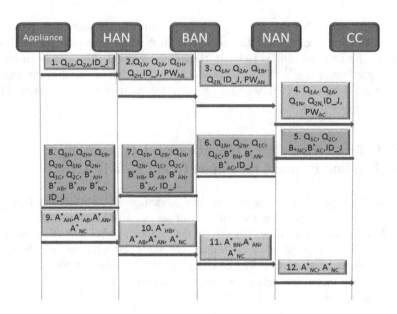

Fig. 3. The SG-EJPAK protocol

3.1 Phase I: Forward/Upstream Flow

1. First packet (Appliance → HAN):

Appliance generates two random numbers $d_{A1} \in [0, p - 1]$ and $d_{A2} \in [1, p - 1]$. These random numbers work as private key of appliance. Using these random numbers appliance computes two points on elliptic curve (EC), $Q_{1A} = d_{A1} * G$ and $Q_{2A} = d_{A2} * G$. It uses the password PW_{AH} and identity of itself and HAN, to generate the temporary key k_{AH}^t.

$$k_{AH}^t = H(ID_A, PW_{AH}, ID_H) \tag{3}$$

Appliance inserts its own ID in the identity vector as $ID_J.[A] = ID_A$. The identity vector collects IDs of all controllers in the path from appliance to control center. Finally, appliance generates the packet P_{AH} encrypted by k_{AH}^t containing Q_{1A}, Q_{2A}, ID_J and sends the packet to HAN.

$$P_{AH} = enc_{\{kAH\}}^t(Q_{1A}, Q_{2A}, ID_J) \tag{4}$$

2. Second packet (HAN → BAN):

HAN utilizes PW_{AH} to calculate temporary key k^t_{AH} and decrypts the message P_{AH}.

$$(Q_{1A}, Q_{2A}, ID_J) = dec^t_{\{kAH\}}(P_{AH}) \tag{5}$$

HAN generates two random numbers $d_{H1} \in [0, p - 1]$ and $d_{H2} \in [1, p - 1]$ as private key. Elliptic Curve points are computed as $Q_{1H} = d_{H1} * G$ and $Q_{2H} = d_{H2} * G$. HAN inserts its ID in the identity vector and computes password PW_{AB} using ID of BAN and k^t_{AH}.

$$PW_{AB} = H(k^t_{AH}|ID_B) \tag{6}$$

With the help of shared key k_{AB}, HAN encrypts the information and sends the packet to BAN.

$$P_{HB} = enc_{\{kHB\}}(Q_{1A}, Q_{2A}, Q_{1H}, Q_{2H}, ID_J, PW_{AB}) \tag{7}$$

3. Third packet (BAN → NAN):

With the help of k_{HB}, BAN decrypts the message P_{HB} and extract Q terms and ID of appliance and verify ID of HAN from identity vector. It calculates EC points based on self-generated random numbers $d_{B1} \in [0, p - 1]$ and $d_{B2} \in [1, p - 1]$ as $Q_{1B} = d_{B1} * G$ and $Q_{2B} = d_{B2} * G$. BAN adds its ID in identity vector, ID_J, and also generates the password PW_{AN}.

$$PW_{AN} = H(PW_{AB}|ID_N) \tag{8}$$

BAN encrypts $Q_{1A}, Q_{2A}, Q_{1B}, Q_{2B}, ID_J$ and PW_{AN} with shared key k_{BN}, and sends the packet to NAN.

$$P_{BN} = enc_{\{kBN\}}(Q_{1A}, Q_{2A}, Q_{1B}, Q_{2B}, ID_J, PW_{AN}) \tag{9}$$

4. Fourth packet (NAN → CC):

NAN obtains $Q_{1A}, Q_{2A}, Q_{1B}, Q_{2B}, ID_J, PW_{AN}$ by decryption of P_{BN}, get Q terms and ID of appliance. It generates points on elliptic curve using self-generated random numbers $d_{N1} \in [0, p - 1]$ and $d_{N2} \in [1, p - 1]$ as $Q_{1N} = d_{N1} * G$ and $Q_{2N} = d_{N2} * G$. It inserts its own ID in identity vector and computes PW_{AC}.

$$PW_{AC} = H(PW_{AN}|ID_C) \tag{10}$$

NAN creates packet containing Q terms, identity vector, PW_{AC} and sends to Control center.

$$P_{NC} = enc_{\{kNC\}}(Q_{1A}, Q_{2A}, Q_{1N}, Q_{2N}, ID_J, PW_{AC}) \tag{11}$$

3.2   Phase II: Backward/Downstream Flow

This phase contains messaging from CC to appliance. Public keys of second party are sent in backward direction from CC to appliance. At the same time, based on J-PAKE protocol, each controller calculates $B^\star$ terms, related with respective controller. Session keys are calculated using these $B^\star$ terms in the third phase.

1. Fifth packet (CC → NAN):

Control center decrypts the message received from NAN and obtains Q_{1A}, Q_{2A}, Q_{1N}, Q_{2N}, ID_J, PW_{AC}. Now, CC has ID of appliance. CC adds its ID in the ID list, ID_J. ID vector is used for verification of communicating controllers. CC finds two random numbers $d_{C1} \in [0, p - 1]$ and $d_{C2} \in [1, p - 1]$ and compute $Q_{1C} = d_{C1} * G$ and $Q_{2C} = d_{C2} * G$. CC has all values to calculate $B^\star$ terms related with NAN and appliance. Using $B^\star$ terms, NAN and appliance are able to calculate the respective session key. CC calculate $B^\star_{NC}$ related with NAN as well as calculates $B^\star_{AC}$ related with appliance.

$$B^\star_{NC} = (Q_{1N} + Q_{2N} + Q_{1C}) * (Q_{2C} * PW_{AC}) \tag{12}$$

$$B^\star_{AC} = (Q_{1A} + Q_{2A} + Q_{1C}) * (Q_{2C} * PW_{AC}) \tag{13}$$

Finally CC creates packet P_{CN} and forwards to NAN.

$$P_{CN} = enc_{\{kNC\}}(Q_{1C}, Q_{2C}, B^\star_{NC}, B^\star_{AC}, ID_J) \tag{14}$$

2. Sixth packet (NAN → BAN):

NAN decrypts P_{CN}, and extract values from the packet. It can find $B^\star_{BN}, B^\star_{AN}$ related with BAN and appliance respectively.

$$B^\star_{BN} = (Q_{1B} + Q_{2B} + Q_{1N}) * (Q_{2N} * PW_{AN}) \tag{15}$$

$$B^\star_{AN} = (Q_{1A} + Q_{2A} + Q_{1N}) * (Q_{2N} * PW_{AN}) \tag{16}$$

NAN sends $B^\star_{BN}$ and $B^\star_{AN}$ to BAN. It also carry forward data sent by CC in backward direction.

$$temp1 = \left(Q_{1N}, Q_{2N}, Q_{1C}, Q_{2C}, B_{BN}^{\star}, B_{AN}^{\star}, B_{AC}^{\star}, ID_J\right) \tag{17}$$

$$P_{NB} = enc_{\{kBN\}}(temp1) \tag{18}$$

3. Seventh packet (BAN → HAN):

BAN decrypts the packet P_{NB} using shared key k_{BN} and receives parameters Q_{1N}, Q_{2N}, Q_{1C}, Q_{2C}, $B_{BN}^{\star}, B_{AN}^{\star}, B_{AC}^{\star}$ and ID_J. BAN computes $B_{HB}^{\star}$ and $B_{AB}^{\star}$.

$$B_{HB}^{\star} = (Q_{1H} + Q_{2H} + Q_{1B}) * (Q_{2B} * PW_{AB}) \tag{19}$$

$$B_{AB}^{\star} = (Q_{1A} + Q_{2A} + Q_{1B})(Q_{2B} * PW_{AB}) \tag{20}$$

BAN creates packet containing $B_{HB}^{\star}, B_{AB}^{\star}$, and the data related to appliance which is carry forwarded by other controller. It forwards the packet to HAN.

$$temp1 = \left(Q_{1B}, Q_{2B}, Q_{1N}, Q_{2N}, Q_{1C}, Q_{2C}, B_{HB}^{\star}, B_{AB}^{\star}, B_{AN}^{\star}, B_{AC}^{\star}, ID_J\right) \tag{21}$$

$$P_{BH} = enc_{\{kHB\}}(temp1) \tag{22}$$

4. Eighth packet (HAN → Appliance):

HAN decrypts the packet P_{BH} and extract values present in the packet and computes $B_{AH}^{\star}$.

$$B_{AH}^{\star} = (Q_{1A} + Q_{2A} + Q_{1H}) * (Q_{1H} * PW_{AH}) \tag{23}$$

HAN generates packet containing Q terms, $B^{\star}$ terms and identity vector and send to appliance.

$$temp1 = (Q_{1H}, Q_{2H}, Q_{1B}, Q_{2B}, Q_{1N}, Q_{2N}, Q_{1C}, Q_{2C}) \tag{24}$$

$$temp2 = \left(B_{AH}^{\star}, B_{AB}^{\star}, B_{AN}^{\star}, B_{AC}^{\star}, ID_J\right) \tag{25}$$

$$P_{HA} = enc\{kHB\}(temp1, temp2) \tag{26}$$

3.3   Phase III: Verification Phase

At the end of phase II, each controller has private key of itself and public keys of respective controller. Additionally, each controller has $B^{\star}$ terms of second party with which it need to generate the session key. Now appliance generates $A^{\star}$ term related to all remaining controllers. It is also able to generate session keys related to all controllers. HAN, BAN and NAN find $A^{\star}$ values for controllers in forward direction as well as generate keys related with neighbor controller. CC gets $A^\star$ values of appliance and NAN and finds respective session keys.

1. Ninth packet (Appliance $\rightarrow$ HAN):

Appliance decrypts the packet P_{HA} and recognize information about Q terms, $B^\star$ terms and identity vector. Identity vector contains IDs of all controllers. Thus, appliance knows for which ID it is generating the session keys. Appliance computes $A_{AH}^\star, A_{AB}^\star, A_{AN}^\star, A_{AC}^\star$ related with respective controller.

$$A_{AH}^\star = (Q_{1A} + Q_{1H} + Q_{2H}) * (Q_{2A} * PW_{AH}) \tag{27}$$

$$A_{AB}^\star = (Q_{1A} + Q_{1B} + Q_{2B}) * (Q_{2A} * PW_{AB}) \tag{28}$$

$$A_{AN}^\star = (Q_{1A} + Q_{1N} + Q_{2N}) * (Q_{2A} * PW_{AN}) \tag{29}$$

$$A_{AC}^\star = (Q_{1A} + Q_{1C} + Q_{2C}) * (Q_{2A} * PW_{AC}) \tag{30}$$

Now, appliance is ready to compute keys related with each controller. For finding the final session keys with each controller, appliance finds key K related with each controller. This K is point on Elliptic Curve and it can be represented as (xK, yK).

$$\begin{aligned} K_H &= \left[B_{AH}^\star - (Q_{2H} * Q_{2A} * PW_{AH})\right] * Q_{2A} \\ &= (xK_H, yK_H) \end{aligned} \tag{31}$$

$$\begin{aligned} K_B &= \left[B_{AB}^\star - (Q_{2B} * Q_{2A} * PW_{AB})\right] * Q_{2A} \\ &= (xK_B, yK_B) \end{aligned} \tag{32}$$

$$\begin{aligned} K_N &= \left[B_{AN}^\star - (Q_{2N} * Q_{2A} * PW_{AN})\right] * Q_{2A} \\ &= (xK_N, yK_N) \end{aligned} \tag{33}$$

$$\begin{aligned} K_C &= \left[B_{AC}^\star - (Q_{2C} * Q_{2A} * PW_{AC})\right] * Q_{2A} \\ &= (xK_C, yK_C) \end{aligned} \tag{34}$$

Appliance computes session keys as hash value of xK and yK. $K_{H'}, K_{B'}, K_{N'}, K_{C'}$ are session keys related with HAN, BAN, NAN and CC respectively.

$$K_{H'} = H'(xK_H | yK_H) \tag{35}$$

$$K_{B'} = H'(xK_B | yK_B) \tag{36}$$

$$K_{N'} = H'(xK_N | yK_N) \tag{37}$$

$$K_{C'} = H'(xK_C | yK_C) \tag{38}$$

Appliance creates a packet containing $A^{\star}$ values related to HAN, BAN, NAN and CC and sends the packet to HAN.

$$P_{AH} = enc\,enc^t_{\{k\,AH\}}\left(A^{\star}_{AH}, A^{\star}_{AB}, A^{\star}_{AN}, A^{\star}_{AC}\right) \tag{39}$$

2. Tenth packet (HAN $\rightarrow$ BAN):

HAN decrypts the message and find values $A^{\star}_{AH}, A^{\star}_{AB}, A^{\star}_{AN}, A^{\star}_{AC}$. HAN calculates the session key K_H' related with HAN using $A^{\star}_{AH}$.

$$K_H = \left[A^{\star}_{AH} - (Q_{2A} * Q_{2H} * PW_{AH})\right] * Q_{2H} \tag{40}$$

$$K_{H'} = H'(xK_H|\ yK_H) \tag{41}$$

HAN computes the session key K_{HB}' for communication with BAN.

$$\begin{aligned} K_{HB} &= \left[B^{\star}_{HB} - (Q_{2B} * Q_{2H} * PW_{HB})\right] * Q_{2H} \\ &= (xK_{HB}, yK_{HB}) \end{aligned} \tag{42}$$

$$K_{HB'} = H'(xK_{HB}|yK_{HB}) \tag{43}$$

HAN also finds $A^{\star}_{HB}$ and send $A^{\star}_{HB}, A^{\star}_{AB}, A^{\star}_{AN}$, and $A^{\star}_{AC}$ to BAN.

$$A^{\star}_{HB} = (Q_{1H} + Q_{1B} + Q_{2B}) * (Q_{2H} * PW_{AB}) \tag{44}$$

$$P_{HB} = enc\{k_{HB}\}\left(A^{\star}_{HB}, A^{\star}_{AB}, A^{\star}_{AN}, A^{\star}_{AC}\right) \tag{45}$$

3. Eleventh packet (BAN $\rightarrow$ NAN):

BAN decrypts packet and extract $A^{\star}$ terms present in the packet. BAN finds session keys K_B', K_{HB}', K_{BN}' related to appliance, HAN and NAN respectively. These keys are used for actual data transfer during the lifetime of network.

$$K_B = \left[A^{\star}_{AB} - (Q_{2A} * Q_{2B} * PW_{AB})\right] * Q_{2B} \tag{46}$$

$$K_{B'} = H'(xK_B|yK_B) \tag{47}$$

$$K_{HB} = \left[A^{\star}_{HB} - (Q_{2H} * Q_{2B} * PW_{AB})\right] * Q_{2B} \tag{48}$$

$$K_{HB'} = H'(xK_{HB}|yK_{HB}) \tag{49}$$

$$K_{BN} = \left[B^{\star}_{BN} - (Q_{2N} * Q_{2B} * PW_{AN})\right] * Q_{2B} \tag{50}$$

$$K_{BN'} = H'(xK_{BN}|yK_{BN}) \tag{51}$$

BAN generates $A_{BN}^{\star}$ which help NAN to compute session key with BAN.

$$A_{BN}^{\star} = (Q_{1B} + Q_{1N} + Q_{2N}) * (Q_{2B} * PW_{AN}) \tag{52}$$

BAN sends $A_{BN}^{\star}, A_{AN}^{\star}, A_{AC}^{\star}$ to NAN in encrypted manner.

$$P_{BN} = enc_{\{kBN\}}(A_{BN}^{\star}, A_{AN}^{\star}, A_{AC}^{\star}) \tag{53}$$

4. Twelfth packet (NAN $\rightarrow$ CC):

CC decrypts the packet and finds session keys K_N', K_{BN}', K_{NC}' for communication with appliance, BAN and CC respectively.

$$K_N = \left[A_{AN}^{\star} - (Q_{2A} * Q_{2N} * PW_{AN})\right] * Q_{2N} \tag{54}$$

$$K_{N'} = H'(xK_N| yK_N) \tag{55}$$

$$K_{BN} = \left[A_{BN}^{\star} - (Q_{2B} * Q_{2N} * PW_{AN})\right] * Q_{2N} \tag{56}$$

$$K_{BN'} = H'(xK_{BN}|yK_{BN}) \tag{57}$$

$$K_{NC} = \left[B_{NC}^{\star} - (Q_{2C} * Q_{2N} * PW_{AC})\right] * Q_{2N} \tag{58}$$

$$K_{NC'} = H'(xK_{NC}| yK_{NC}) \tag{59}$$

NAN finds value of $A_{NC}^{\star}$ which help CC to compute session key with NAN. It sends $A_{NC}^{\star}$ and $A_{AC}^{\star}$ to CC.

$$A_{NC}^{\star} = (Q_{1N} + Q_{1C} + Q_{2C}) * (Q_{2N} * PW_{AC}) \tag{60}$$

$$P_{NC} = enc_{\{kNC\}}(A_{NC}^{\star}, A_{AC}^{\star}) \tag{61}$$

After receiving packet, CC extracts $A_{NC}^{\star}$, $A_{AC}^{\star}$ and finally generate session key K_C' and K_{NC}' for communication with appliance and NAN respectively.

$$K_C = \left[A_{AC}^{\star} - (Q_{2A} * Q_{2C} * PW_{AC})\right] * Q_{2C} \tag{62}$$

$$K_{C'} = H'(xK_C|yK_C) \tag{63}$$

$$K_{NC} = \left[A_{NC}^{\star} - (Q_{2N} * Q_{2C} * PW_{AC})\right] * Q_{2C} \tag{64}$$

$$K_{NC'} = H'(xK_{NC}|yK_{NC}) \tag{65}$$

Now all parties have their session keys with appliance and adjacent controllers.

4 Analysis

Analysis section includes details of security analysis and communication performance analysis.

4.1 Security Analysis

1. Key Establishment: In the SG-EJPAK, each controller generates key based on four different random values. Out of these random values two values are generated by the controller itself and additional two random values are in the form of EC points. For example, key K_H is generated by the appliance and HAN, using random values d_{A1}, d_{A2}, d_{H1} and d_{H2}. Appliance has information d_{A1}, d_{A2}, Q_{1H}, Q_{2H}. HAN has information about d_{H1}, d_{H2}, Q_{1A}, Q_{2A}. HAN cannot distinguish between cipher text generated by appliance i.e. $A_{AH}^{\star}$ and random number in the group based on Decision Diffie Hellman (DDH) Assumption. Thus other party in communication cannot predict about the actual value of random number.

2. Mutual Authentication: In the proposed protocol, PW_{AH} is mutually decided by appliance and HAN and based on which other passwords PW_{AB}, PW_{AN} and PW_{AC} are calculated. These passwords are used for key formation as well as verification by both respective parties.

3. Replay and Man-in-The-Middle-Attack (MITM) Resilience: SG-EJPAK inherits advantages of PAKE protocols. It is replay attack resilient as it uses random numbers and hash functions for key formation and based on D-H algorithm. The messaging during communication between the appliance are based on password and using temporary key, and hence it is resilient from MITM attack. Further communication between controllers is encrypted with shared keys. Finding any of the passwords, an attacker is not able to have access random values which take part in key formation. The past session keys derived from the protocol remain secure even when the secret s is later disclosed, under the Square Computational Diffie-Hellman (SCDH) assumption.

4. Off-Line Guessing Attack Resilience: The SG-EJPAK protocol is resilient to Off-Line Guessing Attack. Under the DDH assumption, $A^{\star}$ and $B^{\star}$ values do not leak any information for password verification. Values $A^{\star}$ and $B^{\star}$ generated by two parties are not distinguishable from random values under the group. Thus any party is not able to find random values generated by other parties. Passive attacker cannot distinguish between random numbers $A^{\star}$ and $B^{\star}$ and thus for him these are two random independent values.

Table 2. Comparison between authentication protocols for smart grid network

Protocol	Hash	Password	Random numbers	Packets	Keys generated
X.1035/PAKE/EPAKE	5	7	14	39	7
J-PAKE	5	7	28	39	7
SG-MCPAK/MCEPAK	1	1	5	12	4
Proposed SG-EJPAK	1	1	10	12	7

4.2 Performance Analysis

Performance of SG-EJPAK is compared to previous PAKE protocols in terms of communication overhead and computation overhead.

Communication Overhead: SG-EJPAK protocol is multilayer protocol. It takes the advantage for using EC points for generation of keys of neighbour controllers. The EC points are calculated based on the random numbers generated by controllers. The performance of the protocol is compared with PAKE based protocols which are X.1035/PAKE [4], Elliptic Curve Version of PAKE (EPAKE) [7], J-PAKE [11], SG-MCPAK [6] and MCEPAK [7].

Table 2 provides comparison between authentication protocols for smart grid network

- X.1035/PAKE: PAKE protocol require 5 different hash functions. Each controller initiates separate communication for generating key with individual controller. Each communication require 3 phases and thus total number of packet transfer are 3 + 6 +9 + 12 = 30 packets for keys related with the appliance and additionally 3 + 3 + 3 = 9 packets for generation of keys between adjacent controller which turns to total 30 + 9 = 39 packets.
- J-PAKE: As like PAKE, J-PAKE also requires 39 packet transfers while calculating keys with all controllers. Number of random numbers are more as compared to X.1035 and total 28 random numbers are necessary. Both X.1035/PAKE and J-PAKE require separate passwords for each controller. Both first and second case is not efficient as they require 39 packet transmission and increase communication overhead.
- SG-MCPAK/MCEPAK: SG-MCPAK/MCEPAK protocols are multilayer consensus protocols. As shown in Table 2, both protocols need one hash function, one password, five random numbers. Number of packet transfers are 12 where all upstream controller generates the secret key with appliance and thus number of keys generated are 4.
- SG-EJPAK: SG-EJPAK inherits advantage of MCEPAK as well as J-PAKE. SG-EJPAK uses 10 random numbers (two random numbers by each controller) and uses a single password for generation of seven secured keys. It requires 12 packets transmission and thus reduces communication overhead as compared to previous two approaches. Total 7 secret keys are generated using the protocol.

Computation Overhead: SG-EJPAK uses EC points during the key generation process. As compared to PAKE/J-PAKE/SG-MCPAK, it is efficient because PAKE/J-PAKE/SG-MCPAK requires exponential operations. Secondly, number of packet transfers are also less as compared to PAKE/J-PAKE/SG-MCPAK and are in parallel to SG-MCPAK/MCEPAK.

5 Conclusion

In this paper, a novel SG-EJPAK authentication protocol is designed which takes advantage of J-PAKE and ECC. SG-EJPAK combines best of previous PAKE protocols. As compared to previous protocols, it is more secure. It is cost effective as it uses EC point calculation rather than exponential operations. Number of message transfers in SG-MCPAK/MCEPAK and SG-EJPAK are same but during these message transfer SG-MCPAK/MCEPAK generates four keys where SG-EJPAK generates four keys between appliance and upstream controllers and at the same time, it generates pairwise keys between adjacent controllers. Additionally, it reduces communication and computation cost as compared to J-PAKE.

References

1. Greer, C., et al.: NIST Framework and Roadmap for Smart Grid Interoperability Standards, Release 3.0 (No. Special Publication (NIST SP) 1108r3) (2014)
2. Fouda, M.M., Fadlullah, Z.M., Kato, N., Lu, R., Shen, X.: Towards a lightweight message authentication mechanism tailored for smart grid communications. In: IEEE Conference on Computer Communications Workshops (INFOCOM WKSHPS), pp. 1018–1023 (2011)
3. Diffie, W., Hellman, M.: New directions in cryptography. IEEE Trans. Inf. Theory **22**(6), 644–654 (1976)
4. Password-authenticated key exchange (PAKE) protocol, ITU-T Rec. X.1035 (02/2007), Series X, Telecommunication Security. Telecommunication Standardization Sector of International Telecommunication Union (2007). www.itu.int/ITU-T/
5. Bellovin, S.M., Merritt, M.: Encrypted key exchange: password-based protocols secure against dictionary attacks. In: IEEE Computer Society Symposium on Research in Security and Privacy, pp. 72–84 (1992)
6. Nicanfar, H., Leung, V.C.: Smart grid multilayer consensus password authenticated key exchange protocol. In: IEEE International Conference on Communications (ICC), Canada, pp. 6716–6720 (2012)
7. Nicanfar, H., Leung, V.C.: Multilayer consensus ECC-based password authenticated key-exchange (MCEPAK) protocol for smart grid system. IEEE Trans. Smart Grid **4**(1), 253–264 (2013)
8. Jaspan, B.: Dual-workfactor encrypted key exchange: efficiently preventing password chaining and dictionary attacks. In: USENIX Security Symposium (1996)
9. Hao, F., Ryan, P.Y.A.: Password authenticated key exchange by juggling. In: Christianson, B., Malcolm, J.A., Matyas, V., Roe, M. (eds.) Security Protocols 2008. LNCS, vol. 6615, pp. 159–171. Springer, Heidelberg (2011). https://doi.org/10.1007/978-3-642-22137-8_23

10. Hao, F., Ryan, P.: J-PAKE: authenticated key exchange without PKI. In: Gavrilova, M.L., Tan, C.J.K., Moreno, E.D. (eds.) Transactions on Computational Science XI. LNCS, vol. 6480, pp. 192–206. Springer, Heidelberg (2010). https://doi.org/10.1007/978-3-642-17697-5_10

11. Hao, F.: J-PAKE: password authenticated key exchange by juggling. In: Network Working Group, Internet-Draft. Newcastle University, UK (2013)

12. Hao, F.: J-PAKE: password-authenticated key exchange by juggling. No. RFC 8236 (2017)

13. Goldwasser, S., Micali, S., Rackoff, C.: The knowledge complexity of interactive proof systems. SIAM J. Comput. 18(1), 186–208 (1989)

14. Anderson, R., Needham, R.: Robustness principles for public key protocols. In: Coppersmith, D. (ed.) CRYPTO 1995. LNCS, vol. 963, pp. 236–247. Springer, Heidelberg (1995). https://doi.org/10.1007/3-540-44750-4_19

15. Dudhwadkar, V., Agarwal, H., Agarkar, A., Ray, P.: On lightweight authentication for smart grid network. Int. J. Comput. Appl. 123(5), 1–6 (2015)

Motion Detection for Video Surveillance System

Aditi Kumbhar[(⊠)] and P. C. Bhaskar

Department of Technology, Shivaji University, Kolhapur, Maharashtra, India
akaditiak@gmail.com, pcb_tech@unishivaji.ac.in

Abstract. In today's scenario; safety has got more attention and hence there is huge demand for video surveillance and it's optimize performance. In this current generation of technological evaluation, computer vision technology is more preferable than manual monitoring for safety purpose. Indeed video surveillance system whether for indoor and outdoor surveying essential for detection of running objects from video. The vital object monitoring and analysis has major issue to taken into consideration. Extracting the frames from video sequences for image processing is important task in motion detection. Background subtraction is common method in motion detection. In this article, modified version of frame differencing with feature extraction is discussed. The system is intended to work for MPEG 1280 × 720 resolution of video data with selecting 10 frames per second.

Keywords: Video surveillance · Object tracking · Motion detection
Reference frame · Background frame · Current frame · Security
Within-class variance · Between-class variance · Feature extraction
Gray level threshold

1 Introduction

Video surveillance system for motion detection is a security device that is installed in building to detect unauthorized movement in restricted area [2]. Motion estimation in a video scene gives critical and imperative data identified with development and presence of object in a scene. This video surveillance system can be used in jewelers shop, big mall, road, house, public places [10]. Security guards can take immediate action in case of unauthorized activity. To make video surveillance systems, "smart", needs fast, reliable and robust algorithm for moving object detection and tracking [9].

Computer vision has enhanced the evaluation in fields like internet, computational power, and camera technology. Computer vision has taken very important role in the realization of a complete vision based automated video surveillance system for automatic scene analysis, monitoring and generation of security alerts based on relevant motion in a video scene, such as human detection, vehicles detection, threat, security [7]. Various motion detection methods have been extensively investigated in the literature.

Now-a-days, closed circuit television (CCTV) camera based surveillance for security has been widely used in the entire world. Today with the development in

© Springer Nature Singapore Pte Ltd. 2018
M. Singh et al. (Eds.): ICACDS 2018, CCIS 906, pp. 523–534, 2018.
https://doi.org/10.1007/978-981-13-1813-9_52

technology, security and safety are major concerns. To address this concern, the number of surveillance cameras has increased in recent years [4]. Data collected is nevertheless difficult to store and monitor manually on a continual basis. The CCTV cameras are generating huge amount of data. The security system requires large storage and faster processing capabilities [5].

Developing the system for object detection creates nonlinear scenarios between data size and processing time. Algorithm complexities irrespective of high configuration and high requirements are the basic problems associated with the idea. The scenarios are different where motion can be detected [5]. Firstly, recording only when motion is detected or also taking continuous inputs from video devices and another one is suspicious activity detection based on moving objects in the image frame are the main targets considered in this research article [8].

Automated motion detection using video surveillance is possible only because of the factors required for movement identification has developed enormously with the time. There are many articles are published on object detection with different methods. The popular and simple method is background subtraction. The system consists of following parts:

- Capturing live video
- Extract frames from video
- Feature extraction
- Indication of movement detection

Background subtraction is based on pixel by pixel processing with threshold. But for practical condition, video reconnaissance application demand an updating reference frames continuously [10]. So there is need of advancement in current system. Frame differencing with feature extraction can detect presence of object using optimized image which will use for quick result. In this method, extracting the features that are interested is only considered.

2 Related Work

Since multimedia application are happens to be required and emerging in current scenario and consequently motion detection is one of the task in the multimedia application where major focus needs to give. Several software based methods has been discovered for real time moving object detection system. A brief survey has been done regarding motion detection techniques. Amongst them, background subtraction is common approach for motion detection technique. Some of the following methods are discussed for motion detection.

2.1 Background Subtraction Technique

Background subtraction is widely used technique for moving object detection. This method identifies objects in motion by subtracting reference frame and current frame from video. Birmohan Singh et al. [1] presented a moving object detection system using background subtraction technique. Background subtraction using threshold algorithm has been used for object detection (Fig. 1).

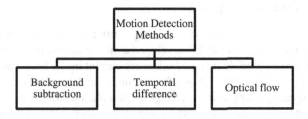

Fig. 1. Types of motion detection

Below Fig. 2 shows background subtraction with blob detection in which a pixel at location (x, y) in current frame N_t is marked as foreground. And Background frame is shown by M_t (x, y) [10].

If $|Nt(x, y) - Mt(x, y)| > Th$
  $f(i, j) = 1$, Where $f(i, j)$ is background detected frame.
else $f(i, j) = 0$.

Fig. 2. Background subtraction method with blob detection

Olugboia et al. [2] developed moving object detection system using Gaussian Mixture Model (GMM), morphological filters. The method uses background subtraction using GMM and threshold method for detecting the moving object. To remove noise in the image, smoothening and morphological filters incorporated in the system.

To grab the exact object, blobs algorithm has been also applied to final processed output image.

2.2   Temporal Difference Method

In temporal difference method, consecutive images from video are subtracted. It is pixel by pixel processing. Shujgen et al. [9] developed a motion detection algorithm based on temporal difference method. In this method, every current image becomes the reference image for next upcoming image. Thus reference image updates dynamically and allows this approach to easily adapt to scene changes. Then obtained differential image is low pass filtered and get translated into binary image. Numbers of such binary image are obtained with gray value information in the image and finally motion is extracted out by applying arithmetic operations on pixels of the binary images.

2.3   Optical Flow Technique

Kanawathi et al. [7] generated optical flow image for motion detection using Horn Schunck algorithm and with the help of few iteration, found out optimum values parameters like smoothing and density. Shirgeri et al. [8] used Lukas–Kanade algorithm in combination with Sobel filter and Gaussian smoothing techniques is used in this paper to compute Optical Flow vectors. With the help of Sobel and Centroid information, object movements in an image can be tracked.

From above discussed technique, background subtraction is common method in terms of its simplicity. But there is need of progression in time consumption and data consumption for processing capability.

3   System Implementation

Video surveillance using motion detection has become more advantageous over manual video surveillance. In recent days, with increase in development of computer vision technology, the security system has developed enormously [9]. In a video, there are fundamentally two sources of data that can be utilized for recognition of object detection is visual features (edge, point, boundary, face, and object) and motion estimation [6].

3.1   Motion Detection System

Detection of moving object from sequence of frames captured from a static camera is widely performed by frames difference method. The objective of this system is to detect the moving objects by comparing reference frame and current frame by using gray level feature for feature extraction with the help of threshold method. Above Fig. 3 shows overview of motion detection system, it will capture sequence of images in video format. Web camera of laptop is going to use for video capturing using MATLAB.

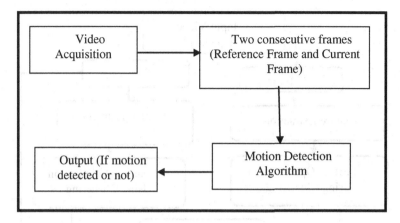

Fig. 3. Overview of motion detection system

3.2   Pyramidal Reduction

Pyramidal hierarchical structure used to represent the image at different resolution levels maintaining information details in frame. Each pyramid level is recursively obtained from its underlying level. Each level is obtained by reducing resolution of previous frame by means of sampling and smoothening.

3.3   Selection of Threshold Value from Gray Level Histogram and Motion Estimation Based upon Gray Level Features

Threshold method is basically simple segmentation, while object is clearly distinguishable from background, there has to be set proper threshold to divide image pixels into different section and segment the objects from background based on their level of distribution [1]. Threshold method creates binary images from gray level image by turning all pixels underneath some limit to zero and all pixels over that threshold to one. Choosing suitable limit of threshold of gray level is very vital in extracting objects from their background. In this case, Otsu's threshold selection, a region based segmentation method is used. Otsu's technique is a kind of adequate threshold in which it depends on gray level estimation of the image. The Otsu's method requires calculating a gray level histogram. The Otsu's strategy depends on interclass variance maximization [3].

Threshold value is used to classify gray level. Ideally, the histogram shows deep and sharp valley between two crests according to objects and background, separately, so that the threshold can be picked at the base of this valley. Threshold is getting to choose according to valley between two crests. Threshold can be chosen by plotting histogram [3]. Work flow for proposed algorithm is shown in Fig. 4.

There is technique to select threshold value, i.e. valley sharpening technique, used to confines the histogram of pixels, calculating value of derivatives of gray level using difference histogram method. Threshold is selected using maximal amount of gray level difference [3].

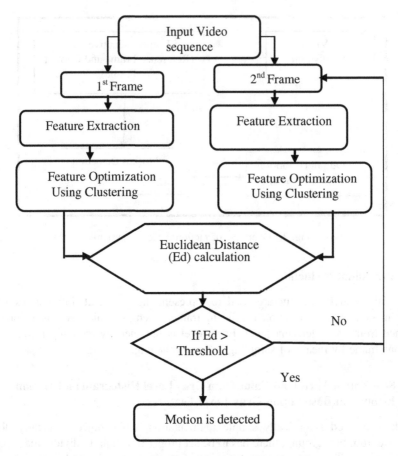

Fig. 4. Work flow for motion detection Algorithm

Assume L gray levels of pixels of image [1,2, ..., L]. n_i: no of pixels at level i
$N = n_1 + n_2 + n_3 + \cdots + n_L$: Total number of pixels
Representation of gray level histogram and probability distribution

$$P_i = n_i/N, \quad P_i \geq 0, \quad \sum_0^L P_i = 1. \tag{1}$$

Consider that dividing total pixels into two classes C_0, C_1 (background and object or vice versa) using threshold at level k.
C_0: [1, ..., k] pixel levels; C_1: [k + 1,..., L] pixel levels.
Probability of class occurrence and class mean level are as follows:

$$\omega_0 = \Pr(C_0) = \sum_{i=1}^{k} P_i = \omega(k) \tag{2}$$

$$\omega_1 = Pr(C_1) = \sum_{i=K+1}^{L} P_i = 1 - \omega(k) \tag{3}$$

$$\mu_0 = \sum_{i=1}^{k} iPr(i|C_0) = \sum_{i=1}^{k} iP_i/\omega_0 = \mu(k)/\omega(k) \tag{4}$$

$$\mu_1 = \sum_{i=k+1}^{k} iPr(i|C_1) = \sum_{i=k+1}^{k} iP_i/\omega_1 = \frac{\mu_T - \mu(k)}{1 - \omega(k)}, \tag{5}$$

Where,

$$\omega(k) = \sum_{i=1}^{k} P_i \tag{6}$$

$$\mu(k) = \sum_{i=1}^{k} iP_i \tag{7}$$

Above equations are zero[th] and first order cumulative moments of the histogram to k level.

$$\mu_T = \mu(L) = \sum_{i=1}^{L} iP_i \tag{8}$$

$$\omega_0 \mu_0 + \omega_1 \mu_1 = \mu_T, \quad \omega_0 + \omega_1 = 1 \tag{9}$$

The class variances are as follows:

$$\sigma_0^2 = \sum_{i=1}^{k} (i - \mu_o)^2 Pr(i|C_0) = \sum_{i=1}^{k} (1 - \mu_0)^2 P_i/\omega_0 \tag{10}$$

$$\sigma_1^2 = \sum_{i=k+1}^{L} (i - \mu_1)^2 Pr(i|C_1) = \sum_{i=k+1}^{L} (1 - \mu_1)^2 P_i/\omega_1 \tag{11}$$

Second cumulative moments (statistics) will require. To calculate threshold value, discriminant criterion measures (or measures of class seperability) will need in discriminant analysis.

$$\lambda = \sigma_B^2/\sigma_W^2, \quad K = \sigma_T^2/\sigma_W^2, \quad \eta = \sigma_B^2/\sigma_T^2 \tag{12}$$

$$\sigma_W^2 = \omega_0 \sigma_0^2 + \omega_1 \sigma_1^2 \tag{13}$$

$$\sigma_B^2 = \omega_0(\mu_0 - \mu_T)^2 + \omega_1(\mu_1 - \mu_T)^2$$
$$= \omega_0 \omega_1 (\mu_1 - \mu_0)^2 \tag{14}$$

According to (9)

$$\sigma_T^2 = \sum\nolimits_{i=1}^{L} (i - \mu_T)^2 P_i \tag{15}$$

Equations (13)–(15) is within class variance, the between class variance and total variance level respectively. To find k threshold, object functions will require (12).

Maximizing λ, K, η will need discriminant criteria. $K = \lambda + 1$ and $\eta = \lambda/\lambda + 1$ in terms of λ.

$$\sigma_W^2 + \sigma_B^2 = \sigma_T^2 \tag{16}$$

σ_W^2, σ_B^2 These are the functions of threshold at level K, but σ_T^2 is independent of K. σ_W^2 is based on class variance. σ_B^2 is based on class means. There is need of η as measures criterion to find k threshold at K level. Using Eqs. (6), (7) or (2)–(5);

$$\eta(k) = \sigma_B^2(K)/\sigma_T^2 \tag{17}$$

$$\sigma_B^2(k) = \frac{[\mu_T \omega(k) - \mu(k)]^2}{\omega(k)[1 - \omega(k)]} \tag{18}$$

The optimal threshold k* is as follows;

$$\sigma_B^2(k^*) = \max_{1 \le k < L} \sigma_B^2(k) \tag{19}$$

$S^* = \{k; \omega_0 \omega_1 = \omega(k)[1 - \omega(k)] > 0, \ or \ 0 < \omega(k) < 1\}$ is range of k, i.e. range of threshold. This is range of the gray level histogram. σ_B^2 or η takes minimum value zero. $0 < \omega(k) < 1$ Means $\omega(k) = 0$ or 1 for $k \in S^*$.

3.4 Calculating Maximum Level of Gray Features

Gray level threshold method is used to convert RGB image into gray image according to threshold [10]. After computing the global threshold level, there is requirement of maximum level of gray level features from gray image because it is going to lead in motion detection. Calculating maximum level of gray feature is going too used in motion detection whether motion is detected or not. It is essential to choose proper threshold values of gray level for extracting the object from the background (Table 1).

Above table indicates the gray levels of given frame and also red, green, blue levels of respective frame. In graph (b) and (c), x-axis indicates the no of frames and y-axis indicated level of gray values present in image. Image shown in figure is last frame showing approximately 148 value of gray level.

Table 1. (a) Frame, (b) Graph of showing gray levels of given frame, (c) Red, Green, Blue levels of given frame.

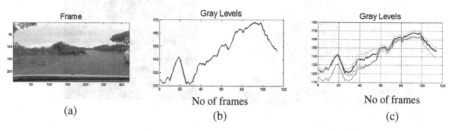

Frame	Gray Levels	Gray Levels
	No of frames	No of frames
(a)	(b)	(c)

4   Results

Frame differencing based gray level feature extraction for motion detection using threshold method is developed on MATLAB 2013a toolbox with Intel Core i3 at 2.4 GHz 4 GB RAM 64-bit operating system. It detects motion of object along with red bar shown below which indicates level of motion of object.

Red bar at the bottom of the result shows level of motion detection in Fig. 5. As the man is sitting in the static position, the minimum level of red bar has been indicated with threshold level 0.3098.

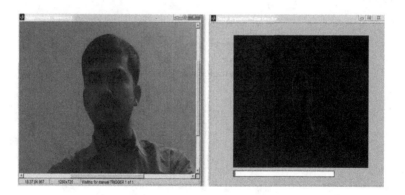

Fig. 5. Sample detected single object with static position.

Figure 6 shows man with hand shaking movement and it is detected with the developed algorithm. As in this case, there are multiple movements; the level of red bar has been increased also threshold level has been changed from 0.3098 to 0.3216.

Figure 7 shows histogram plot for motion present. It has pixel brightness at X-axis and gray level value at Y-axis. From histogram estimation graphs for motion detected frames and no motion frames, it can be seen that the histogram for some points is present at high gray levels in motion frames. When there is no motion then difference image shows zero gray level histogram plots as shown in Fig. 8.

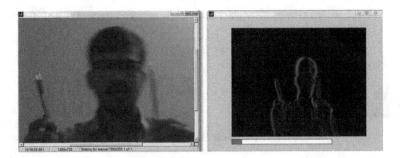

Fig. 6. Hand shaking movement with multiple objects

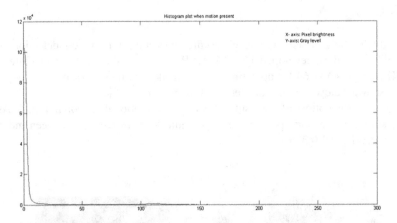

Fig. 7. Histogram plot when motion present

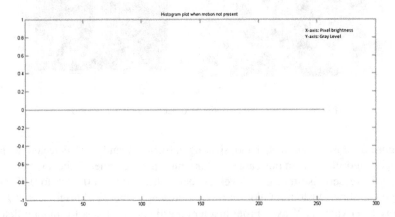

Fig. 8. Histogram plot when motion not present

Below Fig. 9 shows the data from created object file. This has video format, video resolution and time period. As in the.obj file required user data taken in one dimensional array. Timeout is 10 and frames per trigger are 10.

Fig. 9. Obj.mat file

Comparative analysis in table shows comparison of presented technique with existing method. Salt and pepper noise is initially in the video for false detection purpose. Processing time for presented method has less time than others because 10 frames per sec per video are used instead of 30 frames per sec. This leads to reduction in overall processing complexity (Table 2).

Table 2. Comparative analysis with existing techniques

	Proposed method	Approximate median method	Temporal frame difference method
Process time	15.82 s	21 s	17 s
False detection	3%	7%	4.82%
Minimum moving object to frame size ratio	0.3	0.4	0.35
Effect of noise in terms of false detection	5.72	9.82	7.88

5 Conclusion and Future Discussion

This system takes information from video input and shows random movement in video stream. The system takes continuous data in order to set it up for motion detection. This algorithm is able to detect and track, not only the single object in the video but also detects multiple objects in the video. Frame difference is based on global threshold which has value that lies in the range [0, 1]. Hence as discussed in results, better value of threshold is 0.32 in this case. Gray level feature is nothing but feature extraction used to match the same features of image which is relevant for solving the computation task. It matches the same content of reference frame and current frame which can lead to motion detection. For future development of system, it can be design using VLSI architecture implementation on FPGA board. Before that, K-means clustering can be implemented into current algorithm which will able to give faster result in terms of computational time.

References

1. Kumari, S., Kaur, M., Singh, B.: Detection of moving objects in visual surveillance systems. Int. J. Adv. Res. Electr. Electron. Instrum. Eng. **2**(8), 3711–3719 (2013)
2. Olugboja, A., Wang, Z.: Detection of moving objects using foreground detector and improved morphological filter. In: 3rd International Conference on Information Science and Control Engineering, pp. 329–333. IEEE (2016)
3. Otsu, N.: A threshold selection method from gray-level histograms. IEEE Trans. Syst. Man Cybern. **9**(1), 62–66 (1979)
4. Venkatesan, R., Balaji Ganesh, A.: Real time implementation on moving object tracking and recognition using Matlab. Department of TIFAC CORE, Velammal Engineering College, Chennai, India
5. Zarka, N., Alhalah, Z., Deeb, R.: Real-time human motion detection and tracking. Department of Artificial Intelligence. Faculty of Information Technology, University of Damascus, Damascus, Syria
6. Hussien, H.M.: Detection and tracking system of moving objects based on MATLAB. Int. J. Eng. Res. Technol. (IJERT) **3**(10) (2014)
7. Al Kanawathi, J., Mokri, S.S., Ibrahim, N., Hussain, A., Mustafa, M.M.: Motion detection using Horn Schunck algorithm and implementation. In: International Conference on Electrical Engineering and Informatics, Selangor, Malaysia, pp. 83–87 (2009)
8. Shirgeri, S., Naik, P.U., Udupi, G.R., Bidkar, G.A.: Design and development of optical flow based Moving Object Detection and Tracking (OMODT) System. Int. J. Comput. Eng. Res. **3**(4) (2013)
9. Shuigen, W., Zhen, C., Hua, D.: Motion detection based on temporal difference method and optical flow field. In: 2nd International Symposium on Electronics, Commerce, Security. ISECS 2009. IEEE (2009)
10. Shaikh, S.H., Saeed, K., Chaki, N.: Moving Object Detection Approaches, Challenges and Object Tracking. Moving Object Detection Using Background Subtraction. SCS, pp. 5–14. Springer, Cham (2014). https://doi.org/10.1007/978-3-319-07386-6_2

An Android Based Smart Environmental Monitoring System Using IoT

Sangeeta Kumari, Manasi H. Kasliwal$^{(\boxtimes)}$,
and Nandakishor D. Valakunde

Department of Computer Engineering, Vishwakarma Institute of Technology,
Pune, India
{sangeeta.kumari,manasi.kasliwal17,
nandkishor.valakunde}@vit.edu

Abstract. Environmental Monitoring system is the mechanism to provide a means systematic schematic sampling of air, water and soil conditions in order to examine and study the environment.

This proposed prototype provides an IoT based solution to monitors temperature, humidity, Rain Drop, earth quack and also measure light intensity and display. It used to display current status and history in console server ThingSpeak cloud and it can be also accessed through android app globally.

Keywords: Environmental monitoring · IoT · ThingSpeak cloud
Vibration measurements · Temperature monitoring

1 Introduction

Internet of things is connecting physical devices such as vehicles, buildings etc. with internet through which they can exchange and collect data with each other. In general, the IoT promotes an increased level of awareness about our earth. Weather monitoring is also important not just in defining today's climate but also for detecting changes in environment.

The objective of environmental parameters monitoring depends upon situation, like ensuring company compliances with regulations, find risk of human health, animals, factory's machinery. Whether manufacturing factory gas or harmful pollutants emission exceeds permissible range or not, can also checked through continuous monitoring of sensors parameter and if it is beyond permissible range then necessary action can be taken. Gathered humidity data, temperature data and rainfall data can be used by different community like Fishers, farmers, hunters to plan their work and resolve their work dependency on weather. If parameters like Rain fall, earth quack, temperature & humidity are informed in advance then severity of the natural hazard can be reduced.

This paper is organized in the following manner. Section 2 contains literature survey. Proposed prototype contains detailed description of hardware and software we have used in this system along with flowchart of proposed system. Circuit diagram explains the working of proposed prototype along with its connections. The paper has been concluded by results of system and its future scope.

© Springer Nature Singapore Pte Ltd. 2018
M. Singh et al. (Eds.): ICACDS 2018, CCIS 906, pp. 535–544, 2018.
https://doi.org/10.1007/978-981-13-1813-9_53

2   Literature Survey

Several approaches have been found for remote environment monitoring to detect change in temperature, humidity, smoke and motion or the presence of water in data centers and remote sites. Such Proposed system automatically sends progressive alarms if these parameters rise from warning levels to critical alerts.

Kodali and Mandala [1] designed an IoT based weather station using ESP8266 based Wi-Fi module Nodemcu. They used light intensity, temperature, humidity and rain sensor for sensing environmental conditions. Whenever the sensor value exceeds a chosen threshold limit for each a SMS and a tweet post is published which will alert owner to take necessary actions.

Sahoo, Khithani [2] and team developed an environmental monitoring system based on IoT. They have designed a wireless sensor network using raspberry pi as a base station, sensor node as a combination of sensor and controller, and XBee as a networking protocol. They proposed a low-cost, low-power system which contains sensor-logging and location-tracking application and a social-network of things with status updates.

Shewale and Gaikwad [3] have proposed a real-time weather monitoring system using raspberry pi. They have measured different environmental parameters using temperature and humidity sensor, LDR and rain water level measuring sensors. All the sensed data will be sent to ThingSpeak cloud through raspberry pi. His paper get the real-time monitoring of data from sensors Ethernet network.

Author Ugale [4] proposed a system based on IoT for environmental condition monitoring in homes. He used different sensors such as temperature, humidity and level etc. to monitor the environmental conditions. PIC microcontroller is used to monitor and sense the parameters. Sensor will sense the functionality of device. If proposed system is not working properly then email and SMS will be sent to user as well as distributor and this information can be accessed globally.

Roo and Ome developed [5] a IoT based weather monitoring system which sensors environmental parameters such as carbon-monoxide, sound intensity, temperature and light intensity using ATmega328 microcontroller. They have used wi-fi module to upload the data wirelessly onto the cloud.

Rian and Hanif proposed [6] a real time monitoring system based on mobile application using Automatic Weather Station (AWS). The system connects to the AWS contains several sensors for collecting and storing the data to the web server. Data from sensor is taken from the AWS-Davis Instrument using the WeatherLink software. The data is transmitted through the data logger using serial communication, then uploaded via FTP and stored on a web server. The Android application reads the files and displays the information provided by the web server in real-time.

3   Proposed Prototype

In proposed prototype we are using vibration sensor, rain drop detector, DHT22 and light dependent resistor (LDR) and raspberry pi 3 models as main component of hardware. We are also utilizing ThingSpeak cloud and android studio for software. The specifications of all sensors are enlisted one by one in detail in the following subsection.

3.1 Hardware

3.1.1 Raspberry Pi 3 Model

The Raspberry Pi 3 is a third generation model B Raspberry Pi board. It has Broadcom BCM2387 chipset's ARM Cortex-A53 processor. It has inbuilt wireless LAN (802.11 b/g/n) and Bluetooth 4.1. It has clocking speed of 1. 2 GHz. It supports GUI and command line program. Following are the steps for connecting Raspberry-Pi 3 with computer:

- Prepare SD card with OS, then insert it into Raspberry pi 3's SD card slot.
- Connect micro USB cable to Raspberry-pi and laptop to power it up.
- Also connect Ethernet cable from Raspberry pi to laptop for internet connection.
- Make all the circuit connections as per requirement.
- Now power on the Raspberry pi and share your internet connection with raspberry pi over internet.

3.1.2 DHT22

DHT22 stand for 'Digital-output relative Humidity and Temperature sensor/module'. It is also known as AM2302. It has operating range for humidity as 0–100%RH and for temperature as −40 to +80 °C. Single-bus data is used for communication between microcontroller and DHT22.It works on 3.3 V to 6 V of power supply.

3.1.3 Rain Drop Detector

Rain drop detector works like a switch when raindrop falls on the rain drop measuring board and also used for measuring rainfall intensity. It works on 5 V of power supply. The rain drop detector module consists of a rain detector and the control board which are separable for more convenience.

3.1.4 LDR

LDR stands for 'Light Dependent Resistor'. It consists of two cadmium sulphide (cds) photoconductive cells. The cell resistance is inversely proportional to light intensity. It can be used in different applications such as automatic lighting control and burglar alarm system.

3.1.5 Vibration Sensor

Vibration Sensor is used to detect the earthquake. It is consist of vibration sensor to sense the vibrations, adjustable potentiometer to adjust sensitivity and LM393 chip to give an adjustable digital output depending upon vibrations. It works on 3.3 V to 5 V power supply. It can be used in object movement detection, burglary protection system.

3.2   Software

3.2.1   ThingSpeak Cloud

ThingSpeak is an open source Internet of Things (IoT) analytic service. It regains data from things. It also allows user to visualize, aggregate and analyze live data stream in cloud. It has integrated support from computing software MATLAB from MathWorks. It also has a facility to send alert messages to user/customer using social media such as Twitter and Twilio. It allows users to analyze and visualize uploaded data using Matlab. ThingSpeak cloud captures the new data from sensors after every 15 s.

3.2.2   Android Studio

Android Studio is a crossed-platform Integrated Environment Development written in Java. It has gradle based build support. Android studio's editor allows users to drag and drop UI components. It also has built-in support for Google Cloud Platform. It supports windows, macOS and Linux operating systems.

4   Workflow and Circuit Diagram for Sensing of Environmental Parameter

When the raspberry pi 3 gets connected to computer it provides power supply to all other sensors connected to it. Then sensors sense the different environmental parameters and displays the sensed values onto the computer screen as well as it will send data to cloud. When sensed values reach the level where it will harm human beings as well as other creature's health it will start indicating the warning message on screen and will turn ON the LED. This feature will help weather station people to take required measures. The sensed data will be send to cloud and also to mobile application (Fig. 1).

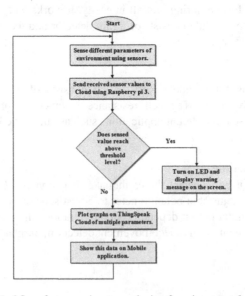

Fig. 1. Workflow from sensing to analysis of environmental parameter

4.1 Circuit Diagram

The proposed system consists of sensors such as LDR, DHT22, vibration sensor and rain drop detector as well as Raspberry-pi 3 model as shown in Fig. 2. The connections are as follows. Rain drop detector's D0 pin is connected to GPIO18 pin of raspberry pi model. Vibration sensor is connected to GPIO17pin of raspberry pi 3 model through D0 pin of sensor and DHT22 is connected to GPIO02 pin of model with the help of 10 KΩ resistor. This resistor is connected in between pin number 1 and 2 of DHT22. LDR is connected to raspberry pi board in series with piezoelectric capacitor at GPIO04 pin. Ground and power supply pins of all the sensors are made common and single connection of ground and Vcc is provided to raspberry pi 3 model B board.

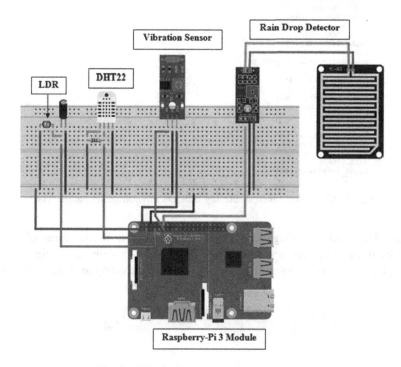

Fig. 2. Circuit diagram of proposed system

5 Result Analysis

All the sensors connected to raspberry pi board collects data from environment and send it to raspberry pi board. Raspberry pi 3 model B board operates in data acquisition mode as well as a web server mode. Raspberry pi 3 collects data from all the sensors and sends that data to cloud via internet. It displays collected sensor values and warning messages on the screen as shown in the Fig. 3. Here we can see whenever there is any movement happened before earthquake it will display a message "Movement Detected!" Also, when it's not raining it will display as "not raining" and when the rain drops detector plate senses water droplets on it, it will display as "Raining". That (200, OK) message indicates that sensor data has been successfully dent to cloud.

```
Python 2.7.9 (default, Sep 17 2016, 20:26:04)
[GCC 4.9.2] on linux2
Type "copyright", "credits" or "license ()" for more information.
>>> ============================= RESTART
=================================
>>>
Light intensity: 814
Temp=26.1*C humidity=47.0%
Not raining :)
Movement Detected!
Movement Detected!
Movement Detected!
(200, 'OK')
Light intensity: 767
Temp=26.1*C humidity=47.0%
Not raining :)
(200, 'OK')
Light intensity: 815
Movement Detected!
Temp=26.1*C humidity=47.0%
Not raining :)
Movement Detected!
(200, 'OK')
Light intensity: 824
Temp=26.1*C humidity=47.0%
Not raining :)
(200, 'OK')
Light intensity: 840
Temp=26.1*C humidity=47.0%
Not raining :)
(200, 'OK')
Light intensity: 756
```

Fig. 3. Computer screen displaying different environmental parameters.

The data send to ThingSpeak cloud will display it in the form of graphs. ThingSpeak cloud accepts new values after every 15 s. As show in the Fig. 4 it plots the graph in form of date vs. parameter which we are providing as input to the cloud.

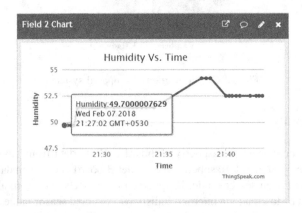

Fig. 4. Humidity vs. Time graph plotted on ThingSpeak cloud

It indicates new input value plotted in the form of dot onto the graph. When we place cursor on that point it will show the input parameter name and its value, time, date and day on which that input value has been plotted. Thus, it helps user to keep track of record of environmental parameters conditions.

Following Fig. 5 shows the graph of LDR values. It is showing the light intensity on different dates. Similarly, another figure shows the temperature variation on different times of the day (Fig. 6).

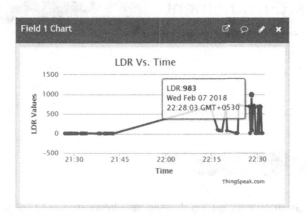

Fig. 5. Light intensity vs. time graph plotted on ThingSpeak cloud

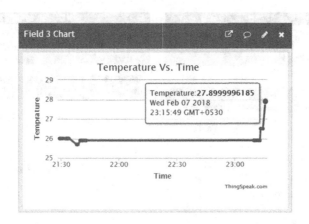

Fig. 6. Temperature vs. time graph plotted on ThingSpeak cloud

These information and graphs are very helpful for weather experts to predict next coming days environment.

The android app that we have designed represents the author's name the one who created that channel and readings as shown in following Figs. 7 and 8.

The table given below shows the comparison between different systems which are already been proposed. Figure 9 compares different systems with the help of parameters such as parameters measured, microcontroller used and output received on which devices.

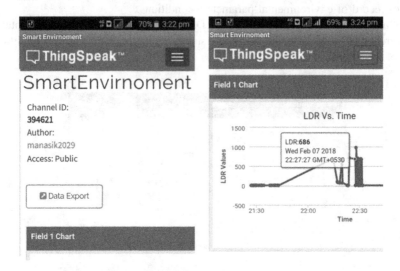

Fig. 7. Smart environment app showing basic information and LDR readings.

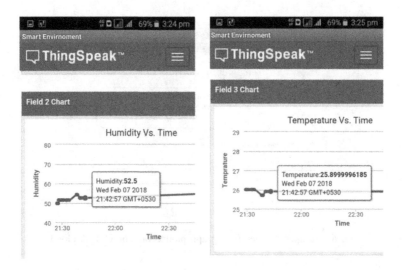

Fig. 8. Smart environments app showing readings of humidity and temperature respectively.

Sr. No.	Paper Name	Parameters Measured	Microcontroller used	Output displayed/Received on?
1.	IoT based weather station using ESP8266 based Wi-Fi module Nodemcu.	Light intensity, temperature, humidity and rain sensor.	Nodemcu.	Tweeter and Email.
2.	An environmental monitoring system based on IoT.	Temperature, Humidity, CO2, Vibration.	Raspberry Pi 3 model, Arduino Mega Board, ZigBee.	Arduino Serial Software.
3.	A real-time weather monitoring system using raspberry pi.	Temperature and humidity sensor, LDR and rain water level.	Raspberry Pi 3 Model.	ThingSpeak Cloud.
4.	IoT for environmental condition monitoring in homes.	Temperature, humidity.	Microcontroller.	Xilinx 14.1 Software.
5.	IoT based weather monitoring system.	Carbon-monoxide, sound intensity, temperature and light intensity.	ATmega328 Microcontroller.	Web Page.
6.	A real time monitoring system based on mobile application using Automatic Weather Station (AWS).	Rain sensor, temperature sensor, humidity sensor, wind speed sensor and a solar radiation sensor.	-	Android Application.
7.	Proposed Model	DHT22, LDR, Rain drop detect sensor, Vibration sensor, Alcohol level detection, Carbon dioxide.	Raspberry Pi 3 Model.	ThingSpeak Cloud, Android Application, Web Page.

Fig. 9. Comparison of different systems.

6 Conclusion and Future Scope

Environmental parameter monitoring may be undertaken for numerous reasons but generally it is done to get information about the present levels of harmful pollutants in the environment. Because of these harmful pollutants not only affect our surrounding environment but also affect animals & Human Beings consequently.

Apart from the pollutant monitoring in drinking water, sampling may be done for river water, lakes water, sea water in order to estimate an overall indication of water quality and preventive action can be taken in advance.

Keeping a check of humidity and temperature can also be useful for numerous applications like smart agriculture, home automation & most importantly smart factory.

References

1. Kodali, R.K., Mandal, S.: IoT based weather station. In: International Conference on Control, Instrumentation, Communication and Computational Technologies (ICCICCT). IEEE, Washington (2016)
2. Sahoo, G., Pawar, P., Malvi, K., Jaladi, A., Khithani, K.: Environment monitoring system based on IoT. Int. J. Innov. Res. Comput. Commun. Eng. 5(1) (2017)
3. Shewale, S.D., Gaikwad, S.N.: An IoT based real-time weather monitoring system using raspberry pi. Int. J. Adv. Res. Electr. Electron. Instrum. Eng. 6(6), 4242–4249 (2017)
4. Ugale, N., Navale, M..: Implementation of "IoT" for environmental condition monitoring in homes. Int. J. Eng. Appl. Technol. (2016)
5. Rao, B.S., Rao, K.S., Ome, N.: Internet of Things (IOT) based weather monitoring system. Int. J. Adv. Res. Comput. Commun. Eng. 5(9), 312–319 (2016)
6. Munandar, A., et al.: Design of real-time weather monitoring system based on mobile application using automatic weather station. In: 2017 2nd International Conference on Automation, Cognitive Science, Optics, Micro Electro-Mechanical System, and Information Technology (ICACOMIT), Jakarta, Indonesia, 23 October 2017

Detection of Fruit Ripeness Using Image Processing

Anuprita Mande[✉], Gayatri Gurav, Kanchan Ajgaonkar,
Pooja Ombase, and Vaishali Bagul

Department of Electronics and Telecommunication Engineering,
Vishwakarma Institute of Technology, Pune, India
anuprita.mande@vit.edu

Abstract. Humans depend on their vision quality to check whether the fruit is ripe or unripe. They grade the maturity level of a fruit based on their vision based features that lead to inaccuracy, inconsistency and inefficiency in the results. There are numerous methods to detect the ripeness of fruits. The proposed work consists of two main steps; one is color image segmentation and other is comparison. For comparison purpose, we have used correlation and histogram matching techniques. The main technique used for image segmentation is region of interest based color segmentation, in which the red color region of image is separated. All the techniques use color images of fruits as input data. In the proposed work, all the images are first converted into LAB color space and then segmented both, the reference image and the input data image. With the help of correlation and histogram comparison of these images, the maturity level of a given fruit is determined.

Keywords: Correlation · Image segmentation · Region of interest
Ripeness

1 Introduction

Human beings rely on their vision quality to check ripeness of a fruit. But this is a very time consuming and inefficient method. Also there was a high error rate due to distraction, illness and other factors. In addition, picking of fruits by hand is very tedious method, so to overcome these errors, humans started to invent new technology methods.

Among many of the techniques, Digital image processing is the most efficient one to analyze the color fruit images. The most useful technique provided by digital image processing is segmentation. Therefore, automation and use of image processing methods in agriculture have become a major trend in recent years [1]. The first major task is to recognize the ripe fruit. Image segmentation is the process of separating an object of interest from the background. The color images can be segmented and compared on the basis of their colors and other features. This project uses digital image processing as a tool since the whole project is based on the color images, their segmentation and comparisons. The techniques used in this project are masking, thresholding, histogram comparison, converting the images to gray scale and correlate them. Correlation provides the similarity between the reference image and the input image.

© Springer Nature Singapore Pte Ltd. 2018
M. Singh et al. (Eds.): ICACDS 2018, CCIS 906, pp. 545–555, 2018.
https://doi.org/10.1007/978-981-13-1813-9_54

2 Pre-requisites

2.1 Image Segmentation

In computer vision, Segmentation is used to divide or segment the images so as to make it easier to analyze. The first objective is to decompose the image into parts for further analysis and second objective of segmentation is to perform a change of representation. Image segmentation algorithms are primarily based on one of two basic properties of intensity values of the image pixels: discontinuity and similarity. Image segmentation can be obtained with number of approaches. Mostly, all these approaches are based either on the similarity criteria or discontinuity criteria. The methods of image segmentation can be broadly classified into six groups [2].

2.1.1 Edge Detection

This is the first approach in which the partition of an image is based on abrupt changes in intensity values.

Edges can be defined as the sudden changes of discontinuities in an image or notable transitions in an image. An edge is nothing but a curve that can be identified as a path of rapid change in image intensity. To find edges, we have used the edge function. The intensity changes are detected using this function.

In the matrix returned, the 1's indicate the edges. The Canny method has two different thresholds for strong and weak edges. Canny edge detection is less susceptible to noise and also accuracy of edge detection is more [3].

An edge detection method is said to be efficient when it detects the global edges which are continuous in nature.

The major disadvantage of the edge detection technique is that it does not work well when images have many edges because in that case the segmentation method produces an over segmented result, and it cannot easily identify a closed curve or boundary. The thresholding method overcomes most of these drawbacks [3].

Figure 1 shows the effect of edge detection algorithm on an input image.

Fig. 1. (a) Input image, (b) Image after edge detection

2.1.2 Thresholding

Thresholding is a technique which produces segments with pixels having similar intensities. It is a useful technique to establish boundaries in the images which contain solid objects which is resting on a contrast background. Thresholding technique requires that an object should have a homogeneous intensity and a background with a different intensity level. Such image can be segmented into two regions just by a simple thresholding.

This way of partitioning an image into a foreground and background isolates the objects by converting gray scale images into binary images. This technique is most effective in the images with high levels of contrast. The most commonly used image thresholding algorithms include histogram and multi-level thresholding. These algorithms cannot completely eliminate the background from the object. Thresholding gives best results if the objects of interest have a uniform interior gray level and rest on a background of unequal but a relatively uniform gray level. Thresholding plays an important role in one of the initial steps of operations of image processing. Only two classes can be generated in this technique however they cannot be applied for multi-channel images.

For this project, thresholding technique is not that effective as it is not able to remove the background of the real time images [4].

Figure 2 shows the effect of thresholding on an input image.

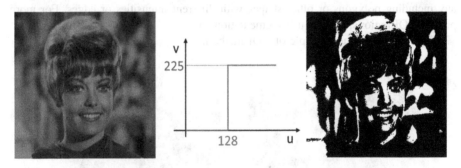

Fig. 2. (a) Input image, (b) Thresholding level, (c) Output image

2.1.3 Histogram Comparison Method

Histogram-based methods have less complexity when compared to other image segmentation methods. In histogram comparison technique, a histogram plots pixels with respect to its tonal value. Clusters are formed depending on its intensity levels ranging from 0 to 256 which give rise to peaks and valleys.

One major disadvantage of this method is that it is cannot work properly if the image has no gray level histogram peak. The second disadvantage is that it cannot ensure the continuity of the segmented regions. The histogram based method can be used efficiently if we focus on the histogram peaks [5].

Figure 3 shows histogram comparison method.

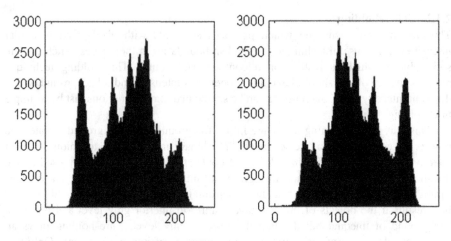

Fig. 3. Histogram comparison

2.1.4   Region of Interest

A region of interest (ROI) is a region of an image that is to be filtered or processed. A binary mask of same size as the image to be processed is used to define the ROI.

The pixels corresponding to the ROI are set to 1 and all other pixels to 0.

More than one ROI can be processed in an image. The regions of interest can be any including polygons or other shapes with different intensities or edges. For more precise ROI regions, we can use segmentation [6].

Figure 4 shows the example of ROI method.

Fig. 4. (a) Input image (b) Image showing selection of region of interest

2.1.5   Masking

A mask is a filter. Concept of masking is also known as spatial filtering. Every pixel in the mask have a value either of 0 (black) or 1 (white). Mask is nothing but a black white version of an original image with same dimensions.

The major problem of separation of the object from the background is solved using the masking technique. In image masking, the object of interest is separated from the image from its background.

Masking can be done in one of two ways:

Using an image as a mask and/or using a set of ROIs as the mask. The ROIs for each slice are used to define the mask. In this project, the ROI is used as a mask [7].

2.2 Color-Based Segmentation Using l*a*b* Color Space

The goal of image segmentation is to group the pixels that have similar feature in an image from the standard point of human visual system. There are many techniques for gray image segmentation but these techniques cannot be applied to color images directly as the color image is a multi-dimensional vector. For color image, Color has always been considered as a strong tool for image segmentation.

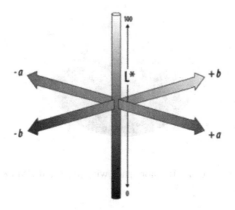

Fig. 5. L*A*B* color space.

The capability of Color image segmentation to enhance the image analysis process is more as compare to the other methods discussed previously. This results into improvement of the segmentation. For color based segmentation, a proper color space is needed. A color space is nothing but a representation of colors in digital as well as analog processes. This project is implemented in the L*A*B* color space.

In L*A*B* color space, channel 1 is for Luminance (Lightness) and other two color channels are 'a' and 'b' are the chromaticity layers. The a* layer indicates where the color falls along the red green axis, and b* layer indicates where the color falls along the blue-yellow axis. a* negative values indicate green while positive values indicate red; and b* negative values indicate blue and positive values indicate yellow. LAB color space is device independent meaning its colors do not change on any devices. Figure 5 shows the coordinates of l*a*b* color space. In Fig. 5, the vertical axis represents lightness (L*). L* can take values from 0 (black) to 100 (white). The horizontal 'a' axis indicates red (positive 'a') and green (negative 'a') and the horizontal 'b' axis indicates yellow (positive 'b') and blue (negative 'b'). The zero represents neutral gray for both the axes. From the co-ordinate system, it is seen that a color can either be red or green and blue or yellow but not both at the same time [8].

Figure 6 shows the comparison of RGB, CMYK and LAB color spaces.

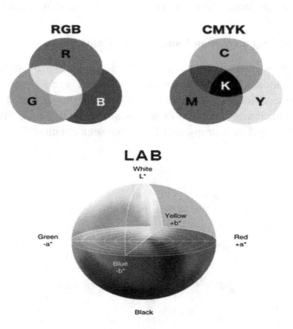

Fig. 6. Comparison of LAB color space with RGB and CMYK color spaces.

3 Methodology

In this project, main aim is to remove the background from the object as it is contributing to the correlation of the images. As our main interest lies in the comparison of the object and not the object with the background, removal of background using image segmentation techniques is the first step to be followed. For this purpose, we are working in the L*A*B* color space. After acquiring the images, the first step is to transform the input image with RGB color space to L*a*b* space and separate the three channels of L*a*b* color space in an image. Select a single channel based on the color under consideration.

Flowchart (See Fig. 7)

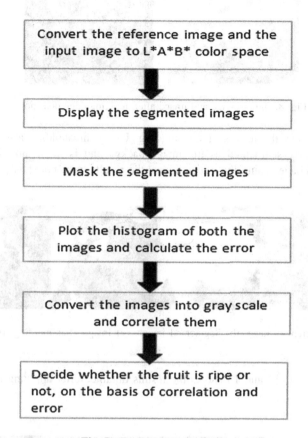

Fig. 7. Proposed methodology.

4 Results and Discussions

Here separation of the red components is done, as we have selected apple as the fruit whose ripeness is to be detected. After masking and calculation of histogram error, the image is converted to gray scale image. After this, both the images are correlated.

A fully ripened fruit is taken as the reference image and the input images will be compared with this reference image. Finally, depending on the correlation value and the histogram error, the decision is taken whether the fruit is ripe, unripe or partially ripe.

Figure 8 shows the results for image segmentation using edge detection. As the background is not uniform, the edge detection feature will capture all the edges from the image and hence it is difficult to detect the object of interest.

Fig. 8. Input image and image after applying edge detection.

Figure 9 shows the results of thresholding. Using thresholding also, the images were not properly segmented as the image background is not plain. So when we correlated the images using these techniques, the results were not satisfying.

Fig. 9. (a) Reference image. (b) Segmented image. (c) Image after masking. (d) Gray scale image of (c).

Figures 10, 11, 12 and 13 shows the results obtained after applying the proposed algorithm.

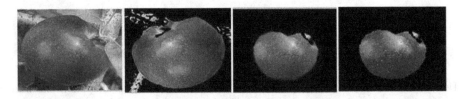

Fig. 10. (a) Reference image. (b) Segmented image. (c) Image after masking. (d) Gray scale image of (c).

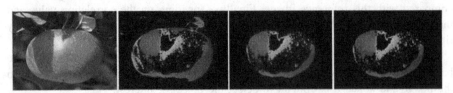

Fig. 11. (a) Input image 1. (b) Segmented image. (c) Image after masking. (d) Gray scale image of (c).

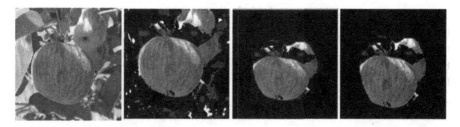

Fig. 12. (a) Input image 2. (b) Segmented image. (c) Image after masking. (d) Gray scale image of (c).

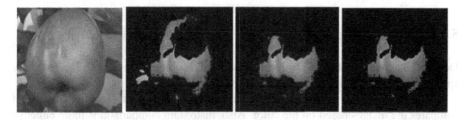

Fig. 13. (a) Input image 3. (b) Segmented image. (c) Image after masking. (d) Gray scale image of (c).

Figure (a) shows the reference image. Figure (b) consists of only the red components of the image and all other objects from the background are eliminated. So the further processing of image is simplified as the main issue of background removal is solved to some extent. In figure (c), a mask for the region of interest is created and so now only the object of interest is extracted. Correlating these extracted images, provided better results as compared to the edge detection and thresholding. Detection of the maturity level of the fruit is taken on the correlation and error values generated using the proposed methodology. These values and their corresponding results are given in Table 1.

Table 1. Indicates how the decisions are taken on the basis of correlation and error.

Correlation (S) of input image with reference image	Error (E) from histogram comparison	Decision (S&&F)
$S == 1$	$E == 0$	Fruit is fully ripped
$S >= 0.6$	$E <= 0.2$	Fruit is ripped and ready to be picked
$0.5 <= S <= 0.6$	$E <= 0.2$	Fruit is almost ripened and can be picked
$0.2 <= S <= 0.5$	$E >= 0.2$	Fruit is about to ripped and must not be picked
Otherwise	Otherwise	Fruit is raw

Table 2. Results

Images	Correlation (w.r.t. reference image)	Error	Decision
Figure 11	0.6223	0.0151	Apple is ripe & ready to be picked
Figure 12	0.6653	0.0034	Apple is ripe & ready to be picked
Figure 13	0.5096	0.0202	Apple is raw

Table 2 displays the correlation values, the error calculated from histogram matching and decision taken based on these two factors. The decision is taken completely based on the color properties of the images.

5 Conclusion and Future Scope

Detecting the maturity level of fruit ripeness based on color processing in L*a*b* color space provides the better results as compared to edge detection method.

Correlation of two color segmented images provides better results because it compares the images based on the color. Also, histogram comparison is more effective as it increases the contrast of images due to which intensities can be distributed properly on histogram. And from both the comparisons the decision is taken, whether the fruit is ripe or unripe. The processing time required for segmentation upon the size of an image.

This project is implemented at software level in MATLAB. This work is proposed for single fruit image but we can extend it for different fruits. This work can be implemented in open CV python and by interfacing camera, real time images from the field can be taken. Further the process of harvesting the ripe fruits can be automated by implementing a robot. With robotics and computer vision complete automation can be implemented in farming.

References

1. Dadwal, M., Banga, V.K.: Color image segmentation for fruit ripeness. In: 2nd International Conference on Electrical, Electronics and Civil Engineering (ICEECE'2012), Singapore, April 28–29 (2012)
2. Kwok, M.N., Ha, P.Q., Fang, G.: Effect of color space on color image segmentation. In: 2nd/International Congress on Image and Signal Processing, CISP'09, Tianjin, 17–19 October 2009
3. Salem, S.A., Kalyankar, N.V., Khamitkar, S.D.: Image segmentation by edge detection. Int. J. Comput. Sci. Eng. 2(3), 804–807 (2010)
4. Ojeda-Magana, B., Ruelas, R., Quintanilla-Domingvez, J., Andina, D.: Colour image segmentation by partitional clustering algorithms. In: IECON 2010 – 36th Annual Conference on IEEE Industrial Electronics Society, 7–10 November, Glendale, AZ, pp. 2828–2833 (2010)

5. Mohamad, F.S., Manaf, A.A., Chuprat, S.: Histogram matching for color detection: a preliminary study. In: 2010 International Symposium in Information Technology (ITSim), Kuala Lumpur, vol. 3, pp. 1679–1684. IEEE (2010)
6. Colm, K., Andrew, P.J.: Survey on the image segmentation. Financ. Rev. **41**, 29–48 (2000)
7. Gonzalez, R.C., Woods, R.E.: Digital Image Processing. Pearson Education, London (2002)
8. Boral, D.J., Gupta, A.K., Khan, F.A.: Comparing the performance of L*A*B* and HSV color spaces with respect to color image segmentation. Department of Computer Science & Applications Barkatullah University, Bhopal

Comparative Study of Different Approaches to Inverse Kinematics

Ayush Gupta[✉], Prasham Bhargava, Sankalp Agrawal,
Ankur Deshmukh, and Bhakti Kadam

Department of Electronics and Telecommunication, VIT, Pune, India
{ayush.gupta15, prasham.bhargava15, sankalp.agrawal15,
ankur.deshmukh15, bhakti.kadam}@vit.edu

Abstract. Finding solutions to inverse kinematics is often the most critical part in designing any robotic system. There exist multiple ways to find a solution for the inverse kinematics. In this paper, a geometric approach to compute Inverse Kinematics is presented. This geometric approach is compared with the Pseudo-Inverse Jacobian Method and the results are discussed. The geometric approach outperforms the Jacobian method in terms of substantially reduced computational complexity and therefore enabling its implementation on a less powerful microcontroller.

Keywords: Forward kinematics · Inverse kinematics · Robotic arm
DoF · Processing · MATLAB · D-H parameters · Inverse pseudo Jacobian

1 Introduction

Designing of any robotic system is based the solutions computed using forward and inverse kinematics. In forward kinematics, the value of the joint angles decides the position of the end-effector. On the other hand, in the case of inverse kinematics, the reverse mechanism is followed. Knowing the position where the end- effector is supposed to move, the values by which the different joint angles must move are calculated. Inverse kinematics has more practical significance over forward kinematics because in all practical cases the position where the end-effector is supposed to move is known and based upon it the appropriate values of various joint angles have to be calculated.

Finding solutions to forward kinematics is easier because it generally has a unique solution defined. In contrast to, inverse kinematics not only involves much higher computational complexity, but also it usually has multiple solutions for the same position of the end-effector. Several methodologies have been proposed to find solutions to problem relating to inverse kinematics. These include algebraic methods, iterative methods which includes the Jacobian Inversion method, the optimization based methods, Cyclic coordinate descent (CCD), Jacobian Transpose method and Genetic programming to name a few [1].

One of the methods to solve the inverse kinematics problem is Artificial Intelligence and Neural networks. ARJ. Almusawi, LC. Dulger, S. Kapucu discusses the use of Artificial Neural Networks in finding the solution of inverse kinematics using Backpropagation technique [10].

© Springer Nature Singapore Pte Ltd. 2018
M. Singh et al. (Eds.): ICACDS 2018, CCIS 906, pp. 556–563, 2018.
https://doi.org/10.1007/978-981-13-1813-9_55

One more method to approach the inverse kinematics is using the geometric approach which involves the use of trigonometric formulae to compute the result. This geometric approach is compared with the pseudo-inverse Jacobian method and the results are presented.

This paper is organized as follows. Section 2 briefs about literature survey for various approaches to inverse kinematics. Section 3 explains the proposed method of geometric approach to inverse kinematics. Section 4 discusses the inverse pseudo-Jacobian method. Experimental results are presented in Sect. 5. Section 6 concludes the paper with the future scope.

In the Fig. 1 the conversion between Joint Space and Cartesian Space is given. To convert Joint Space variable in to Cartesian Space Variables Forward Kinematics is used. Inverse Kinematics is used to find Joint space variables if Cartesian space is given

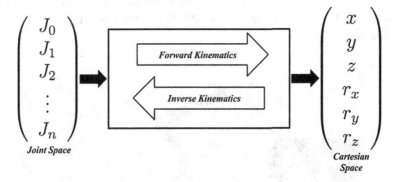

Fig. 1. Block diagram representation of conversion of joint space and Cartesian space

2 Literature Survey

Multiple methods have been discussed and presented to compute the solution to the problems based on inverse kinematics. Takahashi and Kawamura have proposed the simple modified Jacobian Matrix Method using the Newton Raphson Method which simplifies the computation by replacing some of the elements of the Jacobian matrix with zero [1]. Das, Slotine, and Sheridan proposed a solution pertaining to kinematically redundant systems, where the system possesses more degree of freedoms than required to position the end-effector. The method employed by them employs an optimization technique to find the result [2]. Pechev proposed a method to solve inverse kinematics without using matrix inversion operation. This was done by taking a feedback in a closed-loop system. Due to the elimination of matrix inversion operation, the computational time was greatly reduced [3]. Olaru, Olaru, and Mihai approached using the technique Iterative Pseudo Inverse Jacobian Matrix Method (IPIJMM) coupled with Sigmoid Bipolar Hyperbolic Tangent Neural Network with Time Delay and Recurrent Links (SBHTNN-TDRL) [4]. Barakat and Bozed performed the kinematics analysis using the Denavit-Hartenberg algorithm (D-H algorithm) followed by the simulation of the 6 DoF arm using MATLAB [5]. Tokarz and Manger have discussed geometric as well as a rough set approach for the inverse kinematics. The geometric approach has so developed that the same can be implemented on a low-source microcontroller. It also discusses how the combination of rough set theory accompanied with machine learning techniques can be used to calculate a solution to inverse kinematics [6]. Meredith and Maddock discussed Jacobian based inverse kinematics solver and the techniques which can be used to implement it efficiently in real- time inverse kinematics solving [7]. Liu et al. discussed the geometric approach to the inverse kinematics and how it reduces the computational complexity [8]. Fang, Mei, Chen, and Zhao presented an iterative method for inverse kinematics of redundancy robot to obtain a unique solution for inverse kinematics, instead of obtaining multiple solutions for the same configuration [9].

All the above methods involve high complexity in finding a solution to the inverse kinematics. This issue is being addressed by formulating and using geometric approach to compute inverse kinematics. This approach greatly reduces the computational complexity and thereby enabling the implementation on a less powerful microcontroller (Fig. 2).

Fig. 2. A 3 DoF arm CATIA design

3   Robotic Arm

Number of Links: 2
Number of Motors: 3

1. Base Motor
2. Shoulder Motor
3. Elbow Motor

Degree of Freedom: 3
Configuration: Articulated Type.

4 Proposed Method

In this method to reduce the complexity of the system, the links are considered as lines. For further simplification, the arm can be transferred from the 3 dimensions Cartesian frame (xyz frame) to the 2 dimensional (ρz frame). It gives the freedom to visualize the problem in the less complex system. The simplified version of the robotic arm is shown in Fig. 3.

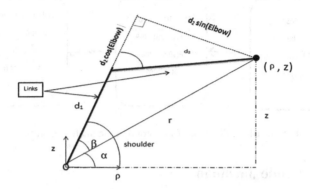

Fig. 3. A 3 DoF arm represented by lines

where,

Base, Shoulder, and Elbow are the 3 joint angles
x, y, z are the end-effector's coordinates.
d_1 and d_2 are link lengths
r is the distance of the end-effector co-ordinate from the origin
(in the reference frame of manipulator/controller)

In our previous work, mathematical relations were formulated between joint angles, link lengths and end-effector's coordinates using simple trigonometric results. The inverse kinematics formulas for the mentioned robotic arm configuration are [11]

$$r = \sqrt{(x^2 + y^2 + z^2)}. \tag{1}$$

$$\text{Base} = tan^{-1}\left(\frac{y}{x}\right). \tag{2}$$

$$\text{Elbow} = -cos^{-1}\left(\frac{x^2 + y^2 + z^2 - d_1^2 d_2^2}{2d_1 d_2}\right). \tag{3}$$

$$\text{Shoulder} = sin^{-1}\frac{z}{r} + tan^{-1}\left(\frac{d_2 \sin(Elbow)}{d_1 + d_2 \cos(Elbow)}\right). \tag{4}$$

In Fig. 1, only two of the three joints are visible (the shoulder and the elbow joint). This is done by rotating the base motor by the value of the angle calculated obtained from Eq. 2. This operation reduces the problem complexity by 1 dimension, and all the three points i.e., the shoulder, the elbow joint, and the destination point lie in the same plane which gives the freedom to apply general trigonometric results to obtain the solution geometrically (Fig. 4).

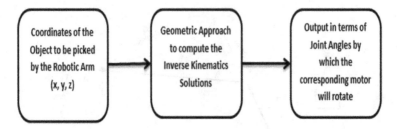

Fig. 4. Block diagram of the proposed geometric approach

5 Inverse Pseudo Jacobian

The end-effector coordinates are known so according to the above equation the error is calculated and a feedback is given to the controller, which is responsible for the movement of end-effector. This method is followed repeatedly until the end-effector is at its destined place. Due to this feedback loops, these methods are called as iterative methods as they keep repeating the same step until they get to the desired location. One of the iterative techniques is described below:

Jacobian matrix is the matrix of all first-order partial derivatives of a vector-valued function. It is a matrix of determinants and it is strictly a square matrix.

$$J = \begin{bmatrix} \dfrac{\partial f}{\partial x_1} \cdots \dfrac{\partial f}{\partial x_n} \end{bmatrix} = \begin{bmatrix} \dfrac{\partial f_1}{\partial x_1} & \cdots & \dfrac{\partial f_1}{\partial x_n} \\ \vdots & \ddots & \vdots \\ \dfrac{\partial f_m}{\partial x_1} & \cdots & \dfrac{\partial}{\partial x_n} \end{bmatrix}. \tag{5}$$

Previously the coordinates were calculated using the joint angles (Fig. 5):

$$X = f(\theta). \tag{6}$$

In the Inverse Kinematics method, We Have
The technique described over here is called the pseudo-inverse of Jacobian. In this method, the end effector tries to reach the target position by moving towards it incrementally or in steps. The objective of this method is to find the joint angles based off of the target position. [7]

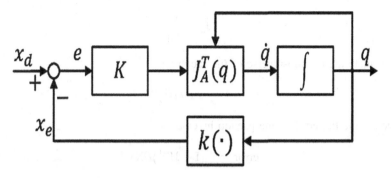

Fig. 5. Block diagram for the inverse pseudo Jacobian

By taking the inverse of Eq. (6) we can get the following equation:

$$\theta = f^{-1}(X). \tag{7}$$

The Jacobian is derived from (6) by taking the partial derivative of it.

$$\partial X = J(\theta)\partial\theta. \tag{8}$$

where,

$$J_{ij} = \frac{\delta f_j}{\delta x_i}.$$

We can write the Eq. (8) in the same fashion as (7):

$$\partial\theta = J^{-1}(\partial X). \tag{9}$$

The problem with this equation is that it needs to be square but the problem is that the matrix hardly turns out to be square and so the pseudo-inverse of the Jacobian matrix needs to be taken.

Steps for Pseudo inverse of Jacobian

(1) Calculate the difference between the goal position and the actual position of the end- effector:

$$\partial X = X_g - X. \tag{10}$$

where,

$$X_g = \text{target coordinates.}$$

(2) Calculate the Jacobian matrix using the current joint angles:

$$J_{ij} = \frac{\delta f_j}{\delta x_i}.$$ (11)

(3) Calculate the pseudo-inverse of the Jacobian:

$$J^{-1} = J^T (JJ^T)^{-1}.$$ (12)

(4) Determine the error of the pseudo-inverse

$$\text{error} = \| (I - JJ^{-1}) \partial X) \| .$$ (13)

(5) If error > e then

$$\partial X = \frac{\partial X}{2}.$$ (14)

goto step 4.
(6) Calculate the updated values for the joint orientations and use these as the new current values:

$$\theta = \theta + J^{-1} \partial X.$$ (15)

(7) Using forward kinematics determine whether the new joint orientations position the end-effector close enough to the desired absolute location. If the solution is adequate, then terminate the algorithm otherwise go back to step 1.

6 Experimental Results

The geometric approach presented in this paper is compared with the inverse pseudo-Jacobian method. The first basis for comparison is the complexity of the code involved. The proposed geometric algorithm has a worst case complexity defined as $\Theta(1)$ since it doesn't involve the execution of any iterative loops, whereas the complexity of the inverse pseudo-Jacobian method involving iterations is $\Theta(n)$ and hence involves a greater execution time. The geometric approach eliminates complex matrix computations, thereby enabling the implementation of the arm on a relatively less powerful microcontroller thereby greatly reducing the hardware cost. The Jacobian Method often leads to multiple solutions, in contrast with our method where a unique solution is obtained. The geometric method also eliminates the possibility of singular solutions, wherein all the joints of a robotic arm get aligned in a straight line. The singular solutions are invalid since they cannot perform the intended task.

The drawback of the geometric method is that in case of a change in the link lengths or offsets, which happens when the mechanical setup is changed, an entirely new set of formulae need to be derived. This problem can be tackled using the Jacobian method.

7 Conclusion and Future Work

The geometric approach is presented which is less computationally expensive, accurate up to a certain point and can be reliably implemented on a less powerful microcontroller. There exists a trade-off between the two methods in terms of reduced computational complexity and the accuracy of the solution obtained. Therefore, a hybrid approach can be developed which not only simplifies the calculations involved but also produces more accurate results. The geometric approach developed for the 3-DoF can be further extended to obtain the results for a higher order of degree of freedom.

References

1. Takahashi, T., Kawamura, A.: High-speed numerical calculation method for on-line inverse kinematics of robot manipulators. In: IEEE (1999)
2. Das, H., Slotine, J.-J.E., Sheridan, T.B.: Inverse kinematics algorithms for redundant systems. In: IEEE (1988)
3. Pechev, A.N.: Inverse kinematics without matrix inversion. In: 2008 IEEE International Conference on Robotics and Automation Pasadena, CA, USA, 19–23 May 2008
4. Olaru, A., Olaru, S., Mihai, N.: Application of a new iterative pseudo-inverse Jacobian neural network matrix technique for controlling geckodrive DC motors of manipulators. In: Proceedings of the 3rd RSI International Conference on Robotics and Mechatronics, Tehran, Iran, 7–9 October 2015
5. Barakatl, A.N., Gouda, K.A., Bozed, K.A.: Kinematics analysis and simulation of a robotic arm using MATLAB. In: Proceedings 2016 4th International Conference on Control Engineering & Information Technology (CEIT-2016), Hammamet, Tunisia, 16–18 December 2016
6. Tokarz, K., Manger, C.: Geometric and rough set approach to inverse kinematics for arm manipulator. Int. J. Math. Models Methods Appl. Sci. 5(1), 1–8 (2011)
7. Meredith, M., Maddock, S.: Real-time inverse kinematics: the return of the Jacobian. https://staffwww.dcs.shef.ac.uk/people/S.Maddock/publications/MeredithMaddock2004_CS0406.pdf
8. Liu, Y., et al.: Geometric approach for inverse kinematics analysis of 6-Dof serial robot. In: Proceeding of the 2015 IEEE International Conference on Information and Automation Lijiang, China, August 2015
9. Fang, J., Mei, T., Chen, J., Zhao, J.: An iteration method for inverse kinematics of redundancy robot. In: Proceedings of 2014 IEEE International Conference on Mechatronics and Automation, Tianjin, China, 3–6 August 2014
10. Almusawi, A.R.J., Dülger, L.C., Kapucu, S.: A new artificial neural network approach in solving inverse kinematics of robotic arm (Denso VP6242). Comput. Intell. Neurosci. (2016)
11. Gupta, A., Bhargava, P., Agrawal, S., Deshmukh, A., Chourikar, S.: A geometric approach to inverse kinematics of a 3 DoF robotic arm. Int. J. Res. Appl. Sci. Eng. Technol. 6(I), 3524–3530 (2018)

Semitransparency Effect in a Video Using Deep Learning Approach

Pavan Dongare[(✉)] and M. Sridevi

Department of Computer Science and Engineering,
National Institute of Technology, Tiruchirappalli 620015, India
dongare.pavan25@gmail.com, msridevi@nitt.edu

Abstract. Online learning platforms deliver huge amount of content through video lectures. In academic videos, content written on surface is often obscured by the instructor. This problem is addressed using either pen digitizers or frame averaging method. However, method using pen digitizer requires costly setup while method using frame averages has certain use case limitations. This paper uses deep learning approach to achieve semi transparency effect with better quality and also removes drawbacks of previous works. The experimental results showed that the proposed method works well on different type of videos.

Keywords: Deep learning · Semi transparency · Image segmentation
Deep residual networks · Video

1 Introduction

Online education has seen huge growth in recent years. Individual users as well as institutions are adopting online modes of education. NPTEL initiative by IITs, Edx by Harvard, MIT are some institute driven platforms while Khan academy, Udacity are independent organizations teaching through online platform. Most of these platforms predominantly teach curriculum content through video lectures. Videos once recorded, need to be processed before uploading into the platform. Video processing is crucial task of many online learning services. Parameters like length of video, background format have shown correlation with student engagement [1]. Research on online learning technologies involve two main aspects, namely student engagement and content delivery style. Some of the research aimed to remove problems associated with video-based lessons. One problem with video-based lessons is content obscuring due to instructor's hand and body. Udacity [2] solved content obscuring problem using digitizer pen-tablet. However, solution was only useful to videos produced using a special costly setup. In [3], a new method is proposed to achieve semitransparency effect on a normal recorded video. Hence, this work focuses on achieving better quality and accuracy of semitransparency using deep learning approach.

© Springer Nature Singapore Pte Ltd. 2018
M. Singh et al. (Eds.): ICACDS 2018, CCIS 906, pp. 564–573, 2018.
https://doi.org/10.1007/978-981-13-1813-9_56

2 Related Work

Academic videos often have content obscured by instructor hand and body. In [2], authors used pen digitizer to solve content obscuring problem. Using pen digitizers is simplest yet costly way to solve this problem. Two different videos are recorded. One with tablet screen capture and another with camera placed over top of hand. Screen capture video is processed to remove all white pixels by setting opacity to zero. A new video is created which includes only written content pixels. These two videos are overlaid to achieve semitransparency effect. This method is useful only for videos recorded using costly setup which require digitizer tablet as shown in Fig. 1.

Fig. 1. Pen digitizer setup

In [3], authors created two different videos from a single video. Background segmentation is done to create second video. There are extensive literatures on background modeling [4, 5]. Dynamic background segmentation is done using frame averaging method [3]. Different types of averaging methods are used namely accumulated, lookahead and running average and classification of pixels are performed based on the result of the three averaging values. New video is created with only background pixels. Each frame of new video is overlaid to original video to achieve semitransparency effect using single video. This approach solved content obscuring problem for many types of videos including paper or whiteboard based videos. This is not possible with just pen digitizers. However, frame averaging approach has limitations in certain use cases. For example, when obscuring object is steady in video for long duration, resulting frame averages cannot differentiate foreground and background pixels. This results in misclassification of pixels in intermediate steps.

In [3], background segmentation is most crucial task. Improving accuracy of background segmentation and removing stable obscuring limitations can provide better results. Segmentation can be done using conventional image processing techniques as well as deep learning based method. Image processing method of segmentation involve problem specific features extraction and algorithms. Deep learning networks are trained end to end without extensive feature extractors. Deep learning based segmentation uses special type of neural network architectures known as Convolution Neural Network (CNN). In [4], CNN was first used for image classification problem which yields higher accuracy than previous works. Variations of [6] were later used to achieve high performance on many image related tasks. Fully Convolutional Networks (FCN) [7] improves image segmentation results by huge margin over previous works. Later, many CNN based architectures were used to improve segmentation accuracy. Hence, this work uses variation of Deep residual network [8] for segmenting academic videos.

The remainder of the sections are organized as follows: Sect. 3 explains the proposed semitransparency effect model. Experimental results are shown in Sect. 4. Section 5 concludes the paper.

3   Proposed Method

To create semitransparency effect in a video, a new video with only content pixels is generated from input. Content pixels are separated using image segmentation. In [3], frame averaging algorithm is used to achieve semitransparency effect. In frame averaging algorithm, pixels of are misclassified if obscuring object is at same position for long duration. Hence, proposed method uses deep learning for background subtraction. Each pixel in every frame of a video is labeled zero or one depending on whether it belongs to background content or foreground obscuring object. Segmentation is used to obtain semitransparency effect using workflow shown in Fig. 2.

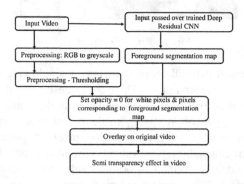

Fig. 2. Workflow for obtaining semitransparency effect using Residual Learning

This work uses simplified version of Deep residual network [8] for image segmentation task. Sections 3.1, 3.2 and 3.3 explains Dataset augmentation, Neural network architecture, Choice of hyperparameters respectively. Algorithm used in proposed method, training and testing is explained in Sects. 3.4 and 3.5 respectively.

3.1   Dataset Augmentation

Most deep learning approaches require labelled dataset to perform the classification task. A labelled dataset contains set of many input along with output. Image classification dataset can be labelled manually on looking the pictures and storing the class label for the picture. However, for achieving semitransparency in a video, image segmentation is required. Image segmentation datasets are hard to create manually because it requires labelling of all pixels of an image. Open source datasets are created manually [9]. Manual labeling requires many hours of effort. Additionally, those datasets are not suitable for segmentation of academic videos due to limited object classes which don't include objects like hand, pen, duster. Hence this work proposes a dataset generation and augmentation method using Algorithm 1 to create dataset for segmentation of academic videos.

Algorithm 1: Generation of dataset

1. Record a video with bright white background and placing objects over it like pen, duster, hand, marker.
2. Split recorded video into frames.
3. Remove white pixels in frames by setting opacity parameter to zero and save as 'm' new frames.
4. Use another set of 'n' images having different types of background like blackboard, whiteboard, paper.
5. Randomly select the images created from step 3 and overlay them the images formed in step 4. Introduce variation in position of object, orientation of image, brightness, contrast, size.
6. Number of images generated >= m*n
7. Pixels in images from step 6 are labelled as follows.
   - Pixels at the location corresponding to active pixels in step 3 are labelled as '1' indicating foreground objects.
   - Rest all pixels are labelled as '0' indicating background objects
8. Labels corresponding to pixels in images are stored in a text file.

Example of training sample created by using Algorithm 1 is shown in Figs. 3, 4, 5 and 6.

Fig. 3. Background frame

Fig. 4. Foreground frame

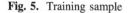

Fig. 5. Training sample　　　　**Fig. 6.** Labelling of pixel

3.2　Neural Network Architecture

Adjacent layers A_1 and A_2 in a neural network can be represented by Eqs. (1) and (2). Function 'G' in Eq. (1) represents linear transformation function and 'F' in Eq. (2) represents nonlinear transformation. In traditional neural networks, 'G' is matrix multiplication between weights and activation layer and choice of 'F' is sigmoid activation function. In CNN, function 'G' is convolution operation and 'F' is Rectified linear unit (Relu). CNN has sparse connection and weight sharing and is computationally efficient than the neural network. Networks with more number of layers usually perform better than networks with few number of layers. However, after 20 layers, adding more hidden layers drastically reduces the performance. This problem is called as vanishing gradient problem. It occurs due to slow learning rate of earlier layers in a deep CNN. Deep residual network [6] uses skip connection to avoid vanishing gradient problem. Figure 7 represents basic unit of Residual CNN. Multiple units are stacked one after another to create Residual network.

$$z_1 = G(A_1, W_1, b) \tag{1}$$

$$A_2 = F(z_1) \tag{2}$$

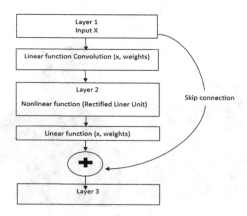

Fig. 7. Residual network unit

3.3   Choice of Hyper Parameters

Hyperparameters are network parameter values which are set explicitly. They are different from weight parameters. Weight parameters are learned by training neural network on dataset. Choice of hyperparameters affects learning rate and accuracy. Hyperparameters values for Residual network are listed below.

  I. **Number of layers:** Among n = 50 layers, 1 to n − 1 layers contain activation units and K * K kernel associated with it. n^{th} layer is FCN.

 II. **Shortcut or skip connections:** Skip connection added after every alternate layer as shown in Fig. 5.

III. **Bias and kernel initialization**: kernel of dimension K * K is used with K = 3 for intermediate layers and L * B kernel for final FCN is used where L and B are dimensions of $n − 1^{th}$ layer. Kernel and bias values are initialized in random manner.

 IV. **Zero padding:** Layers are padded using same padding. In same padding, input dimensions are preserved across adjacent layers using zeros padded around current layer. Zero padding is applied around the layer spatially as shown in Fig. 8.

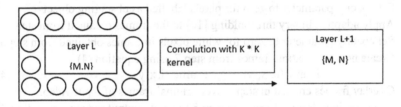

Fig. 8. Zero padding with equal output size

  V. **Stride:** Stride is size of kernel shift in convolution operation. Higher values of stride result in reducing input image size. Thus, stride parameter is set to one. Input size should be preserved across adjacent layer. Substituting s = 1 and k = 3, value of is computed as 1 using Eq. (3). Thus, one row of zero padding required around every network layer.
     Dimension of Layer 1: {n, m, d} Kernel: {k, k, d} Number of kernels: v
     Dimension of Layer 2:

$$\left\{ \frac{n + 2p - k}{s} + 1, \frac{m + 2p - k}{s} + 1, v \right\} \tag{3}$$

 VI. **Spatial dimension and width of network:** Spatial dimension is kept constant across adjacent layers. Images are RGB coded. Input dimensions are L * B * C. L is length of input image, B is breath of input image. C is number of channels. Number of input channels is three because RGB coded images are used.

3.4   Training and Testing

Synthetic dataset created using augmentation is used for training Residual network. Dataset is divided into training, cross validation and testing set. Cross validation set is used for optimizing parameters and learning rate. Choice of error function used to optimize weights is normalized pixel-wise cross-entropy loss [7]. Adams optimization algorithm [11] is used for reducing training time. Learning rate and training parameters suggested in [12] are used. Testing is done to produce segmentation of images into foreground and background.

3.5   Method to Achieve Semitransparency Effect

Residual network architecture is trained with hyperparameters described in Sect. 3.3. Synthetic dataset described in Sect. 3.1 is used. This network obtains segmentation map for input frames of the video. The proposed method uses Algorithm 2.

Algorithm 2: Semitransparency effect

1. Create Deep residual network with selected hyperparameters.
2. Split the input video in frames.
3. Test the network and label every pixel as foreground or background.
4. Set opacity parameter to zero for pixels labelled as obscuring object
5. Apply adaptive binary thresholding [10] to the frames obtained from step 5.
6. Set opacity parameter to zero for white pixels in frames obtained from step6.
7. Create new summation frames from step 7 using equation (4)

$$\text{Frame } (n, x, y) = \sum_i^n \text{Frame } (i, x, y) \tag{4}$$

8. Overlay frames created in step 7 over original frames of input video.
9. Use combined frames formed in step 8 to create output video with audio taken from input video.
10. Output video is generated with semitransparency effect.

4   Results and Experimental Setup

The proposed method is experimented with following setup: (1) Computer with core i7 processor and 8 GB RAM (2) Programming language Python with library OpenCV Library for dataset generation (3) Deep learning library Pytorch [13] for building and training Residual network. Pixel prediction accuracy is optimized on training dataset of 300 images. For a video with input frame as shown in Fig. 9, intermediate frames generated are shown in Figs. 10, 11 and 12, and resulting output video frame is shown in Fig. 13.

Fig. 9. Input frame from a video

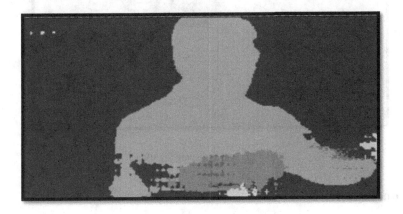

Fig. 10. Segmentation map obtained

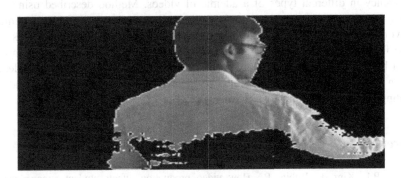

Fig. 11. Obscuring object

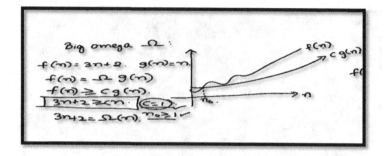

Fig. 12. Combined content frame

Fig. 13. Semitransparency effect

5 Conclusion

It is evident from the results that deep learning based segmentation approach gives better semi transparency effect when compared to previous work such as using digitizer tablet or frame averaging method. This work is more suitable for achieving semi transparency in different types of academic of videos. Method described using deep learning based segmentation does not have limitations of frame averaging technique. This work is cost effective and robust compared to using pen digitizer tablet. This work can be further extended to cover complex use cases like erasing content or moving camera by splitting video and applying this method to individual parts of video. In future a method has to be incorporated to identify the instances of video and also providing suitable algorithm for each instance.

References

1. Guo, P.J., Kim, J., Rubin, R.: How video production affects student engagement: an empirical study of MOOC videos. In: Proceedings of the First ACM Conference on Learning, Scale Conference, pp. 41–50. ACM (2014)

2. Reichelt, K.A.: System and method for combining computer-based educational content recording and video-based educational content recording. U.S. Patent No. 9049482 (2015)
3. Dongare, P., Sridevi, M.: A novel method for semi transparency effect in academic videos. In: 2017 8th International Conference on Computing, Communication and Networking Technologies (ICCCNT), Delhi, pp. 1–5 (2017)
4. Hassanpour, H., Sedighi, M., Manashty, A.R.: Video frame's background modeling: reviewing the techniques. J. Sig. Inf. Process. **2**(02), 72–78 (2011)
5. Bouwmans, T.: Traditional and recent approaches in background modeling for foreground detection: an overview. Comput. Sci. Rev. **11**, 31–66 (2014)
6. Lecun, Y., Bottou, L., Bengio, Y., Haffner, P.: Gradient-based learning applied to document recognition. In: Proceedings of the IEEE, vol. 86, no. 1, pp. 2278–2324 (1998)
7. Long, J., Shelhamer, E., Darrell, T.: Fully convolutional networks for semantic segmentation. In: Proceedings of the IEEE Conference on Computer Vision and Pattern Recognition, Boston, pp. 3431–3440 (2015)
8. He, K., Zhang, X., Ren, S., Sun, J.: Deep residual learning for image recognition. In: IEEE Conference on Computer Vision and Pattern Recognition (CVPR), Las Vegas, pp. 770–778 (2016)
9. Lichman. Image segmentation dataset. UCI machine learning repository
10. Huang, Z.-K., Chau, K.-W.: A new image thresholding method based on Gaussian mixture model. Appl. Math. Comput. **205**(2), 899–907 (2008)
11. Kingma, D.P., Ba, J.: Adam: a method for stochastic optimization. arXiv preprint arXiv: 1412.6980 (2014)
12. Pakhomov, D., Premachandran, V., Allan, M., Azizian, M., Navab, N.: Deep residual learning for instrument segmentation in robotic surgery. arXiv preprint arXiv:1703.08580 (2017)
13. Paszke, A., et al.: Automatic differenciation in pytorch. In: NIPS (2017)

Author Index

Agarkar, Aarti II-507
Agarwal, Arun II-298
Aggarwal, Apeksha II-370
Agnihotram, Gopichand II-167
Agrawal, Himanshu II-507
Agrawal, Navneet I-290
Agrawal, Sankalp II-556
Ahamad, Maksud II-239
Ahmad, Nesar II-239
Ahuja, Laxmi II-380
Ajgaonkar, Kanchan II-545
Ajitha Shenoy, K. B. II-489
Alam, Mirza Mohtashim I-381, II-269
Ali, Rashid I-165, II-98
Allayear, Shaikh Muhammad I-381
Ambigavathi, M. I-144
Anand, Deepa I-279
Anjan Babu, G. II-359
Archana, N. I-302, I-312
Arockiam, L. II-77
Arote, Seema Vitthal I-520
Awasthi, Amit I-208

Badhani, Shikha II-442
Bagchi, Menaxi J. I-270
Bagul, Vaishali II-545
Bansal, Ashu I-372
Bansal, Komal G. II-423
Baruah, Arup I-35
Basu, Subhadip II-66
Bedase, Deepak I-499
Bhagwanti II-388
Bhalla, Saurabh II-413, II-423
Bhanegaonkar, Gauri II-471
Bhanu, S. Mary Saira II-24
Bhargava, Prasham II-556
Bhargavi, B. I-124
Bhargavi, K. II-177
Bhaskar, P. C. II-523
Bhattacharya, Jhilik II-138
Bhorge, Siddharth I-499
Bijalwan, Anchit I-208

Bisht, Rashmi I-175
Borah, Pranjal Protim I-35
Budhiraja, Meenal II-479

Chamoli, Vivek I-401
Chandra, Satish I-411
Chaudhary, Krista I-431
Chaudhary, Prashant I-208
Chauhan, D. K. I-431
Chauhan, D. S. II-336
Chauhan, Rahul I-239
Chauhan, Siddhartha II-34, II-88
Chavan, Mahesh S. I-461
Chavan, Shamkumar B. I-461
Chickerur, Satyadhyan II-108
Chitode, J. S. I-509

Dahiya, Priyanka II-279
Dargar, Shashi Kant II-454
Das, Amit Kishor II-269
Das, Priyojit II-129
Dash, Bodhisattva I-270
Deepshikha II-88
Deshmukh, Ankur II-556
Deshpande, Mangesh Sudhir I-489, I-520
Deshpande, Mangesh I-471
Dev, Amita II-298
Devarakonda, Naga Raju I-196
Dey, Kashi Nath II-129
Dhar, Dhruv II-108
Dhayaleni, G. T. II-288
Dias, Cifha Crecil II-479
Dongare, Pavan II-564

Fandango, Armando II-433
Fernandes Dimlo, U. M. II-205

Garg, Amit Kumar II-197
Garg, Harshi II-249
Garg, Ishan I-228
Gauns Dessai, Kissan G. I-84
Gaur, Anu I-65

Geetha, K.   II-288
Genta, Addisalem   II-402
Ghadekar, Premanand   I-530
Ghosh, Anupam   II-129
Girish, G.   I-249
Goap, Amarendra   II-309
Gopalan, Sundararaman   I-279
Goyal, Riya   I-260, II-119
Gupta, Ayush   II-556
Gupta, Jyoti   II-346
Gupta, P. K.   I-543
Gupta, Punit   II-55
Gupta, Rishab   I-321
Gupta, Shayon   II-158
Gurav, Gayatri   II-545

Hanji, Bhagyashri R.   I-74
Hegde, Lakshana   II-108
Hossain, Syeda Sumbul   I-381
Husain, Adil   I-95

Islam, Md. Baharul   II-269
Islam, Md. Kabirul   II-269
Iyer, Sahasra   I-481

Jagadev, Alok Kumar   II-187
Jagan, Balaji   II-167
Jain, Kanupriya   II-11
Jain, Mohit   I-321
Jain, Praphula Kumar   II-327
Jain, Subhi   I-239
Jalnekar, R. M.   I-509
Jena, Junali Jasmine   I-249
Jindal, Ayush   II-55
Joshi, Garima   I-65

Kabir, S. Rayhan   I-381
Kadam, Bhakti   II-556
Kaliamoorthy, Sathish   II-24
Kalra, Karan   I-260, II-119
Kamat, Venkatesh V.   I-84
Kamath, Surekha   II-479
Kanani, Pratik   I-54
Kandwal, Akhilesh   I-401
Kaonain, Md. Shamsul   II-269
Kapoor, Amita   II-433
Kapoor, Chandan   II-55
Karmakar, Kamalesh   II-158

Kasliwal, Manasi H.   II-535
Kaur, Navneet   II-217
Kaur, Prabhjot   I-208
Kaur, Sanmeet   I-218, I-228, I-260, I-372,
    II-119
Kerani, Mampi   I-362
Khan, Aysha   II-98
Khan, Muneeb H.   I-95
Khan, Nafisuddin   II-43
Krishna, C. Rama   II-309
Kshama, S. B.   I-185
Kshirsagar, Umesh A.   I-461
Kulkarni, Anagha   I-481
Kulkarni, Parag   I-352
Kumar, Gautam   II-205
Kumar, Manoj   I-134
Kumar, Parteek   I-260, II-119
Kumar, Puli Kishore   I-342, I-392
Kumari, Sangeeta   II-535
Kumbhar, Aditi   II-523
Kundeti, NagaPrasanthi   I-196

Lal, Niranjan   II-217, II-249
Lathashree, H.   II-177
Lobiyal, D. K.   II-402

Madhusudanan, V.   II-317
Mahalakshmi, N.   I-302, I-312
Majhi, Banshidhar   I-270
Mande, Anuprita   II-545
Mangaiyarkarasi, P.   I-44
Manjula Shenoy, K.   II-489
Mary, A. Jenifer Jothi   II-77
Maryam, Amrah   I-165
Maulik, Ujjwal   I-25
Mehta, Rachna   I-290
Minakshi, Sharma   II-148
Modi, Shatrughan   II-138
Mohan, Aditya   II-43
Mohanty, Figlu   I-270
Mohanty, Sachi Nandan   II-187
Mohiuddin, Karishma   II-269
Moka Katte, Niveditha J.   II-177
Mollah, Ayatullah Faruk   II-66
Mondal, Jayanta   I-421
Mukherjee, Tanmoy   II-158
Munna, Md Tahsir Ahmed   I-381
Muttoo, Sunil K.   II-442

Nagaraju, V.   II-317
Naik, Pandurang   II-167
Nanmaran, R.   I-44
Nasipuri, Mita   II-66
Natu, Ira   I-481
Nigam, Nitika   I-154
Nijhawan, Rahul   II-11
Nyati, Aradhana   II-454

Ombase, Pooja   II-545

Padole, Mamta   I-54
Pamula, Rajendra   II-327, II-336
Panda, Devee Darshani   I-421
Pandey, Vijay   II-158
Patel, Maulika S.   II-498
Patil, Kajol   I-481
Patil, Mahesh S.   II-108
Patil, Pooja   I-481
Patil, Ravindra   II-1
Patro, Manisha   I-249
Pawan Kumar, K.   II-479
Pawar, Rupali V.   I-509
Pooja, K. P.   II-177
Pradeep, S.   II-317
Pradhan, Gayadhar   I-342, I-392
Purushothaman, A.   I-279

Quamer, Waris   II-327

Raghuwanshi, Ghanshyam   I-449
Rahman, Sheikh Shah Mohammad Motiur   I-381
Rajak, Ranjit   I-331
Rajpal, Rohini   I-218
Raju, G.   I-1
Ramesh, Vani   II-227
Ramola, Ayushman   I-401
Rana, Poonam   I-543
Rana, Prashant Singh   II-138
Rani, Asha   I-321
Rani, K. Swarupa   I-124
Rao, M. V. P. Chandra Sekhara   I-196
Rao, V. Sudarsan   I-12
Ravi, Vidya   II-1
Revathi, A.   I-312
Rup, Suvendu   I-270

Saha, Sujay   II-129
Sahai, Seema   II-463
Saini, Hemraj   II-205
Saini, Himanshi   II-197
Saraswat, Pavi   II-55
Sasikaladevi, N.   I-302, I-312, II-288
Sathish Babu, B.   II-177
Satyanarayana, N.   I-12
Sawant, Sai   I-471
Sawant, Vinaya   I-104
Sen, Poulomi   II-158
Sen, Sagnik   I-25
Seth, Jitendra Kumar   I-411
Shah, Ketan   I-104
Shakya, Amit Kumar   I-401
Sharda, Sandeep   II-454
Sharma, Anamika   II-34
Sharma, Arun   I-114
Sharma, Deepak   II-309
Sharma, Deepika   I-114
Sharma, Dilip Kumar   II-336
Sharma, Harish   II-388
Sharma, Nirmala   II-388
Sharma, Shifali   II-138
Sharma, Vineet   I-543
Sharmila   I-362
Sheenu   I-65
Shettar, Rajashree   I-74
Shobha, K. R.   I-185
Shristi   II-187
Shrivastava, Nilay   I-321
Shukla, A. K.   II-309
Shukla, Ashish K.   II-413, II-423
Shukla, Praveen Kumar   II-259
Singh, Gurinder   II-463
Singh, Mayank   I-114, I-431, I-439
Singh, Shweta   I-175
Singh, Vijander   I-321
Singh, Vivek Kumar   II-259
Sonal, Chawla   II-148
Sonam   I-134
Sridevi, M.   II-564
Sridharan, D.   I-144
Srinivas, Kankanala   I-342, I-392
Srinivas, Nagapuri   I-342, I-392
Srivastava, Devesh Kumar   II-279
Srivastava, Viranjay M.   I-431, I-439

Sugandhi, K.   I-1
Swain, Debabala   I-421
Swathi, M.   I-279

Talukdar, Gitimoni   I-35
Tapas Bapu, B. R.   II-317
Tarar, Sandhya   I-431
Thakkar, Pooja K.   II-413
Thirugnanam, G.   I-44
Thommandru, Suresh   I-196
Tirumala, Sreenivas Sremath   II-359
Tiwari, Anurag   II-259
Toshniwal, Durga   II-370
Trivedi, Suyog   II-167
Tyagi, Vipin   I-449

Valakunde, Nandakishor D.   II-535
Veena, K. M.   II-489
Vibhute, Pritish Mahendra   I-489
Vidhate, Deepak A.   I-352
Vijay, Ritu   I-175

Wahid, Farha Fatina   I-1
Wajg, Dipak   II-471
Wajgi, Rakhi   II-471

Yadav, Divakar   I-154

Zhu, Janet   II-359

Printed in the United States
By Bookmasters